# Advancing Information Management through Semantic Web Concepts and Ontologies

Patricia Ordóñez de Pablos
*University of Oviedo, Spain*

Héctor Oscar Nigro
*Universidad Nacional del Centro de la Provincia de Buenos Aires, Argentina*

Robert Tennyson
*University of Minnesota, USA*

Sandra Elizabeth González Císaro
*Universidad Nacional del Centro de la Provincia de Buenos Aires, Argentina*

Waldemar Karwowski
*University of Central Florida, USA*

T0338723

Information Science
REFERENCE

| | |
|---|---|
| Managing Director: | Lindsay Johnston |
| Editorial Director: | Joel Gamon |
| Book Production Manager: | Jennifer Romanchak |
| Publishing Systems Analyst: | Adrienne Freeland |
| Development Editor: | Myla Merkel |
| Assistant Acquisitions Editor: | Kayla Wolfe |
| Typesetter: | Travis Gundrum |
| Cover Design: | Nick Newcomer |

Published in the United States of America by
Information Science Reference (an imprint of IGI Global)
701 E. Chocolate Avenue
Hershey PA 17033
Tel: 717-533-8845
Fax: 717-533-8661
E-mail: cust@igi-global.com
Web site: http://www.igi-global.com

Copyright © 2013 by IGI Global. All rights reserved. No part of this publication may be reproduced, stored or distributed in any form or by any means, electronic or mechanical, including photocopying, without written permission from the publisher. Product or company names used in this set are for identification purposes only. Inclusion of the names of the products or companies does not indicate a claim of ownership by IGI Global of the trademark or registered trademark.

Library of Congress Cataloging-in-Publication Data

Advancing information management through Semantic Web concepts and ontologies / Patricia Ordóñez de Pablos ... [et a].
    p. cm.
  Includes bibliographical references and index.
  Summary: "This book provides an analysis and introduction on the concept of combining the areas of semantic web and web mining, emphasizing semantics in technologies, reasoning, content searching and social media"--Provided by publisher.
  ISBN 978-1-4666-2494-8 (hardcover) -- ISBN 978-1-4666-2495-5 (ebook) -- ISBN 978-1-4666-2496-2 (print & perpetual access) 1. Semantic Web. 2. Data mining. 3. Ontologies (Information retrieval) 4. Information resources management. I. Ordóñez de Pablos, Patricia, 1975-
  TK5105.88815.A528 2012
  006.3'12--dc23
                                2012023343

British Cataloguing in Publication Data
A Cataloguing in Publication record for this book is available from the British Library.

All work contributed to this book is new, previously-unpublished material. The views expressed in this book are those of the authors, but not necessarily of the publisher.

# Editorial Advisory Board

César Luis Alvargonzález, *University of Oviedo, Spain*
Rauber Andreas, *Vienna University of Technology, Austria*
Rojalin Behura, *Centre for Development of Advanced Computing, India*
Constanta-Nicoleta Bodea, *Academy of Economic Studies, Romania*
Ricardo Colomo-Palacios, *Universidad Carlos III de Madrid, Spain*
Maria-Iuliana Dascalu, *Academy of Economic Studies, Romania*
Heinz Dreher, *Curtin University, Australia*
Josef Froschauer, Vienna *University of Technology, Austria*
Markus Gärtner, *Vienna University of Technology, Austria*
Jose Emilio Labra Gayo, *University of Oviedo, Spain*
Jose María Álvarez Gutiérrez, *University of Oviedo, Spain*
Berger Helmut, *QuantaSeek - Search and Text Analytics Solutions, Austria*
Weena Jimenez, *University of Oviedo, Spain*
Piet A. M. Kommers, *University of Twente, The Netherlands*
Uwe Laufs, *Fraunhofer IAO, Germany*
Adina Lipai, *Academy of Economic Studies, Romania*
Miroslav Minović, *University of Belgrade, Serbia*
Ingo Seidel, *Vienna University of Technology, Austria*
Michaël F. Steehouder, *University of Twente, The Netherlands*
Pablo Abella Vallina, *University of Oviedo, Spain*
Dengya Zhu, *Curtin University, Australia*
Jan Zibuschka, *Fraunhofer IAO, Germany*

# Table of Contents

# Detailed Table of Contents

**Chapter 1**
Understanding Children's Private Speech and Self-Regulation Learning in Web 2.0: Updates of
Vygotsky through Piaget and Future Recommendations........................................................ 1
    *Adel M. Agina, University of Twente, The Netherlands*
    *Robert D. Tennyson, University of Minnesota, USA*
    *Piet A. M. Kommers, University of Twente, The Netherlands*

Web 2.0 offers the Zeitgeist to update seminal research concerning children's Private Speech (PS) and Self-Regulation Learning (SRL) for application in social networks. Contemporary literature holds a body of research from the Vygotsky through Piaget to constructive theories that can be applied to theoretical foundations of Web 3.0 designs. Specifically, the purpose of the present chapter is to be present an index based on valuable and effective research concerning the subject matter in which a historical overview of both PS and SRL have demonstrated significant complexities and the most significant critiques that exist in the literature. The chapter does not mean to include detailed research methodology and results but, instead, to be used as an indexing review of PS and SRL for possible theoretical foundations in applications in the expanding world of social media. Finally, the conclusion provides a reflection on the future of our children's PS and SRL and what we should do next to enhance these concepts.

**Chapter 2**
Emergent Ontologies by Collaborative Tagging for Knowledge Management................................... 54
    *Weena Jimenez, University of Oviedo, Spain*
    *César Luis Alvargonzález, University of Oviedo, Spain*
    *Pablo Abella Vallina, University of Oviedo, Spain*
    *Jose María Álvarez Gutiérrez, University of Oviedo, Spain*
    *Patricia Ordoñez de Pablos, University of Oviedo, Spain*
    *Jose Emilio Labra Gayo, University of Oviedo, Spain*

The massive use of Internet and social networks leads us to a new dynamic environment with huge amounts of unstructured and unclassified information resources in continuous evolution. New classification, compilation, and recommendation systems based on the use of folksonomies and ontologies have appeared to deal with the requirements of data management in this environment. Nevertheless, using ontologies alone has some weaknesses due to the need of being statically modeled by a set of experts in a specific domain. On the other hand, folksonomies show a lack of formality because of their implicit ambiguity and flexibility by definition. The main objective of this chapter is to outline and evaluate a new way to exploit Web information resources and tags for bridging the gap between ontology modeling and folksonomies.

# Chapter 3

The chapter reports the implementation and validation of the knowledge process visualization technology that extends the basic capabilities of the Semantic MediaWiki platform. The Design Project Visualizer has been developed in the ACTIVE Integrating Project of the Seventh Framework Programme of the European Union for the case study in the engineering design in Microelectronics and Integrated Circuits. The concept of knowledge process visualization is based on the paradigm of project navigation. The knowledge workers in this domain are design project managers, designers, and design support engineers. The visualization suggests optimized performance, points to the bottlenecks in executions, and fosters collaboration in development teams. The authors describe the software prototype architecture and implementation. The components and the solution for process knowledge transformation between ontological representations as well as the visualization are presented in detail. Validation results indicate that the solution is helpful in providing expert assistance to design project managers performing their typical tasks of project planning and execution management.

# Chapter 4

The multimedia information system represents a specific form of information system. This research area suffered many changes in direction due to technology shifts. The general problem is that few years back, multimedia technologies had been limited to relatively simple, stand-alone applications, but multimedia systems, particularly Web-based systems grew in complexity and intervened with many critical issues for development. In this chapter, a specific focus will be cast on existing methodology approaches, their upsides and downsides, and on the surveys and research done by distinguished authors in this area on what sort of methodologies are used in practice. Afterwards, the focus of this chapter will be on whether existing development methodologies can be applied to multimedia systems and if there is any need to adapt them for that specific purpose.

# Chapter 5

This chapter examines the ethical questions and actions emerging from academic social networking. Academics have always been involved in rigorous discourse across multiple contexts, involving generation, exploration, analysis, evaluation, and application of ideas through a process of thought, research, peer validation, and publication. The argument is that the concept of collective intelligence is changing the traditional hierarchical "rules" associated with academic dialogue. Collective intelligence is defined as a mix of formal and informal conversational contexts, and the storing and sharing of ideas and information through multiple public online contexts. The meta-concept of collective intelligence presents a number of ethical dilemmas and questions related to privacy, and ownership and control of net-generated data, ideas, and information. The purpose of this chapter is to identify and describe these ethical issues and actions in relation to academic social networking.

## Chapter 6

*Ricardo Colomo-Palacios, Universidad Carlos III de Madrid, Spain*

*Diego Jiménez-López, Egeo IT, Spain*

*Marcos Ruano-Mayoral, Egeo IT, Spain*

*Joaquín Fernández-González, Egeo IT, Spain*

*David Mayorga Martín, PMO partners, Spain*

*Alberto López Fernández, PMO partners, Spain*

*Rocío Vega Alonso, PMO partners, Spain*

The increasing strength and usefulness of semantic technologies have led to innovative decision support processes and management of partners and R&D call for proposals. This book chapter introduces the SEM-IDi project, an architecture that integrates R&D processes with project management software and semantic customized environments. This SEM-IDi platform is composed by two main modules: General Management Module (GMM) which will be responsible for general management of diverse initiatives and projects, and the Semantic and Competence Module (SCM) which will provide functionalities related mainly to decision making.

## Chapter 7

*Jan Aalmink, University of Oldenburg, Germany*

*Timo von der Dovenmühle, University of Oldenburg, Germany*

*Jorge Marx Gómez, University of Oldenburg, Germany*

Cloud Computing is finding its way into the architecture of current IT landscapes. The present chapter depicts an algorithm-based methodology supporting the Root-Cause-Analysis in the context of malfunctioning Federated ERP (FERP) software in Enterprise Clouds. The challenge is to standardize the error-finding procedure and increase the efficiency. For a given error symptom it is shown that the error location is approximated iteratively with help of generic operators in a semiautomatic manner. This approach of Semantic Debugging outperforms classical methods of Technical Debugging in efficiency regarding prerequisite knowledge and time consumption. Semantic integration and maintainability correlate strongly. The Delta-Operator enables the reconstruction of semantic FERP integration in the course of the error reproduction session. In combination with the Join-Operator, the defect approximation can be performed along the dependencies of semantic artifacts.

# Chapter 8

Semantic Web database is an RDF database due to increased use of Semantic Web in real life applications; one can find heavy growth in RDF database. As there is a tremendous increase in RDF data, performance and scalability issues are of main concern. This chapter discusses improving and scaling up query performance for increasingly growing Semantic Web. It discusses current Semantic Web data storage techniques, which have been found to scale poorly and have poor query performance. It discusses the partitioning techniques vertical and horizontal partitioning to improve query performance. To further improve the query performance, along with these partitioning techniques, various compression techniques can also be used. Relational data offers faster execution of queries as compared to RDF data. To demonstrate these ideas, semantic data is converted to relational data and then query performance improvement techniques are applied. The scaling up of Semantic Web data is also discussed.

# Chapter 9

This chapter proposes a mechanism for mapping domain ontologies to metamodels by a direct mechanism; this proposal is necessary because there is no formal mechanism for obtaining requirements in model driven engineering. Specifically, here the authors propose the use of a domain ontology as the main input for defining metamodels. They define a point in common between domain ontologies and metamodels to apply a method of direct conversion between domain ontology and the metamodel. At the end of the chapter, the authors present a real case study in which they use the technique described and the conclusions of the investigation.

# Chapter 10

This chapter describes two conceptual frameworks for the analysis of online knowledge building: outsideness and developing adaptive expertise. The affordances of the metaphor of outsideness are outlined in relation to the construction of knowledge through the sharing and exploration of personal and cultural perspectives, asking questions to resolve doubt, and as a driver of purposeful academic conversation. Developing expertise is examined through the identification of the knowledge and skills for idea generation and evaluation in online environments, and optimal engagement in these learning contexts. A case study is provided of higher education students from three countries working together using a wiki to construct knowledge about teaching and learning. The authors present these two frameworks in order to increase understanding of the knowledge and skills needed by students in higher education to engage with the affordances of collective intelligence systems.

*Hisham Assal, California Polytechnic State University, USA*

*Franz Kurfess, California Polytechnic State University, USA*

*Kym Pohl, California Polytechnic State University, USA*

*Emily Schwarz, California Polytechnic State University, USA*

*John Seng, California Polytechnic State University, USA*

Natural Language Processing (NLP) provides tools to extract explicitly stated information from text documents. These tools include Named Entity Recognition (NER) and Parts-Of-Speech (POS). The extracted information represents discrete entities in the text and some relationships that may exist among them. To perform intelligent analysis on the extracted information a context has to exist in which this information is placed. The context provides an environment to link information that is extracted from multiple documents and offers a big picture of the domain. Analysis can then be provided by adding inference capabilities to the environment. The ODIX platform provides an environment for bringing together information extraction, ontology, and intelligent analysis. The platform design relies on existing NLP tools to provide the information extraction capabilities. It also utilizes a Web crawler to collect text documents from the Web. The context is provided by a domain ontology that is loaded at run time. The ontology offers limited inference capabilities and external intelligent agents offer more advanced reasoning capabilities. User involvement is key to the success of the analysis process. At every step of the process, the user has the opportunity to direct the system, set selection criteria, correct errors, or add additional information.

*Constanta-Nicoleta Bodea, Academy of Economic Studies, Romania*

*Adina Lipai, Academy of Economic Studies, Romania*

*Maria-Iuliana Dascalu, Academy of Economic Studies, Romania*

The chapter presents a meta-search tool developed in order to deliver search results structured according to the specific interests of users. Meta-search means that for a specific query, several search mechanisms could be simultaneously applied. Using the clustering process, thematically homogenous groups are built up from the initial list provided by the standard search mechanisms. The results are more user-oriented, thanks to the ontological approach of the clustering process. After the initial search made on multiple search engines, the results are pre-processed and transformed into vectors of words. These vectors are mapped into vectors of concepts, by calling an educational ontology and using the WordNet lexical database. The vectors of concepts are refined through concept space graphs and projection mechanisms, before applying the clustering procedure. The chapter describes the proposed solution in the framework of other existent clustering search solutions. Implementation details and early experimentation results are also provided.

## Chapter 13

*Dengya Zhu, Curtin University, Australia*
*Heinz Dreher, Curtin University, Australia*

Short-term queries preferred by most users often result in a list of Web search results with low precision from a user perspective. The purpose of this research is to improve the relevance of Web search results via search-term disambiguation and ontological filtering of search results based on socially constructed search concepts. A Special Search Browser (SSB) is developed where semantic characteristics of the socially constructed knowledge repository are extracted to form a category-document set. kNN is employed with the extracted category-documents as training data to classify Web results. Users' selected categories are employed to present the search results. Experimental results based on five experts' judgments over 250 hits from Yahoo! API demonstrate that utilizing the socially constructed search concepts to categorize and filter search results can improve precision by 23.5%, from Yahoo's 41.7% to 65.2% of SSB based on the results of five selected ambiguous search-terms.

## Chapter 14

*Nikos Kirtsis, Patras University, Greece*
*Paraskevi Tzekou, Patras University, Greece*
*Jeries Besharat, Patras University, Greece*
*Sofia Stamou, Patras University, Greece & Ionian University, Greece*

Wikipedia is one of the most successful worldwide collaborative efforts to put together user-generated content in a meaningfully organized and intuitive manner. Currently, Wikipedia hosts millions of articles on a variety of topics, supplied by thousands of contributors. A critical factor in Wikipedia's success is its open nature, which enables everyone to edit, revise, and/or question (via talk pages) the article contents. Considering the phenomenal growth of Wikipedia and the lack of a peer review process for its contents, it becomes evident that both editors and administrators have difficulty in validating its quality on a systematic and coordinated basis. This difficulty has motivated several research works on how to assess the quality of Wikipedia articles. In this chapter, the authors propose the exploitation of a novel indicator for the Wikipedia articles' quality, namely information credibility. In this respect, the authors describe a method that captures the polarized (i.e., biased) information across the article contents in an attempt to infer the amount of credible (i.e., objective) information every article communicates. This approach relies on the intuition that an article offering non-polarized information about its topic is more credible and of better quality compared to an article that discusses the editors' (subjective) opinions on that topic.

## Chapter 15

*Leonardo Balduzzi, Universidad Nacional del Centro de la Provincia de*
*Buenos Aires, Argentina*
*Ignacio Cuesta, Universidad Nacional del Centro de la Provincia de Buenos Aires, Argentina*

The major aim of the chapter is to propose and study the use of ontology-based optimization for positioning websites in search engines. In this sense, using heterogeneous inductive learning techniques and ontology for knowledge representation, a knowledge-based system which is capable of supporting the activity of SEO (Search Engine Optimization) has been designed and implemented. From its knowledge base, the system suggests the most appropriate optimization tasks for positioning a pair (keyword, website) on the first page of search engines and infers the positioning results to be obtained. The system evolution and learning capacity allows optimizing the productivity and effectiveness of the SEO process.

The research in the field of opinion mining has been ongoing for several years, and many models and techniques have been proposed. One of the techniques that can address the need for automated information monitoring to help to identify the trends and patterns that matter is sentiment mining. Existing approaches enable the analysis of a large number of text documents, mainly based on their statistical properties and possibly combined with numeric data. Most approaches are limited to simple word counts and largely ignore semantic and structural aspects of content. Conversation plays a vital role in expressing and promoting an opinion. In this chapter, the authors discuss the concept of ontology and propose a framework that allows the incorporation of information on conversation structure in the models for sentiment discovery in text.

# Chapter 17

This chapter presents a software tool that helps the Competitive Intelligence process by collecting and analyzing texts published on the Internet. The goal is to automatically analyze indicators of the sentiment present in texts about a certain theme, whether positive or negative. The sentiment analysis is made through a probabilistic process over keywords present in the texts, using as reference a task ontology with positive and negative words defined with a degree of confidence.

# Chapter 18

In this chapter, the authors discuss an ontology-based approach to opinion mining exploiting the possibility to represent commonly shared meaning of linguistic relations by ontologies. The ontology definitions are used as a standard to which sentences extracted from texts are compared. Unlike conventional text mining, which is based on objective topics aiming to discover common patterns of user opinions from their textual statements automatically or semi-automatically, it will extract opinion from subjective locations.

*Jan Zibuschka, Fraunhofer IAO, Germany*
*Uwe Laufs, Fraunhofer IAO, Germany*
*Wolf Engelbach, Fraunhofer IAO, Germany*

This chapter presents the architecture of an intermediary platform for networked open innovation management, as well as a surrounding sustainable business ecosystem. The instantiation presented here is tailored towards SMEs, both as stakeholders in the platform and as contributors in the modular ecosystem. It enables SMEs to work together in creating innovative products, increasing both reach and agility of their innovation processes. The chapter also describes to some detail the technical realization of the system, including the representation and automatic acquisition of relevant information. Selected business aspects are also addressed. It specifically focuses on the role of ontologies and how they contribute to the overall business value of the system.

# Preface

## INTRODUCTION

This book provides an introduction and in-depth analysis of the important concepts that underpin this change. It covers semantics: the technologies, the deep Web, reasoning, content searching, Voice-Video-Speech (VVS) searching, multimedia, social media, domain-oriented applications, and others.

The Semantic Web is a vision for the future in which Web content can be manipulated by automated systems for analysis and synthesis. Contrast this with the current Web, where information is published mainly for human consumption; for, although pages are human readable, browsers are able only to interpret HTML mark-up in order to visualize its content. The three most difficult tasks—content interpretation, selection, and management—can currently only be done by humans. The Semantic Web will redress the balance between machine and human, bringing these three most difficult tasks within the remit of the automatic.

Semantic Web mining aims to combine the development of two research areas, namely Semantic Web and Web mining. Web mining extracts information from the content of the pages, its structure of relationships (links), and the users' browsing records.

Both areas are collaborating in different ways:

1.  Mining Web techniques can help create a Semantic Web. A very important portion of Semantic Web is the ontologies. The ontology is represented as a set of concepts and their relevant interrelations for certain domains of knowledge. The challenge is to learn ontologies and/or their concepts, in order to make a scalable solution for a wide range of Semantic Web technologies.
2.  Knowledge in the form of ontologies, or other forms of representation of knowledge, can be used to improve the process and the results of mining Web. Knowledge provided by the ontology is useful in defining the structure and the scope for Web content mining.

In the interaction between ontologies and Web mining, we can mention the following applications:

1.  Sentiment analysis, also called opinion mining, is responsible for classifying words, texts, or documents of opinion, and emotions or feelings that express agreement. It works in tagging texts and their components, which indicate if the expression is positive, negative, or neutral, and in the field of the subjectivity of texts, as well. The area is called affective computing, i.e., the development of means to enable machines to detect and to respond in an appropriate manner to the emotions of users.

2. Optimization in search engines is criteria that must be taken into account in order to plan a campaign of positioning a Web page, its life cycle, and a selection of tools to help analyze the positioning of a site, as well as give keys to improve it. The study of the various basic attributes of an individual Web resource is not sufficient to infer the different strategies of positioning of a search engine. The fundamental problem is the relationship between the different elements of the page and weight that each one brings to the final positioning. The application of various techniques of inductive learning can be a starting point for the optimization of the Web positioning.

3. Web Intelligence (WI) is a research paradigm aimed at exploration of the fundamental interactions between Artificial Intelligence (AI), advanced engineering, and Advanced Information Technology (AIT). Engineering, here, is a general term referring to (a) a new area, for example, informatics of the brain, IA human level, intelligent agents, and intelligence social networks, and (b) classics, such as engineering knowledge, representation, planning, discovery, and data extraction.

The ontologies will give semantic richness to the Web mining process; thus, they will facilitate the understanding of the results obtained and the whole process performance.

The subject area is a combination of Semantic Web, business, management, and information systems.

## OBJECTIVE OF THE BOOK

The book intends to be an international platform to bring together practitioners, academics, researchers, decision makers, those in government, policy makers, and practitioners from different backgrounds to share new theories, research findings, and case studies, enhancing understanding and collaboration in Semantic Web and the role of information technologies and analyses of recent developments in theory and practice.

In addition, this publication comprises the state-of-the-art, innovative theoretical supports, advanced and successful implementations, as well as the latest empirical research findings in the iteration field of ontologies and Web mining.

## CONTENTS OF THE BOOK

Currently, key technologies include those for the fine-grained description of electronically served content. With fine-grained descriptions, automated processing is possible. One proposed vocabulary is RDF, which enables the description of resources and the relationships between them. The main point of RDF is that the relationships between resources are globally identified by URIs. The Semantic Web approach breaks the concept of a Web page as the smallest unit of information to enable the creation of resource descriptions with finer granularity. For example, instead of the homepage of a person, it would be possible to refer to the phone number of that person. In the case of textual information, that break-up is more affordable, although not easy, given that it is possible to access to paragraphs, words, etc. facilitating syntactic searches from keywords. In this way, traditional search engines do a reasonably good job to access text-based information.

Novel and interesting researches in the interaction of Web mining and ontologies are presented, such as ODIX platform, a meta-search tool to deliver search results structured according to the specific users' interests, ontology-based optimization for positioning websites in search engines, improvement of the relevance of Web search results via search-term disambiguation, and ontological filtering of search results based on socially constructed search concepts, and sentiment analysis or opinion mining with ontologies.

## Target Audience

The audience for such a book includes politicians, policy makers, government officers, students (undergraduate, postgraduate, master, PhD level), corporate heads of firms, senior general managers, managing directors, board directors, academics and researchers in the field both in universities and business schools, information technology directors and managers, and libraries and information centres serving the needs of the above, among others.

## Recommended Topics

Topics include, but are not limited to, the following: digital libraries, hypertext and hypermedia semantic, information security in semantic processing, knowledge management, languages (RDF, RDF Schema, OWL, etc.), learning (individual, group, organizational level, industry-academia), ontology for semantic interoperability, ontology learning, ontology mapping and visualization, ontology-based evaluation, progressive ontologies, scalability to the Web level, semantic applications/platforms/tools, semantic blogs, semantic content searching, theoretic foundations on Web mining ontologies-based approach, ontologies in Web mining process, ontology-based interpretation and validation of mined knowledge, interaction from ontologies to Web mining, ontology-based optimization in search engines, opinion mining with ontologies, real study cases, implementing Web mining based on ontologies, and other topics.

*Patricia Ordoñez de Pablos*
*University of Oviedo, Spain*

*Héctor Oscar Nigro*
*Universidad Nacional del Centro de la Provincia de Buenos Aires, Argentina*

*Robert D. Tennyson*
*University of Minnesota, USA*

*Sandra Elizabeth González Císaro*
*Universidad Nacional del Centro de la Provincia de Buenos Aires, Argentina*

*Waldemar Karwowski*
*University of Central Florida, USA*

# Acknowledgment

We wish to express our sincere gratitude to Dr. Mehdi Khosrow-Pour and Jan Travers, whose enthusiasm motivated us to accept their invitation for taking on this project, for the opportunity they have given us.

Special thanks also go to all the staff at IGI Global, whose contributions throughout the whole process from inception of the initial idea to final publication have been invaluable. In particular, to Joel A. Gamon, Development Manager, and Myla R. Merkel, Development Editor, for their help in advising us how to solve some problems and for their guidance and professional support. As well, we thank our first assigned Assistant Development Editors, Hannah Abelbeck and Christine Bufton.

Most of the authors of the chapters included in this book also served as referees for articles written by other authors, without whose support the project could not have been satisfactorily completed. Thanks go to all those who provided constructive and comprehensive reviews.

Once again, as editors we would like to thank all the contributing authors for their excellent papers and patience with the process. Making this kind of compilation is a huge responsibility and involves people with very different experiences and analyses.

Finally, we want to thank our families and friends for their love and support throughout this project.

*Patricia Ordoñez de Pablos*
*University of Oviedo, Spain*

*Héctor Oscar Nigro*
*Universidad Nacional del Centro de la Provincia de Buenos Aires, Argentina*

*Robert D. Tennyson*
*University of Minnesota, USA*

*Sandra Elizabeth González Císaro*
*Universidad Nacional del Centro de la Provincia de Buenos Aires, Argentina*

*Waldemar Karwowski*
*University of Central Florida, USA*

*May 2012*

# Chapter 1

# Understanding Children's Private Speech and Self-Regulation Learning in Web 2.0:
## Updates of Vygotsky through Piaget and Future Recommendations

**Adel M. Agina**
*University of Twente, The Netherlands*

**Piet A. M. Kommers**
*University of Twente, The Netherlands*

**Robert D. Tennyson**
*University of Minnesota, USA*

## ABSTRACT

*Web 2.0 offers the Zeitgeist to update seminal research concerning children's Private Speech (PS) and Self-Regulation Learning (SRL) for application in social networks. Contemporary literature holds a body of research from the Vygotsky through Piaget to constructive theories that can be applied to theoretical foundations of Web 3.0 designs. Specifically, the purpose of the present chapter is to be present an index based on valuable and effective research concerning the subject matter in which a historical overview of both PS and SRL have demonstrated significant complexities and the most significant critiques that exist in the literature. The chapter does not mean to include detailed research methodology and results but, instead, to be used as an indexing review of PS and SRL for possible theoretical foundations in applications in the expanding world of social media. Finally, the conclusion provides a reflection on the future of our children's PS and SRL and what we should do next to enhance these concepts.*

## INTRODUCTION

By and large, the research of children's Private Speech (PS) and Self-Regulation Learning (SRL) remains one of the noblest researches in the literature given the fact that it is about a century since the seminal research of the children's behavioral regulation started by Vygotsky in 1920s, followed by Piaget in 1950s and still continues so far by the subsequent researches. Accordingly, the current researchers must realize the fact that children nowadays are completely different

DOI: 10.4018/978-1-4666-2494-8.ch001

Copyright © 2013, IGI Global. Copying or distributing in print or electronic forms without written permission of IGI Global is prohibited.

compared with the previous generations and the fact that the computer and social networks, in all terms, was not definitely as nowadays given the scientific fact that embedding the powerful of both mathematics and Artificial Intelligent (AI) through the sophisticated programming languages may come with different and novel criteria and measurements for both PS and SRL.

Remarkably, during your navigation in the literature, you will be most probably wondering why the research of PS and SRL remains one of the noblest researches, what the previous and subsequent researches did, and what might be expected to happen for both PS and SRL in terms of modern research. Thus, the present chapter was aimed to gather the most valuable and effective researches associated with most complexities and latest findings with the most significant critiques concerning PS and SRL. However, the present chapter does mean to include the detailed information and results of those studies but, instead, to be used as a review of the literature and simultaneously as an index to the most effective and valuable studies in the literature so far.

## PRIVATE SPEECH (PS)

### Historical Overview

The seminal research regarding the contemporary inner speech investigations was began in 1920s with the early work of the Russian psychologist Lev Semenovich Vygotsky and his colleagues Luria, Leontiev, and Levina. Vygotsky et al. (1929) conducted a series of experiments on the egocentric speech of children and found that egocentric speech was a function that directly connected to thought and problem solving. Stated differently, in Vygotsky's view, private speech represents a stage in the gradual internalization of interpersonal linguistic exchanges whose final ontogenetic destination is inner speech, or verbal thought (Fernyhough & Fradley, 2005).

Piaget (1959) stated the basic observations of children's egocentric speech and this research has been integrated by Luria (1959, 1961), which conducted a number of experiments that based on involving a bulb-squeezing tasks for children aged 1.5 and 5.5 young and her studies found that children aged between 3-5.5 young were perfectly able to complete the tasks when the number of squeezes matched the number of words in the verbalization and the situation is opposite when there was inequality between the number of squeezes and words (for instance, the two statements 'Squeeze two times' and 'Squeeze twice' make the child to squeeze three and tow times respectively that means one squeezing for each word).

In the 1960s, the findings of Luria have been replicated by other researchers who used the same tasks to test the coordination of the speech-action of young children (Lovaas, 1961, 1964; Birch, 1966; Meichenbaum & Goodman, 1969a, 1969b). In sum, those studies emphasized that shifting from motoric to semantic aspects of speech is being functional occurring at almost the same time and this is matching as the Vygotskyian's hypothesis (Vygotsky, 1987) that the internalization of private speech from other to self, from overt (i.e., aloud to self and that is what currently known as self-talk) to covert (i.e., quiet with lip movements that is what currently known as thinking aloud).

In the 1970s and 1980s, Vygotsky (1978, 1986, 1987) in his subsequent research argued that private speech is a form of thinking, problem-solving, and self-regulation. Sokolov's (1972) study provides empirical evidence for the notion that inner speech becomes abbreviated during reading tasks, which are familiar or do not pose a cognitive challenge, and that inner speech becomes expanded when cognition is challenged. From experimental point of view, some other researchers such as Wozniak (1975), Balamore and Wozniak (1984), Goodman (1981), and Tinsley and Waters (1982) proposed new kind of tasks that involved children tapping sequences of different colored pegs with a hammer toy while they are listening to produce various verbal instructions during and before the tapping. Wozniak (1972) found that the verbal instructions affect the children's motor behavior with increasing the children's age.

In sum, those studies concluded that when things have been given to children to verbalize to themselves, these children were delayed longer when they have been given cues as in which time to speak and this result is very clear when these children have been compared with those children who have been given less and specific instructions. Frauenglass and Diaz (1985, p. 358) reviewed the literature concerning private speech and self-regulation and they observed and noticed that that there has been a tendency on the part of researchers to assume that the use of private speech by children should have a positive effect on task performance. Frawley and Lantolf (1986) published a commentary article concerning the study of Frauenglass and Diaz (1985) and concluded that the authors point out that because empirical studies have not consistently uncovered a positive effect of private speech on task performance, some have challenged Vygotsky's claim on the function of private speech in cognitive activity.

By the 1990s, new researchers such as Diaz and Berk (1995) and Winsler (1998) followed the track and reviewed a number of studies concerning the efficacy of self-instructional training programs and they concluded that the failure was mostly because of several unfounded assumptions. Diaz and Berk (1995), in a review of 13 studies on the efficacy of self-instructional training programs, and others (Winsler, 1998) concluded that the failure of these programs was likely due to several unfounded assumptions. At 2000s, Matuga (2003) noticed that private speech has been hypothesized to serve as a form and function of cognitive and behavioral self-regulation. Although Vygotsky and Luria did not generate a list of specific functions or forms of private speech, several researchers interested in sociocultural theory have. Few studies have, to date, successfully confirmed or disconfirmed

the Vygotskian prediction that private speech accompanies then serves a planning function to task-related activity (Beaudichon, 1973; Berk, 1992). It will remain difficult to even address this hypothesis given that the current categorization of private speech does not take into account the temporal sequencing of private speech and task-related activity. The temporal sequencing of private speech and task-related action (i.e., behavior) is just one of many dimensions of private speech investigated by researchers over the past 30 years. In 1968, Kohlberg, Yaeger, and Hjertholm conducted the first studies of private speech from a Vygotskian perspective to appear in an American journal. In their article, put forth six private speech hypotheses concerning the development, form, and function of private speech. These six hypotheses have been adopted by contemporary private speech researchers and have remained relatively unchanged since 1968.

Ehrich (2006) summarize the mechanisms of private speech based on the perspective of the Vygotskian inner speech and the reading process as a product of higher thought arises through a series of developmental stages, going from the external world and travelling inwards, its genesis a result of an initial need to solve problems. This inner speech constitutes a separate language function that is centered on word sense and meaning and has its own syntactic structure. Therefore, a number of researchers (Winsler, et al., 2000a, 2000b, 2003) were working on the self-regulatory difficulties of children's private speech such as ADHA (Attention-Deficit/Hyperactivity Disorder) where the most recent study concerning ADHA has been published by Corkum et al. (2008). Winsler et al. (2007) concluded that the normal developmental trajectory for private speech between the ages of 3.5 and 5.5 appears to be one of decreasing private speech overall accompanied by increasing task success with silence, a pattern from which children at-risk for ADHD deviate. These investigators also found that high and increasing amounts over time of task-irrelevant private speech are linked with poor child behavior both at home and at school.

Therefore, Winsler et al. (2007) clarified the main current aspects of research concerning children's private speech "A variety of different aspects of children's private speech have now been explored, including ontogentic and microgenetic developmental trajectories (Berk, 1986; Berk & Spuhl, 1995; Duncan &Pratt, 1997; Winsler, et al., 2000a), links with adult–child interactions (Berk & Spuhl, 1995; Winsler, et al., 1999), task and situational influences (Frauenglass & Diaz, 1985; Krafft & Berk, 1998; Winsler, et al., 2000b; Winsler & Diaz, 1995), children's awareness of such speech (Winsler & Naglieri, 2003), and private speech use within special populations of children (Berk & Landau, 1993; Berk & Potts, 1991; Winsler, 1998). However, an early and central theme of inquiry in this area has been determining the extent to which private speech is helpful to children in terms of either guiding motor behavior or enhancing task performance (Fernyhough & Fradley, 2005)."

The article by van Daal et al. (2007) offered a brief overview concerning the research of language from another point of view that numerous studies have examined the relations between phonological working memory and problematic language development. In doing this, phonological working memory has been tested in different manners. In some studies, children have been asked to repeat a number of words (e.g., Balthazar, 2003; Montgomery, 2000a, 2000b; Nation, et al., 1999; Rosenquist, et al., 2003). In other studies, children have been asked to either repeat nonsense words (Adams & Gathercole, 1996; Bishop, et al., 1996; Ellis-Weismer, et al., 2000; Gathercole, et al., 1994; Marton & Schwartz, 2003; Montgomery, 2003; Norrelgen, et al., 2002). And in other studies, children have been asked to repeat sentences, parts of sentences or lists of numbers and words presented aurally, sometimes presented at different speaking rates or with different serial positions

(e.g., Adams & Gathercole, 1996; Allen, et al., 1991; Ardila & Rosselli, 1994; Bain, 1993; Fazio, 1996; Gillam, et al., 1995; Isaki & Plante, 1997; Mainela-Arnold & Evans, 2005; Martin & Saffran, 1997; Marton & Schwartz, 2003; Montgomery, 2000a, 2000b, 2004). The relations between the visual aspect of working memory and language development factors have also been studied (Hale, et al., 1996, 1997). With respect to the relation between the central-executive memory functioning of children and their language development, it has been shown that problems switching between different aspects of information processing can correlate with language development problems (Baddeley & Della Sala, 1998; Baddeley, et al., 1998). Research on the central-executive problems of children with specific language impairment is quite scarce, but recent studies have shown the efficiency of children's executive memory functions to constrain their language development (Hoffman & Gillam, 2004; Numminem, et al., 2001; Marton & Schwartz, 2003).

On 2011, Agina and his colleagues (Agina, Kommers, & Steehouder, 2011a, 2011b, 2011c, 2011d, 2011e: hereafter 'Aginian's studies') introduces a serious of studies with a novel computer-based methodology, which is currently known in the literature as Aginian's methodology, that does not allow any human-human interaction, social intervention, or any external regulation while the young children can simultaneously talk, think and act alone during learning computer-based tasks through an isolated, computer learning system that acts as a standalone learning environment.

## Children's Meta-Cognitive Abilities

In many various and different studies such as Flavell (1976), Brown (1978), Baker (1991), Schraw and Dennison (1994), Bransford et al. (2000), and many others, the aspect of self-monitoring has been considered as one of the main strategies of children's metacognitive developmental ability.

Self-monitoring is very important to problem solving in order to manage problem complexity and to evaluate progress towards goals (Cox, 2005). By and large, children are daily engaging and interacting in various and different learning processes at school and home alike and learn as they play and play as they learn to spontaneously get more knowledge and, therefore, they usually ask questions to understand meanings and names especially at early age. Francis (1982) and Paris and Winograd (1990) revealed that young children's understand of their own learning is potentially linked to educational motivations and activities. Simply put, when children engage in the design process of their stimulus materials, they will be already self-motivated to act and react.

The published studies at 1990s such as Presley and Ghatala (1990) and Jones et al. (1995) and at 2000s such as Carroll (2007) concerning metacognitive abilities concluded that the learners who are aware of their metacognitive abilities are more effective and they are also able to increase the achievement when they have been compared with the others (i.e. learners at the average). Bransford et al. (2000) mentioned that the ability to monitor one's approach to problem solving—to be metacognitive—is an important aspect of the expert's competence. Schraw and Dennison (1994) defined metacognition as the ability of individuals to reflect, understand, and control their own learning. According to this definition, Sa´nchez-Alonso and Vovides (2007) explained that this ability implies, on the one hand, knowledge about one's self, about strategies that can be used, and about the application of such strategies (knowledge about cognition and self-monitoring). And on the other hand, implies control about the process of learning, which includes some kind of evaluation (regulation of cognition or control aspect). These general issues of metacognition have been analyzed in detail and broken down in very specific components, such as declarative knowledge, procedural knowledge, planning, monitoring, and more.

Flavell (1976) refers to metacognition as one's knowledge concerning one's own cognitive processes and products or anything related to them. In addition, it involves the active monitoring and consequent regulation and orchestration of these processes in relation to the cognitive objects or data on which they bear, usually in the service of some concrete goal or objective. Therefore, Flavell (1979) refers to Metacognitive Knowledge (MK) as a declarative knowledge about cognition, which we derive from long-term memory. It comprises implicit or explicit knowledge or ideas, beliefs, and 'theories' about the person him/herself and the others as cognitive beings, and their relations with various cognitive tasks, goals, actions, or strategies. It also comprises knowledge of tasks (i.e., categories of tasks and their processing) as well as knowledge of strategies (i.e., general ways of task processing).

In terms of process, Flavell (1979, 1987) defined metacognition as the executive process that monitors and controls one's cognitive processes, and is often defined in terms of metacognitive knowledge and metacognitive experiences. As a result, the assessment of the metacognitive abilities of children is still requiring more attention. In term of learning process, this research will be very valuable for each single learner to set up the proper tasks that fit the individual and improve the learner's skills, strategies and reflection enhancement as well as increasing the self-monitoring. The learner reflection, (Boud, et al., 1985), is defined as a generic term for those intellectual and affective activities in which individuals engage to explore their experiences in order to lead to a new understanding and appreciation. In the literature, a massive body of evidences such as Schön (1983), Boud (1985), Schön (1987), and many others suggest that the effectiveness of learning can be improved especially when learners pay more attention to their experiences of learning through their reflection on the state of their knowledge and learning process. Schön (1983, 1987) identified three types of learner reflection, which are reflection-in-action, reflection-on-action and reflection-on-reflection that may occur in any learning experience.

Regarding the meta-cognitive processes, Cox (2005) examined specific studies that emphasize cognitive self-monitoring such as the importance of explicit representation, higher-order problem-solving, the function of understanding one's own memory system, and data demonstrating a person's ability to assess (or not) the veracity of their own responses and learning. Sun et al. (2006) noticed that meta-cognitive processes have often been portrayed as explicit processes that involve deliberate reasoning (e.g., Mazzoni & Nelson, 1998; Metcalfe & Shimamura, 1994). However, evidence has been mounting that metacognitive processes may not be entirely explicit. For example, Reder and Schunn (1996) argued that there were likely to be implicit processes, for the simple reason of avoiding using up limited cognitive resources (such as attention) and interfering with regular processes. Thus, they argued that, while meta-cognitive strategies themselves might be explicit, and/or explicitly learned, the selection (and use) of meta-cognitive strategies was implicit.

Sun et al. (2006) and Sun and Mathews (2003) believed that meta-cognitive knowledge is neither necessarily explicit, nor necessarily implicit. Meta-cognition is likely a combination of implicit and explicit processes, the same as regular cognitive processes, as has been argued amply before (Mathews, et al., 1989; Sun, 1999, 2002; Sun, Merrill, & Peterson, 2001, 2005; Wegner & Bargh, 1998). In relation to computational cognitive modeling, it is worth noting that in much currently popular cognitive architecture, there is the lack of a sophisticated and sufficiently complex built-in meta-cognitive mechanism. However, a sophisticated and sufficiently complex metacognitive mechanism is important. It is an essential part of cognition, and without it, human cognition may not function properly (Mazzoni & Nelson, 1998; Metcalfe & Shimamura, 1994). In cognitive psychology, meta-cognitive processes have been routinely conceived as being carried out by specialized mechanisms that are separate and standalone for the specific purpose of monitoring and controlling regular cognitive processes. Such a conception has been explicitly stated in some theoretical treatments (Darling, et al., 1998; Nelson & Narens, 1990), as well as implied in many experimental designs (Metcalfe, 1994; Schneider, 1998).

Concerning the effect of self-assessment on metacognition skills, Kay et al. (2007) clarified generally that student self-assessment contributes to the development of meta-cognitive skills; in that it can help learners develop the capacity to identify their strengths and weaknesses and direct their study to areas that require improvement. Tang et al. (2007) offered a brief introduction concerning the evidences of children's understanding over the past two decades that the researchers have offered mixed evidence regarding young children's understanding of their own knowledge acquisition, with some evidence suggesting that 4- and 5-year-olds have a basic appreciation of knowledge acquisition (e.g., Gopnik & Graf, 1988) and other evidence suggesting that children of this age may still have difficulty in even recognizing the occurrence of a learning event (e.g., Esbensen, Taylor, & Stoess, 1997; Taylor, et al., 1994). The topic is of theoretical interest as well as pragmatic interest, pertinent to issues of the mechanisms involved in children's acquisition of an understanding of knowledge, learning, and the workings of the human mind and bearing on source monitoring and source memory (e.g. Roberts, 2002).

Pragmatically, young children's understanding of their own learning is potentially linked to educational motivations and activities (Francis, 1982; Paris & Winograd, 1990). Therefore, Tang et al. (2007) concluded that despite ubiquitous learning in the lives of young children, we still know relatively little about 'children's understanding' of their own learning experiences.

Regarding children's metacognitive developmental ability, Panaoura and Philippou (2007) offered a brief introduction over the last two decades that children's early understanding of their own as well as of others mental states has been intensively investigated, reflecting growing interest for this construct (Bartsch & Estes, 1996). In particular, metacognition has received increased attention in cognitive psychology (Guterman, 2003; Hennessey, 1999; Pappas, Ginsburg, & Jiang, 2003). In psychological literature, the term metacognition refers to two distinct areas of research: knowledge about cognition and regulation of cognition (Boekaerts, 1997; Fernadez-Duque, et al., 2000). According to Desoete et al. (2001) with age children become increasingly more conscious of their cognitive capacities, strategies for processing information, and task variables that influence performance. Although there is a rather general feeling that children gradually develop higher metacognitive abilities, as they get older, our knowledge about this process is very limited (Carr, 1998). Furthermore, it seems that we know little about the relationship between cognitive and metacognitive processes. Veenman et al. (2004) investigated whether metacognitive ability develops within or beyond the boundaries of intellectual growth. They found a significant growth of skill with age from childhood to early adulthood, even though metacognitive growth does not exclusively depend on cognitive growth.

In the literature, there are several techniques used in measuring metacognition and Self-Regulation such as standardized achievement scores, meta-cognitive training programs, interview technique, monitoring checklists, self-report inventories and calibration techniques as clarified by Sperling et al. (2002). Therefore, they stated that each of the methods of measurement has advantages and disadvantages. The main reason for many disadvantages is that it is difficult to capture metacognitive processing via direct observation. Most importantly, they mentioned that the think-aloud protocol measures are often similarly cumbersome in administration and scoring. In this context, it is a question that why the researchers do not work on developing new methodologies that can simultaneously be self-reporting, self-training and self-motivating to measure self-regulation through meta-cognitive with young children?

## CURRENT DEFINITIONS AND MODELS

In the literature, private speech has been named by different terms such as inner speech (Vygotysky, 1986), self-verbalization (Duncana & Cheyne, 2002), and recently as self-talk (Winsler, et al., 2007), and many others. In sum, Nielsen et al. (2002) stated a brief explanation of the naming problem concerning private speech that thinking aloud is described under many names: verbal reports, concurrent verbal protocols, retrospective verbal protocols, after think aloud and verbal protocols. Even the name think-aloud sometimes seems to embed an uncertainty: the concept is placed in brackets: "think aloud" without any explanations as to why (Koenemann-Belliveau, et al., 1994).

The children's private speech, or sometimes children's language, has been a common topic of considerable studies and researches over the years (Diaz & Berk, 1992). Duncana and Cheyne (2002) pointed out that the term "private speech" refers to overtly vocalized speech that is not addressed to anyone other than the speaker. Private speech has been studied almost exclusively in children, based on the Vygotskian assumption that the overt use of this speech form is the equivalent of a developmental stage ending during the early school years. The commonplace occurrence of self-verbalization in adults has been all but overlooked.

The first model of private speech can be considered through the early work of Leontiev, which is already a colleague of Vygotsky's. Leontiev (1978) argued that inner speech as a cognitive process has a direct memory function and described inner speech as having two codes: a code to plan speech and to retain content in the Short-Term-Memory (STM), and as a code to solve problems. Baddeley (1986) introduced another model of private speech based on the mechanism of working memory by describing the process of rehearsing information as a phonological code to prevent decay. This model involves a central executive processor and two slave processors. In the two salve processors, verbal information is stored in the phonological store and visual information is stored in the visual cache. Verbal information is rehearsed within the phonological store through a mechanism referred to as the phonological loop, which functions to prevent memory loss in the working memory.

The researcher van Daal et al. (2007) described the use of Baddely's model that the model of Baddeley is often used to describe the operation of working memory (Baddeley, 2002, 2003; Baddeley & Hitch, 1974; Baddeley, Gathercole, & Papagno, 1998; Burgess & Hitch, 1992; Hoffman & Gillam, 2004; Just & Carpenter, 1992; Martin & Saffran, 1997; Martin, Lesch, & Bartha, 1999) and involves two basic aspects where phonological and visual information are briefly and statically retained, namely the phonological loop and the visual sketchpad. The processing of phonological information is thought to have an inner rehearsal aspect (the articulator loop) which allows the phonological information needed for the process of language comprehension to be retained longer in memory. A third more central aspect of Baddeley's model is the central-executive system, which constitutes the control mechanism to coordinate the storage and processing of basic information.

## Significant Research Findings

The findings concerning the functions of children's private speech are in different and various directions based on the researchers background and perspectives. Importantly to note, a number of the subsequent researchers from 1970s until

2000s have been affected by the seminal work of Vygotsky concerning the functions of inner speech whereas a number of his theoretical approaches and perspectives have been examined and validated by those researchers such as the cognitive role of inner speech in terms of problem solving (e.g., Sokolov, 1972; Frawley & Lantolf, 1985; Appel & Lantolf, 1994; Roebuck, 1998; Anton & DiCamilla, 1999), the developmental nature of inner speech (e.g., de Guerrero, 1994, 1999), and inner speech is a crucial language acquisition device (e.g., Ushakova, 1994; McQuillan & Rodrigo, 1995; Upton & Lee-Thompson, 2001; de Guerrero, 2004). Nevertheless, Fernyhough and Fradley (2005) pointed out that the assumption of a linear relation between private speech and task difficulty has not gone unchallenged.

Particularly, it has been suggested that Vygotsky's ideas are more suggestive of a quadratic relation between these variables, with private speech being most likely to occur when the task is pitched within the ability range, or 'zone of proximal development' (Vygotsky, 1987), of the participant (Behrend, et al., 1989). Other studies at 1980s have concluded that inner speech is a highly efficient and effective generator of language such as inner speech can be generated at a much faster rate than overt speech (Mackay, 1981; Anderson, 1982). Other studies such as Yaden (1984) concluded that Vygotskian inner speech as a predicated structure may reduce meaning to its most essential unit and hence facilitate rapid reading. Frauenglass and Diaz (1985) addressed what is perhaps one of the most controversial issues to arise in Vygotskian psycholinguistic theory (i.e. the relation between cognition and private speech).

Beggs and Howarth (1985) introduced and argued that an important function of inner speech during silent reading is to provide access to prosodic elements such as rhythm, stress, and intonation. They introduced three different experiments where the first two experiments children's recall of homophones and non-homophones were examined in a Short-Term Memory (STM) task by asking the children to recall the word sets in the correct serial order of their presentation. They hypnotized that if the children were acoustically encoding the words in order to remember them, they would have greater difficulty with the homophone set than with the non-homophone set and they concluded that children who were normal readers begin to acoustically encode written words at around 8 or 9 years. In their third experiment, they investigated the effect of 'prosocial' enhanced texts on children's reading comprehension and they found that when children read aloud the 'prosocial' enhanced passages they performed significantly better on the comprehension questions than when they read aloud passages without prosodic enhancement. Therefore, when the elements associated with social speech, such as intonation, stress and rhythm are utilized in reading; children demonstrate a greater understanding of what is being read.

The subsequent studies at 1990s such as Cowan and Kail (1996) and Flavell et al. (1996) concluded that young children can store information as phonological codes but the actual silent rehearsal of this phonological information does not arise until around 7 years, which provides an important link between the rehearsal of the phonological activations (also known as subvocal rehearsal) as a mechanism to retain verbal information in the short-term memory and Vygotskian inner speech perspective, which is also consistent with the dual code description of inner speech by Leontiev's (1978). Other studies such as Abramson and Goldinger (1997) and early such as McCutchen and Perfetti (1982) provided evidence that the phonological activation of words during silent reading acts in a similar way to overt speech. Concerning the ability of vocabulary size of children, Werker et al. (2002) argued that vocabulary size is an indicator of word learning ability. Children who have a larger vocabulary may be better word learners because they have more capacity than their peers.

Therefore, they have the resources necessary to represent fine phonetic detail, which allows them to detect those words.

Fennell and Werker (2004) found another preliminary result that supports the resource limitation account is that if children are given extensive time to play with the so-called 'to-be-labeled' objects beforehand, they attend to subtle phonemic differences when learning the objects' names. Regarding the children's phonemic ability during task performance, Thiessen (2007) concluded that when engaged in word-learning tasks, though, children appear not to take advantage of distinctions that are perceptible to them, and phonemic in their language (Merriman & Schuster, 1991; Shvachkin, 1973; Stager & Werker, 1997). By definition, words that differ by one or more phonemes mean something different. If two words differ by one or more phonemes, they cannot refer to the same object.

## SELF-REGULATION LEARNING (SRL)

### Historical Overview

The term Self-Regulated Learning (SRL) became popular in the 1980s because it emphasized the emerging autonomy and responsibility of students to take charge of their own learning (Paris & Paris, 2001). As a general term, it subsumed research on cognitive strategies, metacognition, and motivation in one coherent construct that emphasized the interplay among these forces. It was regarded as a valuable term because it emphasized how the "self" was the agent in establishing learning goals and tactics and how each individual's perceptions of the self and task influenced the quality of learning that ensued. A great deal of research has focused on a constructivist perspective on SRL (e.g., Paris & Byrnes, 1989), on social foundations of SRL (e.g., Pressley, 1995; Zimmerman, 1989), on developmental changes in SRL (e.g., Paris &

Newman, 1990), and on instructional tactics for promoting SRL (e.g., Butler & Winne, 1995). The integrative nature of SRL stimulated researchers to study broader and more contextualized issues of teaching and learning while also showing the value of SRL as an educational objective at all grade levels. Interested readers can trace the history and various theoretical orientations to SRL in a volume by Schunk and Zimmerman (1989). What is important for teacher educators is that SRL can help describe the ways that people approach problems, apply strategies, monitor their performance, and interpret the outcomes of their efforts.

Paris and Paris (2001) have stated a brief historical overview during the past 30 years as the research on students' learning and achievement has progressively included emphases on cognitive strategies, meta-cognition, motivation, task engagement, and social supports in classrooms. SRL emerged as a construct that encompassed these various aspects of academic learning and provided more holistic views of the skills, knowledge, and motivation that students acquire. The complexity of SRL has been appealing to educational researchers who seek to provide effective interventions in schools that benefit teachers and students directly. SRL, as the three words imply, emphasizes autonomy and control by the individual who monitors, directs, and regulates actions toward goals of information acquisition, expanding expertise, and self-improvement. The main characteristics of the Self-Regulated children learners are that children possessing good self-regulatory skills recognize the importance of instructions, monitor their own progress, seek instruction when they have difficulty, actively involved in classroom activities, and demonstrate an awareness of their own thinking (Loper, 1980; Schunk, 1986; Cross & Paris, 1988; Schraw, 1994).

Patrick and Middleton (2002) concluded an insight about the self-report survey technique, which was the common one used to measure SRL, as the researchers typically conceptualized self-regulated learning as an aptitude—"a relatively enduring attribute of a person that predict future behavior" (Winne & Perry, 2000, p. 534). They also mentioned that, survey methods have produced significant advances in the understanding of self-regulated learning. They are also efficient; surveys are economical in terms of labor, relatively fast and inexpensive to administer and score, and the ensuring research has shown consistent findings among construct. Because surveys typically require respondents to average across situations or occasions, this methodology is particularly oriented toward the stability of perceptions and behaviors. It also emphasizes generalizability to populations (Denzin, 1978). Survey approaches to investigating self-regulated learning are compatible with implicit assumptions that the constructs reside within the individual and are relatively stable, and they de-emphasize contextual and temporal variability.

Rozendaal et al. (2003) discussed and analyst SRL from another point of view, which is the information-processing type and gender differences in the interplay between motivational aspects, and as they found that the two common information-processing modes, surface- and deep-level processing, should not be viewed as ends of the same continuum, but rather as discrete independent dimensions. They also stated a brief historical overview of the information-processing as in the last 20 years the research in the field of learning patterns has identified several characteristic ways of information processing (e.g., Biggs, 1987; Entwistle, 1988; Marton & Sa¨ljo¨, 1984; Pask, 1988; Vermunt, 1992). With the exception of Pask's (1988) research, whose typologies differ from those of other researchers, two broad characteristics in information processing are recurrent in relevant research. They refer to the first as 'surface-level processing,' which comprises information-processing strategies such as memorizing, repetition, and analyzing. The second they refer to as 'deep-level processing,' and comprises information-processing strategies such as relating, structuring, and critical thinking. Inspection of the strategy descriptions in both information-processing modes reveals that conceptually, a sense of regulation is embedded in each information-processing mode.

More specifically, students who tend to stick to and memorize the material presented to them by the teacher (a characteristic of the surface approach; see Schmeck, Geiser-Bernstein, & Cercy, 1991) rely on a form of external regulation. In contrast, students who process knowledge critically by thinking along with authors, teachers, and fellow students, verifying the coherence between the knowledge presented and their prior knowledge (a characteristic of deep-level processing; see Vermunt & Verloop, 1999) show initiative and are likely to be more self-regulating. The relation between information-processing modes and regulation is also retrieved empirically (cf. Boekaerts, Otten, & Simons, 1997; Entwistle, 2001; Pintrich, 1999; Slaats, 1999; Vermunt, 1992). A preference for surface-level processing is related to a need for external regulation of the learning process by teachers or fellow students. A preference for deep-level processing is often accompanied by self-regulation of the learning process.

Martic (2004) mentioned a brief historical overview of SRL as during the past 2 decades, a large body of literature in educational psychology has discussed various theories of Self-Regulated Learning (SRL) such as Pintrich (1995), Schunk and Zimmerman (1998), and Zimmerman and Schunk (1989). Research on SRL has targeted the knowledge, motivation, and volition that learners require to engage in SRL in relation to a wide variety of academic subjects, tasks and learning environments (with respect to both classroom learning and studying). Numerous schematic models of SRL have been proposed that include relationships among task environment and learners' behavioral, cognitive, meta-cognitive, effective, and volitional systems, operations and strategies. Some of these have been used to guide the development of extensive research programs

and to design instructional-learning materials, systems, and environments. What educational psychologists in the area of SRL hope to achieve in knowledge is a combination of academic learning skills and self-control that makes learning easier, so learners are more motivated; in other words, they have the skill and will to learn.

Lakes and Hoyt (2004) pointed out the main two types of SRL failure, according to theorists (e.g., Carver & Scheier, 1981); there are two types of self-regulation failure: under-regulation and mis-regulation. Under-regulation occurs when the self fails to change its response to that which brings the best outcome. Under-regulation is often manifested in procrastination, violence, and binge patterns. Mis-regulation involves efforts that do not bring about the best outcomes, perhaps because of a lack of understanding. Cleary and Zimmerman (2004) described generally the main characteristics of the self-regulated learners as they are proactive learners who incorporate various self-regulation processes (e.g., goal setting, self-observation, self-evaluation) with task strategies (e.g., study, time-management, and organizational strategies) and self-motivational beliefs (e.g., self-efficacy, intrinsic interest). It is assumed that these types of learners will regulate their academic behaviors and beliefs in three cyclical phases: forethought (i.e., processes that precede any effort to act), performance control (i.e., processes occurring during learning efforts), and self-reflection (i.e., processes occurring after learning or performance).

The forethought processes influence the performance control processes, which in turn influence self-reflection phase processes. A cycle is completed when the self-reflection processes impact forethought phase processes during future learning attempts. It should be noted that these phases are cyclical in that feedback from previous performances is used to make adjustments during future learning efforts and attempts (Zimmerman, 2000a). Schunk (2005) clarified the main aspects of the modern and early research on SRL as the research on academic self-regulated learning began as an outgrowth of psychological investigations into self-control among adults and its development in children (Zimmerman, 2001). Much early self-regulation research was therapeutic in nature; researchers taught participants to alter dysfunctional behaviors such as aggression, addictions, and behavioral problems. Researchers now apply self-regulatory principles to academic studying and other forms of learning, such as social and motor skills (Boekaerts, Pintrich, & Zeidner, 2000; Zimmerman & Schunk, 2001a).

Bodrova and Leong (2006) stated the main processes involved in SRL as they can be divided into two broad classes: social-emotional and cognitive self-regulation. The former makes it possible for children to conform to social rules and to benefit in various social contexts, while the later allows children to use cognitive processes necessary for problem solving and related abilities. Kramarski and Gutman (2006) offered a brief overview of the main focuses of SRL during the recent years as the role of self-regulated learning in education that has elicited considerable interest. Research has focused on students' SRL skills in addition to subject matter knowledge for the successful acquisition of knowledge in school. Students are self-regulated to the degree that they are metacognitively, motivationally, and behaviorally active participants in their own learning process (Zimmerman & Schunk, 2001b; Zimmerman, 1998; PISA, 2003).

Simonds, et al. (2007) concluded the main levels of studying SRL as at multiple levels, including: (1) observed regulation of social behavior, (2) parent or self-reports of temperamental effortful control, and (3) executive attention as assessed on cognitive tasks. These findings lead, in turn, to consider the theory of Personality Systems Interaction (PSI) of Julius Kuhl (2001; and see also Kuhl, 2000) where Calero et al. (2007) clarified briefly what is meant by PSI as it is an integrative theory of personality that deals, among other things, with individual differences in self-regulation or

self-control. Self-regulation can be equated to a democratic and self-control to an autocratic form of executive control. Self-regulation is related to affect regulation, that is, to the ability to increase a positive or reduce negative affect under stressful conditions in order to carry out one's intentions.

## Current Definitions and Models

Over the past 30 years (Butler, 2002), definitions of SRL have become increasingly encompassing. Self-regulation has been defined in several and different directions that differ from one study to another and from one area of knowledge to another based on the researchers background and perspective and has emerged not only as a multidisciplinary, but also as an interdisciplinary research (Agina, 2008). In philosophy the definition was based on self-control (e.g., Shonkoff & Phillips, 2000), in psychology the definition was based on self-management (e.g., Stright, et al., 2001), in cognitive science the definition was based on self-generated (e.g., Zimmerman & Schunk, 1989) and in motivational learning the definition was based on self-motivation (e.g., Boekaerts, 1999).

Early descriptions characterized self-regulated learners as metacognitively aware, planful, and strategic (Flavell, 1976; Brown, 1987; Butler, 1998). Subsequently, through the 1980s and 1990s, conceptions of SRL evolved to comprise interactions between students' knowledge (e.g. metacognitive, domain specific, and epistemological), metacognitive skill (e.g. planning and monitoring), motivation (e.g. self-efficacy beliefs and attributions), and cognition (e.g. application of a cognitive strategy; Alexander & Judy, 1988; Butler, 1998; Schommer, 1990; Borkowski & Muthukrishna, 1992; Schunk, 1994; Butler & Winne, 1995). An emphasis has been on how SRL is a function of the knowledge and skill that students construct over time (Paris & Byrnes, 1989). At the same time, evolving definitions of SRL focus on how enactment of self-regulated approaches to learning depends on individuals acting in social contexts (e.g. Zimmerman, 1995; Paris & Paris, 2001; Patrick & Middleton, 2001). This perspective emphasizes that self-regulated learning emerges from more than just individual knowledge and skill. Rather, self-regulation also involves a social aspect that includes interactions with peers and teachers (Patrick & Middleton, 2001), who shape students' task engagement by 'co-regulating' learning (Meyer & Turner, 2002).

Paul R. Pintrich, which is considering as a leading figure in the field of self-regulated learning in education and educational psychology, defined Self-Regulated Learning or Self-Regulation (Pintrich, 2000, p. 453) as an active, constructive process whereby learners set goals for their learning and then attempt to monitor, regulate, and control their cognition, motivation, and behaviour, guided and constrained by their goals and the contextual features in the environment. Zimmerman and Schunk (1989) defined SRL as a learning process in which self-generated thoughts, feelings and actions are systematically oriented towards attainment of the student's own goals. The PISA (2003), the Programme for International Student Assessment, describes SRL as a style of activities for problem solving that includes three phases: Analyzing tasks and setting goals; thinking of strategies and choosing the most appropriate strategy for solving the problem; and monitoring and controlling behaviors, cognitions, and motivations by enlisting strategies such as attention control, encoding control, and self-instruction.

Puustinen and Pulkkinen (2001) clarified that two kinds of definitions of SRL seem to emerge, a goal-oriented definition and a metacognitively weighted definition. Boekaerts, Pintrich, and Zimmerman define SRL as a goal-oriented process. They emphasize the constructive or self-generated nature of SRL and agree that monitoring, regulating, and controlling one's own learning includes cognitive but also motivational, emotional, and social factors. Borkowski and Winne, on the other hand, defined SRL as a metacognitively governed

process aimed at adapting the use of cognitive tactics and strategies to tasks. It is important to add, however, that even if Borkowski and Winne do not include goal orientations in their definitions, they both assume self-regulated learners (or good information users, as Borkowski puts it) to be intrinsically motivated and goal oriented. Borkowski's good information users are assumed to have mastery goals and in Winne's model goals are described as internal standards or criteria to which all attainments are compared. Finally, both Borkowski and Winne assume SRL to include cognitive but also motivational, emotional and social factors. In sum, the differences in the definitions become blurred when one examines the models in more detail, suggesting that it is the relative weight given to the component parts, more than the components themselves that varies from one model to another. Boekaerts (1999) considered the main layers of SRL as the competencies that make a student capable of self-regulated learning reside in three different layers, namely, that of the regulation of information-processing modes, that of the regulation of the learning process and that of the regulation of the self. Currently, self-regulated learning, by definition, is now thought to occur when students are motivated to reflectively and strategically engage in learning activities within environments that foster self-regulation. While Pintrich and Zusho (2002, p. 279) came up with a new consideration to define the dimensions of SRL and as they concluded that Self-regulation is not just afforded or constrained by personal cognition and motivation, but also privileged, encouraged, or discouraged by the contextual factors. Recently, Agina and Kommers (2008) introduced a new definition of SRL in computer gaming as "the learners' ability to direct their verbalization process and, simultaneously, monitoring their learning process's goals."

Puustinen and Pulkkinen (2001) introduced the latest models of SRL that have been developed over the past two decades including Boekaerts'

Model of Adaptable Learning, Borkowski's Process-oriented Model of Metacognition, Pintrich's General Framework for SRL, Winne's Four-stage Model of Self-regulated Learning, and Zimmerman's Social Cognitive Model of Self-regulation. Therefore, they compared those models based on a number of criteria and as they concluded that the models were compared on four criteria: the background theories of the authors, the definitions of SRL, the components included in the models and the empirical research conducted by the authors. They found that the two models that resembled each other more than any other two models (i.e., Pintrich and Zimmerman) were inspired by the same background theory (i.e., social cognitive theory) and the models that differed most from the other models (i.e. Borkowski and Winne) were also theoretically the farthest removed ones.

Azevedo, et al. (2002) clarified, generally, the shared certain basic assumptions among the current models of SRL that the models of SRL share certain basic assumptions about learning and regulation, despite the fact that each model proposes different constructs and mechanisms (for recent reviews see Boekaerts, Pintrich, & Zeidner, 2000; Zimmerman & Schunk, 2001a). Pintrich (2000) has recently summarized five assumptions shared by all SRL models. One assumption, derived from the cognitive perspective of learning, is that learners are active, constructive participants in the learning process. Learners construct their own meanings, goals, and strategies from the information available from both the internal (i.e., cognitive system) and the external (i.e., context) environment. A second assumption is based on the idea that learners are capable of monitoring, controlling, and regulating aspects of their own cognition, motivation, behavior, and context (e.g., the learning environment). Third, biological, developmental, contextual, and individual constraints can impede or interfere with a learner's ability to monitor or control his or her cognition, motivation, behavior, or context. Fourth, all models assume that there is a goal,

criterion, or standard against which the learner makes comparisons in order to assess whether the process should continue or if some type of change (e.g., in strategies) is necessary.

In a learning situation, a learner sets goals or standards to strive for in his or her learning, monitors progress toward these goals, and then adapts and regulates cognition, motivation, behavior, and context to reach the goals. Fifth, self-regulatory activities are mediators between personal and contextual characteristics and actual achievement or performance. In other words, it is not just the learner's cultural, demographic, or personality features that influence achievement and learning directly, or only contextual characteristics of the classroom that shape achievement, but it is the learner's self-regulation of his or her cognition, motivation, and behavior that mediates these relationships. Boekaerts and Corno (2005) stated briefly a comparison among the models of SRL in education as Pintrich (2000) came up to the conclusion that each model emphasizes slightly different aspects of SR. Corno, for example, emphasizes volitional aspects of SR, whereas Winne emphasises the cognitive aspects of SR, and McCaslin and Hickey emphasize the sociocultural aspects of SR. Nevertheless, all of the models share some basic assumptions. Gillespie and Seibel (2006) mentioned that "Shonkoff and Phillips (2000) define self-regulation as a child's ability to gain control of bodily functions, manage powerful emotions, and maintain focus and attention."

## Current Significant Complexities

Puustinen and Pulkkinen (2001) noticed that the empirical research has often been conducted using questionnaires and inventories designed to evaluate the central concepts of the models. However, it has been demonstrated that self-report measures do not necessarily give a reliable picture of the self-regulation tactics students actually engage in Winne et al. (2000). More naturalistic and empirically valid methods will certainly result in a more dynamic and diversified appreciation of the nature of the SRL phenomenon. Therefore, Butler (2002) noticed that a profitable area for further research could center on strategies for engaging collaborative teams of researchers, teachers, and students in co-constructing theories of SRL. Recently, Agina (2008) has briefly formulated what Puustinen and Pulkkinen (2001) and Butler (2002) concluded as an empirical research question "the general research question of self-regulation in all areas of knowledge is that how learners become strategic decision makers rather than strategic planner?" The answer of this question makes self-regulation to involve several and different subjects (multidisciplinary) in different areas of knowledge (interdisciplinary) that, in turn, makes it hard to be considered through only one-definition and one-model.

Cleary and Zimmerman (2004) concluded that self-regulation is a complex, multifaceted process that integrates key motivational variables and self-processes. Although different theories of self-regulation have been developed over the past 20 years, they all share many similar features and characteristics (Zeidner, Boekarts, & Pintrich, 2000). In general, self-regulation involves learners who proactively direct their behavior or strategies to achieve self-set goals. They also rely on affective, cognitive, motivational, and behavioral feedback to modify or adjust their strategies and behaviors when unable to initially attain their goals (Zimmerman, 1989). In terms of defining-complexity, Boekaerts and Corno (2005) stated briefly the most significant problem concerning SRL over the past two decades, in general, as the researchers have struggled with the conceptualisation and operationalisation of self-regulatory capacity, coming to the conclusion that there is no simple and straightforward definition of the construct of SR. The system of self-regulation comprises a complex, superordinate set of functions (see Carver & Scheier, 1990) located at the junction of several fields of

psychological research, including research on cognition, problem solving, decision making, metacognition, conceptual change, motivation, and volition. Each of these research domains has its own paradigms and traditions. In addition, each research community focuses on different content and aspects of the SR process, addressing different components and levels of the construct. Scanning the most recent literature in educational psychology reveals several evolving models of classroom SR (see e.g., Boekaerts, 1997; Corno, 2001; McCaslin & Hickey, 2001; Pintrich, 2000; Schunk & Zimmerman, 1998; Winne, 1995).

In terms of educational context, the main complexities of SRL were clarifying by Schunk (2005) through the work of Pintrich and his colleagues (e.g., Pintrich & De Groot, 1990; Pintrich, Roeser, & De Groot, 1994) and as Schunk concluded that those researchers believed that school contexts contained many complexities; the effects of which had to be determined to know how self-regulation occurred. Schools with children are complex places and much different from controlled laboratory settings with adults. These differences affect self-regulatory processes. A clear example of this complexity is seen in research on help seeking, which is an important self-regulation strategy (Newman & Schwager, 1992). All students require assistance at times, to understand material and when confused about what to do. Seeking help from others (e.g., teachers, peers, and parents) seems like a natural response; yet wide individual differences occur in students' frequency, amount, and type of help seeking. These differences suggest a complex interplay between social and motivational factors. However, Ryan, Pintrich, and Midgley (2001) discussed possible reasons why students might avoid seeking help.

Recently, Agina (2008) clarified, with more details, why naming one definition and stated one model of SRL is complex as each definition of self-regulation in each area of knowledge has been introduced based on the researcher's background and perspective. In philosophy the definition was based on self-control (Shonkoff & Phillips, 2000), in psychology the definition was based on self-management (Stright, et al., 2001), in cognitive science the definition was based on self-generated (Zimmerman & Schunk, 1989) and in motivational learning the definition was based on self-motivation (Boekaerts, 1999). The same of this remarkable perceptive can be applied on all the models of self-regulation. Mostly importantly, all the aforementioned self traits (i.e., self-control, self-management, self-generated, and self-motivation) or any other self trait may raised by any other researcher at any area of knowledge, can be definitely learned and improved by the external regulators while the self-regulation, per se, cannot be learned or improved by the external regulators because it is a result of those self traits acquisition. This means that each trait contributes to the self-regulation acquisition in a different direction that makes each researcher or a group of researchers to focus on one or more factors to promote self-regulation acquisition and that is the main reason why it is quite hard to develop one definition and one model of self-regulation learning.

The learner should acquire and improve the self-regulation by himself that leads to conclude that self-regulation is placed at the top of human self traits, prior to the self-organization indeed, where the other traits are just a set of factors that the learner should first learn and improve to be a self-regulated, which means all self-traits are promoting self-regulation in different directions and that is the reason why the researchers have different point of views concerning the definition and model of self-regulation (Figure 1).

Agina (2008) came up with the conclusion that researchers are defining and modeling self-regulation based on the need of their studies, theoretical background, and perspective. Therefore, they may assume their definitions and models in advance or may conclude them based on the results of their studies. However, assuming a definition of SRL in advance without a practical background (i.e. without an actual experiment) will be academically insufficient. Therefore, Agina and Kommers (2008) have examined the effect of playing the violent games on children's SRL and they concluded that self-monitoring was highly influencing children during learning tasks.

*Figure 1. Why naming one SRL definition and model is complex? (Agina, 2008)*

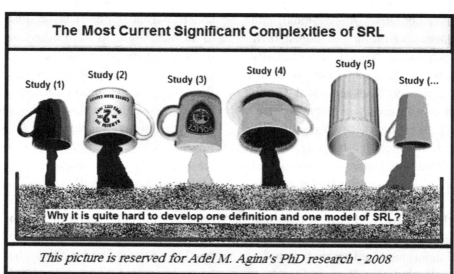

## Significant Findings

Kramarski and Gutman (2006) offered a brief history of the recent general findings concerning SRL and as there are relationships between students' SRL processes and academic achievement (e.g. Pintrich & De Groot, 1990; Zimmerman & Martinez-Pons, 1990; Schoenfeld, 1992; Mevarech & Kramarski, 1997; Zimmerman, 1998; Zimmerman & Schunk, 2001b; Kramarski & Mevarech, 2003; PISA, 2003; Azevedo & Cromley, 2004; Butler & Cartier, 2005). However, research indicated that, knowledge of SRL strategies is usually insufficient in promoting student achievement; students must also be motivated to use the strategies as well as regulate their cognition and effort. Students need to have both the will and the skill to be successful in classrooms, and we need to integrate these components in our models of classroom learning (Pintrich & Groot, 1990, p. 38). This interpretation is in line with the research on self regulation of learning that suggests students must be able to understand the what of cognitive strategies, and the how and when to use strategies appropriately (e.g. Palincsar & Brown, 1984; Pressley, 1986).

Despite the importance of SRL in learning, research indicated that learners have difficulties in SRL behaviour (e.g., Kramarski & Mevarech, 2003; Veenman, 2005). Students often do not realize that they should regulate their ideas and they do not know how to regulate productively. Students forge ahead without considering alternatives of their decisions are bogged down in logistical details of their work and focus on superficial measures of progress. Thus, students need support to identify effective ways to reflect on and regulate their ideas (e.g., Palincsar & Brown, 1984; Kramarski & Mevarech, 2003; Azevedo & Cromley, 2004; Butler & Cartier, 2005).

Kramarski and Gutman (2006) were, also, pointed out the effect of the new technology on SRL and SR-Learners as there are new advances in technology that have brought challenges and opportunities to education and instruction methods. E-learning environments provide students with dynamic, interactive nonlinear access to a wide range of information represented as text, graphics, animation, audio, and video (e.g. Jonassen, 1996; Jacobson & Archodidou, 2000) as well as to self-directed learning in online communication as hypertext, e-mail, and forums. E-learning has the potential to be a powerful learning tool for fostering students' will and skill for learning about complex topics. However, research indicated that very few students are skilled at regulating their learning to optimize self-directed learning (e.g., Veenman, 2005; Azevedo & Cromley, 2004; Kramarski & Mizrachi, 2012).

For the most part, studies have found that students learn little in E-learning environments and they do not deploy key self-regulatory processes and mechanisms such as effective cognitive and metacognitive strategies during learning (e.g., Hadwin & Winne, 2001; Azevedo & Cromley, 2004). The recent study (Renger, 2006) that involved 65 students of a secondary school (grade 7 through 9) confirmed the expectation that action orientation was associated with high levels of motivation, which can result in higher achievement. Liebermann et al. (2007) explained the recent findings of SRL from another point of view and as the development of different aspects of self-regulation and their developmental relations has received considerable attention where several studies have examined the developmental relations between Executive Function (EF), which is considered as an important aspect of cognitive self-regulation (Bodrova & Leong, 2006), and social cognition (Theory of Mind [ToM]).

However, little is known about the developmental relations between EF and social cognition, or between EF and Emotion Regulation (ER). Furthermore, the extent to which language mediates the relations between EF, social cognition, and ER has received little attention. Vieillevoye and Nader-Grosbois (2007), besides their findings, have also stated the general recent findings as self-regulation abilities develop more accurately during preschool period, it represents a significant cognitive-developmental hallmarks and an important achievement associated with social, behavioral, and academic competence (Bronson, 2000a; Flavell, 1977; Gilmore, Cuskelly, & Hayes, 2003; Kopp, 1982; Pressley, 1995). Preschool children are more and more capable of true inner self-regulation, in using rules, strategies and plans to guide their behavior (Kopp, 1982). Moreover, in this period, they become more and more interested by mastery challenges, they are more and more able to solve problems, and they control task progression more efficiently.

Several authors took an interest in this development during infancy and childhood (Chang & Burns, 2005; De La Ossa & Gauvain, 2001; Gardner & Rogoff, 1990; Hudson, Shapiro, & Sosa, 1995; Nelson-Legall, 1987; Puustinen, 1998; Sethi, Mischel, Aber, Shoda, & Rodriguez, 2000; Stipek, Recchia, & McClintic, 1992; St-Laurent & Moss, 2002; Winnykamen, 1993). According to Bronson (2000), even if the self-regulation evolves with age, there are also individual differences in this development in children at the same age. Vieillevoye and Nader-Grosbois (2007) were also hypothesizing a positive link between mental age and self-regulation level in normally developing children and in children with intellectual disability and their clusters analyses showed that the higher was symbolic behavior in creativity context, the higher was self-regulation.

Recently, Agina and Kommers (2008) introduced an interesting finding concerning self-regulation when children play with violent games and, as they concluded, that playing violent games has a great positive contribution to the children's SRL; in more specific, children' self-monitoring was highly affected especially through engaging those children as design-partners to eliminate the violence from the violent games to be changed as learning tools.

## AGINIAN'S STUDIES: AN OVERVIEW

The most recent research concerning PS and SRL is what IS currently known as Aginian's studies. Findings indicate a number of unique outcomes such as the young children showed higher performance without the presence of the human external regulators than their presence when they talk, think, and act alone during learning tasks, how both PS and SRL spontaneously occur, measuring SRL as a function of task level selection, and, in contrast, measure self-regulation as a function of task level selection and as a function of task precision as a function of task precision, the injudicious use of encouragement cues by the human external regulator during learning tasks hindered the children's regulation behavior, the natural elicitation of PS, social speech, and Thinking Aloud (TA) verbalization are fully different. The different task feedbacks can be applied with young children without the human external regulation. The relationship between children's spontaneous thinking aloud, and children's self-regulation is a reverse, and the computer, as a nonhuman external regulator, can identify those children who hold psychological problems and can integrate the net signed of self-regulation of each child at each task through embedding the powerful of the mathematics integration where the most unique result of the Aginian's studies was that the Aginian's Zone of Children's Motivation (ZCM) that enabled the Vygotskyian's Zone of Proximal Development (ZPD) to be practically applied during learning tasks, and, therefore, the preschool children can spontaneously do diagnostic tests of the psychological problems during learning tasks where the nonhuman external regulator (i.e., the computer) becomes able to analyze children's responses that, in turn, are used for detecting those children with the Developmental Problems (DP) through the Aginian's Zone of Children's Regulation (ZCR) in which a new psychological view was introduced and named as Aginian's view that showed that the natural development process of children's self-regulation was fluctuated among three paradoxical views (Vygotskyian vs. Piagetian vs. Aginian).

## Aginian's Methodology

What makes the Aginian's methodology unique is that it is completely computer-based methodology that has never ever seen before in the literature. This novel methodology involves a number of computer agents in which each agent is responsible for such a specific task or mission as long as long the child acts with the tasks. Therefore, the Aginian's methodology does not require the child to follow any previous training, as it does not allow any human-human interaction, social intervention, or any kind of human external regulation even before, during, or after the progression of learning tasks. The set of tasks, which is a collection puzzles, numbers matching, social activities, and picture-arrangement in the form of problem-solving, were not selected or implemented randomly but, instead, through a number of classroom teachers, evaluated by a number of children, and eventually evaluated by a number of experts in teaching.

## Aginian's ZCM vs. Vygotskyian's ZPD

One of the most valuable and practical outcomes of the Aginian's studies is what currently known in the literature as Aginian's Zone of Children's Motivation (ZCM), which defined as "the gap between self-motivated learning and the need to be motivated to learn." In specific, the progression of the Aginian's stimulus material was based on two paradoxical concepts. The teachers, first, selected the tasks based on the Vygotskyian's Zone of Proximal Development (ZPD) that says "children's private speech only occurs when the task is located within the range of their ability and will be less frequent or absent when the task is too difficult." Second, the teachers ordered the

tasks based on the Aginian's ZCM that enables the Vygotsyian's ZPD to be practically applied and evaluated in terms of reliability and validity. The Aginian's results showed that the ZPD is not always reliable and valid because children were able to produce private speech even during the tasks that out of the range of their ability and produced more private speech even with the complex tasks regardless the task precision (read the details in Aginian's studies).

## Aginian's Zone of Children's Regulation

The Aginian's Zone of Children's Regulation (ZCR), which defined as "the equilibrium point in the self-regulation's development process that controls the child to be either a self-Vygotskyian's learner, self-Piagetian's learner, or self-Aginian's learner during learning tasks" might be the most powerful outcome of the Aginian's studies that enabled the young children to be able to spontaneously diagnosis themselves in terms of holding or not holding developmental problem based on their natural responses and without any human's intervention during the time of learning tasks. In terms of innovation, the reviewers of the Aginian's studies during the publication process were highly expecting that the ZCR, through more deeply investigations, will come up with more powerful and unique results that may lead to a new revolution concerning the research of children's PS and SRL.

## CRITIQUES ON CHILDREN'S SPEECH AND SELF-REGULATION

### Theoretical Critique on the Current Findings

Interestingly enough, the first leaders of the seminal research regarding children's behavioral regulation, Vygotsky in 1920s and Piaget in 1950s, were paradoxical with each other in their final outcomes especially their views of the natural development of children's Self-Regulation Learning (SRL)! However, despite the ubiquity and notoriety of the Vygotskyian's and Piagetian's perspectives, they have received little or no attention as a criticize research given the fact that the computer nowadays, as a technology, is not like a hundred years ago, and children, themselves, are a different generation because of the modern schools and sophisticated educational systems, TV channels, video games, toys and tools, parents' educational level, and so on. Nevertheless, the current research in the literature still follows even Vygotsky or Piaget with no major change in the outcomes or the methodologies used.

Vygotsky's believed that social factors are central in development is well known where Piaget was often misunderstood as viewing the child as a lonely scientist apart from the social context (e.g., Damon, 1981; Haste, 1987; New, 1994; Lubeck, 1996; Santrock, 1997), and his research was mostly focused on individuals in a laboratory setting. However, it is important to distinguish between Piaget's statements as an epistemologist and his statements as a psychologist. Epistemologically, Piaget's main goal was to explain how knowledge develops but not how the child develops where Piaget psychologically emphasized the central role of social factors in the construction of knowledge.

According to Piaget (1968) and the subsequent work (e.g., Flavell, 1966), social speech, as distinct from private speech, is addressed to a partner, whereas private speech lacks a target person. Vygotsky's (1978, 1986, 1987) research claimed that private speech constitutes a kind of thinking—i.e., problem solving—and enhances task performance and self-regulation, which has recently figured in research as a major concept described by various definitions and models. However, each definition and model of self-regulation in each area of knowledge was defined and introduced based on the researchers'

theoretical background, perspective, and the need of their studies and they may also assume their definitions and models in advance or concluded them based on the results of their studies (Agina, 2008). In philosophy, for instance, the definition was based on self-control (e.g., Shonkoff, et al., 2000), in psychology the definition was based on self-management (e.g., Stright, et al., 2001), in cognitive science the definition was based on self-generated (e.g., Zimmerman & Schunk, 1989), in motivational learning the definition was based on self-motivation (e.g., Boekaerts, 1999), and recently in computer-gaming and self-regulation the definition was based on self-control (e.g., Agina & Kommers, 2008).

Remarkably, the first branch of the studies on children's speech use and self-regulation (e.g., Fernyhough & Fradley, 2005; Girbau, 2002; Muraven, 2010; Tang, et al., 2007, Winsler, & Abar, et al., 2007) followed the Vygotskyian view that self-regulation is behavioral, appears after and as a result of regulation by others in a specific task and is promoted by external regulators. Those studies still employed external intervention to instruct and guide the participants even before/during/after the experiment, typically in the form of prior training on how to use the material, encouragement through the external regulators to keep talking during the performance, or a questionnaire after the session. The second branch of research (e.g., DeVries, & Zan, 1992; Kamii & DeVries, 1980) followed the Piagetian view that self-regulation is promoted by giving children extensive opportunities to make choices and decisions but still with external intervention through offering instructions and guidance to the participants—despite the fact that Piaget (1965) argued that regulation by others hinders the development of self-regulation.

To date, researchers continue to support their participants with explicit instructions during learning tasks to talk aloud and prompt them when they are silent for long periods. This practice is not recommended, as it places artificial constraints on the situation, changes the cognitive processes and task activities required, and distorts the natural spontaneous emergence of private speech, which is usually the desired behavior under study (Daugherty, et al., 1994). In terms of cognitive load, it is important that the subject does not feel that he is taking part in a human-human interaction or social intervention with the external regulators. This sense should be avoided or, at least, reduced to a minimum (Bernardini, 1999). However, there is another cause for concern: if the subject is silent for a long time, the verbalization obtained becomes useless because significant parts of the cognitive process may not be investigated and might change the actual information to some extent. In addition, emotional and motivational factors can also produce a cognitive process different from the one that would take place without thinking aloud. The researchers usually tried to sidestep this problem by reminding the subject to think aloud (Krahmer & Ummelen, 2004), but this "thinking aloud"—as a method of eliciting data—is not the same as "thinking aloud" in the everyday sense, which entails something other than sitting people down next to tape recorder and asking them to talk (Jääskeläinen, 1999). Stated differently, the participants who were asked to think aloud, as part of a research method, will not talk to themselves spontaneously but instead, talk to themselves because they have been instructed to do so. Therefore, the presence of another person, as an external regulator, creates the problem of separating social speech from private speech (Fuson, 1979). Subsequent research (e.g., Schraw, 1994; Schunk, 1986; Stright, et al., 2001) described the good self-regulation learners as those who can recognize the importance of instructions, monitor their own progress, and seek additional instruction when they have difficulty.

Self-regulation inherently relies upon a multidimensional construct that has traditionally been difficult to operationalise (Boekaerts, 1996; Boekaerts & Corno, 2005). Because of this difficulty, many researchers have examined only limited aspects of SRL and have relied exclusively on self-reports to measure SRL. It is worth to question that how can self-report be used with children at an early age and why do not develop such a measurement that can be inherently used without distorting children's natural spontaneous to respond? To understand children's development more fully, a few studies (e.g., Sektnan, et al., 2010) have suggested that attention must be given to specific aspects of a child's environment that may influence the successful mastery of early academic skills. In particular, children's behavioral regulation—the ability to control, direct, and plan behavior—has been shown to be an important predictor of early academic achievement (McClelland, et al., 2007). The literature, however, still lacks such a practical standalone learning environment that does not allow the external intervention before/after/during learning tasks that, in turn, leads to human-human interaction and social intervention.

In sum, the differences between the theories of Vygotskyian and Piagetian can be realized and discussed in terms of the nature of the stimulus, the nature of knowledge and psychological instruments, the origin of the nature of self-regulation, the nature of novelty in intellectual development, the direction of development, the concept of social development, and the role of language in development (for more details see DeVries, 2000).

## Theoretical Critique on the Task Feedback with Young Children

In the literature, many types of task feedback have been investigated by the researchers (see the "Power of Feedback," John-Hattie & Timperley, 2007). The most common types are Knowledge of Performance (KP), e.g., "you solved 90% of the problems correctly," Knowledge of Result/Response (KR), i.e.," your answer is correct/incorrect," Knowledge of the Correct Response (KCR), i.e., provides the correct answer to the given task, Answer-Until-Correct (AUC), i.e., providing KR and offers the opportunity of further tries with the same task until the task is answered correctly, Multiple-Try Feedback (MTF) provides KR and offers the opportunity of a limited number of further tries with the same task, and Elaborated Feedback (EF) provides additional information besides KR or KCR.

However, the question of whether young children, especially at an early age, are able to assimilate or even to understand the meaning of these types of feedback remains challenged. Some studies (e.g., Gottfried, et al., 1994) concluded that if a child, on one hand, completes a task simply to receive a grade and the grade is not what he thought it should be, then he will be disappointed and provide less effort in the future. On the other hand, a child who completes a task to satisfy his curiosity and receives an average grade will provide more effort in the future to quench his curiosity or master a skill. However, numerous studies have ranged from extremely positive, through no effect; to strong negative effects and the feedback sign positive/negative does not explain the large variance in the effects (Kluger & DeNisi, 1996).

## Methodological Critiques on the Current Self-Regulation's Contexts and Settings

Many studies (e.g., Pintrich & De Groot, 1990; Pintrich, Roeser, & De Groot, 1994; Schunk, 2005) have clarified the main complexities of SRL in the school contexts as the effects of which had to be determined to know how self-regulation occurred and, therefore, schools with children are complex places and much different from controlled laboratory settings with adults. A clear example of this complexity is seen in research on help seeking, which is an important self-regulation strategy whereas all students require assistance at times, to understand material, and when confused about what to do (Newman & Schwager, 1992). Seeking help from others (e.g., teachers, peers, and parents) seems like a natural response; yet wide individual differences occur in students' frequency, amount, and type of help seeking. These differences suggest a complex interplay between social and motivational factors.

Importantly, at both educational and controlled laboratory settings the researchers (e.g., Fernyhough & Fradley, 2005; Girbau, 2002; Muraven, 2010; Tang, Bartsch, & Nunez, 2007; Winsler, Abar, Feder, Schunn, & Rubio, 2007) up to date, are still continuing to support their participants with explicit instructions before/during/after learning tasks to regulate themselves and prompt them to talk/act when they are silent for long periods. This external intervention was typically in the form of prior training on how to use the material, encouragement through the external regulators to keep talking during the performance, or a questionnaire after the session. These practices are not recommended as they place artificial constraints on the situation, changes the cognitive processes and task activities required, and distort the natural spontaneous emergence of self-regulatory behavior (Daugherty, White, & Manning, 1994).

Remarkably, all the affordable studies (e.g., Fernyhough & Fradley, 2005; Tang, Bartsch, & Nunez, 2007; Vygotsky, 1987) still involve the external regulators to instruct and guide the participants before/during/after the experiment in which all of them still followed either Vygotsky's views or Piaget's views. On one hand, such external intervention, which is a form of social interaction, may influence children to verbalize their actual regulation behavior and direct their cognitive process towards undesirable verbalization. Precisely, this external regulation may cause children to divide their cognitive capacity between the present task and understating the external instructions, thereby forcing their cognitive process to work in different directions (i.e., towards a task focus process vs. an external focus process), which is so-called extraneous cognitive load of learners that should be minimized during the learning process (Sweller, 1998). On the other hand, the children's silence during task performance is also a cause for concern, especially for long time where the verbalization becomes invaluable and could lead to undesirable speech either.

However, some researchers (e.g., Branch, 2000; Hoppmann, 2009; Stratman & Hamp-Lyons, 1994) have criticized the Thinking Aloud (TA) technique for the fact that TA and the limited capacity of memory hinder the participant's cognitive processes, thus, affecting performance if the tasks involve a high cognitive load especially that the presence of the external regulator (Duncana & Cheyne, 2002), to a great extent, creates the problem of separating PS and TA verbalization from the undesirable speech. When the external regulators, on one hand, interfere insufficiently to guide the participants, their verbal/nonverbal cues during the performance might result in an inappropriate level of verbalization in which their verbalization is, mostly, a feedback to the environment rather than to those instructions. On the other hand, when the external regulators interfere sufficiently the participants who were asked to think aloud, as part of a research method, will not talk to themselves spontaneously, but instead, because they have been instructed to do so. However, despite, many types of task feedback have been investigated (e.g., John-Hattie & Timperley, 2007); too many theoretical critiques on the task feedback with young children still challenged (e.g., Gottfried, Fleming, & Gottfried, 1994; Kluger & DeNisi, 1996).

## Theoretical Critiques on Reporting Children's DP

Over the past several decades (e.g., Chang, Sanna, Riley, Thornburg, Zumberg, & Edwards, 2007; for a review see: Chang, D'Zurilla, & Sanna, 2004; D'Zurilla, 1986; D'Zurilla & Maydeu-Olivares, 1995; Heppner, 1988; Heppner & Peterson, 1982; Nezu & Ronan, 1988; Nezu, Nezu, & Perri, 1989;

Spivack, Platt, & Shure, 1976; Tisdelle & St. Lawrence, 1986; Nezu, 1986; Dixon, Heppner, & Anderson, 1991), researchers found a significant link between problem solving and various measurements of psychological adjustment. Other researchers (e.g., Zumberg, Chang, & Sanna, 2008) have become increasingly interested in looking at the link between social problem solving and adjustment (Chang, D'Zurilla, & Sanna, 2004; D'Zurilla, Nezu, & Maydeu-Olivares, 2004; Nezu, 2004) whereas a few studies have shown that social problem solving is also related to important positive psychological variables such as positive affect (Baker, 2006; Chang & D'Zurilla, 1996), life satisfaction (Chang, 2003; Chang, et al., 2007), and psychological well-being (Chang, Downey, & Salata, 2004) and also there has been a small, but growing literature, implicating a link between social problem solving and various health outcomes (e.g., Baker, 2006; Lesley, 2007).

However, the major issue for mental health professionals is how to identify children's DP at an early age because children, by themselves, cannot offer self-reports to report their mental status, and their external regulators' views are not entirely objective as they are mostly subjective (e.g., Clarke-Stewart, Allhusen, McDowell, Thelen, & Call, 2003; Zeanah, Boris, & Scheeringa, 1997; Ling-Yi, et al., 2011). Therefore, most young children are not evaluated by a psychologist or psychiatrist until their problems come to the attention of someone of the external regulators. Noteworthy, when the symptoms of the DP reach the level of a diagnosable disorder in school-age children, they are relatively resistant to treatment (Hinshaw, 1994; Kazdin, 1993), and thus, the interventions aimed at preschool children may be more effective than those targeted at older children, both because the disruptive behavior is less entrenched and because behavioral control is emerging during this developmental period (Keenan & Wakschlag, 2000). Behavior problems that become entrenched frequently lead to long-standing and severe life problems (Rutter, 1989).

## Theoretical Critiques on Using the Computer as a Nonhuman External Regulator

From a technical point of view, when using the computer in the studies concerning DP, the young children, generally people, with DP are usually facing difficulties using standard input devices (i.e., mouse, keyboard, trackball) especially with pointing tasks. In specific, common pointing problems for children with DP include inability to aim at small targets, difficulty moving the pointing device, and difficulty controlling the pointer's buttons such as the inability to press the buttons or moving the cursor from the target after clicking. One of the main reasons to explain the computer's inaccessibility to these individuals is that most computer standard input devices are designed for the mainstream population without taking into account the fact that the input devices might also be used by people with DP who generally face computer operation problems (Abascal & Nicolle, 2005; Brodwin, Star, & Cardoso, 2004; Cook & Hussey, 2002; Wong, Chan, Li-Tsang, & Lam, 2009). Thus, such people have limited access to the growing number of well-designed programs available to computer users, unless their computers have specialized alternative input devices (Shih, 2011; Shih, Shih, & Pi, 2011).

## Methodological Critiques on Human and Nonhuman-Based Methodologies

From an experimental point of view, one of the most common experimental steps that appears as an inevitable in the previous work of children's behavioral regulation is that the researchers (e.g., Bridges & Cicchetti, 1982; Rothbart & Bates, 1998; Bailey, Hatton, Mesibov, Ament, & Skinner, 2000; Kau, Reider, Payne, Meyer, & Freund, 2000; Nygaard, Smith, & Torgersen,

2002; Klein-Tasman & Mervis, 2003; Fidler, Most, Booth-LaForce, & Kelly, 2006; Gartstein, Marmion, & Swanson, 2006; Konstantareas & Stewart, 2006; Stoneman, 2007; Shanahan, Roberts, Hatton, Reznick, & Goldsmith, 2008) were usually specified and divided the samples in advance either by primary diagnosis, or between children with and without such a status/condition in the form of condition-A versus condition-B to test such a hypothesis that already proposed and stated in advance too without realizing the fact that the individual and intellectual characteristics are changeable during learning tasks in which the child's mental status may or may not be intellectually changing from one task to another during the progression.

From a human-based methodological point of view, there are also two branches of human-based studies of children's self-regulation learning either be followed the Vygotskyian's view of SRL (e.g., Ericsson & Simon, 1993; Fernyhough & Fradley, 2005; Girbau, 2002; Muraven, 2010; Tang, Bartsch, & Nunez, 2007; Winsler, Abar, Feder, Schunn, & Rubio, 2007 followed) or Piagetian's view of SRL (e.g., DeVries & Zan, 1992; Flavell, 1966; Kamii & DeVries, 1980). For the nonhuman-based methodology for studying children's SRL, however, there is a great gap needs to be filling up given the fact that the use of the computer, per se, in the early developmental investigations concerning children's speech use, thinking aloud, self-regulation, and especially for the symptomatology of children's DP in terms of detection, classifications, identification, and diagnosis has not potentially emerged in the literature yet despite the large and huge body of the research that usually and regularly used the computer in the form of games and/or educational/learning tools to investigate various and different aspects/concepts and ideas.

Thus, the most appropriate question probably is not whether a machine can do psychotherapy or even whether it can do psychotherapy as perfect as a human does and, therefore, it is certainly not whether a computer should do therapy (Spero, 1978). Instead, what precisely we need to know is whether a machine, as a nonhuman external regulator, can do anything useful/valuable for children who need help with the sorts of DP that bring them to the specialists and counselors at an early age for whatever the machine process may be called.

## CONCLUSION AND REFLECTION

Generally, this review started with the seminal research on PS and SRL since the time of Vygotsky in 1920s, through Piaget in 1950s, until state-of-the-art in the 2000s. What the present review would potentially like to clarify is that the researchers must realize the fact that it is about a century since the seminal research concerning PS and SRL started and they have to move from vision to practice given the fact that the world nowadays, in all terms, is completely different and the fact that our children are completely different generation compared not only with the previous generations but also with us (their parents). The first issue that should be taken into account and consideration to move from vision to practice is to solve the problem of the diversity of defining and modeling PS, SRL, or any other concept in which the researches are mostly, if not completely, still using their alternatives (i.e., they only changed the English words) to describe or the explain the same concept/phenomenon without any practical value or even explaining why those alternatives (e.g., the definitions of private speech).

In this context, it is highly expected to see new terms, definitions, and models, and so on to describe such a concept but without any valuable or major changes that may lead, or at least inspire, the researchers to seriously moving from vision to

practice to start a revolution in studying PS and SRL. In more specific language, what valuable will be added with new terminologies of the same phenomenon more than confusing the readers and the researcher as well especially during searching the literature (Have you faced this problem? I faced it as a reader and as a researcher.).

Innovatively, since the seminal research started in 1920s, the subsequent researches really introduced many innovative aspects that neither Vygotsky nor Piaget did. In specific, the highest innovative things are the models of SRL that have been developed over the past two decades including: (1) Boekaerts' Model of Adaptable Learning, (2) Borkowski's Process-Oriented Model of Metacognition, (3) Pintrich's General Framework for SRL, (4) Winne's Four-Stage Model of Self-Regulated Learning, and (5) Zimmerman's Social Cognitive Model of Self-Regulation.

In terms of innovative methodology, since the time of the seminal research concerning PS and SRL started in 1920s until 2010, all the researches and studies and without any exception concerning PS and SRL are completely relying on human-based methodology where the participants still receive encouragement cues to talk, think and act during learning tasks. However, the only one innovative nonhuman-based methodology has recently introduced by Agina and his colleagues (Aginian's studies), which is currently known in the literature as Aginian's methodology that completely prevents any human external regulation. This nonhuman-based mythology has supported by a number of computer agents that produce the final result in points, which is readable for all the readers, and are inline with the statistical tests especially ANOVA and ANCOVA, which both are not easy for most of the readers to understand or even to read the context of their written numerical result as they only understand the related text in terms of level of the significant, slight, or no significant condition.

In terms of computer programming and networking, the present review chapter could simply invite all the specialists to think about the future in very simple way. First, let us imagine a global network where all the specialists are connected together all over the world with all children and their human external regulators (parents, teachers, etc.) either through their schools, kindergartens, homes, or wherever they are available, even in such an Internet-coffee, and second, when children use and play the game/games, the computer, as a nonhuman external regulation, starts to measure and evaluate each single child whereas the specialists can monitor and offer the treatment through the computer itself in which the computer saves that treatment for the similar cases with other children in the future (we may simply call this: Online Treatment of Children's Developmental Problems Through Play).

As a result, the computer becomes very expert in very short time to detect, identify, diagnosis, and even treat all children with developmental problems through playing computer-based games. However, one may wonder why establishing this network all over the world and what exactly the benefit will be. The answer is not hard to be realized given the fact that the computer is already an immortal soul that never died in which it can hold all kinds of the symptomatology and treatments of all developmental problems, and the fact that the computer's time response is faster than human's response that can deal with huge database of all those kinds of the symptomatology and treatments as well as the fact that the computer can simultaneously deal with unlimited number of children at a time.

Stated differently, with this global network we can help our children all over the world 24 hours per day, 7 days per week, and it does not matter where the specialist or the child is on this earth (do we really realize how many children need our help on this earth?).

## REFERENCES

Abascal, J., & Nicolle, C. (2005). Moving towards inclusive design guidelines for socially and ethically aware HCI. *Interacting with Computers*, *17*, 484–505. doi:10.1016/j.intcom.2005.03.002

Abramson, M., & Goldinger, S. D. (1997). What the reader's eye tells the mind's ear: Silent reading activates inner speech. *Perception & Psychophysics*, *59*, 1069–1068. doi:10.3758/BF03205520

Adams, A.-M., & Gathercole, S. E. (1996). Phonological working memory and spoken language development in young children. *The Quarterly Journal of Experimental Psychology*, *49*, 216–233.

Agina, A. M. (2008). Towards understanding self-organization: How self-regulation contributes to self-organization? *International Journal of Continuing Engineering Education and Lifelong Learning*, *18*, 366–379. doi:10.1504/IJCEELL.2008.018838

Agina, A. M., Kommers, P. A., & Steehouder, F. (2011a). The effect of the external regulator's absence on children's speech use, manifested self-regulation, and task performance during learning tasks. *Computers in Human Behavior*. Retrieved from http://doc.utwente.nl/76592/

Agina, A. M., Kommers, P. A., & Steehouder, F. (2011b). The effect of nonhuman's versus human's external regulation on children's speech use, manifested self-regulation, and satisfaction during learning tasks. *Computers in Human Behavior*. Retrieved from http://doc.utwente.nl/76593/

Agina, A. M., Kommers, P. A., & Steehouder, F. (2011c). The effect of the nonhuman external regulator's answer-until-correct (AUC) versus knowledge-of-result (KR) task feedback on children's behavioral regulation during learning tasks. *Computers in Human Behavior*. Retrieved from http://www.deepdyve.com/lp/elsevier/the-effect-of-the-nonhuman-external-regulator-s-answer-until-correct-dKZHxc0Ehi

Agina, A. M., Kommers, P. A., & Steehouder, F. (2011d). The effect of nonhuman's external regulation on detecting the natural development process of young children's self-regulation during learning tasks. *Computers in Human Behavior, 28*(2), 527–539. doi:10.1016/j.chb.2011.10.025

Agina, A. M., & Kommers, P. A. M. (2008). The positive of violent games on children's self-regulation learning. In *Proceedings of the IADIS Multi Conference on Computer Science and Information Systems,* (pp. 141-145). Amsterdam, The Netherlands: University of Twente Press.

Alexander, P. A., & Judy, J. E. (1988). The interaction of domain-specific and strategic knowledge in academic performance. *Review of Educational Research, 58*, 375–404.

Allen, M. H., Lincoln, A. J., & Kaufman, A. S. (1991). Sequential and simultaneous processing abilities of high functioning autistic and language-impaired children. *Journal of Autism and Developmental Disorders, 21*, 483–502. doi:10.1007/BF02206872

Anderson, R. E. (1982). Speech imagery is not always faster than visual imagery. *Memory & Cognition, 10*, 371–380. doi:10.3758/BF03202429

Annett, J. (1969). *Feedback and human behavior*. Oxford, UK: Penguin Books.

Anton, M., & DiCamilla, F. J. (1999). Socio–cognitive functions of L1 collaborative interaction in the L2 classroom. *Modern Language Journal, 83*, 233–247. doi:10.1111/0026-7902.00018

Appel, G., & Lantolf, J. P. (1994). Speaking as mediation: A study of L1 and L2 text recall tasks. *Modern Language Journal, 78*, 437–452. doi:10.1111/j.1540-4781.1994.tb02062.x

Ardila, A., & Rosseli, M. (1994). Development of language, memory, and visual spatial abilities in 5- to 12-year-old children using a neuropsychological battery. *Developmental Neuropsychology, 10*, 97–120. doi:10.1080/87565649409540571

Azevedo, R., & Cromley, J. G. (2004). Does training of self-regulated learning facilitate student's learning with hypermedia? *Journal of Educational Psychology, 96*, 523–535. doi:10.1037/0022-0663.96.3.523

Azevedo, R., Guthrie, J. T., & Seibert, D. (2004). The role of self-regulated learning in fostering students' conceptual understanding of complex systems with hypermedia. *Journal of Educational Computing Research, 30*, 87–111. doi:10.2190/DVWX-GM1T-6THQ-5WC7

Azevedo, R., Ragan, S., Cromley, J. G., & Pritchett, S. (2002). *Do different goal-setting conditions facilitate students' ability to regulate their learning of complex science topics with RiverWeb?* Paper presented at the Annual Conference of the American Educational Research Association. New Orleans, LA.

Baddeley, A., Gathercole, S., & Papagno, C. (1998). The phonological loop as a language learning device. *Psychological Review, 105*, 158–173. doi:10.1037/0033-295X.105.1.158

Baddeley, A. D. (1986). *Working memory*. Oxford, UK: Oxford University Press.

Baddeley, A. D. (2002). Is working memory still working? *European Psychologist, 7*, 85–97. doi:10.1027//1016-9040.7.2.85

Baddeley, A. D. (2003). Working memory and language: An overview. *Journal of Communication Disorders, 36*, 189–208. doi:10.1016/S0021-9924(03)00019-4

Baddeley, A. D., & Della Sala, S. (1998). Working memory and executive control. In Roberts, A. C., & Robbins, T. W. (Eds.), *The Prefrontal Cortex: Executive and Cognitive Functions* (pp. 143–162). Oxford, UK: Oxford University Press. doi:10.1093/acprof:oso/9780198524410.003.0002

Baddeley, A. D., Emslie, H., Kolondny, J., & Duncan, J. (1998). Random generation and the executive control of working memory. *Quarterly Journal of Experimental Psychology, 51*, 819–852.

Baddeley, A. D., & Hitch, G. (1974). Working memory. In Bower, G. A. (Ed.), *Recent Advances in the Psychology of Learning and Motivation* (Vol. 8, pp. 263–302). New York, NY: Academic Press.

Bailey, D. B. Jr, Hatton, D. D., Mesibov, G., Ament, N., & Skinner, M. (2000). Early development, temperament, and functional impairment in autism and fragile X syndrome. *Journal of Autism and Developmental Disorders, 30*, 49–59. doi:10.1023/A:1005412111706

Bain, S. K. (1993). Sequential and simultaneous processing in children with learning disabilities: An attempted replication. *The Journal of Special Education, 27*, 235–246. doi:10.1177/002246699302700206

Baker, L. (1991). Metacognition, reading, and science education. In Santa, C. M., & Alvermann, D. E. (Eds.), *Science Learning-Processes and Applications* (pp. 2–13). Newark, DE: International Reading Association.

Baker, S. R. (2006). Towards an idiothetic understanding of the role of social problem solving in daily event, mood and health experience: A prospective daily diary study. *British Journal of Health Psychology, 11*, 513–531. doi:10.1348/135910705X57647

Balamore, U., & Wozniak, R. H. (1984). Speech–action coordination in young children. *Developmental Psychology, 20*, 850–858. doi:10.1037/0012-1649.20.5.850

Balthazar, C. H. (2003). The word length effect in children with language impairment. *Journal of Communication Disorders, 36*, 487–505. doi:10.1016/S0021-9924(03)00033-9

Bartsch, K., & Estes, D. (1996). Individual differences in children's developing theory of mind and implications for metacognition. *Learning and Individual Differences, 8*, 281–304. doi:10.1016/S1041-6080(96)90020-5

Beaudichon, J. (1973). Nature and instrumental function on private speech in problem solving situations. *Merrill-Palmer Quarterly, 19*, 117–135.

Beggs, W. D. A., & Howarth, P. N. (1985). Inner speech as a learned skill. *Journal of Experimental Child Psychology, 39*, 396–411. doi:10.1016/0022-0965(85)90048-7

Behrend, D. A., Rosengren, K., & Perlmutter, M. (1992). The relation between private speech and parental interactive style. In Diaz, R. M., & Berk, L. E. (Eds.), *Private Speech: From Social Interaction to Self-Regulation* (pp. 85–100). Hillsdale, NJ: Erlbaum.

Behrend, D. A., Rosengren, K. S., & Perlmutter, M. (1989). A new look at children's private speech: The effects of age, task difficulty, and parent presence. *International Journal of Behavioral Development, 12*, 305–320.

Berk, L. E. (1986). Relationship of elementary school children's private speech to behavioral accompaniment to task, attention, and task performance. *Developmental Psychology, 22*, 671–680. doi:10.1037/0012-1649.22.5.671

Berk, L. E. (1992). Children's private speech: An overview of theory and the status of research. In Diaz, R. M., & Berk, L. E. (Eds.), *Private Speech: From Social Interaction to self-Regulation* (pp. 17–53). Hillsdale, NJ: Erlbaum.

Berk, L. E., & Garvin, R. A. (1984). Development of private speech among low-income Appalachian children. *Developmental Psychology, 20*, 271–286. doi:10.1037/0012-1649.20.2.271

Berk, L. E., & Landau, S. (1993). Private speech of learning disabled and normally achieving children in classroom academic and laboratory contexts. *Child Development, 64*, 556–571. doi:10.2307/1131269

Berk, L. E., & Potts, M. K. (1991). Development and functional significance of private speech among attention-deficit hyperactivity disordered and normal boys. *Journal of Abnormal Child Psychology, 19*, 357–377. doi:10.1007/BF00911237

Berk, L. E., & Spuhl, S. T. (1995). Maternal interaction, private speech, and task performance in preschool children. *Early Childhood Research Quarterly, 10*, 145–169. doi:10.1016/0885-2006(95)90001-2

Berk, L. E., & Winsler, A. (1995). *Scaffolding children's learning: Vygotsky and early childhood education*. Washington, DC: National Association for the Education of Young Children.

Bernardini, S. (1999). *Using think-aloud protocols to investigate the translation process: Methodological aspects*. Bologna, Italy: University of Bologna.

Biggs, J. (1987). *Student approaches to learning and studying*. Hawthorn, Australia: Australian Council for Educational Research.

Bilodeau, E. A. (1969). *Principles of skill acquisition*. New York, NY: Academic Press.

Birch, D. (1966). Verbal control of nonverbal behavior. *Journal of Experimental Child Psychology, 4*, 266–275. doi:10.1016/0022-0965(66)90027-0

Bishop, D. V. M., Aamodt-Leeper, G., Creswell, C., McGurk, R., & Skuse, D. H. (2001). Individual differences in cognitive planning on the Tower of Hanoi task: Neuropsychological maturity or measurement error? *Journal of Child Psychology and Psychiatry, and Allied Disciplines, 42*, 551–556. doi:10.1111/1469-7610.00749

Bishop, D. V. M., North, T., & Dnlan, C. (1996). Nonword repetition as behavioural marker for inherited language impairment: Evidence from a twin study. *Journal of Child Psychology and Psychiatry, and Allied Disciplines, 37*, 391–404. doi:10.1111/j.1469-7610.1996.tb01420.x

Bivens, J. A., & Berk, L. E. (1990). A longitudinal study of the development of elementary school children's private speech. *Merrill-Palmer Quarterly, 36*, 443–463.

Bjorklund, D. F., & Douglas, R. N. (1997). The development of memory strategies. In Cowan, N. (Ed.), *The Development of Memory in Childhood* (pp. 201–246). Hove, UK: Psychology Press.

Bloom, B. (1976). *Human characteristics and school learning*. New York, NY: McGraw-Hill.

Bodrova, E., & Leong, D. J. (2006). Self-regulation as key to school readiness: How early childhood teachers promote this critical competency. In Zaslow, M., & Martinez-Beck, I. (Eds.), *Critical Issues in Early Childhood Professional Development* (pp. 203–224). Baltimore, MD: Brookes.

Boekaerts, M. (1996). Self-regulated learning and the junction of cognition and motivation. *European Psychologist, 1*, 100–112. doi:10.1027/1016-9040.1.2.100

Boekaerts, M. (1997). Self-regulated learning: A new concept embraced by researchers, policy makers, educators, teachers and students. *Learning and Instruction*, *7*, 161–186. doi:10.1016/S0959-4752(96)00015-1

Boekaerts, M. (1999). Self-regulated learning: Where we are today. *International Journal of Educational Research*, *31*, 445–457. doi:10.1016/S0883-0355(99)00014-2

Boekaerts, M., & Corno, L. (2005). Self-regulation in the classroom: A perspective on assessment and intervention. *Applied Psychology*, *54*, 199–231. doi:10.1111/j.1464-0597.2005.00205.x

Boekaerts, M., Otten, R., & Simons, R. (1997). Een onderzoek naar de bruikbaarheid van de ILS leerstijlen in de onderbouw van het voortgezet onderwijs. [Exploring the utility of Vermunts' ILS learning style construct for high school students]. *Tijdschrift voor Onderwijsresearch*, *22*, 15–36.

Boekaerts, M., Pintrich, P. R., & Zeidner, M. (Eds.). (2000). *Handbook of self-regulation*. San Diego, CA: Academic Press.

Borkowski, J. G., & Muthukrishna, N. (1992). Moving metacognition into the classroom: "Working models" and effective strategy teaching. In Pressley, M., Harris, K. R., & Guthrie, J. T. (Eds.), *Promoting Academic Competence and Literacy in School* (pp. 477–501). Toronto, Canada: Academic Press.

Boud, D., & Keogh, R. (1985). Promoting reflection in learning: A model. In D. Boud, R. Keogh., & D. Walker (Eds.), *Reflection: Turning Experience into Learning,* (pp. 18-40). London, UK: Kogan.

Bracken, C. C., & Lombard, M. (2004). Social presence and children: Praise, intrinsic motivation, and learning with computers. *The Journal of Communication*, *54*, 22–37. doi:10.1111/j.1460-2466.2004.tb02611.x

Bransford, J., Brown, A. L., & Cocking, R. R. (Eds.). (2000). *How people learn: Brain, mind, experience, and school*. Washington, DC: Academic Press.

Braten, I., & Olaussen, B. S. (2005). Profiling individual differences in student motivation: A longitudinal cluster-analytic study in different academic contexts. *Contemporary Educational Psychology*, *30*, 359–396. doi:10.1016/j.cedpsych.2005.01.003

Bridges, F. A., & Cicchetti, D. (1982). Mothers' ratings of the temperament characteristics of Down syndrome infants. *Developmental Psychology*, *18*, 238–244. doi:10.1037/0012-1649.18.2.238

Brodwin, M. G., Star, T., & Cardoso, E. (2004). Computer assistive technology for people who have disabilities: Computer adaptations and modifications. *Journal of Rehabilitation*, *70*, 28–33.

Bronson, M. B. (2000a). *Self-regulation in early childhood: Nature and nurture*. New York, NY: Guilford.

Bronson, M. B. (2000b). Recognizing and supporting the development of self-regulation in young children. *Young Children*, *55*, 32–37.

Brown, A. L. (1978). Knowing when, where and how to remember: A problem of metacognition. In Glaser, R. (Ed.), *Advances in Instructional Psychology* (pp. 165–177). Hillsdale, NJ: Erlbaum.

Brown, A. L. (1987). Metacognition, executive control, self-regulation, and other more mysterious mechanisms. In Weinert, F. E., & Kluwe, R. H. (Eds.), *Metacognition, Motivation, and Understanding* (pp. 65–116). Hillsdale, NJ: Erlbaum.

Burgess, N., & Hitch, G. L. (1992). Towards a network model of the articulatory loop. *Journal of Memory and Language*, *31*, 429–460. doi:10.1016/0749-596X(92)90022-P

Butler, D. L. (1998). Metacognition and learning disabilities. In Wong, B. Y. L. (Ed.), *Learning about Learning Disabilities* (2nd ed., pp. 277–307). Toronto, Canada: Academic Press.

Butler, D. L. (2002). Qualitative approaches to investigating self-regulated learning: Contributions and challenges. *Educational Psychologist, 37*, 59–63.

Butler, D. L., & Cartier, S. C. (2005). *Multiple complementary methods for understanding self-regulated learning as situated in context.* Paper presented at the Annual Meeting of the American Educational Research Association. Montreal, Canada.

Butler, D. L., & Winne, P. H. (1995). Feedback and self-regulated learning: A theoretical synthesis. *Review of Educational Research, 65*, 245–281.

Byrne, D. (1971). *The attraction paradigm.* New York, NY: Academic Press.

Calero, M. D., García-Martín, M. B., Jiménez, M. I., Kazén, M., & Araque, A. (2007). Self-regulation advantage for high-IQ children: Findings from a research study. *Learning and Individual Differences, 17*(4). doi:10.1016/j.lindif.2007.03.012

Cameron, J., & Pierce, W. D. (1994). Reinforcement, reward, and intrinsic motivation: A meta-analysis. *Review of Educational Research, 64*, 363–423.

Campbell, M. C., & Kirmani, A. (2000). Consumers' use of persuasion knowledge: The effects of accessibility and cognitive capacity on perceptions of an influence agent. *The Journal of Consumer Research, 27*, 69–83. doi:10.1086/314309

Carnegie, D. (1964). *How to win friends and influence people.* New York, NY: Simon & Schuster.

Carr, M. (1998). Metacognition in mathematics from a constructivist perspective. In Hacker, D., Dunlosky, J., & Graesser, A. (Eds.), *Metacognition in Educational Theory and Practice* (pp. 69–81). New York, NY: Academic Press.

Carroll, D. J., Apperly, I. A., & Riggs, K. J. (2007). Choosing between two objects reduces 3-year-olds' errors on a reverse-contingency test of executive function. *Journal of Experimental Child Psychology, 98*, 184–192. doi:10.1016/j.jecp.2007.08.001

Carver, C. S., & Scheier, M. F. (1981). *Attention and self-regulation: A control-theory approach to human behavior.* New York, NY: Springer-Verlag.

Carver, C. S., & Scheier, M. F. (1990). Principles of self-regulation: Action and emotion. In Higgins, E. T., & Sorrentino, R. M. (Eds.), *Handbook of Motivation and Cognition: Foundations of Social Behavior* (*Vol. 2*, pp. 3–52). New York, NY: Guilford.

Catano, V. M. (1975). Relation of improved performance through verbal praise to source of praise. *Perceptual and Motor Skills, 41*, 71–74. doi:10.2466/pms.1975.41.1.71

Chang, E. C. (2003). A critical appraisal and extension of hope theory in middle-aged men and women: Is it important to distinguish agency and pathways components? *Journal of Social and Clinical Psychology, 22*, 121–143. doi:10.1521/jscp.22.2.121.22876

Chang, E. C., & D'Zurilla, T. J. (1996). Relations between problem orientation and optimism, pessimism, and trait affectivity: A construct validation study. *Behaviour Research and Therapy, 34*, 185–194. doi:10.1016/0005-7967(95)00046-1

Chang, E. C., D'Zurilla, T. J., & Sanna, L. J. (2004). Introduction: Social problem solving for the real world. In Chang, E. C., D'Zurilla, T. J., & Sanna, L. J. (Eds.), *Social Problem Solving: Theory, Research, and Training* (pp. 3–7). Washington, DC: American Psychological Association. doi:10.1037/10805-000

Chang, E. C., Downey, C. A., & Salata, J. L. (2004). Social problem solving and positive psychological functioning: Looking at the positive side of problem solving. In Chang, E. C., D'Zurilla, T. J., & Sanna, L. J. (Eds.), *Social Problem Solving: Theory, Research, and Training* (pp. 99–116). Washington, DC: American Psychological Association. doi:10.1037/10805-006

Chang, E. C., Sanna, L. J., Riley, M. M., Thornburg, A. T., Zumberg, K. M., & Edwards, M. C. (2007). Relations between problem-solving styles and psychological adjustment in young adults: Is stress a mediating variable? *Personality and Individual Differences, 42*, 135–144. doi:10.1016/j.paid.2006.06.011

Chang, F., & Burns, B. (2005). Attention in preschoolers: Associations with effortful control and motivation. *Child Development, 76*, 247–263. doi:10.1111/j.1467-8624.2005.00842.x

Cherry, K. E., Matson, J. L., & Palawskyj, T. R. (1997). Psychopathology in older adults with severe and profound mental retardation. *American Journal of Mental Retardation, 101*, 445–458.

Cheung, P. P. P., & Siu, A. M. H. (2009). A comparison of patterns of sensory processing in children with and without developmental disabilities. *Research in Developmental Disabilities, 30*, 1468–1480. doi:10.1016/j.ridd.2009.07.009

Chiang, H. M. (2009). Differences between spontaneous and elicited expressive communication in children with autism. *Research in Autism Spectrum Disorders, 3*, 214–222. doi:10.1016/j.rasd.2008.06.002

Childs, C. P., & Greenfield, P. M. (1980). Informal modes of learning and teaching: The case of Zinacanteco weaving. In Warrenk, N. (Ed.), *Studies in Cross-Cultural Psychology* (*Vol. 2*, pp. 269–316). London, UK: Academic Press.

Clarke-Stewart, K. A., Allhusen, V. D., McDowell, D. J., Thelen, L., & Call, J. D. (2003). Identifying psychological problems in young children: How do mothers compare with child psychiatrists? *Applied Developmental Psychology, 23*, 589–624. doi:10.1016/S0193-3973(03)00006-6

Cleary, T. J., & Zimmerman, B. J. (2004). Self-regulation empowerment program: A school-based program to enhance self-regulation and self-motivation cycles of student learning. *Psychology in the Schools, 41*, 143–168. doi:10.1002/pits.10177

Collies, B., DeBoer, W., & Slotman, K. (2001). Feedback for web-based assignments. *Journal of Computer Assisted Learning, 17*, 306–313. doi:10.1046/j.0266-4909.2001.00185.x

Cook, A. M., & Hussey, S. M. (2002). *Assistive technologies: Principles and practice*. St. Louis, MO: Mosby.

Copeland, A. P. (1979). Types of private speech produced by hyperactive and nonhyperactive boys. *Journal of Abnormal Child Psychology, 7*, 169–177. doi:10.1007/BF00918897

Corkum, P., Humphries, K., Mullane, J. C., & Theriault, F. (2008). Private speech in children with ADHD and their typically developing peers during problem-solving and inhibition tasks. *Contemporary Educational Psychology, 33*, 97–115. doi:10.1016/j.cedpsych.2006.12.003

Corno, L. (2001). Volitional aspects of self-regulated learning. In Zimmerman, B. J., & Schunk, D. H. (Eds.), *Self-Regulated Learning and Academic Achievement: Theoretical Perspectives* (2nd ed., pp. 191–226). Mahwah, NJ: Erlbaum.

Cowan, N., & Kail, R. (1996). Covert processes and their development in STM. In Gathercole, S. E. (Ed.), *Models of Short-Term Memory* (pp. 29–50). Hove, UK: Psychology Press.

Cox, M. T. (2005). Metacognition in computation: A selected research review. *Artificial Intelligence, 169*, 104–141. doi:10.1016/j.artint.2005.10.009

Cross, D. R., & Paris, S. G. (1988). Developmental and instructional analysis of children's metacognition and reading comprehension. *Journal of Educational Psychology, 80*, 131–142. doi:10.1037/0022-0663.80.2.131

D'Zurilla, T. J. (1986). *Problem-solving therapy: A social competence approach to clinical intervention*. New York, NY: Springer.

D'Zurilla, T. J., & Maydeu-Olivares, A. (1995). Conceptual and methodological issues in social problem-solving assessment. *Behavior Therapy, 26*, 409–432. doi:10.1016/S0005-7894(05)80091-7

D'Zurilla, T. J., Nezu, A. M., & Maydeu-Olivares, A. (2004). Social problem solving: Theory and assessment. In Chang, E. C., D'Zurilla, T. J., & Sanna, L. J. (Eds.), *Social Problem Solving: Theory, Research, and Training* (pp. 11–27). Washington, DC: American Psychological Association. doi:10.1037/10805-001

Da Fonseca, D., Santos, A., Bastard-Rosset, D., Rodan, C., Poinso, F., & Deruelle, C. (2009). Can children with autistic spectrum disorders extract emotions out of contextual cues? *Research in Autism Spectrum Disorders, 3*, 50–56. doi:10.1016/j.rasd.2008.04.001

Damon, W. (1981). *The social world of the child*. San Francisco, CA: Jossey-Bass.

Darling, S., Sala, S., Gray, C., & Trivelli, C. (1998). Putative functions of the prefrontal cortex. In Mazzoni, G., & Nelson, T. (Eds.), *Metacognition and Cognitive Neuropsychology* (pp. 42–69). Mahwah, NJ: Erlbaum.

Daugherty, M., White, C., & Manning, B. (1994). Relationships among private speech and creativity measurements of young children. *Gifted Child Quarterly, 38*, 21–26. doi:10.1177/001698629403800103

David, P., Lu, T., & Cai, L. (2002). *Computers as social actors: Testing the fairness of man and machine*. Paper presented to the Fifth Annual International Workshop, Presence 2002, Universidade Fernando Pessoa. Porto, Portugal.

de Geurrero, M. C. M. (2004). Early stages of L2 inner speech development: What verbal reports suggest. *International Journal of Applied Linguistics, 14*, 90–112. doi:10.1111/j.1473-4192.2004.00055.x

de Guerrero, M. C. M. (1994). Form and functions of inner speech in adult second language learning. In Lantolf, J. P., & Appel, G. (Eds.), *Vygotskian Approaches to Second Language Research* (pp. 83–115). Upper Saddle River, NJ: Ablex Pub.

de Guerrero, M. C. M. (1999). Inner speech as mental rehearsal: The case of advanced L2 learners. *Issues in Applied Linguistics, 10*, 27–55.

De La Ossa, J. L., & Gauvain, M. (2001). Joint attention by mothers and children while using plans. *International Journal of Behavioral Development, 25*, 176–183. doi:10.1080/01650250042000168

Deci, E. L., & Ryan, R. M. (1985). *Intrinsic motivation and self-determination in human behavior*. New York, NY: Plenum Press.

Deniz, C. B. (2004). Early childhood teachers' beliefs about, and self-reported practices toward, children's private speech. *Dissertation Abstracts International. A, The Humanities and Social Sciences, 64*(9-A), 3185.

Denzin, N. K. (1978). *The research act: A theoretical introduction to socio-logical methods.* New York, NY: McGraw-Hill.

Desoete, A., Roeyers, H., & Buysse, A. (2001). Metacognition and mathematical problem solving in grade 3. *Journal of Learning Disabilities, 34*, 435–449. doi:10.1177/002221940103400505

Dev, P. C. (1997). Intrinsic motivation and academic achievement: What does their relationship imply for the classroom teacher? *Remedial and Special Education, 18*, 12–19. doi:10.1177/074193259701800104

DeVries, R. (2000). Vygotsky, Piaget, and education: A reciprocal assimilation of theories and educational practices. *New Ideas in Psychology, 18*, 187–213. doi:10.1016/S0732-118X(00)00008-8

DeVries, R., & Zan, B. (1992). *Social processes in development: A constructivist view of Piaget, Vygotsky, and education.* Paper presented at the annual meeting of the Jean Piaget Society. Montreal, Canada.

Diamond, K. E. (1993). The role of parents' observations and concerns in screening for developmental delays in young children. *Topics in Early Childhood Special Education, 13*, 68–81. doi:10.1177/027112149301300108

Diaz, R. M., & Berk, L. E. (Eds.). (1992). *Private speech: From social interaction to self-regulation.* Hillsdale, NJ: Erlbaum.

Diaz, R. M., & Berk, L. E. (1995). A Vygotskian critique of self-instructional training. *Development and Psychopathology, 7*, 369–392. doi:10.1017/S0954579400006568

Diaz, R. M., Winsler, A., Atencio, D. J., & Harbers, K. (1992). Mediation of self-regulation through the use of private speech. *International Journal of Cognitive Education and Mediated Learning, 2*, 1–13.

Dichtelmiller, M., Meisels, S. J., Plunkett, J. W., Bozynski, M. E. A., Claflin, C., & Mangelsdorf, S. C. (1992). The relationship of parental knowledge to the development of extremely low birth weight infants. *Journal of Early Intervention, 16*, 210–220. doi:10.1177/105381519201600302

Dick, W., Carey, L., & Carey, J. O. (2001). *The systematic design of instruction.* New York, NY: Addison, Wesley, Longman.

Dixon, W. A., Heppner, P. P., & Anderson, W. P. (1991). Problem-solving appraisal, stress, hopelessness, and suicide ideation in a college population. *Journal of Counseling Psychology, 38*, 51–56. doi:10.1037/0022-0167.38.1.51

Duncan, D., Matson, J. L., Bamburg, J. W., Cherry, K. E., & Backley, T. (1999). The relationship of self-injurious behavior and aggression to social skills in persons with severe and profound learning disability. *Research in Developmental Disabilities, 20*, 441–448. doi:10.1016/S0891-4222(99)00024-4

Duncan, R. M., & Pratt, M. W. (1997). Microgenetic change in the quantity and quality of preschoolers' private speech. *International Journal of Behavioral Development, 20*, 367–383. doi:10.1080/016502597385388

Duncana, R. M., & Cheyne, J. A. (2002). Private speech in young adults task difficulty, self-regulation, and psychological predication. *Cognitive Development, 16*, 889–906.

Ehrich, J. F. (2006). Vygotskian inner speech and the reading process. *Australian Journal of Educational & Developmental Psychology, 6*, 12–25.

Ellis-Weismer, S. E., Tomblin, J. B., Zhang, X., Buckwalter, P., Chynoweth, J. G., & Jones, M. (2000). Nonword repetition performance in school-age children with and without language impairment. *Journal of Speech, Language, and Hearing Research: JSLHR, 43*, 865–878.

Embregts, P. J. C. M., Didden, R., Schreuder, C., Huitink, C., & van Nieuwenhuijzen, M. (2009). Aggressive behavior in individuals with moderate to borderline intellectual disabilities who live in a residential facility: An evaluation of functional variables. *Research in Developmental Disabilities, 30*, 682–688. doi:10.1016/j.ridd.2008.04.007

Entwistle, N. (1988). Motivational factors in student's approaches to learning. In Schmeck, R. R. (Ed.), *Learning Strategies and Learning Styles* (pp. 21–51). New York, NY: Plenum.

Entwistle, N. (2001). *Scoring key for the approaches and study skills inventory for students (ASSIST)*. Unpublished paper. Edinburgh, UK: University of Edinburgh.

Ericsson, K. A., & Simon, H. A. (1993). *Protocol analysis: Verbal reports as data* (2nd ed.). Cambridge, MA: MIT Press.

Esbensen, B. M., Taylor, M., & Stoess, C. (1997). Children's behavioral understanding of knowledge acquisition. *Cognitive Development, 12*, 53–84. doi:10.1016/S0885-2014(97)90030-7

Faber, A., & Mazlish, E. (1995). Praise that doesn't demean, criticism that doesn't wound. *American Educator, 19*, 33–38.

Farmer, C. A., & Aman, M. G. (2009). Development of the children's scale of hostility and aggression: Reactive/proactive (C-SHARP). *Research in Developmental Disabilities, 30*, 1155–1167. doi:10.1016/j.ridd.2009.03.001

Farson, R. E. (1963). Praise reappraised. *Harvard Business Review, 41*, 61–66.

Fazio, B. B. (1996). Serial memory in children with specific language impairment: Examining specific content areas for assessment and intervention. *Topics in Language Disorders, 17*, 58–71. doi:10.1097/00011363-199611000-00007

Fennell, C. T., & Werker, J. F. (2004). *Applying speech perception to word learning at 14 months: Effects of word knowledge and familiarity*. Paper presented at the 28th Annual Boston University Conference on Language Development. Boston, MA.

Fernadez-Duque, D., Baird, J., & Posner, M. (2000). Awareness and metacognition. *Consciousness and Cognition, 9*, 324–326. doi:10.1006/ccog.2000.0449

Fernyhough, C., & Fradley, E. (2005). Private speech on an executive task: Relations with task difficulty and task performance. *Cognitive Development, 20*, 103–120. doi:10.1016/j.cogdev.2004.11.002

Fidler, D. J., Most, D. E., Booth-LaForce, C., & Kelly, J. F. (2006). Temperament and behaviour problems in young children with Down syndrome at 12, 30, and 45 months. *Down Syndrome, Research & Practice, 10*, 23–29.

Fischer, M., Rolf, J. E., Hasazi, H. E., & Cummings, I. (1984). Follow-up of a preschool epidemiological sample: Cross-age continuities and predictions of later adjustment with internalizing and externalizing dimensions of behavior. *Child Development, 55*, 137–150. doi:10.2307/1129840

Fitts, P. M. (1962). Factors in complex skill training. In Glaser, R. (Ed.), *Training Research and Education* (pp. 177–197). Pittsburgh, PA: University of Pittsburgh Press.

Flavell, J. H. (1966). Le langage privé. *Bulletin de Psychologie, 19*, 698–701.

Flavell, J. H. (1976). Metacognitive aspects of problem solving. In Resnick, L. B. (Ed.), *The Nature of Intelligence* (pp. 231–236). Hillsdale, NJ: Erlbaum.

Flavell, J. H. (1977). *Cognitive development*. Englewood Cliffs, NJ: Prentice-Hall.

Flavell, J. H. (1979). Metacognition and cognitive monitoring—A new era of cognitive-developmental inquiry. *The American Psychologist, 34*, 906–911. doi:10.1037/0003-066X.34.10.906

Flavell, J. H. (1987). Speculations about the nature and development of metacognition. In Weinert, F. E., & Kluwe, R. H. (Eds.), *Metacognition, Motivation, and Understanding* (pp. 21–29). Hillsdale, NJ: Erlbaum.

Flavell, J. H., Beach, D. R., & Chinsky, J. M. (1996). Spontaneous verbal rehearsal in a memory task as a function of age. *Child Development, 37*, 283–299. doi:10.2307/1126804

Fogg, B. J. (2002). *Persuasive technology: Using computers to change what we think and do*. San Francisco, CA: Kaufmann.

Francis, H. (1982). *Learning to read*. London, UK: Allen & Unwin.

Frauenglass, M. H., & Diaz, R. M. (1985). Self-regulatory functions of children's private speech: A critical analysis of recent challenges to Vygotsky's theory. *Developmental Psychology, 21*, 357–364. doi:10.1037/0012-1649.21.2.357

Frawley, W., & Lantolf, J. P. (1985). Second language discourse: A Vygotskian perspective. *Applied Linguistics, 6*, 19–44. doi:10.1093/applin/6.1.19

Frawley, W., & Lantolf, J. P. (1986). Private speech and self-regulation: A commentary on Frauenglass and Diaz. *Developmental Psychology, 22*, 706–708. doi:10.1037/0012-1649.22.5.706

Fuson, K. C. (1979). The development of self-regulating aspects of speech: A review. In Zivin, G. (Ed.), *The Development of Self-Regulation through Private Speech* (pp. 135–217). New York, NY: Wiley.

Gardner, W., & Rogoff, B. (1990). Children's deliberateness of planning according to task circumstances. *Developmental Psychology, 26*, 480–487. doi:10.1037/0012-1649.26.3.480

Gartstein, M. A., Marmion, J., & Swanson, H. L. (2006). Infant temperament: An evaluation of children with Down syndrome. *Journal of Reproductive and Infant Psychology, 24*, 31–41. doi:10.1080/02646830500475237

Gaskill, M. N., & Díaz, R. M. (1991). The relation between private speech and cognitive performance. *Infancia y Aprendizaje, 53*, 45–58.

Gathercole, S. E., Willis, C. S., Baddeley, A. D., & Emslie, H. (1994). The children's test of nonword repetition: A test of phonological working memory. *Memory (Hove, England), 2*, 103–127. doi:10.1080/09658219408258940

Gillam, R. B., Cowan, N., & Day, L. S. (1995). Sequential memory in children with and without language impairment. *Journal of Speech and Hearing Research, 38*, 393–402.

Gillespie, L. G., & Seibel, N. L. (2006). Self-regulation: A cornerstone of early childhood development. *Journal of the National Association for Education of Young Children, 12*, 142–161.

Gilmore, L., Cuskelly, M., & Hayes, A. (2003). Self-regulatory behaviors in children with Down syndrome and typically developing children measured using the Goodman lock box. *Research in Developmental Disabilities, 24*, 95–108. doi:10.1016/S0891-4222(03)00012-X

Girbau, D. (2002). A sequential analysis of private and social speech in children's dyadic communication. *The Spanish Journal of Psychology, 52,* 110–118.

Glascoe, F. P. (1994). It's not what it seems: The relationship between parents' concerns and children with global delays. *Clinical Pediatrics, 33,* 292–296. doi:10.1177/000992289403300507

Glascoe, F. P., & MacLean, W. E. (1990). How parents appraise their child's development. *Family Relations, 39,* 280–283. doi:10.2307/584872

Goodman, S. H. (1981). The integration of verbal and motor behavior in preschool children. *Child Development, 52,* 280–289. doi:10.2307/1129241

Gopnik, A., & Graf, P. (1988). Knowing how you know: Young children's ability to identify and remember the sources of their beliefs. *Child Development, 59,* 1366–1371. doi:10.2307/1130499

Gottfried, A. E., Fleming, J., & Gottfried, A. W. (1994). Role of parental motivational practices in children's academic intrinsic motivation and achievement. *Journal of Educational Psychology, 86,* 104–113. doi:10.1037/0022-0663.86.1.104

Goudena, P. P. (1992). The problem of abbreviation and internalization of private speech. In Diaz, R. M., & Berk, L. E. (Eds.), *Private Speech: From Social Interaction to Self-Regulation* (pp. 215–224). Hillsdale, NJ: Erlbaum.

Gunawardena, C., & Zittle, F. (1997). Social presence as a predictor of satisfaction within a computer mediated conferencing environment. *American Journal of Distance Education, 11,* 8–26. doi:10.1080/08923649709526970

Guterman, E. (2003). Integrating written metacognitive awareness guidance as a 'psychological tool' to improve student performance. *Learning and Instruction, 13,* 633–651. doi:10.1016/S0959-4752(02)00070-1

Hadwin, A., & Winne, P. (2001). CoNoteS2: A software tool for promoting self-regulation. *Educational Research and Evaluation, 7,* 313–334. doi:10.1076/edre.7.2.313.3868

Hale, S., Bronik, M. D., & Fry, A. F. (1997). Verbal and spatial working memory in school-age children: Developmental differences in susceptibility to interference. *Developmental Psychology, 33,* 361–371. doi:10.1037/0012-1649.33.2.364

Hale, S., Myerson, J., Rhee, S. H., Weiss, C. S., & Abrams, R. A. (1996). Selective interference with the maintenance of location information in working memory. *Neuropsychology, 10,* 228–240. doi:10.1037/0894-4105.10.2.228

Haste, H. (1987). Growing into rules. In Bruner, J., & Haste, H. (Eds.), *Making Sense* (pp. 163–195). New York, NY: Metheun.

Henderlong, J. (2000). *Beneficial and detrimental effects of praise on children's motivation: Performance versus person feedback.* (Unpublished Doctoral Dissertation). Stanford University. Palo Alto, CA.

Hennessey, G. (1999). *Probing the dimensions of metacognition: Implications for conceptual change teaching-learning.* Paper presented at annual meeting of the national association for research in science teaching. San Francisco, CA.

Heppner, P. P. (1988). *The problem-solving inventory.* Palo Alto, CA: Consulting Psychologist Press.

Heppner, P. P., & Peterson, C. H. (1982). The development and implications of a personal problem solving inventory. *Journal of Counseling Psychology, 29,* 580–590. doi:10.1037/0022-0167.29.6.580

Higgins, E. T. (1997). Beyond pleasure and pain. *The American Psychologist, 52,* 1280–1300. doi:10.1037/0003-066X.52.12.1280

Hinshaw, S. P. (1994). Conduct disorder in childhood: Conceptualizing, diagnosis, comorbidity, and risk status for antisocial functioning in adulthood. In Fowles, D., Sutker, P., & Goodman, S. (Eds.), *Progress in Experimental Personality and Psychopathology Research: Special Focus on Psychopathology and Antisocial Personality, a Developmental Perspective* (pp. 3–44). New York, NY: Springer.

Hoffman, L. M., & Gillam, R. B. (2004). Verbal and spatial information processing constraints in children with specific language impairment. *Journal of Speech, Language, and Hearing Research: JSLHR, 47*, 114–125. doi:10.1044/1092-4388(2004/011)

Holding, D. H. (1965). *Principles of training.* Oxford, UK: Pergamon Press.

Hudson, J. A., Shapiro, L. R., & Sosa, B. B. (1995). Planning in the real world: Preschool children's scripts and plans for familiar events. *Child Development, 66*, 984–998. doi:10.2307/1131793

Isaki, E., & Plante, E. (1997). Short-term and working memory differences in language/learning disabled and normal adults. *Journal of Communication Disorders, 30*, 327–437. doi:10.1016/S0021-9924(96)00111-6

Jääskeläinen, R. (1999). *Tapping the process: An explorative study of the cognitive and affective factors involved in translating.* Joensuu, Finland: University of Joensuu.

Jacobson, M., & Archodidou, A. (2000). The design of hypermedia tools for learning: Fostering conceptual change and transfer of complex scientific knowledge. *Journal of the Learning Sciences, 9*, 149–199. doi:10.1207/s15327809jls0902_2

John-Hattie, J., & Timperley, H. (2007). The power of feedback. *Review of Educational Research, 77*(1), 81–112. doi:10.3102/003465430298487

Jonassen, D. (1996). *Computers as mind tools for schools.* Columbus, OH: Merrill.

Jones, M. G., Farquhar, J. D., & Surry, D. W. (1995). Using metacognitive theories to design user interfaces for computer-based learning. *Educational Technology, 35*, 12–22.

Just, M., & Carpenter, P. (1992). A capacity theory of comprehension: Individual differences in working memory. *Psychological Review, 99*, 122–149. doi:10.1037/0033-295X.99.1.122

Kamii, C., & DeVries, R. (1980). *Group games in early education: Implications of Piaget's theory.* Washington, DC: National Association for the Education of Young Children.

Katz, I., Assor, A., Kanat-Maymon, Y., & Bereby-Meyer, Y. (2006). Interest as a motivational resource: Feedback and gender matter, but interest makes the difference. *Social Psychology of Education, 9*, 27–42. doi:10.1007/s11218-005-2863-7

Kau, A. S. M., Reider, E. E., Payne, L., Meyer, W. A., & Freund, L. (2000). Early behavior signs of psychiatric phenotypes in fragile X syndrome. *American Journal of Mental Retardation, 105*, 286–299. doi:10.1352/0895-8017(2000)105<0286:EBSOPP>2.0.CO;2

Kay, J., Li, L., & Fekete, A. (2007). *Learner reflection in student self-assessment.* Paper presented at the Ninth Australasian Computing Education Conference (ACE 2007). Ballarat, Australia.

Kazdin, A. E. (1993). Treatment of conduct disorder: Progress and directions in psychotherapy research. *Development and Psychopathology, 5*, 277–310. doi:10.1017/S0954579400004399

Keenan, K., Shaw, D. S., Delliquadri, E., Giovannelli, J., & Walsh, B. (1998). Evidence for the continuity of early problem behaviors: Application of a developmental model. *Journal of Abnormal Child Psychology, 26*, 441–454. doi:10.1023/A:1022647717926

Keenan, K., & Wakschlag, L. S. (2000). More than the terrible twos: The nature and severity of behavior problems in clinic-referred preschool children. *Journal of Abnormal Child Psychology, 28,* 33–46. doi:10.1023/A:1005118000977

Klein-Tasman, B. P., & Mervis, C. B. (2003). Distinctive personality characteristics of 8-, 9-, and 10-year-olds with Williams syndrome. *Developmental Neuropsychology, 23,* 269–290.

Kluger, A. N., & DeNisi, A. (1996). The effects of feedback interventions on performance: A historical review, a meta-analysis, and a preliminary feedback intervention theory. *Psychological Bulletin, 119,* 254–284. doi:10.1037/0033-2909.119.2.254

Koenemann-Belliveau, J., Carroll, J. M., Rosson, M. B., & Singley, M. K. (1994). *Comparative usability evaluation: Critical incidents and critical threads, in human factors in computing systems.* New York, NY: ACM Press.

Kohlberg, L., Yaeger, J., & Hjertholm, E. (1968). Private speech: Four studies and a review of theories. *Child Development, 39,* 691–736. doi:10.2307/1126979

Konstantareas, M. M., & Stewart, K. (2006). Affect regulation and temperament in children with autism spectrum disorder. *Journal of Autism and Developmental Disorders, 36,* 143–154. doi:10.1007/s10803-005-0051-4

Kopp, C. B. (1982). Antecedents of self-regulation: A developmental perspective. *Developmental Psychology, 18,* 199–214. doi:10.1037/0012-1649.18.2.199

Kouijzer, M. E. J., de Moor, J. M. H., Gerrits, B. J. L., Congedo, M., & van Schie, H. T. (2009). Neurofeedback improves executive functioning in children with autism spectrum disorders. *Research in Autism Spectrum Disorders, 3,* 145–162. doi:10.1016/j.rasd.2008.05.001

Krafft, K. C., & Berk, L. E. (1998). Private speech in two preschools: Significance of open-ended activities and make-believe play for verbal self-regulation. *Early Childhood Research Quarterly, 13,* 637–658. doi:10.1016/S0885-2006(99)80065-9

Krahmer, E., & Ummelen, N. (2004). *Thinking about thinking aloud: A comparison of two verbal protocols for usability testing.* Tilburg, The Netherlands: Tilburg University.

Kramarski, B., & Gutman, M. (2006). How can self-regulated learning be supported in mathematical e-learning environments? *Journal of Computer Assisted Learning, 22,* 24–33. doi:10.1111/j.1365-2729.2006.00157.x

Kramarski, B., & Mevarech, Z. R. (2003). Enhancing mathematical reasoning in the classroom: Effects of cooperative learning and metacognitive training. *American Educational Research Journal, 40,* 281–310. doi:10.3102/00028312040001281

Kramarski, B., & Mizrachi, N. (2006). Online discussion and self-regulated learning: Effects of four instructional methods on mathematical literacy. *The Journal of Educational Research, 99*(4), 218–230. doi:10.3200/JOER.99.4.218-231

Kuhl, J. (2000). The volitional basis of personality systems interaction theory: Applications in learning and treatment contexts. *International Journal of Educational Research, 33,* 665–703. doi:10.1016/S0883-0355(00)00045-8

Kuhl, J. (2001). *Motivation und persönlichkeit: Interaktionen psychischer systeme.* Göttingen, Germany: Hogrefe.

Lakes, K. D., & Hoyt, W. R. (2004). Promoting self-regulation through school-based martial arts training. *Applied Developmental Psychology, 25,* 283–302. doi:10.1016/j.appdev.2004.04.002

Lee, E.-J. (1999). The effects of five-year-old preschoolers' use of private speech on performance and attention for two kinds of problems-solving tasks. *Dissertation Abstracts International. A, The Humanities and Social Sciences, 60*(6-A), 1999.

Lee, E.-J. (2003). Effects of gender of the computer on informational social influence: The moderating role of task type. *International Journal of Human-Computer Studies, 58,* 347–362. doi:10.1016/S1071-5819(03)00009-0

Leontiev, A. A. (1978). Some new trends in Soviet psycholinguistics. In Wertsch, J. V. (Ed.), *Recent Trends in Soviet Psycholinguistics* (pp. 10–20). White Plains, NY: Sharpe.

Lepper, M. R., Greene, D., & Nisbett, R. E. (1973). Undermining children's intrinsic motivation with extrinsic reward: A test of the "overjustification" hypothesis. *Journal of Personality and Social Psychology, 28,* 129–137. doi:10.1037/h0035519

Lepper, M. R., & Woolverton, M. (2002). The wisdom of practice: Lessons learned from the study of highly effective tutors. In Aronson, J. (Ed.), *Improving Academic Achievement: Contributions of Social Psychology* (pp. 135–158). Orlando, FL: Academic Press. doi:10.1016/B978-012064455-1/50010-5

Lepper, M. R., Woolverton, M., Mumme, D. L., & Gurtner, J. (1993). Motivational techniques of expert human tutors: Lessons for the design of computer-based tutors. In Lajoie, S. P., & Derry, S. J. (Eds.), *Computers as Cognitive Tools* (pp. 75–105). Hillsdale, NJ: Erlbaum.

Lesley, M. (2007). Social problem solving training for African Americans: Effects on dietary problem solving skill and DASH diet-related behavior change. *Patient Education and Counseling, 65,* 137–146. doi:10.1016/j.pec.2006.07.001

Lester, J., Converse, S., Kahler, S., Barlow, S., Stone, B., & Bhogal, R. (1997). The persona effect: Affective impact of animated pedagogical agents. In *Proceedings of CHI 1997,* (pp. 359-366). ACM Press.

LeVine, R. A. (1989). Cultural environments in child development. In Damon, W. (Ed.), *Child Development Today and Tomorrow* (pp. 52–68). San Francisco, CA: Jossey-Bass.

Liebermann, D., Giesbrecht, G. F., & Muller, U. (2007). Cognitive and emotional aspects of self-regulation in preschoolers. *Cognitive Development, 22,* 511–529. doi:10.1016/j.cogdev.2007.08.005

Ling-Yi, L., Cherng, R., Lee, I., Chen, Y., Yang, H., & Chen, Y. (2011). The agreement of caregivers' initial identification of children's developmental problems with the professional assessment in Taiwan. *Research in Developmental Disabilities, 32,* 1714–1721. doi:10.1016/j.ridd.2011.02.026

Loper, A. B. (1980). Metacognitive development: Implications for cognitive training. *Exceptional Education Quarterly, 1,* 1–8.

Lovaas, O. I. (1961). Interaction between verbal and nonverbal behavior. *Child Development, 32,* 329–336.

Lovaas, O. I. (1964). Cue properties of words: The control of operant responding by rate and content of verbal operants. *Child Development, 35,* 245–256.

LoVullo, S. V., & Matson, J. L. (2009). Comorbid psychopathology in adults with autism spectrum disorders and intellectual disabilities. *Research in Developmental Disabilities, 30,* 1288–1296. doi:10.1016/j.ridd.2009.05.004

Lubeck, S. (1996). Deconstructing child development knowledge and teacher preparation. *Early Childhood Research Quarterly*, *11*, 147–167. doi:10.1016/S0885-2006(96)90003-4

Luria, A. R. (1959). The directive functions of speech in development and dissolution: Part 1: Development of the directive functions of speech in early childhood. *Word*, *15*, 341–352.

Luria, A. R. (1961). Chapter. In Tizard, J. (Ed.), *The Role of Speech in the Regulation of Normal and Abnormal Behavior* (pp. 163–197). New York, NY: Liveright.

Mackay, D. G. (1981). The problem of rehearsal or mental practice. *Journal of Motor Behavior*, *13*, 274–285.

MacNeil, B. M., Lopes, V. A., & Minnes, P. M. (2009). Anxiety in children and adolescents with autism spectrum disorders. *Research in Autism Spectrum Disorders*, *3*, 1–21. doi:10.1016/j.rasd.2008.06.001

Mainela-Arnold, E., & Evans, J. L. (2005). Beyond capacity limitations: Determinants of word recall performance on verbal working memory span tasks in children with SLI. *Journal of Speech, Language, and Hearing Research: JSLHR, 48*, 897–909. doi:10.1044/1092-4388(2005/062)

Martic, J. (2004). Self-regulated learning, social cognitive theory and agency. *Educational Psychologist*, *39*, 135–145. doi:10.1207/s15326985ep3902_4

Martin, N., & Saffran, E. M. (1997). Language and auditory-verbal short-term memory impairment: Evidence for common underlying processes. *Cognitive Neuropsychology*, *14*, 641–682. doi:10.1080/026432997381402

Martin, R. C., Lesch, M. F., & Bartha, M. C. (1999). Independence of input and output phonology in word processing and short-term memory. *Journal of Memory and Language*, *41*, 3–29. doi:10.1006/jmla.1999.2637

Marton, F., & Sa¨ljo¨, R. (1984). Approaches to learning. In Marton, F., Hounsell, D., & Entwistle, N. (Eds.), *The Experience of Learning* (pp. 36–55). Edinburgh, UK: Scottish Academic Press.

Marton, K., & Schwartz, R. G. (2003). Working memory capacity and language processes in children with specific language impairment. *Journal of Speech, Language, and Hearing Research: JSLHR, 46*, 1138–1153. doi:10.1044/1092-4388(2003/089)

Mathews, R., Buss, R., Stanley, W., Blanchard-Fields, F., Cho, J., & Druhan, B. (1989). Role of implicit and explicit processes in learning from examples: A synergistic effect. *Journal of Experimental Psychology. Learning, Memory, and Cognition*, *15*, 1083–1100. doi:10.1037/0278-7393.15.6.1083

Matson, J. L., & Shoemaker, M. (2009). Intellectual disability and its relationship to autism spectrum disorders. *Research in Developmental Disabilities*, *30*, 1107–1114. doi:10.1016/j.ridd.2009.06.003

Matson, J. L., Smiroldo, B. B., Hamilton, M., & Baglio, C. S. (1997). Do anxiety disorders exist in persons with severe and profound mental retardation? *Research in Developmental Disabilities*, *18*, 39–44. doi:10.1016/S0891-4222(96)00036-4

Matuga, J. M. (2003). Children's private speech during algorithmic and heuristic drawing tasks. *Contemporary Educational Psychology*, *28*, 552–572. doi:10.1016/S0361-476X(02)00061-9

Maynard, A. (2002). Cultural teaching: The development of teaching skills in Maya sibling interactions. *Child Development*, *73*, 969–982. doi:10.1111/1467-8624.00450

Mazzoni, G., & Nelson, T. (Eds.). (1998). *Metacognition and cognitive neuropsychology*. Mahwah, NJ: Erlbaum.

McCaslin, M., & Hickey, D. T. (2001). Educational psychology, social constructivism, and educational practice: A case of emergent identity. *Educational Psychologist, 36,* 133–140. doi:10.1207/S15326985EP3602_8

McClelland, M. M., Cameron, C. E., Connor, C. M., Farris, C. L., Jewkes, A. M., & Morrison, F. J. (2007). Links between behavioral regulation and preschoolers' 705 literacy, vocabulary, and math skills. *Developmental Psychology, 43,* 947–959. doi:10.1037/0012-1649.43.4.947

McCutchen, D., & Perfetti, C. (1982). The visual tongue-twister effect: Phonological activation in silent reading. *Journal of Verbal Learning and Verbal Behavior, 21,* 672–687. doi:10.1016/S0022-5371(82)90870-2

McKay, J. (1992). Building self-esteem in children. In McKay, M., & Fanning, P. (Eds.), *Self-Esteem* (2nd ed., pp. 239–271). Oakland, CA: New Harbinger.

McQuillan, J., & Rodrigo, V. (1995). A reading "din in the head": Evidence of involuntary mental rehearsal in second language readers. *Foreign Language Annals, 28,* 330–336. doi:10.1111/j.1944-9720.1995.tb00802.x

Meichenbaum, D., & Goodman, J. (1969a). Reflection-impulsivity and verbal control of motor behavior. *Child Development, 40,* 785–797.

Meichenbaum, D., & Goodman, J. (1969b). The developmental control of operant motor responding by verbal operants. *Journal of Experimental Child Psychology, 7,* 553–565. doi:10.1016/0022-0965(69)90016-2

Merriman, W. E., & Schuster, J. M. (1991). Young children's disambiguation of object name reference. *Child Development, 62,* 1288–1301. doi:10.2307/1130807

Metcalfe, J. (1994). A computational modeling approach to novelty monitoring, metacognition, and frontal lobe dysfunction. In Metcalfe, J., & Shimamura, A. (Eds.), *Metacognition: Knowing about Knowing* (pp. 211–263). Cambridge, MA: MIT Press.

Metcalfe, J., & Shimamura, A. (Eds.). (1994). *Metacognition: Knowing about knowing.* Cambridge, MA: MIT Press.

Mevarech, Z. R., & Kramarski, B. (1997). IMPROVE: A multidimensional method for teaching mathematics in heterogeneous classrooms. *American Educational Research Journal, 34,* 365–394.

Meyer, D. K., & Turner, J. C. (2002). Using instructional discourse analysis to study the scaffolding of student self-regulation. *Educational Psychologist, 37,* 5–13.

Montgomery, J. W. (2000a). Verbal working memory and sentence comprehension in children with specific language impairment. *Journal of Speech, Language, and Hearing Research: JSLHR, 43,* 293–308.

Montgomery, J. W. (2000b). Relation of working to off-line and real-time sentence processing in children with specific language impairment. *Applied Psycholinguistics, 21,* 117–148. doi:10.1017/S0142716400001065

Montgomery, J. W. (2003). Working memory and comprehension in children with specific language impairment: What we know so far. *Journal of Communication Disorders, 36,* 221–231. doi:10.1016/S0021-9924(03)00021-2

Montgomery, J. W. (2004). Sentence comprehension in children with specific language impairment: Effects of input rate and phonological working memory. *International Journal of Language & Communication Disorders, 39*(1), 115–133. doi:10.1080/13682820310001616985

Moon, Y., & Nass, C. (1996). How "real" are computer personalities? Psychological responses to personality types in human-computer interaction. *Communication Research, 23*, 651–674. doi:10.1177/009365096023006002

Mueller, C. M., & Dweck, C. S. (1998). Praise for intelligence can undermine children's motivation and performance. *Journal of Personality and Social Psychology, 75*, 33–52. doi:10.1037/0022-3514.75.1.33

Müller, U., Zelazo, P. D., Hood, S., Leone, T., & Rohrer, L. (2004). Interference control in a new rule use task: Age-related changes, labeling, and attention. *Child Development, 75*, 1594–1609. doi:10.1111/j.1467-8624.2004.00759.x

Munde, V. S., Vlaskamp, C., Ruijssenaars, A. J. J. M., & Nakken, H. (2009). Alertness in individuals with profound intellectual and multiple disabilities: A literature review. *Research in Developmental Disabilities, 30*, 462–480. doi:10.1016/j.ridd.2008.07.003

Muraven, M. (2010). Building self-control strength: Practicing self-control leads to improved self-control performance. *Journal of Experimental Social Psychology, 46*, 465–468. doi:10.1016/j.jesp.2009.12.011

Murphy, O., Healy, O., & Leader, G. (2009). Risk factors for challenging behaviors among 157 children with autism spectrum disorders in Ireland. *Research in Autism Spectrum Disorders, 3*, 474–482. doi:10.1016/j.rasd.2008.09.008

Nass, C., Fogg, B. J., & Moon, Y. (1996). Can computers be teammates? *International Journal of Human-Computer Studies, 45*, 669–678. doi:10.1006/ijhc.1996.0073

Nass, C., & Steuer, J. (1993). Voices, boxes, and sources of messages: Computers and social actors. *Human Communication Research, 19*, 504–527. doi:10.1111/j.1468-2958.1993.tb00311.x

Nass, C., Steuer, J. S., & Tauber, E. (1994). Computers are social actors. In *Proceedings of the CHI Conference,* (pp. 72-77). Boston, MA: CHI.

Nation, K., Adams, J. W., Bowyer-Crane, C. A., & Snowling, M. J. (1999). Working memory deficits in poor comprehenders reflect underlying language impairments. *Journal of Experimental Child Psychology, 73*, 139–158. doi:10.1006/jecp.1999.2498

Nelson, T., & Narens, L. (1990). Meta-memory: A theoretical treatment and new findings. In Bower, G. (Ed.), *The Psychology of Learning and Motivation (Vol. 26*, pp. 125–140). New York, NY: Academic Press.

Nelson-Legall, S. (1987). Necessary and unnecessary help-seeking in children. *The Journal of Genetic Psychology, 148*, 53–62. doi:10.1080/00221325.1987.9914536

New, R. (1994). Culture, child development, and developmentally appropriate practices. In Mallory, B., & New, R. (Eds.), *Diversity and Developmentally Appropriate Practices* (pp. 65–83). New York, NY: Teachers College Press.

Newman, R. S., & Schwager, M. T. (1992). Student perceptions and academic help seeking. In Schunk, D. H., & Meece, J. L. (Eds.), *Student Perceptions in the Classroom* (pp. 123–146). Hillsdale, NJ: Erlbaum.

Nezu, A. M. (1986). Negative life stress and anxiety: Problem solving as a moderator variable. *Psychological Reports, 58*, 279–283. doi:10.2466/pr0.1986.58.1.279

Nezu, A. M. (2004). Problem solving and behaviortherapy revisited. *Behavior Therapy, 35*, 1–33. doi:10.1016/S0005-7894(04)80002-9

Nezu, A. M., Nezu, C. M., & Perri, M. G. (1989). *Problem-solving therapy for depression: Theory, research, and clinical guidelines.* New York, NY: Wiley.

Nezu, A. M., & Ronan, G. F. (1988). Social problem solving as a moderator of stress-related depressive symptoms: A prospective analysis. *Journal of Counseling Psychology, 35*, 134–138. doi:10.1037/0022-0167.35.2.134

Nielsen, J., Clemmensen, T., & Yssing, C. (2002). Getting access to what goes on in people's heads? Reflections on the think-aloud technique. In *Proceedings of NordiCHI*. NordiCHI.

Norrelgen, F., Lacerda, F., & Forssberg, H. (2002). Temporal resolution of auditory perception and verbal working memory in 15 children with language impairment. *Journal of Learning Disabilities, 35*, 540–546. doi:10.1177/00222194020350060501

Numminem, H., Service, E., Ahonen, T., & Ruoppila, I. (2001). Working memory and everyday cognition in adults with Down syndrome. *Journal of Intellectual Disability Research, 45*, 157–168. doi:10.1046/j.1365-2788.2001.00298.x

Nygaard, E., Smith, L., & Torgersen, A. M. (2002). Temperament in children with Down syndrome and in prematurely born children. *Scandinavian Journal of Psychology, 43*, 61–71. doi:10.1111/1467-9450.00269

O'Leary, K. D., & O'Leary, S. G. (1977). *Classroom management: The successful use of behaviour modification* (2nd ed.). New York, NY: Pergamon Press.

Okonkwo, C., & Vassileva, J. (2001). Affective pedagogical agents and user persuasion. In Stephanidis, P. (Ed.), *Universal Access in Human-Computer Interaction* (pp. 397–401). New Orleans, LA: UAHCI.

Oliver, J. A., Edmiaston, R., & Fitzgerald, L. M. (2003). Regular and special education teachers' beliefs regarding the role of private speech in children's learning. In Winsler, A. (Ed.), *Awareness, Attitudes, and Beliefs Concerning Children's Private Speech*. Tampa, FL: Academic Press.

Palincsar, A., & Brown, A. (1984). Reciprocal teaching of comprehension fostering and monitoring activities. *Cognition and Instruction, 1*, 117–175. doi:10.1207/s1532690xci0102_1

Panaoura, A., & Philippou, G. (2007). The developmental change of young pupils' metacognitive ability in mathematics in relation to their cognitive abilities. *Cognitive Development, 22*, 149–164. doi:10.1016/j.cogdev.2006.08.004

Pappas, S., Ginsburg, H., & Jiang, M. (2003). SES differences in young children's metacognition in the context of mathematical problem solving. *Cognitive Development, 18*, 431–450. doi:10.1016/S0885-2014(03)00043-1

Paris, S., & Newman, R. (1990). Developmental aspects of self-regulated learning. *Educational Psychologist, 25*, 87–102. doi:10.1207/s15326985ep2501_7

Paris, S. G., & Byrnes, J. P. (1989). The constructivist approach to self-regulation and learning in the classroom. In Zimmerman, B. J., & Schunk, D. H. (Eds.), *Self-Regulated Learning and Academic Achievement: Theory, Research, and Practice* (pp. 281–321). New York, NY: Springer-Verlag. doi:10.1007/978-1-4612-3618-4_7

Paris, S. G., & Paris, A. H. (2001). Classroom applications of research on self-regulated learning. *Educational Psychologist, 36*, 89–101. doi:10.1207/S15326985EP3602_4

Paris, S. G., & Winograd, P. (1990). Promoting metacognition and motivation of exceptional children. *Remedial and Special Education, 11*, 7–15. doi:10.1177/074193259001100604

Paris, S. G., & Winograd, P. (2001). *The role of self-regulated learning in contextual teaching: Principles and practices for teacher preparation*. Retrieved from http://www.ciera.org/library/archive/2001-04/0104parwin.htm

Pask, G. (1988). Learning strategies, teaching strategies, and conceptual or learning style. In Schmeck, R. R. (Ed.), *Learning Strategies and Learning Styles* (pp. 83–100). New York, NY: Plenum.

Pastor, D. A., Barron, K. E., Miller, B. J., & Davis, S. L. (2007). A latent profile analysis of college students' achievement goal orientation. *Contemporary Educational Psychology, 32*, 8–47. doi:10.1016/j.cedpsych.2006.10.003

Patrick, H., & Middleton, M. J. (2002). Turning the kaleidoscope: What we see when self-regulated learning is viewed with a qualitative lens. *Educational Psychology, 37*, 27–39.

Piaget, J. (1959). *The language and thought of the child*. London, UK: Routledge.

Piaget, J. (1965). *The moral judgement of the child*. London, UK: Free Press.

Piaget, J. (1968). *Le langage et la pensée chez l'enfant: Études sur la logique de l'enfant* (7th ed.). Neuchâtel, Switzerland: Delachaux et Niestlé. [The language and thought of the child]

Picard, R., & Klein, J. (2001). Computers that recognize and respond to user emotion: Theoretical and practical implications. *Interacting with Computers, 3*, 3–14.

Pierce, E. W., Ewing, L. J., & Campbell, S. B. (1999). Diagnostic status and symptomatic behavior of hard-to-manage preschool children in middle childhood and early adolescence. *Journal of Clinical Child Psychology, 28*, 44–57. doi:10.1207/s15374424jccp2801_4

Pintrich, P. (1999). The role of motivation in promoting and sustaining self-regulated learning. *International Journal of Educational Research, 31*, 459–470. doi:10.1016/S0883-0355(99)00015-4

Pintrich, P. R. (Ed.). (1995). Current issues in research on self-regulated learning: A discussion with commentaries. *Educational Psychologist, 30*, 171–232. doi:10.1207/s15326985ep3004_1

Pintrich, P. R. (2000). The role of goal orientation in self-regulated learning. In Boekaerts, M., Pintrich, P. R., & Zeidner, M. (Eds.), *Handbook of Self-Regulation* (pp. 451–502). San Diego, CA: Academic Press. doi:10.1016/B978-012109890-2/50043-3

Pintrich, P. R., & De Groot, E. V. (1990). Motivational and self-regulated learning components of classroom academic performance. *Journal of Educational Psychology, 82*, 33–40. doi:10.1037/0022-0663.82.1.33

Pintrich, P. R., Roeser, R., & De Groot, E. (1994). Classroom and individual differences in early adolescents' motivation and self-regulated learning. *The Journal of Early Adolescence, 14*, 139–161. doi:10.1177/027243169401400204

Pintrich, P. R., & Zusho, A. (2002). The development of academic self-regulation: The role of cognitive and motivational factors. In Wigfield, A., & Eccles, J. S. (Eds.), *Development of Achievement Motivation* (pp. 249–284). San Diego, CA: Academic Press. doi:10.1016/B978-012750053-9/50012-7

PISA. (2003). *Literacy skills for the world of tomorrow*. Paris, France: PISA.

Presley, M., & Ghatala, E. S. (1990). Self-regulated learning: Monitoring learning from text. *Educational Psychologist, 25*, 19–33. doi:10.1207/s15326985ep2501_3

Pressley, M. (1986). The relevance of the good strategy user model to the teaching of mathematics. *Educational Psychologist, 21*, 139–161.

Pressley, M. (1995). More about the development of self-regulation: Complex, long-term, and thoroughly social. *Educational Psychologist, 30,* 207–212. doi:10.1207/s15326985ep3004_6

Puustinen, M. (1998). Help-seeking behavior in a problem-solving situation: Development of self-regulation. *European Journal of Psychology of Education, 13,* 271–282. doi:10.1007/BF03173093

Puustinen, M., & Pulkkinen, L. (2001). Models of self-regulated learning: A review. *Scandinavian Journal of Educational Research, 45,* 21–46. doi:10.1080/00313830120074206

Reder, L., & Schunn, C. (1996). Metacognition does not imply awareness: Strategy choice is governed by implicit learning and memory. In Reder, L. (Ed.), *Implicit Memory and Metacognition* (pp. 63–92). Mahwah, NJ: Erlbaum.

Reeves, B., & Nass, C. (1996). *The media equation: How people treat computers, television, and new media like real people and places.* Cambridge, UK: Cambridge University Press.

Reich, S. (2005). What do mothers know? Maternal knowledge of child development. *Infant Mental Health Journal, 26,* 143–156. doi:10.1002/imhj.20038

Renger, S. (2006). *Evaluation eines trainings zur selbststeuerung.* [Evaluation of a training program in self-government]. (Unpublished Masters Thesis). University of Osnabrück. Osnabrück, Germany.

Rheinberg, F., Vollmeyer, R., & Rollett, W. (2002). Motivation and self-regulated learning: A type analysis with process variables. *Psychologia, 45,* 237–249. doi:10.2117/psysoc.2002.237

Richman, N., Stevenson, J., & Graham, P. (1982). *Preschool to school: A behavioral study.* New York, NY: Academic Press.

Roberts, K. (2002). Children's ability to distinguish between memories from multiple sources: Implications for the quality and accuracy of eyewitness statements. *Developmental Review, 22,* 403–435. doi:10.1016/S0273-2297(02)00005-9

Roebuck, R. (1998). *Reading and recall in L1 and L2: A sociocultural approach.* Stamford, CT: Ablex Publishing.

Rose, E., Bramham, J., Young, S., Paliokostas, E., & Xenitidis, K. (2009). Neuropsychological characteristics of adults with comorbid ADHD and borderline/mild intellectual disability. *Research in Developmental Disabilities, 30,* 496–502. doi:10.1016/j.ridd.2008.07.009

Rosenquist, C., Conners, F. A., & Roskos-Ewoldsen, B. (2003). Phonological and visuospatial working memory in individuals with intellectual disability. *American Journal of Mental Retardation, 108,* 403–413. doi:10.1352/0895-8017(2003)108<403:PAVWMI>2.0.CO;2

Rozendaal, J. S., Minnaert, A., & Boekaerts, M. (2003). Motivation and self-regulated learning in secondary vocational education: Information-processing type and gender differences. *Learning and Individual Differences, 13,* 273–289. doi:10.1016/S1041-6080(03)00016-5

Rutter, M. (1989). Pathways from childhood to adult life. *Journal of Child Psychology and Psychiatry, and Allied Disciplines, 30,* 23–52. doi:10.1111/j.1469-7610.1989.tb00768.x

Ryan, A. M., Pintrich, P. R., & Midgley, C. (2001). Avoiding seeking help in the classroom: Who and why? *Educational Psychology Review, 13,* 93–114. doi:10.1023/A:1009013420053

Salisbury-Glennon, J. D., Gorrell, J., Sanders, S., Boyd, P., & Kamen, M. (1999). *Self-regulated learning strategies used by the learners in a learner-centered school.* Paper presented at the Annual Meeting of the American Educational Research Association. Montreal, Canada.

Sanchez-Alonso, S., & Vovides, Y. (2007). Integration of metacognitive skills in the design of learning objects. *Computers in Human Behavior, 23*, 2585–2595. doi:10.1016/j.chb.2006.08.010

Santrock, J. (1997). *Life-span development* (6th ed.). Dubuque, IA: Brown & Benchmark Publishers.

Schall, U., Johnston, P., Lagopoulos, J., Jüptner, M., Jentzen, W., & Thienel, R. (2003). Functional brain maps of Tower of London performance: A positron emission tomography and functional magnetic resonance imaging study. *NeuroImage, 20*, 1154–1161. doi:10.1016/S1053-8119(03)00338-0

Schmeck, R., Geiser-Bernstein, E., & Cercy, S. (1991). Self-concept and learning: The revised inventory of learning processes. *Educational Psychology, 11*, 343–362. doi:10.1080/0144341910110310

Schneider, W. (1998). The development of procedural metamemory in childhood and adolescence. In Mazzoni, G., & Nelson, T. (Eds.), *Metacognition and Cognitive Neuropsychology* (pp. 143–171). Mahwah, NJ: Erlbaum.

Schoenfeld, A. H. (1992). Learning to think mathematically: Problem solving, metacognition, and sense making in mathematics. In Grouws, D. A. (Ed.), *Handbook of Research on Mathematics Teaching and Learning* (pp. 165–197). New York, NY: MacMillan.

Schommer, M. (1990). Effects of beliefs about the nature of knowledge on comprehension. *Journal of Educational Psychology, 82*, 498–504. doi:10.1037/0022-0663.82.3.498

Schön, D. A. (1983). *The reflective practitioner*. New York, NY: Basic Books.

Schön, D. A. (1987). *Educating the reflective practitioner*. San Francisco, CA: Jossey-Bass.

Schraw, G. (1994). The effect of metacognitive knowledge on local and global monitoring. *Contemporary Educational Psychology, 19*, 143–154. doi:10.1006/ceps.1994.1013

Schraw, G., & Dennison, R. S. (1994). Assessing metacognitive awareness. *Contemporary Educational Psychology, 19*, 460–475. doi:10.1006/ceps.1994.1033

Schunk, D. H. (1986). Vicarious influences on self-efficacy for cognitive skill learning. *Journal of Social and Clinical Psychology, 4*, 316–327. doi:10.1521/jscp.1986.4.3.316

Schunk, D. H. (1994). Self-regulation of self-efficacy and attributions in academic settings. In Schunk, D. H., & Zimmerman, B. J. (Eds.), *Self-Regulation of Learning and Performance: Issues and Educational Applications* (pp. 75–99). Hillsdale, NJ: Erlbaum.

Schunk, D. H. (2005). Self-regulated learning: The educational legacy of Paul R. Pintrich. *Educational Psychologist, 40*, 85–94. doi:10.1207/s15326985ep4002_3

Schunk, D. H., & Zimmerman, B. J. (1988). *Self-regulated learning: From teaching to self-reflective practice*. New York, NY: Guilford.

Sektnan, M., McClellanda, M., Acocka, A., & Morrisonb, J. (2010). Relations between early family risk, children's behavioral regulation, and academic achievement. *Early Childhood Research Quarterly*. Retrieved from http://www.ncbi.nlm.nih.gov/pmc/articles/PMC2953426/

Sethi, A., Mischel, W., Aber, J. L., Shoda, Y., & Rodriguez, M. L. (2000). The role of strategic attention deployment in development of self-regulation: Predicting preschoolers' delay of gratification from mother-toddler interactions. *Developmental Psychology, 36*, 767–777. doi:10.1037/0012-1649.36.6.767

Shanahan, M., Roberts, J., Hatton, D., Reznick, J., & Goldsmith, H. (2008). Early temperament and negative reactivity in boys with fragile X syndrome. *Journal of Intellectual Disability Research, 52*, 842–854. doi:10.1111/j.1365-2788.2008.01074.x

Shih, C. (2011). Assisting people with developmental disabilities to improve computer pointing efficiency through multiple mice and automatic pointing assistive programs. *Research in Developmental Disabilities, 32*, 1736–1744. doi:10.1016/j.ridd.2011.03.002

Shih, C., Shih, C. T., & Pi, P. (2011). Using an extended automatic target acquisition program with dual cursor technology to assist people with developmental disabilities in improving their pointing efficiency. *Research in Developmental Disabilities, 32*, 1506–1513. doi:10.1016/j.ridd.2011.01.043

Shonkoff, J., & Phillips, D. (2000). *From neurons to neighborhoods: The science of early childhood development*. Washington, DC: National Academies Press.

Shvachkin, N. K. (1973). The development of phonemic speech perception in early childhood. In Ferguson, C., & Slobin, D. (Eds.), *Studies of Child Language Development* (pp. 91–127). New York, NY: Holt, Rinehart, & Winston.

Siegler, R. S., & Stern, E. (1998). Conscious and unconscious strategy discoveries: A microgenetic analysis. *Journal of Experimental Psychology. General, 127*, 377–397. doi:10.1037/0096-3445.127.4.377

Simonds, J., Kieras, J. E., Rueda, M. R., & Rothbart, M. K. (2007). Effortful control, executive attention, and emotional regulation in 7–10-year-old children. *Cognitive Development, 22*, 474–488. doi:10.1016/j.cogdev.2007.08.009

Slaats, A. (1999). Learning styles in secondary vocational education: Disciplinary differences. *Learning and Instruction, 9*, 475–492. doi:10.1016/S0959-4752(99)00007-9

Sokolov, A. N. (1972). *Inner speech and thought.* New York, NY: Plenum. doi:10.1007/978-1-4684-1914-6

Sperling, R. A., Howard, B. C., Miller, L. A., & Murphy, C. (2002). Measures of children's knowledge and regulation of cognition. *Contemporary Educational Psychology, 27*, 51–79. doi:10.1006/ceps.2001.1091

Spero, M. (1978). Thoughts on computerized psychotherapy. *Psychiatry, 41*, 279–288.

Spivack, G., Platt, J. J., & Shure, M. B. (1976). *The problem-solving approach to adjustment.* San Francisco, CA: Jossey-Bass.

St-Laurent, D., & Moss, E. (2002). Le developpement de la planification: Influence dune attention conjointe. *Enfance, 4*, 341–361. doi:10.3917/enf.544.0341

Stager, C. L., & Werker, J. F. (1997). Infants listen for more phonetic detail in speech perception than in word-learning tasks. *Nature, 388*, 381–382. doi:10.1038/41102

Stipek, D., Recchia, S., & Mcclintic, S. (1992). Self-evaluation in young children. *Monographs of the Society for Research in Child Development, 57*, 84–87. doi:10.2307/1166190

Stoneman, Z. (2007). Examining the Down syndrome advantage: Mothers and fathers of young children with disabilities. *Journal of Intellectual Disability Research, 51*, 1006–1017. doi:10.1111/j.1365-2788.2007.01012.x

Stright, A. D., Neitzel, C., Sears, K. G., & Hoke-Sinex, L. (2001). Instruction begins in the home: Relations between parental instruction and children's self-regulation in the classroom. *Journal of Educational Psychology*, *93*, 456–466. doi:10.1037/0022-0663.93.3.456

Sun, R. (1999). Accounting for the computational basis of consciousness: A connectionist approach. *Consciousness and Cognition*, *8*, 529–565. doi:10.1006/ccog.1999.0405

Sun, R. (2002). *Duality of the mind*. Mahwah, NJ: Erlbaum.

Sun, R., & Mathews, R. (2003). Explicit and implicit processes of metacognition. In Shohov, S. (Ed.), *Advances in Psychology Research* (pp. 3–18). Hauppauge, NY: Nova Science Pub.

Sun, R., Merrill, E., & Peterson, T. (2001). From implicit skills to explicit knowledge: A bottom-up model of skill learning. *Cognitive Science*, *25*, 203–244. doi:10.1207/s15516709cog2502_2

Sun, R., Slusarz, P., & Terry, C. (2005). The interaction of the explicit and the implicit in skill learning: A dual-process approach. *Psychological Review*, *112*, 159–192. doi:10.1037/0033-295X.112.1.159

Sun, R., Zhang, X., & Mathew, R. (2006). Modeling meta-cognition in a cognitive architecture. *Cognitive Systems Research*, *7*, 327–338. doi:10.1016/j.cogsys.2005.09.001

Sweller, J. (1998). Cognitive load during problem solving: Effects on learning. *Cognitive Science*, *12*, 257–285. doi:10.1207/s15516709cog1202_4

Tang, C. M., Bartsch, K., & Nunez, N. (2007). Young children's reports of when learning occurred. *Journal of Experimental Child Psychology*, *97*, 149–164. doi:10.1016/j.jecp.2007.01.003

Taylor, M., Esbensen, B. M., & Bennett, R. T. (1994). Children's understanding of knowledge acquisition: The tendency for children to report that they have always known what they have just learned. *Child Development*, *65*, 1581–1604. doi:10.2307/1131282

Taylor, R. (1987). Selecting effective courseware: Three fundamental instructional factors. *Contemporary Educational Psychology*, *12*, 231–243. doi:10.1016/S0361-476X(87)80028-0

Thiessen, E. D. (2007). The effect of distributional information on children's use of phonemic contrasts. *Journal of Memory and Language*, *56*, 16–34. doi:10.1016/j.jml.2006.07.002

Thorndike, E. L. (1913). *Educational psychology: The psychology of learning*. New York, NY: Teachers College Press. doi:10.1037/13051-000

Tinsley, V. S., & Waters, H. S. (1982). The development of verbal control over motor behavior: A replication and extension of Luria's findings. *Child Development*, *53*, 746–753. doi:10.2307/1129388

Tisdelle, D. A., & St. Lawrence, J. S. (1986). Interpersonal problem-solving competency: Review and critique of the literature. *Clinical Psychology Review*, *6*, 337–356. doi:10.1016/0272-7358(86)90005-X

Tsao, R., & Kindelberger, C. (2009). Variability of cognitive development in children with Down syndrome: Relevance of good reasons for using the cluster procedure. *Research in Developmental Disabilities*, *30*, 426–432. doi:10.1016/j.ridd.2008.10.009

Tu, C. H., & McIsaac, M. S. (2002). An examination of social presence to increase interaction in online classes. *American Journal of Distance Education*, *16*, 131–150. doi:10.1207/S15389286AJDE1603_2

Upton, T. A., & Lee-Thompson, L. (2001). The role of the first language in second language reading. *Studies in Second Language Acquisition, 23*, 469–495.

Ushakova, T. N. (1994). Inner speech and second language acquisition: An experimental theoretical approach. In Lantolf, J. P., & Appel, G. (Eds.), *Vygotskian Approaches to Second Language Research* (pp. 135–156). Upper Saddle River, NJ: Able.

Van Daal, J., Verhoeven, L., van Leeuwe, J., & Balkom, H. (2007). Working memory limitations in children with severe language impairment. *Journal of Communication Disorders, 41*(2), 85–107. doi:10.1016/j.jcomdis.2007.03.010

Vansteenkiste, M., & Deci, E. L. (2003). Competitively contingent rewards and intrinsic motivation: Can losers remain motivated? *Motivation and Emotion, 27*, 273–299. doi:10.1023/A:1026259005264

Veenman, M., Wilhelm, P., & Beishuizen, J. (2004). The relation between intellectual and metacognitive skills from a developmental perspective. *Learning and Instruction, 14*, 89–109. doi:10.1016/j.learninstruc.2003.10.004

Veenman, M. V. J. (2005). The assessment of metacognitive skills: What can be learned from multi-method designs? In Moschner, B., & Artelt, C. (Eds.), *Lernstrategien und Metakognition: Implikationen für Forschung und Praxis* (pp. 75–97). Berlin, Germany: Waxmann.

Vermunt, J. (1992). *Leerstijlen en sturen van leerprocessing in het hoger onderwijs: Naar procesgerichte instructie en zelfstandig denken* [Learning styles and regulation of learning processes in higher education: Towards process-guided instruction and independent reasoning]. Amsterdam, The Netherlands: Swets & Zeitlinger.

Vermunt, J., & Verloop, N. (1999). Congruence and friction between teaching and learning. *Learning and Instruction, 9*, 257–280. doi:10.1016/S0959-4752(98)00028-0

Vieillevoye, S., & Nader-Grosbois, N. (2007). Self-regulation during pretend play in children with intellectual disability and in normally developing children. *Research in Developmental Disabilities, 29*(3), 256–272. doi:10.1016/j.ridd.2007.05.003

Vygotsky, L. S. (1978). *Mind in society: The development of higher psychological processes.* Cambridge, MA: Harvard University Press.

Vygotsky, L. S. (1978). Chapter. In Cole, M., John-Steiner, V., Scribner, S., & Souberman, E. (Eds.), *Mind in Society: The Development of Higher Mental Processes* (pp. 36–47). Cambridge, MA: Harvard University Press.

Vygotsky, L. S. (1986). *Thought and language.* Cambridge, MA: MIT Press.

Vygotsky, L. S. (1987). Thinking and speech. In Rieber & A. Carton (Eds.), *The Collected Works of L. S. Vygotsky: Vol 1: Problems of General Psychology,* (pp. 39–285). New York, NY: Plenum Press.

Vygotsky, L. S., Luria, A., Leontiev, A., & Levina, R. (1929). The function and fate of egocentric speech. In *Proceedings of the 9th International Congress of Psychology.* Princeton, NJ: Psychological Review.

Wager, W., & Wager, S. U. (1985). Presenting questions, processing responses, and providing feedback in CAI. *Journal of Instructional Development, 8*(4), 2–8. doi:10.1007/BF02906047

Walther, J. B. (1992). Interpersonal effects in computer-mediated interaction: A relational perspective. *Communication Research, 19*, 52–90. doi:10.1177/009365092019001003

Wegner, D., & Bargh, J. (1998). Control and automaticity in social life. In Gilbert, D., Fiske, S. T., & Lindzey, G. (Eds.), *Handbook of Social Psychology* (4th ed., pp. 446–496). New York, NY: McGraw-Hill.

Werker, J. F., Fennell, C. T., Corcoran, K. M., & Stager, C. L. (2002). Infants' ability to learn phonetically similar words: Effects of age and vocabulary size. *Infancy*, 3, 1–30.

Wiener, N. (1954). *The human use of human beings: Cybernetics and society*. Oxford, UK: Houghton Mifflin.

Winne, P. H. (1995). Inherent details in self-regulated learning. *Educational Psychologist*, 30, 173–187. doi:10.1207/s15326985ep3004_2

Winne, P. H. (2001). Self-regulated learning viewed from models of information processing. In Zimmerman, B., & Schunk, D. (Eds.), *Self-Regulated Learning and Academic Achievement: Theoretical Perspectives* (pp. 153–189). Mahwah, NJ: Erlbaum.

Winne, P. H., Hadwin, A. F., Stockley, D. B., & Nesbit, J. C. (2000). *Traces versus self-reports of study tactics and their relations to achievement*. Unpublished.

Winne, P. H., & Perry, N. E. (2000). Measuring self-regulated learning. In Boekaerts, M., Pintrich, P. R., & Ziedner, M. (Eds.), *Handbook of Self-Regulation: Theory Research and Applications* (pp. 531–566). San Diego, CA: Academic Press.

Winnykamen, F. (1993). Gestion socio-cognitive du recours a` l'aide d'autrui chez l'enfant. *Journal of Instructional Psychology*, 28, 645–659. doi:10.1080/00207599308246949

Winsler, A. (1998). Parent-child interaction and private speech in boys with ADHD. *Applied Developmental Science*, 2, 17–39. doi:10.1207/s1532480xads0201_2

Winsler, A., Abar, B., Feder, M. A., Schunn, C. D., & Rubio, D. A. (2007). Private speech and executive functioning among high-functioning children with autistic spectrum disorders. *Journal of Autistic Development Disorder*, 37, 1617–1635. doi:10.1007/s10803-006-0294-8

Winsler, A., Carlton, M. P., & Barry, M. J. (2000b). Age-related changes in preschool children's systematic use of private speech in a natural setting. *Journal of Child Language*, 27, 665–687. doi:10.1017/S0305000900004402

Winsler, A., De Le'on, J. R., Wallace, B., Carlton, M. P., & Willson-Quayle, A. (2003). Private speech in preschool children: Developmental stability and change, across-task consistency, and relations with classroom behavior. *Journal of Child Language*, 30, 583–608. doi:10.1017/S0305000903005671

Winsler, A., & Diaz, R. M. (1995). Private speech in the classroom: The effects of activity type, presence of others, classroom context, and mixed-age grouping. *International Journal of Behavioral Development*, 18, 463–488.

Winsler, A., Diaz, R. M., Atencio, D. J., McCarthy, E. M., & Chabay, L. A. (2000). Verbal self-regulation over time in preschool children at risk for attention and behavior problems. *Journal of Child Psychology and Psychiatry, and Allied Disciplines*, 41, 875–886. doi:10.1111/1469-7610.00675

Winsler, A., Diaz, R. M., McCarthy, E. M., Atencio, D. J., & Chabay, L. A. (1999). Mother-child interaction, private speech, and task performance in preschool children with behavior problems. *Journal of Child Psychology and Psychiatry, and Allied Disciplines*, 40, 891–904. doi:10.1111/1469-7610.00507

Winsler, A., Diaz, R. M., & Montero, I. (1997). The role of private speech in the transition from collaborative to independent task performance in young children. *Early Childhood Research Quarterly*, 12, 59–79. doi:10.1016/S0885-2006(97)90043-0

Winsler, A., Fernyhough, C., McClaren, E. M., & Way, E. (2005). *Private speech coding manual.* Fairfax, VA: George Mason University. Retrieved from http://classweb.gmu.edu/awinsler/Resources/PsCodingManual.pdf

Winsler, A., Manfra, L., & Diaz, R. M. (2007). Should I let them talk? Private speech and task performance among preschool children with and without behavior problems. *Early Childhood Research Quarterly, 22,* 215–231. doi:10.1016/j.ecresq.2007.01.001

Winsler, A., & Naglieri, J. (2003). Overt and covert verbal problem-solving strategies: Developmental trends in use, awareness, and relations with task performance in children aged 5 to 17. *Child Development, 74,* 659–678. doi:10.1111/1467-8624.00561

Wong, A. W. K., Chan, C. C. H., Li-Tsang, C. W. P., & Lam, C. S. (2009). Competence of people with intellectual disabilities on using human-computer interface. *Research in Developmental Disabilities, 30,* 107–123. doi:10.1016/j.ridd.2008.01.002

Wozniak, R. (1972). Verbal regulation of motor behavior: Soviet research and non-Soviet replications. *Human Development, 44,* 13–47. doi:10.1159/000271226

Wozniak, R. H. (1975). A dialectical paradigm for psychological research: Implications drawn from the history of psychology in the Soviet Union. *Human Development, 18,* 18–34. doi:10.1159/000271473

Yaden, D. B. Jr. (1984). Inner speech, oral language, and reading: Huey and Vygotsky revisited. *Reading Psychology: An International Quarterly, 5,* 155–166. doi:10.1080/0270271840050118

Zeanah, C. H., Boris, N. W., & Scheeringa, M. S. (1997). Psychopathology in infancy. *Journal of Child Psychology and Psychiatry, and Allied Disciplines, 38,* 81–99. doi:10.1111/j.1469-7610.1997.tb01506.x

Zeidner, M., Boekarts, M., & Pintrich, P. R. (2000). Self-regulation: Directions and challenges for future research. In Boekaerts, M., Pintrich, P., & Seidner, M. (Eds.), *Self-Regulation: Theory, Research, and Applications* (pp. 749–768). Orlando, FL: Academic Press.

Zimmerman, B. J. (1989). A social cognitive view of self-regulated academic learning. *Journal of Educational Psychology, 81,* 329–339. doi:10.1037/0022-0663.81.3.329

Zimmerman, B. J. (1995). Self-regulation involves more than metacognition: A social cognitive perspective. *Educational Psychologist, 30,* 217–221. doi:10.1207/s15326985ep3004_8

Zimmerman, B. J. (1998). Academic studying and the development of personal skill: A self-regulatory perspective. *Educational Psychologist, 33,* 73–86.

Zimmerman, B. J. (2000a). Attaining self-regulation: A social-cognitive perspective. In Boekaerts, M., Pintrich, P., & Seidner, M. (Eds.), *Self-Regulation: Theory, Research, and Applications* (pp. 13–39). Orlando, FL: Academic Press.

Zimmerman, B. J. (2000b). Self-efficacy: An essential motive to learn. *Contemporary Educational Psychology, 25,* 82–91. doi:10.1006/ceps.1999.1016

Zimmerman, B. J. (2001). Theories of self-regulated learning and academic achievement: An overview and analysis. In Zimmerman, B. J., & Schunk, D. H. (Eds.), *Self-Regulated Learning and Academic Achievement: Theoretical Perspectives* (2nd ed., pp. 1–38). Mahwah, NJ: Erlbaum.

Zimmerman, B. J., & Martinez-Pons, M. (1990). Student differences in self-regulated learning: Related grade, sex, and giftedness to self-efficacy and strategy use. *Journal of Educational Psychology, 82*, 51–59. doi:10.1037/0022-0663.82.1.51

Zimmerman, B. J., & Schunk, D. H. (1989). *Self-regulated learning and academic achievement.* New York, NY: Springer-Verlag. doi:10.1007/978-1-4612-3618-4

Zimmerman, B. J., & Schunk, D. H. (Eds.). (2001a). *Self-regulated learning and academic achievement: Theoretical perspectives* (2nd ed.). Mahwah, NJ: Erlbaum.

Zimmerman, B. J., & Schunk, D. H. (2001b). Reflections on theories of self-regulated learning and academic achievement. In Zimmerman, B. J., & Schunk, D. H. (Eds.), *Self-Regulated Learning and Academic Achievement: Theoretical Perspectives* (2nd ed., pp. 289–307). Mahwah, NJ: Erlbaum.

Zumberg, K. M., Chang, E. C., & Sanna, L. J. (2008). Does problem orientation involve more than generalized self-efficacy? Predicting psychological and physical functioning in college students. *Personality and Individual Differences, 45*, 328–332. doi:10.1016/j.paid.2008.04.017

# Chapter 2
# Emergent Ontologies by Collaborative Tagging for Knowledge Management

**Weena Jimenez**
*University of Oviedo, Spain*

**César Luis Alvargonzález**
*University of Oviedo, Spain*

**Pablo Abella Vallina**
*University of Oviedo, Spain*

**Jose María Álvarez Gutiérrez**
*University of Oviedo, Spain*

**Patricia Ordoñez de Pablos**
*University of Oviedo, Spain*

**Jose Emilio Labra Gayo**
*University of Oviedo, Spain*

## ABSTRACT

*The massive use of Internet and social networks leads us to a new dynamic environment with huge amounts of unstructured and unclassified information resources in continuous evolution. New classification, compilation, and recommendation systems based on the use of folksonomies and ontologies have appeared to deal with the requirements of data management in this environment. Nevertheless, using ontologies alone has some weaknesses due to the need of being statically modeled by a set of experts in a specific domain. On the other hand, folksonomies show a lack of formality because of their implicit ambiguity and flexibility by definition. The main objective of this chapter is to outline and evaluate a new way to exploit Web information resources and tags for bridging the gap between ontology modeling and folksonomies.*

## INTRODUCTION

Throughout human history, knowledge has been stored to cover different needs like education, improvement of scientific knowledge, legal support, and entertainment. However, this trend to store resources turns out a need for systems that are able to recover the information in a rapid and effective way.

Currently, according to the statistics presented on the World Wide Web Size (Miniwastts Marketing Group, 2012) about 30% of the world

DOI: 10.4018/978-1-4666-2494-8.ch002

Copyright © 2013, IGI Global. Copying or distributing in print or electronic forms without written permission of IGI Global is prohibited.

population is a Web user and taking into account the statistics of January 2012 Internet World Stats (Kunder, 2012) there are about 7 billion pages indexed in search engines like Google, Bing and Yahoo. Taking these data as an indicative number of resources that could be contained by the World Wide Web, it can be said that the Internet is the largest knowledge repository in human history.

The growth of quantity of the information offered through the Internet has resulted in the need for classification and retrieval systems. Ontologies and folksonomies try to answer to the need to classify, but their approaches are completely different. An ontology is a specification of a shared conceptualization (Gruber, 1995), it is a formal description of concepts and relationships involved in knowledge domain. On the other hand, a folksonomy (Wal, 2007) is the result of free classification, unstructured and informal, collaboratively created by a group of users through Web-based systems of tagging different kind of resources like the case of Delicious, Flickr, etc.

The use of ontologies offers several advantages as stated in Uschold and Gruninger (1996), which recognizes the ability of ontologies to improve the communication between systems and to reduce ambiguity. It also offers the advantage to provide interoperability for systems and allows reusability and building standards for different areas of knowledge.

Despite the advantages presented by the use of ontologies, Adam Mathes (2004) stated that the metadata created by professionals are considered to be high quality, however, in terms of time and effort they are very expensive to create, which makes it very difficult to scalability and continuous updating. In the same line of reasoning Brewster, Ciravegna, and Wilks (2003) argue that the creation of ontologies is a slow process, like lexicography, once the product is finished it is rarely updated, which generates a high maintenance cost.

Some studies confirm that user participation and influence of the context are important

indicators of success in ontology effectiveness. In *The Ontolingua Server: A Tool for Collaborative Ontology Construction,* Farquhar, Fikes, and Rice (1996) identified three important indicators of success of ontologies use, when it becomes a commonplace for people in a broad spectrum of communities to build and use ontologies on a day to day basis as spreadsheets and e-mails nowadays. Another indicator of success will be the availability and widespread use of large-scale repositories of reusable ontologies in diverse disciplines. These indicators of success should emerge when the technology has progressed enough so that the benefits provided by using ontologies significantly outweigh the costs of developing them.

In this way, in *Some Ideas and Examples to Evaluate Ontologies,* Pérez (1995) proposes that the natural evaluators of ontologies will be the developers and users taking into account utility as the first criteria. Farquhar, Fikes, and Rice (1996) propose that not only experts have the experience necessary for the construction of ontologies, users must be part as evaluators and are a critical part in the process. In the same way, Thomas and Griffin (1998) argued that those who often use the contents are not those who have or who make it, so, experts and creators are not necessarily the best to describe their content.

The human element is important to define the classification structures (Thomas & Griffin, 1998). As a response to the need for user participation folksonomies appeared. According to Mathes (2004), the most important strength of a folksonomy is that it directly reflects the vocabulary of users, represents a fundamental shift in that it is derived not from professionals or content creators, but from the users and documents. A folksonomy directly reflects the terminology of content users. This faithful reflection of the users terminology increases the importance of context, since, as stated in Benz, Hotho, and St (2010), the same term may be used by different communities with different meanings.

As shown, ontologies and folksonomies have pros and cons. Ontologies are presented as robust, accurate but expensive whereas folksonomies are presented as light elements adapted but highly inaccurate. Then, as outlined in Bateman, Brooks, and McCalla (2006), it is necessary to find an easier way to create and use ontologies. We think that the answer to this problem is building a hybrid approach. In the following sections, we describe this proposal.

## BACKGROUND

Combining ontologies and folksonomies is a challenge for several groups of researchers, several groups are focusing on mixing ontologies and folksonomies and others are focusing on creating one from the other. Different kinds of tools are used to do this, we can name the use of statistics models, artificial intelligence, natural language processing, and others. In this section we describe some of these projects related with our own proposal. Farquhar, Fikes, and Rice (1996) proposed making ontologies by a collaborative process. The process was integrated by a Web system called Ontolingua which was able to create and update ontologies by user collaboration. The main contribution was to create a collaborative system to create, update, share, and show ontologies.

Talking about metadata, Greenberg & Pattuelli (2001) argued about the importance of the authors in the process of metadata creation, they affirm that not only the experts have the knowledge to describe the resources. They also build an experiment where they show that metadata created by the authors of contents is as good as metadata created by experts.

Concerned about the high cost of creating and updating ontologies (Brewster, Ciravegna, & Wilks, 2003) propose an automatic process to build it. This process consists in the use of external data sources and natural language processing tools for extracting resources described by texts.

The proposed process have the following steps: identify a text resource to analyze, identify related terms, extract relevant terms, query external data sets, identify relevant terms depending on one domain, and finish with user evaluated results. After applying the prototype, they concluded that the use of external data sets is very important to find interesting information from resources described by texts.

With the same objective that previous research about to build better and more easy updating metadata, Bateman, Brooks, and McCalla (2006) propose a prototype for creating and updating ontologies by collaborative tagging using the language ontology WordNet as evaluator terms. The main objective of this research was to create ontologies to facilitate the emergence of adaptive e-learning systems and to facilitate the creation of metadata.

Taking into account the importance of human elements in the definition of metadata in Guy and Tonkin (2006) analyzed the trends of users to create convergence terms. Through the analysis of generated data in collaborative tagging systems like Deliciuos and Flickr they concluded that the culture and the context are a big influence in tagging actions. The authors suggested that there are two main ways in which improvements can be made. Firstly, much can be done at the point at which new resources are contributed to the system. Simple error-checking potentially accounts for a number of tag errors although rather fewer misspellings occur than may be expected.

Related with social impact in metadata and taxonomies definitions process, Suchanek, Vojnovic, and Gunawardena (2008) conducted an experiment with a group of Microsoft employees to analyze the influence of different tag suggestion methodologies. Their conclusions are a) presentation of top popular tags have a high impact in tagging, b) the meaning of tags is directly proportional to the number of taggers that use it, c) tags applied to a document typically intersect more with the queries and the title than with the content, and d) up to 1 in 3 tags may be induced purely by presence of tag suggestions. This result implies that the popularity of tags observed in existing systems with tag suggestions may be skewed. On the positive side, it implies that tag suggestions could provide an effective control over the tags.

A related line of research is proposed by Tang and Dewei (2009) to create ontologies by a semi-automatic process applying learning from folksonomies. The process of their methodological proposal has three steps. The first one uses a probabilistic model to define the relation between terms and resources, then estimate the possible relations between tags, and finally determine the relation between tags and construct a hierarchical structure. Benz & Hotho (2010) propose an automatic process to building ontologies but their proposal is different to the previous one because this commitment with collaborative tagging tools to do an inference process and then to build the ontology. Thanks to their experiments, they conclude that folksonomies have an implicit semantic meaning.

As a proof of the advantages of implementing structured tools like ontologies to resource and knowledge management, Kayed, El-Qawasmeh, and Qawaqneh (2010) propose to use ontologies in Web search. Their proposal consists in using ontologies as a base tool to re-ranking search results; they apply their proposal and conclude that ontologies are a useful tool to improve the Web search process.

## PROPOSAL

In the previous section, we can see three kinds of research lines; one of them is to find the creation of methodological processes doing inferences and building ontologies in an automatic or semi-automatic way from folksonomies. The second group of projects uses ontologies as a base to improve semantics in folksonomies and the last one support uses of the collaborative tools as a better way for building metadata and ontologies.

After having analyzed the conclusions of these projects, we consider that the three approaches have advantages for building and updating ontologies. The main objective of this research is to present a proposal to build ontologies using a mixture of tools like collaborative tagging, natural language processing, and retrieval.

In general, the main process to model and update an ontology is a cyclic process which follows general headlines like identifying the purpose and scope, building the ontology, coding, sharing and integrating, evaluating and documentation (Figure 1). In this process, all of the actors need to have formal knowledge about the domain and related technologies.

In other way, the process of building folksonomies is simpler because only three steps are necessary to create and update terms. The first step is building a collaborative tagging system, and then this system is offered to users and the end users building the folksonomy thanks to their interaction with the system (Figure 2).

Our proposal is mixing both methodologies to build a new one. The methodology proposed has as main objective to make the building ontology process simpler by using collaborative tagging and other techniques. In the results of the experiments of Suchanek, Vojnovic, and Gunawardena (2008), the researchers concluded that the users tend to think in categories when tagging and

*Figure 1. Generic process for building ontologies*

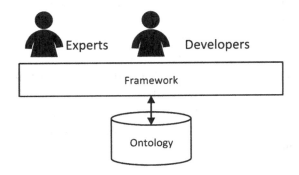

*Figure 2. Generic process for building folksonomies*

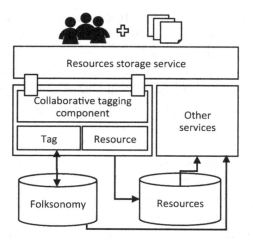

for this reason we consider that it could be a good idea to use generated tags like basing an ontology or another type of formal taxonomy.

Emerging ontology from collaborative tagging implies integrating the collaborative element in building it, this option is supported by Benz, Hotho, and St (2010) where it confirms that it is possible to generate concepts by interactive models. In the same line of reasoning and for the result of their experiments, Suchanek, Vojnovic, and Gunawardena (2008) concluded that the generated tags were useful and for this reason we think it is possible to use it to build and update ontologies.

The collaborative concept has the advantage to turn easier to adapt ontologies to the needs of users. As is confirmed with Bateman, Brooks, and McCalla (2006), the taggers generate concepts thinking about final uses. In this line, Pérez (1995) argues that if the ontology is not adapting for user needs its effectiveness is reduced.

We recognize disadvantages of taxonomies generated by collaborative tagging systems. As stated in Mathes (2004), the problems inherent in an uncontrolled vocabulary lead to a number of limitations and weaknesses in folksonomies. Ambiguity of the tags can emerge as users apply the same tag in different ways. At the opposite

end of the spectrum, the lack of synonyms control can lead to different tags being used for the same concept, precluding collocation. However, it is possible to improve the result generated by collaborative tagging; as stated in Guy and Tonkin (2006), tagging could be improved in two main ways in which improvements can be made. Firstly, a lot of things can be done at the point at which new resources are contributed to the system. Simple error checking potentially accounts for a number of tag errors although rather fewer misspellings occur than may be expected.

For this reason, the methodology proposes to integrate a suggestion system. According to the results obtained in Suchanek, Vojnovic, and Gunawardena (2008), 1 of 3 tags was in the suggested tags. In the same research 2 kinds of systems were suggested:

1. The standard Top Popular method (TOP), which to any user suggests the set of the most popular tags. This complicates the learning of a user's true preference of tags for an object.

2. Frequency Move-To-Set (FMTS) is a method that behaves similarly to TOP. It works as follows: For each document, it maintains a frequency vector of tags. The method will always suggest the top k tags in that vector for the document. After a tagging event, the method increments the frequencies of those tags in the vector that were applied by the user, but did not appear in the suggestion set. In this way, the method facilitates the rise of previously unpopular tags while still biasing towards the popular tags in general. This method, allows even completely unpopular tags to appear in the suggestion set.

Suchanek, Vojnovic, and Gunawardena (2008) show that the abuse of a suggestion tags system could generate passive users and for this we propose also to integrate queries to external data sets to minimize this feature.

Following Ciravegna (2001), the integration of the information extraction task has four important features: a) domain system adaptation through uses of extraction information techniques like lexical tools, knowledge bases, etc.; b) jargon and grammatical adaptation; c) adaptation of different kind of domain specifics text like medical texts or news texts; and d) adaptation of different kind of resources generated in Web systems like blogs, comments, image, state comments, and others.

On other hand, the use of external information datasets is shown to be an important source of dynamism and enrichment (Lee, Neve, Plataniotis, & Ro, 2010) of the knowledge management system.

Integrating the previous concepts, in order to obtain a taxonomy, it is necessary to add an element that defines the hierarchical relationships between the new generated terms.

Keeping in mind all of previous elements, our proposal can be described by the following steps (Figure 3):

1. Integrate collaborative tagging tools to create basic concepts in the ontology
2. Store tags in digital machine accessible language.

*Figure 3. Proposal methodological for building ontologies*

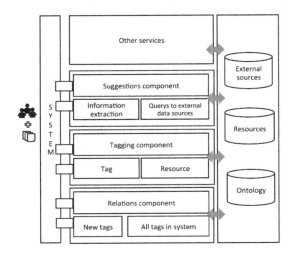

3. Integrate a suggestion system
   a. Implement the FMTS
   b. Using extraction from resources
   c. Integrate data of external datasets like other ontologies or folksonomies
4. Integrated interface which is able to define the relationship between terms

## PROTOTYPE: AUTOMATIC COLLABORATIVE TAGGING (ACOTA)

Following the specifications of the proposed methodology to build ontologies described in the previous section, we have implemented a prototype of one part of the methodology.

This methodology can be compared with a second case of possible uses stated in Berrueta (2006) where the authors found a way to update ontology by tagging tools. For our proposal, we use a mix of these.

In this way, we add a new classification of techniques to integrate folksonomies and ontologies using semi-automatic and collaborative work. This technique uses probabilistic analysis, part of speech detection, and collaborative task by users.

The prototype that applies our proposal is called ACOTA (Automatic Collaborative Tagging); this component has, as a main objective, to be a useful tool for tag suggestion.

The architecture can be seen in (Figure 4) and it is composed of the following main phases:

1. Tagging
2. Suggestion
3. Definition of relationships

In the following sections, we will describe each of those phases.

## Tagging Component

The tagging system is the simplest component of ACOTA. The task of this is to store the users resources and register the tags employed by each one. Three elements are necessary for this process:

1. Users: the user selects the tags for each resource and provides feedback to the system to improve the suggestion patterns in future actions.
2. Resources: a resource is anything that can be described, for example news, knowledge, people, task, images, Web sites, etc. For this system, three elements are necessary: a) Title, main description of the resource; b) Description, content of the resource; c) Url, Web address where the resource can be found.
3. Tags: it is the textual term associated with a resource. The goal is to create or associate concepts into the ontology related with those tags.

## Suggestion Component

Following our methodology, this component consists of a mix of information retrieval and natural language processing tools. To make a suggestion we implement the method of Frequency Move To Set (FMTS) defined by Suchanek, Vojnovic, and Gunawardena (2008) and generate a vector with possible tags and its ranking, this ranking depends of where the term is provided from.

The suggestions component has as input a resource and a user and its result is a list of terms ordered by its relevance (Figure 5). The relevance of each term is defined by its weight expressed in numbers and the weight depends of the relevance of providers, part of speech, users' preferences, and other elements.

In summary the suggestion process is comprised by the following steps:

*Figure 4. Automatic collaborative tagging architecture*

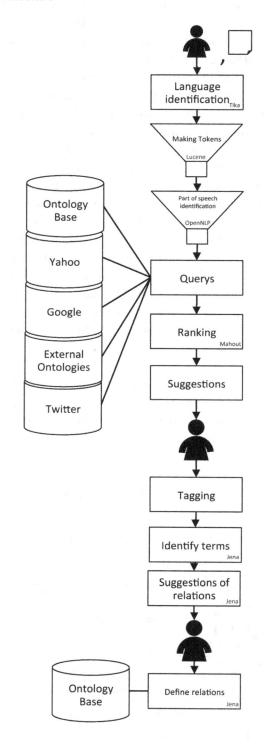

1. Information extraction
2. Query of externals datasets
3. Ranking and visualization of suggestions to users

In the process of information extraction, the prototype makes the first list of terms to complete the next task:

1. Language recognition using the Apache library Tika
2. Tokenize and remove of stop words by Apache Lucene
3. Remove words depending of the part of speech. For this task we use Open NLP

In Figure 6, we present an example of vector of suggested terms done by ACOTA.

After the information extraction process, the component uses the first list of generated terms and does a query to external data sources. In this prototype, we use folksonomies like Google, Yahoo, or Twitter. The definition of external sources is a configuration parameter and can be changed depending on the needs of specific systems.

*Figure 5. Summary of source and result of suggestions process of the prototype*

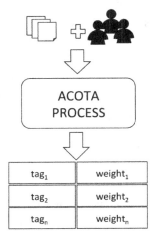

*Figure 6. Example of a resource and its suggestions*

The last task of the suggestion component is to rank the results and to show the list of suggestions to the user. In this point, the system orders the list of tags depending on their relevance. Afterwards, using the library Apache Mahout it compares the list with past preferences of each user and finally show a ranking list.

## Define Relationships Component

The last component of our prototype is responsible for detecting new concepts and providing the interface for generating relationships between new concepts and old concepts contained in the ontology. This task is work in progress.

The ACOTA prototype is a live project development by the WESO research group and its components are offered as a Web service in http://www.weso.es/acota-web.

## METHODOLOGY

With the aim to evaluate the suggestion component and its ability to extract relevant information from resources and to do successful suggestions we did two experiments.

The experiments compare a group of 600 resources previously tagged by users with an automatic list of suggestions done by the suggestion component of ACOTA.

## Boolean Experiments

The first group of experiments tried to check there was or not one successful suggestion, so we called this group Boolean experiments; the only possible result of each comparison was yes or not. With the goal to evaluate each element integrated in the suggestion component the Boolean experiment had four different parts using all components or a mixture of them.

### Boolean Experiment: All Elements

In this case, we compared the obtained tag with the suggestion list done using all the elements of the suggestion component; identify language, tokenize, part of speech analysis, and query to external datasets. The results of this experiment are shown in Figure 7.

### Boolean Experiment: Tokenize

In the same group of experiments and with the objective to assess the difference between using one element or another, this experiment tried to compare the same resources of the previous experiment but adding a different mix of tools. In this case, it used the suggestion list to identify the language and tokenize. For this mix, the component had more than 30% successful suggested tags (Figure 8).

### Boolean Experiment: Tokenize + POS

A part of our proposal is to integrate a query to external datasets with the goal to obtain new concepts. In this experiment, we removed the query to external datasets to study what was the impact. The suggestion list done using language recognition, tokenize and Part Of Speech analysis (POS) had around 30% of successful suggested tags (Figure 9).

## Boolean Experiment: Tokenize + Query

In the same line of the previous experiments and with the goal to evaluate the impact of part of speech analysis, we compared the group of tagging resources with the list of suggestions removing that step. This experiment obtains more than 30% of successful suggested tags (Figure 10).

Taking into account the previous groups of experiments we could affirm that the suggestion component had 30% of successful suggested tag in average (Figure 11). Making a more detailed analysis about the results, we observed:

- The best mix of tools was to employ tokenize and query to externals datasets
- Independently of the mix, the tool of information extraction had relatively good results

## Relevant Positions Experiment

The second group of experiments tried to assess the position of the successful tag, we called Relevant Position Experiments. This data is important because the main objective of the suggestion component is to turn easier the tagging task and for this reason, the list of suggestions has to be short. In the second group of experiments, we did the same classification as the first one, four experiments using all or a mix of the elements of the suggestion component.

### Relevant Position Experiment: All Elements

In this case study, we compared the resources preciously tagged by users with the suggestion

*Figure 7. Boolean experiment using all elements of the suggestions component*

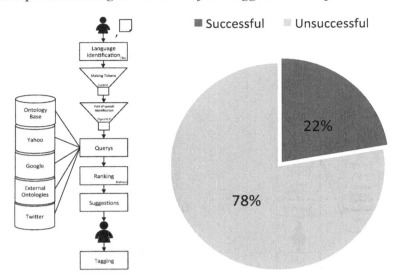

*Figure 8. Boolean experiment only using tokenize*

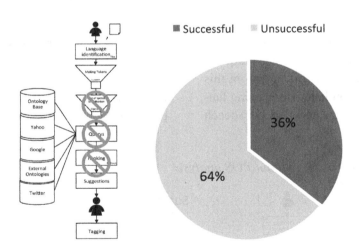

list done using all elements of the suggestion component; identify language, tokenize, part of speech analysis and query to external data sets. The main objective was to identify the position of each successful tag. The results of this experiment are shown in Figure 12.

## Relevant Position Experiment: Tokenize

As the first group of experiments, this one had as a main objective to assess the differences between the uses of all elements in the suggestions list by identifying the language and tokenizing. For this mix, the component had the results expressed in Figure 13.

*Figure 9. Boolean experiment without querying external datasets*

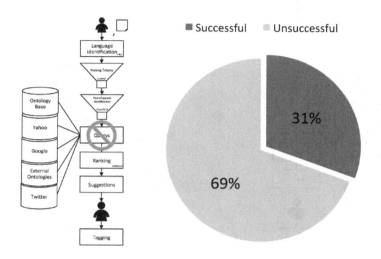

## Relevant Position Experiment: Tokenize + POS

With the main objective to determinate the impact of queries to externals datasets on the relevant position, in this experiment we removed the query to external datasets task. For this reason in this experiment the suggestion list is done using language recognition, tokenize and Part Of Speech analysis (POS). This experiment obtains more than 25% of suggested tags in the first position (Figure 14).

## Relevant Position Experiments: Tokenize + Query

In the same line as the previous group of experiments and with the objective to evaluate the

*Figure 10. Boolean experiment without POS analysis*

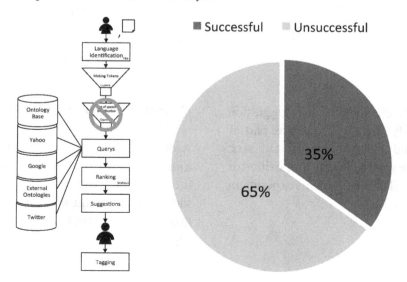

*Figure 11. Compare between Boolean experiments*

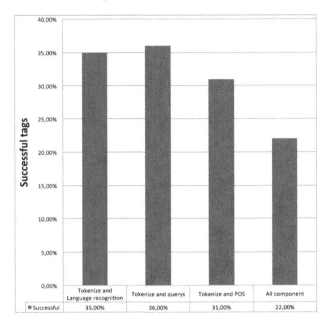

impact of part of speech analysis, we compared the tagging resources with the list of suggestions done without POS analysis. The result of this experiment obtained more than 30% of successful suggested tags in the first position (Figure 15).

Talking into account the results of all of relevant position experiments, we observed that of all of the possible combination of tools obtains good results about the first position, in all cases this position had around 25% of all successful suggested tags. Talking about the rest of positions, we determined that around 80% of successful tags are in the 10 first positions of the list done with the suggestion component (Figure 16).

*Figure 12. Relevant position using all elements of the suggestion component*

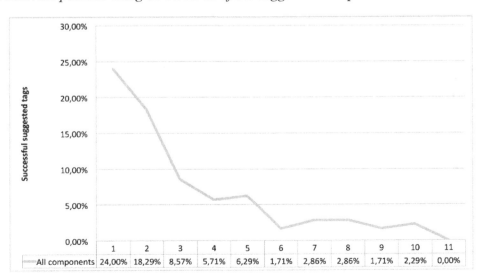

*Figure 13. Relevant position using only tokenizer*

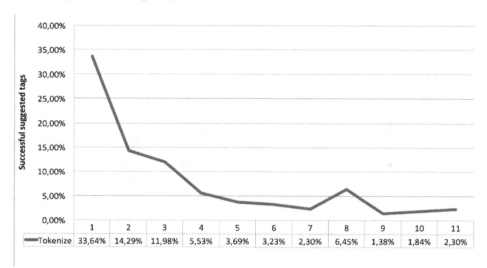

| | 1 | 2 | 3 | 4 | 5 | 6 | 7 | 8 | 9 | 10 | 11 |
|---|---|---|---|---|---|---|---|---|---|---|---|
| Tokenize | 33,64% | 14,29% | 11,98% | 5,53% | 3,69% | 3,23% | 2,30% | 6,45% | 1,38% | 1,84% | 2,30% |

For this reason, we notice that in a real case the suggestion component integrated in any kind of tagging system could do suggestions that could be accepted like good ones by users and in addition the order of the list presented to the user could help the user in the tagging task. Another features are interesting:

- Like in the previous groups of experiments, the most successful combination of tools was adding extraction information and queries to external data sources.
- The most successful tool was the tokenizer, which helped to define the importance of extraction information tools in the task to define relevant terms in the text.

*Figure 14. Relevant position without querying to external datasets*

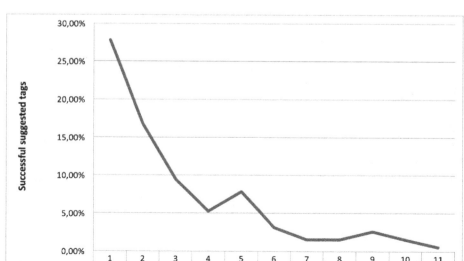

| | 1 | 2 | 3 | 4 | 5 | 6 | 7 | 8 | 9 | 10 | 11 |
|---|---|---|---|---|---|---|---|---|---|---|---|
| Tokenize + POS | 27,75% | 16,75% | 9,42% | 5,24% | 7,85% | 3,14% | 1,57% | 1,57% | 2,62% | 1,57% | 0,52% |

*Figure 15. Relevant position experiment without POS analysis*

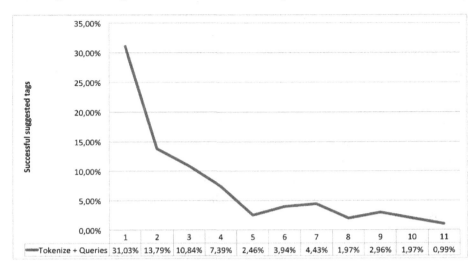

| | 1 | 2 | 3 | 4 | 5 | 6 | 7 | 8 | 9 | 10 | 11 |
|---|---|---|---|---|---|---|---|---|---|---|---|
| Tokenize + Queries | 31,03% | 13,79% | 10,84% | 7,39% | 2,46% | 3,94% | 4,43% | 1,97% | 2,96% | 1,97% | 0,99% |

*Figure 16. Comparison between relevant position experiments*

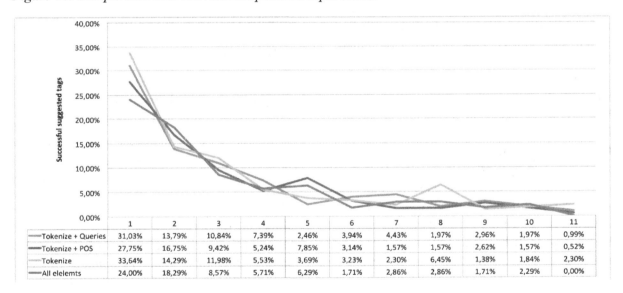

| | 1 | 2 | 3 | 4 | 5 | 6 | 7 | 8 | 9 | 10 | 11 |
|---|---|---|---|---|---|---|---|---|---|---|---|
| Tokenize + Queries | 31,03% | 13,79% | 10,84% | 7,39% | 2,46% | 3,94% | 4,43% | 1,97% | 2,96% | 1,97% | 0,99% |
| Tokenize + POS | 27,75% | 16,75% | 9,42% | 5,24% | 7,85% | 3,14% | 1,57% | 1,57% | 2,62% | 1,57% | 0,52% |
| Tokenize | 33,64% | 14,29% | 11,98% | 5,53% | 3,69% | 3,23% | 2,30% | 6,45% | 1,38% | 1,84% | 2,30% |
| All elelemts | 24,00% | 18,29% | 8,57% | 5,71% | 6,29% | 1,71% | 2,86% | 2,86% | 1,71% | 2,29% | 0,00% |

## CONCLUSION

The present document has identified the need of dynamic information structures that put up a solid foundation for developing classification systems, data collection and search of resources and information in the Web. Currently two approaches have been implemented to address this need: the use of formal structures such as ontologies and the use of more flexible structures such as folksonomies. The use of ontologies as a basic approach for classification, collection, and search is considered as an appropriate choice due to the possibility of establishing clear, reusable, interoperable, and precise terms; it also provides a high level of formality. Nevertheless, this option has a weakness, the lack of adaptability and capability to add new terms as quickly as they arise in areas of continuous innovation like science and technology.

On the other hand, folksonomies show a fully dynamic and adaptive structure, which is constantly renewed by the participation of a large number of users. However, the diversity of participants and the lack of formal restrictions on the creation of terms leads to problems of ambiguity, synonymy, clarity, and formality.

The main objective of this research is to unify the two concepts drawing on the strengths of each one and trying to minimize their weaknesses. Thus, the creation of ontologies from a collaborative tagging system will be modeled as an information classification structure, which is updated dynamically and constantly.

In conclusion, although the collaborative creation of information classification structures is not a new topic (Farquhar, Fikes, & Rice, 1996), it is important to emphasize that the main contribution of the current project is the integration of terms from folksonomies or other ontologies automatically with the goal to integrate and expand the original ontology. Additionally, the participation of users in the process of creating and maintaining the ontology will generate a structure adapted to their context. In future work, we will try to develop dynamic evaluation methods. The collaborative process of creating terms will provide a transition state of new terms where it is expected that consensus, censorship, or modification by other users could affect the information management process. This system could be defined automatically or by user profiles with different responsibilities.

## REFERENCES

Bateman, S., Brooks, C., & McCalla, G. (2006). Collaborative tagging approaches for ontological metadata in adaptive e-learning systems. In *Proceedings of the International Workshop on Applications of Semantic Web Technologies for E-Learning (SW-EL 2006)*, (pp. 3-12). Dublin, Ireland: SW-EL.

Benz, D., Hotho, A., & St, S. (2010). Semantics made by you and me: Self-emerging ontologies can capture the diversity of shared knowledge. In *Proceedings of the 2nd Web Science Conference (WebSci 2010)*. Raleigh, NC: WebSci.

Berrueta, D. (2006). *MORFEO-MyMobileWeb: Tecnologías avanzadas de software abierto para el desarrollo de la Web Móvil: 1.0, 2.0 y 3.0.* CETIC Fundation.

Brewster, C., Ciravegna, F., & Wilks, Y. (2003). Background and foreground knowledge in dynamic ontology construction: Viewing text as knowledge maintenance. In *Proceedings of the Semantic Web Workshop, SIGIR August 2003.* Toronto, Canada: SIGIR.

Ciravegna, F. (2001). Challenges in information extraction from text for knowledge management. In *Proceedings of the IEEE Intelligent Systems and their Applications*. IEEE Press.

Farquhar, A., Fikes, R., & Rice, J. (1996). The ontolingua server: A tool for collaborative ontology construction. *Knowledge Systems, 46*, 707–727.

Greenberg, J., & Pattuelli, M. (2001). Author-generated Dublin core metadata for web resources: A baseline study in an organization. *Journal of Digital Information, 2*, 38–46.

Gruber, T. R. (1995). Toward principles for the design of ontologies used for knowledge. *International Journal of Human-Computer Studies, 43*, 907–928. doi:10.1006/ijhc.1995.1081

Guy, M., & Tonkin, E. (2006). Folksonomies tidying up tags? *D-Lib Magazine, 12*, 1–14.

Kayed, A., El-Qawasmeh, E., & Qawaqneh, Z. (2010). Ranking web sites using domain ontology concepts. *Information & Management, 47*, 350–355. doi:10.1016/j.im.2010.08.002

Kunder, M. D. (2012). *World wide web size.* Retrieved january 2012, from http://www.worldwidewebsize.com/

Lee, S., Neve, W. D., Plataniotis, K. N., & Ro, Y. M. (2010). MAP-based image tag recommendation using a visual folksonomy. *Pattern Recognition Letters, 31*, 976–982. doi:10.1016/j.patrec.2009.12.024

Mathes, A. (2004). *Folksonomies - Cooperative classification and communication through shared metadata the creation of metadata: Professionals, content creators, users*. Retrieved from http://www.adammathes.com/academic/computer-mediated-communication/folksonomies.html

Miniwastts Marketing Group. (2012). *Internet world stasts*. Retrieved 01 20, 2012, from http://www.internetworldstats.com/stats.htm

Pérez, A. G. (1995). Some ideas and examples to evaluate ontologies. In *Proceedings of the Eleventh Conference on Artificial Intelligence for Applications,* (pp. 299-305). IEEE Press.

Suchanek, F., Vojnovic, M., & Gunawardena, D. (2008). Social tags: Meaning and suggestions. In *Proceeding of the 17th ACM Conference on Information and Knowledge Management,* (pp. 223-232). New York, NY: ACM Press.

Tang, H.-F. L., & Dewei, L. (2009). Towards ontology learning from folksonomies. In *Proceedings of the 21st International Joint Conference on Artificial Intelligence (IJCAI),* (pp. 2089-2094). IJCAI.

Thomas, C. F., & Griffin, L. S. (1998). Who will create the metadata for the internet?. *First Monday: A Peer-Reviewed Journal on the Internet, 3*.

Uschold, M., & Gruninger, M. (1996). Ontologies: Principles, methods and applications. *The Knowledge Engineering Review, 11*, 93–136. doi:10.1017/S0269888900007797

Wal, T. V. (2007). *Folksonomy*. Retrieved january 2012, from http://vanderwal.net/folksonomy.html

# Chapter 3
# Visualizing Design Project Knowledge on a Collaborative Web 2.0 Platform

**Vadim Ermolayev**
*Zaporozhye National University, Ukraine*

**Frank Dengler**
*Karlsruhe Institute of Technology, Germany*

## ABSTRACT

*The chapter reports the implementation and validation of the knowledge process visualization technology that extends the basic capabilities of the Semantic MediaWiki platform. The Design Project Visualizer has been developed in the ACTIVE Integrating Project of the Seventh Framework Programme of the European Union for the case study in the engineering design in Microelectronics and Integrated Circuits. The concept of knowledge process visualization is based on the paradigm of project navigation. The knowledge workers in this domain are design project managers, designers, and design support engineers. The visualization suggests optimized performance, points to the bottlenecks in executions, and fosters collaboration in development teams. The authors describe the software prototype architecture and implementation. The components and the solution for process knowledge transformation between ontological representations as well as the visualization are presented in detail. Validation results indicate that the solution is helpful in providing expert assistance to design project managers performing their typical tasks of project planning and execution management.*

## INTRODUCTION

In the knowledge economy (Powell & Snellman, 2004) knowledge workers (Drucker, 1969) are central to an organisation's success—yet the tools they use often stand in the way of increasing their

performance. A remedy to the defects of those tools has recently become in demand across industries. This is why it became a major research and development theme in the ACTIVE project[1]—the three case studies in consulting, telecommunications, and engineering design have been driven

DOI: 10.4018/978-1-4666-2494-8.ch003

Copyright © 2013, IGI Global. Copying or distributing in print or electronic forms without written permission of IGI Global is prohibited.

by this requirement. In this chapter, we focus on presenting our accomplishments in developing a collaborative tool for the knowledge workers who manage projects and take part in performing informal processes (Warren, et al., 2009) in microelectronic engineering design (MIC). This case study has been lead by Cadence Design Systems GmbH (www.cadence-europe.com), a provider of software, hardware, IP, and Services in MIC domain.

The goal of the case study is providing a software tool for design project managers that will articulate and facilitate sharing knowledge about good development practices in this domain. An objective of a project manager as a knowledge worker is finding a reasonable balance between the available and the achievable in order to meet the requirements of a customer and accomplish development in his project with the highest possible productivity. The complexity of this task in modern design environments is beyond the analytical capabilities of even an experienced individual. A manager has to find an optimum in a solution space that has many facets: product structure comprising possibilities for block reuse; the compositions of the development team involving required roles and capabilities of the available individuals; the choices of the tools for performing design and corresponding design methodologies; the resources available for the project; project constraints and business policies; etc. One more complication may appear in the course of the execution of the—the circumstances may change because of external events. Hence, a previously good plan may turn out to be not acceptable for the follow-up. Re-planning may therefore be required at any moment.

Project managers use their working experience and intuition for taking planning decisions under these complex conditions. In fact, they rely on following good practices and exploiting the suggested development methodologies that they used in the past and which constitute their tacit working

knowledge of project management. Our working hypothesis in this research was that offering a software tool for making the tacit knowledge of project managers within a company explicit will decrease the complexity of making decisions and increase the robustness of knowledge work.

For checking this hypothesis, the software tool prototype of a Design Project Visualizer has been developed in the case study. The tool implements a project navigation metaphor. Project navigation helps a knowledge worker decide about a productive execution path through the state space of an engineering design project—very similarly to the decisions made by a driver using a car navigation system.

The Design Project Visualizer, like a car navigation system, provides the visualized views of the basic "terrain" map. These views are product structures, methodology flows that are either generic or bound to a particular product structure, Work Breakdown Structures (WBS). These representations are essentially provided by a project manager in a top-down fashion when he plans and kicks-off the project. The tool also assists in finding out where the project is on the "terrain" at a specific point in time. The knowledge about the execution of the project is mined from the available project log datasets, transformed to the terms of the used ontology, stored to the knowledgebase, and superimposed onto the project execution plans.

Unlike a car navigation system the Design Project Visualizer is a tool for team work. It provides the infrastructure and the functionality for moderated discussions attached to a visualized representation of any kind of a project constituent. By that, it facilitates making more informed decisions that are also more transparent to the team members and are elaborated and approved with their active participation.

The tool we developed in ACTIVE goes beyond the existing performance management solutions by providing the functionalities of the following two kinds: (1) at the back-end, the learning of design process execution knowledge from distributed datasets of acquired knowledge; and (2) at the front-end, design project knowledge articulation and sharing – by providing a lightweight and user friendly collaboration platform. In this chapter, we present the solutions for visualizing project elements.

The remainder of the chapter is structured as follows. Section 2 surveys the related work in informal process representation and visualization. It also outlines the unsolved problems that are further addressed in our work. Section 3 elaborates on the architecture and implementation of our software prototype. Section 4 explains in more detail our solutions for visualizing design project knowledge. Section 5 presents the procedure for and the results of the validation of the implemented software tool in an industrial setting. Section 6 discusses the results and draws some conclusions.

## RELATED WORK

The work presented in this chapter contributed to several interrelated aspects relevant to managing and productively using informal process knowledge. Our contributions that are reported in this chapter comprise the representation of informal process knowledge in the form of ontologies, the methods for informal process knowledge articulation, and sharing using a visualization and superimposition approach.

### Informal Process Knowledge Representation

The mainstream in process modeling is represented by enterprise and business process representations—in the form of ontologies or languages. Among the ontologies the following results have to be mentioned: the Enterprise Ontology (Uschold, et al., 1998), Toronto Virtual Enterprise

Ontology (TOVE) (Grüninger, et al., 2000), and more recently the theoretical work by Dietz (2006) and the reference ontology for business models developed in Interop, an EU FP6 Network of Excellence (Andersson, et al., 2006). The business process modeling community has developed a variety of languages with the major objective of representing business processes as the executable orchestrations of activities. The most prominent examples of such languages are: PSL (Bock & Grüninger, 2005), BPEL and more recently WS-BPEL (docs.oasis-open.org/wsbpel/2.0/OS/wsbpel-v2.0-OS.pdf), BPML and more recently BPDM (www.omg.org/spec/BPDM/1.0/). A more comprehensive approach to semantic business process modeling and management has been developed in the FP6 SUPER project (Hepp & Roman, 2007). A major shortcoming of the listed results is that they are not supposed to provide a means to model informal processes as denoted by Warren et al. (2009).

One of the relevant approaches to modelling and representing informal processes has been developed in the FP6 Nepomuk project (Grebner, et al., 2006). A shortcoming of the process representation in Nepomuk ontologies is the limitation of the scope only to the tasks performed on the computer desktop.

Our approach to informal process representation builds on the work in dynamic engineering design process modeling of the PSI and PRODUKTIV+ projects (Ermolayev, et al., 2008). Our contribution in ACTIVE is the lightweight knowledge process representation for engineering design that is essentially a micro ontology (Ell, et al., 2010) providing a simplified yet sufficiently expressive view of a design process to be visualized for articulation and sharing. This micro ontology is aligned with the ACTIVE Knowledge Process Model (Tilly, 2010) through the PSI Upper-Level Ontology where the latter is used as a semantic bridge (Ermolayev, et al., 2008).

## Informal Process Knowledge Articulation and Sharing

The spiral of knowledge (Nonaka & Takeuchi, 1995) introduces different knowledge conversions which is a fundamental part of sharing knowledge. People can share tacit knowledge with each other (socialization), but this is a rather limited form of sharing knowledge. Knowledge articulation within companies is the process of making tacit knowledge explicit (externalization). This explicit knowledge can be combined with other explicit knowledge (combination) and shared throughout an organization. Other employees extend and reframe their tacit knowledge with explicit knowledge by internalizing it (internalization). There are different ways to articulate and share informal process knowledge, but in all cases, the informal process knowledge has to be made explicit. For instance, process knowledge can be visualized manually or with tool support. In contrast to the visualization approach, the process knowledge can also be stored and shared within the system by using it directly for recommendations (Dorn, et al., 2010).

## Articulation and Sharing using Visualization Approach

It is natural for a human to use visualized representations of artifacts in general and of processes in particular. Research in psychology, human memory models, image recognition and perception reveals that graphical representations are comprehended much easier and with lower effort than equivalent textual ones (Crapo, et al., 2000). Therefore, process visualization is one of the mature instruments to articulate processes thus enabling users to easily understand the logic of a process.

Most process visualization techniques are included in process modeling activities, which can be centralized or decentralized. An abundance of modeling methods and tools like ARIS (Scheer & Jost, 2002) and IDEF3 (Mayer, et al., 1995) have been developed to ease the standardization, storage, and sharing of process visualization. Unfortunately, these tools are not sufficient for modeling collaborative, decentralized processes. Therefore, other approaches like CPM (Ryu & Yücesan, 2007) have been introduced.

In the area of knowledge processes additional methods and tools like KMDL (Gronau, 2005), PROMOTE (Woitsch & Karagiannis, 2005), and CommonKADS (Schreiber, et al., 1999) have been developed extending the methods and tools mentioned above. In addition, semantic wikis combine the collaborative aspects of wikis (Leuf & Cunningham, 2001) with Semantic Web technology to enable large-scale and inter-departmental collaboration on knowledge structures. Such features of semantic wikis have been extended to support process development (Dengler, et al., 2009), enterprise modelling (Ghidini, et al., 2009), and workflows (Dello, et al., 2008). Our contribution in process visualization is the enhancement of the existing Semantic MediaWiki (SMW) (Krötzsch, et al., 2007) process development approach (Dengler, et al., 2009; Ermolayev, et al., 2011) to visualize and discuss informal processes.

Our project navigation approach is based on offering a collaboration platform to knowledge workers that facilitates socializing, externalizing, and internalizing design project knowledge using visualization. Visualization of project knowledge helps to combine and internalize explicit project knowledge in a way that suggests productive continuations of project execution.

## PROTOTYPE ARCHITECTURE AND IMPLEMENTATION

The architecture of the software prototype of the ACTIVE Design Project Visualizer is pictured in Figure 1. It comprises both the back-end and the front-end components and involves several ACTIVE technologies. Design process knowl-

*Figure 1. The configuration of software components in ACTIVE design project visualizer. The SMW connector and the active front-end components are explained in detail. The rest of the back-end is described in Ermolayev et al. (2011).*

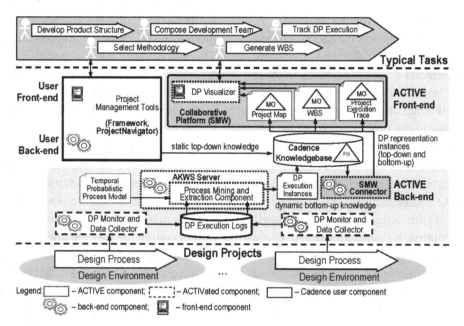

edge acquisition is done mainly at the back-end while the functions of knowledge articulation and sharing are offered by the front-end. As shown in Figure 1, the prototype helps users to perform their typical tasks of design project management. The tool monitors the environments of the managed engineering design project, that are design systems, and allows for run-time extraction of the process-related knowledge in a bottom-up fashion. The normative, methodological, and static parts of project knowledge are provided via the external tools in a top-down manner. The external tools are the ProjectNavigator and the Flow Infrastructure Framework—c.f. Figure 1. Hence, the prototype exploits the superimposition of the top-down and bottom-up project knowledge for making its articulation and sharing more efficient and effective. The fusion of the bottom-up and top-down knowledge is done by transforming those to the instances of the PSI Suite of Ontologies, which are stored in the knowledgebase.

Articulation and sharing are done by visualizing different facets of design project knowledge in the collaborative front-end using the SMW as a platform—the ACTIVE Design Project Visualizer. Visualization functionality is structured around the typical tasks that design project managers perform in their everyday business (upper part of Figure 1). The kinds of visualization pages are those for product structures, generic methodologies, product-bound methodologies[2], tools, and actor roles. These primary functionalities are supported by decision-making instruments for conducting moderated discussions—the discussion component as an extension of SMW and LiveNetLife (www.livenetlife.com), an application for contextualized interactive real-time communication between the users of a website.

A challenge in the development of knowledge representation for the case study and the software prototype of the Design Project Navigator was finding a proper balance between:

- The background result, the PSI Suite of Ontologies for MIC Engineering Design domain used at Cadence, and the model of a Knowledge Process (KPM) developed in ACTIVE (Tilly, 2010).
- The expressive power of the knowledge representation of the Cadence knowledgebase (PSI Ontologies) and the lightweight character of the enterprise knowledge structures developed in ACTIVE caused by the lightweight character of the SMW used for the prototype development.

The first aspect was essentially a harmonization problem. For harmonizing the KPM with the PSI Suite of Ontologies (isrg.kit.znu.edu.ua/ontodocwiki/) the PSI Upper Level ontology (PSI-ULO) has been used as a semantic bridge (Ermolayev, et al., 2010b). The harmonization process was bidirectional. On one hand, the Suite of PSI Ontologies has been refined by cleaning the representations of process patterns and processes. This work led to fixing the v.2.3 release of the PSI Suite. On the other hand, the KPM has been revised by aligning it to the PSI-ULO. This work led to the final release of the KPM.

The second problem was the selection of the minimal required part of the PSI Core Ontologies v.2.3 as the lightweight knowledge representation for the Design Project Visualizer. For that the requirements based on the analysis of the typical user tasks and use cases have been applied and resulted in the development of the micro ontology for the case study (Ell, et al., 2010).

The front-end—ACTIVE Design Project Visualizer—for process visualisation and discussion of design projects is based on SMW and has been implemented by extending the existing process visualization approach (Dengler, et al., 2009) and by developing additional result printers for SMW to visualize and export the WBS—namely the Gantt chart and the XML export result printers that are the part of the Mediawiki Semantic Project Management extension (www.mediawiki.org/wiki/Extension:Semantic_Project_Management). The screenshots of the characteristic features of the Design Project Visualizer are shown in Figures 6-8.

This extension builds on the capability to query for semantic properties, which is provided by SMW and displays query results as process graphs, Gantt charts, or XML-files containing the WBS in XML schema to be further imported into MS-Project. For the back-end, a software connector has been developed that imports the knowledge stored in the knowledgebase into the SMW pages (Figure 1).

Each element of the micro ontology is represented as a wiki page containing annotated links to other wiki pages (properties). These properties are queried via an inline query language provided by SMW and the result is rendered into the destination format required by the different visualization libraries.

For supporting collaboration the functionality for working with talk pages has been developed as another SMW extension. Talk pages corresponding to visualized project elements can be created to discuss pros and cons of different project elements. Discussion summary icons indicate open discussions attached to the visualized project elements (Figure 5). The numbers correspond to the pro and con counters for the discussion.

## PRODUCT AND PROCESS KNOWLEDGE VISUALIZATION

A connector component (SMW Connector, Figure 1) has been developed as a Java application to convert instances from PSI Core Ontologies into the micro ontology used in ACTIVE Design Project Visualizer. Each class of the micro ontology is represented in the application as a Java class with the corresponding properties. The application uses the OWL API (Horridge & Bechhofer, 2009) for loading the PSI Ontologies provided as multiple OWL files. The required instances of the PSI Ontologies are processed and transformed into the Java class structure. As not all knowledge is explicitly stored within these ontologies, the missing parts have to be inferred during this transformation. For instance, the PSI Ontologies do not have explicit successor properties between *GenericTask* instances. These properties are derived by using the property connections via *DAStatePatterns* and *InputConfig*. In the following, we illustrate the transformations for *DesignArtifacts*, *GenericTasks*, and *Tasks*, where the source representations are respective Core Ontologies of the PSI Suite of Ontologies v.2.3 (isrg.kit.znu.edu.ua/ontodocwiki/index.php/PSI_Suite_of_Ontologies) and the target is the ACTIVE micro ontology representation.

*DesignArtifacts:* The classes and properties of the PSI Core Design Artifact Ontology are pictured in Figure 2 as a UML class diagram. In fact, only a fragment of a broader and more expressive PSI Design Artifact ontology is used. The complete specification of this PSI ontology may be retrieved from the OntoDocWiki (isrg.kit.znu. edu.ua/ontodocwiki/index.php/PSI_Core_Design_Artifact_ontology). A *DesignArtifact* may comprise the other *DesignArtifacts* connected using the *hasChild* property. It can further have a *DAType* (*hasDAType* property) and may belong to a *DALibrary* (*belongsToDALibrary* property). In the PSI Design Artifact Ontology, a *Design-Artifact* can have multiple relations to the other

*Figure 2. DesignArtifact context mapping from the PSI core design artifact ontology v.2.3 to the ACTIVE micro ontology. PSI concepts used in the micro ontology are shaded gray. The properties introduced in the micro ontology are bold with the names shaded gray.*

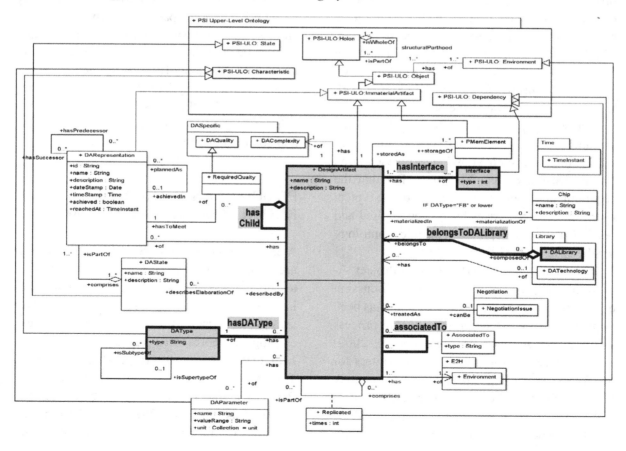

*DesignArtifact* class instances via the property represented by an association class *AssociatedTo*. In the ACTIVE micro ontology, we ignore the additional properties of the *AssociatedTo* class and only use a property *associatedTo* between *DesignArtifacts*. Furthermore, a *DesignArtifact* can have a *hasInterface* property relating it to the *Interface* class.

*GenericTasks: GenericTasks* in the ACTIVE micro ontology are a means to represent development methodologies. Please refer to the visualization of those methodologies in Figure 7. The context of the PSI Core Process Pattern Ontology v.2.3 describing the class *GenericTask* is pictured in Figure 3. The complete Process Pattern Ontol-

ogy is documented at the OntoDocWiki (isrg.kit. znu.edu.ua/ontodocwiki/index.php/PSI_Core_ Process_Pattern_ontology).

A *GenericTask* as a pattern is related to the concept of a *Task,* which may belong to a *GenericTask.* The pattern specification by a *GenericTask* contains also a requirement of involving a specific *Role. GenericTask* data properties of *id* and *name* are ported to the micro ontology without transformations. The *hasSuccessor* property between *GenericTasks* is inferred by using the bolded path via *DAStatePatterns* and *InputConfig* back to *GenericTask* (Figure 3).

*Tasks: Tasks* in the ACTIVE micro ontology are a means to represent development processes.

*Figure 3. GenericTask context mapping from the PSI process pattern ontology v.2.3 to the ACTIVE micro ontology. PSI concepts used in the micro ontology are shaded gray. The properties introduced in the micro ontology are bold with the names shaded gray.*

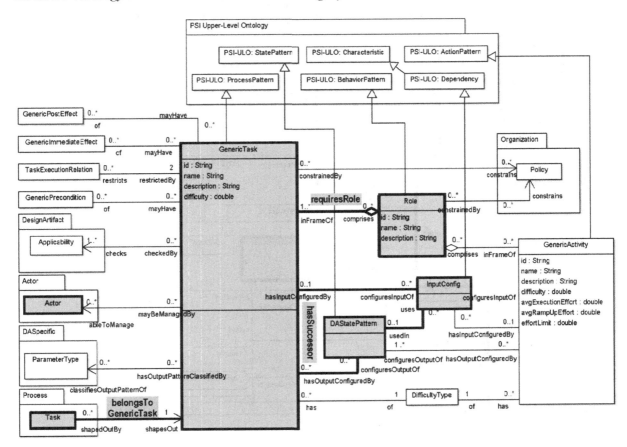

Please refer to the visualization of those methodologies in Figure 8. The context of the PSI Core Process Ontology v.2.3 containing the classes and properties used for the description of a *Task* are shown in Figure 4. The complete Process Ontology is documented at the OntoDoc-Wiki (isrg.kit.znu.edu.ua/ontodocwiki/index.php/

PSI_Core_Process_ontology). The *hasSuccessor* object property between the instances of a *Task* is also inferred by using the bolded path via an *Activity* and a *DARepresentation* back to a *Task*. A *Task* can belong to a *GenericTask* and every *Task* has an *Actor*. A *Task* can have subtasks, connected with the property *belongsToTask*. The

*Figure 4. Task context mapping from the PSI process pattern ontology v.2.3 to the ACTIVE micro ontology. PSI concepts used in the micro ontology are shaded gray. The properties introduced in the micro ontology are bold with the names shaded gray.*

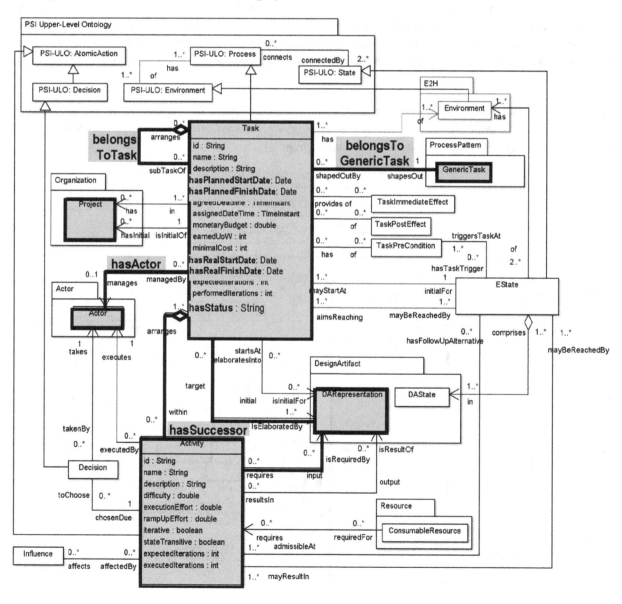

datatype properties of the class *Task* are mapped as follows: *startingDateTime* to *hasPlannedStart Date*, *agreedDateTime* to *hasPlannedFinishDate*, *realStart* to *hasRealStartDate*, *realEnd* to *hasRealFinishDate* and *status* to *hasStatus*.

In a second step, the created Java class model containing all the instances of the micro ontology is imported into the ACTIVE Design Project Visualizer by using the Java Wiki Bot Framework (JWBF; jwbf.sourceforge.net)[3]. Therefore, each Java class contains a method, which translates each instance into wiki text using a MediaWiki template structure. With the help of the JWBF, a wiki page including the generated wiki text is created in the ACTIVE Design Project Visualizer. A new wiki page is created for each instance.

As instances can have the same value for the name property, we use the ontology instance URIs as wiki page names to avoid name conflicts. An example code snippet translating the class *GenericTask* into wiki text using a MediaWiki template structure is presented in Figure 5. Similar snippets have been implemented for performing the transformations of all required classes.

The product and process knowledge stored within the ACTIVE Design Project Visualizer is visualized in various ways.

Product structures are visualized by showing the dependencies of the different *DesignArtifacts* in a graph as illustrated in Figure 6. The individuals of a *DesignArtifact* are displayed as boxes containing the name and the type of the *DesignArtifact*

*Figure 5. Example code snippet translating the class GenericTask into wiki text using a MediaWiki template structure*

```
public void WriteToWiki(MediaWikiBot bot){
   // Create wiki page using the ontology instance URIs as
   // wiki page name
   Article sa = new Article(bot,this.getWikiName());
   // Start adding template text
   sa.addText("{{GenericTask");
   sa.addTextnl("| Version=1");
   // Add value of the name property
   sa.addTextnl("| Name=" + this.name);
   // Add GenericTask successors
   if (this.GenTaskSuccessors.size()!=0)
     sa.addTextnl("| has Successor=");
   int j = 1;
   for (GenTask successor : this.GenTaskSuccessors) {
       sa.addText(successor.getWikiName());
     if (this.GenTaskSuccessors.size()!=j) sa.addText("; ");
       j++;
     }
   ...
   // Close template
   sa.addTextnl("}}");
   // Save article into the wiki
   sa.save();
}
```

instance. A *DesignArtifact* can either be atomic or composed of other *DesignArtifacts*. This feature is visualized using a hierarchy structure (top to bottom) with lines as connectors.

Generic Development Methodologies consist of *GenericTasks* connected in a way to cover the complete technological cycle and present all possible development paths. For the visualization, a graph is created by using the successor relations between the *GenericTasks*. A rectangle containing the corresponding name of the *GenericTask* individual is displayed for each *GenericTask* instance. The successor relation is expressed with an arrow between these rectangles. For a better overview, only one successor is displayed in the graph, because the predecessors are more important for the users. Since many *GenericTasks* exist to de-

velop a specific design product, the user can select how many predecessors are shown in the graph, which also improves clarity and, therefore the usability of the ACTIVE Design Project Visualizer tool. An example is illustrated in Figure 7.

Product-Bound Methodologies are visualized as Work Breakdown Structures with superimposed execution status as shown in Figure 8. The different *Tasks*, which constitute a particular Work Breakdown Structure, have dedicated attributes like planed and real start and end dates, status as well as a resource executing the task. For the Gantt chart visualization, the Javascript library jsGantt (jsgantt.com) is used for rendering the Gantt charts. The data stored in the ACTIVE Design Project Visualizer are transformed into the jsGantt format. For the status visualization different colors are

*Figure 6. Characteristic features of the design project visualizer: product structure visualization as a hierarchy of DesignArtifacts specified by the micro ontology*

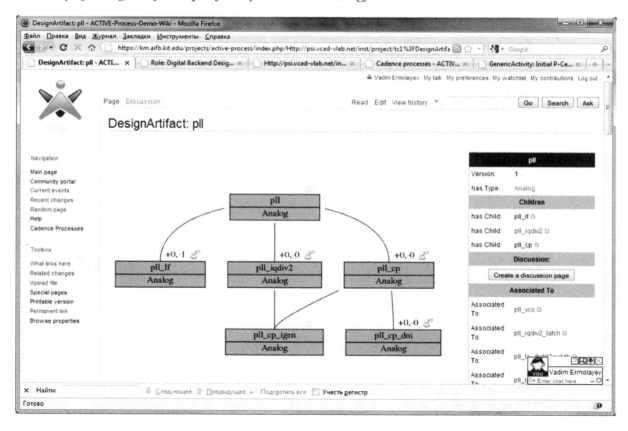

*Figure 7. Characteristic features of the design project visualizer: generic development methodology context visualization as a PERT diagram containing the chosen number of the predecessor GenericTasks of the highlighted GenericTask*

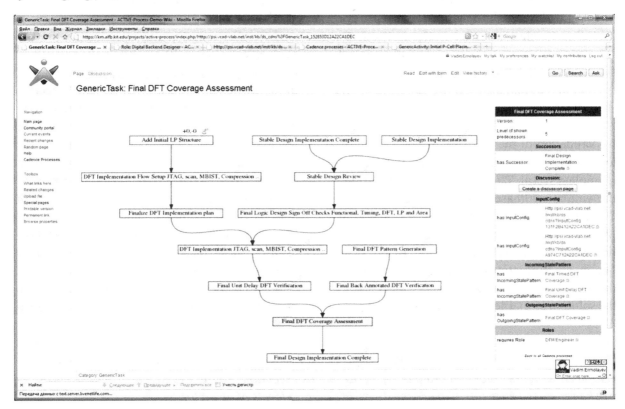

used. Similar to the Gantt chart, the data can be transformed to MS Project XML schema. The XML output generated using this functionality may further be used and modified in MS Project.

## VALIDATION SETUP AND RESULTS

The development of the software prototype was performed as an iterative process, which was strongly focused on user needs and the organizational requirements for the application. A MIC design process is very demanding in terms of adherence to detailed technical requirements and standards, consequently we had to emphasise testing detailed user and design processes. Different types of tests were carried out throughout the development process (Melchior & Bösser, 2011).

Each software version was tested repeatedly in a sequence of tests, where as a general rule the subsequent level of test was carried out after the lower level test returned a satisfactory result, usually after a number of iterations:

- **T1: Dry Runs and Technical Appropriateness:** Experts and user representatives who are familiar with the application context assess if the software is bug-free and consistent with the requirements (Ermolayev, et al., 2010), and suggest design improvements.
- **T2: Usability in representative user tasks:** User representatives and experts assess the software in representative tasks according to quality-of-use criteria and conformance to requirements.

- **T3: Information quality for users:** Experienced users assess the quality of information generated by the application.
- **T4: User satisfaction, acceptance:** Representative samples of users use the application in a realistic working context. User satisfaction and indicators for the likely acceptance of the application are measured.

Validation of the software prototype and the technologies used in its development was planned (Ermolayev, et al., 2011) in two phases. The results the validation Phase 1 that focused on T1 and T2 test types are presented in Ermolayev et al. (2011). Here we report the results of the validation Phase 2 which objectives were to assess the quality of information provided to a user (T3) and the degree of user acceptance and satisfaction by the solution (T4). Eleven test persons, all of them experienced IC designers or project managers who were previously not familiar with the Design Project Visualizer software, were involved in this validation phase.

For information quality assessment, the test persons carried out 20 separate validation tasks (i.e. a task-based evaluation). In each of these tasks, they retrieved different kinds of design project related information in graphical representation using the Design Project Visualizer. After each task the test persons were asked to rate the quality of the retrieved information by filling in the Information Quality Questionnaire. The information quality has been rated using 6 discrete graphic scales with 9 levels. The extremes are marked with descriptive terms such as "not useful at all" and "most useful." These are translated into values from -4 to +4 for the quality ratings.

Finally, after accomplishing all 20 validation tasks, the same test persons assessed the added

*Figure 8. Characteristic features of the design project visualizer: product bound methodology and development process execution progress visualization as execution progress status superimposed over the work breakdown structure comprising Tasks of different levels of granularity*

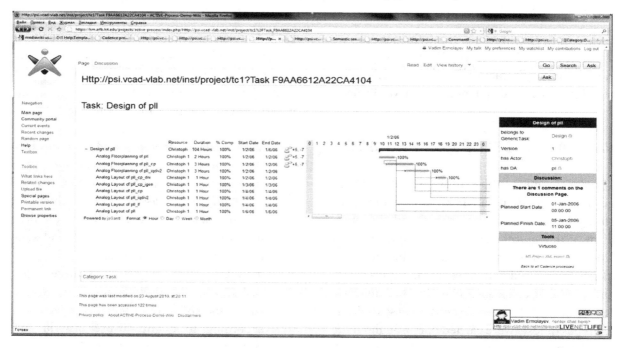

value of the Design Project Visualizer. It was explicitly stated in the instructions, and implicit in the test procedure, that the subjects compare the Design Project Visualizer to the standard Cadence tools, which they use in their daily work and with which they are very familiar. The test persons were asked to fill in the Added Value Questionnaire.

The results of the validation of software prototype indicate that the solution is helpful in providing expert assistance to design project managers performing their typical tasks of project planning and execution management.

The assessments of the information quality provided by and the added value of the developed solution indicate that the Design Project Visualizer software prototype is mature and can be used to perform the intended tasks in MIC engineering design. One of the strong features of the prototype is the quality of information representation. Especially the visualization of project status in the form of Gantt charts is recognized by the test users as a valuable feature. The main problems which were identified are the slow performance of the application and the weakness of the solution in assisting the reuse of the information from the previous projects. The first issue may be dealt with as a technical implementation problem while the second requires the extension and the refinement of the functionality. Both issues have to be dealt with in future work.

The main benefit expected from the Design Project Visualizer is a more predictable management of IC design processes, based on the monitoring of the process status with the Design Project Visualizer. An adaptation of the work procedures based on using the Design Project Visualizer is an issue, which must be justified at the organizational and management level. The total cost / benefit improvement remains to be vindicated taking into account both organizational objectives and the fact that for some users, notably design engineers, additional overhead may be created by the tools.

## CONCLUSION

The chapter presented the results of the case study of the ACTIVE integrated project on the development of a Design Project visualization approach based on the project navigation paradigm. We also presented the implementation of the Design Project Visualizer tool developed in the ACTIVE project with a focus on the design project knowledge transformation and visualization components. The tool has been validated in the industrial setting. The results of the validation confirm that the solution is helpful in providing expert assistance to design project managers performing their typical tasks of project planning and execution management and the quality of the information delivered to users is appropriately good.

## ACKNOWLEDGMENT

The research leading to these results has been funded in part by the European Union's Seventh Framework Programme (FP7/2007-2013) under grant agreement IST-2007-215040.

## REFERENCES

Andersson, B., Bergholtz, M., Edirisuriya, A., Ilayperuma, T., Johannesson, P., & Gordijn, J. … Weigand, H. (2006). Towards a reference ontology for business models. In *Proceedings of the 25th International Conference on Conceptual Modeling*. Berlin, Germany: Springer-Verlag.

Bock, C., & Grüninger, M. (2005). PSL: A semantic domain for flow models. *Software & Systems Modeling, 4*(2), 209–231. doi:10.1007/s10270-004-0066-x

Crapo, A. W., Waisel, L. B., Wallace, W. A., & Willemain, T. R. (2000). Visualization and the process of modeling: A cognitive-theoretic view. In *Proceedings of the 6th ACM SIGKDD International Conference on Knowledge Discovery and Data Mining*. New York, NY: ACM Press.

Dello, K., Nixon, L., & Tolksdorf, R. (2008). Extending the makna semantic wiki to support workflows. In *Proceedings of the 3rd Semantic Wiki Workshop*. IEEE.

Dengler, F., Lamparter, S., Hefke, M., & Abecker, A. (2009). Collaborative process development using semantic MediaWiki. In *Proceedings of the 5th Conference of Professional Knowledge Management*. Solothurn, Switzerland: IEEE.

Dietz, J. L. G. (2006). *Enterprise ontology: Theory and methodology*. Berlin, Germany: Springer Verlag. doi:10.1007/3-540-33149-2

Dorn, C., Burkhart, T., Werth, D., & Dustdar, S. (2010). Self-adjusting recommendations for people-driven ad-hoc processes . In Hull, R., Mendling, J., & Tai, S. (Eds.), *Business Process Management*. Berlin, Germany: Springer-Verlag. doi:10.1007/978-3-642-15618-2_23

Drucker, P. F. (1969). *The age of discontinuity: Guidelines to our changing society*. London, UK: Heinemann.

Ell, B., Dengler, F., Djordjevic, D., Garzotto, F., Krötzsch, M., & Siorpaes, K. … Wögler, S. (2010). *Conceptual models for enterprise knowledge – Final models and evaluation*. New York, NY: ACTIVE Project.

Ermolayev, V., Dengler, F., Fortuna, C., Tajner, T., Bösser, T., & Melchior, E.-M. (2011). Increasing predictability and sharing tacit knowledge in electronic design . In Warren, P., Simperl, E., & Davies, J. (Eds.), *Context and Semantics in Knowledge Management* (pp. 189–212). Berlin, Germany: Springer Verlag. doi:10.1007/978-3-642-19510-5_10

Ermolayev, V., Jentzsch, E., & Fortuna, C. (2010). *Requirements for fully functional prototype*. New York, NY: ACTIVE Project.

Ermolayev, V., Keberle, N., & Matzke, W.-E. (2008). An upper level ontological model for engineering design performance domain. In *Proceedings of the 27th International Conference on Conceptual Modeling*. Berlin, Germany: Springer-Verlag.

Ermolayev, V., Ruiz, C., Tilly, M., Jentzsch, E., & Gomez-Perez, J. M. (2010b). A context model for knowledge workers. In *Proceedings of the 2nd International Workshop on Context, Information and Ontologies (CIAO 2010)*. Retrieved from http://ceur-ws.org/

Ghidini, C., Kump, B., Lindstaedt, S., Mahbub, N., Pammer, V., Rospocher, M., & Serafini, L. (2009). Moki: The enterprise modelling wiki . In *The Semantic Web: Research and Applications*. Berlin, Germany: Springer-Verlag. doi:10.1007/978-3-642-02121-3_65

Grebner, O., Ong, E., Riss, U., Brunzel, M., Bernardi, A., & Roth-Berghofer, T. (2006). *Task management model*. NEPOMUK Project.

Gronau, N., Müller, C., & Korf, R. (2005). KMDL – Capturing, analysing, and improving knowledge-intensive business processes. *Journal of Universal Computer Science*, *11*(1), 452–472.

Grüninger, M., Atefy, K., & Fox, M. S. (2000). Ontologies to support process integration in enterprise engineering. *Computational & Mathematical Organization Theory*, *6*(4), 381–394. doi:10.1023/A:1009610430261

Hepp, M., & Roman, D. (2007). An ontology framework for semantic business process management . In Oberweis, A., Weinhardt, C., Gimpel, H., Koschmider, A., Pankratius, V., & Schmizler, B. (Eds.), *eOrganisation: Service-Prozess, Market-Engineering* (*Vol. 1*). Karlsruhe, Germany: Universitaetsverlag Karlsruhe.

Horridge, M., & Bechhofer, S. (2009). *The OWL API: A Java API for working with OWL 2 ontologies*. Paper presented at the 6th OWL Experiences and Directions Workshop. Chantilly, VA.

Krötzsch, M., Vrandecic, D., Völkel, M., Haller, H., & Studer, R. (2007). Semantic wikipedia. *Journal of Web Semantics*, *5*(4), 251–261. doi:10.1016/j.websem.2007.09.001

Leuf, B., & Cunningham, W. (2001). *The wiki way: Collaboration and sharing on the internet*. Reading, MA: Addison-Wesley.

Mayer, R., Menzel, C., Painter, M., Witte, P. D., Blinn, T., & Perakath, B. (1995). *Information integration for concurrent engineering (IICE) IDEF3 process description capture method report*. New York, NY: Knowledge Based Systems Inc.

Melchior, E.-M., & Bösser, T. (2011). *Results of the field trials: User acceptance, business benefits, and organizational impact of ACTIVE technology*. ACTIVE Project.

Nonaka, I., & Takeuchi, H. (1995). *The knowledge-creating company*. Oxford, UK: Oxford University Press.

Powell, W. W., & Snellman, K. (2004). The knowledge economy. *Annual Review of Sociology*, *30*, 199–220. doi:10.1146/annurev.soc.29.010202.100037

Ryu, K., & Yücesan, E. (2007). CPM: A collaborative process modeling for cooperative manufacturers. *Advanced Engineering Informatics*, *21*(2), 231–239. doi:10.1016/j.aei.2006.05.003

Scheer, A.-W., & Jost, W. (2002). *ARIS in der praxis*. Berlin, Germany: Springer Verlag. doi:10.1007/978-3-642-55924-2

Schreiber, G., Akkermans, H., Anjewierden, A., de Hoog, R., Shadbolt, N., van de Velde, W., & Wielinga, B. (1999). *Knowledge engineering and management: The CommonKADS methodology*. Cambridge, MA: MIT Press.

Tilly, M. (2010). *Dynamic models for knowledge processes: Final models*. ACTIVE Project.

Uschold, M., King, M., Moralee, S., & Zorgios, Y. (1998). The enterprise ontology. *The Knowledge Engineering Review*, *13*(1), 31–89. doi:10.1017/S0269888998001088

Warren, P., Kings, N., Thurlow, I., Davies, J., Bürger, T., & Simperl, E. (2009). Improving knowledge worker productivity – The ACTIVE integrated approach. *BT Technology Journal*, *26*(2), 165–176.

Woitsch, R., & Karagiannis, D. (2005). Process oriented knowledge management: A service based approach. *Journal of Universal Computer Science*, *11*(4), 565–588.

## ENDNOTES

1. ACTIVE – Enabling the Knowledge Powered Enterprise (active-project.eu) is the accomplished EU FP7 Integrating Project.
2. A product bound methodology is a superimposition of the segments of the generic methodologies appropriate for the particular types of functional blocks in the structure of the product to be designed.
3. The library provides methods for reading and modifying the collections of articles using the MediaWiki API.

# Chapter 4
# Multimedia Systems Development

**Miloš Milovanović**
*University of Belgrade, Serbia*

**Velimir Štavljanin**
*University of Belgrade, Serbia*

**Miroslav Minović**
*University of Belgrade, Serbia*

**Dušan Starčević**
*University of Belgrade, Serbia*

## ABSTRACT

*The multimedia information system represents a specific form of information system. This research area suffered many changes in direction due to technology shifts. The general problem is that few years back, multimedia technologies had been limited to relatively simple, stand-alone applications, but multimedia systems, particularly Web-based systems grew in complexity and intervened with many critical issues for development. In this chapter, a specific focus will be cast on existing methodology approaches, their upsides and downsides, and on the surveys and research done by distinguished authors in this area on what sort of methodologies are used in practice. Afterwards, the focus of this chapter will be on whether existing development methodologies can be applied to multimedia systems and if there is any need to adapt them for that specific purpose.*

## INTRODUCTION

People have many senses that are used to perceive the world around them. Aside from traditional five senses (sight, hearing, smell, taste, touch) there are others such as kinesthetic or motion sense and vestibular sense commonly known as a sense of balance. As computer technology advances, the means of communication between human and computer broadens to include more senses. At the beginning interaction was based solely on human sight, by reading the output of rather primitive screens that had low number of colors. Soon another form of interaction included arousing the sense of hearing by using sound as a medium for passing information.

Today's technology advances enables stimulating almost every human sense. Using touch as a form of input as well as for reception of feedback is a part of many widely used mobile

DOI: 10.4018/978-1-4666-2494-8.ch004

Copyright © 2013, IGI Global. Copying or distributing in print or electronic forms without written permission of IGI Global is prohibited.

equipment (Kim, Kim, & Lee, 2007). There are many examples of successful use of sound in human computer interaction, and there was even research in the direction of converting sound to data for the purpose of communication and interpretation (Asrim, Ibrahim, & Hunt, 2006). This is done by the use of the technique called sonification. Efforts to include all human senses in human computer interaction went so far to using scent as a form of communication. It is now possible to purchase off-the shelf, easily controllable hardware for aroma output, and incorporate scent into HCI (Kayem, 2004).

All the scientific and industry achievements cast a completely different perspective to using computer technology. During the 90s of the past century, rapid development of the Internet alongside the development of the processor power, including graphical processors, were the main driving power for the development of multimedia information systems. Advances in multimedia technologies make it possible now for us to provide instant information access to any type of information one desires—text, data, still image, motion picture, and sound (Chen, 1992). The technology served as a tool to enhance the ability of well established procedures people already used multimedia for. Let us take this hypothetic situation for example. If a neurosurgeon suspects a brain tumor in a patient, he completes a set of tomography, magnetic resonance imaging, and positron emission tomography scans of the patients' head (Grosky, 1994). Now, a surgeon can use the power of computer to process the images, use prewritten algorithms to translate the images that were previously digitized and construct the 3D model that would give him a proper insight in were the tumor is, if it is present.

Multimedia information system represents a specific form of information systems. This research area suffered many changes in direction due to technology shifts. This can be seen by simply reviewing what was the standard grasp of multimedia systems at the initial steps back in 1991: "Multimedia systems are systems enabling the usage of multiple sensory modalities and multiple channels of the same or different modality (for example both ears, both hands, etc.), and as systems enabling one user to perform several tasks at the same time. That is, multimedia is viewed as a multisensory, multichannel, multitasking, and multi-user approach to system design. In addition, multimedia systems put the user in control, i.e. could be described as a user centered approach" (Marmolin, 1991).

Even though most of this definition still applies, we can argue that performing several tasks simultaneously is not reserved for multimedia systems. Additionally, the user centered approach is now a paradigm mostly connected to Human Computer Interaction that is closely connected to MMS but not exclusive.

Right from the very beginning of such systems there is no clear definition or a clear line separating these systems from other information systems. The main problem is that the development in technology constantly influenced the shift in this area. With the invention of World Wide Web and Hypertext Markup Language (HTML), many researchers and professionals linked multimedia informational systems to Web applications. If we put this in the appropriate time frame, it is quite understandable. World Wide Web set a new ground in multimedia. Hyper-linking text, images, and sound was a technological breakthrough in multimedia. However, if we compare a Web application to some other form of multimedia information system such as medical multimedia information system we can acknowledge many differences that are structural, resource vise, and definitely can be identified in development process.

The general problem is that a few years back, multimedia technologies have been limited to relatively simple, stand-alone applications (Barry & Lang, 2003). However, multimedia systems, particularly Web-based systems grew in complexity and intervened with many critical issues for development. Firstly, it is important to identify crucial differences and whether they influence the development course between "traditional" and multimedia information systems.

## TRADITIONAL VS. MULTIMEDIA INFORMATION SYSTEMS

When developing an information system one must take in to account all the specifics of such system. Each developer as a first step in development must decide on the development methodology. Most developers are true to one methodology and rarely take in to account the specifics of the system to be developed. However, when it comes to multimedia information systems, many authors claim that they are fundamentally different from traditional information systems (Carstensen & Vogelsang, 2001; Nanard & Nanard, 1995; Russo & Graham, 1999). Additionally, some authors claim that developing multimedia information systems by use of traditional methods established in area of information systems is not the best way to go (Nanard & Nanard, 1995; Lowe & Hall, 1999; Murugesan, et al., 1999).

This last statement is clearly debatable. Just because of the fact that there are clear differences between multimedia and traditional information systems it does not necessary apply that same development methodology is not applicable. Information industry as well as academia is known to suffer from the syndrome of "newness" (Keen, 1991; Pressman, et al., 1998). With every new advance in technology researchers are looking for new approaches in dealing with it even though in many cases well established principles still apply. The problem is sometimes in not honoring a scientific method of research. A lot of times the background of the technology is not properly attended which leads to simply skipping to the part of generating ideas.

For that exact purpose in this chapter a specific focus will be cast on existing methodology approaches, their upsides and downsides and on the surveys and research done by extinguished authors in this area on what sort of methodologies are used in practice. Afterwards, the focus of this chapter will be on whether existing development methodologies can be applied to multimedia systems and if there is any need in adapting them for that specific purpose.

## STATE OF THE ART

Since multimedia information systems hyped during mid 90s of the last century, it was evident that by early 2000s researchers noticed significant level of entropy when it comes to developing them. Initially researchers and practitioners struggled in following the technology that allowed MMIS to constantly reach new levels of complexity. As a result several development methodologies were created that target specifically multimedia information systems, for example, RMM (Balasubramanian, Bieber, & Isakowitz, 2001; Isakowitz, Kamis, & Koufaris, 1997; Isakowitz, Stohr, & Balasubramanian, 1995), OOHDM (Rossi & Schwabe, 2001; Schwabe, Guimaraes, & Rossi, 2002; Schwabe & Rossi, 1995), WSDM (De Troyer, 2001; De Troyer & Leune, 1998), or HDM (Garzotto, Mainetti, & Paolini, 1995; Garzotto & Paolini, 1993). In spite of this fact there seems to lack consensus among practitioners on which of these existing methodologies to use, if any. The impression is that these methodologies were developed and proposed by academia but are not commonly used in practice.

Barry and Lang (2003) conducted a study among 100 Irish companies that work in Multimedia industry and also among the top 1000 Irish companies in General industry. As a tool for they study they used a survey that was distributed among the companies employees. The goal of the study was to identify how respondents approach multimedia systems development. They compared companies that deal in traditional information systems development with the ones developing multimedia systems. The purpose was finding in what amount they use same methodologies, and if they are not in which areas or disciplines do they overlap.

Firstly, let us concentrate on the results they acquired regarding traditional information systems development. Highest number of respondents stated that they use In-house method, 56.9% of them. This is understandable, since the software industry is quite unstructured, and also it can be claimed that some companies decided to hide their approach behind in-house choice. Second highest response was that they are not using any development methodology, as high as 24.6%. Next in line, and first of the standardized methodologies was Structured Systems Analysis and Design Method (SSADM) with 16.9% of respondents. SSADM is essentially a waterfall like methodology that is based on Structural System Analysis that serves the purpose of analyzing the system. In spite recent popularization of rapid development methodologies in this survey structural methodologies are in front of Rapid Application Development that had 13.8%. Following are UML, Information engineering, etc.

Techniques used in development of traditional information systems are edging System Flowcharts and Data Flow Diagrams that had 70% and 52.9% responses, respectively.

When it comes to Multimedia industry, their responses on which methodology they use were slightly different. Highest ranking had prototyping based methodologies, almost 60%. Next in line were Production-oriented approaches, nearly 53%. Third in line was semi-structured approach, 40%. Analysis of this data drives us to a conclusion that multimedia industry uses different approaches in comparison to general industry. However, upon insight in to what techniques are used there seems to be a certain amount of inconsistency. As in general industry, System Flowcharting is very commonly used, responses reaching 68%. The difference is in using story boarding, that does not occur in general industry and here it reaches 58%. This is understandable since this technique is common in game development.

Results of this survey study clearly state that practitioners are not using methodologies developed specifically for multimedia, probably due to the fact that there was always a significant gap between academia and industry. In addition, we can argue that both industries tend to use similar or same techniques even though methodologies sometimes differ.

Barry and Lang (2001) in another paper that describes the results of the same study stated the conclusion that developers need new techniques that capture requirements and integrate them within a systems development framework. This is an interesting proposition derived from the fact that it is obvious that companies feel comfortable using traditional methods and techniques, and that maybe they can be improved or broadened to better fit requirements of multimedia.

Another statement in favor of such approach comes from Osswald (2003) that conducted a survey out of a basis of 3000 enterprises in Germany that work in interactive media sector. The results were astonishing. According to the survey over 80% of companies uses "waterfall model" when it comes to development of multimedia projects.

In order to complete the image on what methodology is adequate for multimedia systems development it is necessary to also take a look at what can be used in low level development (implementation) and what is actually used in practice.

Three classes of multimedia development tools exist: (1) automated design software, (2) programming languages, and (3) authoring languages. In order to develop multimedia software using programming languages, the developer composes complex codes to create commands for text, graphics, sound, video, hyper-linking, and interactivity. Commercial authoring languages, on the other hand, combine some of the capabilities of the automated instructional design software with the flexibility of programming languages, usually in an object-oriented format.

The survey done by Moshinskie (1998) targeted the specific matter of the ratio in which these technologies are used in practice. This survey was developed by the ten national leaders of the Instructional Technology Forum of the American Society of Training and Development (ASTD). This body has vast experience in working with specialized instructional software that represents a specific form of multimedia information system. The investigators mailed the questionnaires to all 2,481 ASTD members who indicated on their ASTD membership application that their primary job role involved multimedia technology. Researchers received 481 completed surveys for a 20% return rate, significantly higher than the 10% rate that ASTD reported on similar surveys. Surprisingly, 76% of the participants reported they did not use any type of multimedia authoring tools. The main reason cited was lack of knowledge about multimedia authoring. Other reasons included the costs involved, the time involved, the task not being applicable to their job, the required learning curve, outsourcing authoring to outside developers, and a fear of technology. Those 24% who did use an authoring tool ranked convenience as their main reason, followed by the time saved, the availability of simulations, the costs involved, update ability, use for distance education, and record keeping capabilities.

We can conclude that in practice a majority of implementation work in multimedia development is done by programming. This can be contributed to the fact that problems are often specific and generic nature of automated tools is not applicable. In addition, strong issue presents lack of education in the matter.

# EXISTING DEVELOPMENT METHODOLOGIES FOR MULTIMEDIA INFORMATION SYSTEMS

With the development of the Web multimedia system advanced, and researchers noticed that there is a void in development methodologies that would require facilitation of specifics of multimedia. As a result, there were several proposals on how to develop multimedia systems that differed from traditional methodologies. At the time multimedia systems were gaining on popularity, most popular approach to traditional information systems development was waterfall. There was significant improvement in iterative-incremental approach to information systems development, while agile approach was in its beginnings.

The problem many authors faced when it comes to proposing new methodology is the obvious diversity of multimedia systems. That is why some of the proposed methods focused for instance only on Web (Koch, et al., 2003), or maybe for medical information systems (Agarwal & Son, 1993). Another issue was how to differentiate between developing multimedia content and multimedia applications. Even though multimedia applications require interactivity and contain multimedia content, the dividing border is not always so clear. For example, games can be viewed as multimedia content as well as multimedia applications. They have script; require design and development of models, but also characters. On the other hand, they have algorithms that take care of game-play and also present a software solution.

## Relationship Management Methodology (RMM)

Authors of this methodology started on the already set notion that hypermedia projects may involve people with very different skill sets: authors, librarians, content designers, artists, and musicians, as

*Table 1. Usefulness of RMM approach*

| Volatility of information | | | |
|---|---|---|---|
| | | High | Low |
| Structure | High | Medium usefulness [e.g., Kiosk Application] | High usefulness [e.g., Product catalog, DBMS interface] |
| | Low | Not useful [e.g., Literary work] | Low usefulness [e.g., Multimedia news service] |

well as programmers (Garzotto & Paolini, 1993). One of the main ideas was that hypermedia applications have volatile data that requires frequent updating, and some means to routine and automate both the initial development and subsequent update process is needed. This methodology brings benefit to applications that have lower rate of structure, while in case of highly structured ones it is less pronounced (see Table 1).

Main idea of this methodology is to be used as a constructing part in a surrounding software development methodology. The user does not state applicability of this method in different approaches to software development but it is clear that it can be applied to waterfall model and maybe as a part of some iterative incremental methodology such as spiral approach (Boehm, 1986).

The process is of RMM is strongly incorporated in to wrapping software development methodology There is a three step design process that can be clearly distinguished from the rest of the steps of software development methodology, but the rest of the process is close interlaced. Methodology is based on a specifically developed model called Relationship Management Data Model (RMDM). The authors constructed their own model that is based on entity relationship model. Essentially, the idea is that you use initial design steps to accommodate multimedia requirements of the application. Authors are introducing a new domain primitive in E-R modeling. That domain is *Slice*. This enables the division of existing enti-

ties. Since multimedia systems are strongly based on presentation by doing this we enable different presentation forms of entities based on users current needs. For example, if you are accessing information on certain professor, u can read about his personal information, his research activities, or view a video of his address. Although all this data represent entity of one professor, by slicing the data according to needs we can better manage presentational forms.

It can clearly be stated that this approach is characteristic to Web development. It is based on different forms of presentation, which is far from distinguishing multimedia systems from traditional. However, the authors state that this methodology targets hypermedia design, which is obviously applications based primarily on hypertext. The problem is that many times developing multimedia is not for Web. And also the primary purpose is not always viewing of the data. With the development of Web, the dynamics became one of the cornerstones of Web. In order to develop multimedia the process is often joined with writing of algorithms, and the code cannot be separated. This is emphasized when games are in question. This is why this development methodology does not provide full support for developing a wide variety of multimedia information systems.

## Hypertext Design Model (HDM)

With the initial expansion of Hypertext Markup Language and the World Wide Web, one of the first methodologies for developing websites was HDM. The general idea of this approach is to embrace the new paradigm of navigation that was new to Web. Since the occurrence of first operating systems that had the ability to accommodate applications with graphical user interface development methodologies were based mostly on the flow of the work done on this applications. Use cases enabled transforming of real business processes captured by system analysis and converted in to the flow of data inside the application, and the shifts of displayed screens containing information. Completing tasks in a Web application included a different chain of actions. Initial Web applications were mostly a repository of information that can be accessed remotely. The primary purpose was not to complete a business task but to get informed on a certain topic. This is because of the non-dynamic nature of the initial Web. Since the type of usage differs substantially from rich client applications, it was suggested that different approach to development is necessary. The main problem was navigation. A totally new perspective was added with creation of hyperlinks. In enabled switching from one resource to another on a website, or even outside it. This brought a new issue in design. The problem was how to shift from viewing an application as a tool to execute a task through preconceived flow to an open paradigm that allows people to navigate according to their needs and the links between resources.

This specific design model is meant to provide a language for specifying an application. It is suppose to enable reuse of resources. This particular model is rather similar to E-R model. However, it is more specific, and it is expanded in order to accommodate primitives that are characteristic to hypermedia. The authors decided on a compromise course: some of the terms are new; others are taken from preexisting models in the database or hypertext field. Preexisting terms should be understood with the caveat that the reader should never assume that use of some term exactly corresponds to the notion that he is already aware of.

HDM application is built by using building blocks called entities. Further, entities are grouped in to entity types. Entities are autonomous pieces of information and are not conditioned by other entities. There are also components and units. Components that are hierarchically ordered compose an entity. Units provide the content for component under a particular perspective. Units are smallest chunks of information in this design model.

In HDM information structures can be interconnected through the use of links. There are three types of links in this model:

- Structural links that interconnect components belonging to the same entity.
- Perspective links that interconnect units that correspond to the same component.
- Application links that can interconnect components and entities, which are not the same and are a part of the authors design.

An HDM specification of a hypertext application consists of a schema definition and a set of instances definitions. A schema definition specifies a set of entity types and link types. Instances are allowed to be inserted in the application only if they obey the constraints specified by the schema.

As seen on Figure 1. Application links enable the developer to interconnect different entities or components together. This specific approach enabled the developers of planning the execution of Web applications. Schema is a tool derived

*Figure 1. Different types of links in HDM model schema*

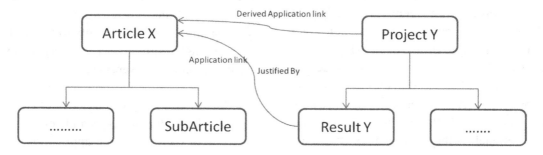

from use in database modeling, and similarly it provides in this case the developer to plan the structure of hypermedia.

Since this is one of the early models for designing multimedia, it suffers from many issues. One of the greatest issues is that it does not offer anything else but a design language. Development methodology must be viewed as a composition of several aspects, some of which are organizational like resource planning. Another serious issue comes from its navigational focus. Although this provides a good foundation when it comes to developing Web applications, it is not that applicable to other types of multimedia systems such as wide area multimedia systems as identified by some researchers (Hitz & Werthner, 1993).

## Object-Oriented Hypermedia Design Model (OOHDM)

This methodology of design was meant to surpass some of the disadvantages of the previous design models. In general object-oriented design methods do not provide primitives for specifying navigation, while hypermedia design approaches emphasize structural aspects, ignoring computational behavior (Hitz & Werthner, 1993).

General idea of this method is to honor the diversity of Web applications when it comes to navigation but to respect the notions of software engineering and object oriented development.

Authors are proposing the conduct of development through several disciplines that are well established in software engineering but with added values that regard the specific nature of Web applications.

As seen on Table 2 important added aspect to the software lifecycle is navigational design. Due to the specific nature of the Web applications navigation plays an important part. Conceptual design ensures the proper development of business logic of the system. This is done by use of design patterns base on object-oriented paradigm. When it comes to navigational design, the developer invests an effort to model the behavior of future application. It provides the view towards the business logic of the system. During the interface

*Table 2. Disciplines in OOHDM*

| Activities | Products | Formalisms | Mechanisms | Desing Concerns |
|---|---|---|---|---|
| Requirements Gathering | Use Cases, Annotations | Scenarios, User Interaction Diagrams; Design Patterns | Scenario and Use Case Analysis, Interviews, UID mapping to Conceptual Model | Capture the stakeholder requirements for the application |
| Conceptual Design | Classes, sub-systems, relationships, attribute perspectives | Object-oriented modeling constructs; Design patterns | Classification, aggregation, generalization and specialization | Model the semantics of the application domain |
| Navigational Design | Nodes, links, access structures, navigational contexts, navigational transformations | Object-oriented views, Object-oriented State charts; Context Classes; Design Patterns, User | Classification, Aggregation, Generalization and Specialization | Takes into account user profile and task; Emphasis on cognitive aspects; Build the navigational structure |
| Abstract Interface Design | Abstract interface objects, responses to external events, interface transformations | Abstract Data Views; Configuration Diagrams; ADV-Charts; Design Patterns | Mapping between navigation and perceptible objects | Model perceptible objects, implementing choosen metaphors, describe interface for navigational objects |
| Implementation | Running application | Those supported by the target environment | Those provided by the target environment | Performance, Completeness |

design, it is necessary to honor the navigational aspect of the design.

Navigational model provides the specific view for the conceptual model. It is also schema based, and the schema is created according to the presentational needs of the data. Schema contains different perspective of the conceptual model that is accommodated for presentational purposes. In addition, it contains links that provide navigational perspectives of the application.

This model is a significant improvement of the HDM model, since it provides a mean to manage a complete software lifecycle. Also, object oriented paradigm is honored that provides the reusability and scalability of the created applications. The issue that this model did not solve is diversity of multimedia systems. Those that are not Web-based can only be burdened by the navigational aspect of this methodology.

## WSDM: Web Semantic Design Method

This development methodology was a created to fill a void that other existing technologies left. More than other methods, WSDM is a methodology, i.e. it not only provides modeling primitives that allow a Web developer to construct models that describe the website/application from different perspectives and at different levels of abstraction, but it also provides a systematic way to develop the Web application (De Troyer, 2008).

The two basic characteristics of WSDM are the audience driven approach, and the explicit conceptual design phase. With the first characteristic, the audience driven approach, WSDM puts, already in a very early stage of the development, the emphasis on the different kind of users (called audience classes) (De Troyer & Casteleyn, 2003). WSDM starts the design with the identification of the different audience classes, their needs, and requirements. These different audiences and their requirements will drive the entire development process. The second important characteristic

is the explicit conceptual design phase. First a conceptual design free of any presentation or implementation detail is made. This allows for different presentations for different users and/or platforms (see Figure 2).

Initial phase is creation of mission statement. In the mission statement, the purpose, the subject, and the targeted users of the website are specified. In addition, it defines the borders of the design. Upon that designer can decide which functionalities to include in the final product and how to present it.

Next phase is audience modeling. It involves primary an audience classification. This process requires classifying of different types of users that will visit the website, according to their needs and requirements. During Audience Characterization relevant characteristics are specified for each audience class. Next to the fact that different types of users may have different information and functional requirements, it may be necessary to represent the (same) information or functionality in different ways to different kinds of users.

Next, the conceptual design is built. It consists out of two processes. One is task and information modeling. This is similar to the well-known process of working through use cases. As a result, object-oriented model is created along with relational model. The goal of the navigational design is to define the conceptual structure of the Web system and to model how the members of the different audience classes can navigate through the Web system and perform their tasks. Because of the audience driven approach of WSDM, a navigation track is created for each audience class. Such an audience track can be considered as a sub-site containing all and only the information and functionality needed by the members of the associated audience class.

Upon completion of the conceptual design the implementation design is performed. This phase is somewhat similar to the design phase of the waterfall method in software engineering. The difference is that it is more specific and adapted

*Figure 2. Five design phases of WSDM, and the output model(s) produced in each phase*

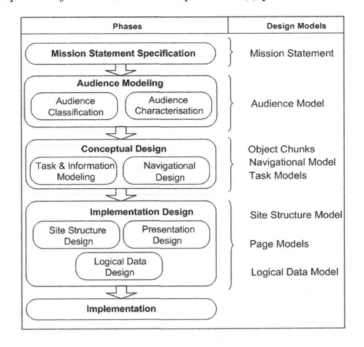

to website design. Major activity is the development of site structure design, mostly based on navigational design. This structure rests also on logical data design, and it influences the presentational design.

Final stage is implementation. Implementation is done according to the implementation design.

This methodology as oppose to previously analyzed, offers the most guidelines when it comes to design of Web applications. It offers a complete methodology by combining organizational aspects along with development tools and languages. Still there are evident deficiencies even in this methodology. Initial problem derives from the fact that this methodology is uses audience driven approach. It focuses on potential users and what are their potential needs. The problem is that most of the times websites are commissioned by companies or third party people, that have their own needs and requirements. This methodology lacks the obviously needed step of defining the requirements. Additionally, it is somehow pre-

sumed that the designer is well acquainted with the business process that lies behind the future website, and most of the time this is not the case. For that, specific purpose traditional methods such as SSADM offer the designer an analysis toll and method to get familiar with the business process by using Structured System Analysis. Finally, this methodology is applicable only on Web development, which is only a part of multimedia systems.

## MULTIMEDIA METADATA

Metadata became very important concept in retrieving multimedia data from databases, especially today when the databases are complex and effective data management is imperative. Web additionally raised the importance of metadata. In multimedia databases, metadata is used to describe individual objects. This type of metadata is termed as associative metadata. Metadata supports processing, improves performance, and is used in indexing. Metadata supports all three types of retrieval—attribute, text, and content-based. Dunckley (2003) identified the purposes of metadata as administrative, descriptive, preservation, technical, and usage. Different metadata standards are developed to date. Standards are important for common representation of data and are basis for interoperability of the systems.

## ISO/IEC 11179

Standard provides description of metadata and process that enable organizations to describe common understanding of data across organizational entities and between different organizations. The standard has six parts: framework, classification, registry metamodel and basic attributes, formulation of data definition, naming, and identification principles, and registration of data elements. Standard provides unique identifiers and standard structure of attributes. It provides a set of 10 attributes: name, identifier, version, registration authority, language, definition, obligation, datatype, maximum occurrence, and comment. Information is held in data registry. Standard divides data elements into three parts: object class, property, and representation.

## Dublin Core

Was developed in order to provide simple resource description for usage in online libraries accessed by the Internet. Updated version provides link to ISO/IEC 11179. Dublin Core provides a simple structured record that can be mapped to complex records. The standard was originally developed for textual documents, but now is used for Web documents description. The shortage is that standard can only define the existence of image in a document. In addition to ISO/IEC 11179 attributes, 15 metadata elements has been presented in 1.1 version. These elements are Title, Creator, Subject, Description, Publisher, Contributor, Date, Type, Format, Identifier, Source, Language, Relation, Coverage, and Rights.

## RDF (Resource Description Framework)

RDF was developed by W3 Consortium as a framework for representing information in the Web. RDF has a number of objectives (Dunckley, 2003): resource discovery, cataloging, content rating, describing intellectual property, expressing privacy preferences and policies, and digital signatures. However, the aim is to provide a foundation for processing metadata and allowing interoperability between applications. Language for writing RDF schemas is XML. Basic RDF data model is represented by resources, properties, and statements. Resources are different thing that can be described using RDF (Web page, some HTML element, multimedia object). Properties describe a resource. In addition, statements are resources with specific property values.

## MPEG-7

MPEG-7 is standard developed by MPEG group for multimedia data description. MPEG-7 is standardized in ISO/IEC 15938 standard. The aim is to make standard framework for describing different aspects of multimedia object content (Dunckley, 2003): low-level description of individual objects on scene, high level description of scene, objects contains and events, and audio information. Standard consists of 12 parts: System, Description definition language, Visual, Audio, and Multimedia description schemes, Reference software, Conformance testing, Extraction and use of MPEG-7 description, Profiles and levels, Schema definition, MPEG-7 profile schemas, and Query format. Standard defines descriptor—D as feature of an object. Objects could be described by using several descriptors. Structure and semantics of relations between descriptors is defined by Description Schemes. DDL (Description Definition Language based on XML) is used for writing Descriptor Schemes. Main benefit of using MPEG-7 is better searchability of multimedia objects, and interoperability.

# METHODOLOGIES FOR DEVELOPING MULTIMEDIA CONTENT

Multimedia systems are specific because of their use of multimedia content. Development process of multimedia systems as an essential part must provide the proper means to develop multimedia content that will be used in the system. This content can be a variety of text, audio, images, video, etc. Some multimedia systems contain a significant amount of multimedia content while others maybe use it only in certain functionalities. Since none of the existing methodologies was found to me adequate for the entire process and for all types of multimedia systems development, maybe integrating some multimedia content development techniques with software engineering techniques can produce a satisfactory result.

Authors of these methodologies usually claim that they can be used to develop multimedia projects, regardless whether they are movies, podcasts, games, or other complex multimedia systems. Although this may be true, the results of this approach are not always satisfactory. The general problem is that these methodologies do not poses the engineering practice required to develop something as complex as some software systems are. In addition, the paradigm of software engineering is significantly different than in multimedia content producing. In addition, participating roles are quite different even though they sometime overlap.

One author attempted to instate the methodology to develop multimedia systems based on his experience in a movie and multimedia game industries (Elin, 2000). These industries are great examples on how to manage large projects that as a result have a multimedia product. During the conduct and development movie industry produced a strict process on how a movie is made, starting from script writing, then storyboarding, directing, and producing. Larry Elin (2000) suggested on using well-established principles due to the fact that the processes are quite similar. He proposed development process of four phases: Discovery, Design, Prototype, and Production. The purpose of initial phase is development agreement between parties (client and developer) involved. Parties must agree about product, development time, and price. After agreement, developer writes functional specification, document that contains details about product components, content organization, product behavior, look and feel, and user controls. In addition to functional specification, in design phase, many other design and business documents are created. In prototype phase goal is to produce prototype and test various aspects of product design, technology, and development process. At the end, after the tests were completed, team is ready for creation of final multimedia assets and programming. Elin proposed, in addition to development process, Interactive Design Process as a series of iterative steps which goal is final design documentation. Interactive Design takes place during initial phases, Discovery and Design, of the development process. Developing multimedia content has a generic process on which most of the authors concur consisted out of four phases (Ivers & Baron, 2002). Some author offer alternative and go up to 9 phases (Web1, 2011; Web2, 2011) but essentially they can be grouped in to four. Those phases are: Decide, Design, Develop, and Evaluate. Interactive design process and Elin development proces goes deeper on to the process of initial steps in multimedia content development. The Interactive design process is shown in Table 3.

This design process provides a good basis for management of such specific projects, but it lacks the engineering paradigm in order to solve some of the constantly occurring issues in software development, such as scalability, reusability, communication breakdown, and similar.

*Table 3. Interactive design process*

| Activities | Product | Mechanisms |
|---|---|---|
| Concept design | Concept design document | Goal market, production capabilities, product subject |
| Concurrent analysis | Competitive matrix | Competition research |
| Top level design | Top level design document | Product components description, estimates |
| Cost/benefit analysis | Cost/benefit analysis document | Resource planing, expected revenue |
| Functional specification | Functional specification document | User interviews, dient interviews |

## DETECTED ISSUES AND POSSIBLE SOLUTIONS

As a result of previous work, many different issues were detected when studying existing approaches to multimedia systems development and also when analyzing specifically proposed methodologies for this purpose. When combining the outputs from different approaches we can form several principles and guidelines on which methodology for multimedia systems development should be based. They can be identified as:

- Honor the diversity between many different forms of multimedia systems.
- Provide proper organizational guidelines in managing such projects.
- Provide adequate tools and languages to aid in planning and development.
- Provide the engineering practice required for all aspects of such systems.

The approach attempted here will be to explore the possibilities of using existing methodologies for developing "traditional information systems" and add value to them that will adapt them to multimedia systems development. The reason for this is the fact that people are primarily used to using these methodologies, especially in industry (Barry & Lang, 2003). In addition, it is important to state that "traditional information systems" development methodologies are rather successful (Ambler, 2010). Since software development industry is an extremely risky business ground that suffers from many influences inside and outside of the organization, conclusions gathered from several different surveys speak in favor of established methodologies (Ambler, 2010). Conclusions are as follows:

- **Ad-hoc projects:** 49% are successful, 37% are challenged, and 14% are failures.
- **Iterative projects:** 61% are successful, 28% are challenged, and 11% are failures.
- **Agile projects:** 60% are successful, 28% are challenged, and 12% are failures.
- **Waterfall projects:** 47% are successful, 36% are challenged, and 17% are failures.

Even though iterative project are most successful, with agile approach following, one can argue that success rate is pretty high when all things are considered.

The other aspect that must be considered aside from the success of these methodologies is the amount of similarity between these projects and multimedia systems development projects. Although this gap widens and constricts from one project to another, still large amount is usually the same. This is why maybe there should only be added value to existing methodologies to deal with specific aspects of multimedia systems. But also multimedia systems differ among themselves, so sometimes even different approaches will be necessary.

One possible solution is to combine the benefits of two or more methodologies. Combining two or more development methodologies is a well-known practice. Usually in companies that deal with software development it is quite common to use some combination form of different methodologies. This is usually done due to the lacking each methodology exhibits in real environment in one way or the other. Survey done among European organizations indicated that almost 60% of them use some combination of waterfall and agile development (Web3, 2010). In this case, we can combine software development methodologies with specific aspects of multimedia content development methodologies.

The question that emerges is how to combine existing methodologies? Initially we should take a glance at how this is usually done in an example of some multimedia systems, such as game development. Developers usually combine different methodologies without even knowing it. They actually use the best practices derived from their previous experiences. Most of them agree on major steps in game development process. They are pre-production, production, and post-production.

During pre-production step, they identify concepts and create a main design, usually materialized as a design document. During production step, implementation is done according to previously defined design. Finally, post-production includes testing and deployment. This is general guideline of game development process. However, usually when it comes to implementation, software nature of games rises to surface. Most of the time when production starts approach shifts towards some software engineering methodology, usually waterfall or unified process or some agile development. Finally, during the conduct of that software engineering methodology, some principles from multimedia content development are implemented (see Figure 3).

This approach proved appropriate in games development. Unfortunately, advances in technology shift the work from programmers towards designers and modelers. More and more activities are automated and now programming is often replaced with drawing and modeling. Upon that, patterns of movement are usually generated automatically. So now, focus should be more on multimedia than on software engineering. Maybe if we could concurrently perform the work as-

*Figure 3. Approaches in developing multimedia systems (example games) in combining multimedia and software development methodologies*

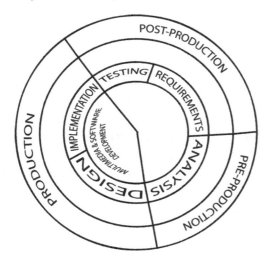

*Figure 4. Concurrently developing multimedia and software engineering aspects of the project*

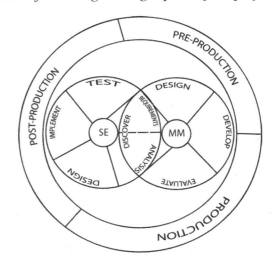

signed to SE and MM we can find the winning formula. One solution is to combine the efforts in initial steps and then work semi independently (see Figure 4).

This approach provides good basis for separation of work and ability to focus on separate aspects of the project. Although using this formula provides solution on paper on how this type of project can be managed, it is very important to see the implications on each step of the software life cycle. We need to define tools and procedures for specific aspects and processes. Let's attempt to clarify the idea by going step by step in software lifecycle.

## Requirements

During the initial phases if the requirements it is important to properly record the clients' needs. This can be the first step in indentifying the future multimedia requirements of the system. This step can include some specifics of the interactive design process (Elin, 2000). Specifically it is to create a concept document to provide the insight in to multimedia needs of the system. The purpose is to discover the subject, target market, theme, educational goals etc. of the future product.

## Analysis

Performing analysis in a software development process is an extensive and extremely important part of the work. Analysis is done in order to development team gets better introduced to business process. The more complex the process is analysis is performed more thoroughly. It can be done using structured approach or object approach.

Structured approach, defined in SSADM (Malcom, 1994) rests on Structured System Analysis. It is performed in order to identify processes and how data flows through the system. It is done by the use of Data Flow diagrams. It is very useful in complex systems when object oriented approach derives too many outputs (Lazarevic, et al., 2006).

Upon SSA we can identify multimedia documents, and content and describe it by applying interactive design process. As output, we can create Top Level Design document, which contains the description of the main aspects of multimedia. In addition, a first glance can be cast on the user interface, since we can clearly identify users, and also according to concept document their preferences.

Object oriented approach rests on the definition of Use Cases. Upon notation of user's requirements, we can differentiate all the cases of use. This is particularly handy when using iterative process, since you can develop partial outputs base on specific use cases. Multimedia content and procedures can be identified through this process, by analyzing the signals that travel between user and the system. Then we can recognize their multimedia nature and describe it in Top Level Design Document. This approach distinguishes aspects of user interface even more clearly, so now we can focus even more on that aspect of TLD document.

Since this can still be considered early stages, it can be a good time to perform a Cost/Benefit analysis that is also an integrating part of the interactive design process (Elin, 2000) to decide on using some multimedia functionalities in our project or to simply disregard them if they are not of great importance and if they greatly influence the overall cost.

## Design

Design phase is very important stage in development. Result of this stage should be models and guidelines to be used in implementation stage. It should address both the logical design as well as physical design. It is the built of conceptual model that represents the simplified model of the system based on classes, application logic base described by the use of collaboration or activity diagrams and finally as a result of previous two, design of the complete logical system through complete class diagrams. Physical design must propose the database model, inclusion of generic specific components such as patterns, design of the user interface and hardware architecture.

This stage should also be intensive on multimedia content and functionalities. Since multimedia development now runs its course through discover, design, develop and evaluate this is when multimedia team must be involved. Design stages are run concurrently and multimedia team designs the specific aspects of multimedia. Main tools are storyboarding, dataflow etc. In many aspects activities overlap. In definition of the class model and also database model, it is important to include specifics of multimedia. Some attributes and functions must be declared as needed multimedia types. Choosing database system must include decision on whether some multimedia database functions are necessary and how to implement them.

Also in this stage, we should consider the specific aspect of the multimedia systems being developed and consider introduction of the specific tools and techniques. For example in case of websites or games, we can consider the use of the map of nodes since these systems are oriented towards navigation. We can even use the language introduced in (Garzotto & Paolini, 1993) to describe the navigational aspects of these systems.

In case of systems such as medical systems, we need to consider the handling of different standards and solve interoperability issues.

## Implementation

Implementation should be done according to the outputs of the design stage. During the implementation multimedia developers develop models, do graphical work, create images, record and edit sounds, and prepare other forms of multimedia content. Two teams must cooperate in writing functions to deal with searching, storing, and managing of multimedia content. In case the system requires they also must contribute in provide the conversion of unstructured knowledge in to structured form.

At the final stages of implementation an integration must be performed in order to complete the intermediary or final product depending on whether it is iterative approach or not. As a result of that integration a completed product is a result, which combines multimedia with the application functionalities.

## Test

Testing stage must be slightly altered to accommodate the needs of multimedia. It is very important to test the performances of the application along with its functionalities. Multimedia is very high on requirements in hardware performance. It usually requires high-end graphic processing, quality of sound output and last but not least the capabilities of network capacity. In case the system has streaming functionalities, it is important to test the network optimization.

Testing multimedia performance is extremely difficult test. It requires practically a fully developed environment for deployment in order to properly test. It can be performed in laboratory environment, but it can never be a good picture on what will occur when the system is in production and under the full stress. This is why it is important to continue on one of the main activities of multimedia development and that is quality of service. This is main part of the evaluation stage in multimedia design. It is important to continuously monitor the functioning of the system and if necessary return to design stages and work on optimization.

## CONCLUSION

Focus of this chapter was on trends in multimedia systems development. Many researchers are active in this area. It is one of the fast changing areas and this brings many problems.

We can notice that with the development of the technology and the abilities of multimedia, researchers started to explore different ways on managing projects that involve multimedia systems development. This chapter reviewed some of the most widely used methodologies. After the review, many issues were discovered.

One of the main problems identified is the researchers shift towards developing brand new methods for multimedia systems development while disregarding the already established methods used in developing "traditional information systems." Academia is known to suffer from the syndrome of "newness" (Keen, 1991; Pressman, et al., 1998). With every new advance in technology, researchers are looking for new approaches in dealing with it even though in many cases well-established principles still apply.

Most of the reviewed methodologies focused only on one specific form of multimedia systems such as Web applications. Even though some authors stated that their ideas can be easily applied to other types of MMS that is just not the case. Nevertheless, some proposed methodologies had some interesting contributions to tools and languages that can clearly be used to aid traditional information system development methodologies. This is why in a final section of the chapter a new approach was proposed. It was based on the notion that industry is rather successful and used to using traditional methods that was confirmed by many studies. The general idea is to use existing methodologies for developing "traditional information systems" and enrich them with the tools and practices that are fit to developing multimedia content. Since developing multimedia content is not new and there are successful methods of developing derived mostly form movie and game industry all that was needed was to find the way to integrate them.

This chapter was an attempt to introduce an approach that is widely used in practice but it was not formalized. The conduct of this method was left to project manager and his creativity.

Finally, we can state that even though this area of research is by no means young, it is still very interesting and in trend. This is mostly because of the fact that changes in technology constantly change the way we look at multimedia systems and it is necessary to attempt to catch up the progress of technology with the theoretical basis.

# REFERENCES

Agarwal, N., & Son, S. H. (1993). *Experiences with the development of a multimedia information system for medical applications. Technical Report.* Charlottesville, VA: University of Virginia.

Ambler, S. W. (2010). *Surveys: What they tell us, 2010 IT project success rates.* Retrieved from http://drdobbs.com/architecture-and-design/226500046

Asrim, A. M., Ibrahim, A., & Hunt, A. (2006). An HCI model for usability of sonification applications. In *Proceedings of the 5th International Conference on Task Models and Diagrams for Users Interface Design (TAMODIA 2006)*, (pp. 245-258). Berlin, Germany: Springer-Verlag.

Balasubramanian, V., Bieber, M., & Isakowitz, T. (2001). A case study in systematic hypermedia design. *Information Systems, 26*(4), 295–320. doi:10.1016/S0306-4379(01)00022-9

Barry, C., & Lang, M. (2001). A survey of multimedia and web development techniques and methodology usage. *IEEE MultiMedia, 8*(2), 52–60. doi:10.1109/93.917971

Barry, C., & Lang, M. (2003). A comparison of traditional and multimedia information systems development practices. *Information and Software Technology, 45*(4), 217–227. doi:10.1016/S0950-5849(02)00207-0

Boehm, B. (1986). A spiral model of software development and enhancement. *SIGSOFT Software Engineering Notes, 11*(4), 14–24. doi:10.1145/12944.12948

Carstensen, P. H., & Vogelsang, L. (2001). Design of web-based information systems —New challenges for systems development? In *Proceedings Ninth European Conference on Information Systems*. Bled, Slovenia: IEEE.

Chen, C. (1992). Understanding multimedia information systems: Consequences for today and possibilities for tomorrow. In *Proceedings of NIT 1992: The 5th International Conference on New Information Technology*, (pp. 49-62). Hong Kong, China: NIT.

De Troyer, O. (2001). Audience-driven web design . In *Information Modeling in the New Millennium* (pp. 442–461). Hershey, PA: IGI Global. doi:10.4018/978-1-878289-77-3.ch022

De Troyer, O. (2008). Audience-driven design approach for web systems . In *Encyclopedia of Information Science and Technology* (2nd ed., pp. 274–278). Hershey, PA: IGI Global. doi:10.4018/978-1-60566-026-4.ch047

De Troyer, O., & Casteleyn, S. (2003). Modeling complex processes for web applications using WSDM. In *Proceedings of the Third International Workshop on Web-Oriented Software Technologies*. Oviedo, Spain: IEEE.

De Troyer, O. M. F., & Leune, C. J. (1998). WSDM: A user centered design method for web sites. In *Proceedings of Seventh International World Wide Web Conference*. Brisbane, Australia: ACM.

Elin, L. (2000). *Designing and developing multimedia: A practical guide for the producer, director, and writer*. Needham Heights, MA: Allyn & Bacon, Inc.

Garzotto, F., Mainetti, L., & Paolini, P. (1995). Hypermedia design, analysis, and evaluation issues. *Communications of the ACM, 38*(8), 74–86. doi:10.1145/208344.208349

Garzotto, F., & Paolini, P. (1993). HDM—A model-based approach to hypertext application design. *ACM Transactions on Information Systems, 11*(1), 1–26. doi:10.1145/151480.151483

Grosky, W. I. (1994). Multimedia information systems. *IEEE MultiMedia, 1*(1), 12–24. doi:10.1109/93.295262

Hitz, M., & Werthner, H. (1993). Development and analysis of a wide area multimedia information system. In *Proceedings of the 1993 ACM/SIGAPP Symposium on Applied Computing: States of the Art and Practice (SAC 1993)*, (pp. 238-246). New York, NY: ACM Press.

Isakowitz, T., Kamis, A., & Koufaris, M. (1997). Extending the capabilities of RMM: Russian dolls and hypertext. In *Proceedings of 30th Hawaii International Conference on System Sciences (HICSS-30)*. Maui, HI: IEEE.

Isakowitz, T., Stohr, E. A., & Balasubramanian, P. (1995). A RMM: Methodology for structured hypermedia design. *Communications of the ACM, 38*(8), 34–44. doi:10.1145/208344.208346

Ivers, K. S., & Baron, A. (2002). *Multimedia projects in education: Designing, producing, and assessing*. Wesport, CT: Teacher Ideas Press.

Kayem, J. J. (2004). Making scents: Aromatic output for HCI. *Interaction, 11*(1), 48–61.

Keen, P. G. W. (1991). Relevance and rigor in information systems research: Improving quality, confidence, cohesion and impact . In *Information Systems Research: Contemporary Approaches and Emergent Traditions* (pp. 27–49). Amsterdam, The Netherlands: Elsevier Science Publishers.

Kim, S. G., Kim, J. W., & Lee, C. W. (2007). Implementation of multi-touch tabletop display for HCI (human computer interaction). In *Proceedings of the 12th International Conference on Human-Computer Interaction: Interaction Platforms and Techniques (HCI 2007)*, (pp. 854-863). Berlin, Germany: Springer-Verlag.

Koch, N., Kraus, A., Cachero, C., & Meliá, S. (2003). Modeling web business processes with OOH and UWE. In *Proceedings of the Third International Workshop on Web-oriented Software Technology (IWWOST 2003)*, (pp. 27-50). IWWOST.

Lazarević, B., Marjanović, Z., Aničić, N., & Babarogić, S. (2006). *Databases*. Faculty of Organizational Sciences. Belgrade, Serbia: University of Belgrade.

Lowe, D., & Hall, W. (1999). *Hypermedia and the web: An engineering approach*. Chichester, UK: Wiley.

Malcom, E. (1994). *SSADM version 4: A user's guide* (2nd ed.). New York, NY: McGraw-Hill, Inc.

Marmolin, H. (1991). Multimedia from the perspectives of psychology. In *Proceedings of the Eurographics Workshop on Multimedia*, (pp. 39-52). Springer-Verlag.

Moshinskie, J. F. (1998). A survey of multimedia developers concerning the use of automated instructional design software. *Journal of Instruction Delivery Systems, 12*(2), 26–32.

Murugesan, S., Deshpande, Y., Hansen, S., & Ginige, A. (1999). Web engineering: A new discipline for development of web-based systems. In *Proceedings of First ICSE Workshop on Web Engineering, International Conference on Software Engineering (ICSE 1999)*. Los Angeles, CA: ACM.

Nanard, J., & Nanard, M. (1995). Hypertext design environments and the hypertext design process. *Communications of the ACM, 38*(8), 49–56. doi:10.1145/208344.208347

Osswald, K. (2003). *Konzeptmanagement: Interaktive medien – interdisziplinäre projekte*. Berlin, Germany: Springer.

Pressman, R. S., Lewis, T., Adida, B., Ullman, E., DeMarco, T., & Gilb, T. (1998). Can internet-based applications be engineered? *IEEE Software, 15*(5), 104–110. doi:10.1109/MS.1998.714869

Rossi, G., & Schwabe, D. (2001). Object-oriented web applications modeling . In *Information Modeling in the New Millennium* (pp. 463–483). Hershey, PA: IGI Global. doi:10.4018/978-1-878289-77-3.ch023

Russo, N. L., & Graham, B. R. (1999). A first step in developing a web application design methodology: Understanding the environment. In *Proceedings of Sixth International BCS Information Systems Methodologies Conference*. London, UK: Springer.

Schwabe, D., Guimaraes, R. M., & Rossi, G. (2002). Cohesive design of personalized web applications. *IEEE Internet Computing, 6*(2), 34–43. doi:10.1109/4236.991441

Schwabe, D., & Rossi, G. (1995). The object-oriented hypermedia design model. *Communications of the ACM, 38*(8), 45–48. doi:10.1145/208344.208354

Schwabe, D., & Rossi, G. (1998). An object oriented approach to web-based applications design. *Theoretical Practice and Object Systems, 4*(4), 207–225. doi:10.1002/(SICI)1096-9942(1998)4:4<207::AID-TAPO2>3.0.CO;2-2

Web1. (2011). *A development process for a multimedia project*. [Web log]. Retrieved from http://www.squidoo.com/multimedia-development-process

Web2. (2011). *Multimedia development life cycle: DIMACC interactive media project*. Retrieved from http://www.dimacc.com/lifecycle.shtml

Web3. (2010). *A CA technologies survey, balancing agility with governance: A survey of portfolio management for agile IT*. Retrieved from http://www.ca.com/~/media/files/supportingpieces/ppm-summit-agile-research-oct-2010.aspx

# Chapter 5
# Ethical Tensions Emerging from the Application of the Collective Intelligence Concept in Academic Social Networking

**Craig Deed**
*La Trobe University, Australia*

**Anthony David Edwards**
*Liverpool Hope University, UK*

## ABSTRACT

*This chapter examines the ethical questions and actions emerging from academic social networking. Academics have always been involved in rigorous discourse across multiple contexts, involving generation, exploration, analysis, evaluation, and application of ideas through a process of thought, research, peer validation, and publication. The argument is that the concept of collective intelligence is changing the traditional hierarchical "rules" associated with academic dialogue. Collective intelligence is defined as a mix of formal and informal conversational contexts, and the storing and sharing of ideas and information through multiple public online contexts. The meta-concept of collective intelligence presents a number of ethical dilemmas and questions related to privacy, and ownership and control of net-generated data, ideas, and information. The purpose of this chapter is to identify and describe these ethical issues and actions in relation to academic social networking.*

## INTRODUCTION

Academics have always been involved in rigorous discourse across multiple contexts including conferences, teaching, academic writing, and research. Having a sense of curiosity about ideas, asking clarifying questions as part of a critiquing process and seeking congruence when dealing with different perspectives about complex problems; these are conventional aspects of a fertile academic life.

DOI: 10.4018/978-1-4666-2494-8.ch005

Copyright © 2013, IGI Global. Copying or distributing in print or electronic forms without written permission of IGI Global is prohibited.

The emergence of Web 2.0, and in particular the social networking phenomenon have impacted significantly on who, how, when, where and why academics can engage in learning conversations. Networking for knowledge generation is not confined to academics because the social imperative to exchange in this form of exchange, although originally academic, now comes from the broader commercial and government community. Web 2.0 has emerged as a creative driver of "reworking hierarchies, changing social divisions, creating possibilities and opportunities, informing us, and reconfiguring our relations with objects, spaces, and each other" (Beer & Burrows, 2007, p. 2). Social networking technologies have introduced permeable, public, and participatory elements to academic conversations that are disruptive and invigorating.

Here, academic social networking is conceptualized as extending traditional formal academic scholarship into a blend of ordered and informal social practices characterized by collaboration, sharing, and conversation that values openness and deliberate seeking of outside perspectives and difference. This is consistent with the views of Greenhow, Robelia, and Hughes (2009, p. 253), who argue that participation in social networking by academics "Capitalizes on the learning ecology perspective, bridging scholarship and advocacy well beyond traditional, formal university spaces."

Examples of academic engagement in social networking spaces include formal and informal learning management spaces; attending virtual conferences; writing, editing, rating, and commenting on digital material including journal papers and texts; participation in online special interest groups; use of blogs and wikis; online forums; collaborative writing; Facebooking with students and colleagues; sharing multi-media; contributing to and linking with databases e.g. iTunesU; e-portfolios and individual Web pages.

Features of social networking that act as a framework for this chapter are interconnection, content creation, and interactivity (based on Greenhow, et al., 2009). Web 2.0 tools allow interconnection limited only by an individual's technical and Internet access capability; afford content creation through access to ideas, information and data; and through interaction with either information or others, share, remix, edit, create, or reframe knowledge.

Three broad sociological issues are apparent when considering the impact of social networking on academic knowledge generation (See for example Beer & Burrows, 2007). In a sense these issues have always existed regardless of the nature of exchange but the key difference now is these communities of learners are no longer entirely exclusive as they were in the past. First, when an academic posts a blog entry, edits a wiki, or tweets; they are both producing and consuming ideas and information, more so as others interact with these postings. This generates ethical issues around the role of the individual as part of the process of active knowledge production. Second, information that may have been relatively private through the exchange of personal correspondence or even a handwritten journal is now frequently publicly available. For instance, interaction on a blog produces a range of information in addition to the actual content—number of visitors, frequency of visits and postings, key words used in postings, and so on. Popular topics and interest groups can readily be identified by commercial data trawlers or e-researchers. Ethical issues here related to privacy and use of data by third parties, and questions about consent and identity become important. One ethical question concerns the possible vulnerability of individuals who may be unaware of the public status of using Web 2.0 technology. Finally, the public nature of online social networking has lead to a discourse of democratization of knowledge. This has led to ethical concerns about respect for diverse opinions and cultural representation and positioning.

The purpose of this conceptual paper is to identify and describe ethical issues, questions, and actions that have practical and functional application in academic social networking. Collective intelligence is the construct used as a basis for identifying affordances of virtual conversational spaces.

Ethics are a dynamically constructed, or imagined, set of moral principles peculiar to a specific context. An ethical action is one that is congruent with these principles (Wendell, 2000). As an illustrative example, there are well-accepted ethical values around plagiarism and known teachable actions to assist students avoid this accusation. Yet, what ethical framework can be unarguably and universally placed around collaborative processes to deliberately share and remix knowledge in an open and informal virtual learning space.

This example demonstrates how the use of Web 2.0 tools are "changing the way we as researchers and educators think about learners' participatory and creative practices ... especially about what, how, with whom, and for what purposes learning occurs through such practices" (Greenhow, et al., 2009, p. 249). By addressing the ethical dilemmas associated with the use of 21st century learning mechanisms, this chapter contributes to discourse around the effective and efficient deployment of such tools within contemporary learning environments.

## THEORETICAL FRAMEWORK

### Collective Intelligence

Levy (1997, p. 9) posed the question "What then will our new communication tools be used for?" and then suggested the answer was sharing of "mental abilities in the construction of collective intellect of imagination."

Web 2.0 tools that have enabled what is termed *collective intelligence* are typified by the interactive practices used by wikis and blogs, hyper-linking, Rich Site Summary (RSS) and Google (O'Reilly, 2007). Although the general features of collective intelligence are described

below, it is not possible to definitively articulate this dynamic meta-concept. It remains important to explore this concept as it provides a framework of explanatory and analytical ideas that can increase understanding of knowledge building in contemporary learning environments.

Numerous examples of collective intelligence are in day-to-day use in modern society, formed through semantic and social processes in structured and informal ways. One common element is that any individual may deliberately seek, draw together, and engage with a collective intelligence system by assembling ideas, data, or knowledge through the use of a number of disparate Web 2.0 tools and practices. This may range from a simple personal blog with hyperlinks and interaction with followers; to the more formally ordered and comprehensive online specialist community.

Levy (1997, p. 13) defined collective intelligence as "a form of universally distributed intelligence, constantly enhanced, coordinated in real time, and resulting in the effective mobilization of skills." It is also referred to as distributed intelligence, innovation communities or crowd wisdom (Brabham, 2008).

The collective intelligence concept is used in biology and psychology to describe massed contextual behaviour of animals (See for example Sulis, 1997). Sulis commented that collective intelligence is characterized by a lack of hierarchical organisation. Thus, individuals are simultaneously inside and outside any specific decision or action; and may adapt to context through individual or socially interactive activity.

Gruber (2007) identifies the main elements of collective knowledge systems as (1) user-generated content through participative social interaction; and (2) a synergy between people—the source of experience and ideas—and computers—providing a means of linking people and storing searchable data—resulting in a rapid increase in the volume of information being constructed online. This is apparent in sites such as Wikipedia where the more people accessing and using the site increases the validity and usefulness of the information; leading to gains in knowledge and understanding beyond the collected information.

In education settings, collective intelligence structures are evident in multiple variants, including academics interacting with known and unknown peers, sharing ideas and hyperlinks to useful resources and ideas, generating and exploring ideas—learning within and about the process of collaborative knowledge construction in digital contexts.

An example of collective intelligence in an academic social network is Methodspace (http://www.methodspace.com). The purpose of the website is to connect members of the (albeit loosely defined) academic research community. Any individual can join and create a personal profile page and join discussion of research methods, join a method group, respond to method blogs, questions, and discussion forums. Resources are available for members including article and book of the month, as well as links to relevant journals and texts. Members can contact each other through public or private spaces.

It could be argued that this is an academic variant of Facebook, with many of the same features. If the Methodspace site is viewed from a data harvesting perspective, there is academic information in the form of in-depth discussion about methodological questions, including suggested references and hyperlinks to further reading; and semantic data about popular topics, individuals with specific interests, as well as page and topic visit and use data. This demonstrates how a mix of how stored data (the Semantic Web) can be linked to the experiences and interests of individual and sub-groups of individuals (the social Web). This example demonstrates how collective intelligence can be construed as a means of rapid gathering, representing and exploring ideas from a global information system that the user has a part in constructing and shaping.

Lee and Lan (2007) and others make the claim that knowledge emerging through Web-based interaction challenges the notion of top-down expertise. Expertise is thought of, in terms of collective intelligence, as more expansive and distributed although available online via formal and informal means. Interaction between novices and experts provides experience and practice in development and use of contextual language, building knowledge deemed useful and relevant by practitioners within defined contexts, and learning strategies.

The notion of expertise in professions has been considered by Sternberg (1999) and others. While there is no precise and encompassing definition of expertise, it can perhaps be conceived of as the reflective, "... wise *and* intelligent use of knowledge" (Sternberg, 2003). As an example, Sternberg and Horvath (1995) suggest that an expert teacher can be differentiated from a novice by the amount of subject and pedagogical knowledge they use to respond to their teaching context; the efficiency with which they resolve emerging problems during their teaching; and the insight they apply to devise innovative and workable solutions to teaching issues (Sternberg & Horvath, 1995). This view of expertise is characterized by a dynamic capacity to adapt practice to local contexts, involving constant reflective monitoring and reinvestment of learnt professional practice knowledge and skills (Matthew & Sternberg, 2009).

The generation and re-generation of professional practice knowledge is at the centre of what it means to be an adaptive expert. This is consistent with Sharples, Taylor, and Vavoula (2007, p. 222) comment that "We learn across space as we take ideas and learning resources gained in one location and apply or develop them in another." Our argument is that expertise should include consideration of the ethical nature of all knowledge generation activities, especially the seeking, drawing upon, and sharing ideas accessed from professional dialogue across real and virtual networks. Table 1 offers a comparison between hierarchical and collective intelligence models of academic interaction.

*Table 1. A comparison of hierarchical and collective intelligence models of academic interaction*

|  | **Hierarchical model** | **Collective intelligence** |
|---|---|---|
| Interconnection | Centrality of expert; critique; sensorial; prescriptive | Open; distributed expertise; creativity; disruptive |
|  | Respect for expertise | Expertise questioned |
| Content creation | Formal; structured; defensible | A mix of formal and informal; ideas are of varying quality |
|  | Expert structures and formally presents ideas | Individual must locate, interpret, interact with, and assess usability of information |
| Interactivity | Expert provides and reports models of interrogation | Each individual conducts analytical and evaluative processes |
|  | Academic; largely text based; conventional | Multi-modal, including 'txt' |
|  | Procedural and expert-directed within set time and space e.g. classroom | Individual opts in and out; varying intensity of effort |

While the collective intelligence model may be conceived of as an extension of the hierarchical model, it also includes newly imagined and emerging social networking experiences. This model is offered here as a basis for discussion about emergent ethical issues and deliberately constructed to show how, in a collective intelligence system, the responsibility for effortful seeking, translating and judging information, in order to construct knowledge, moves from a formal procedure to an openly self-regulated system. Expert knowledge remains a key component of both systems, although within a collective intelligence system the 'expertise' has been fragmented through time and space.

Moving from the rigid strictures of a traditional hierarchical model to a process that can be characterized as chaotic or even disruptively democratic introduces uncertainty about how to interact with and judge information. The question of the future role and place of the expert is raised by Bothos, Apostolou, and Mentzas' (2009) assertion that rich interaction requires a degree of expert input to moderate uncertainty involved in evaluation of ideas. Similarly, Lee and Lan (2007) note the need for not only vigorous interaction, but a process to resolve conflicting perspectives. Siemens (2005, p. 4), commenting on contemporary learning models afforded through digital landscapes indicated that:

*Learning is a process that occurs within nebulous environments of shifting core elements—not entirely under the control of the individual. Learning ... is focused on connecting specialized information sets, and the connections that enable us to learn more are more important than our current state of knowing.*

There is already considerable overlap between the social constructivist ideals of a collective intelligence system, and the co-regulated or blended learning formats of many contemporary approaches to learning in higher education. The principal influence is the loss of hierarchical control over the learning context.

## Academic Social Networking: The Affordances of Conversation

Online interaction has often been conceived in terms of conversation (Bothos, et al., 2009; Laurillard, 2009; Sharples, et al., 2007). Sharples et al. (2007, p. 225), for example, assert that:

*Conversation is the driving process of learning. It is the means by which we negotiate differences, understand each other's experiences and form transiently stable interpretations of the world.*

Laurillard (2009) provides a conversational framework or map explicating the process of collaborative learning in online environments. This framework assumes a purpose and intensity that defines academic conversation. For instance, interaction characterising knowledge building may include posting comments, ideas and asking questions of other participants, adapting explanations or ideas in response to feedback, peer-based discussion, representation of collective ideas and personal and critical reflection on the experience. Academic conversation may include interactions that are considered, strategic, informal, and reactive, moments of intensity mixed with disengagement; as well as tangential mental abstraction. Conversely, academic conversation may be terse, lacking civility, or shaped by the bureaucratic or pragmatic need to reach a resolution. Moving from the generation and exploration of ideas to coherent and credible end-points remains a fundamental although complex part of academic conversation; necessary to bind the anarchic tendencies of informal Web-based social dialogic interaction (Riedl, Blohm, Leimeister, & Krcmar, 2010).

The purpose of academic conversation is potentially at odds with the inherent strength of the collective intelligence concept, as illustrated by Bonabeau's (2009) comment that online academic conversations may be better at generating ideas than evaluation; although this may be mediated if participants actively resolved issues of motivation and purpose, diversity, accuracy and quality.

Collective intelligence is defined here as the deliberate employment of Web 2.0 tools across a distributed, although loose, network of peers and information in order to enact a purposeful academic conversation concerned with generating, exploring and evaluating knowledge. A number of affordances can be identified in relation to what collective intelligence offers for academic conversation; and the skills and knowledge required to harvest this potential. These affordances are outlined in Table 2. Affordances are features of a context that allow or potentially contribute to the resultant activity (Greeno, 1994). Affordances and the ability and perceptions of individuals are integrated. Therefore, affordances are realized through the individual's perceptions about what and how something can be done and their enactment capacity.

Drawing upon, monitoring and refining knowledge is a constructive process that can be aided by accessing and interacting with a range of perspectives. Deliberately seeking other perspectives by communicating, to use the example of educators, with the wider academic community, in order to informally and formally reflect on and build knowledge of one's own professional practice can be a significant component of building knowledge (Trigwell, Martin, Benjamin, & Prosser, 2000).

The main affordances are the accessing and interplay of a variety of ideas, where questioning and imagining multiple possible interpretations and applications, raise questions and doubt about

*Table 2. Affordances of academic conversation through online social interaction*

|  | **Affordances** |
|---|---|
| Interconnection | Representation and communication of ideas to distant peers<br>Learning perceived as dynamic, involving formal and informal sources |
| Content creation | Progressively cycling through sharing, explanation and questioning, based on a sense of doubt, applying higher standards of analysis and evaluation to make sense of new ideas and experiences, leading to idea building and refinement |
| Interactivity | Purposeful conversation to share, explore and build ideas<br>Deliberately seeking outside ideas and diverse perspectives |

the ideas being discovered and examined. The affordances of collective intelligence has been considered and outlined in previous work by the authors (Deed & Edwards, 2011a). This prior work utilized the metaphor of outsideness to consider online engagement with distant peers; and as a means of differentiating digital and non-digital collective intelligence systems. Outsideness was conceived of as a key influence in online environments where geographically and culturally distant peers have the potential to engage in rich, thoughtful, and purposeful conversational moments.

Laurillard (2009) emphasized that social learning using technology employ multi-pathway dialogue. This involves participants presenting, commenting on and comparing ideas; seeking and providing feedback; generating or resolving questions; reflecting on experience; and adapting practice. Effective dialogue needs to balance description with the nuanced questioning and affective hints that form part of multi-directional and reciprocal conversation (Enyedy & Hoadley, 2006). Thus, the principal activity becomes the discussion, adaptation and agreed meaning given to ideas and actions as a result of participation in social learning environments (Cassidy, et al., 2007; Deed & Edwards, 2010).

Expressing an idea may be a starting point for conversation involving description, explanation and exploration of ideas (Pask, 1975). Each idea expressed in an online social space is dense with potential meaning; conversation may occur if group members seek to question the multiple interpretations of shared ideas (Enyedy & Hoadley, 2006).

Novel ideas—perhaps emerging from the different cultures and perspectives to be found among distant peers—are likely create tensions, arguments, contradictions that will act as a starting point for dialogue. This increased sense of doubt may be heightened by working with outside peers, leading to asking questions about ideas and meaning ascribed to those ideas (Deed & Edwards, 2011a).

This is coherent with Palincsar's (1998) argument that the process of discourse, where learning is purposefully social, involves the interplay of ideas with cycles of display, validation, and refinement of meaning, where progressively higher standards of argument are applied to idea creation and potential application.

Engestrom (1987) has written extensively about expansive learning. In relation to collective intelligence, expansive learning involves co-construction of ideas as an adaptive and dynamic production of knowledge, with no definitive endpoint. This affords opportunity for engaging with varied loosely bound communities of practice through access to multi-disciplinary teams and repositories of expert knowledge.

While the purpose of collaboration in a formal system may be to devise new knowledge, Engestrom et al. (1997) assert that the driving influence in expansive learning is disturbance, unexpected events and a lack of coordination. Kangasoja (2002) makes clear that whereas "the idea of disturbance assumes a script … (this) has little meaning in settings where there are no established practices of collaborating." This is only partially relevant in communities of practice where participants construe ideas, problems, and purposes of collaborating differently; although separately devising an outcome specific to their own context (Kangasoja, 2002). One possibility is that expansive systems may disintegrate into disparate individual pockets, depending on the capacity of individual participants to reassert meaning over and between the fragments.

Adding to the complexity of academic conversation in virtual spaces is that the nature of communication is usually through text. Emig (1977, p. 124) asserted that "Because writing is often our representation of the world made visible, embodying both process and product, writing is more readily a form and source of learning than talking."

Writing online does afford an opportunity to be deliberate when communicating ideas, but raises questions about the balance between 'txting' language and academic conventions. Writing is an actively rational process "… of constructing, creating and making" (Badley, 2009, p. 211). Freinet (1969, pp. 54-55) stated that "Writing makes no sense unless one is obliged to resort to it in order to communicate beyond the reach of our voice, outside of the limits of school."

Yet, when a person writes they simultaneously project multiple meanings and different levels of understanding by using past, current and future interpretations of experience. Words are re-imagined and interpreted by others, who may ask questions, leading to further writing and re-thinking. Written conversation can become a social interaction where meaning is interpreted through local contextual understanding (Enyedy & Hoadley, 2006).

As Emig (1977, p. 124) noted however, "Writing is stark, barren, even naked as a medium ..." This barrenness is accented in online environments, where communication prompts such as facial expression are absent, means the text has to attempt to convey the explicit sense of the writer. Adding complexity to the starkness of writing in an online context is that each word is dense with potential meaning.

Dialogue is afforded when community participants seek to constrain the multiple interpretations of each key word (Enyedy & Hoadley, 2006). A written dialogue thus needs to balance description with the nuanced questioning and affective hints that form part of normal conversation.

Outsideness influences the construction of knowledge in online collaborative contexts through the sharing and exploration of personal and cultural perspectives; asking questions to resolve doubt; and as a driver of purposeful conversation. In a technologically-infused context outsideness refers to an individual's sense of cultural differences among peers as a stimulus for a rich, interactive and complex learning conversation. Thus, collective intelligence affords rich online collaborative spaces where knowledge may be actively and individually constructed.

The principal affordance of collective intelligence, using the analytical framework of outsideness, relate to a sense of doubt about the process of effortful learning required, and the purposeful engagement in making meaning out of uncertainty. The affordance of uncertainty, even allowing for geographic, disciplinary, methodological, and cultural barriers, is about ensuring that multiple interpretations of meaning are acknowledged and explored in order to create new and appropriate knowledge.

The argument here is that collective intelligence provides a means to improve professional practical knowledge, beyond—although connected to—traditional procedures. This is afforded by the use of technology as a means of moving from individual to social learning; having a view of expertise as collective and located in individuals that are globally distributed; and willingly entering a space where learning is open and dynamic (Lankshear & Knobel, 2007).

## ETHICAL ISSUES EMERGING FROM COLLECTIVE INTELLIGENCE

The purpose here is to identify ethical questions and the practical application of possible ethical actions in the specific context of online social interaction. Ethical questions, rather than a definite set of ethics, are raised because of the difficulty of conceptualizing the complexity of working in new online contexts.

*Ethical questions concern ... what serves as a 'standard' or 'norm' of human conduct, what is 'demanded' of us; or, finally, to name it by the oldest, simplest word, ethical questions concern the 'good' (Schlick, 1939, pp. 2-3).*

Ethical actions are identified, not as a means of regulating possible activity, but to encourage further questions and dialogue about behaviors that support the long-term interests of online interactions among professional colleagues.

Ethics are peculiar to a specific group within a defined context. An ethical action is one that can be recognised as consistent with a dynamically constructed, or imagined, set of moral principles thought to apply to activities within that context.

The discussion here is congruent with Wendel's (2000, p. 201) argument that "ethical decisions can never become completely theorized and predictable." It is assumed that academics function as ethical agents in relation to knowledge producing activities. Thus, it is possible to identify ethical dilemmas in new spaces by examining ethical frameworks that are used in traditional spaces, given similar purposes in activity. This is consistent with Wendel's (2000, p. 198) statement that:

*Ethical agents are not decision makers that approach each choice anew, bound to decide on a course of action based solely on the facts as they present themselves in that case. Instead, they approach ethical choices as persons who have lived lives shaped in particular ways by past decisions and commitments.*

However, it is possible that the new context for academic conversation may provide new ethical choices that cannot be simply resolved through consideration of precedent. Further, the new space may afford new activities or exposure to different sets of "authentic human value commitments, both of which are morally worthy," leading to a "plurality of right answers, none of which is impersonally better" (Wendel, 2000, p. 202).

Table 3 summarizes the ethical issues identified and described here. Each set of ethical dilemmas is then examined below using the categories of interconnection, content creation and interactivity. These ethical dilemmas are mired in the widespread use of new technology and previously un-imagined ways of conducting the business of knowledge creation. Wholesale harnessing of Web-based data from academic interaction for research and commercial purposes is already taking place, largely in the absence of agreed legal and ethical frameworks. In the main, ethical dilemmas emerge from the relative meaning and understanding ascribed by individuals to the nature and implications of public comment.

## Interconnection

One ethical issue is the frequently raised concern about accessibility of online interaction. There are certain technical and socio-cultural tools required to participate in social networking; and while important, this is our main concern. Indeed, ethical issues identified here largely emerge from the pervasive adoption of Web 2.0 technology in higher education, enabling extensive participation in knowledge construction. This is particularly relevant for social networking, as knowledge and related conversational process are the currency of academic life.

Take the important example of publishing. New models of participatory publishing can be seen as an extension of social networking. SAGE Open (http://sgo.sagepub.com/) is an example of peer reviewed academic publishing in an open-access format. In addition to a variety of sharing

*Table 3. Ethical dilemmas associated with academic conversation through online social interaction*

|  | **Ethical dilemmas** |
|---|---|
| Interconnection | Accessibility<br>Public conversation<br>Risk taking (ideas 'in-play') |
| Content creation | Privacy and consent<br>Vulnerability of naïve individuals<br>Ownership of socially generated and semantic data |
| Interactivity | Clarity of purpose<br>Effortful collaboration<br>Engaging with diverse experiences and perspectives |

and linking options, interactivity with readers is encouraged by the provision of a comments function. Thus, the author and readers can interact about published ideas.

This raises the ethical issue of the difference between offline academic writing and formal publishing and online public drafting of ideas. If the author uses a number of informal, yet incisive, comments to redraft a further version of the paper using the ideas 'in-play' through the interactive commentary of readers, is might reasonably be asked – who does the primary author then acknowledge and cite?

The main ethical action in an interconnected conversational environment may be awareness that knowledge is a social (and no longer a privileged) currency—it is both the means and outcome of academic work. It is sought and traded, reworked and re-traded. This is particularly so in online networking contexts. Like the commercial use of monetary currency, knowledge has tacit structural and transactional 'rules.'

There are certain natural barriers to the production, movement, and standard of knowledge in academic contexts—these relate to the building of defensible knowledge. A key ethical consideration is control of knowledge—it may be traditionally vested in 'privileged' locations (possibly established hierarchical networks among English-speaking academic publications). However, online networking allows the flow, revision, application, and re-shaping by those in distant and diverse locations. Any expert or established knowledge base can be accessed by any individual with the technical expertise to achieve their purpose through the use of a computer and an Internet connection. Certainly, there is exposure to new socio-cultural ideas within a networked conversation. Rather than trying to break in to established knowledge networks, new ways of doing business (e.g. free access academic publishing) are perhaps introducing pressure on the bastions of traditional hierarchies. Enduring questions remain though, including how

these diverse perspectives and opportunities to be reconciled (even validated) with the established practices of knowledge production?

We suggest that a primary ethical action is to engage with the affordances of online interactivity, to share ideas and participate in knowledge generation through collective intelligence systems.

## Content Creation

There are multiple levels and types of content created through even basic forms of online interaction. This raises the ethical question of how to retain control of the public nature of content creation in online academic networks.

Take for example an online discussion among a group of academics with experience or expertise in a specific methodological approach to research. There are at least five layers of data being continually produced including (a) the process of knowledge construction as the discussion weaves among group member postings (for an example of an analytical framework for online discussion see Deed & Edwards, 2011b); (b) the final resolution or end points of the discussion (for example see Korfiatis, Poulos, & Bokos, 2006); (c) online text data, including citations, linkages, track-backs and use of key words (for example of the use of text-crawling data collection in blogs see Adar & Adamic, 2005); (d) user activity data, including popularity of networks, level of participation, tagging of content, the 'flow' of activity around certain sites and discussions (O'Reilly, 2007); and (e) identification of individuals involved.

Ethical considerations here are generally related to ownership and control of generated information. A primary question concerns the users' awareness of the public nature of their postings and interaction. Rosenblum (2007, p. 48) comments that "There is little that can be done from a technical point of view to change the intrinsically porous nature of a digital medium" meaning "… there is no longer an expectation of privacy in the sphere that traditionally has been at the core of our self-conceived private lives."

Regardless of an individual's belief in the restricted privacy of their activity, any online social interaction leaves a durable digital footprint. However, the expectation of a level of privacy or ownership over public activity persists. Ethical actions therefore include a personal awareness of the public nature of online interaction, possibly leading to manipulation of private and public boundaries (including setting access controls). This however may reduce the very potential and purpose of online interaction—to converse with unknown, distant, colleagues.

There are differences between online and offline, synchronous and asynchronous, conversation. These differences require more detailed consideration. One difference examined here is where online academic conversation is conducted using text. While this affords deliberateness, it also simultaneously projects multiple meanings and different levels of understanding as words are re-imagined and interpreted by others—similar to conventional offline writing. However, the often brief nature of online exchange, and the contextual and cultural differences between online peers may exacerbate the tendency for some text may be taken out of context or be misinterpreted. Thus, it is not possible to control the use of online postings as they are fragmented and distributed across cyberspace.

A second ethical action is to actively consider participant expectations of privacy when using online social interactions as source material. Information in an online space may be used by data-miners. Academics frequently research their own and their peers' actions, particularly in relation to knowledge generation. When research occurs in online contexts, complex and currently unresolved (and perhaps unresolvable) ethical issues emerge. The question of what expectations participants in a conversation have about privacy has no ethically coherent answer. Barnes (2006, p. 3) labels this a privacy paradox. That is, some individuals freely post personal information online because they are often "not aware of the public nature of the internet." One solution is to argue that individuals capable of exercising personal responsibility about what they place on social networking sites can be said to have no expectations of privacy. However, this raises the question of what constitutes a capacity for responsibility specific to the use of the internet. Thus, a more realistic solution may be to argue that social networking participants need continual reminding of the public nature of their networking activities, and that unanticipated actions may occur at any time in the future related to the use of their public postings.

## Interactivity

Prior research by the authors examined the nature of interactivity among pre-service teacher education students working in groups made up of members from three countries (see Deed & Edwards, in press). The requirements of the task reported, i.e. an academic conversation involving generation, exploration and creation of knowledge, meant that the findings could be considered in relation to a discussion of academic networked dialogue.

The students in the reported study indicated a high level of internet access and familiarity with social interaction in online contexts, although a lack of experience with academic dialogue in a wiki environment. Although personal and cultural narratives were shared, there was variation in the degree of explanation and exploration of group member's ideas. Overall, there were minimal attempts at active exploration, and unevenness in the distribution of postings among group members. Rather than Laurillard's (2009) multi-pathway dialogue, the transcript analysis showed a somewhat linear set of postings. Wiki dialogue tended to move rapidly from idea description to final product, bypassing the nuances associated with social construction of knowledge. The paucity of exploratory postings indicated a gap between the potential of collective intelligence and the individuals' capacity to converse using text in an academic social networking space.

While the participants in that study may have been empathetic to different cultural perspectives, they were unable, or lacked capacity, to enact a collaborative effort in order to deepen the extent of their inquiry.

This reflected the tension between the dual sense of outsideness and insideness—a key point when considering the ethical issues related to interactivity in academic social networking. Each member of an academic social network conducted in virtual space is both known and unknown to each other in terms of individual purpose and prior experience. For example, three academics with extensive background and knowledge of (for example) grounded theory may be members of a group that discusses the intricacies of this methodological approach. A fourth individual may join the group and pose a relatively naive question. The purpose of the new member's question is to access the distributed expertise of the existing group members. The purpose of the existing group members may be to continue to explore complex knowledge and creatively examine abstract principles related to their expertise (rather than offer assistance to a novice).

Thus, they can respond to the novice's question in a number of ways. They could 'flame' the new member by being cleverly sarcastic. They may use deliberately obscure jargon-laden language to alienate or minimize ongoing discussion. Alternatively, they may offer assistance by suggesting some rudimentary readings on the topic.

The central ethical question is whether they will engage with the individuals from outside their tacitly bounded club. The term engage is used with some caution, as it is a meta-concept, although in this case it is used to refer to the members making an investment in building and supporting the development of knowledge and building an academic community of practice. An initial indicator of effortful activity would be the deliberate and purposeful seeking and interaction with multiple perspectives. In terms of academic conversation, investment would include using clear language to explore, analyze, evaluate, and apply ideas as part of either construction or reconstruction of knowledge. Ethical actions related to interactivity concern the level of effortful cognitive activity as evidenced through the multimodal representation and communication of ideas with peers. Multimodality is suggested here in order to facilitate engagement with individuals from different language and cultural backgrounds.

Interactivity is based on the primal concept of uncertainty and doubt. Seeking and sharing ideas with other distant peers will inevitably result in a collision between diverse perspectives and cultural experiences. These differences can be subtle or dramatic.

Table 4 provides a summary of the ethical actions identified in the above discussion. These ethical actions are related to academic social interaction in online contexts, but are also relevant to other professionals who interact with distant colleagues.

Academic conversation has at its core a need for defensibility. That is, the pursuit of an arguable case in support, or as critique, of an idea. This means that diverse opinions are examined, or critiqued, and one primary solution determined. The rigor of this process, conducted in the raw and artificial environment of online interaction, becomes an ethical issue when the question of cultural values is considered.

A suggested ethical activity here emerges from the practice of argument. Ethical activity can be determined by the efficiency with which individuals resolve emerging or potential abstract conflict through insightful and creative identification and application of innovative and workable local solutions; and acknowledgement of the workability of alternative resolutions in different contexts. In sum, it is the exploration of ideas that is the ethical act, not a single-minded determination to find an ultimate solution.

*Table 4. Ethical actions suggested for academic conversation through online social networking*

| | **Suggested personal ethical actions** |
|---|---|
| Interconnection | Awareness that knowledge is a social commodity<br>Awareness of possible outcomes of online interaction<br>Responsiveness to collective intelligence opportunities |
| Content creation | Awareness of public nature of online interaction<br>Awareness of differences between online and offline dialogue<br>Consider participant expectations of privacy when using online social interactions as source material |
| Interactivity | Purposeful seeking and interacting with multiple perspectives<br>Use of strategies for interaction in multiple contexts, including use of multimodal representation and communication of ideas<br>Exploration of uncertainty and doubt rather than seeking a single solution |

## CONCLUSION

The traditions of academic discourse include sharing, explaining, and questioning as part of reviewing and building ideas (Palincsar & Herrenkohl, 2002). Making connections, assembling networks among colleagues—these are the activities used to forge a critical path through the chaos and uncertainty of contemporary academic life. Web 2.0 tools afford an extension—although in modified form—of these conventions into a virtual context.

It is reasonable to argue that a disposition to engagement with ideas is a precursor to effortful investment with ideas, knowledge, and perspectives on a global scale. Perhaps this is a rather optimistic view of the potential of academic social networking, but we are reminded of Dewey's (1916, pp. 5-6) comment that:

*To be a recipient of a communication is to have an enlarged and changed experience ... Except in dealing with commonplaces and catch phrases one has to assimilate, imaginatively, something of another's experience in order to tell him intelligently of one's own experience.*

Learning and development occur in specific contexts, which constantly evolve in response to technological and social change. As Dede (2009) makes clear, the social use of immersive collaborative media has led to an emphasis on active and reflective learning characterised by fluency in multiple media; collective seeking, sorting, and interpreting varied experiences; and representation and communication using multi-modal forms.

We have only considered social networking from an academic users' perspective, and thus have been more concerned with the ethics of conversation. Other perspectives need to be examined, particularly social, commercial and government implications of questions about ethical use of public production and consumption of information.

Academics need to further consider the ethical implications of applying traditional discourse conventions in each new social networking context. This includes the conceptualization of knowledge as distributed across time and space; leading to ethical questions concerning interconnection, content creation and interactivity.

Here we have identified differences between traditional and collective intelligence models of academic social networking that support knowledge production. Ethical questions—concerning the nuances of standards of conduct required—emerge from these differences. While these questions are not fully resolved, some ethical activities can be identified based on the translation of conventional conduct by taking account of the properties of alternative and emerging dialogic contexts.

We have indicated a number of ethical dilemmas emerging from the widespread tendency of academics to engage in online social networking. Many more philosophical and sociological issues require ongoing examination and debate.

## REFERENCES

Adar, E., & Adamic, L. A. (2005). Tracking information epidemics in blogspace. In *Proceedings of the IEEE/WIC/ACM International Conference on Web Intelligence*. IEEE/WIC/ACM.

Badley, G. (2009). Academic writing as shaping and re-shaping. *Teaching in Higher Education, 14*(2), 209–219. doi:10.1080/13562510902757294

Barnes, S. B. (2006). A privacy paradox: Social networking in the United States. *First Monday, 11*(9).

Beer, D., & Burrows, R. (2007). Sociology and, of and in Web 2.0: Some initial considerations. *Sociological Research Online, 12*(5). doi:10.5153/sro.1560

Bonabeau, E. (2009). Decisions 2.0: The power of collective intelligence. *MIT Sloan Management Review, 50*(2), 45–52.

Bothos, E., Apostolou, D., & Mentzas, G. (2009). Collective intelligence for idea management with internet-based information aggregation markets. *Internet Research, 19*(1), 26–41. doi:10.1108/10662240910927803

Brabham, D. C. (2008). Crowdsourcing as a model for problem solving: An introduction and cases. *Convergence: The International Journal of Research into New Media Technologies, 14*(1), 75–90. doi:10.1177/1354856507084420

Cassidy, C., Christie, D., Coutts, N., Dunn, J., Sinclair, C., & Skinner, D. (2007). Building communities of educational enquiry. *Oxford Review of Education, 34*(2), 217–235. doi:10.1080/03054980701614945

Dede, C. (2009). *Determining, developing and assessing the capabilities of 'future-ready' students*. Retrieved from http://www.fi.ncsu.edu/assets/research_papers/brown-bag/determining-developing-and-assessing-the-capabilities-of-future-ready-students.pdf

Deed, C., & Edwards, A. (2010). Using social networks in learning and teaching in higher education: An Australian case study. *International Journal of Knowledge Society Research, 1*(2), 1–12. doi:10.4018/jksr.2010040101

Deed, C., & Edwards, A. (2011a). The role of outside affordances in developing expertise in online collaborative learning. *International Journal of Knowledge Society Research, 2*(2), 27–38. doi:10.4018/jksr.2011040103

Deed, C., & Edwards, A. (2011b). Unrestricted student blogging: Implications for active learning in a virtual text-based environment. *Active Learning in Higher Education, 12*(1). doi:10.1177/1469787410387725

Deed, C., & Edwards, A. (2012). Knowledge building in online environments: Constraining and enabling collective intelligence. In de Pablos, P. O., Lytras, M. D., Tennyson, R. D., & Gayo, J. E. L. (Eds.), *Cases on Open-Linked Data and Semantic Web Applications*. Hershey, PA: IGI Global.

Dewey, J. (1916). *Democracy and education*. New York, NY: MacMillan.

Emig, J. (1977). Writing as a mode of learning. *College Composition and Communication, 28*(2), 122–128. doi:10.2307/356095

Engestrom, Y. (1987). *Learning by expanding: An activity-theoretical approach to developmental research.* Helsinki, Finland: Orienta-Konsultit.

Engestrom, Y., Brown, K., Christopher, L. K., & Gregory, J. (1997). Coordination, cooperation and communication in the courts: Expansive transitions in legal work . In Cole, M., Engestrom, Y., & Vasquez, T. (Eds.), *Mind, Culture and Activity: Seminal Papers from the Laboratory of Comparative Human Cognition.* Cambridge, UK: Cambridge University Press.

Enyedy, N., & Hoadley, C. M. (2006). From dialogue to monologue and back: Middle spaces in computer-mediated learning. *Computer-Supported Collaborative Learning, 1,* 413–439. doi:10.1007/s11412-006-9000-2

Freinet, C. (1969). *Pour l'ecole du peuple: Guide pratique pour l'organisation materielle, technique et pedagogique de l'ecole populaire* [For a school of the people: A practical guide for the material, technical, and pedagogical organization of a popular school]. Barcelona, Spain: Editorial Laia.

Greenhow, C., Robelia, B., & Hughes, J. E. (2009). Web 2.0 and classroom research: What path should we take now? *Educational Researcher, 38*(4), 246–259. doi:10.3102/0013189X09336671

Greeno, J. G. (1994). Gibson's affordances. *Psychological Review, 101*(2), 336–343. doi:10.1037/0033-295X.101.2.336

Gruber, T. (2007). Collective knowledge systems. In *Proceedings of the 5th International Semantic Web Conference.* IEEE.

Kangasoja, J. (2002). *Complex design problems: An impetus for learning and knotworking.* Retrieved 21 May, 2011, from http://www.edu.helsinki.fi/activity/publications/files/47/ICLS2002_Kangasoja.pdf

Korfiatis, N., Poulos, M., & Bokos, G. (2006). Evaluating authoritative sources using social networks: An insight from Wikipedia. *Online Information Review, 30*(3), 252–262. doi:10.1108/14684520610675780

Lankshear, C., & Knobel, M. (2007). Researching new literacies: Web 2.0 practices and insider perspectives. *E-Learning and Digital Media, 4*(3).

Laurillard, D. (2009). The pedagogical challenges to collaborative technologies. *Computer-Supported Collaborative Learning, 4,* 5–20. doi:10.1007/s11412-008-9056-2

Lee, M. R., & Lan, Y. (2007). From web 2.0 to conversational knowledge management: Towards collaborative intelligence. *Journal of Entrepreneurship Research, 2*(2), 47–62.

Levy, P. (1997). *Collective Intelligence: Mankind's Emerging World in Cyberspace* (Bononno, R., Trans.). New York, NY: Plenum.

Matthew, C. T., & Sternberg, R. J. (2009). Developing experience-based (tacit) knowledge through reflection. *Learning and Individual Differences, 19,* 530–540. doi:10.1016/j.lindif.2009.07.001

O'Reilly, T. (2007). What is web 2.0: Design patterns and business models for the next generation of software. *Communications & Strategies, 65,* 17–37.

Palincsar, A. S. (1998). Social constructivist perspectives on teaching and learning. *Annual Review of Psychology, 49,* 345–375. doi:10.1146/annurev.psych.49.1.345

Palincsar, A. S., & Herrenkohl, L. R. (2002). Designing collaborative learning contexts. *Theory into Practice, 41*(1), 26–32. doi:10.1207/s15430421tip4101_5

Pask, G. (1975). *Conversation, cognition and learning: A cybernetic theory and methodology.* Amsterdam, The Netherlands: Elsevier.

Riedl, C., Blohm, I., Leimeister, J. M., & Krcmar, H. (2010). Rating scales for collective intelligence in innovation communities: Why quick and easy decision making does not get it right. In *Proceedings of the 31st International Conference on Information Systems*. IEEE.

Rosenblum, D. (2007). What anyone can know: The privacy risks of social networking sites. In *Proceedings of the IEEE Security and Privacy*, (pp. 40-49). IEEE Press.

Schlick, M. (1939). *Problems of ethics*. New York, NY: Prentice-Hall.

Sharples, M., Taylor, J., & Vavoula, G. (2007). A theory of learning for the mobile age . In Andrews, A., & Haythornthwaite, C. (Eds.), *The Sage Handbook of e-Learning Research* (pp. 221–247). London, UK: Sage Publications Ltd. doi:10.1007/978-3-531-92133-4_6

Siemens, G. (2005). *Connectivism: A learning theory for the digital age*. Elearnspace.

Sternberg, R. J. (1999). Intelligence as developing expertise. *Contemporary Educational Psychology, 24*, 359–375. doi:10.1006/ceps.1998.0998

Sternberg, R. J. (2003). What is an expert Student? *Educational Researcher, 32*(5), 5–9. doi:10.3102/0013189X032008005

Sternberg, R. J., & Horvath, J. A. (1995). A prototype view of expert teaching. *Educational Researcher, 24*(6), 9–17.

Sulis, W. (1997). Fundamental concepts of collective intelligence. *Nonlinear Dynamics Psychology and Life Sciences, 1*(1), 35–53. doi:10.1023/A:1022371810032

Trigwell, K., Martin, E., Benjamin, J., & Prosser, M. (2000). Scholarship of teaching: A model. *Higher Education Research & Development, 19*(2), 155–168. doi:10.1080/072943600445628

Wendel, W. B. (2000). Value pluralism in legal ethics. *Washington University Law Quarterly, 78*, 113–213.

# Chapter 6
# Sem—IDi:
## Research and Development Management Enabled by Semantics

**Ricardo Colomo-Palacios**
*Universidad Carlos III de Madrid, Spain*

**Joaquín Fernández-González**
*Egeo IT, Spain*

**Diego Jiménez-López**
*Egeo IT, Spain*

**David Mayorga Martín**
*PMO partners, Spain*

**Marcos Ruano-Mayoral**
*Egeo IT, Spain*

**Alberto López Fernández**
*PMO partners, Spain*

**Rocío Vega Alonso**
*PMO partners, Spain*

## ABSTRACT

*The increasing strength and usefulness of semantic technologies have led to innovative decision support processes and management of partners and R&D call for proposals. This book chapter introduces the SEM-IDi project, an architecture that integrates R&D processes with project management software and semantic customized environments. This SEM-IDi platform is composed by two main modules: General Management Module (GMM) which will be responsible for general management of diverse initiatives and projects, and the Semantic and Competence Module (SCM) which will provide functionalities related mainly to decision making.*

## INTRODUCTION

The general definition of Research & Development advanced in the Frascati Manual currently reads as follows (OECD, 1993, paragraph 57): "Research and experimental development (R&D) comprise creative work undertaken on a systematic basis in order to increase the stock of knowledge, including knowledge of man, culture, and society, and the use of this stock of knowledge to devise new applications." R&D is seen as an indicator of development in countries (Lee, 2009; Sahaym,

DOI: 10.4018/978-1-4666-2494-8.ch006

Copyright © 2013, IGI Global. Copying or distributing in print or electronic forms without written permission of IGI Global is prohibited.

Steensma, & Barden, 2010) and the rate of growth in productivity of the firms was positively correlated with their research and development expenditures (Minasian, 1969).

Howels (2006) defined an intermediary as an entity assuming the role of an agent or broker in an innovation process between some parties. This author claims that the role of intermediaries covered ten functions in all including foresight and diagnostics, scanning and information processing, knowledge processing and combination/recombination, gate-keeping and brokering, testing and validation, accreditation, validation and regulation, protecting the results, commercialization, and evaluation of outcomes. Wright, Clarysse, Lockett, and Knockaert (2008) divides innovation intermediaries in two types: internal intermediaries and external intermediaries. The first ones are entities like the Technology Transfer Offices (OTT) that guide researches in institutions like universities and perform an intermediary role between these research institutions and the industry. The second kind of intermediaries (external) groups entities with the required expertise to guide the first steps of a company in R&D processes. One example of these intermediaries is Collective Research Centres (CRC). Sawhney, Prandelli, and Verona (2003) defined the role of innomediators (i.e., intermediary innovators) that connect, recombine, and disseminate the ideas of different pools of knowledge that otherwise would not be connected. The emergence of innomediaries parallels the development of infomediaries, a term coined by Hagel and Rayport (1997). Infomediaries are seen as third parties that mediate between customers seeking to make buying decisions and the companies that want to reach them. Infomediaries gather and organize information on products and services for individuals who are considering a purchase; they also organize communities of customers on the basis of common interests or specific industries (Sawhney, Prandelli, & Verona, 2003).

Returning to innovation itself, despite the benefits obtained from intermediaries by the Industry, the growth in number and nature of these professionals (Howels, 2006) and the heterogeneity of partnership cases (Hagedoorn, Link, & Vonortas, 2000) and research domains may create confusion for new clients in these scenarios. At times, consulted intermediaries will not always be able to offer them proper advices regarding potential consortium members or proper projects to present in the appropriate call for proposals.

It is easy to perceive R&D initiatives of an innovative company or innovation intermediary as a project portfolio, where managers have to prioritize those initiatives considered appropriate in each situation, analyzing factors such as risks involved, or the return of investment. Since the 1970s, business portfolios and portfolio management have been portrayed as a powerful and pervasive tool (Roussel, Saad, & Erickson, 1991). There are many project portfolio management models that propose the use of success factors to evaluate and approach strategic selection processes, such as those proposed by Zhao (2007), Wang and Hwang (2007), or Meskendahl (2010). It would be interesting to address management issues from innovative companies from a Project Portfolio Management (PPM) perspective, as it would lead intermediaries and companies to a more efficient and profitable R&D initiatives management.

Partnership selection is one of the most important factors in a R&D project success (Spekman, Isabella, MacAvoy, & Forbes, 1996). Several authors have analyzed and proposed alternatives to efficiently manage partnership selection and relationships (e.g. Barnes, Pashby, & Gibbons, 2006; Hagedoorn, et al., 2000).

The aforementioned heterogeneity of partnerships along with the wide range of domains within R&D represent a challenge for intermediaries, when counselling R&D entities and taking decisions about e.g. presentation of certain proposal to certain call or recommendation of known entities as partners for a project. The decision making process could be implemented using Semantic Technologies, a truly relevant trend in the last years.

This chapter presents SEM-IDi. This tool is designed for R&D projects portfolio management. SEM-IDi is based on Semantic Web technologies and provides decision support regarding financing programmes and call for proposals selection and overall about partnership formation and project management.

## BACKGROUND

Semantic, from Greek sēmantikos, having significance, from sēmainein to signify, from sēma a sign, is of or relating to meaning or arising from distinctions between the meanings of different words or symbols. Now, semantic technology research relies on a number of key methodologies such as knowledge representation languages or reasoning algorithms (Hitzler & Janowicz, 2011). The application of ontologies for expressing semantics of data does not restrict any longer exclusively on Semantic Web or semantic Web services (Vrba, et al., 2011). On the technological side, the Semantic Web aims at adding semantic information to Web contents in order to create an environment in which software agents will be capable of doing tasks efficiently (Berners-Lee, Hendler, & Lassila, 2001). The Semantic Web proposes the idea that Web contents are defined and linked not only for visualization but for being used by applications (Castellanos-Nieves, et al., 2011).

Semantic technologies, based on ontologies (Fensel, 2002), provide a common framework that enables for data integration, sharing and reuse from multiple sources. An ontology can be defined as "a formal and explicit specification of a shared conceptualisation" (Studer, et al., 1998). Ontologies provide a formal, structured knowl-edge representation, with the advantage of being reusable and shareable. Ontologies also provide a common vocabulary for a domain and define—with different levels of formality—the meaning of the terms and the relations between them. Ontologies based on description logics (Gruber, 1995) or related formalisms provide the added benefit of enabling certain kinds of reasoning over the terms, relations, and axioms that describe the domain. Ontology formalizes knowledge meaning and facilitates the search for contents and information (Jiang & Tan, 2009). Knowledge in ontologies is mainly formalized using five kinds of components: classes, relations, functions, axioms, and instances (Gruber, 1993). Classes in the ontology are usually organized into taxonomies. In computer science scenario, instances are equivalent to individuals in ontology terminology (Gómez-Pérez, Fernández-López, & Corcho, 2001). Ontologies provide information systems with a semantically rich knowledge base for the interpretation of unstructured content (Mikroyannidis & Theodoulidis, 2010). Languages such as RDF and OWL (McGuinnes & Van Harmelen, 2004) have been developed; these languages allow for the description of Web resources, and for the representation of knowledge that will enable applications to use resources more intelligently (Horrocks, 2008). These languages, and the tools developed to support them, have rapidly become de facto standards for ontology development and deployment; they are increasingly used, not only in research labs, but in large scale IT projects (Horrocks, 2008).

In the past years our community has seen continuous, sustained growth in the deployment of Semantic Web inventiveness in large and small organizations of many types (Cardoso, 2007) and as a result of this, various industries have adopted SW technologies (Lytras & García, 2008). According to Breslin et al. (2010), industry has begun to watch developments with interest and a number of large companies have started to experiment with Semantic technologies to ascertain if these new technologies can be leveraged to add more value for their customers or internally within the company, while there are already several offers of vendors of Semantic solutions on the market. Moreover, according to Ding (2010), Semantic Web is fast moving in a multidisciplinary way. Thus, Semantic Web has emerged to be a new and highly promising context for knowledge and data engineering (Vossen, Lytras, & Koudas, 2007).

As a consequence of the popularity and applicability of semantic technology solutions, literature reported wide range of applications: tourism (e.g. Garcia-Crespo et al., 2011), customer relationship management (e.g. Garcia-Crespo et al., 2010), research and development activities (Colomo-Palacios, et al., 2010), human resources development (e.g. Fernandez-Breis, et al., 2009; Soto-Acosta, et al., 2010), eGovernment (e.g. Alvarez-Sabucedo, et al., 2010), health domain (e.g. Garcia-Sanchez, et al., 2008), multimedia (e.g. Paniagua-Martin, et al., 2011), financial (e.g. Rodriguez-Gonzalez, et al., 2011), or media (e.g. García, et al., 2008).

## THE SEM-IDi APPROACH

The SEM-IDi platform is an integrated solution for managing research and development initiatives that is based on Semantic Web technologies to support decision-making at all stages of these initiatives lifecycle, and can be used by individual R&D agents or more complex R&D promotion offices.

This SEM-IDi platform is composed by two main modules: General Management Module (GMM) which will be responsible for general management of diverse initiatives and projects, and the Semantic and Competence Module (SCM) which will provide functionalities related mainly to decision making. Both modules will be discussed in following paragraphs.

## Semantic and Competence Module (SCM)

To perform those decision-making functionalities, SCM module will process the data provided by GMM about each R&D idea in all states along their lifecycle; as initiative, proposal, or project. Decision support processes will require two types of information:

- Explicit information related to non-Ieasoning processes, info that will be stored in a conventional database. Representatives of this type of information are the legal nature and the nationality of a research entity.
- Implicit information related to semantic reasoning processes that will be stored in a OWL ontology. For example, competency of an entity extracted from its description and inferred from its participation in previous projects.

The differentiation of the two types of information stems from the optimization of the processing to be performed on the ontology and thus, explicit information has been extracted out of the ontology.

The lifecycle of a research initiative has been divided into three different phases, each of which will be supported on different functionalities provided by the SEM-IDi platform. These phases are the following:

- **Opportunity:** this phase includes all tasks regarding a research initiative usually performed before a fully-fledged proposal is generated. In this phase, the opportunity can be obtained by an exogenous channel (ideas generated by external entities that are submitted to the promotion office) or by endogenous channel (ideas generated by the R&D office/agent themselves). By the end of this phase, the funding mechanism should have been identified/evaluated and generally, the consortium should have been drafted, although it could be easily modified in subsequent phases.

- **Proposal:** this phase embraces all tasks required for the elaboration of a project formal proposal. The sub-phases and the generated documentation for the proposal will be dependent on inherent characteristics of the programme to which the proposal shall be finally submitted. At the end of this phase and depending on specific programme requirements and criteria any active proposal could be approved or rejected by funding/evaluating entity it has been submitted to or, having been approved, the applicant can still decide if it will (or not) go ahead with this proposal or even in some cases, applicants could split its initial proposal in several ones.

- **Project:** In this phase funding/endorsement has been secured to the project so finally starts development of the research project itself, with SEM-IDi supporting its control and management processes. The SCM does not provide relevant functionalities for this phase since it will be mainly supported by GMM.

Anytime during the lifecycle, active research initiatives can get stuck in a certain phase or can be duplicated. This means that it is possible that a given opportunity does not generate any proposal at all or that it may generate several proposals if it is submitted to different funding/evaluating programmes. This scenario is also feasible during the transition from proposal to project.

The role of promotion offices implies to take decisions at several points of the initiative lifecycle and that will configure the final workflow for that initiative. The decisions supported by SEM-IDi include:

- **Consortium Definition:** Several alternatives for partner selection will be provided to define the consortium that will develop the research initiative.

- **Selection of Funding Mechanism:** Selection of a bunch of funding instruments (and their corresponding calls) suitable for the characteristics of each research initiative.

Initially, one of the intended decisions to be supported by the SEM-IDi platform was a filter to discern between bad and good ideas or opportunities. Being such a fuzzy and relative term, it was not feasible to implement it using semantic technologies. A second approach was focused on the identification of previously founded or partially covered ideas. In order to perform such reasoning access to databases with relevant information is essential, so access to databases with CDTI funded projects information was officially requested but full access was not granted due to privacy and knowledge protection issues. The provided dataset was only populated with a quite scarce info about funded projects (project title, year, applicant, etc.), which makes technically extremely difficult to perform the intended reasoning. This fact, along with the heterogeneity of public data accessible via Web from other repositories (such as CORDIS), forced us to define an implicit filter of the initiatives. Thus, any opportunity or research initiative will be considered relevant if it fits into the requirements of a given call or programme.

The support of the aforementioned decisions requires the processing of data relative to the R&D initiatives themselves as well as relevant information about R&D performers (namely universities, research centres, and companies) and about the targeted calls and programmes. The management of R&D performers is supported by the GMM while the calls and programmes are managed via a Web interface provided by the SCM. Using that interface an administrator can fill in the information and data about explicit eligibility requirements (deadlines, budget limitations, composition of the consortium, etc.) and implicit requirements about the typology of projects covered by the call or programme, that are extracted by the analysis of the description of the call using semantic technologies. Once all the explicit and implicit information has been stored, semantic rules can be applied to perform decision taking supported by semantic reasoning.

For the composition of consortia, an additional mechanism is included in the process that takes into account the evaluation of previous consortium members to suggest future consortium arrangements. Upon the finalization or a collaborative project, consortium members perform a 360-degree evaluation on diverse aspects of the performance evidenced by the different partners during the development of the project. Such evaluation allows determining the weaknesses, strengths, and

competences of each entity, which can be used for the creation of cohesive and complementary consortia. Additionally, the SEM-IDi platform provides an interface to exchange competence data with external competence management systems that shall allow a richer reasoning when building consortia.

## Project Management Module (PMM)

The Project Management Module (PMM) developed for SEM-IDi project is based on a commercial software PPM solution (Daptiv PPM), on which detailed customizations have been made to improve the comprehensive management of R&D initiatives meant for any program, call, project type, or potential user.

This tool covers the complete R&D management flow, allowing ideas and opportunities recollection, management and approval of proposals (team/consortium agreement, economic

*Figure 1. Project management module areas*

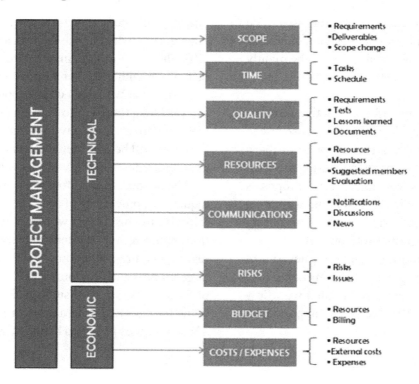

and technical project form preparation…) and project initiation, planning, management and closing. The main market methodologies and project management best practices (PMI, Prince 2, MÉTRICA v3) have been used as a starting point and a series of customized applications have been developed to facilitate a 360° project monitoring and control (including technical and economical point of view). Figure 1 describes the areas of application of this module.

Each of the areas described in the Figure 1 improves R&D project management that covers:

- **Scope Management:** Requirement collection and classification to clearly identify the scope of the project, allowing its breakdown in high-level and detailed requirements. Its approval process and subsequently its change control are thus improved.
- **Time Management:** Identification of project planning WBS, detailing the activities and tasks to be performed, its sequence, duration, dependencies, and assigned resources. The solution allows the storage of multiple planning baselines allowing the subsequent comparison and improvement of project monitoring and control.
- **Quality Management:** Quality Management functionalities the tracking of project specifications / approved requirements through the definition, planning and implementation of different levels (ex. User testing, integrated testing, approval testing, etc.) and testing scenarios. In addition, the systematic collection of lessons learned will be used as a quality indicator, improving system feedback and project management.
- **Resource Management:** It includes both material and human resources. In R&D projects, it is a key element due to the complexity and importance of project team members. To cover this complexity

the customized applications "suggested members," "project members," and lastly the "performance evaluation" (both formal project evaluator and any other project member) were created. This evaluation feeds the semantic module and it conditions later member suggestions for future R&D projects.

- **Communication Management:** Lack of clear and precise communication is one of the key factors in project failure. To avoid this, the solution identifies stakeholders and establishes a set of automatic notifications depending on their project role. In addition, the collaborative aspects from any project are favored through News and Discussions applications.
- **Risk Management:** The early and properly risk identification allows the reduction of the project costs through the implementation of detailed action plans, according to qualitative and quantitative risk categorization.
- **Economic Management:** Constant monitoring on certain cost and expenses values such as budget figures, expected expenses and labor material costs. The tool also allows showing all gathered input in a single location where it may used too for calculations, graphic representation, and budget control.

Quite likely most innovative feature attached to SEM-IDi platform is the easy-to-use and comprehensive integration of opportunities, proposals and projects management processes built on Daptiv with a whole array of semantic tools. By using such efficient integration, users can interact with Daptiv PPM as a driver completes the scope of project management through the suggestion, on the one hand, of potential programs and calls to include ideas and, on the other hand, of the optimum project members for the team (see Figure 2).

## FUTURE RESEARCH DIRECTIONS

In this chapter, the context of the solution has been limited to R&D intermediaries and consortium partners. It is aimed to offer a solution for innovative entities in order for them to manage their low-level tasks and projects. Thus, every innovative company could particularize its own staff as individual clients when forming teams for different projects.

## CONCLUSION

This book chapter illustrates the implantation of an interorganizational information system that uses semantic technology. The SEM-IDi project aims to address all these pitfalls and become a decision support system intended to narrow the gap between large organizations and more modest ones in the R&D context. This project should contribute to level the opportunities to develop R&D ideas, independently of entities resources. Semantic technologies are beginning to be good shape.

*Figure 2. Main modules and interfaces*

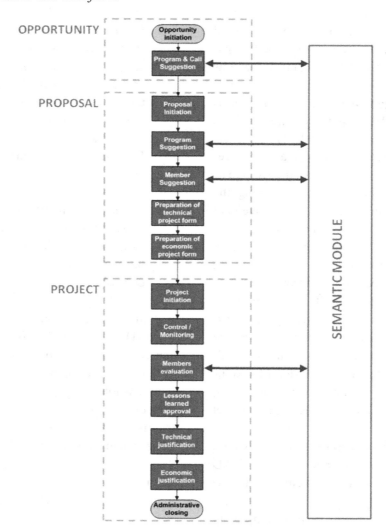

These technologies can be efficiently deployed for domains including Web Services, Enterprise Application Integration, Knowledge Management, and E-Commerce, fulfilling existing gaps in current applications. This book chapter along with several previous efforts linked to SEM-IDi project depicts a real semantics-enabled solution to a real problem: R&D consortia management.

## ACKNOWLEDGMENT

This work is supported by the Centre for the Development of Industrial Technology (CDTI) (Ministry of Science and Innovation) under Sem-IDI project IDI-20091150.

## REFERENCES

Alvarez-Sabucedo, L., Anido-Rifon, L., Corradini, F., Polzonetti, A., & Re, B. (2010). Knowledge-based platform for egovernment agents: A web-based solution using semantic technologies. *Expert Systems with Applications, 37*(5), 3647–3656. doi:10.1016/j.eswa.2009.10.026

Barnes, T. A., Pashby, I. R., & Gibbons, A. M. (2006). Managing collaborative R&D projects development of a practical management tool. *International Journal of Project Management, 24*(5), 395–404. doi:10.1016/j.ijproman.2006.03.003

Berners-Lee, T., Hendler, J., & Lassila, O. (2001). The semantic web. *Scientific American, 284*(5), 34–43. doi:10.1038/scientificamerican0501-34

Breslin, J. G., O'Sullivan, D., Passant, A., & Vasiliu, L. (2010). Semantic web computing in industry. *Computers in Industry, 61*(8), 729–741. doi:10.1016/j.compind.2010.05.002

Cardoso, J. (2007). The semantic web vision: Where are we? *IEEE Intelligent Systems, 22*(5), 22–26. doi:10.1109/MIS.2007.4338499

Castellanos-Nieves, D., Fernández-Breis, J. T., Valencia-García, R., Martínez-Béjar, R., & Iniesta-Moreno, M. (2011). Semantic web technologies for supporting learning assessment. *Information Sciences, 181*(9), 1517–1537. doi:10.1016/j.ins.2011.01.010

Colomo-Palacios, R., García-Crespo, Á., Soto-Acosta, P., Ruano-Mayoral, M., & Jiménez-López, D. (2010). A case analysis of semantic technologies for R&D intermediation information management. *International Journal of Information Management, 30*(5), 465–469. doi:10.1016/j.ijinfomgt.2010.05.012

Ding, Y. (2010). Semantic web: Who is who in the field — A bibliometric analysis. *Journal of Information Science, 36*(3), 335–356. doi:10.1177/0165551510365295

Fensel, D. (2002). *Ontologies: A silver bullet for knowledge management and electronic commerce.* Berlin, Germany: Springer-Verlag.

Fernandez-Breis, J., Castellanos-Nieves, D., & Valencia-García, R. (2009). Measuring individual learning performance in group work from a knowledge integration perspective. *Information Sciences, 179*(4), 339–354. doi:10.1016/j.ins.2008.10.014

Garcia, R., Perdrix, F., Gil, R., & Oliva, M. (2008). The semantic web as a newspaper media convergence facilitator. *Journal of Web Semantics, 6*(2), 151–161. doi:10.1016/j.websem.2008.01.002

García-Crespo, A., Colomo-Palacios, R., Gómez-Berbís, J. M., & Ruiz-Mezcua, B. (2010). SEMO: A framework for customer social networks analysis based on semantics. *Journal of Information Technology, 25*(2), 178–188. doi:10.1057/jit.2010.1

García-Crespo, Á., López-Cuadrado, J. L., Colomo-Palacios, R., González-Carrasco, I., & Ruiz-Mezcua, B. (2011). Sem-fit: A semantic based expert system to provide recommendations in the tourism domain. *Expert Systems with Applications*, *38*(10), 13310–13319. doi:10.1016/j.eswa.2011.04.152

Garcia-Sanchez, F., Fernandez-Breis, J., Valencia-Garcia, R., Gomez, J., & Martinez-Bejar, R. (2008). Combining semantic web technologies with multi-agent systems for integrated access to biological resources. *Journal of Biomedical Informatics*, *41*(5), 848–859. doi:10.1016/j.jbi.2008.05.007

Gómez-Pérez, A., Fernández-López, M., & Corcho, O. (2003). *Ontological engineering*. Berlin, Germany: Springer-Verlag.

Gruber, T. R. (1993). A translation approach to portable ontology specifications. *Knowledge Acquisition*, *5*(2), 199–220. doi:10.1006/knac.1993.1008

Gruber, T. R. (1995). Towards principles for the design of ontologies used for knowledge sharing. *International Journal of Human-Computer Studies*, *43*(5-6), 907–928. doi:10.1006/ijhc.1995.1081

Hagedoorn, J., Link, A. N., & Vonortas, N. S. (2009). Research partnerships. *Research Policy*, *29*(4-5), 567–586. doi:10.1016/S0048-7333(99)00090-6

Hagel, J., & Rayport, J. F. (1997). The coming battle for customer information. *Harvard Business Review*, *75*(1), 53–65.

Hitzler, P., & Janowicz, K. (2011). Semantic web tools and system. *Semantic Web*, *2*(1), 1–2.

Horrocks, I. (2008). Ontologies and the semantic web. *Communications of the ACM*, *51*(12), 58–67. doi:10.1145/1409360.1409377

Howels, J. (2006). Intermediation and the role of intermediaries in innovation. *Research Policy*, *35*(5), 715–728. doi:10.1016/j.respol.2006.03.005

Jiang, X., & Tan, A. H. (2009). Learning and inferencing in user ontology for personalized semantic web search. *Information Sciences: An International Journal*, *179*(16), 2794–2808.

Lee, S., Beamish, P., Lee, H., & Park, J. (2009). Strategic choice during economic crisis: Domestic market position, organizational capabilities and export flexibility. *Journal of World Business*, *44*(1), 1–15. doi:10.1016/j.jwb.2008.03.015

Lytras, M. D., & García, R. (2008). Semantic web applications: a framework for industry and business exploitation - What is needed for the adoption of the semantic web from the market and industry. *International Journal of Knowledge and Learning*, *4*(1), 93–108. doi:10.1504/IJKL.2008.019739

McGuinness, D. L., & Van Harmelen, F. (2004). Owl web ontology language overview: W3C recommendation 10 Feb 2004. *World Wide Web Consortium*. Retrieved from http://www.w3.org/TR/owl-features/

Meskendahl, S. (2010). The influence of business strategy on project portfolio management and its success -- A conceptual framework. *International Journal of Project Management*, *28*(8), 807–817. doi:10.1016/j.ijproman.2010.06.007

Mikroyannidis, A., & Theodoulidis, B. (2010). Ontology management and evolution for business intelligence. *International Journal of Information Management*, *30*(6), 559–566. doi:10.1016/j.ijinfomgt.2009.10.002

Minasian, J. R. (1969). Research and development, production functions, and rates of return. *The American Economic Review*, *59*(2), 80–85.

OECD. (1993). *Proposed standard practice for surveys of research and experimental development: Frascati manual* (5th ed.). Paris, France: OECD.

Paniagua-Martín, F., García-Crespo, Á., Colomo-Palacios, R., & Ruiz-Mezcua, B. (2011). SSAA-MAR: Semantic annotation architecture for accessible multimedia resources. *IEEE MultiMedia, 18*(2), 16–25. doi:10.1109/MMUL.2010.43

Rodríguez-González, A., García-Crespo, Á., Colomo-Palacios, R., Guildrís-Iglesias, F., & Gómez-Berbís, J. M. (2011). CAST: Using neural networks to improve trading systems based on technical analysis by means of the RSI financial indicator. *Expert Systems with Applications, 38*(9), 11489–11500. doi:10.1016/j.eswa.2011.03.023

Roussel, P. A., Saad, K. N., & Erickson, T. J. (1991). *Third generation R&D: Managing the link to corporate strategy.* Boston, MA: Harvard Business School Press.

Sahaym, A., Steensma, H. K., & Barden, J. Q. (2010). The influence of R&D investment on the use of corporate venture capital: An industry-level analysis. *Journal of Business Venturing, 25*(4), 276–388. doi:10.1016/j.jbusvent.2008.12.001

Sawhney, M., Prandelli, E., & Verona, G. (2003). The power of innomediation. *MIT Sloan Management Review, 44*(2), 76–82.

Soto-Acosta, P., Casado-Lumbreras, C., & Cabezas-Isla, F. (2010). Shaping human capital in software development teams: The case of mentoring enabled by semantics. *IET Software, 4*(6), 445–452. doi:10.1049/iet-sen.2010.0087

Spekman, R. E., Isabella, L. A., MacAvoy, T. C., & Forbes, T. III. (1996). Creating strategic alliances which endure. *Long Range Planning, 29*(3), 346–357. doi:10.1016/0024-6301(96)00021-0

Studer, R., Benjamins, V. R., & Fensel, D. (1998). Knowledge engineering: Principles and methods. *Data & Knowledge Engineering, 25*(1-2), 161–197. doi:10.1016/S0169-023X(97)00056-6

Vossen, G., Lytras, M., & Koudas, N. (2007). Editorial: Revisiting the (machine) semantic web: The missing layers for the human semantic web. *IEEE Transactions on Knowledge and Data Engineering, 19*(2), 145–148. doi:10.1109/TKDE.2007.30

Vrba, P., Radakovic, M., Obitko, M., & Marik, V. (2011). Semantic technologies: Latest advances in agent-based manufacturing control systems. *International Journal of Production Research, 49*(5), 1483–1496. doi:10.1080/00207543.2010.518746

Wang, J., & Hwang, W. L. (2007). A fuzzy set approach for R&D portfolio selection using a real options valuation model. *Omega, 35*(3), 247–257. doi:10.1016/j.omega.2005.06.002

Wright, M., Clarysse, B., Lockett, A., & Knockaert, M. (2008). Mid-range universities' linkages with industry: Knowledge types and the role of intermediaries. *Research Policy, 37*(8), 1205–1223. doi:10.1016/j.respol.2008.04.021

Zhao, Y. (2007). A dynamic model of active portfolio management with benchmark orientation. *Journal of Banking & Finance, 31*(11), 3336–3356. doi:10.1016/j.jbankfin.2007.04.007

## ADDITIONAL READING

Blumauer, A., & Pellegrini, T. (2009). *Social semantic web.* Berlin, Germany: Springer. doi:10.1007/978-3-540-72216-8

Breslin, J. G., Passant, A., & Decker, S. (2010). *The social semantic web.* Berlin, Germany: Springer.

Cardoso, J., Hepp, M., & Lytras, M. D. (2008). *The semantic web: Real-world application from industry.* Berlin, Germany: Springer.

Cardoso, J., & Lytras, M. D. (2009). *Semantic web engineering in the knowledge society.* Hershey, PA: IGI Global. doi:10.4018/978-1-60566-112-4

Colomo-Palacios, R., González-Carrasco, I., & López-Cuadrado, J. L. (2012). *Soft computing for collaborative corporate environments: Social and semantic technologies.* Hershey, PA: IGI Global.

Colomo-Palacios, R., Varajao, J., & Soto-Acosta, P. (2011). *Customer relationship management and the social and semantic web: Enabling cliens conexus.* Hershey, PA: IGI Global. doi:10.4018/978-1-61350-044-6

García, R. (2008). *Semantic web for business: Cases and applications.* Hershey, PA: IGI Global. doi:10.4018/978-1-60566-066-0

García-Castro, R. (2010). *Benchmarking semantic web technology.* Dordrecht, The Netherlands: AKA Verlag Heidelberg and IOS Press.

Hitzler, P., Krötzsch, M., & Rudolph, S. (2009). *Foundations of semantic web technologies.* Boca Raton, FL: Chapman & Hall/CRC.

Kalfoglou, Y. (2010). *Cases on semantic interoperability for information systems integration: Practices and applications.* Hershey, PA: IGI Global.

Lytras, M. D., & Ordóñez-De Pablos, P. (2009). *Social web evolution: Integrating semantic applications and web 2.0 technologies.* Hershey, PA: IGI Global. doi:10.4018/978-1-60566-272-5

Lytras, M. D., & Ordóñez de Pablos, P. (2009). *Emerging topics and technologies in information systems.* Hershey, PA: IGI Global. doi:10.4018/978-1-60566-222-0

Lytras, M. D., Ordóñez de Pablos, P., & Damiani, E. (2011). *Semantic web personalization and context awareness: Management of personal identities and social networking.* Hershey, PA: IGI Global. doi:10.4018/978-1-61520-921-7

Lytras, M. D., & Sheth, A. (2010). *Progressive concepts for semantic web evolution: Applications and development.* Hershey, PA: IGI Global. doi:10.4018/978-1-60566-992-2

Matsuo, T., & Fujimoto, T. (2011). *E-activity and intelligent web construction: Effects of social design.* Hershey, PA: IGI Global. doi:10.4018/978-1-61520-871-5

Mika, P. (2009). *Social networks and the semantic web.* Berlin, Germany: Springer.

Murugesan, S. (2010). *Handbook of research on web 2.0, 3.0, and X.0: Technologies, business, and social application.* Hershey, PA: IGI Global.

Naeve, A., & Lytras, M. D. (2006). *Intelligent learning infrastructure for knowledge intensive organizations: A semantic web perspective.* Hershey, PA: IGI Global.

Ordóñez de Pablos, P., Lytras, M. D., Karwowski, W., & Lee, R. W. B. (2011). *Electronic globalized business and sustainable development through IT management: Strategies and perspectives.* Hershey, PA: IGI Global.

Paquette, G. (2010). *Visual knowledge modeling for semantic web technologies: Models and ontologies.* Hershey, PA: IGI Global. doi:10.4018/978-1-61520-839-5

Sheth, A., & Lytras, M. D. (2007). *Semantic web-based information systems: State-of-the-art applications.* Hershey, PA: IGI Global.

Tao, D., Xu, D., & Li, H. (2009). *Semantic mining technologies for multimedia databases.* Hershey, PA: IGI Global. doi:10.4018/978-1-60566-188-9

Zhang, Y. J. (2007). *Semantic-based visual information retrieval.* Hershey, PA: IGI Global.

Zilli, A., Damiani, E., Ceravolo, P., Corallo, A., & Elia, G. (2009). *Semantic knowledge management: An ontology-based framework.* Hershey, PA: IGI Global.

# Chapter 7
# Enterprise Tomography:
## Maintenance and Root-Cause-Analysis of Federated ERP in Enterprise Clouds

**Jan Aalmink**
*University of Oldenburg, Germany*

**Timo von der Dovenmühle**
*University of Oldenburg, Germany*

**Jorge Marx Gómez**
*University of Oldenburg, Germany*

## ABSTRACT

*Cloud Computing is finding its way into the architecture of current IT landscapes. The present chapter depicts an algorithm-based methodology supporting the Root-Cause-Analysis in the context of malfunctioning Federated ERP (FERP) software in Enterprise Clouds. The challenge is to standardize the error-finding procedure and increase the efficiency. For a given error symptom it is shown that the error location is approximated iteratively with help of generic operators in a semiautomatic manner. This approach of Semantic Debugging outperforms classical methods of Technical Debugging in efficiency regarding prerequisite knowledge and time consumption. Semantic integration and maintainability correlate strongly. The Delta-Operator enables the reconstruction of semantic FERP integration in the course of the error reproduction session. In combination with the Join-Operator, the defect approximation can be performed along the dependencies of semantic artifacts.*

## INTRODUCTION

Enterprise Cloud Computing becomes more and more prevalent in the IT and Business Application Industry. The quality of integration, i.e. the extent of vertical and horizontal Business Process Integration and its efficient management is a key IT asset in Enterprise Data Centers. The scientific approach now is to overcome most of the drawbacks of legacy on-premise solutions regarding maintenance. Therefore, existing different research streams, requirements, and semantic perspectives

DOI: 10.4018/978-1-4666-2494-8.ch007

Copyright © 2013, IGI Global. Copying or distributing in print or electronic forms without written permission of IGI Global is prohibited.

need to be converted into one central ubiquitous, optimized, and standardized architectural approach. The goal is to perform on-demand and cross-enterprise business processes in the context of Very Large Business Applications (VLBA). Also in this context, cloud standardization is one of the major challenges of the Open Cloud Manifesto. This chapter discusses and outlines the realization of automated semantic debugging for Federated ERP Systems in Enterprise Clouds. Furthermore, it is discussed, how enterprises can develop and maintain enterprise software solutions in the Cloud Community in an evolutionary, self-organized way complying Cloud Standards. In this context, a metric driven Semantic Service Discovery and the Enterprise Tomograph can be seen as an entry-point to an organic, gradable marketplace of processes exposed by cloud based Service Grids and Data Grids in graded levels of granularity and semantic abstractions.

Regarding Enterprise Cloud Computing, areas of conflict like requirements and design principles need to be resolved. It is possible to observe a convergence of the polymorphic streams towards a shared, cloud-based platform. The main motivation in utilizing Enterprise Cloud Computing for a customer is the reduction of the Total Cost of Ownership (TCO) in different aspects: Pooling of resources and services regarding consumption peaks or simplification of legacy infrastructure from on-premise solutions towards an on-demand solution. From the perspective of an Enterprise Cloud Provider, virtualization with multi-tenancy functionality proves as suboptimal. There is a higher degree of sharing and reuse possible. This leads to federated service-based cloud software, which can grow organically. The scientific challenge is to provide a controllable reference model, which serves as a common standard, where standards overcome the typical vendor-lock-in phenomenon and are prerequisite for acceptance.

In general, FERP Systems based on Web Services are heterogeneous software systems processing business data complying integration rules, so different customers can have different views, i.e. access points to the FERP. Since the typical software ownership (provider-consumer) is transformed from a 1:n relation to a m:n relation (Brehm, Marx Gómez, & Rautenstrauch, 2006, pp. 99-111; Brehm, Luebke, & Marx-Gómez, 2007, pp. 290-305) and the complexity of such information eco-systems is increased in the course of the life cycle, the superordinate goal in the context of Enterprise Cloud Computing is to provide methodologies and mechanisms for streamlining and controlling the integration in FERP systems. The organic growth of interlinked Enterprise Services Networks needs to follow compliance rules. Therefore, semantic deviation-analysis of enterprise service consumption, Monitoring and Tracking becomes essential in distributed consumer-provider networks along the life cycle.

The Enterprise Tomography approach enables monitoring of the complete life cycle of federated Enterprise Software or Corporate Environmental Management Information Systems 2.0 (CEMIS) described in Marx Gómez (2009): With Enterprise Tomography it is possible to make consumption patterns comparable. This comparison is based on a common interlingua represented as lightweight hierarchical ontologies and is succeeded by applying the Delta Operator which determines the status differences between system $A$ and system $B$ in a cloud. To be more precise, the comparison and evolution tracking of integrated business process scenarios in a cloud represented as interlinked enterprise services assemblages is possible. The Enterprise Tomography approach provides the possibility to visualize differences with help of tomograms, which aggregate indicators, metrics and serve as a decision basis in the governance process and Integration Lifecycle Management (ILM) of an Enterprise Cloud (Aalmink & Marx Gómez, 2009).

Figure 1 illustrates an overview of the topology of a Cloud Farm. It shows different aspects and fundamental pillars of the FERP reference model. The procedure, how Enterprise Cloud Evolution can be controlled is outlined in Figure 2.

*Figure 1. Topology of an enterprise cloud computing farm based on FERP and enterprise tomography*

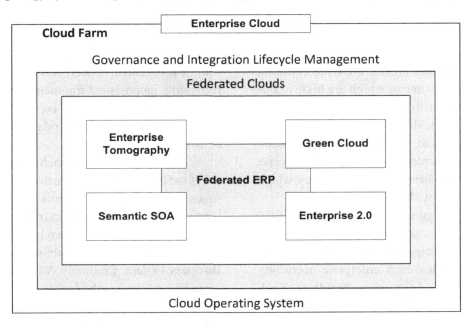

*Figure 2. Enterprise tomography driven governance of FERP in a cloud farm*

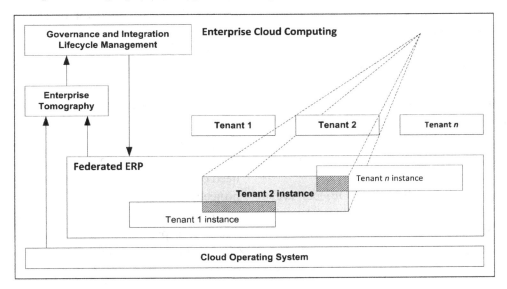

## FEDERATED ERP IN A CLOUD

In reality, on-premise Standard Enterprise Software is widely used within the enterprise community. Standard means, there are common business process patterns, which are highly configurable and extensible according to the business requirements. Typically, this methodology results in similar composed, configured and enhanced CEMI-Systems deployed too many Enterprise Data Centers. Similarity means redundancy, which can be eliminated with the FERP approach.

According to Figure 2, in the cloud-based FERP approach we have one single software instance active for all participating enterprises. A Cloud Tenant encapsulates each enterprise according to the Separation of Concerns Paradigm. Each Tenant is provided a view on the single software and data instance. The software and data instance is a network of shared Business Objects that are projected on columnar In-Memory databases (Plattner, 2009). The In-Memory Databases can be considered as intelligent Caches (Heuser, Alsdorf, & Woods, 2008). In-Memory Columnar Databases significantly reduce the redundancy in the data volume and provides instantaneous access to non-materialized aggregates and business object collections. Aggregates are being calculated on the fly and are exposed as services via endpoints of Data Grids. It is possible to keep the Business Object Network consistent according to the ACID transactional OLTP methodology. Columnar In-Memory Database Models provide extensibility by nature.

Non-frequent used Business Objects are physically stored in a distributed fashion. A read access of a Business Object means data retrieval of distinct fragments for reconstruction of the original Business Object. A Business Object is viewed as a tree serialized to a document. This document is fragmented. The fragments are coded and distributed within the Data Grids. In general, a sequence of numbers, which defines a mathematical polynomial, represents a document. According to the fundamental theorem of algebra, a unique reconstruction of this document is possible, if there are only $n$ distinct fragments (out of a redundant coded set) available. While retrieving, inconsistent fragments can be ignored and substituted by distinct consistent fragment retrieved from remote Data Grids (Heuser, Alsdorf, & Woods, 2007).

Within the FERP approach, technical references to Business Objects are the payload of messages. E.g. if company A wants to send company B an invoice (Business Object) only the reference of the invoice is sent as a payload. In this case, the invoice is a shared and ubiquitous accessible Business Object. Company A has an individual view-based access to the Invoice via the reference only. The same applies to company B. Receiving the message, company B will change the status of the invoice to the value *paid* as soon as the real payment is executed.

Inverted Indexing known in classical Information Retrieval are the base of Columnar Databases. In (Plattner, 2009) it is shown that this algorithmic approach is well suited for parallel multi-core hardware. Systolic arrays are in the position to accelerate string position/value matching even further with the rate of clock frequency speed (Epstein, 2004).

View-based access via references to Business Objects has the great advantage, that no mapping and technical transformation of the Business Objects is required. Within the memory, there is no need of moving Business Objects. Thus, there is no need for asynchronous processing and updating anymore. This leads to tremendous scalability, which is a prerequisite for Cloud Computing. Having immediate services in places, completely new quasi real-time applications will be possible in future.

In addition, the FERP reference model leads to a more data-consistent behavior. The cloud software can become much leaner in comparison to classical stacked on-premise software solutions and is therefore less error-prone. A closed-loop feedback development process ensures a promptly iterative correction cycle. This leads to quality insurance.

## GOVERNANCE OF INTEGRATION LIFECYCLE MANAGEMENT IN ENTERPRISE CLOUDS

The FERP model can be regarded as a central shared and pervasive accessible network based approach. An error in the enterprise cloud software can lead to dramatic consequences and might have serious business impact.

An enterprise client can extend its own business processes or even create and compose its individual business process schemas. Related tenants can share the individual parts of functionality. So FERP leaves the classical software vendor/software client ownership model. Within the FERP approach, each individual tenant can be simultaneously in the role of a service consumer as well as a logical service provider. A Semantic Service Discovery (Heuser, Alsdorf, & Woods, 2008) exposes these services. The essential point here is that each service, composite service, or business process is potentially provided with a set of alternatives distinguished by Quality of Service (QoS) and metrics.

To be more general, the FERP approach can be seen as a definition of a governed service marketplace. Each individual participant can contribute materialized cloud content as shared services and shared (sub-)processes. Each participant can virtually compose his own ERP. In fact, he gets a view on a service of a one software and data instance.

With Enterprise Tomography, it is possible to make similar data contexts comparable. The comparison is based on a common interlingua represented as lightweight ontologies. With a delta operator, it is realizable to determine dynamically the differences between service offering A and service offering B. The Enterprise Tomograph provides the possibility to visualize semantic differences with help of tomograms. A comparison between two services is possible as well as a comparison of a single service between two points in time. E.g. in a project a consulting team implements business processes and therefore customizes or alters the composition of an Enterprise Service Ensemble. This delta is of common interest, e.g. as an indicator for the quality of security evolvement in the last period. Another use-case is to determine the delta after a functional upgrade in the cloud. The delta is calculated between the previous reference version and the active version of Enterprise Service Ensemble. The delta in this case is the equivalent of new or changed functionality. This delta, represented as a hierarchical ontology tree, is a good basis for evaluation of new functionality. Test and training teams therefore can focus on new/changed functionality only. This results automatically in cost containment.

One more interesting use case for Enterprise Tomography is to calculate the data footprint of a selected business transaction or a business process in a cloud. Between two points in time, the update on database is calculated with help of the Delta Operator. Based on the business data delta, IT experts are in the position to measure the correctness of the behavior of the executed business transactions more efficiently. This is a highly efficient diagnostics approach for root cause analysis for given error symptoms. Based on the delta, the undo operator resets the business transaction. This business transaction can be executed again with same preconditions and data contexts. In this way, repetitive testing of business processes is enabled.

The Enterprise Tomography approach allows the construction of an early warning system based on semantic metrics and indicators. If the distance—computed by the Delta Operator—exceeds a threshold, actions (from cloud-based services) can be executed to control the usage of dedicated Enterprise Services. For example, the Enterprise Tomograph can execute process mining. When the quota exceeds a threshold, the enterprise tenant needs to be invoiced for funding the cloud infrastructure he has used. This is a simple example to implement self-organized feedback control system based on the generic Enterprise Tomography approach.

Each participant can contribute service-based software as materialized cloud content. This naturally leads to high redundancy in offerings of business processes. The Enterprise Tomograph can evaluate the services and business processes according real consumption patterns. Business processes with low traffic on the cloud infrastructure are regarded as non-value added processes and will be disabled. The decision of disablement is based on dynamic calculated results of the Enterprise Tomograph. The services with the highest Quality of Services will survive the market competition. This example illustrates how Enterprise Tomography approach can control

the Integration Lifecycle Management (ILM) of Enterprise Clouds and increase the overall quality in an Enterprise Cloud according to free definable metrics while fulfilling requirements in a prioritized manner.

In Figure 3 an advanced VLBA (FERP) across Data Centers of distinct owner (Enterprises) is displayed. The Enterprise Cloud encompasses federated clouds, which exposes services and infrastructures. The Enterprise Tomograph manages the lifecycle of the cross-federated VLBA. Crawling of cloud entities, i.e. of business data, log files, data, metadata, operational data, master data, configuration data, service repositories, and infrastructure content is executed on a permanent basis. Changes in ontologies can be calculated via delta determination of the Enterprise Tomograph. Deviation analysis and metric based rule infringement detection leads to immediate adaptive actions and events.

*Figure 3. Controlled cross-datacenter VLBA residing in an enterprise cloud*

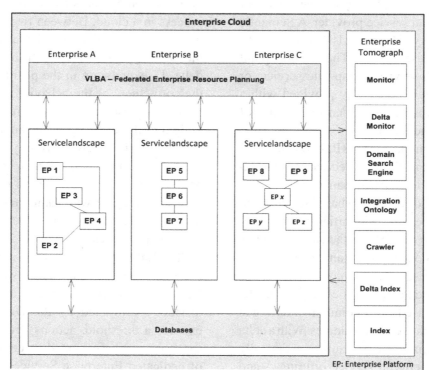

A more business relevant use-case is a partial architectural transformation from real world data centers to virtual data centers as shown in Figure 4. A subset of static infrastructures can be converted in virtual infrastructures. This allows a better sharing and assignment of resources. This enables an adaptive pooling of virtual resources. From user perspective, the transformation is non-transparent. Keeping Hybrid Scenarios in sync according to Business Process Integration requires definition of dedicated compliance rules, which can be enforced with the Enterprise Tomography approach.

Scientific purpose of the research field Enterprise Clouds is analyzing enterprise software within cloud environments for the reduction of company-made environmental pollution. Solutions are worked out, to harmonize legal compliance, environmental compliance, cost indicators, complexity, and the degree of integrating environmental information systems. Centralized cloud solutions are used to avoid isolated views on enterprises. This can result in a federated ERP system enhanced by environmental aspects. The approach is showing similarities to an enhanced Balanced Scorecard model.

Enterprise Tomography approach can be advantageous to identify environmental indicators from ontology based network structures or reference models. A further domain of enterprise tomography is the integration management of environmental information systems (Integration Lifecycle Management). Integration of isolated solutions in virtual cloud environments is in the center of interest.

## Operator-Based Approach for Root-Cause-Analysis in Cloud Environments

Environmental Information Systems do have inherent complex integration concepts. Because of cascading effects, internal errors can accumulate, propagate, and have massive negative impacts

*Figure 4. Hybrid scenarios regarding on-premise and on-demand solutions*

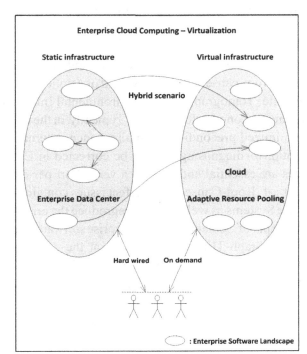

regarding data integrity. Finding the root-cause of error symptoms is time-critical, generally very time consuming and requires high skilled software engineers. The following sections outlines a generic methodology supporting the Root-Cause-Analysis phase using scientific algorithms defined in discrete mathematics, spectral graph-theory, and bio-informatics. An operator-based approach alleviates the error finding procedure in a systematic and efficient way. Semantic Debugging Patterns can be defined upon generic operators provided by an Enterprise Tomography diagnosis system.

In Enterprise Software Engineering, industrialization made significant progress over the last years. However, regarding automation, the progress in Root-Cause-Analysis of Environmental Information Systems Maintenance is far behind. Especially the diagnostics in maintenance is not standardized and provides high potential regarding efficiency. Operative Enterprise Software System Landscapes in their entirety are heterogenic and complex. Defect analysis and corrections in integrated software conglomerates is often extremely difficult and risky, is time consuming, and needs to be performed by highly specialized software engineers on a case-by-case basis. In this section, the procedure of Enterprise Software Maintenance is standardized according to the metaphor Computer Tomography established in medical diagnostics. In medical root-cause and comparative diagnostics Computer Tomography is a de-facto standard, is a generic concept for defect location along with minimized preconditions and non-surgical intervention for diagnosing scenarios. Both characteristics are essential and advantageous in the context of Root-Cause-Analysis of Enterprise Software Systems as well. Dedicated approaches and concepts of Semantic Web, Social Networking, Spectral Graph-Theory, and Bio-Informatics are transferred to Enterprise Software Diagnostics. The resulting approach is called Enterprise Tomography (Aalmink & Marx Gómez, 2011). To increase efficiency in mainte-

nance of Environmental Information Systems, the concepts are adapted individually and combined to a holistic error-approximation concept.

In the present chapter, generic operators are constructed with interdisciplinary algorithms and methods. These operators are in the position to categorize polymorphic integration concepts by semantic views in Enterprise Platforms both, in dimension space and time (Aalmink & Marx Gómez, 2009). The generic operators facilitate repetitive maintenance tasks and point the maintenance engineer in the periphery of the root-cause. In accordance to apparatus supported medical diagnostics, the proposed Enterprise Tomography approach enables localization of semantic integration concepts, enables visualization, and makes the tracking of the semantic integration concepts in dimension time and space possible. A domain-specific delta analysis between Enterprise Platforms is possible as well. The concept Enterprise Tomography contains algorithm-based Semantic Debugging Patterns and enables system-based guidance for defect approximation and defect detection. In this chapter, the scientific contribution is primarily seen in a novel methodology for automation and streamlining of continuous Enterprise Software Maintenance. The presented Enterprise Tomography approach supports the Root-Cause-Analysis and is therefore to be positioned in the context of Application Lifecycle Management for Environmental Information Systems.

Typically, in the context of enterprise software maintenance, externally reported defect issues are to be corrected in Enterprise Software Systems in a very short period with no side effects. The defect issues contains the whole description, how to reproduce the error symptom in the productive enterprise software system or in a reference system hosted at the enterprise software manufacturer site. Reproducing the error symptom means executing business transactions, individual business process steps or performing operations or fine granular enterprise services according to the defect description. All those steps leave a footprint in the system. Assuming, a system at point-in-time $t_0$ before reproducing the error symptom and at point-in-time $t_1$ after reproducing the error symptom is introspected. This results in two system states $S_0$ and $S_1$ respectively. Abstract speaking, the difference of the system states $D = S_1 - S_0$ is a good approximation for the root-cause of the error symptom. This assumption can be made in most cases, because executing a business transaction touches in an enterprise software system a small amount of data in comparison to the whole system. Therefore, it is assumed, that the delta of the system state contains a small amount of data, i.e. in terms of formula $|D| << |S|$ where $S$ denotes the volume of the whole Enterprise Software System data with its associated set of $S_0$ and $S_1$ of artifacts. The delta $D$, i.e. the Delta-Centrality represents the entry-point for the Root-Cause-Analysis with the advantage, being in the environment of the origin error. It is a close periphery of the root-cause for the error symptom. The touched data is a small sub-space $D$ of the full space $S$ with $S$ containing $D$. Intuitively speaking, there are integration paths from the delta $D$ to the origin defect in the space $S$ beyond delta space $D$. In the context of this chapter, the space is modeled as a multi-relational property graph. This graph spans a decision space for the Root-Cause-Analysis. Delta-determination reduces the decision space drastically and therefore this approach of defect location procedure will become more efficient. Technically, the delta can be calculated using algorithms of the virtualization context. With help of virtualization, it is technically an easy task to determine a delta between two different system states in linear time complexity $O(|S|)$. The enterprise software system needs in this case to be virtualized, i.e. needs to be operative in a virtual environment. The big disadvantage here is that the delta contains neither semantic nor structured data that can be evaluated in the course of the Root-Cause-Analysis scenario. The delta in this case is merely a bit-level sequence and therefore not useful for Root-Cause-Analysis purposes. Therefore, an alternative modeling approach is to be established.

## Semantic Representation

The challenge is to model the Environmental Information System integration complexity in an appropriate way. Conclusively, an alternative representation of the physical Environmental Information System covering all relevant aspects for the Root-Cause-Analysis is needed. This model will be a projection, i.e. logical representation of the physical Environmental Information System. The model can be compared as a generalized Semantic Web—a Web of Data enriched by semantics.

Ontologies are good concept to represent the semantic reality of the interior of an Environmental Information System. Ontologies correlate to the Semantic Web in the same way as schemas do for databases. All the logical artifacts are represented with ontology concepts and ontology instances. The elements of the ontologies are in possibly different semantic relationships. Applying these semantic principles on a graph will result in a multi-relational property graph. The nodes contain the artifacts, i.e. the ontology instances and the edges represent the semantic relationship between the nodes. It is worth noting, that there are also multiple edges between two nodes possible. Those edges contain different semantics. Let $V$ denote a finite set of nodes and let $E\sigma$ be a subset of $(V \times V)$ and $\sigma \in M$, and $M$ a finite set of semantic views. In addition to that, let $f_V$ be a function, that maps every node $v \in V$ to a set of 2-tuples of string. $f_V$ assigns each node $v$ a set of key-value pairs to. An individual character of the key-value-pairs is an element of a finite alphabet $\Sigma$. Similarly, let $f_\sigma$ with $\sigma$ in the set of $M$ according to $f_\sigma: E_\sigma \rightarrow D_\sigma$ that assigns in the semantic view $\sigma$ each edge in $E_\sigma$ a subset of key-value pairs in $D_\sigma$.

Furthermore, let $\hat{E} = < E_0, E_1, ..., E_{M-1} >$ be a family of semantic relationships. Then the graph $G = (V, \hat{E}, f_V, f_0, f_1, ..., f_{|M-1|})$ is called a multi-relational property graph. The property graph is a simplistic representation of the Semantic Web of data. The interior of the Enterprise Software System can be mapped to the multi-relational property graph defined before. This is a projection of the real world Environmental Information System status $S_t$ onto a knowledge representation system $G$. For example, business objects like production orders, business partner, customer order, service order or financial accounts can be mapped to a specific semantic view in terms of key-value assignment in the property graph $G$. Business objects are special kinds of ontology instances. Other meaningful semantic views include coding, i.e. the coding artifacts and its relationships to each other. Further examples for semantic views include metadata view based on business objects and its dependencies. The database view with all native data entries of the database tables and their relationships to each other can be a semantic view. Documentation of development artifacts and their relationships is another semantic view to be mapped onto the multi-relational property graph $G$. It is worth noting, that the multi-relational property graph is a systematic textual representation of the integration ontology of an operative Environmental Information System at point-in-time $t_0$. The Root-Cause-Analysis is now reduced to the problem of finding the relevant smallest sub graph in the multi-relational property Graph $G$ causing the error symptom. The aspects of integration of an Environmental Information System are represented as integration paths within the graph: nodes with integrative dependencies are linked via edges to overlapping paths. Dependency trees as spanning sub graph reflect the aspects of integration. Here, the integration can cover different semantic views. This provides huge flexibility in appropriate modeling of integration concepts.

## Traversal in Decision Space

The property graph spans a decision space for the enterprise software maintenance engineer. Contextual traversal along the edges can easily be performed within a semantic view (intra-traversal) as well as between the different semantic views (inter-traversal). It needs to be mentioned, that the decision space is quite big. Therefore, several decision space reduction algorithms are outlined in the course of this chapter. The reduction can either be a sub graph because of delta-determination of a multi-relational property graph $G$ at point-in-time $t_0$ and $t_1$. In terms of discrete mathematics, this means determination of the delta between two similar graphs representing the states of an Environmental Information System at point-in-time $t_1$ and $t_0$. Another decision space reduction is the prioritization of the decision space. This means e.g. that some nodes are more important, if they are connected to important nodes. This definition is recursive and leads to recursive or iterative determination of the relevancy regarding the integration aspects. In the Social Networking research, area a bunch of graph centrality algorithms is defined. Google PageRank is one prominent example. The PageRank can be calculated iteratively based on linear equation system. Other graph centralities are the Eigenvector Centrality defined by Bonacich, the Betweeness Centrality or the Bridging Centrality (Bader, et al., 2007; Bunke, et al., 2007).

Let $G_\sigma = (V, E_\sigma, f_V, f_\sigma)$ be a sub graph of the multi-relational property graph G containing the semantic view $\sigma$. Then an adjacency matrix $A$ can be derived. Linear combinations of term $A^k$, with $k$ a positive natural number, can build a polynomial of matrices according to:

$$p(A)x = (\delta_k A^k + \delta_{k-1} A^{k-1} + \dots + \delta_1 A^1 + \delta_0 A^0)x$$

(1.1)

with

$$\sum_{i \leq k} \delta_i = 1, \; \delta_i \geq 0, \; i = 0, \dots, k$$

(1.2)

The adjacency matrix is a square matrix with dimensions $(|V|, |V|)$. The $k$-times multiplication of the matrix $A$ according to $A^k$ contains in each component *(u, v)* the number of distinct paths from node $u \in V$ to node $v \in V$ in the sub graph $G_\sigma$ with path length *k*. The $\delta_i$ can carry the semantic of weights or damping factors for path traversals. Therefore, the resulting polynomial *p(A)* is a matrix, which can be regarded as weighted composition of integration paths of different length. Above-mentioned centrality algorithms like PageRank or Bridging Centrality can be calculated on basis of the constructed matrix as denoted in Equation 1.1. This definition takes the importance of the path length into consideration. In the context of Root-Cause-Analysis, paths with short length should be higher weighted than paths with greater length. Centrality algorithms, mentioned above, can now prioritize the set of nodes *V* in the semantic view σ respecting path length.

Another, a rather lightweight approach of reduction of decision spaces is the separation of the components of the graph $G_\sigma$. If the software engineer starts Root-Cause-Analysis in node *v* containing in sub graph *P* as subset of $G_\sigma$ and the defect is located in the same component, other non-connected components can be ignored. The spectrum of the Laplace Matrix - a matrix derived from the degrees of the nodes $v \in V$ - represents the number of components: The amount of Eigenvalues = *0* is the number of disconnected components. Therefore, if there are more than one Eigenvalue with value equal to *0* then there is potential for graph reduction, which makes the Root-Cause-Analysis more efficient. The reduction can be done with dedicated standard algorithms from graph theory.

Up to here, only one semantic view $\sigma \in M$ of the multi-relational property graph *G* is taken into consideration for decision space reduction. Taking the different semantics views into consideration, linear combinations of the adjacency matrixes of each individual semantic view can be established. The topology of the multi-relational property graph *G* can be represented not as matrices but as tensors known in discrete mathematics. In our case 3-way tensors with dimensions *(|V|, |V|, |M|)*,

a kind of cuboid of numbers with cells denoting the adjacency between node $u \in V$ and $v \in V$ in semantic view σ in *M* are constructed. Building the linear combinations over the layers of the tensors (weighting of the semantic views) can be done easily. As a result, in Root-Cause-Analysis individual layers, e.g., the coding layer and the database layer can be prioritized and the proportion of e.g. the metadata layer can be decreased. Centrality algorithms now can be applied on basis of weighted matrices.

The tensors and its calculus mentioned above play a significant role in the context of path algebra (Rodriguez & Shinavier, 2009). Searching and finding of relevant integration paths in the multi-relational property graph can be performed with the expressiveness of the path algebra, e.g. find all function modules *a*, that are indirectly called by class method *b* that contain a remote function call *c* in system *Y* that inserts database entries $d_i$ into database table *T*. This example outlines a typical integration path in Root-Cause-Analysis to be identified by a path algebra query.

Path algebra is a mathematical formalized description for retrieval of sub graphs of the multi-relational property graph *G*. The procedure of determining the sub graph based on a path algebra query is therefore a decision space reduction algorithm. The path algebra cannot only determine a sub graph in read mode. The path algebra can enrich or modify the graph in change mode as well. With help of tensor multiplication, addition, subtraction, weighting, etc., it is possible to identify the relevant integration paths in the decision space of the multi-relational property graph *G*. Therefore, the path algebra is a very generic mechanism for reducing the decision space.

One disadvantage needs to be mentioned here: The path algebra is based on matrices, more generally on tensors, which can contain billions of components, i.e. cells. Having operative Environmental Information Systems in mind, a graph derivation leads to multi-relational graphs with billions of nodes and billions of edges in the individual semantic views. The density is not necessarily high, but the resulting tensors are too big for efficient calculation. Recent research is heading in the direction of ring algebra instead of tensor calculation. Regarding performance and efficiency, this seems to become an interesting alternative approach (Rodriguez & Shinavier, 2009).

Up to here, the reduction of the decision space with help of methods of spectral graph theory was discussed. Another algorithmic approach is the evaluation of the structure of the multi-relational property graph $G$. For example dense sub graphs (highly and complex integrated software components) is typically more error-prone than regions with low density sub graphs. Therefore, to increase efficiency in, Semantic Debugging, the detection of such sub graphs with high density is always a good approach. The identified regions are prioritized regions and therefore the decision space is reduced. Algorithms for community detection in the context of Social Networking Research can be applied. A community in a social network is the pendant of a complex integrated subsystem represented as a high-density sub graph within a multi-relational property graph. In addition, $k$-means clustering algorithms can be very useful to exclude subspaces in the decision space. All algorithms need to cope with mass-data, which can be a knockout criterion in the context of Semantic Debugging or Root-Cause-Analysis. Interactivity given in classical technical debuggers are also expected in semantic debuggers. Therefore, algorithms need to be constructed, that work in a relaxative mode without losing the correctness regarding defect location.

The methodology of prioritizing a whole decision space is called ranking. All nodes and edges of a multi-relational property graph are taken into consideration. Another approach is the scoring of a path query. This means sub graphs, resulting from a concrete path algebra query, are ranked e.g. with centrality algorithms. Therefore, the ranking happens in combination with the path algebra query. The ranking takes place only on a sub graph. Depending on the query, the result is ranked. This scoring is very useful in diagnosis scenarios.

The concept of recommendation is also a practice proven approach in Root-Cause-Analysis. When the software maintenance engineer is at a specific stage in the semantic debugging scenario, he has many degrees of freedom to follow paths. This can result in false positive, true negative, positive, or negative hits regarding approaching the defect location. A recommendation engine provides hints in terms of nodes to follow with higher rated root-cause hit rate. This is a probabilistic approach. Recommendations can be calculated on basis of tensors mentioned above. Therefore, recommendations consider different semantic views. This leads to a more efficient routing to the root-cause location. All in all the concept of recommendations leads to decision space reduction. Finally, in category of decision space reduction algorithms, the semantic inference based on multi-relational property graphs needs to be mentioned. Semantic interference in our context means making the implicit knowledge of a specific integration graph $G$ explicit. This can be done with help of interference algorithm used in artificial intelligence. Typically, the interference algorithms do not modify the multi-relational property graph $G$. The graph $G$ is rather extended to $G'$, i.e. in terms of formula $G$ is a subset of $G'$. This set-theoretical inclusion is to be interpreted in the following sense: All information retrievable from the multi-relational property graph $G$ can also be retrieved from the multi-relational property graph $G'$. The graph $G'$ contains more information. In other words, $G'$ can have additional nodes, additional edges, additional semantic views or additional key-values on existing nodes and edges. The time consumption for provisioning of the additional knowledge in the graph $G'$ can be reused in multiple follow-up queries and therefore amortized over the amount of path algebra queries.

## Delta-Operator

In the previous section, a flexible schema-free model for adequate knowledge representation covering integration aspects in an Environmental Information System at point-in-time $t_0$ is discussed. The model is schema-free, because if the integration aspects are extended, or the system states change, the multi-relational property graph is in the position to absorb those crosscutting concerns and represent the data in an appropriate way without the need of static extension of the data model. This section is concerned with the comparison of two similar systems. Basically, two multi-relational property graphs need to be compared. If the comparison is based on graphs with large node sets and edge sets in the range of beyond billions of entities, the comparison cannot be executed in reasonable time. Although mathematically correct and exact, the results are not provided in a reasonable period and therefore this option is not applicable. Nevertheless, the procedure shall be outlined for having a better understanding of the algorithms involved. It is worth noting, that the comparison exceeds the entity-by-entity comparison. The comparison of two similar multi-relational property graphs is rather a structural comparison. Therefore, it needs to be figured out, what is the algorithm for detecting the structural difference of two similar graphs. The involved indices can based upon a graph $G_1$ at $t_0$ and its modified version $G_2$ at $t_1$, i.e. comparison of one Environmental Information System, which changes over a short period of time. The other use case is the comparison of two different Environmental Information Systems. The comparison of a productive system with the test system is based on data close to production system. Test cases can be verified based on this comparison of physical similar systems. The comparison is based on two physical software instances at different locations. The delta is the footprint of the test scenarios executed based on copied productive data.

Especially in the case of physical distributed comparison, the entity-by-entity comparison is not sufficient. Here, the structural comparison is the path forward to go. Alternatively speaking, nodes in different systems with the same semantics can be labeled with different IDs, e.g., the labeling is based on number ranges or based on GUIDs, which is a rather randomized labeling procedure. The probabilistic distribution or the policy-based labeling is different; the semantic relationships are rather invariant. This case of relationship association with different labeling needs to be taken into consideration. Consequently, nodes with the same semantics are belonging cross-system together and therefore need to be structural compared. The structure of two similar systems is nearly invariant, not necessarily the individual labeling of the nodes.

Basically, the comparison reflects the changes of the multilayered represented semantic. If e.g. a business transaction in an Environmental Information System is executed, the semantic in the multi-relational property graph will be modified at point in time $t_{0, \text{which}}$ results in a changed graph $G_2$. The delta is the footprint of the business transaction executed. More generally, the delta is the footprint of any tool, process step, user interaction, service execution, maintenance task. Different layers of the multi-relational property graph represent the delta, which reflects not only the data, i.e. the labeling, but the semantic topology as well. This generic delta-approach embeds inter alia the mathematics of several domain specific topics of applied computer science like Business Process Mining, SAP Standard Proximity (Sekatzek & Krcmar, 2009), Architecture Deviation Analysis or Software-Tracking and Tracing in the context of Software Evolution. The delta in this context is a subset, i.e. a multi-relational sub graph of a multi-relational property graph. It is a holistic semantic representation useful for a family of algorithms in the area of in-depth structural analysis. The Delta-Operator in this context can be seen as a reusable component for those algorithms. This enables significant complexity reduction while simultaneously the quality of the resulting compositions increases. The delta is to be seen as a means for defining a graph centrality in the context of Root-Cause-Analysis. This is comparable to the approaches of Eigenvector Centrality, Closeness Centrality, Bridging Centrality, Google Page-Rank Centrality, or Vitality Centrality inter alia as defined and used in Social Network Analysis or Spectral Graph Theory, respectively. The new Delta Centrality points the software maintenance engineer close to the regions of relevancy in the decision space that is spanned by the multi-relational property graph. To put it in other words, there is an analogon of approaches and the fuzzy Root-Cause-Analysis procedure can be formulized and captured more precisely. This leads to concrete derivation of approximate algorithms.

It is worth noting, that the theory of Software Metrics can build on the abstraction of Delta Centrality as presented in this chapter. In this chapter, the Root-Cause-Analysis is primarily using the Delta Centrality, i.e. for approximation of the defect location. The approximation happens in the decision space spanned by the multi-relational property graph. The Root-Cause-Analysis is therefore based on the indirection of the delta graph centrality.

In the following section the precise mathematical calculus of the Delta-Operator is developed. For the sake of simplicity, the focus is based on one single semantic view $\sigma \in M$. This reduction can be made without loss of generality. Levenshtein has developed the Levenshtein-Distance for two single finite sequences $\tau_1, \tau_2 \in \sum^n$. By the way - a sequence can be seen as a very simplistic chained labeled graph. The positions are the node IDs and the elements of the sequences are the labels.

In the Levenshtein theory, the concept of Edit Script, denoted as $\Pi$, is developed. The length of the minimal Edit Script is defined as the Levenshtein Distance $£(\tau_1, \tau_2) = |\Pi|$. The Edit Script represents a sequence of elementary operation *insert, delete,* and *update* needed to be performed on $\tau_1$ to morph $\tau_1$ sequentially into $\tau_2$. Calculation of the Edit Script and consequently for the Edit Distance can be done with help of the generic Simplex Method known in the theory of Linear Programming for integer based programs. It is possible to formulate the concept of Levenshtein Distance more generically and transfer it to Tree Distance. With help of these Tree Distance Algorithms, a minimum Edit Script will be calculated, representing the shortest sequence of elementary operations on the tree for transforming tree $F$ into tree $H$. Elementary operations may be performed on nodes, edges and the associated labels. Deleting of a node implies deleting of the incident edge. Inserting a node implies inserting of the related edge at the specific parent node. The Tree Edit Script and Tree Edit Distance can be calculated with Simplex Method as well, but the asymptotic time complexity is exponentially in the number of nodes of the tree.

In the context of Root-Cause-Analysis, the Tree-Edit-Distance is generalized to the Graph-Edit-Distance. Referring to the complexity of the Tree-Edit-Distance, the complexity of the Graph-Edit-Distance is much higher, but remains exponential. In addition, the Graph-Edit-Distance can be calculated with help of Simplex Method, well known, that this approach is not necessarily the optimal one regarding time and space complexity.

Let

$$G_1 = (V_1, E_1, f_1, g_1) \text{ and } G_2 = (V_2, E_2, f_2, g_2)$$

be two labeled graphs and $S$ the set of possible Edit Scripts transforming graph $G_1$ morphologically into graph $G_2$. $f_1$ is a label function that maps the node set $V_1$ onto a finite discrete set of labels

*L.* The label function $g_1$ maps the set of edges $E_1$ to the set of labels *L.* Likewise, $f_2$ and $g_2$ maps the set of nodes $V_2$ and the set of edges $E_2$ into *L.* Furthermore, let *c* be a cost function for the set of individual elementary graph operation sequences based on *insert, update, delete,* which maps those sequence sets into the field of positive rational numbers. Then the Graph-Edit-Distance is calculated according to Neuhaus and Bunke (2006):

$$d(G_1, G_2) = min_{<s1,...sk> = s \in S} \sum_{i \in [1:k]} c_i \qquad (1.3)$$

As mentioned before, this definition of distance according to the optimization schema can be generalized to multi-relational graphs. The Graph-Edit-Distance $d(G_1, G_2)$ and the Edit Script is leading to the Graph-Edit-Distance, that is the center of interest. Having the minimal Graph Edit Script in place, the delta sub graph can easily be derived from the source graph $G_1$. This delta sub graph is referred to as Delta or Delta Centrality throughout the chapter. The Delta encompasses the nodes and edges, that are close to the defect location, i.e. most relevant for continuing Root-Cause-Analysis in direction to the error. The Delta-Centrality in generalization can encompass different semantic views in *M.*

Consequently, the error, i.e. the root-cause of the error symptom, can be approached from different angles. The defect itself can also affect different semantic views. Delta determination according to Equation 1.3 is very time consuming, in theory as well as in practice for operational data. Therefore, determination of the Delta, utilizing optimization techniques is not applicable in the context of Root-Cause-Analysis, where in general the graphs have a large extent. Asymptotically with the extent of graphs, the time for semantic debugging would exceed the time for manual Root-Cause-Analysis. To enable drastic acceleration, relaxation techniques to Equation 1.3 are to be applied.

The basic idea of the Delta-Operator is that calculation does not take place on the level of the graphs, but rather on the level of indices. Speaking more precisely, the involved graphs are to be indexed. The index construction algorithms need to fulfill the characteristic of redundancy elimination of the multi-relational property graph to a large extent while preserving the topology structure of the graph. It can be shown, that multi-relational property graphs can be mapped to tensors which, technically speaking, are a homogeneous set of matrices. Those matrices, derived from operational Corporate Environmental Management Information Systems with help of crawlers, are in fact sparse, i.e. have low density in values not equal to 0. Beyond that, it can empirically be shown, that there are patterns in such matrices, e.g. many adjacent equal values. This leads to high redundancy in the set of matrices. This redundancy can easily be removed with help of a multilevel inverted indexing technique. In addition to that, different further redundancy elimination techniques can be applied. Amongst others, interval determination for neighboring positions or codes of label values according to the probabilistic distribution in that way, that the labels with higher frequency will be assigned the codes with smaller length to. This is a very easy but efficient redundancy eliminating technique in combination with inverted indexing. A good, with linear time complexity indexing algorithm for matching subsequences or patterns is the *DCμ* Difference Cover Modulo *μ* algorithm, a generalized indexing algorithm of *DC3* used in bio-informatics (Kärkkäinen, Sanders, & Burkhardt, 2006; Nulens, 2006). The resulting index is a PAT-Array, which is a compact representation of the logically involved PAT-tree. PAT-Arrays allow logarithmic access to the indexed sequence, which is very advantageous for primary access to the inverted index via the lexicon. This sequence-indexing algorithm can be combined with the inverted indexing for defining an index-path to the lexicon of the distinct values of the multi-relational property graph.

Basically, the Delta-Operator compares rather the redundancy-eliminated indices instead of the involved redundant graphs. This leads to performance gains. It constructs the indices of the involved multi-relational property graphs in a first step. A Delta-Index is constructed based on the previously constructed indices. The indices are systematically organized and allow easy light-weight comparison. In the case of high redundancy, as given in Enterprise Software Systems (Plattner, 2009), the Delta-Index is quasi-isomorphic to the Delta of the involved multi-relational property graphs. A small Delta-Index indicates that the involved multi-relational property graphs are similar. The Delta-Operator is an efficient algorithm for handling of similar Enterprise Software Systems or for tracing the changes of an Enterprise Software System over a short period of time.

The efficiency of the Delta-Operator is given only in the case of highly redundant and sparse graphs. The approach of the Delta-Operator is in general not loss-free, i.e. it may result in an incorrect delta-sub graph. Nevertheless, if the characteristics of high redundancy and low density of the involved graphs are given, the resulting Delta is quasi-correct and therefore suitable in most practicable use cases. At the same time, the time and space complexity is reasonable in this situation in the context of Semantic Debugging. In addition to that, the parameter $\mu$ can rebalance time complexity against space complexity to a certain extent.

If the involved graphs are orthogonal to each other, i.e. with high entropy in the set of nodes, edges and labels, then the approach of the Delta-Operator has no value-added advantage in comparison to the optimization approach outlined in Equation 1.3. A comparison of two complete structural different integrated Enterprise Software Systems is suboptimal in conjunction with the Delta-Operator. The decision space will not be reduced significantly. In this situation, the indices degrade and the Delta-Centrality provides non-relevant hints regarding defect location in the context of Semantic Debugging. The Delta-Operator is applicable for similar and redundant Enterprise Software Systems only. Nevertheless, this restriction leaves many options for practicable use-cases in the context of Root-Cause-Analysis.

## Join-Operator

In Root-Cause-Analysis, it is essential to have effective means in place for reducing the decision space in order to approach or at least approximate the defect location. Using multi-relational property graphs in Semantic Debugging implies the need for grouping the nodes and edges according to specific semantic criteria. The nodes may be topologically adjacent via direct or indirect edges or the nodes are distributed, but connected semantically across different semantic views $\sigma \in M$. Those nodes have a semantic link rather than an edge relationship. The nodes are grouped in a semantic bundle. This semantic bundle can be refined iteratively with help of the Join-Operator. As a result, a sub graph of the multi-relational property graph encompasses the defect location or the graph periphery is in the proximity of the defect location. This iteratively approximation is very effective in Semantic Debugging, because there is no need to define a complex path algebra query at the very beginning. The decision space reduction can be done iteratively with help of a sequence of elementary queries. Each intermediate step, i.e. each query depends on the result of the previous semantic grouping. The iteratively constructed sub graphs of the multi-relational property graph can be prioritized. In each individual step all nodes and edges can be prioritized with help of centrality rankings, e.g. the Delta Centrality, Google PageRank Centrality, Bridging Centrality, Betweeness Centrality to name but a few. This is called multi-relational property graph scoring, because the ranking, i.e. prioritizing is depending on the previous query, more precisely on the previous materialized queries executed in a sequence. With help of centralities, the most relevant nodes can be emphasized in the decision space. E.g., Degree Centrality, Bridging Centrality, or the Betweeness Centrality are good means to identify intensive integrated software regions with high correction risks. Defect locations are primarily to be found in areas with high grade of integration. Basically, from the perspective mathematics the algorithms of the Join-Operator are included in the Delta-Operator. In essence, the Join-Operator is executed in the first step for each operand of the Delta-Operator.

The Join-Operator constructs a multilayered inverted index for two multi-relational property graphs. In addition, here the $DC\mu$ Difference Cover Modulo $\mu$ indexing algorithm is involved. As a result, the Join-Operator performs the union of the multi-relational property graphs and constructs a reusable inverted index for efficient query access.

As mentioned before, the Join-Operator enables identification and grouping of distributed elements of the multi-relational property graph. Those elements are bundled. The semantic bundle is a not necessarily connected subspace in the decision space in the context of semantic debugging. There is an analogon to Cross-Cutting Concerns as known from Aspect-Oriented-Programming AOP. More precisely, the Join-Operator is an algorithm for identification of aspects in an Enterprise Software System. The aspects may include Security, Logging, Numerical Precision, Connectivity, Software Enhancements, and Modifications to name but a few. Those aspects are crosscutting and therefore are distributed in the multi-relational property graph. Not to be mentioned, that the aspects can freely be defined by a sequence of elementary queries.

The Join-Operator has two operands and enables iterative refinements of the Cross-Cutting-Concerns in the decision space spanned by the multi-relational property graph. The index is redundancy eliminated, structured, and allows an efficient materialization of the queries, i.e. the reconstruction of the sub graphs implied by the queries.

In summary, the Join-Operator as well as the Delta-Operator spans a subspace in the decision space. This subspace can be prioritized to segregate defect location relevant from the non-relevant subspaces. The queries take place not on the graph level but rather on the level of the inverted index of the involved graph. This indexing procedure is redundancy eliminating to a large extent and enables the reconstruction of the sub graphs. If redundancy of Enterprise Software System can be assumed (Plattner, 2009) and in the case of system similarity, the algorithms work efficient and correct also for multi-relational graphs of a larger extent. This relaxation approach can ensure the quasi-correctness in most practical use-cases. It circumvents the extreme time consumption needed for the exact calculation in the optimization approach mentioned in Equation 1.3.

## SEMANTIC DEBUGGING PATTERNS

In the previous sections, basically, two generic operators for reducing the decision space have been constructed. This paragraph covers the topic of Semantic Debugging Patterns based upon the operators defined before. In this context, Semantic Debugging Patterns are best practice blueprints for defect location approximation. Assuming, an erroneous business process needs to be diagnosed in a Corporate Environmental Management Information System. The business process can be seen as a sequence of individual business process operations leaving a footprint in the Enterprise Software System each. The sequence of business process steps changes the Enterprise Software System from the initial system status $S_{t0}$ to $S_{t1}$ until the final business process step, which transforms the system into the target state $S_{tn}$. In terms of mathematics, this means a trajectory in the decision space. The sequence of system states $< S_{t0}, S_{t1}, ..., S_{tn} >$ represents the set of consecutive intermediate states in the decision space. The Delta of the system states $\Delta_k = S_{tk} - S_{tk-1}$, $k \in [1, n]$ represents the footprint of an individual business process step k. The system deltas $\Delta_k$ can easily be calculated utilizing the Delta-Operator. Overall, the Delta is the incremental composition of the trajectory of the business process in the decision space. The Delta-Centrality points to the periphery of the defect location. Traversal from the individual delta is possible. Elements in the delta-sub graph can be ranked or scored according to the centralities mentioned in the previous sections. With the Join-Operator, it is possible to traverse from an individual delta sub graph $\Delta_k$ to the periphery of the defect location. This can be done in different semantic views $\sigma \in M$ of the multi-relational property graph G. Up to here, a fundamental Semantic Debugging Pattern has been discussed. Another Semantic Debugging Pattern is related to the Join-Operator only. With the aid of Join-Operator, it is possible to refine the decision space of the multi-relational property graph iteratively. This leads, in comparison to a trajectory, to a monotone decreasing sequence of multi-relational sub graphs according to $G = G_{t0} \geq G_{t1} \geq ... \geq G_{tn}$. The relation $\geq$ denotes the inclusion of graphs. A query $q_k$ is based on $G_k$ and results in an indexed multi-relational sub graph $G_{k+1}$. In terms of mathematics, this iteration is the analogy to fixed-point determination or invariant point determination of a graph operator. This allows a very flexible decision space reduction in an easy way. The Join-Operator, the Delta-Operator, and the Inference-Operator of the next section are multivariate operators, respectively. The algorithms can be parameterized and be reused and composed for individual Semantic Debugging Patterns. This enables a specific target-oriented defect location approximation strategy. Enterprise Tomography encompasses the set of Semantic Debugging Patterns based on generic graph operators utilizing redundancy eliminating indexing techniques.

## FUTURE RESEARCH DIRECTIONS: INFERENCE-OPERATOR

A strong limitation of the Delta-Operator and of the Join-Operator is the fact, that approximation for the defect location and for the root cause can be performed iteratively only. For reconstruction and traversal of the integration graph, each individual step requires human interaction and decision. Therefore, this diagnosis approach is semiautomatic.

For Semantic Debugging it would be advantageous to have an operator in place that is in the position to evaluate deep queries based on multi-relational property graphs. The depth, the attributes and the topology of the graph should be taken into consideration. The Inference-Operator, based on path-algebra, should be aligned to techniques mentioned in Rodriguez and Shinavier (2009). Basically, it is an open research question, how to build graph based queries based on path algebra and simultaneously employ the indexing techniques as used for the Delta-Operator and for the Join-Operator. On the one hand, side, the Inference-Operator shall provide more flexibility and generality in the queries and on the other hand side; there is a big potentiality for runtime-efficient algorithms based on graph redundancy eliminating indexing techniques. The research for the Inference-Operator should address the fact, that the graph based queries not to be executed on the extrinsic level of the Multi-relational Property Graph, but rather on the intrinsic level of the graph representation, i.e. on basis of the index representation. In summary, graph theoretic algorithms and the path algebra based queries need to be performed on indices directly. The query results can be materialized to the extrinsic graph representation.

To make the Inference-Operator useful for reducing decision spaces in Semantic Debugging, different Centrality Algorithms shall be applied. The open research question results in finding a good balanced and practice relevant combination of graph traversal and evaluation algorithms, indexing techniques and decision space reduction algorithms with help of centrality prioritization. The compatibility of the operators regarding the operands as indices enables a harmonized approach for Semantic Debugging Patterns. This provides potentiality for standardization in software maintenance as part of Application Lifecycle Management and leads to efficiency in the Root-Cause-Analysis phase.

## RELATED WORKS

The approach Enterprise Tomography driven Governance of Federated ERP in a Cloud is complementary to the research areas Application Lifecycle Management of VLBAs and governance of Semantic SOA respectively. In Semantic SOA, there are dedicated procedures in alignment of semantic entities and semantic services (Panchenko, 2007). The Enterprise Tomography approach generically unifies a set of ontology matching approaches and is primarily based on algorithms for genetic engineering known in Bio-Informatics (Tiun, Abdullah, & Kong, 2001; Haak & Brehm, 2008; Aalmink & Marx Gómez, 2009; Abels, Haak, & Hahn, 2005). The mathematical model of a family of matching algorithms for large data sets in genetic engineering is transformed to semantic matching and delta determination. The delta indicators can be interpreted as generic software metrics in a specific domain called semantic view. The software metrics are the decision basis in the governance procedure. Regarding metrics, service provisioning and consumption (dependency graph), business data as well as meta-data is taken into consideration.

## CONCLUSION

In previous sections, we have outlined the Federated EPR approach in the context of Enterprise Computing. It was discussed how FERP can

increase scalability in a Enterprise Cloud. In addition, we adumbrated the Integration Lifecycle Management of a Federated ERP network in a Cloud. With help of closed-loops the evolution of a shared Federated ERP system can be controlled according to cloud metrics, which are indicators calculated by the Enterprise Tomograph. The Enterprise Tomograph acts as a generic Delta-calculating search engine, which permanently crawls and observes the materialized cloud content. The search engine of the Enterprise Tomograph can be executed in delta mode as well as in full mode. With help of extractors for the Enterprise Tomograph we can have polymorphic search operator or delta operator which delivers the indicators as decision basis in the governance procedure.

This chapter proposes a set of Semantic Debugging Patterns based on generic graph operators as blueprints for efficient Root-Cause-Analysis regarding defect location in Enterprise Software Systems. With help of Enterprise Tomography, it is possible to perform efficient systematic structural system analysis regarding approximation towards defect locations. The decision space can effectively be reduced while simultaneously minimizing the algorithmic time consumption during the diagnosis iteration. The chapter outlines the generic Join-Operator and the Delta-Operator. The Delta-Operator determines and prioritizes the decision space according to the Delta Centrality. The Delta-Centrality is a metric on multi-relational property graphs for defining the periphery and proximity of the defect location. The operator-based approach is applicable for Environmental Information Systems with high redundancy in software and data artifacts. With help of relaxation techniques, the performance of graph algorithms can be increased drastically while preserving the correctness largely. In particular, the Delta-Operator is applicable and efficient only for similar systems. However, these restrictions leave many, in practice useful semantic debugging patterns for large and complex integrated Corporate Environmental Management Information Systems.

# REFERENCES

Aalmink, J., & Marx Gómez, J. (2009). Enterprise tomography - An efficient approach for semi-automatic localization of integration concepts in VLBAs . In Cruz-Cunha, M. M. (Ed.), *Social, Managerial and Organizational Dimensions of Enterprise Information Systems*. Hershey, PA: IGI Global. doi:10.4018/978-1-60566-856-7.ch012

Aalmink, J., & Marx Gómez, J. (2011). Enterprise tomography - An efficient application lifecycle management approach supporting semiautomatic localization, delta-tracking and visualization of integration ontologies in VLBAs . In Kumar, S., Bendoly, E., & Esteves, J. (Eds.), *Frontiers of Research in Enterprise Systems*. Thousand Oaks, CA: SAGE.

Abels, S., Haak, L., & Hahn, A. (2005). Identification of common methods used for ontology integration tasks: Interoperability of heterogeneous information systems. In *Proceedings of the First International Workshop on Interoperability of Heterogeneous Information Systems*, (pp. 75-78). Bremen, Germany: ACM Press.

Bader, D. A., Kintali, S., Madduri, K., & Mihail, M. (2007). Approximating betweeness centrality. *Lecture Notes in Computer Science, 4863*, 124–134. doi:10.1007/978-3-540-77004-6_10

Brehm, N., Lübke, D., & Marx Gómez, J. (2007). Federated enterprise resource planning (FERP) systems . In Saha, P. (Ed.), *Handbook of Enterprise Systems Architecture in Practice* (pp. 290–305). Hershey, PA: IGI Global. doi:10.4018/978-1-59904-189-6.ch017

Brehm, N., Marx Gómez, J., & Rautenstrauch, C. (2006). An ERP solution based on web services and peer-to-peer networks for small and medium enterprises. *International Journal of Information Systems and Change Management, 1*(1), 99–111. doi:10.1504/IJISCM.2006.008288

Bunke, H., Dickinsion, P. J., Kraetzl, M., & Wallis, W. D. (2007). *A graph-theoretic approach to enterprise networks dynamics* (pp. 71–117). Birkhäuser, Switzerland: Birkhäuser Verlag.

Epstein, A. (2004). *Parallel hardware architectures for the life science.* (Doctoral Thesis). Delft University. Delft, The Netherlands.

Grünwald, C., & Marx Gómez, J. (2007). Conception of system supported generation of sustainability reports in a large scale enterprise. In J. Marx Gomez, M. Sonnenschein, M. Müller, H. Welsch, & C. Rautenstrauch (Eds.), *Information Technologies in Environmental Engineering: ITEE 2007 - Third International ICSC Symposium*, (pp. 60-68). Berlin, Germany: Springer Verlag.

Haak, L., & Brehm, N. (2008). *Ontologies supporting* VLBAs semantic integration in the context of FERP. In *Proceedings of the 3rd International Conference on Information and Communication Technologies: From Theory To Applications, ICTTA 2008*, (pp. 1-5). ICTTA.

Heuser, L., Alsdorf, C., & Woods, D. (2007). Enterprise 2.0 - The service grid –User-driven innovation - Business model transformation. In *Proceedings of the International Research Forum 2007, Potsdam, SAP Research*. Evolved Technologist Press.

Heuser, L., Alsdorf, C., & Woods, D. (2008). The web-based service industry – Infrastructure for enterprise SOA 2.0, potential killer applications - Semantic service discovery. In *Proceedings of the International Research Forum 2008, Potsdam, SAP Research*. Evolved Technologist Press.

Kärkkäinen, J., Sanders, P., & Burkhardt, S. (2006). Linear work suffix array construction. *Journal of the ACM, 53*(6), 918–936. doi:10.1145/1217856.1217858

Marx Gómez, J. (2009). Corporate environmental management information systems - CEMIS 2.0. In D. Davcev & J. Marx Gómez (Eds.), *Proceedings of the ICT Innovations Conference 2009*, (pp. 1-4). Ohrid, Macedonia: Springer Heidelberg.

Neuhaus, M., & Bunke, H. (2006). A random walk kernel derived from graph edit distance. *Lecture Notes in Computer Science*, *4109*, 191–199. doi:10.1007/11815921_20

Nulens, R. (2006). *Sequentie analyse*. (Doctoral Thesis). Transnationale Universiteit Limburg. Maastricht, The Netherlands.

Panchenko, O. (2007). Concept location and program comprehension in service-oriented software. In *Proceedings of the IEEE 23rd International Conference on Software Maintenance: Doctoral Symposium, ICSM*, (pp. 513-514). Paris, France: IEEE Press.

Plattner, H. (2009). A common database approach for OLTP and OLAP using an in-memory column database. In *Proceedings of the 35th SIGMOD International Conference on Management of Data*. Providence, RI: ACM Press.

Rodriguez, M. A., & Shinavier, J. (2009). Exposing multi-relational networks to single-relational network analysis algorithms. *Journal of Informetrics*, *4*(1), 29–41. doi:10.1016/j.joi.2009.06.004

Sekatzek, P. E., & Krcmar, H. (2009). Measurement of the standard proximity of adapted standard business software. *Business and Information Systems Engineering*, *1*(3), 234–244. doi:10.1007/s12599-009-0045-4

Tiun, S., Abdullah, R., & Kong, T. E. (2001). Automatic topic identification using ontology hierarchy. In *Proceedings, Computational Linguistic and Intelligent Text Processing, Second International Conference CICLing*, (pp. 444-453). Mexico City, Mexico: Springer.

# Chapter 8
# Semantic Web Data Partitioning

**Trupti Padiya**
*DA-IICT Gandhinagar, India*

**Minal Bhise**
*DA-IICT Gandhinagar, India*

**Sanjay Chaudhary**
*DA-IICT Gandhinagar, India*

## ABSTRACT

*Semantic Web database is an RDF database due to increased use of Semantic Web in real life applications; one can find heavy growth in RDF database. As there is a tremendous increase in RDF data, performance and scalability issues are of main concern. This chapter discusses improving and scaling up query performance for increasingly growing Semantic Web. It discusses current Semantic Web data storage techniques, which have been found to scale poorly and have poor query performance. It discusses the partitioning techniques vertical and horizontal partitioning to improve query performance. To further improve the query performance, along with these partitioning techniques, various compression techniques can also be used. Relational data offers faster execution of queries as compared to RDF data. To demonstrate these ideas, semantic data is converted to relational data and then query performance improvement techniques are applied. The scaling up of Semantic Web data is also discussed.*

## INTRODUCTION

The Semantic Web is an effort by the W3C to enable integration and sharing of data across different applications and organizations. It is a contemplation of combination of different content, information applications, and systems across Internet. There is a tremendous growth in semantic Web data due to its application in real

world. Application which relies on semantics in real life has perceived the importance of RDF (Resource Description Framework) data that is spread across and as a result we can find a rapid growth in semantic Web data. Mostly all semantic applications require fetching the data efficiently which is spread over Internet and hence different Semantic Web applications will often retrieve information dynamically from URLs and merge

DOI: 10.4018/978-1-4666-2494-8.ch008

Copyright © 2013, IGI Global. Copying or distributing in print or electronic forms without written permission of IGI Global is prohibited.

them into a storage system to make the data available. Therefore, data manipulation has to be carried out many times, on the scale of the Web, and it should be done in efficient manner. Researchers are investigating usefulness of RDBMS tools for this purpose. Efficient management of RDF data is an important factor in realizing the semantic Web vision. There is need for efficient query processing as performance and scalability issues are becoming increasingly important as semantic Web technology is applied to real-world applications.

## ISSUES IN ACCESSING SEMANTIC WEB DATA

The Semantic Web data, which is in RDF format <Subject, Property, Object> known as an RDF triple can be stored in database table format. To retrieve data efficiently we can store data tables in two ways: row-by-row or column-by-column. The former approach will keep all information about an entity together. For example in a vendor table, it will store all information about the first vendor and then all information about the second vendor and so on. The later approach will keep all attribute information together: the entire vendor names will be stored consecutively, then the entire vendor addresses and so on. Now as these designs are even handed the choice is based on performance expectations. If it is expected the result should be based the granularity of an entity for, e.g., find a vendor, add a vendor, delete a vendor, etc., then the row-by-row storage is preferable as all of the required information will be stored together. On the other hand, if the expected result tends to read per query only a few attributes from many records will be the result, for, e.g., a query that finds the most common e-mail address domain, then column-by-column storage is preferred as other attributes which are not required for a particular query need not have to be accessed. This is what is said to be partitioning or division

of a logical database or its constituting elements into distinct independent parts, which is done for manageability, performance or availability. These are our basic requirements in order to scale up Semantic Web data.

## Scalability

As the Semantic Web evolves, scalability becomes increasingly important. Triples are used for resource description on the Web. All resources are described with many triples and this makes a complex graph of relationships, which includes references to other resources and the relationships in semantic Web data also have types. It is therefore necessary that triple stores can deal with large numbers of triples in real life. To fetch and store triples also impacts scalability, it brings in the issues of timeliness, caching and other general problems from a distributed system, which can fail or be delayed.

## Performance

Manipulation of data in a triple store is required as triples can be added, modified, and/or removed. This needs support for identifying triples, querying the graph as well as administering the graph— i.e. creating and deleting it and other operations for transferring data to and from the network. Indexes should be created for efficient searching, or for providing specialized searches such as text-based search, or other searches based on properties, sub-properties, logical inference, etc. It is always possible that data from multiple sources will be merged into single graphs of data, and the relationships between them will connect them up and this needs triple-store support in order to handle such merging when the graphs are large enough and also should be possibly separated again later. Such manipulations by applications using semantic Web data will be occurring many times for even simple systems and thus these need to be lightweight, fast, and easy to understand conceptually as well as easy to use via APIs from software or Web methods.

## DATA PARTITIONING TECHNIQUES

The semantic Web data is in RDF format so we need to take a deep insight to improve RDF query performance. As we know that RDF data is a single table, which includes subject, predicate and object as a triple. All details are in this format. So querying such data will include so many self-joins, and it will affect the query performance, depending upon the type of data and the application.

As Semantic Web technology is applied to real-world applications, Performance and scalability issues are becoming crucial day by day. Here we will examine the reasons, why current data management solutions for RDF data scale poorly, and then will explore the fundamental scalability limitations of these approaches.

Structurally RDF is in triple format as <subject, predicate, object>. These triples can then be stored in a relational database with a three-column schema and the advantage of this approach is that it is very general. This data representation is very flexible, but can suffer from serious performance issues, as there is only a single RDF table, and almost all interesting queries will involve many self-joins over this table. So here, it is important to improve RDF query performance as people represent their data in RDF format on the Web. Several research groups feel that relational query processor is likely to be the best performing approach so here we will study all the way through, relational query processor.

There are different organization techniques for RDF data. The first is known as the *property table* technique proposed by Jena Semantic Web toolkit, which is nothing but de normalized RDF tables that are physically stored in a wider, flattened representation more similar to traditional relational schemas. Let us understand how PAR-

TITIONING affects the query performance, as stated in Abadi (2008), through an example with RDF data. Suppose we want to represent details of a book authored by three authors say book named as "Database System Concepts" authored by Silberschatz, Korth, and Sudarshan needs seven triples to represent the data as under:

- person1 isNamed "Silberschatz."
- person2 isNamed "Korth."
- person3 isNamed "Sudarshan."
- book1 hasAuthor person1.
- book1 hasAuthor person2.
- book1 hasAuthor person3.
- book1 isTitled "Database System Concepts."

And now let us consider the same kind of data for another book whose author is Antonio Grigoris and the book title is Semantic Web primer. So now, when we will put it up as a property table it will look as shown in Table 1.

*Table 1. Property table*

| Subject | Predicate | Object |
|---------|-----------|--------|
| ID1 | Title | Database Management Concepts |
| ID2 | Title | Semantic Web Primer |
| ID1 | Type | Book |
| ID2 | Type | Book |
| ID3 | Type | Author |
| ID4 | Type | Author |
| ID5 | Type | Author |
| ID6 | Type | Author |
| ID3 | isNamed | Silberschatz |
| ID4 | isNamed | Korth |
| ID5 | isNamed | Sudarshan |
| ID6 | isNamed | AntonioGrigoris |
| ID1 | has Author | ID3 |
| ID1 | has Author | ID4 |
| ID1 | has Author | ID5 |
| ID2 | has Author | ID6 |

Now let us consider a query "to find out all authors of the books whose title contains the word 'database.' This could be found out by a query that can perform five-way self-join as shown in Figure 1.

This query will be very slow to execute, because as the number of trples in the collection scales, the RDF table may well exceed the size of memory, and each of these filters and joins will require a scan or index lookup. Real world queries involve many more joins, which complicates selectivity estimation and query optimization, and limits the benefit of indices. Even though the representation is very simple and flexible, there are several issues with this property table technique:

- **Attributes having NULL Values**: There are possibilities that there may not be all the properties defined for all the subjects. Therefore, wherever the property is not defined it will contain NULL values and these NULL values in wider tables will result in sparse tables. Hence, many tables will have many sparse attributes and finally it will eventually end up in space overhead.
- **Complexity**: As the data changes, how to cluster data in various groups may change over data. So re-clustering will be required to as data characteristic changes.

- **Multi-Valued Attributes**: Relationship between a book and a author is many-to-many. It is also possible that a book can have multiple authors and an author can write multiple books. So this kind of relationship cannot be represented in a polished way in property tables. RDF dataset mostly will have such kind of data with multiple values and many-to-many relationship. Hence, a way should be found to represent such data.

To address these limitations, different physical organization techniques can be used for RDF data which includes vertical partitioning and horizontal partitioning.

## Vertical Partitioning

Vertical partitioning divides a table into multiple tables that contain fewer columns. The two types of vertical partitioning are normalization and row splitting:

- Normalization is the standard database process of removing redundant columns from a table and putting them in secondary tables that are linked to the primary table by primary key and foreign key relationships.

*Figure 1. Query*

```
SELECT p5.object

FROM propTable  AS p1,propTable AS p2,propTable AS

p3,propTable AS p4,propTable AS  p5

WHERE p1.property='title' AND p1.object like 'database' AND

p1.subject=p2.subject AND p2.property='type' AND

p2.object='book' AND p3.property='type' AND p3.object='author'

AND p4.property='has Author' AND p4.subject=p2.subject AND

p4.object=p3.subject AND p5.property='is Named' AND

p5.subject=p4.object
```

- Row splitting divides the original table vertically into tables with fewer columns. Each logical row in a split table matches the same logical row in the other tables as identified by a unique key column that is identical in all of the partitioned tables.

This approach can be used to store semantic Web data in order to improve query performance. One way to store the data using vertical partitioning is by creating a table for every property with its subject, means every table will have only two columns. One is the subject and the other will be its property. The example in Figure 2 illustrates how data can be partitioned vertically according to our discussed example.

Here it can be seen that each table is sorted by subject, so that particular subjects can be located quickly, and that fast merge joins can be used to reconstruct information about multiple properties for subsets of subjects. The value column for each table can also be indexed as required. The advantages of this approach compared to the property table approach are:

- **Representing Multi-valued attributes**: While using this partitioning technique, It is no more a problem to represent a multi-values attribute. If a subject has more than one object value for a particular property, then each distinct value is listed in a successive row in the table for that property.
- **Reduced I/O Cost:** I/O costs can be substantially reduced as only those properties are accessed by queries which are actually required and hence I/O cost will be less compared to property tables.
- **Representing heterogeneous records**: If there are subjects that do not define a particular property then they are omitted from the table for that property and hence NULL value is not explicitly stored. This is more helpful when data is not well structured.
- **No clustering needed**: As vertical partitioning is straight forward and will not change over time the same thing is applied to the data, no matter what the nature of data is. While in case of property table, it was supposed to be taken care of such that the tables do not become wide.

*Figure 2. Vertically partitioned tables*

**Type**

| ID1 | Book |
|-----|------|
| ID2 | Book |
| ID3 | Author |
| ID4 | Author |
| ID5 | Author |
| ID6 | Author |

**Title**

| ID1 | Database Management Concepts |
|-----|------------------------------|
| ID2 | Semantic Web Primer |

**IsNamed**

| ID3 | Silberschatz |
|-----|--------------|
| ID4 | Korth |
| ID5 | Sudarshan |
| ID6 | AntonioGrigoris |

**hasAuthor**

| ID1 | ID3 |
|-----|-----|
| ID1 | ID4 |
| ID1 | ID5 |
| ID2 | ID6 |

## Horizontal Partitioning

Horizontal partitioning divides a table into multiple tables. Each table then contains the same number of columns, but fewer rows. For example, in a university database a table that contains more than a billion rows can be partitioned horizontally into several other tables, with each smaller table representing data for a specific year. Any queries requiring data for a specific year only reference the appropriate table.

Determining how to partition the tables horizontally depends on how data is analyzed. You should partition the tables so that queries reference as few tables as possible. Otherwise, excessive union queries, used to merge the tables logically at query time, can affect performance.

In case of RDF data as we know it is difficult to partition data row wise as many subjects can have few properties and some may not have the same. So there can be no comparison done on the basis of their properties as they do not exist in either of the table for a particular subject. For e.g. if we consider the same example above we can see that we can construct at least six tables according to subject i.e. ID1 to ID6. Now we can see that a property such as title is there for ID1 and ID6 and missing for the rest of the others. Therefore, this will potentially give a slower result for the query, which we discussed about in the above example. Therefore, because of this reason column store approach is more feasible compared to row store.

## DATA COMPRESSION

In addition to partitioning techniques, we can also use some other techniques that can help improve the query performance. Data compression is an effective technique for saving storage space and network bandwidth. There exist a large number of compression schemes, which are based on character encoding or on detection of repetitive strings. We know that the database performance strongly depends on the amount of available memory, whether it as I/O buffers or as work space for query processing algorithms. Therefore, we can try to use all available memory as effectively as possible and manipulate data in memory in compressed form. We can use the described available techniques in conjunction with the partitioning approach:

## Dictionary Encoding

The most common compression schemes found in databases are Dictionary compression schemes. These schemes replace frequent patterns with smaller codes. We can implement a column-optimized version of dictionary encoding whereas Row-oriented dictionary schemes have the limitation that they can only map attribute values from a single tuple to dictionary entries. The reason behind this is row-stores fundamentally are incapable of mixing attributes from more than one tuple in a single entry if other attributes of the tuples are not also included in the same entry.

## Null Suppression

There exists many variations on the null compression technique, but the basic idea is that consecutive zeros or blanks in the data are deleted and replaced depending on the description of the amount of zeros/blanks were there and the place where they existed. In general, this technique performs well on data sets where zeros or blanks appear frequently. Here, we can allow field sizes to be variable and encode the number of bytes needed to store each field in a field prefix. This allows us in omitting leading nulls required to pad the data to a fixed size. For, e.g. for type integer, instead of using the full 4 bytes to store it, we can encoded the exact number of bytes required using two bits and place these two bits before the integer. We can combine these bits with the bits for three other integers to make a full byte's worth of length information and use a table to decode this length quickly.

## Parsing Into Single Values

As the name implies this scheme degrades gracefully into a single entry per attribute, which is useful for operating directly on compressed data. For example, instead of decoding a 16-bit entry in the above example into the 3 original values, one could instead apply 3 masks and corresponding bit-shifts to get the three single attribute dictionary values. For example:

- $(X000000000100010\ \&\ 0000000000011111) >> 0 = 00010$
- $(X000000000100010\ \&\ 0000001111100000) >> 5 = 00001$
- $(X000000000100010\ \&\ 0111110000000000) >> 10 = 00000$

These dictionary values in many cases can be operated on directly and can be decompressed at the top of the query-plan tree.

## Bit-Vector Encoding

Bit-vector encoding scheme can be most useful when columns have a limited number of possible data values for e.g. states in a country, or flag columns. In this type of encoding, a bit-string is associated with each value with a '1' in the corresponding position if that value appeared at that position and a '0' otherwise. For example, the following data:

- 1 1 3 2 2 3 1

would be represented as three bit-strings:

- bit-string for value 1: 1100001
- bit-string for value 2: 0001100
- bit-string for value 3: 0010010

Since an extended version of this scheme can be used to index row-stores so-called bit-map indices there has been much work on further compressing these bit-maps and the implications of this further compression. One needs the bit-maps to be fairly sparse on the order of 1 bit in 1000 in order for query performance to not be hindered by this further compression.

## Cache-Conscious Optimization

The decision as to whether values should be packed into how many number of bytes is decided by requiring the dictionary to fit in the cache. So depending on the memory and dataset size, we can decide on cache conscious optimization.

## Run-Length Encoding

This encoding scheme compresses runs of the same value in a column to a compact singular representation. Thus, it is well suited for columns that are sorted or that have reasonable-sized runs of the same value. In Abadi (2008), these runs are replaced with triples: (value, start position, run length) where each element of the triple is given a fixed number of bits. When used in row-oriented systems, RLE is only used for large string attributes that have many blanks or repeated characters. But RLE can be much more widely used in column-oriented systems where attributes are stored consecutively and runs of the same value are common especially in columns that have few distinct values. As the C-Store architecture results in a high percentage of columns being sorted or secondarily sorted they can provide many opportunities for RLE-type encoding.

## Heavyweight Compression Schemes

Lempel-Ziv Encoding (Welch, 1984) compression is the most widely used technique for lossless file compression. This is the algorithm upon which the UNIX command gzip is based. Lempel-Ziv takes variable sized patterns and replaces them with fixed length codes. Lempel-Ziv encoding scheme does not require knowledge about pattern frequencies in advance; it builds the pattern table dynamically as it encodes the data. The basic idea is to parse the input sequence into non-overlapping blocks of different lengths while constructing a dictionary of blocks seen thus far. Subsequent appearances of these blocks are replaced by a pointer to an earlier occurrence of the same block.

Some key benefits that compression brings to semantic Web solutions have been discussed in existing literature (Oracle White Paper, 2009). Compression gives up to 3 times or higher reduction in storage costs. These savings also extend to test, development, and backup and disaster recovery environments, further magnifying the cost savings. There is no adverse impact on query performance, as queries read the compressed version of data directly without having to decompress it. In fact, query performance may improve due to improved disk scan rate and reduction in the number of I/Os. It also enhances memory efficiency, as data in memory is in a compressed format. This allows more data to be stored in memory and reduces number of I/Os, which may improve performance.

## DATA CLUSTERING

There is a great impact in performance of a database by the manner in which data is loaded and this is true regardless of when the data is loaded; whether the data is loaded before the application begin accessing the data, or concurrently while the application are accessing the data. This can be achieved by clustering. In plain English, we can say that clustering is grouping of related items held together. In terms of database, this can be stated as a grouping of related items stored together for efficiency of access and resource utilization. Typically, clustering is nothing but collocation of data on the same physical disk page. We know that an index on a collection yields faster query performance. If the index is placed, as it is by default, in the same physical location as the collection itself

and the items in the collection, then poor locality of reference for the index items is likely to occur Or say all the items which are related to the index should be placed in close proximity to one another. All items related to the collection excluding the index should be placed in close proximity to one another. The index items should not be intermixed with the collection nor the items contained within the collection. Therefore, if we cluster the index and all the index items together in an area that is physically distinct from the collection and/or the items in the collection, the index will be faster to fetch. If there are no non-index items intermixed with the index items, then fewer pages will be required to fetch the index to perform a query or update the index.

## COMPARISON OF DATA PARTITIONING TECHNIQUES

In this section comparison between data partitioning techniques through an experiment carried out on a very small dummy RDF data is given. This helps us out to know in detail, how partitioning affects execution time. A database was created in which five subjects, five properties and five objects were considered. It was a dummy FOAF (Friend of a Friend) data set. The properties included in this experiment were name, email, homepage, knows, and interest. In which the first three are single valued attributes where as rest of the two are multi valued attributes. Initially these triples were stored as property table in the database and the following set of queries were executed on it.

- **Query 1:** Find person, the person he knows and 2nd person's homepage.
- **Query 2:** Find person1, person1 email, and person2, person2 email, where person1 knows person2.
- **Query 3:** Find people in their circle with common interest.

The data was partitioned to evaluate query performance. It was partitioned using vertical and hybrid approach. Firstly, the data was partitioned using vertical partitioning. For every property, a table was created. As we have used five properties we created five tables. For each property, these tables will be as shown (see Tables 2-5).

After creating tables and inserting data in these tables, the above queries were executed to evaluate the query performance.

The data was then partitioned using hybrid partitioning technique. For this, properties having single valued attribute were put in a single table with its subject, and rest of the two having multi valued attributes were having separate tables. So the three tables are shown in Tables 3-5).

After creating and populating the tables, the same set of queries was executed on these tables to evaluate query performance. Results of query execution time for all the above discussed technique as depicted in Table 6.

It can be seen from the Figure 3 that after partitioning the data, the query execution time

has decreased compared to flat representation of RDF data in property tables.

As stated in Abadi (2008), a significant amount of excitement and recent work is carried out on column-oriented database systems—"column-stores." These database systems have been shown to perform more than an order of magnitude better than traditional row-oriented database systems—"row-stores" on analytical workloads such as those found in data warehouses, decision support, and business intelligence applications. The reason behind this performance difference is straightforward: column-stores are more I/O efficient for read-only queries since they only have to read from disk or from memory those attributes accessed by a query. It is not impossible for a row-store to achieve some of the performance advantages of a column-store, and in order to achieve the benefits of a column-oriented approach, changes must be made to both the storage layer and the query executor to fully obtain

## DATA PARTITIONING IN PRACTICE

Partitioning can simplify the manageability of large databases. It is used in algorithms for distributed computing and many methods are devised namely Navathe method, Furd method, Furd-Fremandas method (Zorilla, 1999). Vertical Partitioning for a database can be done through graphical techniques (Navathe, 1994). Vertical and horizontal partitioning are used in automated

*Table 2.*

| Subject | Predicate |
|---------|-----------|
|         |           |

*Table 3.*

| Subject | Name | Email | Homepage |
|---------|------|-------|----------|
|         |      |       |          |

*Table 4.*

| Subject | Knows |
|---------|-------|
|         |       |

*Table 5.*

| Subject | Interest |
|---------|----------|
|         |          |

*Table 6. Query execution time for various partitioning techniques*

| Query | Vertical Partitioning (Execution time is in ms) | Hybrid Partitioning (Execution time is in ms) | Property Table (Execution time is in ms) |
|-------|------|------|------|
| Query 1 | 14 | 16 | 16 |
| Query 2 | 15 | 15 | 16 |
| Query 3 | 15 | 16 | 16 |

*Figure 3. Query execution time v/s data partitioning technique*

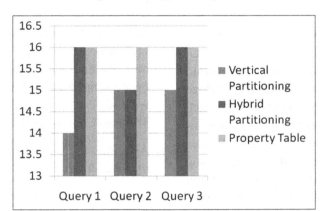

physical database design (Agrawal, 2004). It is used in Semantic Web to improve query performance and scale the semantic database. Researchers are working on how to implement this on clouds to gain maximum out of it. It is also applied on MapReduce in an experiment for HadoopDB (Abouzeid, 2009). It is used in sensor networks for storing and accessing data frequently (Abadi, 2004). This is widely used in data warehousing

as there are number of fetching operations compared to other operations. Data, which is shared and accessed across various application, needs partitioning techniques to improve performance, scale data and utilize storage space. It is used in temporal and transactional databases. Efficient query processing is carried out in split execution environment using partitioning (Pawlikowski, 2011).

*Figure 4. Research methodology*

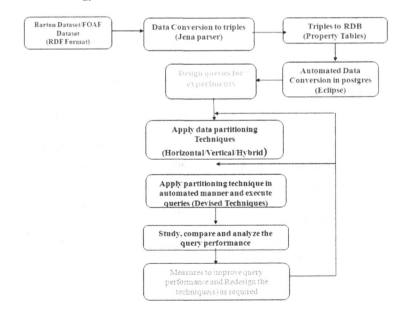

## FUTURE DIRECTION

We are working on scaling up Semantic Web and improve query performance. This research will analyze the query performance and will find ways to improve it. This work will also analyze and devise methods or techniques through which semantic data can be scaled up. The research intends to conduct experiment on Barton libraries dataset as an RDF benchmark data. Partitioning techniques will be applied on this data set and query performance will be evaluated in terms of query execution time and scalability.

Barton data set is to be used as benchmark experiment database, which have 50,000,000 triples. Data is converted to triples using Jena parser. As Barton data set is huge in size that is around 6 G.B after decompression and goes till 750 GB after converting the data to triple. A tool can be created to insert data in postgres. Here postgres will be used as database tool to store or replicate data in vertical or horizontal partitioning. As the data is quite huge at present the work will be carried on FOAF dataset which contains about 201616 triple. The flow of the work is depicted in Figure 4.

## SUMMARY

The chapter shows various techniques which can help in improving query performance for semantic data. It gives glimpse of various compression techniques and clustering which can be used in addition to the partitioning approach in order to improve query performance. A prototype experiment is demonstrated through which comparison between partitioning techniques can be done. Again it will vary from one RDF data to other. Research is going on different aspects of improving query performance and scaling up the semantic Web data.

## REFERENCES

Abadi, D., Lindner, W., Madden, S., & Schuler, J. (2004). An integration framework for sensor networks and data stream management systems. In *Proceedings of the Thirtieth International Conference on Very Large Data Bases*, (pp. 1361-1364). Toronto, Canada: IEEE.

Abadi, D. J. (2008). *Query execution in column-oriented database system.* Cambridge, MA: MIT.

Abadi, D. J., Madden, S. R., & Hachem, N. (2008). Column-stores vs. row-stores: How different are they really? [ACM Press.]. *Proceedings of SIGMOD, 2008*, 967–980. doi:10.1145/1376616.1376712

Abouzeid, A., Bajda-Pawlikowski, K., Abadi, D., Silberschatz, A., & Rasin, A. (2009). HadoopDB: An architectural hybrid of MapReduce and DBMS technologies for analytical workloads. *Proceedings of the VLDB Endowment, 2*(1).

Agrawal, S., Narasayya, V., & Yang, B. (2004). Integrating vertical and horizontal partitioning into automated physical database design. In *Proceedings of the 2004 ACM SIGMOD International Conference on Management of Data.* Paris, France: ACM Press.

Navathe, S., Ceri, S., Wiederhold, G., & Dou, J. (1984). Vertical partitioning algorithms for database design: A graphical algorithm. *ACM Transactions on Database Systems, 9*(4), 680–710. doi:10.1145/1994.2209

Oracle White Paper. (2009). *Advanced performance and scalability for semantic web applications.* Oracle.

Padiya, T., Ahir, M., Bhise, M., & Chaudhary, S. (2012). Data partitioning for semantic web. *International Journal of Computer and Communication Technology, 3*(2), 32–35.

Pawlikowski, K., Abadi, D., Silberschatz, A., & Paulson, E. (2011). Efficient processing of data warehousing queries in a split execution environment. In *Proceedings of the 2011 International Conference on Management of Data, SIGMOD 2011*. ACM Press.

W3. (2001). SWAD-Europe deliverable 10.1: Scalability and storage: Survey of free software/open source RDF storage systems. Retrieved from http://www.w3.org/2001/sw/Europe/reports/rdf_scalable_storage_report/

Welch, T. A. (1984). A technique for high-performance data compression. *Computer*, *17*(6), 8–19. doi:10.1109/MC.1984.1659158

Zorilla, M., Mora, E., Corcuera, P., & Frenandez, J. (1999). Vertical partitioning algorithms in distributed databases. In *Proceedings on Computer Aided Systems Theory, EUROCAST 1999*. EUROCAST.

# Chapter 9
# Metamodels Construction Based on the Definition of Domain Ontologies

**Carlos Enrique Montenegro-Marin**
*Universidad Distrital "Francisco José de Caldas", Colombia*

**Juan Manuel Cueva Lovelle**
*Universidad de Oviedo, Spain*

**Rubén González Crespo**
*Universidad Pontificia de Salamanca, Spain*

**B. Cristina Pelayo García-Bustelo**
*Universidad de Oviedo, Spain*

**Oscar Sanjuán Martínez**
*Universidad Carlos III de Madrid, Spain*

**Patricia Ordóñez de Pablos**
*Universidad de Oviedo, Spain*

## ABSTRACT

*This chapter proposes a mechanism for mapping domain ontologies to metamodels by a direct mechanism; this proposal is necessary because there is no formal mechanism for obtaining requirements in model driven engineering. Specifically, here the authors propose the use of a domain ontology as the main input for defining metamodels. They define a point in common between domain ontologies and metamodels to apply a method of direct conversion between domain ontology and the metamodel. At the end of the chapter, the authors present a real case study in which they use the technique described and the conclusions of the investigation.*

## INTRODUCTION

One of questions of model-driven engineering is how to start building a metamodel. The formal part of the requirements engineering is so important in any software development process and the whole project in general. Many authors have raised the possibility of using ontologies to meet this need.

We propose the use of a domain ontology as the main input for defining metamodels.

Papers such as "Bridging Metamodels and Ontologies in Software Engineering" in which the authors present and investigate the literature on both metamodelling and ontologies in order to identify ways in which they can be made compatible and linked in such a way as to ben-

DOI: 10.4018/978-1-4666-2494-8.ch009

Copyright © 2013, IGI Global. Copying or distributing in print or electronic forms without written permission of IGI Global is prohibited.

efit both communities and create a contribution to a coherent underpinning theory for software engineering. Analysis of a large number of theoretical and semi-theoretical approaches using as a framework a multi-level modelling construct identifies strengths, weaknesses, incompatibilities, and inconsistencies within the extant literature. A metamodel deals with conceptual definitions while an ontology deals with real-world descriptors of business entities and is thus better named "domain ontology." A specific kind of ontology (foundational or high-level) provides "metalevel" concepts for the domain ontologies. In other words, a foundational ontology may be used at the same abstraction level as a metamodel and a domain ontology at the same abstraction level as a (design) model, with each pair linked via an appropriate semantic mapping (Henderson-Sellers, 2011), and "Ontologies, Meta-Models, and the Model Driven Paradigm" that presents meta-modelling hierarchy that is aware of ontologies—that is, an ontology-aware mega-model of MDE. Based on the insight of that the main difference of models and ontologies lies in their descriptive prescriptiveness, the role of ontologies in this meta-pyramid is to describe the existing world, the environment, and the domain of the system (analysis), while the role of system models is to specify and control the system under study itself on various levels of abstraction (design and implementation). Consequently, in this scheme, MDE starts from ontologies, refines, and augments them towards system models, respecting their relationships to prescriptive models on all metalevels (Aßmann, Zschaler, & Wagner, 2006), are the main basis for this proposal.

This chapter presents the reader a formal method to map an ontology in a metamodel. However, more importantly it also presents a methodology for obtaining a domain ontology and with the domain ontology is shown how map it to a metamodel of M1 or M2 level. In addition, it shows a scenario where this methodology was used to obtain an ontology of LMS platforms which was then transformed to a metamodel to finally make a visual domain-specific-language—DSL. With this, we use the DSL for modeling a course to be deployed on any platform specific LMS.

The chapter is organized as follows: first there are some basics on Ontologies, then presents a chapter that describes how ontologies relate to metamodels, then explain the concepts of Model Driven Engineering—MDE—and metamodels, then addresses how to map an ontology to a metamodel, and finally presents a case study and the conclusions.

## ONTOLOGY CONCEPTS

Much information is found regarding the issue of ontology; for this reason, the definitions in the area of ontologies are taken from *Ontology Development 101: A Guide to Creating Your First Ontology* (Natalya & Deborah, 2005). It is official guidance provided by Stanford University and founder of Protege (Stanford Center for Biomedical Informatics Research, 2010), which is the most used tool in the creation of ontologies.

The Semantic Web literature contains several definitions of ontology. In addition, many definitions contradict others definitions. In order to standardize definitions in this chapter, an ontology is a formal and explicit concepts in a specific domain (classes [also called concepts]), properties of these concepts that contain various features and attributes (slots [also called roles or properties]). Finally, also have restrictions on the properties (facets [also called role restrictions]). An ontology together with a group of individuals of classes constitutes a knowledge base. Actually, there is a fine line where the ontology ends and the knowledge base begins. Classes are the focus of most ontologies. And the classes describe concepts in a domain (Natalya & Deborah, 2005).

## Why Use Ontologies?

Ontologies offer several useful features for intelligent systems in the process of knowledge engineering. These features are analyzed below.

## Vocabulary in an Ontology

An ontology provides a vocabulary to describe the different terms in a particular area. Ontologies consist of logical statements that describe the meaning of the terms of vocabulary and how they relate in a way that allow to extend vocabulary. An ontology specifies terms whose meaning is not ambiguous, so that the ontologies use semantics independent of the reader and the context.

## Taxonomy in a Ontology

A taxonomy is a classification of entities in a given domain. A good taxonomy separates its entities in groups and subgroups mutually exclusive and unambiguous.

All ontologies provided a taxonomy in a format suitable to be read and processed by a machine. On the other hand, an ontology is more than its corresponding taxonomy, is a complete specification of a domain. The vocabulary and taxonomy included in the ontology, provides a conceptual framework that is useful for the analysis and information retrieval in a particular domain.

## Reuse of Knowledge Sharing

The main objective of ontologies is not to serve as a vocabulary or taxonomy; the main objective of ontologies is they are used as a source for knowledge sharing and reuse by applications. For this reason, it is essential that all ontology provided a description of the concepts and relationships that exist in a domain, which can be exchanged and reused by other applications.

## Application Areas of Ontologies

There are many possible applications for ontologies, but Ciocoiu, Nau, and Gruninger (2001) shows a number of key application areas:

- **Collaboration**: Different people may have different views on a particular problem when working in a team project. This is really important in interdisciplinary areas, a place where reside specialists from different areas of knowledge. For these specialists the ontologies provide a unified framework of knowledge that can be used as a common reference and unified.
- **Interoperability**: The ontologies allow the integration of information from different systems. As an end user is not interested to know where the information that he use, but he need get the information you need and get the maximum performance. Distributed applications may need to access different formats and levels of detail. However, if all recognize the same ontologies systems. The data conversion and integration of data are easier to carry out automatically.
- **Education**: The ontologies are the result of a broad consensus about the domain it represents; the ontologies are a source of reliable and objective information for those who want to learn about a domain.
- **Model:** The ontologies can serve as pre-fabricated blocks of knowledge that can be used for many applications. For example, an ontology of the clothes could be used on websites selling clothes online, or in education systems to find information about clothing.

# SEMANTIC WEB, ONTOLOGIES, AND RELATIONS WITH THE METAMODELS

The part of the computer science that studies the ontologies is the Semantic Web. There are many definitions on the Semantic Web as "The Web more understandable by machines" (Heflin & Hendler, 2001) or "Semantic Web is about building an appropriate infrastructure for intelligent agents to run around the Web performing complex actions for their users" (Hendler, 2001). Also defined as "Semantic Web is about explicit declaring the knowledge embedded in main Web-based applications, integrant information in a intelligent way, providing semantic-based access to the Internet, and extracting information from text" (Asunci, Mez, & Rez, 2002) or "Semantic Web is about how to implement reliable, large-scale interoperation of Web services, to make such services computer interpretable, to create a Web of machine-understandable and interoperable services that intelligent agents can discover and compose automatically" (McIlraith, Son, & Honglei, 2001). The reason why there are many definitions on the Semantic Web is the heterogeneity of the Web, so that the definitions are adapted according to different contexts where they are used. Currently much of the information on the Web is presented in a natural language that machines cannot understand, the Semantic Web is necessary to express the information in a manner accurate and interpretable by machines.

The reason for using an ontology to model knowledge is that ontologies provide all the features of vocabulary and taxonomy needed to specify a domain of knowledge.

Models are an abstraction of reality bounded, they represent a particular point of view, the models necessarily must be limited and omit details depending the point of view, for example Guizzardi (2005a) defined the models as "A model is an abstraction of reality according to a certain conceptualization." In addition, the meta-model is simply a modeling language. Pardillo and Cachero (2010) show the existence of two metamodels: UML (Unified Model Language) and DI (Diagram Interchange) that covering different purposes. García-Magariño, Fuentes-Fernández, and Gómez-Sanz (2009) suggested that the metamodel is a mechanism for defining the abstract syntax of a modeling language. To determine the validity of the models in these languages the OMG (Object Management Group) explains the relationship between models and metamodels as the definition of a modeling language under the MOF (Meta Object Facility) architecture (Group, 2007).

The affirmation that "an ontology is a metamodel describing how to build models" (Devedzi, 2002), related directly to ontologies with the models, because they are the description of these models. Therefore, with this definition we conclude that from an ontology can get a metamodel, and starting from here, then it will show a methodology to define a metamodel which have a start point in the definition of a specific domain with ontologies. First, we must present the basic concepts of Model Driven Engineering—MDE.

# MODEL DRIVEN ENGINEERING (MDE)

To make a connection between ontologies and models is necessary to talk before of the models in the context of model driven engineering. MDE arises as the response of software engineering to the industrialization of software development, Model Driven Architecture—MDA—is the proposal of OMG, which focuses its efforts to recognize that interoperability is essential and the development of models allows the development of others models. That after to do a process of union, is generated the solution an entire system and independent of the development of specific technologies (Stephen, Kendall, Axel, & Dirk, 2004).

It has been seen as the level of abstraction of the different programming languages has increased for decades; this can be seen as an evolution in programming languages, in this sense before spoken of binary languages, then the assembler, later in procedural languages, then object oriented languages, the latter supported by various artifacts such as UML. Now we talk about building those models like UML; this has been called MDA. Although the level of abstraction increases and is closer to the specific domain on which to work, so anyone could get to make a model using the knowledge of context. And complexity moves to see how this model becomes a functional solution and can be deployed on any specific technology.

A good interpretation of what is a model, a metamodel and a meta-metamodel is shown in García Díaz and Cueva Lovelle (2010). There, a metamodel is defined as those tools that allows the creation of a model; the model is a description of one or more elements of the domain or the real world and finally the meta-metamodel describes these metamodels, generating an extremely high degree of abstraction in which all models agree (see Figure 1).

According to García Díaz and Cueva Lovelle (2010), there are four areas of modeling: baseline levels M0 are the elements of the real world, the levels M1 are classes, UML, software, among others, levels M2 would be the specification of UML, ODM, Java, C #, XML, or other, and finally, levels M3 that are the more abstract. Basically, there are two meta-metamodels raised, on the one hand this MOF and on the other hand this EBNF, as shown in Figure 2.

The idea of generating these levels of abstraction is to provide a common mechanism to allow through transformation from one model to an-

other interoperability of systems. An explicit definition of what is MDA, is found below:

"The Model Driven Architecture (MDA) is a framework for software development defined by the Object Management Group (OMG). Key to MDA is the importance of models in the software development process. Within MDA the software development process is driven by the activity of modeling your software system" (Kleppe, Warmer, & Bast, 2003).

MDA focuses on the generation of models, so their life cycle focuses on creating models and in no way alters the traditional life cycle software development, only that the generation of artifacts is changed, and some of them as the passage of a PIM (Platform Independent Model) to PSM (Platform Specific Model) and then to code is done automatically. This transformations is called "transformations starting from the generated models" so that if there is a change in the system, takes place in the overall model, and for the deployment of the solution is necessary, repeats the process of transformations between models. Figure 3 shows the life cycle of software development with MDA.

The artifact that meets the requirements of the system is called the CIM (Computation Independent Model), the result of modeling this system is a PIM, that is built with a DSL (Domain Specific Language) previously built. This DSL generates through a process of transforming a PSM, which through another transformation becomes in code or Implementation Specific Model—ISM—this process is shown in Figure 4.

*Figure 1. Model, metamodel, and meta-metamodel*

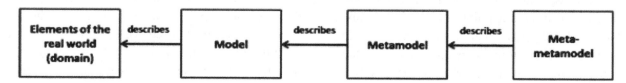

*Figure 2. Model spaces*

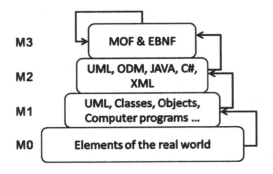

## CONVERSION OF A DOMAIN ONTOLOGY TO METAMODEL

This chapter will describe the proposal to define metamodels from domain ontologies (Guizzardi, 2005b). The first step is to determine a common point between these two concepts metamodels and domain ontologies. This point of convergence in the two cases is that both seek to define a domain specific and limited of concepts that are well

*Figure 3. MDA software development life cycle (Kleppe, et al., 2003)*

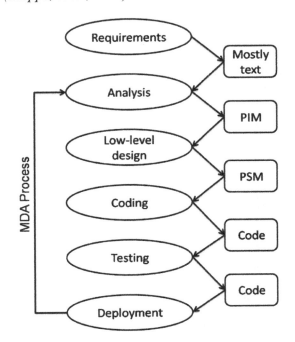

described and well defined structurally for use in computer systems.

Thus, although the ontologies are used in the philosophy, epistemology, artificial intelligence, and Semantic Web, and the metamodels in software engineering. The point of convergence allows us to convert a domain ontology in a metamodel. That defines a concrete modeling space, this need arises because in model driven engineering describe the way how to obtain computing solutions from metamodels, but never describes a way to get these metamodels, in this sense, is where we find that domain ontologies can provide this mechanism of definition, which is necessary in model driven engineering.

Clearly, there are mechanisms and accepted recommendations on how to define ontologies,

*Figure 4. MDA complete deployment process with MDE*

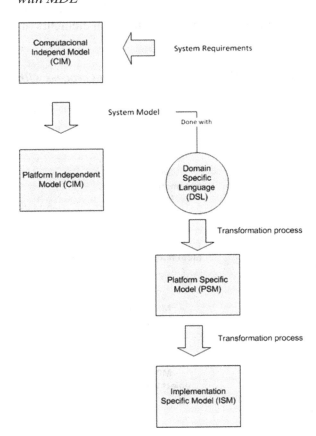

as raised in Natalya and Deborah (2005), this recommendation has seven steps:

1. Determine the domain and scope of the ontology.
2. Consider reusing existing ontologies.
3. Enumerate important terms in the ontology.
4. Define the classes and the class hierarchy.
5. Define the properties of classes—slots.
6. Define the facets of the slots.
7. Create instances.

Of these seven steps, in the sixth stage, we get at the domain ontology, to which we can apply a process of parsing to generate a metamodel. In the process of generation of the metamodel, the knowledge could be transformed to meet the needs of the system. Bringing the metamodel is not an accurate representation of the domain ontology. For the mapping between ontology and metamodel, we used the proposed of Henderson-Sellers (2011), which posits a relationship between elements of the domain ontology and the metamodel; this approach in turn is an adaptation of the proposed of Aßmann et al. (2006). The mapping process can be seen in Figure 5.

Guizzardi (2007) further argues that this approach allows the comparison of conceptualizations as intensional structures and metamodels as represented by logical theories. The real world abstractions are related to a domain ontology while the conceptualizations can be depicted using a foundational ontology. Henderson-Sellers (2011) claims an ontology is a conceptual model, sharing characteristics with more traditional data models.

However, an ontology can be mapped to a metamodel of level M1 or M2 but not both at the same time and this process is done using the methodology proposed in Henderson-Sellers (2011); this proposed used the powertype pattern (Brian, 2008) and this way we can make direct mapping as shown in Figure 6.

*Figure 5. MDA complete deployment process with MDE (Henderson-Sellers, 2011; Aßmann, et al., 2006)*

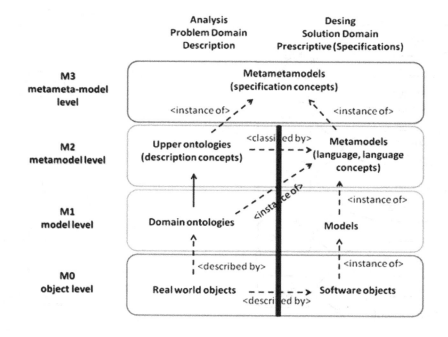

*Figure 6. Integration of the powertype pattern and a semantic mapping between the model and the ontology (Henderson-Sellers, 2011)*

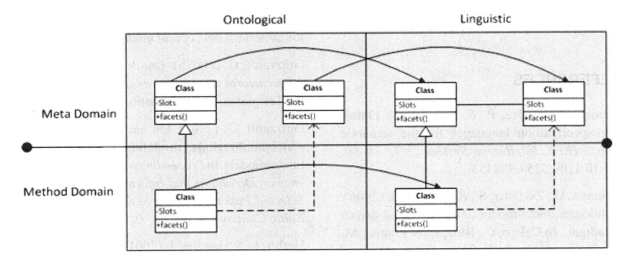

As shown in Figure 6, the mapping between ontology and metamodel is straightforward, but is necessary considering that this mapping can be done for M1 or M2 level of the structure of MDA, in no case can mix the more than one level.

## CASE STUDY: DOMAIN SPECIFIC LANGUAGE FOR THE GENERATION OF LEARNING MANAGEMENT SYSTEMS MODULES

In these research projects have shown that there are LMS platforms with different architectures and inoperative to each other. The most significant contribution of MDE has been the creation of a common meta-metamodel. This meta-metamodel allows transformations between different models. This research work presents a LMS metamodel. The metamodel created is based on the study of five LMS platforms and of the ontology obtained from this study. The LMS metamodel is a global model that makes a bridge for the transformation of modules between the model and different LMS platforms, and it also presents the development

of a Domain Specific Language (DSL) tool to validate the metamodel, the transformation process of the model with our DSL Tool to modules deployed in Moodle, Claroline, and Atutor, and finally testing and validation of creating modules with LMS platforms VS creating modules with our DSL Tool (Montenegro-Marin, Cueva-Lovelle, Martínez, & García-Díaz, 2012; Montenegro-Marin, Cueva-Lovelle, Sanjuan-Martinez, & Neñez-Valdes, 2011).

## CONCLUSION AND FUTURE RESEARCH WORK

In conclusion, the Model Driven Engineering raises no formal mechanism to start the process of modeling domain; this is can be supplied with the application of techniques for defining the domain that ontologies use, since these techniques are quite formal and comprehensive.

For the mapping between the domain ontology and metamodel, we can use the proposed of Henderson-Sellers (2011). However, it is necessary to consider that we cannot mix different levels mapping, and this mapping is done directly.

In this process of mapping, there is a large work area to finally achieve automatic mapping.

## REFERENCES

Asunci, G., & Mez, P., & Rez. (2002). Ontology specification languages for the semantic web. *IEEE Intelligent Systems*, *17*, 54–60. doi:10.1109/5254.988453

Aßmann, U., Zschaler, S., & Wagner, G. (2006). Ontologies, meta-models, and the model-driven paradigm . In Calero, C., Ruiz, F., & Piattini, M. (Eds.), *Ontologies for Software Engineering and Software Technology* (pp. 249–273). Berlin, Germany: Springer. doi:10.1007/3-540-34518-3_9

Brian, H.-S. (2008). *Connecting powertypes and stereotypes*. Retrieved from http://www.jot.fm/issues/issue_2005_09/article3.pdf

Ciocoiu, M., Nau, D. S., & Gruninger, M. (2001). Ontologies for integrating engineering applications. *Journal of Computing and Information Science in Engineering*, *1*(1), 12–22. doi:10.1115/1.1344878

Devedzi, V. (2002). Understanding ontological engineering. *Communications of the ACM*, *45*(4), 136–144. doi:10.1145/505248.506002

García Díaz, V., & Cueva Lovelle, J. M. (2010). *Ingeniería dirigida por modelos* [presentations ]. Oviedo.

García-Magariño, I., Fuentes-Fernández, R., & Gómez-Sanz, J. J. (2009). Guideline for the definition of EMF metamodels using an entity-relationship approach. *Information and Software Technology*, *51*(8), 1217–1230. doi:10.1016/j.infsof.2009.02.003

Group, O. M. (2007). *MOF 2.0/XMI mapping, version 2.1.1* (p. 120). Object Management Group.

Guizzardi, G. (2005a). *Ontological foundations for structural conceptual models*. Enschede.

Guizzardi, G. (2005b). *Ontological foundations for structural conceptual models. CTIT*. Centre for Telematics and Information Technology.

Guizzardi, G. (2007). On ontology, ontologies, conceptualizations, modeling languages, and (meta)models. In *Proceedings of the 2007 Conference on Databases and Information Systems IV: Selected Papers from the Seventh International Baltic Conference*. IEEE.

Heflin, J., & Hendler, J. (2001). A portrait of the semantic web in action. *IEEE Intelligent Systems*, *16*(2), 54–59. doi:10.1109/5254.920600

Henderson-Sellers, B. (2011). Bridging metamodels and ontologies in software engineering. *Journal of Systems and Software*, *84*(2), 301–313. doi:10.1016/j.jss.2010.10.025

Hendler, J. (2001). Agents and the semantic web. *IEEE Intelligent Systems*, *16*(2), 30–37. doi:10.1109/5254.920597

Kleppe, A., Warmer, J., & Bast, W. (2003). *MDA explained: The model driven architecture™: Practice and promise*. Reading, MA: Addison Wesley.

McIlraith, S. A., Son, T. C., & Honglei, Z. (2001). Semantic web services. *IEEE Intelligent Systems*, *16*(2), 46–53. doi:10.1109/5254.920599

Montenegro-Marin, C. E., Cueva-Lovelle, J. C., Sanjuan-Martinez, O., & Neñez-Valdes, E. R. (2011). Towards an ontology to describe the taxonomy of common modules in learning management systems. *International Jorunal of Interactive Multimedia and Artificial Intelligence*, *1*, 47–53.

Montenegro-Marin, C. E., Cueva-Lovelle, J. M., Martínez, O. S., & García-Díaz, V. (2012). Domain specific language for the generation of learning management systems modules. *Journal of Web Engineering, 11*(1), 23–50.

Natalya, F. N., & Deborah, L. M. (2005). *Ontology development 101: A guide to creating your first ontology*. Palo Alto, CA: Stanford.

Pardillo, J., & Cachero, C. (2010). Domain-specific language modelling with UML profiles by decoupling abstract and concrete syntaxes. *Journal of Systems and Software, 83*(12), 2591–2606. doi:10.1016/j.jss.2010.08.019

Stanford Center for Biomedical Informatics Research. (2010). *Protege ontology library*. Retrieved Nov, 2010, from http://protegewiki. stanford.edu/wiki/Protege_Ontology_Library

# Chapter 10
# Knowledge Building in Online Environments:
## Constraining and Enabling Collective Intelligence

**Craig Deed**
*La Trobe University, Australia*

**Anthony David Edwards**
*Liverpool Hope University, UK*

## ABSTRACT

*This chapter describes two conceptual frameworks for the analysis of online knowledge building: outsideness and developing adaptive expertise. The affordances of the metaphor of outsideness are outlined in relation to the construction of knowledge through the sharing and exploration of personal and cultural perspectives, asking questions to resolve doubt, and as a driver of purposeful academic conversation. Developing expertise is examined through the identification of the knowledge and skills for idea generation and evaluation in online environments, and optimal engagement in these learning contexts. A case study is provided of higher education students from three countries working together using a wiki to construct knowledge about teaching and learning. The authors present these two frameworks in order to increase understanding of the knowledge and skills needed by students in higher education to engage with the affordances of collective intelligence systems.*

## INTRODUCTION

Online social interaction is an engaging feature of current technology use among contemporary students in higher education. However, previous research has indicated that while students may be adept at using digital technology to stay in touch, arrange meetings or discuss the latest news; they are less likely to engage in academic purposes unless there is a genuine need to do so (Deed & Edwards, 2011).

DOI: 10.4018/978-1-4666-2494-8.ch010

Copyright © 2013, IGI Global. Copying or distributing in print or electronic forms without written permission of IGI Global is prohibited.

While current dialogue in higher education emphasizes the potential of online learning environments to support learning, there remains uncertainty about how to use Web 2.0 technologies to help students learn (Starkey, 2010). A key concern is how to move higher education students from the potential chaos and idiosyncrasies of Web surfing to a coherent and rich learning experience resulting in generation and exploration of knowledge. Grace-Martin et al. (2001, p. 104) noted that the educational benefits of unfettered network access may exist "for some populations in some contexts, but that characteristics of the user and his/her educational environment may limit or even reverse these benefits when measured in terms of academic performance." Purposeful engagement in a virtual text-based context is likely to be dependent on the extent to which students recognize the distance between potential opportunities and actual capacity to engage in online interactions and the development and application of strategies and working practices to overcome these difficulties.

Two principal questions are examined in this chapter. First, what affords the active participation of higher education students in collective intelligence systems? Then, what knowledge and skills do students need to cope with the dynamics of collective intelligence systems? The first question is addressed through the metaphor of outsideness – engaging with distant peers using Web 2.0 tools. In particular, the affordances of outsideness are identified that support the development of higher education students' capacity to generate and engage with the concept of collective intelligence. Bakhtin (1986, p. 142) suggests this outsideness, which can result from the very act of trying to understand others "… results in mutual change and enrichment."

Here, outsideness is conceived of as a key influence in online environments where students have the potential to engage in rich, thoughtful, and purposeful conversational moments. Outsideness influences the construction of knowledge in online collaborative contexts through sharing and exploration of personal and cultural perspectives; asking questions to resolve doubt; and as a driver of purposeful conversation.

The second question is examined using the concept of adaptive expertise, a term first employed by Hatano and Inagaki (1986) and further developed by Schwartz et al. (2005). A distinguishing feature of adaptive expertise is the application of knowledge to novel or unusual situations. This concept is explored through identification of knowledge and skills for idea generation and evaluation in online environments, and optimal engagement in these learning contexts. A case study is then presented of collective intelligence, using pre-service teaching students and others studying education related degrees from three countries working together using a wiki. Factors that constrained and enabled collective intelligence are identified and implications drawn for learning in higher education.

This chapter contributes to educational discourse about the need to provide a structure that balances providing scope for individuals to make decisive choices about their own learning, and supports students develop conversational capacity in online learning communities.

## COLLECTIVE INTELLIGENCE

Collective intelligence generally refers to the seeking or creation of new knowledge at the intersection of the social and Semantic Web. In sum, the process is afforded through Web 2.0 tools and both draws upon and challenges the notion of the expert and expert knowledge.

The Web 2.0 tools that have enabled collective intelligence—for example: wikis and blogs, hyper-linking, Rich Site Summary (RSS) and Google—are essentially a set of philosophically similar practices and principles that aim to harness the power of the Internet (O'Reilly, 2007). Although the general features of collective intelligence are described below, it is not possible to definitively articulate this dynamic meta-concept.

Gruber (2007) identifies the main elements of collective knowledge systems as (1) user-generated content through participative social interaction; and (2) a synergy between people—the source of experience and ideas—and computers—providing a means of linking people and storing searchable data—resulting in a rapid increase in the volume of information being constructed online. This is evident in sites such as Wikipedia where the more people accessing and using the site increases the validity and usefulness of the information; leading to gains in knowledge and understanding beyond the collected information.

Numerous examples of digital collective intelligence are in day-to-day use in modern society, formed through semantic and social processes in both formal and informal ways. One common element is that an individual has to deliberately seek, draw together, and engage with a collective intelligence system by assembling a number of disparate Web 2.0 tools and practices. This may range from a simple personal blog with hyperlinks and interaction with followers to the more formally structured and comprehensive online specialist community.

An online bookstore is an example of how collective intelligence has been commercially normalized in contemporary society. The more time you spend online in a store the better able the website is able to determine your preferences and make recommendations based on your browsing and buying selections, and make use of other customers with a similar buying history. You have the opportunity to read other customer's reviews of books, and generate and access literary interest groups through links to blogs and other sites (leading to further linkages).

This is a mix of how stored search, browse and purchase data (the Semantic Web) can be linked to the experiences and interests of individual and sub-groups of individuals (the Social Web). This example demonstrates how collective intelligence

can be construed as a means of rapid gathering, representing and exploring ideas from a global information system that the user has a part in constructing and shaping.

In education settings, collective intelligence structures are evident in multiple variants, including students interacting with known and unknown peers, sharing ideas and hyperlinks to useful resources and ideas, generating and exploring ideas—learning within and about the process of collaborative knowledge construction in digital contexts. This chapter is focused on the social interactions that characterise the efforts of higher education students to generate and explore knowledge through Web-based intellectual cooperation, commonly known as an online learning community.

Lee and Lan (2007) and others make the claim that knowledge emerging through Web-based interaction challenges the notion of top-down expertise. Expertise is thought of, in terms of collective intelligence, as more expansive and distributed although available online via formal and informal means. Sharples, Taylor, and Vavoula (2007, p. 222) comment that "We learn across space as we take ideas and learning resources gained in one location and apply or develop them in another."

Table 1 offers a somewhat blunt comparison between traditional models of information transmission compared to the principles of collective intelligence. This model is offered here as a basis for dialogue and questions are invited concerning conceptual similarities and differences. The comparison has been deliberately constructed to show how, in a collective intelligence system, the responsibility for effortful seeking, translating, and judging information, in order to construct knowledge, moves from an expert to the individual higher education student. Expert knowledge remains a key component of both systems, although within a collective intelligence system the 'expert' has been fragmented and scattered through time and cyber-space.

*Table 1. A comparison of two learning models: transmissive and collective intelligence*

| | **Transmissive model** | **Collective intelligence** |
|---|---|---|
| Driving philosophy | Hierarchical; idea interrogation; prescriptive; sensorial | Open; idea generation; disruptive |
| Responsibility for developing meaning | Expert structures, chunks and transmits information | Individual must locate, interpret, interact with, and assess usability of information |
| Questioning | Expert models or provides modes of interrogation | Individual conducts analysis and evaluation |
| Information | Formal; structured; validated | Formal and informal; varying quality; raw ideas are 'in-play' |
| Language | Academic; inter-cultural; largely text based; conventional | Inter- and intra-cultural; multi-modal, including 'txt' |
| Mindset of learner | Respect for expert; waits to be authorised to think and act | Questions expertise; acts within and beyond tacit boundaries |
| Interaction with peers | Orderly and expert-directed within set time and space e.g. classroom | Individual opts in and out; varying intensity of effort; a loose network across time and space |

The notion that knowledge can be gathered in a relatively simple joining-the-dots exercise has been qualified by a number of researchers. Moving from the rigid strictures of a traditional expert to student transmissive model to a chaotic or even disruptively democratic process introduces uncertainty about how to interact with and judge information. The question of the future role and place of the expert can reasonably be raised at this point. Bothos, Apostolou, and Mentzas (2009) argue that strong and rich interaction requires a degree of expert input to moderate uncertainty involved in evaluation of ideas. Similarly, Lee and Lan (2007) note the need for not only vigorous and rich interaction, but a process to resolve conflicting perspectives.

An individual student, for example, researching a topic may access pockets of (what may or may not be) expert knowledge including current research literature, blogs from eminent thinkers or practitioners, a YouTube clip other students have made attempting to explain the topic under investigation—all identified from a Google search; and then attempt to clarify and edit the collected ideas via a wiki with class peers. The possibilities for action and the choices made by the student within this virtual system offer a mix of rich potential and frustrating dead-ends and confusion. Siemens (2005, p. 4), commenting on contemporary learning models afforded through digital landscapes indicated that:

*Learning is a process that occurs within nebulous environments of shifting core elements—not entirely under the control of the individual. Learning ... is focused on connecting specialized information sets, and the connections that enable us to learn more are more important than our current state of knowing.*

This is an influential argument from a pure model of collective intelligence. There is already considerable overlap between the social constructivist ideals of a collective intelligence system, and the co-regulated or blended learning formats of many contemporary approaches to learning in higher education. The principal means of comparison between the traditional and emergent systems of learning is the use of academic conversation to engage with ideas.

Online interaction has often been conceived of in terms of conversation (Bothos, et al., 2009; Laurillard, 2009; Sharples, et al., 2007). Sharples et al. (2007, p. 225), for example, assert that:

*Conversation is the driving process of learning. It is the means by which we negotiate differences, understand each other's experiences and form transiently stable interpretations of the world.*

Laurillard (2009) provides a conversational framework or map explicating the process of collaborative learning in online environments. This framework assumes a purpose and intensity that defines academic conversation. For instance, interaction characterising knowledge building may include posting comments, ideas and asking questions of other participants, adapting explanations, or ideas in response to feedback, peer-based discussion, representation of collective ideas, and personal and critical reflection on the experience. Academic conversation may include interactions that are informal and reactive, moments of intensity mixed with disengagement; as well as tangential mental doodling through imaginative abstract sketches. However, academic conversation among students is frequently bounded or shaped by the pragmatic need to reach a task-focused resolution. Moving from the generation and exploration of ideas to a coherent and credible end-point remains a fundamental although complex part of academic conversation; necessary to bind the anarchic tendencies of informal Web-based social dialogic interaction (Riedl, Blohm, Leimeister, & Krcmar, 2010).

The purpose of academic conversation is potentially at odds with the inherent strength of the collective intelligence concept, as illustrated by Bonabeau's (2009) comment that online academic conversations may be better at generating ideas than evaluation, although this may be mediated if participants actively resolved issues of motivation and purpose, diversity, accuracy and quality.

Collective intelligence is defined here as the deliberate employment of Web 2.0 tools across a distributed, although loose, network of peers and information in order to enact a purposeful academic conversation (concerned with generat-

ing, exploring, and evaluating knowledge). This leads to the following discussion concerning the affordances collective intelligence offers for academic conversation; and the skills and knowledge required to harvest this potential.

# THE AFFORDANCES OF OUTSIDENESS FOR COLLECTIVE INTELLIGENCE

Here the metaphor of outsideness is defined and affordances identified for collective intelligence. A summary of the ideas utilized in this section is shown in Table 2.

Affordances are features of a context that allow or potentially contribute to the resultant activity (Greeno, 1994).

*Table 2. The affordances of outsideness for collective intelligence*

| Outsideness concepts | Affordances for collective intelligence |
|---|---|
| Interscholastic correspondence (Freinet, 1969) | Representation and communication of ideas to distant peers |
| Expansive learning (Engestrom, 1987) | Deliberately seeking tensions, arguments, differences, contradictions etc from peers with diverse perspectives in order to generate ideas |
| Knowledge as distributed and collective (Lankshear & Knobel, 2007) | Learning perceived as dynamic, involving both formal and informal sources, and an openness to new ideas |
| Written conversation in a specific, although open community (Enyedy & Hoadley, 2006) | Purposeful conversation to share, explore and build ideas – seeking agreement within a cohesive community |
| Interplay, interpretation and refining of ideas through exploratory academic conversation (Palincsar, 1998; Yelland, Cope, & Kalantzis, 2008) | Progressively cycling through sharing, explanation and questioning, based on a sense of doubt, applying higher standards of analysis and evaluation to make sense of new ideas and experiences, leading to idea building and revision |

Outsideness serves as a useful metaphor to model how students engage in dialogue through Web 2.0 technology. In a technologically-infused context outsideness refers to an individual's sense of cultural differences among peers as a stimulus for a rich, interactive and complex learning conversation. It is construed as a positive friction that heightens openness to possibility and uncertainty about meaning.

Although the concept of outsideness was primarily developed by the geographer Edward Relph (1976) as a means of explaining an individual's relationship to place and placement, it provides a useful framework for exploring social networks in higher education. Relph's descriptions of outsideness, and indeed its opposite insideness, typifying the range of attitudes and associations towards a situation or place, serve as a useful metaphor to model how students engage in dialogue through Web 2.0 technology. It helps locate outsiders who are alienated, dispassionate, or casual about the emotional and intellectual landscape created through technologies, and insiders who regard them as places of deep significance or as a means of providing vicarious experience (Relph, 1976).

## Interscholastic Correspondence

European educational philosopher, Celestin Freinet, wrote widely on what he referred to as the Modern School Movement, through the 1940s-1960s. His ideas are finding fresh currency today, and in particular being applied to the computer-mediated student writing networks (For example see Sivell, 1994). One key Freinet idea was interscholastic correspondence, the sharing of student writing with others in like-minded schools. This writing includes projects, stories, both individual and collaborative. The idea was that quality of work produced would increase through this process, as other students would ask clarifying questions and make criticisms about the text, and identify preferences of students.

*As for criticisms ... everyone will take these remarks into account for future productions. Those who don't submit their work to the judgment of others cannot benefit from their assistance to achieve new awareness ... Only through collective work will stagnation be avoided (Gervilliers, Bertellot, & Lemery, 1977, pp. 95-96).*

Another reason was to allow students to think more deeply about their local context and to communicate this knowledge to distant peers. This is explained by Gervilliers et al. (1977, pp. 29-30) assertion that

*When we live very close to our surroundings and to people, we eventually come not to see them... But thanks to the questions which emanate from afar [italics added], our eyes are opened, we question, we investigate, we explore more deeply ...*

The suggestion here is that interaction with distance peers affords a space where ideas can be represented and communicated with the purpose of improving the quality through continual sharing, questioning, and revision.

## Expansive Learning

Engestrom (1987) has written extensively about expansive learning. In relation to collective intelligence, expansive learning involves co-construction of ideas as an adaptive and dynamic production of knowledge, with no definitive endpoint. This affords opportunity for engaging with varied loosely bound communities of practice through access to multi-disciplinary teams and expert knowledge.

While the purpose of collaboration in a formal system may be to devise new knowledge, Engestrom et al. (Engestrom, Brown, Christopher, & Gregory, 1997) argue that the driving influence in expansive learning is disturbance, unexpected events and a lack of coordination. Kangasoja (2002) makes clear that whereas "the idea of disturbance assumes a script … (this) has little meaning in settings where there are no established practices of collaborating." Indeed, in communities of practice where participants construe ideas, problems and purposes of collaborating differently and require an outcome specific to their own context (Kangasoja, 2002). Thus, expansive systems may disintegrate into disparate individual pockets, depending on the capacity of individual participants to reassert meaning over the fragments.

This raises the interesting point about the balance between individual and collaborative attempts to harness collective intelligence for academic purposes, and thus allows the question of individual capacity to engage in knowledge construction in these contexts.

## Knowledge as Distributed and Collective

Knowledge is derived from personal experience and refined through interaction with experience. As an example, teachers from around the world are likely to have similar knowledge and skills, or at least similar questions about the knowledge and skills they employ to achieve professional goals. Continually drawing upon, monitoring and refining this knowledge is a constructive process that can be aided by accessing and interacting with a range of perspectives.

Deliberately seeking other perspectives by communicating, to use the example of teachers, with the wider teaching community, in order to informally and formally reflect on and build knowledge of one's own professional practice can be a significant component of building teacher knowledge (Trigwell, Martin, Benjamin, & Prosser, 2000).

The argument here is that collective intelligence is the application of a way of acting to improve personal knowledge. This is afforded by the use of technology as a means of moving from individual to social learning; having a view of

expertise as collective and located in individuals that are globally distributed; and willingly entering a space where learning is open and dynamic (Lankshear & Knobel, 2007).

## Written Conversation in Open Communities

Adding to the complexity of academic conversation in virtual spaces is that the nature of communication is usually through text. Emig (1977, p. 124) asserted that "Because writing is often our representation of the world made visible, embodying both process and product, writing is more readily a form and source of learning than talking."

Writing online does afford an opportunity to be deliberate when communicating ideas, but raises questions about the balance between sms or texting language and academic conventions. Writing is an actively rational process "… of constructing, creating and making" (Badley, 2009, p. 211). Freinet (1969, pp. 54-55) stated that "Writing makes no sense unless one is obliged to resort to it in order to communicate beyond the reach of our voice, outside of the limits of school."

Yet, when a person writes they simultaneously project multiple meanings and different levels of understanding by using past, current and future interpretations of experience. Words are re-imagined and interpreted by others, who may ask questions, leading to further writing and re-thinking. Written conversation can become a social interaction where "Meaning is negotiated, indexical, and context dependent … The text emerges and reflects the bi-directional, reciprocal unfolding of the conversation" (Enyedy & Hoadley, 2006, p. 418).

As Emig (1977, p. 124) noted however, "Writing is stark, barren, even naked as a medium …" This barrenness is accented in online environments, where communication prompts such as facial expression are absent, means the text has to attempt to convey the explicit sense of the writer.

Adding complexity to the starkness of writing in an online context is that each word is dense with potential meaning. Even common words like "classroom" simultaneously contain personal and cultural interpretations and are thus contested among educators.

Dialogue is likely to occur when community participants seek to constrain and question the multiple interpretations of each key word (Enyedy & Hoadley, 2006). A written dialogue thus needs to balance description with the nuanced questioning and affective hints that form part of normal conversation.

## Interplay, Interpretation, and Refining of Ideas

A key idea employed in collective intelligence is moving from brief and informal text-messaging type communication to the inherent complexity of academic conversation. The main affordances are the accessing and interplay of a variety of ideas, where questioning and imagining multiple possible interpretations and applications, raise questions and doubt about the ideas being discovered and examined. This hopefully provides more opportunities for learning through a phenomenon observed by Sadoski and Paivio (2001) in which the "…richer the elaboration…and their defining interconnections, the richer the meaning."

Laurillard (2009) emphasized that social learning tasks using technology employ multi-pathway dialogue. This involves participants presenting, commenting on and comparing ideas; seeking and providing feedback; generating or resolving questions; reflecting on experience; and adapting practice. The key idea is the discussion, adaptation and agreed meaning given to ideas and actions as a result of participation in social learning environments (Cassidy, et al., 2007; Deed & Edwards, 2010).

Expressing an idea is a starting point for conversation involving description, explanation and exploration of ideas (Pask, 1975). Each idea

expressed in an online social space is dense with potential meaning. As Bakhtin (1986) commented

*A meaning only reveals its depths once it has encountered and come into contact with another, foreign meaning: they engage in a kind of dialogue, which surmounts the closedness and one-sidedness of these particular meanings...*

Conversation may occur if group members seek to question the multiple interpretations of each key idea (Enyedy & Hoadley, 2006). Effective dialogue needs to balance description with the nuanced questioning and affective hints that form part of multi-directional and reciprocal conversation (Enyedy & Hoadley, 2006).

Novel ideas—perhaps emerging from the different cultures and perspectives to be found among distant peers—are likely create tensions, arguments, contradictions that will act as a starting point for dialogue. This increased sense of doubt may be heightened by working with outside peers, leading to asking questions about ideas and meaning ascribed to those ideas. The concept of outsideness is coherent with Dewey's (1916, pp. 5-6) comment:

*To be a recipient of a communication is to have an enlarged and changed experience ... one has to assimilate, imaginatively something of another's experience in order to tell him intelligently of one's own experience.*

This is coherent with Palincsar's (1998) argument that the process of discourse, where learning is purposefully social, involves the interplay of ideas with cycles of display, validation and refinement of meaning, where progressively higher standards of argument are applied to idea creation and potential application. This raises the question as to how knowledge generated from a collective intelligence system can be validated as appropriate and credible within an academic context (Yelland, et al., 2008).

## ADAPTIVE EXPERTISE: COPING WITH THE DYNAMICS OF COLLECTIVE INTELLIGENCE

The model of developing expertise put forward here is based on the work of Sternberg (1999). While there is no precise and encompassing definition of expertise, there are similarities or a "family resemblance" of experts within specific fields (Sternberg & Horvath, 1995). This model extends prior accepted versions of expertise, including the reflective practitioner (Schon, 1983).

Table 3 outlines the elements of developing expertise, linked to the knowledge and skills required to enter and use a collective intelligence system. Sternberg and Horvath suggest that an expert can be differentiated from a novice by the amount of subject and pedagogical knowledge they use to respond to their context; the efficiency with which they resolve emerging problems; and the insight they apply to devise innovative and workable solutions to workplace issues (Sternberg & Horvath, 1995).

This view of expertise is characterized by a dynamic capacity to adapt practice to local contexts, involving constant reflective monitoring and reinvestment of learnt professional practice knowledge and skills (Matthew & Sternberg,

2009). Expertise can perhaps be conceived of as the reflective, "... wise *and* intelligent use of knowledge" (Sternberg, 2003).

*The novice works towards expertise through deliberate practice. But this practice requires an interaction of all five of the key elements... Eventually, one reaches a kind of expertise, at which one becomes a reflective practitioner of a certain set of skills (Sternberg, 1999).*

Sternberg's model of developing expertise proposes five interconnected elements that enable the development of context specific expertise, outlined in Table 3, linked to the knowledge and skills for collective intelligence.

Each element of developing expertise has a dual set of knowledge and skills for effective use of collective intelligence systems. The first set relate to the process of individual knowledge construction through the process. A metacognitive question for this set of activities might be: what am I learning? As Siemens' (2005, p. 2) comments "The need to evaluate the worthiness of learning something is a meta-skill that is applied before learning itself begins."

The second set concern strategies used to make the process of engagement in collective

*Table 3. Developing expertise in collective intelligence*

| Elements of developing expertise (Sternberg, 1999) | Knowledge and skills for collective intelligence | |
|---|---|---|
| | Knowledge building | Experience optimization |
| Metacognitive skills: monitoring and evaluation of resource and strategy use | Perceived usefulness of (dis)engaging with collective intelligence systems | Perceived self-efficacy and possibilities of active engagement |
| Learning skills: cognitive learning processes | Seeking and interacting with multiple perspectives | Adaptive interaction in multiple contexts |
| Thinking skills: critical, creative and practical thinking processes | Strategies for progressively higher standards of analysis and evaluation | Strategies for engagement in collective intelligence systems |
| Knowledge: declarative and procedural | Knowledge personally understood and applied in local contexts | Evaluating knowledge quality (detail, completeness and applicability to real contexts) |
| Motivation: achievement and competence | Responding to uncertainty and intrigue about new ideas | Responsiveness to collective intelligence opportunities |
| Context: features of a specific time and space | Knowledge of personal context for action | Adaptive application of ideas across multiple contexts |

intelligence systems efficient and effective. A metacognitive question for these actions may be: what other sources of information could I use? This is consistent with Siemens' (2005, p. 4) comment: "Choosing what to learn and the meaning of incoming information is seen through the lens of a shifting reality."

A key thematic component of expertise development is a capacity to be self-regulating. This is particularly important when considering the emphasis on individual choices made when constructing knowledge through engagement in a collective intelligence system.

Self-regulated learning was defined by Boekaerts and Corno (2005) as the deliberate use of personal strategies to achieve academic and well-being goals. The concept of self-regulation promotes a sense of student autonomy and responsibility for how and what they learn (Boekaerts & Corno, 2005; Butler & Winne, 2005).

A number of researchers have identified instructional formats that support independent learning behavior; although all have the common purpose of overtly involving the individual in making choices about the learning process (for example see Grinsven & Tillema, 2006). Individual learning behavior is a dynamic response to each learning context. Individuals engage and disengage with the purpose and process of a task, informed by perceptions of the context and imagined possible alternative actions (Emirbayer & Mische, 1998). Influences on choices—as individuals exercise their adaptive expertise—within the context of the contemporary learning spaces are multi-faceted and complex. The concept of investment in learning can be used to examine cognitive engagement or mental effort individuals make in order to acquire knowledge and skills, and the tactical choices made when self-regulating to achieve the task demands (Fredricks, Blumenfeld, & Paris, 2004). Making an investment refers to going beyond minimal task completion requirements and includes effort made to understand and master

knowledge and skills. As an example, one indicator of investment in learning is an individual's use of strategies to construct knowledge through online interaction in collective intelligence systems. The context is an important consideration in any study of learning activity, as it is the individual's perspective and experience of the context that influences the way they choose to learn.

## CASE STUDY: ENGAGING WITH CO-CONSTRUCTION OF KNOWLEDGE

### Case Study Context

A case study is reported here of 135 students from three countries tasked as groups to independently interact online. A wiki environment was set up to provide students with a space to exercise autonomy and responsibility for how and what they would learn. Each group had to set up the wiki and ensure all group members were able to access it. Each group member had to provide a narrative of their own childhood experience of school, and then groups had to discuss and agree on five principles of effective teaching and learning environments.

Participants consisted of 54 third-year education students from La Trobe University, Australia; 54 students from Catholic University of Chile; 18 students from Keele University UK, and 9 students from Liverpool Hope University, UK. The students worked in groups over a three-week period in March 2010. There were a total of 27 groups, made up of 13 groups each with two Australian and two Chilean students; and 14 groups each with two Australian, two Chilean, and two UK students. As English was a second language for the Chilean students, each group of two included a bilingual student. Between one to two hours of class time per week, over the three weeks of the project, were allocated to the Australian and Chilean students.

Data was collected from two sources: an online survey completed by students at the end of the project, and a transcript analysis. Both the survey and the submission of the group's wiki transcript were voluntary. At the conclusion of the task, a link to an online survey was emailed to all students. A total of 87 students responded to the invitation to complete the survey. This included 46 Australian, 30 Chilean, and 11 UK students. Students were asked about their internet access; prior experience of social interaction online; expectations of the task prior to working on the wiki; and their experience of working in a distributed collaborative context. Five open-ended questions were asked about the students' perspectives about having a conversation about learning in the wiki environment. Thematic trends were identified by each of the researchers independently analyzing the data and then sharing, discussing and agreeing on the final analytical themes.

Ten randomly selected wiki transcripts were used for analysis. Four analytical categories were identified, based on Pask's (1975) outline of a learning conversation involving description, explanation, and exploration of ideas. A fourth category, that of taking action, was used to code action statements in relation to completing the task requirements. A second level of analysis was then conducted using the categories from the development of expertise, outlined above.

## Case Study Findings and Discussion

Students were asked about their access and use of the internet. The responses indicate a high level of internet access with 84.8% of Australian, 86.7% of Chilean, and 72.7% of UK students using the internet on at least a daily basis. 94.3% of all students were familiar with YouTube and 96.6% familiar with Facebook. In contrast, in response to the question "How often do you use a wiki?" 21.7% of Australian students had never used it

or had no idea what it was, compared to 56.7% of Chilean students and 36.4% of UK students.

Approximately half of the students who responded to the survey made some comment about the influence of working with students from other cultures, usually involving the raising of doubt about the meaning of personal and other experiences. Student 67 commented:

*Working with people likely to have significantly different educational experiences from your own ... made you less likely to succumb to the fallacy of feeling you've had a 'normal' and 'unexciting' experience.*

Students raised a number of issues when asked how this project could be improved—indicators of the metacognitive sense of doubt about task planning, progress and achievement. The majority of comments were about the organization of the task, including the need for more detailed expectations, forcing students to participate, and making sure group members are online to conduct synchronous conversation. These indicate planning and monitoring issues for students. Students identified key problems as participation of group members and potential language barriers, and these are discussed in the context of the following affordances. While many comments were made about the sense of value attached to the task, students generally felt their involvement was rushed, particularly when they were identifying and responding to time differences, language barriers, technical issues in some cases, and organizing the participation of group members.

Learning through seeking and using multiple perspectives were identified by students as the most significant and easily enacted part of expertise development. A number of comments were made about exchanging ideas, sharing experiences and asking questions of each other.

*There is no way students in Australia could have an understanding of ideas, teachings, and schooling in other countries like Chile unless we talk about them… It has widened by thoughts, ideas and mind … (Student 44).*

This potential was influenced by the participation rate and energy of group members. The basis of successfully completing the task required that each student make an investment, not only in reading and making posts, but also in reading, thinking, asking questions, and collaboratively generating ideas. This was the most significant issue identified by students, usually related to the anticipated time commitment.

Students indicated that they built meaning through narrative based exploration of ideas and drawing upon and adapting social and cultural knowledge in response to personal practice. This related to the building of abstract knowledge based on the shared narrative of personal school experience. Although only a small number of students commented on this aspect, it nevertheless was a powerful component of the task. Several students perceived they were using knowledge in a different way, including generating new ideas. One aspect noted was the adaptation of new knowledge to future personal practice.

*… As they have developed a text from their own knowledge [italics added] and learning about the subject in question (Translated from Spanish, Student 1).*

Students indicated that connecting with outside peers to make sense of uncertainty was a source of intrinsic motivation. Several minor themes merged here: the familiar anxieties and questions of pre-service teachers, the advantages of social networking with future colleagues, the opportunity to ask questions in a non-threatening environment, and to engage with different ideas. The sense of uncertainty meant that the conversation had to be closely examined and questioned by group members in order to gain surety about emerging meaning.

*I think it takes more time to discuss what distinguishes his views from ours. There was time for consensus and determine what we agreed but we differ (Translated from Spanish, Student 24).*

Uncertainty may be apparent because of either a language barrier or because of the interrupted nature of the flow of communication in a wiki environment. Therefore, the intended communication was liable to multiple interpretations.

*I just felt (the Chilean students) were afraid to share their thoughts and ideas due to their limited knowledge of the English language (Student 19).*

On one level, the uncertainty was exacerbated by the artificiality of having a written conversation, with no non-textual clues or prompts to clarify meaning. The conversational flow, important when exploring even simple ideas, was perceived as important for adding complexity and depth to idea generation.

*… In some cases leave the conversation for another day and you lose the speed and spontaneity of the conversation (Translated from Spanish, Student 22).*

*The lack of face-to-face contact is a problem for me since oral contact with all the visual clues that come with it is an important part of both molding into a coherent team and in comprehending each other fully (Student 67).*

Students identified that accessing collegial perspectives across time and space provided a challenging but purposeful learning space. This related primarily to the features of asynchronous communication using Web 2.0 tools. These include a learning environment that utilized contemporary multi-media skills of students, speed, and flex-

*Table 4. Transcript analysis*

| Group | Introduction | Descriptive | Explanatory | Exploratory | Taking-action | Total |
|---|---|---|---|---|---|---|
| | | | Coding category | | | |
| A | 3 | 3 | - | - | 1 | 7 |
| B | 5 | 3 | 1 | - | 1 | 10 |
| C | 12 | 5 | - | - | 1 | 18 |
| D | 4 | 6 | - | 1 | 1 | 12 |
| E | 4 | 3 | - | 1 | 1 | 9 |
| F | 4 | 5 | - | 2 | 1 | 12 |
| G | 3 | 4 | 3 | 2 | 2 | 14 |
| H | 10 | 8 | 2 | 1 | 13 | 34 |
| I | 5 | 7 | 2 | 2 | 14 | 30 |
| J | 9 | 2 | 2 | 15 | 7 | 35 |
| Total | 59 (32.6%) | 46 (25.4) | 10 (5.5) | 24 (13.3) | 42 (23.2) | 181 |

ibility of access, and being able to see a record of discussion.

*I think it gives you time to think about what you mean (Translated from Spanish, Student 4).*

*We all have different strategies as teachers and we are learning different ways of learning and teaching through each other [italics added] (Student 39).*

Providing opportunities for online sharing and generating knowledge is an important part of developing expertise. This is consistent with the idea of knowledge continually being drawn upon, and subsequently rebuilt, though interpreting, interaction and reshaping of experience (Connelly, Clandinin, & He, 1997).

Ten transcripts were analyzed, a total of 181 postings. The transcript analysis is outlined in Table 4. As can be seen, all groups made introductory and descriptive postings—32.6% and 24.4% respectively of the postings in the sample of transcripts. Explanatory postings were the least used element of the students' conversations—5.5% of the postings. Explanation is a key middle step in

a conversation, as it signals the movement from 'barren' words to creating shared meaning.

Exploratory postings were also under-represented (13.3%). This is more the case if Group J, who made fifteen exploratory postings, is removed from the analysis. Explorative postings involved more than one connected post and more than one group member interacting in relation to an idea.

Taking-action posts (23.2%) tended to be task oriented and in some cases perhaps reflect the strategic intention of each group to complete the task in a somewhat efficient manner. These posts related to the production of the final product, and are mainly concerned with formalizing agreement on ideas or editing processes. These posts were mainly focused on reaching agreement on ideas or editing processes, and included suggesting principles of teaching and learning environments and summarizing the group's ideas.

The groups in Table 4 are organized from those ranked as making a low level of investment in the task to those groups making a high level. Investment can be said to have increased if a group's postings move from individuals separately posting an opinion to detailed explanation, interpretation of other group member's ideas, asking questions about the group's postings, and engaging in reflective dialogue about task completion and subsequent planned and unplanned learning. In other words, using a range of conversational strategies to explore and idea indicates an increase in investment.

At one end, Groups A – C had no exploratory posts and only one explanatory post in total. Following introductions group members may have suggested ideas but there was no follow up discussion. Conversely, groups H – J had postings distributed across all categories, including some in explanation and exploration. Only one group (J) demonstrated evidence of high-level investment in academic conversation.

In the middle, Groups D – G tended to adopt a strategic approach—deliberate choices to control and regulate their personal investment in learning. There was evidence of strategic posts across the majority of groups, although most apparent in groups D – I. For instance it was noted that the majority of posts were generally brief and to the point; students opting in and out of conversations—making just enough effort; groups making rapid-fire decisions on their final product with no explanatory or exploratory posts; limiting discussion to general ideas, and leaving final wording to one person; clustering posts in a short time frame and quickly agreeing to any return suggestions; not asking questions; and drawing conversations to a close by reminding group members of need to finalize final product.

## Discussion of Case Study Findings

Personal and cultural narratives of childhood school experience were shared on the wikis; although there was variation in the degree of explanation and exploration of group member's ideas about effective teaching and learning. Overall, there were minimal attempts at active exploration, and unevenness in the distribution of postings among group members. Rather than Laurillard's (2009) multi-pathway dialogue, the transcript analysis showed a somewhat linear set of

postings. Online dialogue tended to move rapidly from idea description to final product, bypassing the nuances associated with social construction of knowledge.

The written conversations were conducted in English. This may have limited the capacity of some group members to create personal or shared meaning using words that have multiple contextual meaning. Trying to converse using "... stark, barren, even naked ..." (Emig, 1977) written text provides a reason to unearth and question meaning. The paucity of exploratory postings indicates a gap between the potential influence of outsideness and the student perception of their capacity to interact via writing with other group members ideas.

Although it did not exert significant influence in this case, the concept of outsideness is coherent with the notion that individual learning takes place in socially and culturally shaped contexts (Palincsar, 1998). This can be interpreted in two ways. First, individuals learn with immediate peers in local contexts, and thus struggled to translate those processes to the virtual environment involving distant peers. Alternatively, the virtual environment provided a radically different context where new means of conversational interaction had to be negotiated. A tension may have been created by forcing students to interact with those from another culture and without a shared language. An emerging question is therefore whether insideness or outsideness plays a greater role in determining learning processes in virtual contexts.

In terms of online interaction, the discussion process has internal (personal imaginings) and external (deliberative writing) moments during the construction of individual and shared meaning. It is during the process of interpreting context-specific experiences that learners individually construct knowledge and ideas (Palincsar, 1998). A student may be on the periphery of an online conversation yet still imagine and construct ideas that were influenced by the interaction they observed and the concepts they perceived to be 'in-play.' The survey data indicated that the students anticipated a rich discussion informed by the exchange of culturally diverse perspectives.

While the student participants may have been able to imaginatively conceive and be empathetic to different perspectives they were unable, or lacked capacity, to enact a collaborative effort in order to deepen the extent of their inquiry. This reflects the tension between the dual sense of outsideness and insideness. Degrees of outsideness for the student cohort as a whole varied depending on a number of factors. For some, dialogue was undertaken in a second and perhaps even a third language. For others the means of engaging in dialogue itself may have been unfamiliar and potentially alienating. However, rather than view these differences as a deficit the very process of exchange unexpectedly resulted in the development of a shared sense of achievement in those groups that were able to function well despite the challenges they faced.

## CONCLUSION

While acknowledging collective intelligence as a dynamic meta-concept, here it is conceived of as deliberate academic conversation among a loosely defined set of peers whose purpose is to generate, explore, and evaluate knowledge through use of Web 2.0 tools. Collective intelligence has been characterised here as a disruptive process of social constructivism that challenges the tenets of the traditional expert-to-student transmissive model of learning.

Two questions were posed at the start of this chapter. First, what affords the active participation of higher education students in collective intelligence systems? Second, what knowledge and skills do students need to cope with the dynamics of collective intelligence systems?

A conceptual framework was outlined as one means of resolving the initial question using outsideness—a metaphor referring to how

an individual's sense of beliefs, values, and cultural differences among peers initiates rich academic conversations in online environments. Conceptualized affordances of outsideness for collective intelligence included: representing and communicating ideas to distant peers; generating ideas through deliberately seeking tensions and differences from peers; being open to new ideas from formal and informal sources; seeking agreement through purposeful conversation that shares, explores and builds knowledge; and progressive application of higher standards of analysis and evaluation as part of academic conversation.

The case study provided an example of the complexity of real world application of these concepts. It was demonstrated that outsideness acted simultaneously as a constraint and enabler of participation and learning. Where there is a probability that the constraining elements (as in the case of different first languages) could significantly overpower the enabling mechanisms educators need to create systems and structures that address this imbalance. They should provide enough scope for individuals to make a contribution to their own learning, and support students develop conversational capacity in digital collective intelligence systems. However, eradicating all imbalances will negate the positive affordances of outsideness.

The case provided a snapshot of the lived perspective of a cohort of students from four universities in three countries. This represents a thin slice of time, context, and structure of the incorporation of technology into higher education. While the analytical framework was a useful sensitizing construct that allowed the basic categorization of each group's conversational progress, the authors remained mindful throughout of the limitations of any taxonomy. The case outlined only considered the personal reflective and social interaction components of knowledge building. Individuals are capable of seeking, interpreting, and using perspectives and knowledge from a variety of sources. It is argued that while the metaphor of outsideness provided an explanatory lens when considering the complexity of written conversations with distant peers in collective intelligence systems, accessing fine-grain evidence of both personal and shared sense of outsideness is an area for ongoing research. The focus needs to be on detailed case studies examining the process and influences on the change in group member's ideas in a context where outsideness is a key design element.

Engagement in a task can occur at different behavioral, cognitive, and affective levels, and the process of making meaning is likely to include mindfulness of the context for writing and constructing ideas. Thus, it is the individual's self-regulation of their own learning effort that is a significant variable to be examined in future studies of collective intelligence.

In relation to the second question examined in this chapter, a model for the development of contextually adaptive expertise, drawing on Sternberg (1999) was developed to identify the knowledge and skills needed to enable students to cope with the dynamics of collective intelligence systems.

The model conceptualized key knowledge building skills, including: metacognitive perceptions of the engagement and disengagement with multiple perspectives; strategies for analysis and evaluation; the application of knowledge in local contexts; strategies for responding to uncertainty and doubt about ideas; and knowledge about the personal context for action. Knowledge and skills for optimizing the experience of collective intelligence systems included: metacognitive perceptions of self-efficacy and possibilities for active engagement; capacity for adaptive engagement and interaction across multiple contexts; strategies for evaluating the quality of knowledge generated; a capacity to respond to collective intelligence opportunities; and the application of ideas across a variety of work and learning contexts.

A driver of the enactment of these knowledge and skills is the self-efficacy and motivation of individuals within a learning context. A question emerges here about the balance between allowing students to self manage their own developing expertise and the co-regulation of this development by educators. The balance is most important when expectations of academic conversations move from generation of ideas to the evaluation and application of knowledge—from online interaction to professional practice knowledge.

This chapter has identified two conceptual frameworks, outsideness, and developing adaptive expertise, to explain and analyse the contextual influences and variables operating to drive the strategic decision making of individuals learning in emerging collective intelligence communities through academic conversation. The case study provided a real-life example of the complexities of translating the potential of Web 2.0 tools into higher education learning contexts. Future research should concentrate on more detailed explications of the dynamic learning behavior of individuals as they (dis)engage with contemporary learning contexts. Specifically, on their perceptions of the learning context, their capacity to learn effectively and efficiently in those contexts, and the gap between what they think they are capable of and how they actually act in order to achieve required learning.

# REFERENCES

Badley, G. (2009). Academic writing as shaping and re-shaping. *Teaching in Higher Education*, *14*(2), 209–219. doi:10.1080/13562510902757294

Bakhtin, M. M. (1986). *Speech genres & other late essays*. Austin, TX: University of Texas Press.

Boekaerts, M., & Corno, L. (2005). Self-regulation in the classroom: A perspective on assessment and intervention. *Applied Psychology, 54*(2), 199–231. doi:10.1111/j.1464-0597.2005.00205.x

Bonabeau, E. (2009). Decisions 2.0: The power of collective intelligence. *MIT Sloan Management Review, 50*(2), 45–52.

Bothos, E., Apostolou, D., & Mentzas, G. (2009). Collective intelligence for idea management with internet-based information aggregation markets. *Internet Research, 19*(1), 26–41. doi:10.1108/10662240910927803

Butler, D. L., & Winne, P. H. (2005). Feedback and self-regulated learning: A theoretical synthesis. *Review of Educational Research, 65*, 245–281.

Cassidy, C., Christie, D., Coutts, N., Dunn, J., Sinclair, C., & Skinner, D. (2007). Building communities of educational enquiry. *Oxford Review of Education, 34*(2), 217–235. doi:10.1080/03054980701614945

Connelly, F. M., Clandinin, D. J., & He, M. F. (1997). Teachers' personal practical knowledge on the professional knowledge landscape. *Teaching and Teacher Education, 13*(7), 665–674. doi:10.1016/S0742-051X(97)00014-0

Deed, C., & Edwards, A. (2010). Using social networks in learning and teaching in higher education: An Australian case study. *International Journal of Knowledge Society Research, 1*(2), 1–12. doi:10.4018/jksr.2010040101

Deed, C., & Edwards, A. (2011). Unrestricted student blogging: Implications for active learning in a virtual text-based environment. *Active Learning in Higher Education, 12*(1). doi:10.1177/1469787410387725

Dewey, J. (1916). *Democracy and education*. New York, NY: MacMillan.

Emig, J. (1977). Writing as a mode of learning. *College Composition and Communication, 28*(2), 122–128. doi:10.2307/356095

Emirbayer, M., & Mische, A. (1998). What is agency? *American Journal of Sociology, 103*, 962–1023. doi:10.1086/231294

Engestrom, Y. (1987). *Learning by expanding: An activity-theoretical approach to developmental research*. Helsinki, Finland: Orienta-Konsultit.

Engestrom, Y., Brown, K., Christopher, L. K., & Gregory, J. (1997). Coordination, cooperation and communication in the courts: Expansive transitions in legal work . In Cole, M., Engestrom, Y., & Vasquez, T. (Eds.), *Mind, Culture and Activity: Seminal Papers from the Laboratory of Comparative Human Cognition*. Cambridge, UK: Cambridge University Press.

Enyedy, N., & Hoadley, C. M. (2006). From dialogue to monologue and back: Middle spaces in computer-mediated learning. *Computer-Supported Collaborative Learning, 1*, 413–439. doi:10.1007/s11412-006-9000-2

Fredricks, J. A., Blumenfeld, P. C., & Paris, A. H. (2004). School engagement: Potential of the concept, state of the evidence. *Review of Educational Research, 74*(1), 59–109. doi:10.3102/00346543074001059

Freinet, C. (1969). *Pour l'ecole du peuple: Guide pratique pour l'organisation materielle, technique et pedagogique de l'ecole populaire* [For a school of the people: A practical guide for the material, technical, and pedagogical organization of a popular school]. Barcelona, Spain: Editorial Laia.

Gervilliers, D., Bertellot, C., & Lemery, J. (1977). *Las correspondencias escolares*. Barcelona, Spain: Editorial Laia.

Grace-Martin, M., & Gay, G. (2001). Web browsing, mobile computing and academic performance. *Journal of Educational Technology & Society*, *4*(3), 95–107.

Greeno, J. G. (1994). Gibson's affordances. *Psychological Review*, *101*(2), 336–343. doi:10.1037/0033-295X.101.2.336

Grinsven, L., & Tillema, H. (2006). Learning opportunities to support student self-regulation: Comparing different instructional formats. *Educational Research*, *48*, 77–91. doi:10.1080/00131880500498495

Gruber, T. (2007). *Collective knowledge systems*. Paper presented at the 5th International Semantic Web Conference. New York, NY.

Hatano, G., & Inagaki, K. (1986). Two courses of expertise. In Stevenson, H., Azuma, H., & Hakuta, K. (Eds.), *Child Development and Education in Japan* (pp. 262–272). New York, NY: W. H. Reeman and Company.

Kangasoja, J. (2002). *Complex design problems: An impetus for learning and knotworking*. Retrieved 21 May, 2011, from http://www.edu.helsinki.fi/activity/publications/files/47/ICLS2002_Kangasoja.pdf

Lankshear, C., & Knobel, M. (2007). Researching new literacies: Web 2.0 practices and insider perspectives. *E-Learning and Digital Media*, *4*(3).

Laurillard, D. (2009). The pedagogical challenges to collaborative technologies. *Computer-Supported Collaborative Learning*, *4*, 5–20. doi:10.1007/s11412-008-9056-2

Lee, M. R., & Lan, Y. (2007). From web 2.0 to conversational knowledge management: Towards collaborative intelligence. *Journal of Entrepreneurship Research*, *2*(2), 47–62.

Matthew, C. T., & Sternberg, R. J. (2009). Developing experience-based (tacit) knowledge through reflection. *Learning and Individual Differences*, *19*, 530–540. doi:10.1016/j.lindif.2009.07.001

O'Reilly, T. (2007). What is web 2.0: Design patterns and business models for the next generation of software. *Communications & Strategies*, *65*, 17–37.

Palincsar, A. S. (1998). Social constructivist perspectives on teaching and learning. *Annual Review of Psychology*, *49*, 345–375. doi:10.1146/annurev.psych.49.1.345

Pask, G. (1975). *Conversation, cognition and learning: A cybernetic theory and methodology*. Amsterdam, The Netherlands: Elsevier.

Relph, E. (1976). *Place and placelessness*. London, UK: Pion.

Riedl, C., Blohm, I., Leimeister, J. M., & Krcmar, H. (2010). *Rating scales for collective intelligence in innovation communities: Why quick and easy decision making does not get it right*. Paper presented at the 31st International Conference on Information Systems. New York, NY.

Sadoski, M., & Paivio, A. (2001). *Imagery and text: A dual coding theory of reading and writing*. Mahwah, NJ: Lawrence Erlbaum Associates.

Schon, D. (1983). *The reflective practitioner: How professionals think in action*. New York, NY: Basic Books. doi:10.1080/07377366.1986.10401080

Schwartz, D. L., Bransford, J. D., & Sears, D. (2005). Efficiency and innovation in transfer. In Mestre, J. (Ed.), *Transfer of Learning from a Modern Multidisciplinary Perspective* (pp. 1–51). Greenwich, CT: Information Age Publishing.

Sharples, M., Taylor, J., & Vavoula, G. (2007). A theory of learning for the mobile age. In Andrews, A., & Haythornthwaite, C. (Eds.), *The Sage Handbook of e-Learning Research* (pp. 221–247). London, UK: Sage Publications Ltd. doi:10.1007/978-3-531-92133-4_6

Siemens, G. (2005). *Connectivism: A learning theory for the digital age*. Elearnspace.

Sivell, J. (Ed.). (1994). *Frienet pedagogy: Theory and practice*. New York, NY: The Edwin Mellen Press.

Starkey, L. (2010). Teachers' pedagogical reasoning and action in the digital age. *Teachers and Teaching: Theory and Practice, 16*(2), 233–244. doi:10.1080/13540600903478433

Sternberg, R. J. (1999). Intelligence as developing expertise. *Contemporary Educational Psychology, 24*, 359–375. doi:10.1006/ceps.1998.0998

Sternberg, R. J. (2003). What is an "expert student?". *Educational Researcher, 32*(5), 5–9. doi:10.3102/0013189X032008005

Sternberg, R. J., & Horvath, J. A. (1995). A prototype view of expert teaching. *Educational Researcher, 24*(6), 9–17.

Trigwell, K., Martin, E., Benjamin, J., & Prosser, M. (2000). Scholarship of teaching: A model. *Higher Education Research & Development, 19*(2), 155–168. doi:10.1080/072943600445628

Yelland, N., Cope, B., & Kalantzis, M. (2008). Learning by design: Creating pedagogical frameworks for knowledge building in the twenty-first century. *Asia-Pacific Journal of Teacher Education, 36*(3), 197–213. doi:10.1080/13598660802232597

# Chapter 11
# Enhancing Information Extraction with Context and Inference:
## The ODIX Platform

**Hisham Assal**
*California Polytechnic State University, USA*

**Kym Pohl**
*California Polytechnic State University, USA*

**Franz Kurfess**
*California Polytechnic State University, USA*

**Emily Schwarz**
*California Polytechnic State University, USA*

**John Seng**
*California Polytechnic State University, USA*

## ABSTRACT

*Natural Language Processing (NLP) provides tools to extract explicitly stated information from text documents. These tools include Named Entity Recognition (NER) and Parts-Of-Speech (POS). The extracted information represents discrete entities in the text and some relationships that may exist among them. To perform intelligent analysis on the extracted information a context has to exist in which this information is placed. The context provides an environment to link information that is extracted from multiple documents and offers a big picture of the domain. Analysis can then be provided by adding inference capabilities to the environment. The ODIX platform provides an environment for bringing together information extraction, ontology, and intelligent analysis. The platform design relies on existing NLP tools to provide the information extraction capabilities. It also utilizes a Web crawler to collect text documents from the Web. The context is provided by a domain ontology that is loaded at run time. The ontology offers limited inference capabilities and external intelligent agents offer more advanced reasoning capabilities. User involvement is key to the success of the analysis process. At every step of the process, the user has the opportunity to direct the system, set selection criteria, correct errors, or add additional information.*

DOI: 10.4018/978-1-4666-2494-8.ch011

Copyright © 2013, IGI Global. Copying or distributing in print or electronic forms without written permission of IGI Global is prohibited.

## INTRODUCTION

Over the last decade, advances in search engine technology have made them indispensable tools for many users, be it in their private or professional lives. Their benefits are so obvious and far-reaching that it becomes very easy to overlook some of the limitations that they still have. In this chapter, we investigate the needs of analysts or knowledge workers when trying to find pieces of information and knowledge in distributed document repositories, the most widely available one being the World Wide Web. Our initial target area is intelligence analysis, where an analyst is faced with a mountain of documents that may contain possibly relevant information for a particular problem or domain they are investigating. Our assumption is that the analyst has an initial conceptual or formal model of the domain, reflecting the knowledge they have already acquired. Their task now may have two major components: one, to enhance the domain model by incorporating additional knowledge as they investigate the new documents, and two, to identify interesting knowledge items that may be relevant for a particular purpose. An analyst tasked with examining terrorism financing, for example, will have access to existing and historical investigations of this problem, which are used to form the initial conceptual model. Gaining access to additional sources of information, be it public ones from the World Wide Web, or proprietary ones from intelligence agencies or other organizations, allows the agent to expand the model. In the larger context of dealing with terrorism in general, another task of the agent may be to identify suspicious activities, for example the planning of a specific terrorist activity such as a bombing.

A traditional approach to this problem consists of analysts reading documents, bookmarking and annotating them, and entering important pieces of information into databases. These databases can then be queried during the search for relevant information. If the analyst encounters informa-

tion that may indicate an ongoing plot, an alert could be raised to initiate further investigations. This scenario clearly does not use analysts nor computer systems very effectively, although it apparently was applied by intelligence services for the analysis of the Afghan Wikileaks documents released in the summer of 2010 (Wikileaks, 2010; Schmitt, 2010). The most obvious problem is the amount of time required to read all documents in the repository. This may eventually be necessary in a situation like the Wikileaks documents, but is not practical with a virtually limitless repository such as the World Wide Web. Using the Web as a source requires assistance from a search engine, combined with browsing to follow links on Web pages. Search engines present their results typically as an ordered list of links to documents that are judged to be relevant by their ranking algorithms, again requiring the analyst to read documents, extract information, and enter it in a database. Another limiting factor is the use of databases, which rely on relatively fixed structures for the entries. While it is possible to use databases to store knowledge with a complex internal structure, this structure should be exposed to the user without having to use traditional database methods like database query languages.

Another important aspect where computer support can be essential is the capability to bookmark and cross-reference documents. This can be done with relatively simple means like hyperlinks, but it becomes quickly impractical to do so manually. It is also possible to use search engine technology and create a (reverse) index that lists all occurrences of words (or, to be precise, strings) in the documents. This can be the basis for a Web of metadata linking together entities (e.g. persons, locations) in the documents. The use of natural language processing methods enables a limited degree of named entity recognition, plus the extraction of relationships between entities. This results in a Web of metadata that overlays the original set of documents, possibly incorporating additional knowledge as well. Such an approach was proposed by Tim Berners-Lee and others as the Semantic Web (Berners-Lee, Hendler, & Lassila, 2001), and can be traced back to Vannevar Bush's article "As We May Think" in *The Atlantic* in 1945 (Bush, 1945). An ontology provides a structured network of entities and relationships, and enables the use of metadata for bookmarking and cross-referencing documents. Through these cross-references, it is also straightforward to identify sources of information that was extracted from the original documents. While somewhat more complicated, it can also be used as the basis for tracing knowledge obtained by reasoning (Auer & Lehmann, 2010).

The goal of our system is to support analysts by using computer-based methods to examine the content of documents, extract potentially relevant knowledge items from them, and to incorporate them into a computer-based conceptual model of the domain under investigation. This conceptual model can be captured through an ontology, and we are utilizing natural language processing techniques for the extraction of knowledge items. This approach is not entirely new (see Wimalasuriya & Dou, 2010) for an overview of ontology-based information extraction), but our focus is on computer-assisted knowledge extraction, in contrast to fully automatic approaches such as Lin, Etzioni, and Fogarty (2009).

After the introduction, this chapter will examine the background for the problem of extracting knowledge through Web mining and incorporating that knowledge into an ontology. We will then give an overview of our approach, with separate sections for the main methods and technologies we use: Natural Language Processing (NLP), ontologies, and Service-Oriented Architecture (SOA) as a framework of the overall system design. This is followed by a case study with terrorism financing as the target domain, and a discussion of adapting our approach to other domains.

## BACKGROUND

The task of the aforementioned analyst can be construed as the incremental development of a customized faceted domain model: extracting and deriving information and knowledge from a variety of sources, the analyst assembles a conceptual model of the domain according to the intended purposes and envisioned tasks. Over time, computers have played a variety of supporting roles here: they serve as repositories for source documents and artifacts created when assembling the domain model, assist humans with the efficient retrieval of documents, provide flexible options for presenting documents and query results, and offer a variety of tools and services. In our context, there are four main areas of support: information retrieval, information extraction, domain modeling, and knowledge extraction.

### Information Retrieval (IR)

Although storage capacities and retrieval times were relatively limited compared with current systems, computers were used very early as repositories for digitized documents. Since even computers with a few megabytes of memory can accommodate thousands of documents, strategies had to be developed for efficient and effective retrieval of the documents in such a repository. This led to the development of information retrieval (Baeza-Yates & Ribeiro-Neto, 2011; Manning, Raghavan, & Schütze, 2008; Belew, 2000), where the main objective is to identify a document that contains information sought by the user, and to provide the user access to the document. One of the major outcomes of these approaches was the development of indexing techniques, where a (reverse) index containing all relevant terms that appear in the documents of the repository is constructed at compile time, and serves as an efficient proxy for locating relevant documents at query time. Another important development was the specification of a set of metrics for the comparison of retrieval methods, leading to the widely used precision and recall measures. Many of the IR techniques have been incorporated into search engines, where the repository is often not constrained to one particular computer system or network, but may span the World Wide Web. This expansion also led to significant revisions and refinements; one of the major ones is the importance of ranking the results of the retrieval process in such a way that the document that is most likely to contain the answer is presented to the user at the top of the list. Nevertheless, the main principle remains the same: in response to a query, the computer provides a list of document proxies to the user, and the user has to read one or more of those documents to find the answer to their query. Obviously, in many situations the intended goal of a user query is not to find interesting reading material, but to identify the answer to a question. To do this, the computer not only has to identify a document, but also a smaller unit within the document (such as a paragraph, sentence, word as text units, or images, drawings, sounds, or other media entities).

## Information Extraction (IE)

Suppose a user is interested when the next bus leaves from the university to the train station. Information Retrieval identifies a document with the bus schedule that shows the departure and arrival times. If the computer system is capable of parsing the schedule and determining that the next bus leaves in twelve minutes from the stop closest to the user's current location, it performs Information Extraction (Wimalasuriya & Dou, 2010; Russell & Norvig, 2009; Moens, 2003), and possibly some domain-specific reasoning. One important aspect of IE is *Named Entity Recognition (NER)*, which identifies people, places, objects, and other entities that have a label (the name) to distinguish them from other entities of the same type. In addition

to NER, the computer system may have to be familiar with domain-specific representations of information, and capable of extracting the relevant items. In our bus example, this means that the bus schedule must be represented in such a way that the computer can determine at least two important pieces of information (the current location of the user, and the current time), and then identify the closest bus stop, and calculate the next departure time. Most likely, this will require a computer-readable internal representation of relevant documents such as a map and the bus schedule. This internal representation can serve as the basis both for an IE query where the computer presents an answer to the user, and an IR query, where the user is given a document containing the requested information. The latter document, however, most likely will be significantly different in appearance from the internal representation. Note that even in the relatively simple bus schedule example; some domain-specific knowledge is required to determine the answer to the user's query. While in this particular and many similar cases, a database or spreadsheet in combination with some simple algorithms are sufficient, for more complex domains or queries more sophisticated methods have to be used.

## Domain Modeling (DM)

In contrast to the experimental approach to science (the historically questionable apple falling on Newton's head), the analytical approach to science relies on the construction of abstract models that capture essential aspects of a system under investigation (e.g., Newton's work on celestial mechanics and universal gravitation). In this context, Domain Modeling refers to the development of computer-readable specification of essential aspects of a system, and is often combined with methods that allow the description of dynamical aspects. Although not necessarily under this particular term, domain modeling has long been associated with the specification and implementation of computer programs, be it with the intention of explicitly simulating some aspect of the real world, or in connection with the attempt to capture knowledge about a domain. While in systems design and software engineering there is sometimes a gap between the specification of a domain model (e.g. in UML) and its implementation, this gap is typically less pronounced for knowledge-based systems. In recent years, ontologies have evolved as a domain modeling method for knowledge-centric systems. Here, an important aspect of ontologies is the context they can offer for information and knowledge extraction. In the above bus example, domain aspects like the structure of a bus schedule as consisting of a series of time points associated with locations (the bus stops), together with domain constraints (e.g. that the value of the time points increases in the direction in which the bus travels) can be captured in an ontology. For a more in-depth investigation of this seemingly simple example (see Wang, Ding, & Jiang, 2005; or the IBK-SightSpeeding App for iPhone and Android, which uses the Public Transport ontology to create an efficient route in respect to time and price).

## Knowledge Extraction

The distinction between Information Extraction and Knowledge Extraction (Vargas-Vera, et al., 2001) is somewhat fuzzy. For us, we consider the identification of single items (often named entities) by themselves IE, whereas a concerted effort to extract a set of such entities together with the relationships that tie them together Knowledge Extraction. In practice, IE may happen at a lower level of abstraction or earlier in the pipeline, and KE occurs when many extracted items and relationships are brought together and integrated into an ontology. Knowledge Extraction is also closely related to Knowledge Acquisition in knowledge-based systems; the latter, however, often refers to activities performed by humans, and is not limited to the identification and extraction of knowledge

from documents already in computer-readable format. In many knowledge-based systems, knowledge is represented in the form of rules and facts, into which the structure of the domain is incorporated. Ontologies on the other hand, often make this structure explicit, and rely on a set of core relationships to express this structure. Our focus here is on the extraction of knowledge from text-based documents, and does not include such techniques as rule extraction from neural networks, or via data mining. Although approaches for the automatic generation of ontologies from collections of text documents are under development, often under the term Ontology Learning, our experiences indicate that human knowledge analysts play an important role at this stage. They typically have a significant amount of domain knowledge, are familiar with the expected tasks, and possess valuable common-sense knowledge that still is rather elusive for computers.

An excellent overview of ontology-based information extraction is provided in Wimalasuriya and Dou (2010), and Weikum and Theobald (2010) describe how to harvest entities and relationships from Web sources. Open information extraction on the Web (e.g. Textrunner) (Yates, et al., 2007; Banko, et al., 2007) is the focus of ongoing research at the University of Washington. All these approaches incorporate entities, relationships, and utilize ontologies to describe a domain model; thus, according to our above definition, they fall into the category of Knowledge Extraction.

## Reasoning

The focus of knowledge extraction approaches is usually on the identification and representation of entities and relationships among them. At an informal level, this can be represented and visualized through graphs, and captured in mind maps, concept maps, or more formalized structures such as topic maps and ontologies. While entities and relationships are clearly essential for the construction of a domain model, they are not sufficient. Additional knowledge about the domain is frequently captured through rules. A core set of rules referring to generally accepted key rules and aspects of a domain is often formalized in the form of axioms for the domain. In addition to the axioms, other rules describe more specific aspects of the domain, possibly referring to localized sub-areas in the domain, or expressing viewpoints that are not generally accepted by the community or organization maintaining the domain model. These rules form the basis for reasoning in the domain, and are used to generate new knowledge, to examine relations among existing pieces of knowledge, or to answer queries that cannot be satisfied by simply looking up combinations of facts and relations. Extracting such rules is a major challenge for computer-based systems. Depending on the nature of the source documents, it may be feasible to extract specific rules that are formulated in natural language, but close enough to the representation of rules in computers. For example, a medical textbook may describe a heuristic for diagnosing an illness based on a set of symptoms through a set of if-then statements. Such statements correspond closely to rules, and can be converted with moderate effort. Constructing a set of rules for the axioms of a domain, on the other hand, typically requires a deep understanding of the domain, and the ability to analyze the consequences of incorporating or leaving out some axioms, or of restructuring them. Thus our assumption here is that a core domain model captured as an ontology with the most important concepts and relations, together with a suitable set of axioms, is either already available, or will be developed by skilled analysts in collaboration with knowledge engineers. Once this core domain model is in place, additional rules may be incorporated by analysts, possibly based on candidate rules extracted from source documents. Beyond the computational difficulties of extracting knowledge to be incorporated into the domain model, the task of developing and maintaining such a model requires a well-

defined process, especially if it is conducted in a distributed manner (Giarratano & Riley, 2005).

## VISION

The use of information extraction technology can provide benefits in processing large volumes of text documents and organize or categorize the information. To provide meaningful use of the extracted information it has to be placed in a larger context, which describes the role of every piece of information in the domain. This domain context can also provide help in extracting information from documents and organizing it. The bidirectional relationship between the domain context and the extraction process is necessary for the accuracy and relevance of the extracted information.

The vision of this research work relies on an ontology to provide the context, i.e. the bigger picture, and to be a medium for performing intelligent analysis. A domain ontology describes the entities in the domain and how they relate. The ontology may also include some rules on how new entities emerge or constraints on the way entities relate to each other. Given this detailed description of the domain in terms of its entities and their behavior, a context now exists for the information coming out of this domain. Figure 1 depicts the intended outcome of the system.

Another aspect of the vision is the ability to process the extracted information in an intelligent way. The sophisticated structures of the ontology, along with the rules that describe their behavior offer an opportunity to perform inference on the existing information, which may lead to producing new information.

The ontology can play a guiding role in the extraction and interpretation of information. The entities in the ontology can serve as a target for the extraction process. The extraction tools can take a set of entity types from the ontology and process the repository documents for entities that

*Figure 1. From text to ontology*

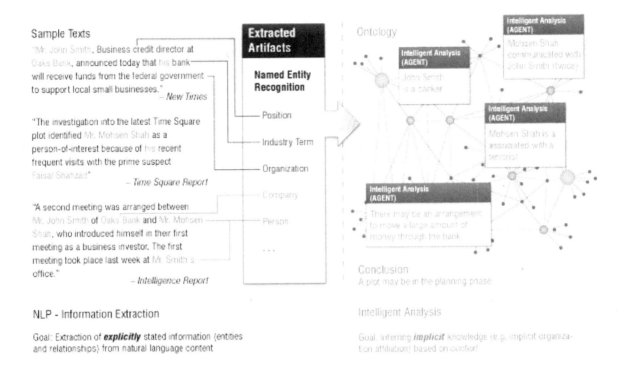

fit the description of the ontology entities. This can make the extraction process more efficient and more accurate. The ontology structure provides guidance for the types of other entities that may be connected to any given entity to make the extraction process more comprehensive.

A key aspect of the vision is the user opportunity for involvement in every step of the process from extraction to interpretation, ontology population, inference, and request for additional information. The interpretation of textual material in natural language is ambiguous and requires user knowledge of the domain to double check the automated work of the system for accuracy and relevance. The user can also provide guidance to the extraction process in the form of rules of extraction (in rule-based extraction) or for adjusting the results of training data (in statistical approaches).

The processing of extracted information may expose the need for more information, which guides the extraction process to look for specific types of entities. The emergence of new entities in the ontology as a result of inference may also trigger the need for more extractions. This iterative nature of the process, along with user involvement is essential to producing meaningful results and can support the complex analysis work for the user.

The objective of the research is to produce a generic platform, which can be configured with external services and a domain ontology to suit the needs of different types of users. There are existing services that provide some of the needed functionality, such as crawling the Web for information that fit given criteria, or extracting generic information from plain text documents. It is important for the success of this system to allow the integration of external services and provide tools to process their results into the domain ontology.

## SYSTEM ARCHITECTURE

The design of the ODIX platform is based on a Service-Oriented Architecture (SOA). There are four initial services, which perform the Web crawling function, the NLP extraction function,

the ontology and inference functions and external support functions as shown in Figure 2.

## Natural Language Processing Technologies

There are several approaches to performing automated extraction of information using natural language text. These approaches often fall into one of two broad categories: rule-based approaches

*Figure 2. System architecture*

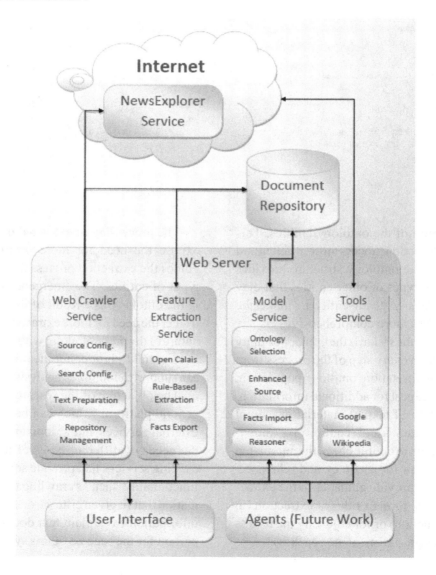

and statistical approaches. In this section, we will provide a short description of each approach and the benefits of each.

In a rule-based approach, an expert specifies exact rules, which a text phrase must match in order to capture an individual extraction. A domain expert knows what patterns are present in speech and how phrases are used in various contexts and the expert specifies these rules usually using some type of rule language. One of the primary advantages of a rule-based approach is that the extractions themselves can be typically very precise. Rule-based approaches tend to be difficult to maintain because of the fact that a human expert is needed to specify the rules and if additional rules are needed, new rules must be created. This makes transferring the information extraction process to and from different domain areas more work in order to create the new rules.

Statistical approaches on the other hand utilize the frequency of various phrasing and sentence patterns in order to build natural statistical models for information extraction. Given a known set of parsed sentences or a set of labeled documents, various machine-learning approaches can be applied to the data in order to build models of the parameters of the data. Given these models, predictions can be performed when a new sentence or document is provided. Statistical approaches can be more general and translate well from domain to domain, but the difficulty lies in providing labeled data sets to build the models.

## Ontologies as a Means of Expressing Context

While computers can accomplish rudimentary processing of data (e.g., presentation, parsing, etc.) without an understanding of its meaning, software intended to intelligently analyze such content requires a representational model capable of expressing the concepts, entities, and relationships that together provide *context*. This can be accomplished utilizing a type of model known as

an *ontology*. Ontologies provide an expressive, cohesive description of a domain that can be used by intelligent software components to answer in-depth questions as to the nature of relevant aspects of a domain. Typically rich with relationships, such domain knowledge is an integral component allowing intelligent software to effectively *reason* about an event or situation within the context in which it occurs.

Ontologies come in a variety of forms differing in their ability to precisely express intricate concepts and characteristics as well as their capacity to accommodate modifications in existing concepts or introduction of wholly new concepts while maintaining overall integrity and consistency. Well-crafted ontologies support these qualities through the exploitation of powerful analysis patterns (Fowler, 1997) that engineer into such models qualities such as expression, flexibility, and extensibility.

## Opportunities and Challenges

Within the last twenty years, research and practical experimentation with ontologies has grown significantly. The establishment of the Workshop on Ontology Patterns in 2009 is evidence that the field is maturing. Hepp et al. (2007) summarizes the six advancements that ontologies provide:

- Use of philosophical guidance for identifying stable and reusable conceptual elements.
- Unique identifiers for conceptual elements.
- Excluding unwanted interpretations by means of informal semantics.
- Excluding unwanted interpretations by means of formal semantics.
- Inferring implicit facts automatically.
- Spotting logical inconsistencies.

It is important to note that the formal semantics are only one reason for the use of ontologies. Informal semantics (textual descriptions and naming conventions, among others) facilitate understanding between the ontology and its users and are important for maintaining consistency within the ontology.

Ontologies, however, are not suitable for all projects. There are significant costs involved with creating and maintaining an ontology as well as computational concerns with implementing reasoning. Ontologies are also inappropriate when the source information they will be used with is largely unstructured (Hepp, et al., 2007). We believe that the richness of natural language knowledge extraction provides an important motivation for the use of ontologies, since this data demands flexibility of storage and is highly structured.

## A Methodology for Ontology Development

Developing the ontological models that provide the context necessary for agents to interpret and reason about data requires an effective system of methods, principles, and rules. Certainly not exclusive, the methodology outlined below provides a process whereby key concepts are initially captured in a form unburdened by concerns for formality, extensibility, or even consistency. Once captured within the fluidity of a Concept Map, model content is progressively engineered with the aid of powerful analysis patterns into an expressive, consistent, and extensible formal Ontology. In some cases, this model may be further processed into a form known as an Implementation Model that adapts model structure in favor of target performance requirements and implementation constraints.

The process of building an ontology consists of a number of steps to ensure the validity and completeness of the final product. While these steps include the significant, yet peripheral activities of model documentation, communication, validation, and potential integration with external models of varying levels of expressiveness, the methodology outlined below focuses on the two core activities of identifying the model's primary purpose and the construction of a model that successfully satisfies such mandate.

## Step 1: Identifying the Purpose

The intended use of the ontology must be defined in some formal way to guide the development process. Without a well-defined purpose of the ontology, development can continue with no apparent end-state, and the ontology can grow in different directions beyond the control of system developers. Some common purposes of ontologies include the representation of knowledge in a given domain of interest, facilitating communication among system components, re-use by other applications, or as a common language for multiple systems within the same domain.

An effective method for defining the purpose of the ontology is by means of use-cases. The intended application of the ontology can be broken down into specific, well-defined types of usage in which actors and actions are identified as well as the perceived components that will be involved in each action. Another tool for identifying the purpose of an ontology is a set of questions, which the ontology is supposed to answer.

The ontology is complete, in the context of a given set of requirements, when all the use-cases are supported by ontology concepts and all the types of questions to be asked can be effectively addressed by the model.

## Step 2: Constructing the Ontology

Once the purpose and scope of the model have been clearly identified, development of the first form of the model (i.e., concept map) can commence. Relevant concepts and relationships are freely described in a form closely aligning with the knowledge acquired from a variety of knowledge acquisition resources including textbooks, interviewing Subject Matter Experts (SME), case studies, analysis reports, and so on. At this stage, little attention is given to engineering this knowledge with the qualities of consistency, extensibility, or formality. One of the primary methods of capturing knowledge in a particular domain is utilizing a subject matter expert to articulate the concepts pertaining to relevant areas of operations. The key knowledge is identifiable as concepts relating to the purpose of the ontology. Such knowledge typically addresses critical questions necessary to support identified use-cases or contributes to the communication among system components. Other concepts that help to relate key concepts to each other or add details to key concepts are considered supporting concepts and are also captured within the concept map. As the concept map evolves, it provides a useful tool to communicate with various stakeholders and where applicable, validate captured knowledge with key experts. Once areas of the concept map have been adequately validated and stabilized, they are candidates to be engineered into a formal ontology.

The task of processing components of the concept map into a formal ontology involves the selection of an appropriate specification method. The language chosen for coding an ontology (e.g., formal logic, Unified Modeling Language [UML], Web Ontology Language [OWL], etc.) must provide the following characteristics:

- **Conceptual distance:** The ability of the language to represent abstract concepts at multiple levels of abstraction.
- **Expressive power:** The ability to represent complex concepts with consistent language constructs.
- **Standards compliant:** The language should follow accepted standards and notations to allow for better communication among development team members.
- **Translatability:** The language constructs have formal structures that can be converted to forms in other languages, without undue ambiguity.

- **Formal semantics:** The intended meaning of each language construct is unambiguous and well-defined.
  - For example, the selected coding language may be OWL to facilitate Web-based interaction. OWL satisfies many of the selection criteria mentioned above.
- **Conceptual distance:** OWL allows the representation of abstract concepts, maintaining its level of abstraction and allowing for details as needed.
- **Expressive power:** OWL employs description logic in a dynamic environment utilizing the open world assumption. Description logic is a powerful mechanism for stating concepts.
- **Standards:** OWL is based on RDF, which is a standard that is becoming more popular with many tools for processing formats.
- **Translatability:** As a formal language with well-defined semantics, OWL can be translated into other implementation languages, especially RDF-based languages. The degree to which the translation preserves all of the ontology features depends on the target language and its supported features.
- **Formal semantics:** OWL has well-defined semantics for language constructs. The semantics capability is supported by *Reasoner* specifications that describe what a valid structure should be.

Once a suitable paradigm and associated specification language has been selected, the concepts and information captured within the concept map must be described within this language and skillfully engineered to be consistent and expressive. The resulting model should also be engineered with enough flexibility to support graceful integration of the additional concepts and features that inevitably occur throughout the model's lifecycle. The form, in which these analysis patterns (Fowler, 1997) exist, and the manner, in which they are applied, tend to differ depending on the modeling paradigm and associated language that is selected. Patterns for models described in more rigid paradigms such as the those supported by the UML will differ in form and application as compared to patterns applicable for more relaxed paradigms such as those supported by OWL. Regardless of the paradigm, selection and effective application of analysis patterns that underpin domain content is crucial to the utility and longevity of the resulting ontology.

Although terminology is important in the formulation of a concept map as a means of capturing domain language in its raw form, it becomes even more critical during the development of the formal ontology. Further, while formality and consistency are important objectives in the formulation of an ontology, these qualities must be engineered in a manner that retains the individual perspectives of key domains (Pohl, 2006). The goal is to closely align the terminology and content pertaining to differing groups of users with the way in which they 'view the world.' Supporting multiple perspectives for concepts and information that may be the basis for communication across user group, or domain boundaries highlights the significance of engineering an ontology with select analysis patterns. For example, the roles pattern is a powerful analysis pattern that can be used to dynamically connect entities with the various contexts they are involved in at any point in time. Although a vehicle may typically behave as something that is used to transport passengers or cargo, in some situations it is the vehicle itself that is being transported. This is a common scenario in military logistics where large-scale deployments involve the seaborne transportation of the vehicles intended to be used as ground transports once they arrive in the theater. In this case it would be highly valuable for users and intelligent software alike to be able to view and interact with such vehicles in terms of the individual contexts. In the context being shipped to the theater, interacting with it as cargo

would be useful. In the context of projecting using the vehicle in various planned deliveries once it arrives, interacting with it as a transport would be desirable. Supporting such expressive qualities is especially important within intelligent information systems that engage in extensive analysis of concepts and characteristics in a rich, domain-centric manner.

It should also be noted that accommodating domain bias goes beyond terminology and also includes structure. Regardless of how it is termed, some features may only be relevant to a subset of perspectives, and may need to be described in individual forms. In the same manner, features that are not relevant to certain domain perspectives should not be represented within the associated description of that concept for that domain group. The need to incorporate such precision while at the same time supporting the flexibility and dynamics of multiple, varying perspectives highlights the importance of engineering powerful analysis patterns into the foundation of the ontology.

The final step in developing a useable ontology is to produce a version of the model that can be directly coded against. This form of the ontology is known as the Implementation Model. Similar to there being many ways to implement a design, many implementation models can be produced that support a single formal ontology. These implementations may differ from one another based on the specifics of the various implementation languages and performance constraints. Translation of analysis patterns into these implementations may also differ depending on the constructs and facilities each implementation paradigm provides.

Since the formal ontology is highly expressive and detailed in nature, there is considerable scope for implementation models to be automatically generated from ontology specifications. This can be a significant time savings in the development process and also allow for inevitable changes in the ontology to be quickly reflected in implementation.

To preserve the integrity and accuracy of the concepts and information represented within the ontology as it is processed into an implementation model, constant attention should be given to avoid prematurely compromising such qualities in favor of implementation concerns. There are typically many ways implementation constraints can be addressed solely at the implementation level by applying various design patterns and techniques (e.g., caching, facades, etc.).

Although modifying the representational purity and intention of the ontology should be a last resort, sometimes it is unavoidable. In such situations where it is important to maintain a distinction between the target ontology that exhibits the true representational accuracy of the domain content and its implementation model variant. Capturing the deviations along with their justification at the time can be useful in tracking exactly what compromise was made, why it was made, and what impact it has on the implementation model's ability to support the intended concept.

## The OWL Representational Paradigm

At the heart of the semantic environment is the context model, or ontology, which contains the concepts necessary to describe and reason about the extracted information fragments produced by the enhanced NLP capability. Particular attention was given to the selection of the appropriate representational paradigm suitable to support the flexibility and inference involved in semantic analysis. This paradigm must provide a somewhat relaxed view of classification along with native support for embedding inference logic within the very concepts that it semantically relates to. Following investigation into several more traditional paradigms, we decided upon OWL as the representational language and execution platform suitable for this research.

OWL is a semantic markup language whose primary purpose is to facilitate the publishing and sharing of ontologies across the World Wide Web (WWW). OWL is intended to be used by software applications that need to process Web-based content in a meaningful manner. That is, OWL-based content is designed to be machine-interpretable.

A typical OWL environment consists of several key components that support both model development as well as subsequent execution. A characteristic OWL execution platform consists of a triple-store where model content is persisted, a reasoner capable of inferring additional concepts based on embedded and externalized logic, and a query engine used to ask questions regarding model content. Together, these components form a cohesive platform for the development and execution of semantic content.

Perhaps the most significant component of any OWL environment is the reasoner and as such warrants a more detailed description of its tasks. As the name implies, the main function of this component is to essentially reason about a given OWL model and its associated content. More specifically, an OWL reasoner processes class definitions, individuals, and rules in an effort to accomplish two primary objectives. The first of these tasks is to identify any logical inconsistencies existing within the model definition and its use. As the platform produced by this research supports user-driven importation of ontologies applicable to the target analysis domain (e.g., intelligence, logistics, command and control, etc.), this feature can be used to verify decidability and logical consistency of such models. The second task performed by the reasoner is to identify any additional knowledge that can be automatically inferred based on the logic accompanying the model definition in conjunction with associated content. This additional knowledge can include subsumption and association relationships along with the adjustment of classification of various scenario content. Although only beginning to emerge within the timeframe of this research, some reasoners are beginning to have the ability to not only infer additional content, but to retract previously inferred content whose truth can no longer be established (i.e., truth maintenance). This is a crucial feature for any practical application of automated reasoning as establishing what is no longer true is as important as the initial inference that produced it.

Above and beyond the components comprising its typical platform, the OWL representational paradigm supports several very powerful concepts that can be successfully exploited by the information extraction process. These concepts provide the flexibility to represent as of yet unclassifiable extractions as well as to repeatedly adjust the definitions of those that can be classified at the present time.

## Multiple Classification

Multiple classification is the ability for something to be simultaneously defined under two or more classifications. This is a very powerful capability and has significant implications on the manner in which representational models are developed. Unlike traditional, more rigid modeling paradigms where inheritance must be employed as a means for the specialization of concepts, OWL modelers enjoy a much more flexible environment without concern for relating classifications in order to support a single entity exhibiting features defined across multiple classifications. Once qualification rules are embedded within class definitions, the management of exactly which classifications are appropriate at any given time can be conveniently offloaded onto the OWL reasoner.

## Dynamic Classification

Dynamic classification is the ability for the classification of something to be adjusted throughout time. In contrast to the traditional approach of re-instantiating an entity under a new classification, dynamic classification offers the means to preserve referential integrity by maintaining the existence of the original entity by only changing which type characteristics are currently applicable. This capability goes hand-in-hand with multiple classification in creating a dynamic environment where extracted facts can effectively mutate throughout their lifecycle as additional knowledge is encountered. Like management of multiple classification, determining exactly what classification(s) an OWL object qualifies for at any point in time is typically the responsibility of the OWL reasoner.

## Logical Assumptions

Traditional database systems operate under a set of assumptions in order to enable the query engine to return meaningful responses. These suppositions include the closed world assumption, the unique name assumption, and the domain closure assumption.

The closed world assumption states that if a statement cannot be proven true, given the information in the database, then it must be false. The unique name assumption states that two distinct constants designate two different objects within the given universe. The domain closure assumption states that there are no other objects in the universe than those designated by constants within the database.

These assumptions were reasonable in a world where a database represented all the information available about a given domain and no external information sources were needed to perform the functions of any database application. Since this time, however, the Internet has become a major source of information with the effectiveness of many applications being based on access to external information from sources that may be unknown at the time of application design. This has required a different kind of knowledge representation, capable of dealing with the openness of the Internet. The open world assumption was adopted to allow for the relaxation of the constraints imposed by the closed world assumption. Along with the open world assumption, the other two assumptions were consequently also relaxed.

Under an open world assumption, all things are possible unless asserted otherwise. This is in stark contrast to traditional decision-support paradigms where the volume and extent of considerations is limited to what is explicitly asserted to be true about the world at any given time. Although operating under an open world assumption has implications on model development, it is primarily model usage and interpretation that is affected since logic operating across such a model must refrain from assuming too much and be receptive to the possibility that some information is yet to be discovered.

## Unconstrained Composition of Features

The ability to describe the characteristics of an entity in a manner unbound by available definitions can be very helpful when dealing with evolving knowledge within an open environment. With environments equipped with such flexibility, information extractions can be characterized and continuously re-characterized in a manner unconstrained by current classification(s) or known concepts. Working in conjunction with dynamic classification, as an entity's characteristics evolve or otherwise change, so may its alignment with available definitions. As described earlier, determining exactly what changes in classification are appropriate is typically the responsibility of the reasoner.

The complementary partnership between this set of representational concepts is one of the most powerful aspects of the OWL paradigm. Collectively, these mechanisms support a progressive and fluid understanding of extracted information fragments within a dynamic and constantly evolving context.

## Capability for Reasoning

In addition to being a powerful description language, OWL provides a useful representation for reasoning. Two types of inference can be preformed over OWL ontologies. The first method is the use of OWL semantics for deriving new knowledge from existing facts, which will be referred to here as OWL inference. The second is to use custom made rules for rule-based reasoning over the triples constructing the ontology.

The OWL language description provides formal semantics for deriving new knowledge from existing facts. Property Characteristics are particularly useful for reasoning, although they are not the only mechanism for reasoning. Property Characteristics allow additional description of an OWL property, such as setting a property to be the inverse of another property. Many OWL tools such as Protégé, Pellet, and Jena, have built in capabilities for performing OWL inference. The result is that the users of OWL need only to properly describe their domain with OWL to allow for inference. Because many facts can be derived this way, users can describe only a subset of the individuals and their properties and allow the reasoning capabilities to create the full set.

In cases where a more general method is needed, it is also possible to reason over the triples with an ontology using rules. Reasoners such as Jena, BigOWLIM, and others, allow for the execution of custom rule sets over an ontology. This is important in the cases where some reasoning cannot be described in OWL. All OWL inference is limited to OWL semantics and is monotonic. In order to reason over an ontology in a non-monotonic fashion (such as reasoning by default, or removing outdated information) rule-based inference needs to be applied. It should also be noted that all OWL inference can be written in the form of rules and is therefore can be seen as a special case of rule-based inference, the case where the rule set describes reasoning over only OWL semantics. Rule-based inference can therefore also be used to extend OWL semantics by adding to the basic OWL inference rule set.

A practical approach for managing the inference related to an ontology is through the use of a community of software agents. Delegating varying inference goals to agents presents an opportunity to increase the overall flexibility of the system. For example, a complex chain of rule-based inference can be encapsulated within an agent to be run at specific times or when specific conditions are met. Dividing large rule sets into agents has the additional benefit of reducing the set of rules stored directly with the ontology, increasing readability and enforcing separation of concerns.

## Service-Oriented Architecture (SOA) Influence

The design of the approach to information extraction presented in this chapter is greatly influenced by a service-oriented methodology. The primary components of the system are architected as services that offer the flexibility and agility inherent in Service-Oriented Architecture (SOA) designs. The decision to architect the information extraction capability in a service-oriented manner was twofold. First, the extraction of information is an activity that is intended to be invoked on a repetitive basis by numerous external users as a part of their larger business processes. As such, it is useful to deploy the information extraction capability as a whole in the form of a discoverable and subsequently invocable service that adheres to applicable Web service standards. Second, the designers felt it useful to have the ability to easily exchange select components of what amounts to a multi-faceted capability with alternative solutions in an effort to experiment with effectiveness and performance. As such, it seemed advantageous to carry the service-oriented concept into the internal architecture as well. It was anticipated that doing so would produce a test bed-like environment where internal capabilities were extensively decoupled and primed for potential replacement or partnering with additional, complementary capabilities.

For our work, we utilize the Unstructured Information Management Architecture (UIMA) document processing framework. This framework handles multiple documents and allows our application to process and annotate several documents during each stage of our information extraction task. The UIMA architecture provides facilities that allow the creation of individual annotators, which can be used to perform specific NLP tasks. In our work, we create an annotator to identify if a particular name in a document is the name of a known terrorist.

For the task of information extraction, we utilize the OpenCalais service provided by Thomson Reuters. This service takes individual documents as input and provides an RDF file, which labels several various entities and relationships. In our application, we focus on the following entities and relationships provided by OpenCalais: Person-Career, PersonCommunication, PersonRelation, and FinancialInstitution. PersonCareer defines the relationship that a person was or currently is an employee of a particular institution. PersonCommunication defines the event that two people plan to communicate with each other. PersonRelation declares that a type of relationship exists between two people. FinancialInstitution is an entity that OpenCalais believes is a financial institution.

Using the extracted entities and relationship that OpenCalais provides for each document, we aggregate the common occurrences across several documents and tabulate the frequency of these occurrences. This information, along with the information extracted from the rule-based UIMA terrorist annotator, shown in Figure 3, is combined and an RDF file is created which contains all of the assertions.

## Model Service

The Model Service is SOAP Web service that hosts the ontology management component of our system. Jena is used as the primary tool for managing and persisting the ontology. Jena's SQL-based storage allows the ontology to be saved over multiple Web sessions. This service contains functionality for loading a domain-specific ontology. This ontology forms the heart of the knowledge representation for the system.

*Figure 3. Extraction example*

**1. Al-Qaeda's top** commander Osama bin Laden

**Extraction rule: (terrorist_organization + "\s+(" + adjectives + "\s+)*" +
person_role + "\s+" + person)**

**2. Osama bin Laden, the top** Al-Qaeda commander

**Extraction rule: (person + ",\s+(a|an|the)\s+(" + adjectives + "\s+)*" +
terrorist_organization + "\s+" + person_role)**

The Model Service also contains the translation functionality to both import extractions from the NLP component and export selected knowledge to the user interface. An importation process is necessary because the NLP extractions are built around the OpenCalais rather than the domain-specific ontology. While it may seem like extra work to translate out of the ontology of the NLP, this process enforces flexibility within the system. It is possible for the Model Service to be configured to read multiple NLP extractions with different underlying ontologies. Likewise, this allows a single configuration of the NLP Service to create extractions for several Model Services, all with different domain-specific ontologies.

While Jena provides a number of options for exporting ontologies, it was also necessary to create a separate export functionality for interfacing with the user interface component. This is because the user interface requires a general object based XML format, and will not accept RDF/XML. This is a common problem for interoperability between ontologies and Web services and is discussed in Akhtar et al. (2008). Our export solution uses a combination of XML templates and SPARQL queries.

## Provenance

Our method for data extraction through NLP can be applied to a variety of textual sources, possibly obtained through the Web. We cannot guarantee the veracity of these sources, so our system must

have the capability to record and manage the trustworthiness of the extraction. For our application, provenance is the process of tracking the source or derivation of a fact within the assertion component (ABox) of our ontology.

To establish provenance, all facts imported from the NLP are connected to a source object via RDF reification. The contents of the source object for NLP imported facts include the name of the file and the offset and length of where the extraction occurred. This information could be supplemented with additional facts relating to a measure of the trustworthiness of the source, confidence in the NLP extraction, or other metadata relating to the fact. All facts are RDF reified since facts relating to the same individual do not necessarily come from the same NLP extraction.

During reasoning, additional source objects are asserted to maintain provenance. Rather than having a source article, these source objects relate the new fact to the ABox facts that were used to derive it, as well as the terminology component (TBox) facts that triggered the reasoning. This ensures that an ABox fact always have source information, regardless of whether it was extracted directly or inferred. We achieve this through a modified version of Jena's OWL inference rules by adding the source manipulation and creation components to the rules themselves. This is a highly experimental approach, although it is similar to Vacura and Svatek (2010). Unlike their approach, our method restricts provenance to the ABox, and thus requires no additional manage-

*Figure 4. Example Inference*

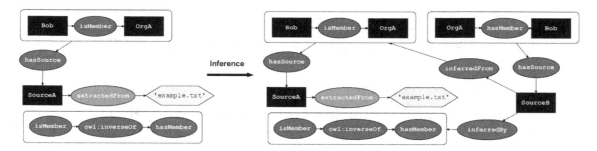

ment outside of a modified rule set. Since RDF reification creates an explosion of additional facts within the ontology, we believe this approach will be best suited to environments that handle named triples without reification, such as BigOWLIM.

Figure 4 shows and example of inference and attached source information.

## CASE STUDY

We present an example of a system that is developed on the ODIX platform to illustrate its main features and to highlight the advantages of our approach. Our case study deals with the analysis of a large volume of text, which is obtained from many news sources, focusing on terrorist activities. Running the inference engine on the extracted entities aims at expanding the ontology by creating new relationships and even new objects. The case study also addresses the user experience and the importance of user involvement throughout the process.

### Collecting Relevant Data

The first task in the analysis process is to collect text documents, which contain information about the subject matter. The user interface, (shown in Figure 5) provides a Web access module, which collects news articles by accessing a news aggregation service. The user can set a date range, a selection of keywords and a maximum number of articles to download. For our case study, we download documents about terrorist attacks within the date range of December 2009 and January 2010. This module also allows the user to manage the document repository, by adding more documents, deleting entire folders, and displaying the text of any selected document. The relevant documents are collected in a folder for processing.

### Extracting Entities and Relationship with NLP

The user can now run the NLP extraction service on all the documents in the selected folder. The result of NLP extraction is a structured RDF file, which contains the entities, which were extracted from all the documents in the folder and the relationships that existed among them. This RDF file is saved on the server for access by other modules. It can also be displayed as a text file in the text display area. The downloading and extraction processes can be repeated as many times as desired, until the user is satisfied with the amount of information.

### Loading an Ontology

Now that the document repository has enough information, the inference engine can be utilized by going to the inference tab (Figure 6). The 'Service Setup' function makes sure that the inference engine is ready. The user can now select an

*Figure 5. ODIX repository control*

OWL model to load for reasoning and an RDF file to load for populating the ontology. We load an ontology, which describes terrorist organizations and financial institutions, along with the concepts of organization membership and person-to-person communication.

## Populating the Ontology with Extracted Entities

When the RDF file is loaded, the user can now examine its content in tabular format and as a graph. The tables on the left-hand side allow the user to see the entities (the upper table) and the relationships (the lower table). The graph area displays the same information as a network of connected entities. For our case study, the loaded

entities contain an organization that is identified as a terrorist organization, a person who is a member of this organization, an organization that is identified as a financial organization (bank), a person who is a member of the bank, and an instance of communication object between the two people.

## Maintaining Source Information

The user now has the opportunity to examine the source documents for any extracted entity or relationship. When the user makes a selection in the object table on the left, some details are presented above the graph area about this object, including a link to the source document, where this object was extracted. If the user wants to look at the source document, they can click on that

*Figure 6. Inference engine*

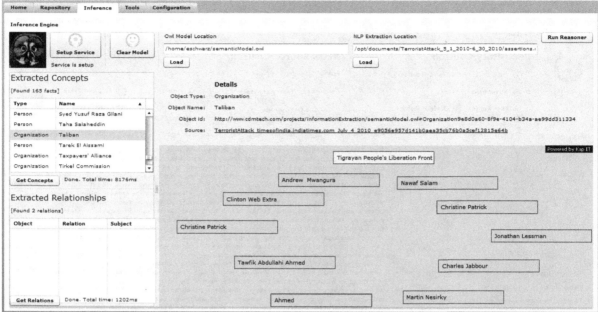

link and the document will be displayed in the text area on the repository tab. It is possible that an entity is extracted from multiple documents. In this case, the detailed information will have a list of links to all the source documents, and the user can examine any one of them.

## Running the Reasoner and Creating New Entities

At this point, the user can see on the graph two organizations, each with one member and the two people are linked with a communications object. The user can run the reasoner to execute any rules that address this situation. The rule set in this case study has a rule that creates a potential terrorist plot, if a person linked to a terrorist organization makes contact with a person linked with a financial organization. When the user runs the reasoner now, a plot object is created and is linked to the two people in question.

## DOMAIN ADAPTATION

The ODIX platform is designed to support the implementation of many domains with the flexibility to provide inference capabilities to any given ontology. The development of a domain-specific system on the ODIX platform requires additional development and configuration tasks.

The first task is to develop a domain ontology, which describes the objects of interest in the given domain and the relationships that exist among them, thus defining the context for the application. The domain ontology may also include basic rules of inference, which determine class membership for objects, or simple property chain inference. An important aspect of the ontology development is to define the types of queries that are needed by the user interface and provide support for fulfilling such queries in a user-friendly manner.

The second task is to develop intelligent agents, which provide the required analysis. Agents operate on ontology objects and need to be aware of the ontology structure. Agent analysis is defined by the requirements for the application.

In addition to development tasks, some configuration may need to take place on the platform. Extraction rules, for example, help classify some of the extracted entities into more specific classes based on the role they play in the text. For example, the role of a person in an organization, or the classification of an organization as a terrorist organization can be defined by extraction rules, which can be added to the platform or even loaded at run-time.

Another configuration element is lists of known entities that may be helpful for the extraction process. For example, in a financial system, a list of known financial institutions and their classification can be added to the platform and used at run-time to identify extracted entities.

Other configuration elements will be added to help fine tune user interaction with the system.

## FUTURE WORK

We plan to extend the ODIX platform to allow more flexibility and power in three areas: ontology, reasoning, and deployment.

## Ontology

The ODIX platform is designed to perform NLP extraction and inference in any domain. The case study presents an example of a domain that relies heavily on text documents, which is intelligence analysis. The objective for the platform is to be domain-independent and flexible to meet the requirements of many domains. The platform allows loading of ontologies at runtime. We plan to implement the ability to edit ontologies within a session to adapt to the analysis requirements of the given domain. We also plan to add a feature to edit the extracted entities to merge instances that refer to the same entity, e.g. different spellings of the same name, or to adjust the identification of

an entity. The future versions of the platform will add a confidence level for the extracted entities, based on the source and the appearance of the same entity in multiple sources. Other factors, such as connections to well-known entities may also contribute to the confidence level.

## Reasoning

The reasoning capabilities of ODIX will be extended to meet the objectives of greater user interaction with agents and better and more flexible truth maintenance. Although agents perform their analysis in an autonomous way, there is a need for the user to ask specific questions of agents or direct their analysis by providing priorities or additional information. The ODIX platform will allow more ways for the user to interact with agents, through an agent UI that is accessible at any time. The user will be able to stop an agent and change the settings on some reasoning mechanisms or set goals for the agents to satisfy.

The current state of truth maintenance keeps track of the dependencies among information items and adjusts them as new information is asserted or retracted to maintain the integrity of the current state of the ontology. This is performed by re-running the reasoner every time instances are added to or removed from the ontology. We plan to enhance this process to allow the platform to deal only with the new information and its dependencies. This will allow truth maintenance to run continuously without the user requesting a reasoner check.

## Deployment

The ODIX platform is designed in an SOA environment and runs on remote servers. We plan to deploy the platform to a cloud computing environment, so that the individual services become available to other applications. Both the NLP extraction service and the inference service are generic and can be used separately or combined to build other applications. The cloud computing environment will also offer other services to the platform and applications that use it. These services include security, single sign-on, intelligent routing, load balancing, and location transparency among other services. The objectives of deployment to the cloud are high availability and the ability to process large volumes of documents.

## CONCLUSION

In this chapter, we presented the ODIX platform, which enhances information extraction by providing context and inference capabilities. The platform is designed with SOA principles to provide the flexibility of utilizing external services and the easily integrate with internal services and other system components. The SOA design facilitates the deployment of the system in a Web based environment for user collaboration. The platform uses existing NLP tools to extract information from text documents, which are collected from the Web. This information is then used to populate a domain ontology that is loaded at run time. The ontology provides basic inference rules and external agents provide more complex rules. User involvement is a key aspect in the system design. The user plays an important role in interpreting the extracted information and deciding where it fits in the ontology.

The ODIX platform is a work-in-progress. Future development will add more capabilities to the system and will allow greater user flexibility in interacting with the information extraction process as well as the inference process.

## REFERENCES

Auer, S., & Lehmann, J. (2010). Creating knowledge out of interlinked data. *Semantic Web*, *1*(1), 97–104.

Baeza-Yates, R., & Ribeiro-Neto, B. (2011). *Modern information retrieval: The concepts and technology behind search* (2nd ed.). Reading, MA: Addison-Wesley Professional.

Banko, M., Cafarella, M. J., Soderland, S., Broadhead, M., & Etzioni, O. (2007). Open information extraction from the web. In *Proceedings Of The 20th International Joint Conference On Artificial Intelligence,* (pp. 2670–2676). San Francisco, CA: Morgan Kaufmann Publishers Inc.

Belew, R. (2000). *Finding out about: a cognitive perspective on search engine technology and the WWW*. Cambridge, UK: Cambridge University Press.

Berners-Lee, T., Hendler, J., & Lassila, O. (2001). The semantic web. *Scientific American*, *284*(5), 34–43. doi:10.1038/scientificamerican0501-34

Bush, V. (1945). As we may think. *Atlantic Monthly*, *176*(1), 101–108.

Fowler, M. (1997). *Analysis patterns, reusable object models*. Reading, MA: Addison Wesley Longman.

Giarratano, J. C., & Riley, G. D. (2005). *Expert systems: Principles and programming*. Pacific Grove, CA: Brooks/Cole Publishing Co.

Hepp, M., De Leenheer, P., & de Moor, A. (2007). *Ontology management: Semantic web, semantic web services, and business applications*. Berlin, Germany: Springer.

Lin, T., Etzioni, O., & Fogarty, J. (2009). Identifying interesting assertions from the web. In *Proceeding of the 18th ACM Conference on Information And Knowledge Management*, (pp. 1787–1790). New York, NY: ACM Press.

Manning, C. D., Raghavan, P., & Schütze, H. (2008). *Introduction to information retrieval*. Cambridge, UK: Cambridge University Press. doi:10.1017/CBO9780511809071

Moens, M. (2003). *Information extraction: Algorithms and prospects in a retrieval context*. Berlin, Germany: Springer-Verlag.

Pohl, K. (2006). Perspective models as a means for achieving true representational accuracy. In *Proceedings of the IEEE Aerospace Conference*. Big Sky, MT: IEEE Press.

Russell, S., & Norvig, P. (2009). *Artificial intelligence: A modern approach* (3rd ed.). Upper Saddle River, NJ: Prentice Hall Press.

Schmitt, E. (2010). US tells WikiLeaks to return Afghan war logs. *New York Times*. Retrieved from http://www.nytimes.com/2010/08/06/world/asia/06wiki.html

Vacura, M., & Svatek, V. (2010). Ontology based tracking and propagation of provenance. [NDT.]. *Proceedings of NDT, 2010*, 489–496.

Vargas-Vera, M., Domingue, J., Motta, E., Buckingham Shum, S., & Lanzoni, M. (2001). Knowledge extraction by using an ontology based annotation tool. In *Proceedings of the Workshop on Knowledge Markup and Semantic Annotation (K CAPA 2001)*. Victoria, Canada: K CAPA.

Wang, J., Ding, Z., & Jiang, C. (2005). An ontology-based public transport query system. In *Proceedings of the International Conference on Semantics, Knowledge and Grid (SKG 2005)*. IEEE Press.

Weikum, G., & Theobald, M. (2010). From information to knowledge: Harvesting entities and relationships from web sources. In *Proceedings of the Twenty-Ninth ACM SIGMOD-SIGACT-SIGART Symposium on Principles of Database Systems of Data*, (pp. 65–76). New York, NY: ACM Press.

Wikileaks. (2010). Afghan war diary. *Wikileaks Organization*. Retrieved from http://wikileaks.org/wiki/Afghan_War_Diary,_2004-2010

Wimalasuriya, D. C., & Dou, D. (2010). Ontology-based information extraction: An introduction and a survey of current approaches. *Journal of Information Science, 36*(3), 306–332. doi:10.1177/0165551509360123

Yates, A., Cafarella, M., Banko, M., Etzioni, O., Broadhead, M., & Soderland, S. (2007). TextRunner: Open information extraction on the web. In *Proceedings of Human Language Technologies: The Annual Conference of the North American Chapter of the Association for Computational Linguistics*, (p. 25–26). Morristown, NJ: ACL.

## ADDITIONAL READING

Alves, A., Antunes, B., Pereira, F. C., & Bento, C. (2009). Semantic enrichment of places: Ontology learning from web. *International Journal of Knowledge-Based and Intelligent Engineering Systems, 13*(1), 19–30.

Bawden, D., & Robinson, L. (2008). The dark side of information: overload, anxiety and other paradoxes and pathologies. *Journal of Information Science, 35*(2), 180–191. doi:10.1177/0165551508095781

Bellifemine, F. L., Caire, G., & Greenwood, D. (2007). *Developing multi-agent systems with JADE*. New York, NY: Wiley. doi:10.1002/9780470058411

Bordini, R. H., Dastani, M., Dix, J., & Seghrouchni, A. E. F. (2006). *Programming multi-agent systems: Third international workshop, ProMAS 2005 revised and invited papers*. Utrecht, The Netherlands: Springer.

Bordini, R. H., Dastani, M., & Seghrouchni, A. E. F. (2010). *Multi-agent programming: Languages, platforms and applications*. Berlin, Germany: Springer.

Buse, D. P., & Wu, Q. (2010). *IP network-based multi-agent systems for industrial automation: Information management, condition monitoring and control of power systems.* Berlin, Germany: Springer.

Carvey, P. M. (1998). *Drug action in the central nervous system.* Oxford, UK: Oxford University Press.

Chen, S., Terano, T., & Yamamoto, R. (2011). *Agent-based approaches in economic and social complex systems VI: Post-proceedings of The AESCS international workshop 2009.* Berlin, Germany: Springer. doi:10.1007/978-4-431-53907-0

Cho, W. C., & Richards, D. (2007). Ontology construction and concept reuse with formal concept analysis for improved web document retrieval. *Web Intelligence and Agent Systems, 5*(1), 109-126. Retrieved from http://iospress.metapress.com/content/187272723XUL1571

Choren, R., Garcia, A., Lucena, C., & Romanovsky, A. (2005). *Software engineering for multi-agent systems III: Research issues and practical applications.* Berlin, Germany: Springer. doi:10.1007/b106347

Croft, B., Metzler, D., & Strohman, T. (2009). *Search engines: Information retrieval in practice.* Reading, MA: Addison Wesley.

d'Inverno, M., & Luck, M. (2010). *Understanding agent systems* (2nd ed.). Berlin, Germany: Springer.

Dou, D. (2010). Ontology-based information extraction: An introduction and a survey of current approaches. *Journal of Information Science, 36*(3), 306–323. doi:10.1177/0165551509360123

Dunin-Keplicz, B. M., & Verbrugge, R. (2010). *Teamwork in multi-agent systems: A formal approach.* New York, NY: Wiley. doi:10.1002/9780470665237

Edmonds, B., & Moss, S. (2011). *Simulating social complexity: A handbook.* Berlin, Germany: Springer.

Feldman, R., & Sanger, J. (2006). *The text mining handbook: Advanced approaches in analyzing unstructured data.* Cambridge, UK: Cambridge University Press. doi:10.1017/CBO9780511546914

Ferber, J. (1999). *Multi-agent systems: An introduction to distributed artificial intelligence.* Reading, MA: Addison-Wesley Professional.

Janowicz, K. (2010). The role of space and time for knowledge organization on the semantic web. *Semantic Web, 1*(1), 25–32.

Kanegsberg, B., & Kanegsberg, E. (2011). *Handbook for critical cleaning: Cleaning agents and systems* (2nd ed.). Boca Raton, FL: CRC Press.

Klusch, M., Ossowski, S., & Shehory, O. (2002). *Cooperative information agents VI: 6th International Workshop, CIA 2002.* Madrid, Spain: Springer.

Konchady, M. (2006). *Text mining application programming.* New York, NY: Charles River Media.

Li, S.-T., & Tsai, F.-C. (2010). Constructing tree-based knowledge structures from text corpus. *Applied Intelligence.* doi:10.1007/s10489-010-0243-2

Lin, H. (2007). *Architectural design of multi-agent systems: Technologies and techniques.* Hershey, PA: IGI Global. doi:10.4018/978-1-59904-108-7

Luck, M., Ashri, R., & d'Inverno, M. (2004). *Agent-based software development.* New York, NY: Artech House Publishers.

Marmanis, H., & Babenko, D. (2009). *Algorithms of the intelligent web.* New York, NY: Manning Publications.

Navarro, V. J. B., & Boggino, A. G. (2008). *ANEMONA: A multi-agent methodology for holonic manufacturing systems*. Berlin, Germany: Springer.

Padgham, L., & Winikoff, M. (2004). *Developing intelligent agent systems: A practical guide*. New York, NY: Wiley. doi:10.1002/0470861223

Polleres, A., Hogan, A., Harth, A., & Decker, S. (2010). Can we ever catch up with the web? *Semantic Web, 1*(1), 45–52.

Preda, N., Kasneci, G., Suchanek, F. M., Neumann, T., Yuan, W., & Weikum, G. (2010). Active knowledge: Dynamically enriching RDF knowledge bases by web services. In *Proceedings of the 2010 International Conference on Management of Data*, (pp. 399–410). New York, NY: ACM Press.

Rehtanz, C. (2010). *Autonomous systems and intelligent agents in power system control and operation*. Berlin, Germany: Springer.

Ríos, S. A., Velásquez, J. D., Yasuda, H., & Aoki, T. (2006). A hybrid system for concept-based web usage mining. *International Journal of Hybrid Intelligent Systems, 3*(4), 219–235. Retrieved from http://iospress.metapress.com/content/6JB1PJ9VVF5F0TW0

Roberson, S., & Dicheva, D. (2007). Semi-automatic ontology extraction to create draft topic maps. In *Proceedings of the 45th Annual Southeast Regional Conference*, (pp. 100-105). New York, NY: ACM Press.

Robinson, E. H. (2010). An ontological analysis of states: Organizations vs. legal persons. *Applied Ontology, 5*(2), 109–125.

Sánchez, D., & Moreno, A. (2006). A methodology for knowledge acquisition from the web. *International Journal of Knowledge-Based and Intelligent Engineering Systems, 10*(6), 453–475. Retrieved from http://iospress.metapress.com/content/9JKFKC0T84Y8A4K1

Shoham, Y., & Leyton-Brown, K. (2008). *Multiagent systems: Algorithmic, game-theoretic, and logical foundations*. Cambridge, UK: Cambridge University Press. doi:10.1017/CBO9780511811654

Spyns, P., Tang, Y., & Meersman, R. (2008). An ontology engineering methodology for DOGMA. *Applied Ontology, 3*(1), 13–39.

Symeonidis, A. L., & Mitkas, P. A. (2011). *Agent intelligence through data mining*. Berlin, Germany: Springer.

Uhrmacher, A. M., & Weyns, D. (2009). *Multi-agent systems: Simulation and applications*. Boca Raton, FL: CRC Press.

Wagner, T. A. (2004). *An application science for multi-agent systems*. Berlin, Germany: Springer. doi:10.1007/b109934

Weiss, G. (2000). *Multiagent systems: A modern approach to distributed artificial intelligence*. Cambridge, MA: The MIT Press.

Weyns, D. (2010). *Architecture-based design of multi-agent systems*. Berlin, Germany: Springer. doi:10.1007/978-3-642-01064-4

White, R., & Roth, R. (2008). *Exploratory search*. San Francisco, CA: Morgan & Claypool Publishers.

Witte, R., Krestel, R., Kappler, T., & Lockemann, P. (2009). Converting a historical encyclopedia of architecture into a semantic knowledge base. *IEEE Intelligent Systems, 25*(1), 58–66. doi:10.1109/MIS.2010.17

Wong, T.-L., Lam, W., & Chen, E. (2005). Automatic domain ontology generation from web sites. *Journal of Integrated Design and Process Science, 9*(3), 29–38. Retrieved from http://iospress.metapress.com/content/EAW8X83GFBQ3FYCQ

Wooldridge, M. (2009a). *An introduction to multiagent systems* (2nd ed.). New York, NY: Wiley.

Zhang, Z., & Zhang, C. (2004). *Agent-based hybrid intelligent systems: An agent-based framework for complex problem solving.* Berlin, Germany: Springer.

Zhu, J., Nie, Z., Liu, X., Zhang, B., & Wen, J.-R. (2009). StatSnowball: A statistical approach to extracting entity relationships. In *Proceedings of WWW 2009.* Madrid, Spain: ACM. Durville, P., & Gandon, F. (2009). Filling the gap between web 2.0 technologies and natural language processing pipelines with semantic web. In *Proceedings of the International Conference on Advances in Semantic Processing,* (pp. 109-112). IEEE Press.

## KEY TERMS AND DEFINITIONS

**Agent-Based Systems:** A system of interacting intelligent agents, embedded within an ontology or information model.

**Information Extraction (IR):** The process of extracting entities and relationships from unstructured documents.

**Knowledge Extraction:** The process of extracting information within a given context, which serves to clarify and disambiguate meaning.

**Natural Language Processing (NLP):** The processing of text in natural language with the purpose of extracting information in a structured manner.

**Ontology:** A formal representation of knowledge as a set of concepts within a domain, and the relationships between those concepts. It is used to reason about the entities within that domain, and may be used to describe the domain.

**OWL:** The Web Ontology Language. A language to describe ontology for sharing and exchanging knowledge on the Web in a machine readable format.

**Provenance:** The property of specifying and tracking the source of information items.

**Service-Oriented Architecture (SOA):** A software design paradigm, which views software components as a set of interoperable services, which can be packaged, configured and reused in multiple systems.

# Chapter 12
# An Ontology–Based Search Tool in the Semantic Web

**Constanta-Nicoleta Bodea**
*Academy of Economic Studies, Romania*

**Adina Lipai**
*Academy of Economic Studies, Romania*

**Maria-Iuliana Dascalu**
*Academy of Economic Studies, Romania*

## ABSTRACT

*The chapter presents a meta-search tool developed in order to deliver search results structured according to the specific interests of users. Meta-search means that for a specific query, several search mechanisms could be simultaneously applied. Using the clustering process, thematically homogenous groups are built up from the initial list provided by the standard search mechanisms. The results are more user-oriented, thanks to the ontological approach of the clustering process. After the initial search made on multiple search engines, the results are pre-processed and transformed into vectors of words. These vectors are mapped into vectors of concepts, by calling an educational ontology and using the WordNet lexical database. The vectors of concepts are refined through concept space graphs and projection mechanisms, before applying the clustering procedure. The chapter describes the proposed solution in the framework of other existent clustering search solutions. Implementation details and early experimentation results are also provided.*

## INTRODUCTION

The Web users are asking for intelligent services in order to discover and access the content they need. The mechanisms for discovering Web documents are powerful search engines, with specialized discovery services, indexes, and databases.

A simple query could have produce hundreds even thousands of results making it practically impossible for the user to check the relevance of all of them. Even when the list of results is ordered by a rank, most of the time it is not sufficient support for the user to identify the most relevant resources. A first solution for this issue

DOI: 10.4018/978-1-4666-2494-8.ch012

Copyright © 2013, IGI Global. Copying or distributing in print or electronic forms without written permission of IGI Global is prohibited.

was to sort the results based on a relevance criteria (the more relevant the result is, the higher in the list it is displayed). Even so, the required result is sometimes hard to find because it is not in the first 20 – 50 displayed results. The algorithm for clustering search results presented in this chapter addresses this issue.

Trying to keep up with the continuous growth of World Wide Web (WWW) the searching tools are engaged in a permanent race for ever faster development in order to reach better performances. In the initial stages the general trend of development was concentrated on bigger databases, bigger document bases, in order to store the web pages accordingly.

When the document storage reached considerable sizes, the problem of better indexation was addressed. The bigger the storage capacity becomes, the more efficient the indexing algorithm had to be in order to keep the Web pages properly ordered. However, the WWW was still growing with increasingly speed, so the crawler module had to be developed to reach higher speed in finding and downloading new pages.

For many years, it was believed that the bigger the database of the search engine is, the more performing it will be. The more and more efficient crawler was downloading pages at a higher speed and proper indexer algorithm was constructing the permanently increasing document base. However, when document bases reached billions and tens of billions of documents, and the crawlers were downloading new documents at a speed of hundreds, or even thousand a day, a new problem appeared. With such large quantity of pages, the indexer was retrieving and presenting to users longer and longer lists as result to queries. The simpler and more common the query is, the more results will be returned, rendering the user unable to check all of them in order to identify the Web pages that best fit his needs. Thus, another efficiency criterion was introduced: easy retrieval of the relevant information within the results provided by the search tool. The "easy retrieval"

is evaluated both from the speed perspective and from the relevance of the results.

## RELATED WORK

## Existing Systems for Search Results Clustering

A result clustering of Web searches represents a technique for retrieving information that had relatively little success in comparison with other techniques used in the Web. The first system which implemented clustering was developed by Scatter and Gather. They proposed a system, which searches documents ordered by clustering. The main drawback of the clustering algorithms is that they are slow, not attractive for Web search applications. To combat this disadvantage, Cutting (1992) proposed algorithms with linear processing time, demonstrating their usefulness in retrieving information. After Scatter and Gather, the Grouper system was designed as an interface for clustering the results of a meta-search engine, named HuskySearch (Zamir, 1999). The algorithm used by Grouper used suffix trees. Two years later, Carrot system has emerged as an infrastructure for the development of new clustering algorithms (Weiss, 2001). As an open source platform, Carrot is currently developed by adding new clustering algorithms. Clustering technology applied to the Web search results still remains partially unknown to the general public, despite numerous research and publications have been made in this direction. Next, we present brief characteristics of some of the existing clustering systems.

## Carrot

It is a search engine that provides results clustering of a meta search. It is located at: www.carrotsearch. com. Search engines used by Carrot system are: Yahoo, Google, MSN, Open Search, Lucene, and Dmoz. It implements several search algorithms including: Lingo, STC (clustering using suffix tree), Rought k-means, HAOG, and FuzzyAnts. Other facilities provided by the system are mechanisms for extracting the roots of words and stop words elimination mechanisms.

Currently Carrot is the most popular system for results clustering. Thanks to the open source license and the flexibility to add new modules, it has been evolving since the appearance in 2001. Carrot infrastructure is designed as a data analysis system with a set of basic modules, such as: components that provide input, components that provide a query on a commercial search engine, modules for results filtering, modules for lexical analysis, and of course a number of modules for clustering.

## Vivisimo/Clusty

Vivisimo has emerged in 2000 (www.vivisimo. com), as a commercial search engine, which clusters the results online. It uses a hierarchical search algorithm that produces clusters of high quality. This quality is explained by the advanced clustering algorithm: it initially finds the description of a cluster, and then formulates group results in that cluster. If a description is not consistent, that cluster will not be formed.

In 2004 the Vivisimo company will launch the search engine called Clusty (Price, 2004). Now all the searches made on Vivisimo are redirected to Clusty.

## Clustering Algorithms for Web-Based Search

Several algorithms which have been successfully used in clustering results, taking into account the characteristics of the searched Web pages are:

## Grouper

It uses the suffix tree-based clustering algorithm and it is based on processing methods of text phrases. Original algorithm identifies a core set of clusters, creating a suffix tree. Each cluster will be associated with a score based on the words contained by the phrase which created the cluster and the documents it contains. Core clusters will be joined by the number of overlapping documents (Zamir, 1999). The algorithm produces overlapped clusters with a high processing speed, but they are slightly influenced by noisy data.

## Scatter/Gather

Initially it was not seen as an appropriate tool for retrieving information. It was brought as a tool for consulting large collections of text documents. The instrument groups the documents into classes with the same or similar themes, presenting a brief description of groups. To achieve this clustering, a segmented algorithm was used.

The algorithm was designed to demonstrate the feasibility of applying clustering methods for ranking results of Web searches. The main objective was to obtain a high processing speed. For achieving this, various optimization methods were used. One of these improvements is the use of Backshot and Fractionation methods for determining the initial cluster centers. The algorithm works by performing successive scatters and gathers of Web documents. Abatement operations are performed by the user to place documents of interest in certain categories and assembly operations are carried out by algorithms to refine the cluster results (Cutting, 1992).

## Lingo

The algorithm was especially designed for clustering the results of Web searches. Thus it focuses on finding high quality labels. The Lingo algorithm searches descriptions of abstract concepts, represented by common phrases in text documents. After identifying these phrases, it will build clusters by testing the concepts' occurrence in documents. The advantage of the method is that it will create clusters with a very good description (Wroblewski, 2003). In terms of performance, Lingo has the characteristics to create a low number of clusters, with a long and precise semantic description. The drawback is that sometimes the description is too long and does not correspond to all the documents in the cluster.

## AHC

It is the algorithm which applies hierarchical agglomeration clustering and it is implemented by Carrot infrastructure. It produces clusters of relatively small size compared with other methods (Wroblewski, 2003). Clusters are disjoint products; a website may belong to a single cluster. In addition, the cluster label has a high degree of generality, making a poor description of the cluster.

## Retriever

The algorithm was implemented to process the results provided by the search engine Lycos. It uses the vector space model to generate the vectors for documents, with weights terms according to the terms of the frequency method - inverted document frequency. To form the clusters, it uses a fuzzy method by medoids: Robust Fuzzy C Medoids (Jiang, 2000).

## Other Search Engines Using Clustering

In addition to well-known search engines dedicated to achieving results' clustering, clustering techniques are implemented on a number of other search engines:

- **WebClust:** The search engine is available at: www.webclust.com. The engine appeared in 2005 and uses technology provided by the Carrot project.
- **Grokker:** The search engine uses the engine index Grooker Yahoo! to generate a list of result clusters.

- **Ask:** The Teoma search engine incorporates a clustering version at: http://www.ask.com/?o=10182.
- **LyGo:** Video search engine offered by Lycos.
- **Cuil:** It is a visual clustering engine, available at: www.cuil.com, which was launched in early 2008 and claimed to be the largest search engine nowadays (Ryan, 2008). Soon after release, there were a number of obvious shortcomings in the implemented technology, following criticism from a number of experts (Ryan, 2008).

Cluuz, BizNet, and Qksearch are three other search engines that use results clustering, but do not fulfill a set of quality criteria. Cluuz is available at www.cluuz.com, it does not have a nice graphical interface and products low quality clusters. BizNet (www.biznetic.com) has both an unfriendly interface structure and a low quality clustering. Qksearch performes a meta search on engines like Yahoo, MSN, AltaVista, Fast, Google, Exalead, and AOL, with the option of result clustering.

Based on our research, a number of search engines exist that successfully implement clustering algorithms, but their popularity is still low: their usefulness is poorly understood among users. On the other hand, in scientific domain there is a greater concern for such tools. At conferences and scientific meetings, there is an increasing number of papers and studies seeking to improve information retrieval on Web, through various techniques of data mining. However such systems are still limited in number and in performance.

## Ontology-Based Clustering of Web Search Results

The difficulties in clustering Web search results which are repeatedly reported are: the big volume, the high dimensionality and the complex semantic of the results. The clustering methods should properly address some or all of these issues.

The semantics is very important, in order to deal in a personalized way with the search results. If the user's needs and preferences are not taken into consideration, the solution for retrieving and presenting the search results is not so useful. Different users might have different views of the same documents, so the search results should be delivered differently for different users. In addition, the user should be assisted to understand the clusters' significance in order to use them efficiently.

Adopting an ontology approach is a common way of dealing with semantics of the Web search results. Most of the existing ontology-based clustering methods identify the conceptual features (or concepts) to be used on the clustering process, instead of the index words occurring in Web documents (Hotho, Staab, & Stumme, 2003; Bloehdorn & Hotho, 2004). The corresponding concepts are identified with the aid of ontology class labels and the WordNet lexical database. In WordNet the terms are organized in synsets, which are sets of synonyms. Using concepts instead of index words could reduce the clustering dimensionality, considering that we can have multiple index words replaced by the same concept. Some methods recommend adding the identified concepts to the index words list, and increasing the process dimensionality (Jing, Zhou, Ng, & Huang, 2006). As consequence, it is not possible to consider the concept-based clustering as an implicit solution for the dimensionality issue. The clustering solution proposed in this chapter is based on the concepts' identification, via WordNet and the replacement of the index words by the corresponding concepts.

For clustering purpose, a document is represented as a vector of index words in a vector space model. The vector components are weights of the correspondent index words showing their relative importance in the document and the entire set of documents. Having the vector collection (all documents represented as vectors), the Euclidean distance, Minkowski distance Manhatten distance, and other distance measures could be used in order to compute the distance or similarity between documents, as part of clustering algorithms, such as k-means. In order to take into consideration the document semantic, different ontology-based measures were defined (Hotho, Maedche, & Staab, 2001). Considering the semantic relationship between each pair of words, as mutual information between terms, Jing, Zhou, Ng, and Huang (2006) proposed the extension of the vector space model with a mutual information matrix, and an Euclidian distance measure considering the correlation between each pair of terms. Using this modeling framework a clustering method, named FW-Kmeans, was defined, which performs better than classical methods.

Hotho, Maedche, and Staab (2001) proposed the COSA (Concept Selection and Aggregation) clustering method. The COSA approach uses the core ontology for restricting the document features needed by the aggregation process. The aggregation result is exploited by K-means algorithm, in order to produce a set of clustering results, considered as a set of views.

An ontology-based clustering framework is proposed by Lula and Paliwoda-Pekosz (2008), giving the possibility of incorporating various kinds of measures to determine similarity between objects and set of objects in the following three dimensions: taxonomic, relationship and attribute. Kogilavani and Balasubramanie (2009) developed a system which revises the user's query by mapping it with synonyms and semantically related concepts using MeSH ontology knowledge source. The system first clusters the terms using a term semantic similarity measure. Then the term is re-weighted to increase the weight of the terms which are more semantically similar. The similarity measures are defined based on information content.

The chapter recommends the relative semantic relevance of a concept with respect to its prerequisites, named the self weight of the concept, to be used in the clustering process. The concept's self-weight is combined with the weight of the corresponding term obtaining the final concept's weight. This measure is used in order to compute the distance or similarity between documents, as part of the clustering algorithms, such as k-means. The measure is used also for the space graph projections, in order to select the concepts, for clustering dimensionality reduction. The self-weight of the concept is defined based on expert opinions. The measure of the concept's self-weight was previous used by authors (Bodea, Trandafir, & Borozan, 2008; Bodea & Dascalu, 2009a, 2009b; Bodea & Lipai, 2009) for adaptive designing of tests based on semantic nets and concept space graphs.

## AN ONTOLOGICAL-BASED APPROACH FOR CLUSTERING THE WEB META-SEARCH RESULTS

Clustering the search results means grouping them into object classes, which are developed using the search results characteristics, with the purpose of simplifying the user work to retrieve the relevant results. Meta-search means the use of more search tools simultaneously for the same query. Organizing search results in clusters is not meant to replace the classical way of presenting results in ranked lists (Brin & Page, 1998). Its purpose is to provide supplementary organization for those results. Clustering is applied after the query results are provided by the search engines. The user interface provides the user's query to different search engines, and takes the list of results offered by traditional Web search.

Generally, the list of results provided by a search engine is composed of the link to the site that meet the query criteria, brief description of the page (usually the selection of page) and the page title. Some search engines return additional information such as: the page size, connection to similar pages, connection to pages in cash, the page indexing date. Using this information, the

user usually goes through the entire list of results to find relevant pages. Even if the results list is sorted by a rank which gives a score of importance of the site, there are cases where the user will have to go through a high number of results (20 to 100 sites) in order to find the desired pages, or because a query was poorly supplied, with insufficient details, or because the desired pages have a low share in the search. For example when performing a search on the keywords "data mining" wishing to obtain sites that include works that present data mining algorithms, will notice that the first results from the list will find such companies that provide economic analysis of data mining, and books on data mining process, and after that a relevant result to the user.

In order to make the user's job easier, the clustering algorithm will divide the list of results in homogenous groups. The user will have to identify the cluster in which the required pages are most likely to be and only search through that cluster, ignoring the other clusters. In Figure 1, we have represented schematically the basic principles of how clustering method operates. The initial results $R_1, R_2, ..., R_n$ make a list, which, after clustering, will become part of one of the clusters $C_1, ..., C_n$. The cluster can differ in size accordingly to what Web pages meet the subject criteria of that cluster. The search results' clusters have the property that the pages inside one cluster are similar to each other, and the pages belonging to different clusters differ from one another. Inside each cluster, the initial ranking order provided will be preserved.

The search results clustering module of a crawler has to meet the following requests:

- It has to simplify the user's work in finding the results.
- The module must not overcrowd the search tool's resources.
- It must not over extend the time needed to find the proper Web page (e.g. if Google of-

*Figure 1. The web search results clustering process*

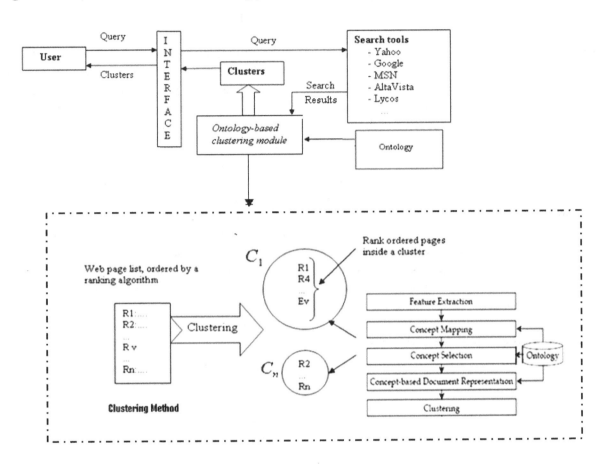

fers results for a query in few milliseconds, a clustering process that will take tens of seconds will be unsatisfactory [Leouski & Croft, 1996]).

The results' clustering module has a unique user interface to take over the search keywords for querying different search engines (Google, Yahoo, MSN search, and so on). The search module will send keywords to different search engines, which will retrieve the results and send them to the clustering module. The clustering algorithm is run on the local machine. The clustering results are presented to the user, together with all the Web documents (the link and the description) included in those clusters. Figure 1 presents the integration of the clustering module in a meta-search process.

User interface has to provide different facilities in order to incorporate the user search preferences, such as:

- Support for specific language.
- Can eliminate / add search engine at will.
- Flexibility in display preferences (for example, the number of links per page).
- The choice of the number of clusters.
- Various filters, such as filters for blogs, adult sites.

The ontology used for results clustering is an educational one. An educational ontology is an explicit formal specification of how to represent learning concepts, learning objects, and other entities and the relationships among them

(Kanellopoulos, Kotsiantis, & Pintelas, 2006). For these ontologies, an important relationship type is *requires(Ci, Cj)*, meaning "Ci requires Cj as prerequisite," where Ci and Cj are two learning concepts. Each concept class of the ontology has its self-weight as class attribute. The attribute value is set using expert opinion.

The *space graph* of concept Ci is the graph which has Ci as the root node and all other concepts directly or indirectly connected to Ci with "requires" links as graph nodes. The relevance of the concept Ci with respect to its prerequisites is measure by, *the self-weight* of the concept. The *prerequisite weight* of concept Ci, is the relative semantic relevance of the prerequisite topics and *the link weight* represents the relative importance of learning concept Cj for learning Ci. For all nodes of the concept space graph, the sum of self-weight and prerequisite weight is 1. The sum of all prerequisite link weights to the child nodes is also 1.

$$W_s(i) + W_p(i) = 1, \forall i \tag{1}$$

$$\sum_{j=1}^{n} l(C_0, C_j) = 1 \tag{2}$$

Figure 2 shows an example of concept space graph (for concept C1.02), with $W_p(i)$ shown on the right side of node and $W_s(i)$ on the left side.

Given a root concept $C_0$ and a projection threshold coefficient $\lambda$, *a projection graph* is defined as a sub-graph with root $C_0$ and all nodes $C_t$, where there is at least one path from $C_0$ to $C_t$ such that node path weight $\eta(C_0, C_t)$ satisfies the condition: $\eta(C_0, C_t) >= \lambda$, where node path weight between $C_0$ and $C_t$ for the path $[C_0, C_1, ..., C_t]$ is:

$$\eta(C_0, C_t) = W_s(t) \prod_{m=n}^{1} l(C_{m-1}, C_m) * W_p(m-1) \tag{3}$$

We consider as an example the concept space graph shown on the upper part of Figure 2. A small value for $\lambda$ parameter has as result a larger projection graph than bigger one, as shown in Table 1.

The projection graphs are used during the concept selection process, in order to reduce the dimension of the extended index concept vector. The result of the concept selection process is the reduced index vector list.

Each concept class has lexical instances, in addition to usual concept instances. The lexical instances are created using the synonym classes of the WordNet and represent synonyms for the concept label. The number of lexical instances is related to the concept self-weight measure. In our experiments, we applied relation (4) to set the lexical instance number for each ontology concept.

$$Li_i = \gamma \cdot e^{W_s(i)} \tag{4}$$

where $Li_i$ is the number of lexical instances for concept class I, $\gamma$ is a positive parameter, greater than 1 (we used $\gamma=10$), and $W_s(i)$ is the self-weight of the concept Ci.

The synonyms of ontology concepts are used on the concept mapping process, to find the corresponding ontological class for each index word. A direct matching between the concept labels and index words is not recommended, because most of the ontology representations have a very limited lexicon, comparing to the Web content, so there is a small chance to find concept labels in the index word list.

## THE SEARCH RESULTS CLUSTERING PROCEDURE

The main steps of the search results clustering are the following:

1. Obtaining the Web page list.
2. Pre-processing of the documents.

*Figure 2. The projection graphs for different values of the λ parameter*

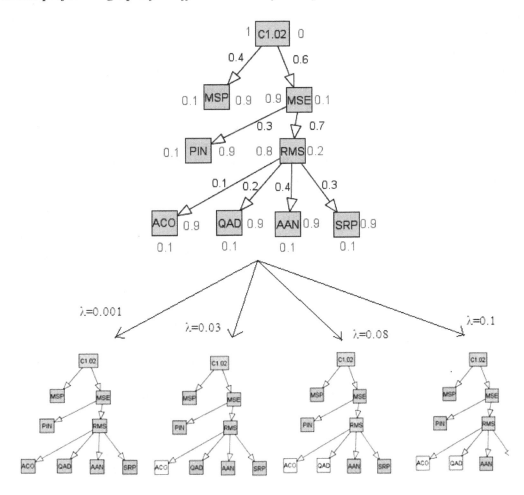

*Table 1. The projection results for different values of the λ parameter*

| R (Root) | N (Node) | η(R,N) | η(R,N) >= (λ=0.001) | η(R,N) >= (λ=0.03) | η(R,N) >= (λ=0.08) | η(R,N) >= (λ=0.01) |
|----------|----------|--------|---------------------|--------------------|--------------------|--------------------|
| C1.02 | MSP | 0.36000 | √ | √ | √ | √ |
| | MSE | 0.06000 | √ | √ | √ | X |
| | PIN | 0.14580 | √ | √ | √ | √ |
| | RMS | 0.07560 | √ | √ | X | X |
| | ACO | 0.02722 | √ | X | X | X |
| | QAD | 0.05443 | √ | √ | X | X |
| | AAN | 0.10886 | √ | √ | √ | √ |
| | SRP | 0.08165 | √ | √ | √ | X |

The results from Table 1 are also presented graphical format in Figure 2. The white nodes of the concept space graph are not included in the projection graphs.

3. Transforming the documents into vector representation.
4. K-means clustering, with adequate adaptations for Web pages.
5. Designing the cluster representation for final results.

## Obtaining the Web Page List

The initial Web page list is obtained putting all results delivered by all search tools in a single list. This list will be used to cluster the results. In order to obtain the Web page list the next steps have to be done:

1. Performing simultaneous queries on multiple search engines through a meta-search interface.
2. Elimination of the multiple links because the results are obtained from more search tools, it's more than likely that the same site will be returned by more than one tool.
3. Calculating the new rank, the formula below will be used.
   a. $Rank_{new} = I_M * NrRez + I_{Rez}$ (5)
   b. where
      i. $Rank_{new}$: the new rank calculated for each Web page
      ii. $I_M$: the index of the search engine which provided this page
      iii. NrRez: total number of results after the duplicates were eliminated
      iv. $I_{Rez}$: the index of the page in the $I_M$ search tool
4. Duplicate Web pages will receive the rank from the search tool with the lowest index

## Pre-Processing of the Documents

The clustering algorithm uses information from the pages in order to determine its subject or characteristics. Most document clustering algorithms use the whole document for this process,

but such approach would slow our Web page clustering algorithm too much. Therefore, the algorithm will only use the snippets provided by the initial search tools. Previous work has showed that snippets provide good quality description of Web pages, thus justifying their use (Leuski & Allan, 2000). The title of the Web page will also be used, if there is one. Title words will become more important for classification than snippet words. Web pages processing is made up by the following operations.

1. **The Tag Cleaning**: It will eliminate the portions of the Web document which are strictly related to the text formatting. The main processes are the following:
2. **The Lexical Analysis**: The purpose of the analysis is to identify distinct words. The process implies eliminating useless characters such as comma, punctuation marks, sometimes numbers, or characters like: #, $...
3. **The Word Root Extraction:** The goal is to obtain a homogenous one-word description of similar but not identical words. The word obtained in the end doesn't have to have a meaning, nor be grammatically correct, but it will contain the description and similarity with all the other words that it represents. For example: *implementing, implementation, implemented* will be described by the root word *implement*.
4. **The Stop Word Elimination:** A stop word is a word that does not have an informational value. In all languages there are a series of words which are considered stop words. For example: "on," "and," "the," "in," etc.
5. **Establishing The Index Words:** An index word is a word that it is representative in the context of the document.

The Figure 3 presents the pre-processing steps.

*Figure 3. Web pages pre-processing steps*

a) Lexical analysis                                   b) Final list after all steps

## Transforming the Documents into a Concept Vector Representation

In order to use the k-means clustering algorithm we need to transform each document into a concept vector. The vectors will have the same size, turning our results' list into a M*N matrix. A line represents one Web page and each column represents a concept. The N dimension represents the total number of concepts that will be used for document clustering, from all documents. The M dimension represents the remaining number of Web pages after the duplicate eliminations, the final search results' list.

Supposing we have:

M Web pages: $d_1, d_2,..., d_M$ and

N indexed concepts from 1 to N

a Web page will be represented in concept vector space using the following formula:

$$d_i = \left[ W_{i1}', W_{i2}',..., W_{iN}' \right] \qquad (6)$$

where $W_{ij}'$ represents the weight of concept j for document $d_i$

Transforming the documents into concept vector space representation requires the following steps:

1. **Index word vector identification and vector space representation:** It implies joining together in one vector all the index word from all the documents. For each document and each index word we will count the number of times one word appears in the same page.

2. **Word weight calculation for each document:** In order to calculate each word weight, the frequency of word in document and the inverted document frequency are used.

3. **The concept mapping:** Each index word is checked against the lexical instances, for all ontology concept classes, starting with those having the greatest. The first successful matching will indicate the parent class as the concept to be assigned to the index word. Having the index word list as input data of the concept mapping process, an extended index concept list will be produced as the result of this process.

4. **The concept selection**: Projection graphs of the concepts included in the extended index concepts' list are used to reduce the dimension of the extended index concepts' vector during the concepts' selection process. The result is a reduced index concepts' vector list.

5. **Concept weight calculation for each document and the concept-based representation of documents**: The concept's weight for a document is the weight of the corresponding word adjusted with the concept's self weight.

We start the concepts' vector space representation of documents with the index words' vector identification. For example, using as search query "data mining" we will have the vector space representation presented by Table 2.

The words 1..L are usually the index words, and they are obtained after the pre-processing the documents. Assigning each word a weight it's crucial in order to distinguish the more relevant words from the less important ones. In the end we will quantify the importance that each concept has for a given Web page.

*The weight of word $t_j$ for a specific* document $d_i$ is calculated using the Formula 7:

$$w_{ij} = fT_{ij} * \log(n \,/\, fd_j) \qquad (7)$$

where:

- $w_{ij}$ is the weight of word $t_j$ for document $d_i$
- $fT_{ij}$ is the frequency of word $t_j$ in $d_i$ document
- $fd_i$ is the total number of Web pages in which the word $t_j$ appears.

The term $\log(n \,/\, fd_j)$ is also called inverted document frequency. The words that have a

*Table 2. Vector space representation of the search results*

| Document / Words | course | Data | Mining | ... | computer |
|---|---|---|---|---|---|
| d1 | 2 | 3 | 3 | | 0 |
| d2 | 0 | 2 | 2 | | 1 |
| d3 | 1 | 3 | 3 | | 0 |

higher frequency in a page will most likely be a better description than the words that have low frequency. In addition, the terms that have high frequency in all documents, will not make good description for differences that appear between pages. The term inverted document frequency intends to minimize the importance of the words that appear frequently in all documents (Chi, 2003).

The weight of concept $C_k$ for the document $d_i$ is calculated using the following Formula 8:

$$W_{ik}^{'} = W_{ik} * \log\left(\frac{1}{W_s(k)}\right) \qquad (8)$$

where:

- $W_{ik}$ is the weight of corresponding word for document $d_i$.
- $W_s(k)$ is the self weight of the concept k.

The Table 3 presents the weights concept-based representation for the previous example.

*Table 3. Concept-based representation of documents*

| Document / Concepts | training | ... | computer |
|---|---|---|---|
| d1 | 0.176 | … | 0 |
| d2 | 0 | … | 0.477 |
| d3 | 0.176 | … | 0 |

## K-Means Clustering with Adequate Adaptations for Web Pages

The classical K-means clustering algorithm uses numerical input to build up distinct clusters. It splits the total data set into exclusive clusters using a measure called "distance." The distance can be calculated using many formulas, but basically having the meaning of metric distance. Just as in traditional k-means clustering, a cluster K will be represented by its centre or centroid (Baeza-Yates & Ribeiro-Neto, 1999). For Web page clustering this centroid will represent a weighted concept document within the vector space documents. This centroid will be called "the representative of cluster $K_k$" noted $R_k$.

In order for $R_k$ to be equivalent with the centre of clusters from the traditional k-means clustering, it must meet the following conditions:

- Each document $d_i$ from $K_k$ has joint concepts with $R_k$.
- The concepts in $R_k$ also appear in the most documents in $K_k$.
- Not all the concepts from $R_k$ have to appear in all the documents from $K_k$.
- The weight of concept $C_j$ from $R_k$ is calculated as an average weight of all the concepts in all documents of $K_k$ (Chi, 2003).

After determining the representatives of the cluster, the Web meta-search results clustering algorithm is as follows:

- **Input data:**
  - *Di* are the Web pages/documents provided by the initial search.
    - l is the number of clusters, accordingly to k-means traditional algorithm.
- **Output data:**
  - l clusters with documents (the clusters can overlap, meaning the same page can be assigned to more than just one cluster, for each distribution there will be a weight assigned to the document).
- **Step 1:** l documents from the Web page list are randomly selected. These l documents will form the starting representatives of the clusters. We have $K_1, K_2, ..., K_l$ clusters and $R_1, R_2, ..., R_k$ as clusters representatives.
- **Step 2:** For each Web page from D $d_i \in D$ and each cluster $K_k$, $k = 1, ..., l$ we calculate the similarity between the Web page and the representative of the cluster $S(d_i, R_k(K_k))$.
- **Step 3:** If the similarity is bigger than a given threshold $S(d_i, R_k(K_k)) > \delta$, than the document $d_i$ will be assigned to cluster $K_k$ with a weight attached, the weight being calculated based upon the similarity value:
  - $m(d_i, K_k) = S(d_i, R_k(K_k))$ (9)
- **Step 4:** For each cluster the representative is re-calculated taking into account the new documents that were assigned to that particular cluster.
- **Step 5:** The process is re-started from step 2 until new modifications are below a given threshold.
- **Step 6:** For each Web page $d_n$ which is not assigned to any cluster the closest neighborhood will be calculated $V(d_u)$. The neighborhood must not contain documents that have similarity measure zero. The $d_n$ Web page will be assigned to the cluster to which the neighborhood $V(d_u)$ belongs to. The weight for $d_n$ assignation to $K_k$ is calculated:
  - $m(d_n, K_k) = m(V(d_u), K_k) * S(d_n, (V(d_u)))$ (10)
- **Step 7:** For each cluster $K_k$ the representative of the cluster $R_k$ is recalculated.

Similarity is calculated using the following formula, also named as Salton's cosine coefficient (Salton, 1989):

$$S(x,y) = \frac{\sum_{i=1}^{t} x_i y_i}{\sqrt{\sum_{i=1}^{t} x_i^2 + \sum_{i=1}^{t} y_i^2}} \quad (11)$$

## Developing the Cluster-Like Representation for the Final Results

1. **Label extraction:** For each cluster, the sequence of words with the highest frequency will be assigned as label for that class. If a sequence of words is not found then a single word will be used instead.
2. **Creating the cluster structure:** It will be done using both the size of the clusters and the weight of the pages inside the cluster.

A measure of the cluster quality will be calculated.

3. **Results delivery:** During the pre-processing phase, we extracted the root for the similar words and we eliminated the stop words, and some other modifications took place in order to make the document suitable for clustering. In order for the user to understand what a page is about it must be presented with a short relevant description of that Web page. In almost all cases the initial search result list provides a short description (the snippet). That description can be kept, and delivered to the user after clusters are developed, but it can also be enhanced with particular characteristics of the cluster.

The Figure 4 presents the results of the query "Data mining," delivered as clusters. On the left side, there are mentioned four clusters induced for this search. On the right side, we can see the links and the related snippets.

*Figure 4. Search results delivered as clusters*

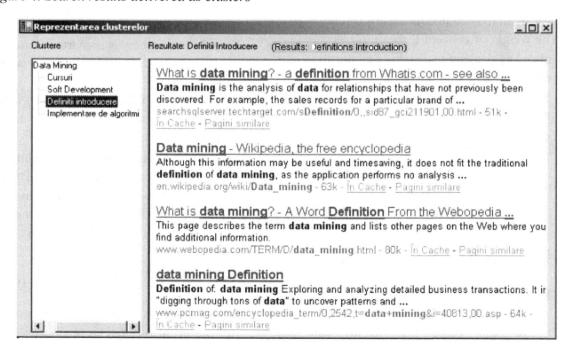

# IMPLEMENTATION OF THE ONTOLOGY-BASED SEARCH CLUSTERING SOLUTION

## Modules and Functionality

Clustering solutions for Web documents which queries search engines must meet the following functions: acquisition of queries from the user, providing one or more query search engines, results acquisition, processing of Web documents, Web documents clustering and results display. The functional components that perform those tasks are presented below.

## User Interface

The user interface has the role of taking the words, which have to be searched, the search engines on which queries will be executed and users' display and clustering preferences, if any. The application interface is represented in Figure 5.

Selecting search engines is made using the right tab. The search begins when all engines were selected and loaded by inserting the keywords and when the button "Initiate Search" is pressed. The browsers within the application are fully functional, so if a search is performed in the browser, it will be taken by the processing module. The disadvantage of using this method of query (by browsers) is that the browsers will not be synchronized. Thus if one wants one meta-search on multiple search engines using the same keywords and same parameters, it is recommended to use the searching and viewing facilities offered by the application. If one wants special preferences offered by a certain search engine, which are not implemented in the application, then it is best to access the browsers.

The application allows the possibility of inserting user-specific preferences for viewing the results and for establishing clustering parameters, such as: search by language, processing a given number of results and choosing a visualization level. Each of these preferences will be further described.

*Figure 5. Ontology-based search clustering application: user interface*

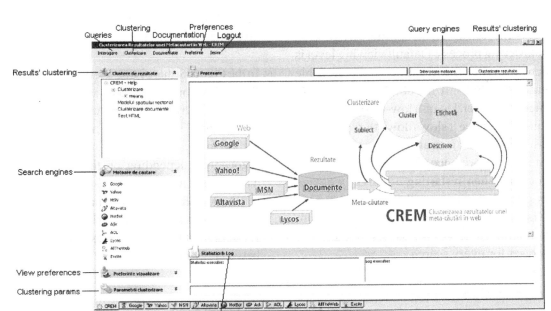

## Language Preferences

The application has the possibility of searching documents in Romanian and in English. The default option is Romanian: so, if one searches for documents in any other language, the results will contain Romanian Web pages. A set of processing are specific to Romanian language: it is expected that the search algorithms will achieve better results on documents written in Romanian, because the preprocessing stage is more detailed.

However, there are many situations that will get poor results due to particularities of the Romanian language to use diacritics. There are several Web sites which don't display correctly these diacritics, so the snippet displayed after processing the search will be grammatically wrong.

## Results Number to be Processed

The application has the possibility of introducing the number of results that are intended to be used. By default, the maximum number of results provided by an engine on first page will be considered, but one can choose a smaller number of results.

## Visualization Level

The user is allowed to see, at runtime, certain steps of the clustering process. Default viewing level is 5, which means that the whole process is invisible to the user. Finally, only the obtained clusters are presented to the user. Using a low-level view is not recommended, since it slows down the computing process. This option is useful when one wants to estimate the performance obtained in the clustering process. When restarting a search, we have the option to keep and use the old results. This option is useful when the user wants an in-depth search for the same keywords. By default, the data is reset for every search.

## Processing Modules

The application is comprised from three major processing modules: module for preprocessing the documents, module for implementing the vector space model and clustering module itself. The processing of documents is essential to obtain qualitative results. The main function of this module is to form a condensed description of the Web search results, by eliminating characters and words that have a low degree of information. The description will be used in the construction of the vector of indexed terms. Using the indexed terms' vector, the "document-terms" matrix will be built, which will be further used to clustering composition. These results are obtained by taking the results from all search engines and eliminating identical ones. The properties of an indexed terms' vector are:

- It does not contain duplicate words.
- It does not contain stop words.
- It does not contain figures or special characters.
- It is composed of all words from unique results.

## Overall Functioning of the Application

In the Figure 6, there is the overall operating flow of the application. The user has access to the interface application, by entering search words and viewing the results. Therefore, the application represents a tool for testing the performance of different algorithms, depending on the processed query. The algorithm used for clustering is "k-means" (Franstrom & Lewis, 2000) and it is customized for calculating the similarity between documents. By default, it will build 6 clusters, but it can build between 2 and 10 clusters.

*Figure 6. Normal flow of execution in the clustering based search application*

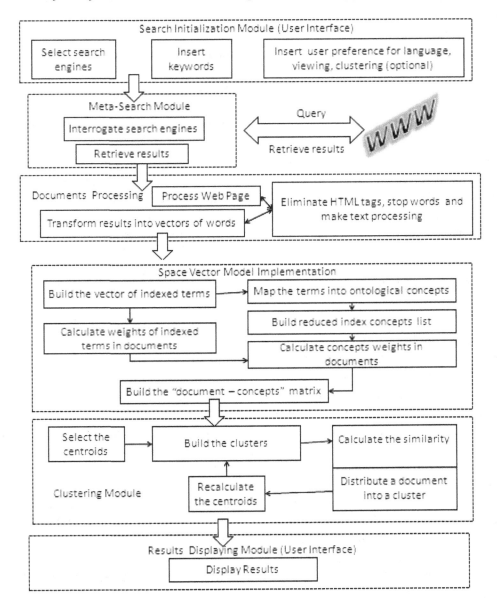

## Documents Preprocessing

Search results are obtained by performing a query on multiple engines. The selection of the engines is made before making the actual search. By default, the system uses Google search.

## HTML Tag Removal

Search results are retrieved from search engines via a browser, by extracting useful content from the HMTL document body. The first step in processing this document is to remove the sequences of letters which have the purpose of formatting the pages in standard HTML, for example, "head," "script," or "style" tags. A removal procedure is used, in order to keep the information between tags for further processing.

## Removal of Duplicate Sites

Since multiple search engines are used, it is inevitable that duplicate results will emerge. The application will retain only one result, taking into account the order of search engines in which the result occurred. Finally, we have a concatenated list of unique results, which will be clustered. Each result has attached the following attributes: title, description, link, and rank.

## Removal of Stop Words and Characters

The stop words do not bring any information in text processing: they are eliminated from the vector of indexed terms. Some examples of stop words are: "end," "with," "in." Stop words are removed entirely from the vector of indexed terms. Still, stop words might bring information about the text structure. This is the reason for which their position in the text is memorized when documents' description is processed. When determining the frequent phrases in the text, this position will be used. A frequent phrase is a pair of two consecutive terms or two consecutive terms separated by the same sequence of stop words. Stop characters are considered any character that delimits a word. These are: { ' ', ',', ';', '.', '-', '/', '|', '\\', '%', '#', '@', '!', '~', '$', '^', '(', ')', '+', '[', ']', '{', '}', '"", ':', '<', '>', '?', '\r', '\n', '*' }.

## Words Root Extraction and Language Processing

Root extraction module has been developed entirely in C #, using basic grammatical rules. The module makes only minimal extraction of roots' level. We believe that more complex processing would be inefficient to implement in terms of

computing time, and not justified by the added quality. For extracting the root level, the following rules have been used: removal of plural forms, removal of standard suffixes, and removal of verbal suffixed. The module is available only for Romanian language.

## Implementing Vector Space Model

The vector space model of documents' processing consists of transforming the string of words in a snippet into a vector of numbers: a document will be represented by a numerical vector of n elements, where n represents the number of unique words in the document. The value of each element of the vector is given by the number of occurrence of that word in the document.

## Building the Vector of Index Terms

Building the vector of index terms is the first step in implementing the vector space model. The vector of index terms is built from individual words contained by the page title or the page description. The entire list of pages/documents is browsed in order to build the vector. The vector of index terms does not contain: stop words, stop characters, single-letter words, numbers of one or two digits and the keywords used to process the search, because these keywords are presented in all the documents.

## Building the Reduced Concept Lists

Each element of the index terms vector is mapped to the educational ontology and then projections are applied to obtain the most relevant lists of concepts for each document.

## Vectoring the Documents

Vectoring the documents is the step in which numerical vectors are built for each document. In the vector space model, each document is represented by a numerical vector of n elements, where n is the number of indexed terms. The value of each word in the numerical vector is calculated using two formulas: word frequency-inverted document frequency and linear inverted document frequency (Wróblewski, 2003).

Vectoring procedure can be described as:

- **Step 1:** Each document will have an array of null values associated with it.
- **Step 2:** For each result:
  - **Step 2.1:** The result is decomposed in individual words using the words' delimiters.
  - **Step 2.2:** The presence of each word is tested in the index vector
  - **Step 2.3:** The occurrence of each word from document is counted into the index vector $f$++.
  - **Step 2.4:** The indexed term- frequency of occurrence in the document is built.
- **Step 3:** For each indexed term, the inverted document frequency in which it appears is calculated.
- **Step 4:** Using the matrix of indexed terms and frequency of word and the vector of indexed terms among all results, we calculate the weight of the word in document .
- **Step 5:** All indexed terms are mapped into ontological concepts and the extended index concept list is obtained.
- **Step 6:** The extended index concept list is transformed into reduced index concept list, through projection.
- **Step 7:** Concept weight is calculated for each document, using the weight of the corresponding word (from Step 4) adjusted with the concept's self weight.

After vectoring the documents and calculating the frequency of words in documents, we will remove the index words that appear in a single document.

## CLUSTERING ALGORITHM IMPLEMENTATION

### Determining the Initial Cluster Centroids

A major disadvantage of k-means method (Franstrom & Lewis, 2000) is the high number of iterations. When clustering results of a search in a network, a high number of iterations means a high computing time. In current study, we implemented three methods for calculating the initial centroids, to be followed by experimental determination of the most successful method l. The three methods are described below.

### The Documents with the Highest Number of Concepts

In this method, the initial centroids are the documents with the highest frequency of occurrence of the index concepts. Based on the method of approximate tolerant sets, our hypothesis is that a document containing a large number of words will be an approximate representation for documents that contain only one set of those concepts.

### The Documents with the Highest Weight of Concepts

Initial centroids will consist of documents that have concepts with the highest weight. Such documents will be representative for a limited set of documents, resulting in compact clusters, with high similarity between clusters.

### Segmented Algorithm

The algorithm consists of dividing the dataset into k groups where k is the number of clusters we want to get. For each of the k groups we calculate the group average. This vector of averages will form the initial centroids. The algorithm is based on the assumption that results will be ranked by page rank. Thus, the first group will be a centroid containing the averages of highly ranked pages. The algorithm is based on clustering by partinioning.

## Clustering Algorithm

Basically, the clustering process means calculating the similarity between each instance and the centroids of each cluster. The main adjustments of k-means algorithm for Web documents are: calculating the similarity as a measure of distance and use a software assignment to obtain clusters. In the end, we will have a set of k+1 overlapping clusters, where the last cluster contains the unclassified documents.

In Figure 7, the logical scheme of the clustering process is presented, starting with calculating the frequency of documents. Clustering will be realized after a predefined number of iterations. This number will be determined experimentally in order to find a compromise between computing time and quality of clusters obtained. By default, we make 6 clusters, the 7th cluster representing unclassified documents and we use a threshold value of 0.3 for classification of instances in clusters.

After each clustering, we recalculate the centroids and we reset the clusters' components. The new centroids are calculated using the average weigh of words reached in that cluster.

## Clusters Representation

After determining the composition of clusters by successive assignments as stated by the k-means algorithm, clusters are displayed. The first step in clusters' display is determining clusters' label. Clusters' label may consist of one, two, or three representative words for that cluster. The label will be chosen according to the centroid's weight for that cluster.

## EXPERIMENTATION AND EVALUATION

In this section, we propose some methods for evaluating the preliminary stages of the ontology-based search using clustering (evaluation of documents processing and evaluation of document vectoring), and methods of evaluation the results' clustering (user method of evaluating the clustering performance and expert method of evaluating the clustering performance). We also present experimental results.

## Methods for Evaluating the Preliminary Stages

### Documents Processing Evaluation

The evaluation of document processing is strictly related to testing and development phases of the application. When running the application, the results of documents processing aren't available, as they are a secondary result of results clustering. Taking into account that the final quality of clustering depends directly on the quality of documents to be classified, the documents processing evaluation is an important activity.

The first step in the processing of documents is to remove HTML tags. It is considered that the text will be unprocessed if HTML tags aren't entirely removed.

The second step is to remove stop words. The indicator of removing stop words can be calculated by performing runs in different queries and calculating the number of stop words in the index in each run, using the following formulas:

$$IICStop = \frac{\sum CuvStopInIndex_i}{n} \qquad (12)$$

and

*Figure 7. Logical scheme of clustering process*

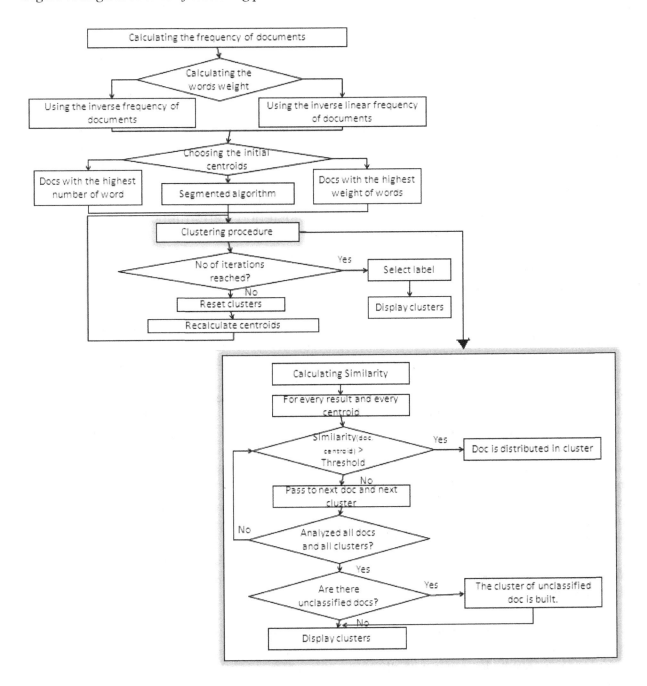

$$CuvStopInIndex = \frac{NoCuvStopIndex}{NrCuvIndex} \quad (13)$$

where

- *IICstop* represents the indicator of removing the stop words.
- *CuvStopInIndex* represents the percent of words having no information value.

- *i* represents one search.
- represents the total number of searches.

The evaluation of root extraction can be done by using the same principle described above: we assess the number of words not represented by root, but presented in the index, at successive runs, using different queries and we make an average.

$$IRCr = \Sigma \, UnrepresentedWord / TestsNo \qquad (14)$$

where

- *IRCr* represents index representation of words by root.
- *UnrepresentedWords*: number of words representations present in the vector index.
- *TestsNo*: number of tests.

## Documents Vectoring Evaluation

There are two methods of calculating the weight of index words in the document. The calculation of the weight will be reflected in the calculation of similarity between documents, which is the function of document distribution in clusters. The only way to determine the best method of calculating the weight is to apply both methods, for the same query, for several times. We noticed that the method which uses the linear inverted document frequency is more suitable for large data sets.

## Methods for Evaluating the Results Clustering

Clustering of Web searches is intended to facilitate the work of a user in retrieving desired Web pages, by ordering the results in groups with different topics. The quality of a clustering can be defined taking account its usefulness. Such a measure is subjective because different users will have different requirements, making the evaluation process difficult. We propose two methods of assessing the results of clustering. The first one evaluates

the usefulness of clustering, from a normal user perspective. Its disadvantage is that it requires a long testing time, with a large number of distinct users to provide statistically accurate results. The expert method of evaluating the usefulness of clustering is the second provided method of evaluation. Its main disadvantage is that it requires a set of data, which is hard to find, because a manual clustering can lead to different results if made by different individuals (Osinski, 2003).

## User Method of Evaluating the Clustering Performance

There are two ways of evaluating the clustering performance by user methods: first is the observation of navigation patterns of clusters in the logs and the second is interrogating the users through specific forms. We used the second method: we defined some quantitative indicators for evaluating the clustering utility, in our users' perspective (Osinski, 2003; Stefanowski, 2003). The utility of a cluster is defined by the need for that cluster and the proper allocation of an instance in that cluster. We consider the following questions to be valuable for finding out whether a cluster is useful or not for a user:

- Do you consider the cluster k to be useful in classifying the set of results returned? (Yes/No)
- Does the document Dk correspond to the description of k cluster label? (Yes/No/Partial)

After collecting the users' responses, one can define the following metrics (Wróblewski, 2003):

- Number of useful clusters of all clusters.
- Number of documents correctly and incorrectly classified in each cluster environment.
- We also consider the following indicators to be important: The quality of cluster la-

bel, measured as the ratio of the number of existing relevant clusters and total clusters (Wróblewski, 2003).

- The quality of document distribution within a cluster, measured by the number of documents correctly classified in the cluster, the number of documents incorrectly classified and the number of documents probably classified correctly; quality distribution of the documents will be better when the number of correctly classified documents is higher and the other two indicators are lower.
- The coverage degree of clustering, which measures the number of classified instances from the total number of instances; we have to take into account that there are instances which remain unclassified (Wróblewski, 2003; Osinski, 2003).
- The overlapping degree of clusters, which can be measured through the total number of documents classified in more than one cluster.

## Expert Method of Evaluating the Clustering Performance

The export method can be performed through:

- Evaluating the clustering on a set of documents from different domains, by applying the „merge than cluster" algorithm (Cho, 2001).
- The hypothesis of true base set or „ground truth hypothesis" (Cho, 2001): a set of data which was manually clustered is used by the application and, after processing, the results are compared.
- Comparison with other available implementations, whose performance is known or benchmarking: the same query is provided for both systems and a series of comparative estimations is conducted.

## Experimentation Results

The current experimentation has several major aims, namely:

1. Determining the performance of the proposed solution.
2. Determining the best parameters for certain situations.
3. Determining the degree of performance for the Romanian language compared with English.
4. Comparison with other clustering methods.

## Preliminary Stages of Preprocessing

The removal of HTML tags was always successful. For three queries ("noaptea," "albă ca zăpada," "anual"), we obtained an indicator of stop words removal having the value of 0.11. Using as a comparison measure the frequency of stop words in an unprocessed document, which ranges between 0.3-0.6, we can say there has been a satisfactory removal of stop words.

## Results Clustering

For testing the clustering algorithms, we use four queries, with the following features:

- **Query 1:** Query string: "Inteligență artificială," query language: Romanian, query specificity: low, number of tested results: 90;
- **Query 1:** Query string: "Data mining," query language: English, query specificity: high, number of tested results: 100;
- **Query 1:** Query string: "Indice refracție," query language: Romanian, query specificity: high, number of tested results: 82;
- **Query 1:** Query string: "Salariu net," query language: Romanian, query specificity: medium, number of tested results: 90;

It should be noted that the evaluation was made using a low number of users, which is not enough to provide statistically plausible results, but enough to give an overview of operating performance. The parameters used in queries are the following:

- **Search engines:** Google, Yahoo!.
- **Number of used results:** Maximum.
- **Language preferences:** Romanian (1,3,4) and Default (2).
- **Similarity threshold:** 0,3.
- **Number of clusters:** 4.
- **Method of calculating the weight:** Inverted document frequency.
- **Method of calculating the initial centroids:** Documents with the highest number of word.

## Results Obtained in Evaluating the Quality of the Cluster Label

In our tests, the quality of the cluster label range between 0.6 and 0.95, with the observation that the quality is higher for queries with low specificity. The average number of useful clusters range between 2.4 and 3.8, which is a very good result, considering the fact that we had only 4 clusters.

## Results Obtained in Evaluating the Quality of Documents' Distribution

The coverage degree for the four queries is:

- **Query 1:** 0.96.
- **Query 2:** 0.88.
- **Query 3:** 0.89.
- **Query 4:** 0.84.

Taking into account the above results and the charts from Figure 8, one can draw the following conclusions:

- The number of incorrectly classified instances is less than the number of correctly classified instances, in all cases.
- The number of partial/medium classified instances is less than the number of correctly classified instances, in all cases.
- Correctly classified instances dominate the clusters.

## Determining the Optimal Combination of Preferences

Resuming testing on the same set of four queries, an expert test was performed on various combinations available in the program. The following parameters were tested:

- The ideal number of clusters to achieve quality.
- The clustering quality when using the three types of initial choice of centroids.
- Preferences which have the lowest speed of clustering.

In addition to the above aims, another target was to find the weight that would provide a high degree of clustering purity.

The tests revealed the following:

- The best clustering, in terms of the usefulness of clusters, will be obtained for a number of 4 clusters.
- The most efficient choice of initial centroids is segmented algorithm.
- The two formulas for calculating the weights have similar performance.
- The clustering average speed is 10 seconds, for 50 results.
- The components that have the greatest effect on are clustering are the root extraction modules and replacement of stop words.

*Figure 8. Indicators of documents classification: empirical results*

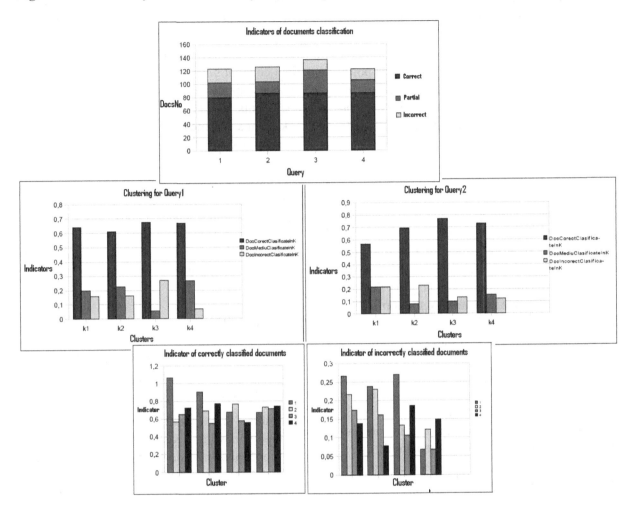

## Comparison with Other Similar Applications

After comparing the performance of our solution to other three similar applications, available on the market (Carrot, Clusty, and WebClust), we came to these conclusions:

- Our application has the highest average number of clusters for a query in Romanian language; for query in English, Carrot system will have a higher performance.
- The quality of cluster label is higher than the one from other implementations for the Romanian language and is comparable for English to the one from Carrot engine; it is better than the ones from Clusty and WebClust.
- We will have a lower number of correctly classified documents than Carrot system for queries in English; in the same time, we will have a lower number of incorrectly classified documents for English.
- For queries in Romanian we will get the largest number of correctly classified documents and the lowest number of incorrectly classified documents.

- The coverage degree is lower than at Carrot system, being higher in one example out of four queries.

In conclusions, we can say that the proposed system has a very high performance of clustering documents in Romanian language and an acceptable performance of clustering English documents.

## FUTURE DEVELOPMENT

Although using ontological approaches brings more refined clustering results, our application currently uses only the educational ontology. A module which permits the connection to any ontology would be a nice improvement: after the user inserts the features of the ontology, the application should be able to map the indexed words to the concept structure from that particular ontology. Another targeted improvement is to be able to use multiple ontological representations at the same time: the value of the results would be considerably increased. In order to increase the usability of the solution, we should migrate the clustering process on the Web and go for a distributed architecture: the ontology can stay on a machine, the clustering process on other machine and so on.

## CONCLUSION

The chapter presented a clustering tool for Web search. The chapter started by presenting the circumstances in which the need for Web search result clustering algorithm appeared and it presented the characteristics that a clustering module needs to meet in order to be practically efficient. After that, we presented a classical approach of k-means clustering algorithm, and the modifications it undertook in order to be adapted to a Web page clustering process. The chapter recommends the relative semantic relevance of a concept with

respect to its prerequisites, named the self-weight of the concept, to be used in the clustering process. The concept's self-weight is combined with the weight of the corresponding term obtaining the final concept's weight. This measure is used in order to compute the distance or similarity between documents, as part of clustering algorithms, such as k-means. The measure is used also for the space graph projections, in order to select the concepts, for clustering dimensionality reduction. The Web page clustering process was than described in detail starting with the initial document processing steps, and moving to the clustering process itself. In the end, it was presented the representation requirements that the clustering module must meet in order to be efficient in a Web search.

## REFERENCES

Baeza-Yates, R., & Ribeiro-Neto, B. (1999). *Modern information retrieval*. New York, NY: Addison Wesley.

Blochdorn, S., & Hotho, A. (2004). Text classification by boosting weak learners based on terms and concepts. In *Proceedings of the 4th IEEE International Conference in Data Mining*, (pp. 331-334). Brighton, UK: IEEE Press.

Bodea, C., & Dascalu, M. (2009a). Designing project management tests based on semantic nets and concept space graphs. In *Proceedings of the 12th International Business Information Management Association Conference (IBIMA)*, (pp. 1232-1236). Kuala Lumpur, Malaysia: IBIMA.

Bodea, C., & Dascalu, M. (2009b). A parameterized web-based testing model for project management. In *Proceedings of the 8th International Conference on Advances in Web Based Learning*, (pp. 68-72). Aachen, Germany: Springer.

Bodea, C., & Lipai, A. (2009). Development of a meta-search tool for the web using a clustering algorithm. In *Proceedings of the 12th International Business Information Management Association Conference (IBIMA),* (pp. 729-733). Kuala Lumpur, Malaysia: IBIMA.

Bodea, C., Trandafir, I., & Borozan, A. M. (2008). Assessment of project management knowledge using semantic networks in the SinPers system. In *Proceedings of the 22nd IPMA World Congress on Project Management.* Rome, Italy: IPMA.

Brin, S., & Page, L. (1998). The anatomy of a large-scale hypertextual web search engine. In *Proceedings of the Seventh International World Wide Web Conference,* (pp. 107-117). Brisbane, Australia: Elsevier Science Publishers.

Chi, N. L. (2003). *A tolerance rough set approach to clustering web search results.* (Master Thesis). Warsaw University. Warsaw, Poland.

Cho, J. (2001). *Crawling the web: Discovery and maintenance of large-scale web data.* (PhD Thesis). Stanford University. Stanford, CA.

Cutting, D. R., Karger, D. R., Pedersen, J. O., & Tukey, J. W. (1992). Scatter/gather: A cluster-based approach to browsing large document collections. In *Proceedings of the 15th International Conference on Research and Development of Information Retrieval (SIGIR),* (pp. 318-329). Copenhagen, Denmark: ACM.

Franstrom, F., & Lewis, J. (2000). *CiteSeer.* Retrieved December 27, 2009, from http://citeseerx.ist.psu.edu/viewdoc/summary?doi=10.1.1.36.7008

Hotho, A., Maedche, A., & Staab, S. (2001). Ontology-based text clustering . In *Proceedings of Text Learning: Beyond Supervision, IJCAI.* Seattle, WA: IJCAI.

Jiang, Z., Joshi, A., Krishnapuram, R., & Yi, L. (2000). *Retriever: Improving web search engine results using clustering.* Baltimore, MD: University of Maryland Baltimore County.

Jing, L., Zhou, L., Ng, M., & Huang, J. Z. (2006). Ontology-based distance measure for text mining. In *Proceedings of the Sixth SIAM International Conference on Data Mining (SDM).* Bethesda, MD: SIAM.

Kanellopoulos, D., Kotsiantis, S., & Pintelas, P. (2006). Ontology-based learning applications: A development methodology. In *Proceedings of the 24th IASTED International Multi-Conference Software Engineering,* (pp. 27-32). Innsbruck, Austria: IASTED.

Kogilavani, A. A., & Balasubramanie, P. (2009). Ontology enhanced clustering based summarization of medical documents. *International Journal of Recent Trends in Engineering, 1.*

Leouski, A., & Croft, W. (1996). *An evaluation of techniques for clustering search results.* Amherst, MA: University of Massachusetts.

Leuski, A., & Allan, J. (2000). Improving interactive retrieval by combining ranked list and clustering. In *Proceedings of RIAO,* (pp. 665-681). Paris, France: RIAO.

Lula, P., & Paliwoda-Pekosz, G. (2008). An ontology-based cluster analysis framework. In *Proceedings of the First International Workshop on Ontology-Supported Business Intelligence,* (pp. 1-6). Karlsruhe, Germany: IEEE.

Osiński, S. (2003). *An algorithm for clustering of web search results.* (Master Thesis). Poznań University of Technology. Poznań, Poland.

Price, G. (2004). *Reducing information overkill.* Retrieved January 28, 2010, from http://searchenginewatch.com/showPage.html?page=3415071

Ryan, K. (2008). *What's wrong with being cuil?* Retrieved February 13, 2010, from http://searchenginewatch.com/showPage.html?page=3630382

Salton, G. (1989). *Automatic text processing: The transformation, analysis and retrieval of information by computer.* Reading, MA: Addison-Weslay Logman Publishing.

Stefanowski, J., & Weiss, D. (2003). Carrot2 and language properties in web search results clustering. In *Proceedings of the First International Web Intelligence Conference,* (pp. 240-249). Madrid, Spain: Springer.

Weiss, D. (2001). *A clustering interface for web search results in Polish and English.* (Master's Thesis). Poznan University of Technology. Poznan, Poland.

Wróblewski, M. (2003). *A hierarchical WWW pages clustering algorithm based on the vector space model.* (Master Thesis). Poznań University of Technology. Poznań, Poland.

Zamir, O. (1999). *Clustering web documents: A phrase-based method.* (PhD Thesis). University of Washington. Seattle, WA.

Zamir, O., & Etzioni, O. (1998). Web document clustering: A feasibility demonstration. In *Proceedings of the 19th International Computer Research and Development of Information Retrieval (SIGIR),* (pp. 46-54). Melbourne, Australia: ACM.

## ADDITIONAL READING

Andrews, N., & Fox, E. (2007). *Recent developments in document clustering technical.* Report TR-07-35. Blackburg, VA: Virginia Tech.

Bradley, P., Fayyad, U., & Reina, C. (1998). Scaling clustering algorithms to large database. In *Proceedings of Fourth International Conference on Knowledge,* (pp. 9 – 15). AAAI Press.

Dhillon, I. S., & Modha, D. S. (2001). Concept decompositions for large sparse text data using clustering. *Machine Learning, 42*(1-2), 143–175. doi:10.1023/A:1007612920971

Dubin, D. (2004). The most influential paper Gerard Salton never wrote. *Library Trends, 52*(4), 748–764.

Dunham, M. H. (2002). *Data mining: Introductory and advanced topics.* Upper Saddle River, NJ: Prentice Hall.

Jain, A. K. (2000). Date clustering: A review. *ACM Computing Surveys, 31*(3), 264–323. doi:10.1145/331499.331504

Johnson, N. (2008). *Microsoft top display advertiser for June 2008.* Retrieved January 28, 2010, from http://blog.searchenginewatch.com/blog/080827-090357

Kim, H., & Loh, W. (2003). Classification trees with bivariate linear discriminant node models. *Journal of Computational and Graphical Statistics, 12*, 512–530. doi:10.1198/1061860032049

Lawrence, S., & Giles, L. (1999). Accessibility of information on the web. *Nature, 400.*

Lingras, P. (2002). Rough set clustering for web mining. In *Proceedings of IEEE International Conference on Fuzzy Systems.* IEEE Press.

Najork, N., & Heydon, A. (2001). *High-performance web crawling.* Palo Alto, CA: System Research Center.

Nicholson, S. (2000). A proposal for categorization and nomenclature for web search tools. *Journal of Internet Cataloging.* Retrieved from http://bibliomining.com/nicholson/classify.html

Nilsson, J. N. (1996). *Introduction to machine learning.* Stanford, CA: Stanford University.

Northern Light Enterprise Search Engine. (2004). *Overview white paper.* Retrieved December 17, 2009, from http://www.northernlight.com

Online Computer Library Center. (2008). *Web characterization: Size and growth statistics.* Retrieved December 21, 2009, from http://www.oclc.org/research/projects/archive/wcp/stats/size.htm

Pawlak, Z. (1994). Rough sets present state and further prospects. In *Proceedings of the Third International Workshop on Rough Set and Soft Computing (RSSC 1994)*, (pp. 72–76). RSSC.

Pawlak, Z. (1997). Rough sets, rough relations and rough functions. *Fundamenta Informaticae*. Retrieved from http://chc60.fgcu.edu/images/articles/PawlakReport94-24.pdf

Rastogi, R., & Shim, K. (1999). Scalable algorithm for mining large database. In *Proceedings of the Conference on Knowledge Discovery*, (pp. 73 - 140). IEEE.

Salton, G., Wong, A., & Yang, C. (1975). A vector space model for automatic indexing. *Communications of the ACM, 18*(11), 613–620. doi:10.1145/361219.361220

## KEY TERMS AND DEFINITIONS

**Cluster Centroid:** Is the concept or word which appears in all the documents from the same cluster.

**Clustering Algorithms:** Are methods through which a set of entities are grouped into subsets, called clusters, so that observations in the same cluster are similar, according to some predefined criteria.

**Concept Space Graphs:** Are hierarchical representations of concepts, in which mathematical relationships can be computed, based on the power of explanation of the root concept by the child nodes concepts.

**Documents Vectoring:** Represents the method by which numerical vectors are built for each document, according to the frequency of each word in a document; stop words (such as "and," "or," "in") and characters are not included.

**Graph Projection:** Represents the method by which, in concept space graphs, the root node concept can be explained by one or many child nodes concepts; it depends on a threshold value, established by a set of experts in the domain in which the concept space graph is defined.

**Meta-Search:** Means the use of more search tools simultaneously for the same query.

**Ontology:** Is a formal representation of the knowledge by a set of concepts within a domain and the relationships between those concepts.

# Chapter 13
# Exploring Semantic Characteristics of Socially Constructed Knowledge Repository to Optimize Web Search

**Dengya Zhu**
*Curtin University, Australia*

**Heinz Dreher**
*Curtin University, Australia*

## ABSTRACT

*Short-term queries preferred by most users often result in a list of Web search results with low precision from a user perspective. The purpose of this research is to improve the relevance of Web search results via search-term disambiguation and ontological filtering of search results based on socially constructed search concepts. A Special Search Browser (SSB) is developed where semantic characteristics of the socially constructed knowledge repository are extracted to form a category-document set. kNN is employed with the extracted category-documents as training data to classify Web results. Users' selected categories are employed to present the search results. Experimental results based on five experts' judgments over 250 hits from Yahoo! API demonstrate that utilizing the socially constructed search concepts to categorize and filter search results can improve precision by 23.5%, from Yahoo's 41.7% to 65.2% of SSB based on the results of five selected ambiguous search-terms.*

DOI: 10.4018/978-1-4666-2494-8.ch013

Copyright © 2013, IGI Global. Copying or distributing in print or electronic forms without written permission of IGI Global is prohibited.

# INTRODUCTION

The introduction and subsequent explosion of the Web has dramatically changed our approach to access and use of information. Internet is becoming a part of life for most people in the world. However, as indicated by Baeza-Yates and Ribeiro-Neto (1999), most users have difficulties in expressing their information needs in search-term format: they prefer short queries instead of the Boolean expressions (Jansen & Spink, 2006). To address this issue, most search engines encourage users to enter very short search terms as queries, and then return a list of search results which are ranked by technologies such as traditional information retrieval models and PageRank (Page, et al., 1998), according to the relevance degree of the results with respect to a given query. However, as the volume of information on the Web is becoming unbelievably huge, short search terms based Web search usually leads to search engines return a list of thousands, even millions of search results. Searchers are thus frustrated when facing such a long list of results especially when half of the search results are irrelevant to their information needs (Gauch, Chaffee, & Pretschner, 2003). It is now commonly recognized that information search services are far from perfect. The challenges of search engines are summarized in Table 1.

The first challenge for search engines is the *Information overload* (C1). What does "1-10 of 55,400,000 for jaguar" mean? Can we really access 55,400,000 information items about jaguar? Are all of the items are relevant to my information need? Oh my God, how can manage to read all of them. It seems that search engines prefer to present a number of search results as huge as this for short queries. However, as research indicated (Jansen & Spink, 2006), the tendency is fewer results pages are browsed. Therefore, millions of search results are a kind of information overload for users.

The second challenge of search engines is *Mismatching hits* (C2). The performance of an information retrieval system is usually measured by precision and recall. Precision is an evaluation of how retrieved results of the information retrieval system are relevant; whereas the recall is an evaluation of how the relevant results are retrieved (Baeza-Yates & Ribeiro-Neto, 1999). While millions of search results being retrieved, meaning that the recall is very high, precision remains low, because most the retrieved results are irrelevant. For example, the top ten search results of a Chinese name "Wei Liu" are about ten different persons (Zhu, 2007), and you are lucky if the person you are searching for is among the top ten results; or on the other hand, the information you are looking for is located on the tenth page.

The third issue of search engines is that search results are presented in the form of a *flat list* (C3). The flat list of results is suitable for a small amount of results because it provides an easy and quick way to locate a relevant information item. However, when there are hundreds or even thousands of retrieved results returned, users have to do re-search amongst the returned items; they need to go through page by page to pick up useful information items. Finding relevant information

*Table 1. Challenges of web search engines (Zhu, 2007)*

|  | Challenges | Phenomena |
|---|---|---|
| **C1** | Information overload | Millions of Web hits |
| **C2** | Mismatching hits | High recall, low precision, many irrelevant results |
| **C3** | Flat list of results | Results are presented in a flat list, users have to pick up useful items among the list, like finding a needle in haystack |
| **C4** | Mismatching mental model | Automatically formed hierarchy used to re-organize Web hits usually mismatches human mental model |
| **C5** | Homogeneity | Search engines present "the same for all" hits, not personalized |
| **C6** | Low recall of Web navigation | Web navigation is more accurate, but the recall is very low |

items is somewhat like finding a needle in haystack (Baeza-Yates & Ribeiro-Neto, 1999).

Another issue of so called clustering engines is that the automatically generated labels for the clusters usually *mismatch mental model* (C4). Clusty.com is an example of a successful clustering engine which groups search results based on some common properties shared among each of the generated groups, and at the same time, assigns each of the groups a label which is believed the most concise and informative description of the group. However, since the label is generated automatically by an algorithm, the generated label has the potential to mismatch the user's mental model. For instance, the generated labels by Clusty.com for search results of jaguar include "Car for sale," "Car Models," and "Land Rover" (retrieved on 2nd March, 2010). However, the common sense is that "Land Rover" is only one of "Car models," so the automatically generated labels are sometimes confusing.

. "The same for all" or *Homogeneity* (C5) is another challenge of search engines. When a search term is submitted to a search engine, different users have different information needs; and even the same user may have different information needs at different times. Taken jaguar as an example again, if the user is an environmentalist, when jaguar is the query, the information need for the user should be about the information of animal jaguar; this information need is different from that of a computer engineer who is using Apple's jaguar operating system. In the future, the environmentalist may want to buy a jaguar car; at this time, the information need is about the automobile named jaguar. The "Same-for-All" policy of search engines cannot solve this issue.

Web directory such as *Yahoo! Directory* provides an alternative approach for users to access Web information. Users can follow the predefined hierarchical structure to gradually refine the search scope and thus obtain accurate information. Obviously, the precision of the results of Web navigation is almost 100% if the Web directory

is well constructed and the submitted websites are properly indexed by human editors. However, since it is almost impossible to manually index all the Web pages into a Web directory for the reason of the huge and rapidly growing number of websites, therefore, the recall of the results of Web navigation is very poor. This is a last challenge facing by search engines (C6), *Low recall of Web navigation*.

Behind these phenomena, the polysemous and synonymous characteristics of natural languages, the huge amounts of information available on the Web, and the lack of personalization (Ferragina & Gulli, 2005; Micarelli, et al., 2007) are the main reasons for the low quality of Web searching.

In this research, a Special Search Browser (SSB) was developed which addresses the above issues by categorizing Web search results into the Open Directory Project categories (ODP) (www. dmoz.org or www.dmoz.com). The semantics of each category in the ODP is manifested by forming a *category-document* (Zhu, 2007). *Yahoo! Search Web Services API* is used to obtain search results. *k Nearest Neighbors* classifier (Cover & Hart, 1967) is employed to group the Web results by using *category-documents* as training document set; similarity distance are measured by Lucene (Gospodnetić & Hatcher, 2005) which uses a modified Vector Space Model (Baeza-Yates & Ribeiro-Neto, 1999). In this research, personalization is the direct interaction process, which allows users to explicitly select an interest or relevant category, and the SSB consequently presents each user with ontologically filtered and categorized Web results based on the user's selection.

This research differs from other clustering based approaches (Ferragina & Gulli, 2005; Zeng, et al., 2004) that groups Web search results by comparing the similarities only amongst the returned search results set. Furthermore, clustering algorithms automatically assign labels to the formed clusters making them difficult to understand; and as discussed above, hierarchies formed by clustering engines such clusty.com often exhibit a mismatch with the human mental model of the search user.

The contribution of this research is two-fold. First, we propose to manifest the semantics of the ODP categories by analyzing and selectively utilizing the ODP meta-data; whereas other research (Dumais & Chen, 2000; Frommholz, 2001; Klas & Fuhr, 2000) downloaded all referenced Web pages (the ODP referenced more than four million pages at present) in these categories. This is not only computationally expensive but also noise-prone as some pages are not correctly linked. Second, while other researchers classify Web documents in full length by using *Yahoo! Directory* (Mladenic, 1998) or LookSmart Web directories (Chen & Dumais, 2000), our research uses the ODP *category-documents* to classify Web search results that are much less informative than the full length text documents, with the resultant algorithm being more efficient.

## RELATED WORK

One of the early researchers who employed *Yahoo! Directory* to reorganize Web search results is Mladenic (1998). Experiments are based on three top levels *Yahoo! Directory*, *Reference*, *Education*, and *Computers and Internet*. Documents are represented as feature vectors which contain not only single words, but also up to 5-gram phrases. Low frequency (lower than 3) features are removed, and Odd ration feature selection algorithm (Forman, 2003) is utilized to reduce the high feature dimension. Naïve Bayes classifier (Mitchell, 1997) is trained to assign a test document to one of the three categories. Experimental results demonstrate that more than half of the testing documents can be correctly arranged by the trained classifier with the highest predicated probability.

*Yahoo! Directory* is also employed by Klas and Fuhr (2000) to categorize Web pages which are quite different from the text documents in the document collection such as Reuters or OHSUMED in that documents in the latter collection have a similar structure and are about the same length whereas the content of Web pages are heterogeneous and variable length. Classic text categorization algorithms that perform well in Reuters or OHSUMED need to be modified to obtain acceptable performance results for Web documents set. To address the issue, all the Web pages indexed under the Yahoo! categories are downloaded to generate a *megadocument* set by concatenating the texts of all the downloaded documents for each of the categories. By using this approach, each of the categories will have a corresponding *megadocument*. Features are selected based on the tf-idf (term frequency-inverse document frequency) (Baeza-Yates & Ribeiro-Neto, 1999) values in a descending order. Probability information retrieval model (Baeza-Yates & Ribeiro-Neto, 1999) is used to evaluate the similarities between *megadocuments* and Web pages. Experimental results demonstrate that the proposed *megtadocument* approach performs very well for Web document categorization (Klas & Fuhr, 2000).

Frommholz (2001) also uses *Yahoo! Directory* to categorize Web pages and in his research *Yahoo! Directory* is taken as a directed acyclic graph. The proposed approach consists of two steps, pre-classification and post-classification. The first step (pre-classification) classifies the Web results by using the *megadocument* approach suggested by Klas and Fuhr (2000) to obtain a categorization result by a non-hierarchical classifier; the second step (post-classification) intends to improve the obtained results by exploring the hierarchical information of the *Yahoo! Directory*. The motivation is somewhat similar to that of majority voting rule where a final decision is not simply decided by the top ranked category but by the majority voting results of the top k ranked categories. In the scenario of *Yahoo! Directory*, the question is for two categories C and C', how to estimate the probability P(C'|C), that is, given a category C, the probability of C implies C'. To estimate the probability, let C be a set of documents grouped in C, C' $\subseteq$ C is a subset of C, then P(C'|C) can be estimated as |C $\cap$ C'| / |C|. Since it is almost impossible to estimate all the category pairs (for a category set with N elements, there are $2^N$ such pairs), for the case of *Yahoo! Directory*, the probability P(C'|C) is only calculated for C and C' which hold a subcategory-supercategory relationship which is derived from *Yahoo! Directory* hierarchy. The calculated probability is referred to as local implication probability and thus a global implication probability can be estimated by taking into consideration of the acyclic graph of the *Yahoo! Directory*. Experimental results show a marginal improvement is obtained when compared with the results of Klas and Fuhr (2000).

Dumais and Chen (2000) suggest a Support Vector Machine (SVM) (Joachims 1998) based classifier which is trained by using the hierarchical structure of *Looksmart Web directory*. Binary vector is employed to represent the Web pages. 1000 features with the highest mutual information are selected for each category. The categories at the top two levels of the *Looksmart* knowledge hierarchy are considered, the hierarchical information is expressed by multiplicative function which multiplies P(C1) and P(C2) where P(C1) and P(C2) are the probability that a document be assigned to category C1 and C2, where C2 is a subcategory of C1. Experiments data show the proposed approach can marginally improve the performance of Web site categorization, compared with the flat, non-hierarchical algorithms.

Labrou and Finin (1999) argue that Web categories like *Yahoo! Directory* provide a "standardized and universal way" for depict real world, and propose using *Yahoo! Directory* as an ontology to automatically categorize Web documents by an n-gram based classifier which compares the cosine similarities between two representation vectors. The title of each category, especially a brief description of the submitted Web pages, actually represents the semantic content and can be taken advantage of.

Instead of categorizing Web search results directly, some researchers categorize Web queries. Compared with Web search results and full-length text documents, Web queries which usually contain fewer words are more noisy and ambiguous, and their meanings are changing over time. A two-phase text categorization algorithm referred to as *query enrichment* is proposed by Shen et al. (2006) to address the issues of Web query classification which assigns Web queries into a predefined category hierarchy. The proposed approach first maps a query Q into a set of Web pages, which is then mapped into the target categories, or alternatively, the query Q is submitted to a meta search engine to obtain a list of results which are categorized by a statistical classifier into an intermediate taxonomy such as the Open Directory Project. Since the intermediate category set is different from the target categories, the obtained intermediate categories are then mapped onto the target categories. The second step combines the categorization results aforementioned to obtain an ensemble based approach. In the 2005 ACM Knowledge Discovery and Data Mining competition (http://www.sigkdd.org/kddcup/index.php), the proposed algorithm won the championship with best $F_1$ and precision as high as 44.4% and 42.4%, and other outstanding performances.

The shortcomings of the ensemble-based approach suggested by Seng et al. (2006) are that it must use an external knowledge base while queries being submitted to a metasearch engine, and obviously more time consuming and thus not suitable for demanding operational environments. Beitzel et al. (2007) propose a query enrichment technique which not only addresses the query classification issues as discussed previously, but also tries to overcome the drawbacks of approach proposed by Seng et al.. The suggested technique utilizes an unlabeled query log of a search engine to assist improving the automatic query classification. A rule-based classifier is developed which conducts co-occurrence analysis on the unlabeled query log to establish associations between query terms and particular categories. A manually classified query set and a weighted automatic classifier is also trained. These three types of results are then combined together to provide better results. Experimental results of this approach are comparable to the results of Seng et al. (2006) but more computationally efficient.

In our research, the main purpose is to improve the relevance of Web searching. When an ambiguous search term is submitted to a search engine, an effective approach to refine the results is to get assistance from the users themselves to indicate which category is of interest. Therefore, the focus of this research is to automatically re-arrange the returned results into an easily un-

derstood knowledge hierarchy such as the ODP, and allow the users to make their own decision of category relevance. To automatically assign an ODP category to a search result, a *category-document* set is constructed similar to Labrou and Finin (1999) to represent the ODP categories; however, we also explore the information from the ODP "Description" link which is not presented in *Yahoo! Directory* employed by Labrou and Finin.

As the largest, most comprehensive human-edited Web directory, the ODP has a range of applications in personalization, categorization, feature selection, and others. Table 2 summarizes the usage of the ODP. It can be found that although the idea of using a Web directory to categorize

*Table 2. The usage of the ODP*

| Usage | Work | Description | Similarity measure |
|---|---|---|---|
| Catego-rization | Zhu (2007) | Semantic features of ODP categories form a *category-document* set, re-orga-nize Web search result based on the ODP categories, and let users to select an interesting category to filter irrelevant results. | kNN |
| | Seng et al. (2006) | Categorize queries and Web search results to the ODP categories, these results are then mapped into another predefined category set | SVMs (Hearst, et al., 1998) |
| | Kules et al. (2006) | Search results are arranged into the ODP category based on an assumption that the highest ranking pages in search results would oftern be cataloged in the ODP | Looking up in ODP by prefix matching |
| person-alization | Chirita et al. (2005) | Using ODP to define user profiles, to produce ODP-biased PageRank (Page et al. 1998), to personalize search results. | Biased-PageRank |
| | Gauch et al. (2003) | ODP is used as a reference ontology to weight users search preference based on a super-document set formed by ODP data | Vector Space Model |
| | Pitkow et al. (2002) | Create user profile based on top 100 ODP categories. Search terms are aug-mented by using user profile information. | Vector Space Model |
| | Tanudjaja and Mui (2002) | ODP is used as a Web taxonomy to model user search preference which is compared with a result by extended HITS (Kleinberg, 1999) | Extended HITS |
| Hyper-link-based usage | Chakrabarti et al. (1999) | ODP topics and links are used as canonical taxonomy to train a classifier, which is then used to administrate a "focused crawler" | Naïve Bayes classifier |
| | Ester et al. (2004) | Links in ODP are used as training data for topic focused crawling | |
| | Haveliwala (2002) | Top 16 ODP categories are used to produce biased PageRank | PageRank |
| Feature selec-tion | Gabrilovich (2006) | Using ODP and Wikipedia data to enrich document representation to improve the performance of text categorization | SVMs |
| Spam filter | Kolesnikov et al. (2003) | Classify URLs in emails into ODP categories to detect spam | |
| | Williamson (2003) | Using ODP to create a whitelist which is of interesting | |

Web search pages or search results is not novel in itself, our approach is distinct from others in that it extracts the semantic aspect of the ODP categories to form a *category-document* set, which is then used as a training data set to train a classifier to group Web snippets; and we allow users to choose which category is of interest and can thus accurately disambiguate search terms.

## SEMANTIC CHARACTERISTICS OF SOCIALLY CONSTRUCTED KNOWLEDGE REPOSITORY

The ODP is the most widely distributed socially constructed Web directory classified by humans. It now has nearly one million categories; more than 4.7 million submitted Web pages; and over 87,000 human editors world-wide (as of September 2010). The directory is arranged in a hierarchical tree structure (Chirita, et al., 2005) with symbolic links which make the directory look like a directed acyclic graph (Perugini, 2008).

Most categories in the ODP contain four parts, the *topic* of the category; subcategories; the *description* of the category, which is usually a further explanation of the meaning of the category (Open Directory Project, 2008); and a *list of submitted Web pages*, each with a title and concise and accurate description of the submitted website which tells end users what they will find when the site is visited. The information described above in a given category can be used to represent the semantic characteristics of the category, which can then be utilized to categorize and filter search results (Zhu, 2007). Other links such as "help" which gives editorial or instructional information that is not related to the semantic characteristics of a category will not be discussed. "See also" part includes some links to other categories will not be considered neither because they are simply a list of links to other categories and contain no semantic features of the category. "This category

in other languages" includes list of non-English languages which involve multilingual problem and are not considered in this research.

We propose to combine the *topic* of the category, the *description* of the category, and the *submitted Web pages* under this category (title and brief description of each page) to form a *category-document* to represent the semantic characteristics of the category. For example, in the ODP, there is a category "Flora and Fauna" with the *topic* "Science: Biology: Flora and Fauna;" the *description* of the category is:

- This category is intended for websites about the biology of … plus Viruses…

Two samples of *submitted Web sites* under this category are:

- Flora and Fauna of the Grate [sic] Lakes – provides access to … of specimens.
- HabitasOnline – Information on the plants, … Museum Sciences Division.

The *category-document* of the category "Flora and Fauna" is thus composed of the above three elements.

As suggested by Dumais and Chen (2000), this research also considers the top two level ODP categories to arrange search results. There are 15 top level ODP categories (exclude category "World") and more than 500 second level categories, this is enough for Web snippet categorization purpose because too many categories will distract users' attention and take their time to browse amongst the huge number of categories.

All the *category-documents* that belong to a second level ODP category are taken as positive training instances of this category. For example, *category-document* "Recreation: Outdoors: Fishing: Salmon and Steelhead" is a training instance of category "Recreation: Outdoors."

*Figure 1. Main components of the SSB (Zhu, 2007)*

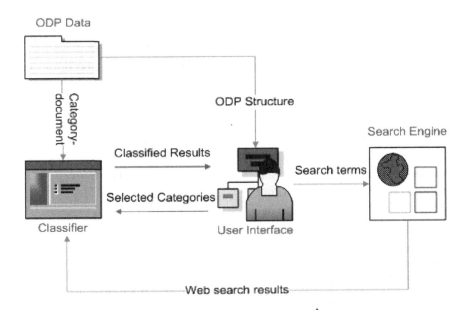

## CONCEPTUAL FRAMEWORK

The Special Search Browser consists of four parts as illustrated in Figure 1. The 'Search Engine' component utilizes *Yahoo! Search Web Services APIs* to obtain search results directly from Yahoo! Web search databases. The input of this part is users' search-terms (query), using the two Yahoo! API functions: WebSearchRequest (String query), and SearchClient. WebSearch (WebSearchRequest request), Yahoo! returns a list of search result for a given query and stores the result list in an instance of class WebSearchResults. Each query gets 50 search results for non-commercial license which is publicly available from *Yahoo! Developer Network* (http://developer.yahoo.com/).

The 'ODP Data' part analyzes and extracts semantic characteristics of each category in the ODP by utilizing Java API for XML Processing (JAXP) to create a *category-document* set as described in the previous section. The ODP data can be downloaded directly from the ODP Web site under the Open Directory License (http://www.dmoz.org/license.html). The hierarchy of the ODP is also extracted and represented by a JTree component of Java and is used to form an instance of the class Document Object Model (DOM). The node data of the DOM object is then adapted and taken as input by the object of the JTreeModel class. The JTreeModel object can then be used by the JTree object to display the hierarchical structure of the ODP data. Another way to display the hierarchical ODP category is to create the JTree by utilizing items in a text file to form the nodes of the tree. A more detailed description of how semantic characteristics are extracted from ODP and how the *category-document* set is constructed is presented by Zhu and Dreher (2009).

The ODP knowledge hierarchy is human edited, and is therefore much more easily understood than that of the automatically created hierarchy of cluster engines such as Clusty.com; Challenge C4)—mismatch of mental model of automatically constructed cluster hierarchies—is thus alleviated. Since the results are arranged according to a tree structure, Challenge C3)—flat list presentation of search results—is consequently addressed.

"Classifier" component implements term indexing, searching, and non-overlapping search results categorizing based on top two level categories in the ODP. Lucene (Gospodnetić & Hatcher, 2005) is employed to achieve the objectives. Web results and *category-document* are represented as vectors with terms weighted by tf-idf scheme. Stop words are removed and terms are stemmed by Snowball. k-nearest *category-document* neighbors are selected, and a modified Majority Voting strategy as shown in Figure 2 is employed to determine the most appropriate *category-document*. The category which is represented by the voted *category-document* will be marked in the corresponding position in the JTree to inform the user how the returned search results are classified according to the ODP knowledge structure. The user can then select an interesting category, which causes the results to be appropriately filtered and presented. Note that one search result is assigned only one category, although multi-categories are sometime more appropriate.

The similarity distance *s* between Web search results $\vec{q}$ and *category-document* $\vec{d}$ is measured by:

$$s(\vec{q}, \vec{d}) = coord(\vec{q}, \vec{d}) \cdot queryNorm(\vec{q}) \cdot$$
$$\sum_{t \in q} (tf(t \ in \ d) \cdot idf(t)^2 \cdot$$
$$t.getBoost() \cdot norm(t, d))$$

where tf(t in d) is the term frequency of term t in document $\vec{d}$ which takes value of sqrt(frequency); idf is inverse document frequency calculated by

$$1 + \log(\frac{number \ of \ documents}{document \ frequency + 1});$$

$coord(\vec{q}, \vec{d})$ is a score factor which gives a document a higher value if the document contains more terms in a given query; for example, the value can be maximum 1 for a document if it contains all terms in the query; $queryNorm(\vec{q})$ does not affect the ranking of documents (the same for all documents) but to make scores between queries comparable, the default value of the factor is 1/sqrt(SumOfSquaredWeights); t. boost() is used to boost a term in the query. Lastly, norm(t, d) consists of three parts,

$$norm(t, d) = doc.getBoost() \cdot$$
$$lengthNorm(field) \cdot$$
$$\prod_{field \ f \ in \ d \ named \ as \ t} f.getBoost()$$

doc.getBoost() boosts a document before adding the document to the Lucene indexer; lengthNorm(field) factor makes sure short length field will not be ignored when calculating similarity socres; f.getBoost() will boost field *f* before the field is added to a document. Note that in Lucene a document object is a collection of field objects which is <name, value> pair (http://lucene.apache. org/java/3_0_1/).

Organizing search results under the ODP categories can address Challenge C1), the information overload problem, because relevant documents which are usually similar which each other are grouped under the same categories, and thus are well organized; meanwhile, Challenge C2), mismatching search results, is also alleviated because under a given category, most of the results are relevant to the semantics of that category.

The Challenge C5), assumption of homogeneity, can be addressed by allowing user to select interest categories from the ODP hierarchy. User navigates the ODP category tree just like they are using the Yahoo! Directory to access high precision information, Challenge C6), the low recall of Web navigation is thus addressed because the search results are from one of the most popular search engine, Yahoo! which provides high recall search results.

*Figure 2. Flow chart of majority voting algorithm*

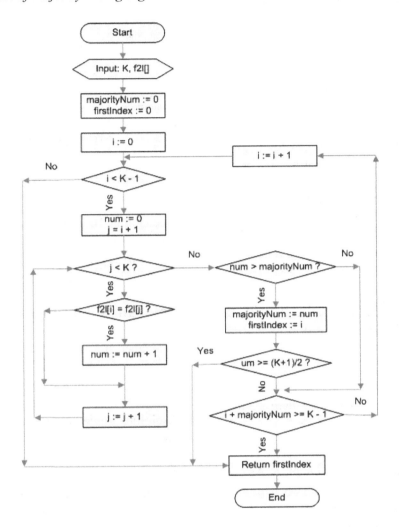

## EXPERIMENTAL RESULTS AND ANALYSIS

### Search-Term Selection

Three principles are followed when selecting queries in the experiment. The first one is that search-terms should not only be motivated by genuine user information need, but should also come directly from users. The second consideration is that the selected queries should cover a wide range of subject material. Zeng et al. (2004) classify 30 queries selected from MSN search log file into three types, namely, Ambiguous queries, Entity names, and General terms. Last but not least thing needs to bear in mind is that as the purpose of this study is to disambiguate search-terms, the selected search-terms should have more than one meaning, and should easily cause search engines to retrieve different categories of information. Based on the above considerations, five search terms are selected in this experiment, as shown in Table 3. The five search terms are all from the 30 queries provide by Zeng et al. (2004) although they use the search terms for Web search result clustering purposes.

## Evaluation of the Effectiveness of SSB

The selected queries are submitted to Yahoo! API to obtain 50 search results for each of the five search terms, and this will produce all together 250 search results from Yahoo!. The SSB then categorizes the returned results under the appropriate top two levels categories of the ODP by using a k-nearest neighbor classifier. The search results from Yahoo! and the categorized results under different categories are recorded in different log files, which are subsequently used to calculate the recall and precision, the two widely used measures to evaluate the effectiveness of an information retrieval system.

$$precision = \frac{number\ of\ relevant\ doucments}{number\ of\ documents\ returned}$$

$$recall = \frac{number\ of\ relevant\ doucments}{number\ of\ all\ relevant\ documents\ in\ an\ informatoin\ retrieval\ system}$$

Search results are presented to users according to their relevant degree to a given query. As users examine the ranked list from the very beginning, the number of relevant documents are changing, and consequently the precision and recall. To evaluate the ranked list of results, precision is plotted against recall when latter changes from 0 to 1.0 with a step of 0.1 to produce an 11 standard recall levels. With the corresponding values of precision at the 11 standard recall level, a curve can be drawn to illustrate the how an information retrieval system performs.

For Web search results evaluation, because it is almost impossible to know all the relevant documents for a given query in search engines, therefore, it is usual to consider only the top n returned results and to count how many results are relevant. For example, for the top ten returned results, if six of them are relevant, we say that

*Table 3. Search-terms used in this experiment*

| Type (Zeng, et al., 2004) | Query | Information Need |
|---|---|---|
| Ambiguous | jaguar | animal jaguar |
| | UPS | How Uninterruptible Power Supply works; UPS specification |
| Entity name | Clinton | The American president William J. Clinton |
| | Ford | Henry Ford, the founder of the Ford Motor Company |
| General term | health | How can one keep healthy |

precision at 10 is 60%, or, P@10 is 0.6. In this research, the performance of SSB is evaluated based on the precision-recall curve at the standard 11 recall levels, P@5, and P@10.

## Relevance Judgment

Relevance judgment, inherently subjective and based on psychological factors (Harter, 1992), has been the central of information retrieval research from the beginning (Harter, 1992) of this discipline. Subjectiveness of relevance judgment implies that, for a given document or a Web search result, different people, even the same people at different times, may make different decisions on whether the document or Web search result is relevant or not. In this research, since all the search terms are ambiguous, we therefore postulate an information need for each of the five selected queries. For each of the returned search results, we need to know whether it is relevant to the postulated information need or not.

To obtain relevance judgments and to alleviate the bias introduced by the subjectiveness of individuals, five experts from our faculty are employed. Furthermore, graded relevance categories are utilized to quantify the judgments. Judges are presented with the five queries with the stipatulated information needs as shown in Table 3. They are then asked to make a judgment on whether each of the listed search results is relevant (R), partially relevant (P), irrelevant to the information need (I),

*Table 4. Relevance judgment score*

| Relevance Judgment | Relevant | Part Relevant | Irrelevant | No Sufficient Information |
|---|---|---|---|---|
| Weighting | 3 | 1 | -3 | 0 |

or not sufficient information provided to make a decision (N). After the relevance judgment results are collected, each relevance judgment category is assigned a number as shown in Table 4. This number is a weighting schema for the purposes of arriving at an overall score.

To make a final binary relevance judgment decision (relevant or not relevant), for each of the search results, the weighting scores of the five judges are accumulated into a final weighted score; if the score is larger than zero, the returned item will be treated as relevant; if the score is less than zero, the Web search result will be treated as irrelevant; if the number equals zero, the search result is determined as neutral. We find that less than 1% of the relevance judgments are neutral and thus can be ignored and are not further discussed. By summing the relevance judgment score for each of the returned items, a final binary relevance judgment decision can be obtained.

## Performance Comparison

Based on the relevance judgment results from the five judges, the recall-precision curve for the search results of Yahoo! and SSB are shown in Figure 3 and Figure 4.

During the categorization process, relevant search results may be placed into several different categories. The categorized search results are usually associated with a higher precision, but at a relatively lower recall. Therefore, to address the low recall issue, for each search-term, two categories with the most relevant search results are selected with the assumption that users are familiar with the hierarchy of the ODP and can easily pick up the two categories. The combined categorized search results of the two selected categories are compared with the Yahoo! search results.

The overall average precisions at the standard 11 recall level of Yahoo! search results (0.0 to

*Figure 3. Precision-recall curve of the search results of Yahoo!*

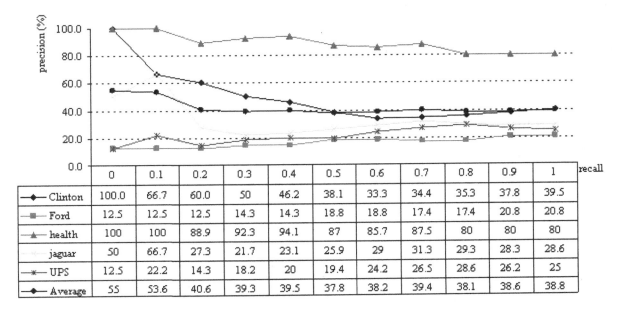

| | 0 | 0.1 | 0.2 | 0.3 | 0.4 | 0.5 | 0.6 | 0.7 | 0.8 | 0.9 | 1 |
|---|---|---|---|---|---|---|---|---|---|---|---|
| Clinton | 100.0 | 66.7 | 60.0 | 50 | 46.2 | 38.1 | 33.3 | 34.4 | 35.3 | 37.8 | 39.5 |
| Ford | 12.5 | 12.5 | 12.5 | 14.3 | 14.3 | 18.8 | 18.8 | 17.4 | 17.4 | 20.8 | 20.8 |
| health | 100 | 100 | 88.9 | 92.3 | 94.1 | 87 | 85.7 | 87.5 | 80 | 80 | 80 |
| jaguar | 50 | 66.7 | 27.3 | 21.7 | 23.1 | 25.9 | 29 | 31.3 | 29.3 | 28.3 | 28.6 |
| UPS | 12.5 | 22.2 | 14.3 | 18.2 | 20 | 19.4 | 24.2 | 26.5 | 28.6 | 26.2 | 25 |
| Average | 55 | 53.6 | 40.6 | 39.3 | 39.5 | 37.8 | 38.2 | 39.4 | 38.1 | 38.6 | 38.8 |

*Figure 4. Precision-recall curve of the search results of SSB*

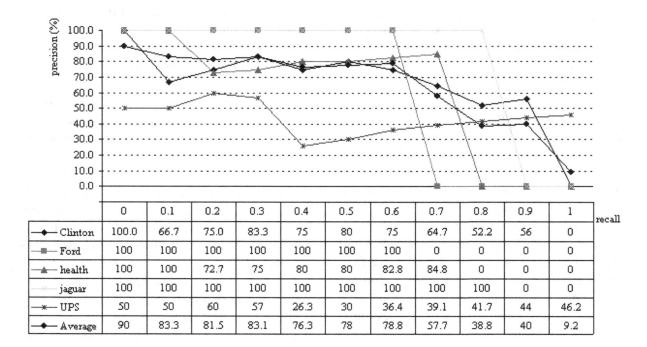

| | 0 | 0.1 | 0.2 | 0.3 | 0.4 | 0.5 | 0.6 | 0.7 | 0.8 | 0.9 | 1 | recall |
|---|---|---|---|---|---|---|---|---|---|---|---|---|
| —◆— Clinton | 100.0 | 66.7 | 75.0 | 83.3 | 75 | 80 | 75 | 64.7 | 52.2 | 56 | 0 | |
| —■— Ford | 100 | 100 | 100 | 100 | 100 | 100 | 100 | 0 | 0 | 0 | 0 | |
| —▲— health | 100 | 100 | 72.7 | 75 | 80 | 80 | 82.8 | 84.8 | 0 | 0 | 0 | |
| —✳— jaguar | 100 | 100 | 100 | 100 | 100 | 100 | 100 | 100 | 100 | 0 | 0 | |
| —✳— UPS | 50 | 50 | 60 | 57 | 26.3 | 30 | 36.4 | 39.1 | 41.7 | 44 | 46.2 | |
| —◆— Average | 90 | 83.3 | 81.5 | 83.1 | 76.3 | 78 | 78.8 | 57.7 | 38.8 | 40 | 9.2 | |

1.0), and categorized results of the special search browser, are illustrated in Figure 5. This figure demonstrates that our proposed approach can improve precision by 23.5% when measured by the standard 11 point recall-precision interpolated curve. The averaged precision of the 50 search results of Yahoo! API over the 11 recall levels is 41.7%, while averaged precision of categorized search results of the special search browser over the 11 recall levels is 65.2%, as shown below.

*Figure 5. Average precision-recall curves of Yahoo! and SSB over the five queries*

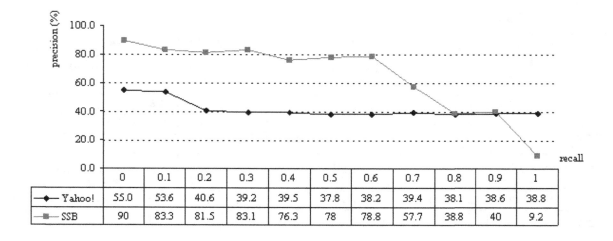

| | 0 | 0.1 | 0.2 | 0.3 | 0.4 | 0.5 | 0.6 | 0.7 | 0.8 | 0.9 | 1 | recall |
|---|---|---|---|---|---|---|---|---|---|---|---|---|
| —◆— Yahoo! | 55.0 | 53.6 | 40.6 | 39.2 | 39.5 | 37.8 | 38.2 | 39.4 | 38.1 | 38.6 | 38.8 | |
| —■— SSB | 90 | 83.3 | 81.5 | 83.1 | 76.3 | 78 | 78.8 | 57.7 | 38.8 | 40 | 9.2 | |

*Table 5. P@5 and P@10 comparison*

|  | **P@5** | **P@10** | **Average** |
|---|---|---|---|
| Yahoo! | 46.7 | 42.0 | 44.4 |
| SSB | 85.0 | 70 | 77.5 |
| Improvement | 38.3 | 28.2 | 33.2 |

- (55.0+53.6+40.6+39.2+39.5+37.8+38.2+39.4+38.1+38.6+38.8)/11 = 41.7 (bottom line of Figure 3).
- (90.0+83.3+81.5+83.1+76.3+78.0+78.8+57.7+38.8+40.0+9.2)/11 = 65.2 (bottom line of Figure 4).

The P@5 and P@10 measures and the mean values of the two measurements are shown in Table 5. The data demonstrate that the averaged P@5 and P@10 is 44.4% and 77.5% for Yahoo! and the Special Search Browser respectively. The improvement of P@5 is 38.3%, and the improvement for P@10 is 28.2%, an averaged improvement of 33.3% is achieved.

Figure 6 illustrates the averaged precision over the 11 recall levels for each of five queries for Yahoo! and SSB. The figure reveals that SSB outperforms Yahoo! for four out of five queries; however, Yahoo! reaches the highest precision for search term "health." For query "Ford," the 16.4% precision of Yahoo! is the poorest.

## A CASE STUDY

Figure 7 is a screenshot of SSB which shows the search results of "clinton." As can be seen from the figure, there are 50 search items presented on the right part of the figure. On the left is the list of the top 15 ODP categories, and five of them (Business, Kids and Teens, News, Regional, Society) are highlighted with the color aqua. The highlighted categories indicate that the 50 returned search results are categorized under the five categories. When "Highlighted" check box above the 15 ODP categories is selected, only the five categories will be presented and the rest categories will not be shown.

Figure 8 shows how the 50 search results are the categorized by Special Search Browser into the second level ODP categories when "Highlighted" check box is selected. As can be seen from the figure, search results under category "Business" are further categorized into a subcat-

*Figure 6. Averaged precision of Yahoo! and SSB for the five queries*

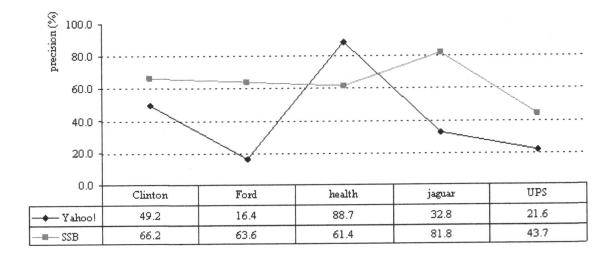

|  | Clinton | Ford | health | jaguar | UPS |
|---|---|---|---|---|---|
| Yahoo! | 49.2 | 16.4 | 88.7 | 32.8 | 21.6 |
| SSB | 66.2 | 63.6 | 61.4 | 81.8 | 43.7 |

*Figure 7. Search results of "clinton" presented by special search browser*

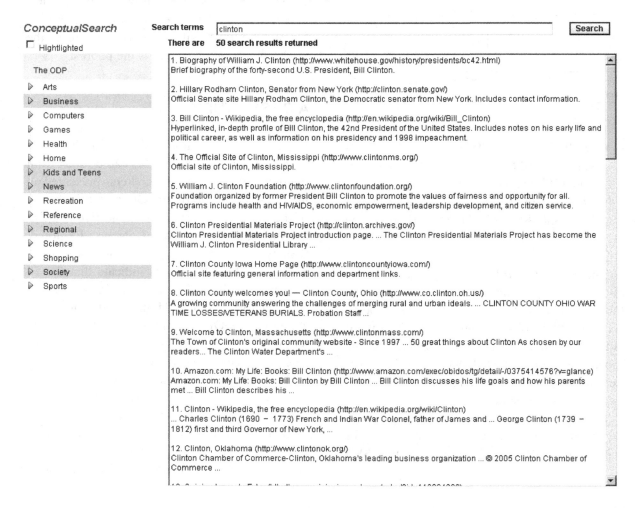

egory (second level ODP category) "Investing." The results presented in this figure are that when category "Society" is selected. There are 15 search results categorized under "Society" and the 15 results are further categorized under a subcategory "History."

## DISCUSSION

We found that in our experiment, for a given query, if the five judges tended to agree with each other on their relevance judgments, the Special Search Browser performs well; on the other hand, if the

five judges have less agreement on their relevance judgment decisions for the search results, our search-browser does not perform consistently. This is the case when searching for "health": the precision of Yahoo!'s search results is 88.7%; while SSB is only 61.4%.

It is therefore suggested that if the judgment of human judges is convergent, or the convergent degree (Zhu, 2007) is higher, the relevance judgment decision made by an algorithm should perform better as well; on the other hand, if the judgment of human judges is divergent, that is, the convergent degree is lower; it is arguable to

*Figure 8. Categorized search results of "clinton" under category "society"*

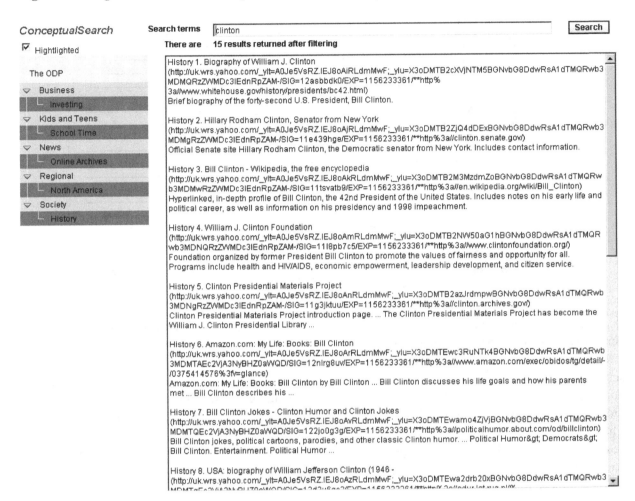

use the data to evaluate a categorization (or IR) algorithm.

Based on this intuition, Figure 9 demonstrates the relationship between the relevance judgment convergent degree and the precision improvement of this research (Zhu, 2007).

The relevance judgment convergent degree of the search-term "Health" is the smallest in the five convergent degrees. Among the 200 (50 results times 4 possible judgment values) possible relevance judgments, there is only one agreement of all the five judges; on the other hand, the five judges give 114 different judgments for the 50 search results. These figures reveal that the human

judges disagree with each other on relevance judgment of search results of this search-term. Therefore, this negative precision improvement should not be regarded as a fault of the proposed approach, but should be regarded as one of the advantages of the proposed approach because it is sensitive to the low relevance judgment convergent degree.

On the other hand, the experimental data also demonstrate that there is still space for the improvement of the performance of SSB in terms of precision and recall. Possible reasons which prevent a more desirable results include that the kNN text classifier may not be the suitable one

*Figure 9. Relationship between precision improvement and relevance judgment convergent degree*

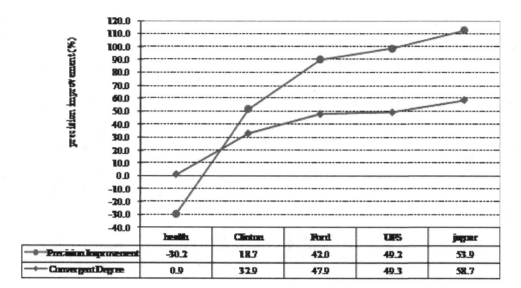

| | health | Clinton | Ford | UPS | jaguar |
|---|---|---|---|---|---|
| Precision Improvement | -30.2 | 18.7 | 42.0 | 49.2 | 53.9 |
| Convergent Degree | 0.9 | 32.9 | 47.9 | 49.3 | 58.7 |

to carry out Web snippet categorization task, the similarity measure algorithm employed is not as effective as expected, a more informative feature set is needed when constructing the *category-documents*, one search result should be assigned more than one category in some circumstances. These issues are to be addressed in our next research stage by combining text categorization, clustering, and feature selection techniques, and assigning more than one category to one search result and others.

## LIMITATION AND FUTURE WORK

One limitation of this research is that only five queries are used in the experiment. This is mainly because the relevance judgment involves much human labor and it is inherently a subjective activity; furthermore, it is very difficult for users to categorize Web search results into the first two level ODP categories (there are more than 500 categories in second level), and then use the labeled Web results as training data. The second limitation is the absence of category recommendation feature of the SSB which at the moment requires

user interaction. In the future, other categorization algorithms, such as Naïve Bayesian and Support Vector Machines, are to be evaluated. We are also planning to merge all training instances belonging to a second level ODP category into a single training instance, and then reduce the high concept-dimensionality of the instance by utilizing feature select / extraction algorithms, such as chi-square, mutual information, information gain, odds ratio or others and then pick up one that gives best performance.

## SUMMARY

The chapter proposed the utilization of text categorization techniques to group Web search results obtained by Yahoo! API. Based on the users' interaction with SSB, irrelevant results were ontologically filtered to boost the performance of Web search. The ODP directory was used as the pre-defined, socially constructed knowledge hierarchy for categorizing Web search. The semantic features of the categories in the ODP were used to build a *category-document* set. The similarities between the Web search results and the *category-documents* were evaluated by employing a modified vector space information retrieval model provided by Lucene. A Special Search Browser was developed to accomplish the above objectives and address the six challenges discussed in the introduction part of this chapter.

The preliminary experimental results demonstrated the proposed search model improved precision by 23.5%, from 41.7% of Yahoo! API, to 65.2% of our algorithm. The mean value of P@5 and P@10 was also increased from Yahoo's 44.4% to the SSB's 77.5%; a 33.2% improvement was achieved. Our next research stage will combine text categorization, clustering, feature selection, and personalization techniques to address the remaining issues as discussed in the introduction.

# REFERENCES

Baeza-Yates, R., & Ribeiro-Neto, B. (1999). *Modern information retrieval*. Harlow, MA: Addison Wesley.

Beitzel, S. M., Jensen, E. C., Lewis, D. D., Chowdhury, A., & Frieder, O. (2007). Automatic classification of web queries using very large unlabeled query logs. *ACM Transactions on Information Systems, 25*(2). doi:10.1145/1229179.1229183

Chakrabarti, S., Berg, M. V. D., & Dom, B. (1999). Focused crawling: A new approach to topic-specific web resource discovery. *Computer Networks: The International Journal of Computer and Telecommunications Networking, 31*(11-16), 1623-1640.

Chen, H., & Dumais, S. (2000). Bringing order to the web: Automatically categorizing search result. In *Proceedings of the SIGCHI Conference on Human Factors in Computing Systems CHI 2000*. The Hague, The Netherlands: ACM Press.

Chirita, P.-A., Nejdl, W., Paiu, R., & Kohlschütter, C. (2005). Using ODP metadata to personalize search. In *Proceedings of the 28th Annual International ACM SIGIR Conference on Research and Development in Information Retrieval*. Salvador, Brazil: ACM Press.

Cover, T. M., & Hart, P. E. (1967). Nearest neighbour pattern classification. *IEEE Transactions on Information Theory, 13*(1), 21–27. doi:10.1109/TIT.1967.1053964

Dumais, S. T., & Chen, H. (2000). Hierarchical classification of web content. In *Proceedings of the 23rd Annual International ACM SIGIR Conference on Research and Development in Information Retrieval*. Athens, Greece: ACM Press.

Ester, M., Kriegel, H.-P., & Schubert, M. (2004). Accurate and efficient crawling for relevant websites. In *Proceedings of the 30th International Very Large Data Bases Conference*. Toronto, Canada: Morgan Kaufmann.

Ferragina, P., & Gulli, A. (2005). A personalized search engine based on web-snippet hierarchical clustering. In *Proceedings of the Special Interest Tracks and Posters of the 14th International Conference on World Wide Web*. Chiba, Japan: ACM Press.

Forman, G. (2003). An extensive empirical study of feature selection metrics for text classification. *Journal of Machine Learning Research, 3*, 1289–1305. Retrieved from http://jmlr.csail.mit.edu/papers/volume3/forman03a/forman03a_full.pdf

Frommholz, I. (2001). Categorizing web documents in hierarchical catalogues. In *Proceedings of the 23rd European Colloquium on Information Retrieval Research (ECIR 2001)*. Darmstadt, Germany: British Computer Society

Gabrilovich, E. (2006). *Feature generation for textual information retrieval using world knowledge.* (PhD Dissertation). Israel Institute of Technology. Haifa, Israel. Retrieved from http://www.cs.technion.ac.il/~gabr/pubs.html

Gauch, S., Chaffee, J., & Pretschner, A. (2003). Ontology-based personalized search and browsing. *Web Intelligence and Agent System, 1*(3-4), 219–234.

Gospodnetić, O., & Hatcher, E. (2005). *Lucene in action.* Greenwich, CT: Manning Publications.

Harter, S. P. (1992). Psychological relevance and information science. *Journal of the American Society for Information Science American Society for Information Science, 43*(9), 602–615. doi:10.1002/(SICI)1097-4571(199210)43:9<602::AID-ASI3>3.0.CO;2-Q

Haveliwala, T. H. (2002). Topic-sensitive PageRank. In *Proceedings of the 11th International Conference on World Wide Web (WWW 2002).* Honolulu, HI: ACM Press.

Hearst, M. A., Dumais, S. T., Osuna, E., Platt, J., & Schölkopf, B. (1998). Support vector machines. *IEEE Intelligent Systems, 13*(4), 18–28. doi:10.1109/5254.708428

Jansen, B. J., & Spink, A. (2006). How are we searching the world wide web? A comparison of nine search engine transaction logs. *Information Processing & Management, 42*(1), 248–263. doi:10.1016/j.ipm.2004.10.007

Joachims, T. (1998). Text categorization with support vector machines: Learning with many relevant features. In *Proceedings of the 10th European Conference on Machine Learning (ECML 1998).* Chemnitz, Germany: Springer-Verlag.

Klas, C.-P., & Fuhr, N. (2000). A new effective approach for categorizing web documents. In *Proceedings of the 22nd Annual Colloquium of the British Computer Society Information Retrieval Specialist Group (BCSIGSG 2000).* Cambridge, UK: British Computer Society.

Kleinberg, J. M. (1999). Authoritative sources in a hyperlinked environment. *Journal of the ACM, 46*(5), 604–632. doi:10.1145/324133.324140

Kolesnikov, O., Lee, W., & Lipton, R. (2003). *Filtering spam using search engines.* Retrieved from ftp://ftp.cc.gatech.edu/pub/coc/tech_reports/2003/GIT-CC-03-58.pdf

Kules, B., Kustanowitz, J., & Shneiderman, B. (2006). Categorizing web search results into meaningful and stable categories using fast-feature techniques. In *Proceedings of the 6th ACM/IEEE-CS Joint Conference on Digital Libraries (JCDL 2006).* Chapel Hill, NC: ACM Press.

Labrou, Y., & Finin, T. (1999). Yahoo! as an ontology - Using Yahoo! categories to describe documents. In *Proceedings of the Eighth International Conference on Information and Knowledge Management, 1999.* Kansas City, MO: ACM Press.

Micarelli, A., Gasparetti, F., Sciarrone, F., & Gauch, S. (2007). Personalized search on the world wide web . In Brusilovsky, P., Kobsa, A., & Nejdl, W. (Eds.), *The Adaptive Web* (pp. 195–230). Berlin, Germany: Springer-Verlag. doi:10.1007/978-3-540-72079-9_6

Mitchell, T. M. (1997). *Machine learning.* New York, NY: McGraw-Hill Companies.

Mladenic, D. (1998). Turning Yahoo into an automatic web-page classifier. In *Proceedings of the 13th European Conference on Artificial Intelligence Yong Research Paper.* Brighton, UK: John Wiley & Sons.

Open Directory Project. (2008). *Website.* Retrieved from www.dmoz.org

Page, L., Brin, S., Motwani, R., & Winograd, T. (1998). *The pagerank citation ranking: Bring order to the web*. Retrieved from http://citeseer.ist.psu.edu/page98pagerank.html

Perugini, S. (2008). Symbolic links in the open directory project. *Information Processing & Management, 44*(2), 910–930. doi:10.1016/j.ipm.2007.06.005

Pitkow, J., Schütze, H., Cass, T., Cooley, R., Turnbull, D., & Edmonds, A. (2002). Personalized search: A contextual computing approach may prove a breakthrough in personalized search efficiency. *Communications of the ACM, 45*(9), 50–55.

Shen, D., Pan, R., Sun, J.-T., Pan, J. J., Wu, K., Yin, J., & Yang, Q. (2006). Query enrichment for web-query classification. *ACM Transactions on Information Systems, 24*(3), 320–352. doi:10.1145/1165774.1165776

Tanudjaja, F., & Mui, L. (2002). Persona: A contextualized and personalized web search. In *Proceedings of the 35th Hawaii International Conference on System Sciences (HICSS-35 2002)*. Big Island, HI: IEEE Computer Society.

Williamson, M. (2003). *Using DMOZ open directory project lists with novell bordermanager*. Retrieved from http://www.novell.com/coolsolutions/feature/7930.html

Zeng, H.-J., He, Q.-C., Chen, Z., Ma, W.-Y., & Ma, J. (2004). Learning to cluster web search results. In *Proceedings of the 27th Annual International ACM SIGIR Conference on Research and Development in Information Retrieval*. Sheffield, UK: ACM Press.

Zhu, D. (2007). *Improving the relevance of search results via search-term disambiguation and ontological filtering*. (Master Dissertation). Curtin University of Technology. Perth, Australia. Retrieved from http://adt.curtin.edu.au/theses/available/adt-WCU20080331.163016

Zhu, D., & Dreher, H. (2009). Discovering semantic aspects of socially constructed knowledge hierarchy to boost the relevance of web searching. *Journal of Univeral Computer Science, 15*(8), 1685–1710.

## ADDITIONAL READING

Arasu, A., Cho, J., Garcia-Molina, H., Paepcke, A., & Raghavan, S. (2001). Searching the web. *ACM Transactions on Internet Technology, 1*(1), 2–43. doi:10.1145/383034.383035

Baeza-Yates, R. (2003). Information retrieval in the web: Beyond current search engines. *International Journal of Approximate Reasoning, 34*(2-3), 97–104. doi:10.1016/j.ijar.2003.07.002

Chen, J., Huang, H., Tian, S., & Qu, Y. (2009). Feature selection for text classification with Naïve Bayes. *Expert Systems with Applications, 36*(3), 5432–5435. doi:10.1016/j.eswa.2008.06.054

Cutting, D. R., Karger, D. R., Pedersen, J. O., & Tukey, J. W. (1992). Scatter/gather: A cluster-based approach to browsing large document collections. In *Proceedings of the 15th Annual International ACM/SIGIR Conference on Research and Development in Information Retrieval*. Copenhagen, Denmark: ACM Press.

Gordon, M., & Pathak, P. (1999). Finding information on the world wide web: The retrieval effectiveness of search engines. *Information Processing & Management, 35*(2), 141–180. doi:10.1016/S0306-4573(98)00041-7

Han, J., & Kamber, M. (2006). *Data mining: Concepts and techniques* (2nd ed.). San Francisco, CA: Morgan Kaufmann.

Hawking, D., Craswell, N., Bailey, P., & Griffiths, K. (2001). Measuring search engine quality. *Information Retrieval, 4*(1), 33–59. doi:10.1023/A:1011468107287

Jones, K. S. (2003). Document retrieval: Shall data, deep theories; historical reflections, potential directions. In F. Sebastiani (Ed.), *Advances in Information Retrieval, 25th European Conference on IR Research, ECIR 2003,* (Vol. 2633, pp. 1-11). Berlin, Germany: Springer-Verlag.

Lam, W., Ruiz, M., & Srinivasan, P. (1999). Automatic text categorization and its application to text retrieval. *IEEE Transactions on Knowledge and Data Engineering, 11*(6), 865–978. doi:10.1109/69.824599

Lewis, D. D. (1995). Evaluating and optimizing autonomous text classification systems. In *Proceedings of the 18th Annual International ACM SIGIR Conference on Research and Development in Information Retrieval.* Seattle, WA: ACM Press.

Lewis, D. D., Yang, Y., Rose, T. G., & Li, F. (2004). RCV1: A new benchmark collection for text categorization research. *Journal of Machine Learning Research, 5,* 361–397.

Manning, C. D., Raghavan, P., & Schütze, H. (2008). *Introduction to information retrieval.* Cambridge, UK: Cambridge University Press. doi:10.1017/CBO9780511809071

Mitchell, T. M. (1997). *Machine learning.* New York, NY: McGraw-Hill Companies.

Mizzaro, S. (1997). Relevance: The whole history. *Journal of the American Society for Information Science American Society for Information Science, 48*(9), 810–832. doi:10.1002/(SICI)1097-4571(199709)48:9<810::AID-ASI6>3.0.CO;2-U

Osiński, S., & Weiss, D. (2005). A concept-driven algorithm for clustering search results. *IEEE Intelligent Systems, 20*(3), 48–54. doi:10.1109/MIS.2005.38

Rijsbergen, C. J. V. (1979). *Information retrieval* (2nd ed.). London, UK: Butterworths.

Salton, G., & Buckley, C. (1988). Term-weighting approaches in automatic text retrieval. *Information Processing & Management, 24*(5), 513–523. doi:10.1016/0306-4573(88)90021-0

Salton, G., Wong, A., & Yang, C. S. (1975). A vector space model for automatic indexing. *Communications of the ACM, 18*(11), 613–620. doi:10.1145/361219.361220

Sebastiani, F. (2002). Machine learning in automated text categorization. *ACM Computing Surveys, 34*(1), 1–47. doi:10.1145/505282.505283

Sherman, C. (2000). *Humans do it better: Inside the open directory project.* Retrieved from http://www.infotoday.com/online/OL2000/sherman7.html

Uschold, M., & Gruninger, M. (1996). Ontologies: Principles, methods and applications. *The Knowledge Engineering Review, 11*(2), 93–136. doi:10.1017/S0269888900007797

Voorhees, E. M., & Harman, D. K. (2005). *TREC: Experiment and evaluation in information retrieval.* Cambridge, MA: The MIT Press.

Witten, I. H., Moffat, A., & Bell, T. C. (1999). *Managing gigabytes: Compressing and indexing documents and images.* San Diego, CA: Morgan Kaufmann. doi:10.1109/TIT.1995.476344

Yang, Y. (1999). An evaluation of statistical approaches to text categorization. *Information Retrieval, 1*(2), 69–90. doi:10.1023/A:1009982220290

Yang, Y., Chute, C. G., & Clinic, M. (1994). An example-based mapping method for text categorization and retrieval. *ACM Transactions on Information Systems, 12*(3), 252–277. doi:10.1145/183422.183424

Yang, Y., Zhang, J., & Kisiel, B. (2003). A scalablity analysis of classifiers in text categorization. In *Proceedings of the 26th Annual International ACM Conference on Research and Development in Information Retrieval.* Toronto, Canada: ACM Press.

Zhu, D. (2009). *Improving the relevance of search results: Search-term disambiguation and ontological filtering*. Saarbrucken, Germany: VDM Verlag.

Zhu, D., & Dreher, H. (2008). Improving web search by categorization, clustering, and personalization. *Lecture Notes in Artificial Intelligence, 5139*, 659–666.

## KEY TERMS AND DEFINITIONS

**DOM:** The Document Object Model, "is a platform- and language-neutral interface that will allow programs and scripts to dynamically access and update the content, structure and style of documents" (http://www.w3.org/DOM/).

**Information Retrieval:** Is the science of searching for documents, for information within documents, and for metadata about documents, as well as that of searching relational databases and the World Wide Web.

**JAXP:** Java API for XML Processing. JAXP is set of Java APIs for XML programming. It can be used to validating and parsing XML documents.

**JTree and JTreeModel:** Two Java APIs to manage and show a tree-based data structure.

**k-Nearest Neighbors (kNN):** Is a categorization algorithm for classifying objects based on k training examples which are closest to test object. kNN is a kind of lazy learning or instance-based learning for which there is no training phrase, and all computation is deferred until classification.

**n-Gram Phrase:** An n-gram phrase is sequence of n words from a given document.

**Open Directory Project (ODP):** Or sometimes dmoz, "is the largest, most comprehensive human-edited directory of the Web. It is constructed and maintained by a vast, global community of volunteer editors" (http://www.dmoz.org/docs/en/about.html).

**Reuters/OHSUMED:** Two labeled document sets frequently used by text categorization researcher as benchmark document collection to evaluate text categorization algorithms.

**Search Engine:** Is a kind of information retrieval system designed to search for information on the World Wide Web. Search results of search engines are usually presented in a flat list based on some ranking algorithms.

**Snowball:** Is a small string processing language designed for creating stemming algorithms for use in information retrieval (http://snowball.tartarus.org).

**Text Categorization:** Is the process of automatically assign predefined categories to free-text documents.

# Chapter 14
# Identifying Polarized Wikipedia Articles

**Nikos Kirtsis**
*Patras University, Greece*

**Jeries Besharat**
*Patras University, Greece*

**Paraskevi Tzekou**
*Patras University, Greece*

**Sofia Stamou**
*Patras University, Greece & Ionian University, Greece*

## ABSTRACT

*Wikipedia is one of the most successful worldwide collaborative efforts to put together user-generated content in a meaningfully organized and intuitive manner. Currently, Wikipedia hosts millions of articles on a variety of topics, supplied by thousands of contributors. A critical factor in Wikipedia's success is its open nature, which enables everyone to edit, revise, and/or question (via talk pages) the article contents. Considering the phenomenal growth of Wikipedia and the lack of a peer review process for its contents, it becomes evident that both editors and administrators have difficulty in validating its quality on a systematic and coordinated basis. This difficulty has motivated several research works on how to assess the quality of Wikipedia articles. In this chapter, the authors propose the exploitation of a novel indicator for the Wikipedia articles' quality, namely information credibility. In this respect, the authors describe a method that captures the polarized (i.e., biased) information across the article contents in an attempt to infer the amount of credible (i.e., objective) information every article communicates. This approach relies on the intuition that an article offering non-polarized information about its topic is more credible and of better quality compared to an article that discusses the editors' (subjective) opinions on that topic.*

## INTRODUCTION

Wikipedia is one of the most popular social media websites that enables users to create content in a collaborative manner. As Wikipedia increases in both size and popularity, there is an urgent need to come up with effective quality assessment methods that would guarantee the value of its contents. Such need is primarily imposed by Wikipedia's open nature, which enables everyone contribute new or modify existing content on a variety of topics, without any pre-requisite that

DOI: 10.4018/978-1-4666-2494-8.ch014

Copyright © 2013, IGI Global. Copying or distributing in print or electronic forms without written permission of IGI Global is prohibited.

content insertions and/or modifications undergo a peer review process. Wikipedia's open nature has led to its remarkable growth, but at the same time, it has raised skepticism about the quality of its contents, considering that anyone can become a Wikipedia editor. In light of the above, numerous researchers over the last few years attempted to design methods and techniques that would capture the article features that signify quality and thus be able to quantify the overall quality of Wikipedia (Stvilia, et al., 2005b; Blumenstock, 2008a).

Most of existing Wikipedia quality assessment efforts, estimate the articles' value based on the study of their internal characteristics such as their contextual elements (Stvilia, et al., 2005a), their linkage in the Wikipedia graph (Kamps & Koolen, 2009), their length (Blumenstock, 2008b), their factual accuracy (Giles, 2005), the formality of their language (Emigh & Herring, 2005), and many more. Additionally, over the last couple of years researchers proposed methods for the automatic identification of controversial or vandalized Wikipedia articles (Vuong, et al., 2009; Potthast, et al., 2008) in an attempt to alleviate administrators from the laborious process of manually removing malicious content from the Wikipedia collection and at the same time assist readers discriminate between commonly accepted and disputed content.

In this chapter, we build upon existing Wikipedia quality assessment efforts and propose a novel method for automatically identifying articles that need undergo revisions and/or repair in order for their contents to reach good quality levels. Our method applies text mining and lexical analysis to the Wikipedia article contents in order to firstly capture highly polarized content in the articles' body and therefore deduce the credibility of the information that Wikipedia articles communicate to readers. In our work, the distinction between credible and polarized articles is defined as follows. A credible article is one that contains unbiased and objective information on the topic being discussed, whereas a polarized article is one that presents the personal viewpoints of its editors about the topic under discussion. Considering that Wikipedia is more than a Web 2.0 information source, we believe that the contents of its hosting articles should communicate reliable and solid information and not serve as a forum of misleading and disputable content. Therefore, via the exploitation of our proposed technique we aspire to assist Wikipedia administrators detect articles of subjective content and either repair or flag them as polarized.

In brief, our proposed technique operates as follows. Given a set of Wikipedia articles, we process their contents in order to discriminate between articles of objective and articles of subjective content. Note that articles of objective content are perceived as communicators of credible information, while articles of subjective content are perceived as communicators of biased information. Articles' processing is applied at two distinct yet complementary levels: lexical and semantic. Lexical processing of the article contents concerns parsing the articles to remove markup and then apply tokenization, part-of-speech tagging, and lemmatization to the article textual elements. Having represented the article contents into canonical sequences of word tokens, we proceed with the identification of the article tokens that might express personal opinions. To that end, we explore the words' *semantic orientation*[1] as introduced in Hatzivassiloglou and McKeown (1997); a factor used to discriminate between words of positive and negative sentiments. The main idea is that not all words in a text serve as good indicators of the text's polarity. Thus, we rely on the observations of Hatzivassiloglou and McKeown (1997) and Turney and Littman (2003) that people use adjectives and adverbs to evaluate a topic or verbalize an opinion and try to infer the polarity of the Wikipedia articles as follows. Based on the article sentences that contain adjectives and/or adverbs, we apply shallow syntactic parsing and where needed anaphora resolution to their contents in order to identify whether the later refer to the topics being discussed in their respective articles. Based on the output of the syntactic parser we pick the articles containing phrases with adjectives and/or adverbs, which refer to the article's topic and we further process them. The article adjectives/adverbs and their referential tokens formulate the co-called opinion phrases about the article.

Having identified the article-related opinion phrases, our next step is to deduce whether the opinions expressed in an article entail polarity or rather they are neutral. In our approach, polarized opinions are those that indicate the editors' positive or negative stance towards the article's discussed topic, while neutral opinions are those that refer to the topic under discussion neither positively nor negatively. To discriminate between polarized and neutral opinion phrases, we rely on SentiWordNet[2] (Baccianella, et al., 2010), a lexical resource for opinion mining that assigns to every WordNet (Fellbaum, 1998) synset three sentiment scores: positivity (+), negativity (-) and objectivity (=). Based on the highest weighted average sentiment score assigned in SentiWordNet to the identified adjectives and adverbs, we cluster the articles' opinion phrases into two groups: polarized and non-polarized opinion phrases. Polarized opinion phrases are those whose contained adjectives and/or adverbs have either a dominant positive or negative sentiment orientation according to SentiWordNet, whereas non-polarized opinion phrases are those that according to SentiWordNet contain adjectives and/or adverbs that entail a dominant neutral sentiment orientation.

Having clustered opinion phrases, we deduce the polarity of the articles in which they appear by accounting for the distribution of polarized opinion phrases across the articles' body. Then, depending on the distribution of polarized phrases an article contains, we may infer the degree of its content subjectivity and therefore deduce if the information it communicates is reliable (i.e., non-polarized) or not (i.e., polarized). The findings of our study might help Wikipedia editors

and administrators track content that needs be revised in order to reach good objectivity levels.

The remainder of the chapter is organized as follows. We begin our discussion with an overview of relevant studies that try to estimate the Wikipedia articles' quality. In Section 3, we describe how articles' polarity can serve as implicit indicator of reliable information for the Wikipedia contents and we present the details of the method we propose towards identifying highly polarized content within the Wikipedia articles. In Section 4, we present a preliminary experiment we carried out in which we assess the amount to which a subset of the Wikipedia articles communicate polarized information about their discussed topics. Obtained results shed light on the article features to be considered in forthcoming Wikipedia quality assessment efforts. We conclude the chapter in Section 5 where we also sketch our plans for future research.

## RELATED WORK

Wikipedia is one of the most successful Web 2.0 paradigms that employ the so-called crowd-sourcing model defined as the *creation of collective intelligence* (O'Reilly, 2005). Conversely, to conventional websites each edited by a single user, Wikipedia engages a huge network of editors, who generate content collaboratively in an unsupervised manner. User-generated content, although useful and of increasing popularity over the last years, needs to undergo quality control, as the traditional expert review model is not applicable to such seer volumes of continuously evolving data. Wikipedia, being a Web 2.0 resource, needs more than ever quality control mechanisms that would guarantee the value of the information it delivers.

Based on the above observations, a large number of researchers proposed several methods for assessing the quality of Wikipedia articles. In this respect, researchers have suggested a number of article features that signify quality, such as their survival period (Cross, 2006), the number and frequency of their edits (Wilkinson & Huberman, 2007), their revision history (Adler & de Alfaro, 2007), the amount of outbound citations to 'trusted' material, e.g. scientific publications (Nielsen, 2007), the dedication of their editors (Riehle, 2005), and so forth. A complete analysis of the Wikipedia features is provided in Voss (2005).

Besides studying the article contextual elements that signal quality, researchers have also explored the properties and evolution of the Wikipedia link graph for assessing the impact of global and local link topology structure on information retrieval tasks (Buriol, et al., 2006; Koolen & Kamps, 2009). The above studies reveal two interesting trends regarding Wikipedia's link structure: first, that Wikipedia links are good indicators of relevance for the article topics and second that there is a strong correlation between the link degree and the document length in the Wikipedia collection.

Another interesting area of research is that of capturing the reputation of the article contributors as implicit indicators of the respective articles' quality (Adler & de Alfaro, 2007; Hu, et al., 2007; Lim, et al., 2006). This body of research does not interpret the article contents but rather it focuses on the articles' edit histories, which record the collaborations between contributors and, based on the mutual reinforcement principle models, the reputation of contributors in order to infer the quality of their generated content. Experimental results in this research direction showed that content contributed by low-reputation authors is more likely to suffer from low quality and vise versa. In a similar direction, researchers proposed a set of page metrics (e.g., number of revisions, internal links, number of distinct editors, etc.) as features for learning whether a Wikipedia article contains controversial information (Kittur, et al., 2007; Vuong, et al., 2008). Experimental results showed that the proposed controversy identification models can effectively determine controver-

sial articles and their performance can be further enhanced when accounting also for the articles' survival over time (i.e. age).

Although our work relates to the above studies that investigate the Wikipedia article contents for inferring their quality, it is different in a significant way. Unlike previous works that estimate the quality of articles based on their lexical elements, we take a step further and account for the article's sentiment orientations. That is, we introduce a novel model for capturing the Wikipedia articles' quality, namely the polarity of their contents. In this respect, we delve into the article semantics and seek for the polarity orientation of their elements. In fulfilling our goal we employ a recently developed resource for opinion mining, namely SentiWordNet, which to the best of our knowledge is the first time it is explored towards capturing biased content in the Wikipedia collection.

## CAPTURING POLARITY IN WIKIPEDIA ARTICLES

In this section, we present our approach for capturing potentially polarized content within the Wikipedia article collection. We begin our discussion by justifying the motivation for our study and we continue with the description of the method we propose for estimating information polarity in the contents of Wikipedia articles. Figure 1 illustrates that overall architecture of the model we propose toward capturing polarized content within Wikipedia articles. The functionality of our model is described in the next paragraphs.

### Motivation

Wikipedia is the largest free-content online encyclopedia. Although there are no specialized qualifications set forth in order for someone to become editor, there exist precise editing instructions with respect to what should or could be part of an article, how to organize the article contents

*Figure 1. Identification of polarized opinion phrases within the Wikipedia articles*

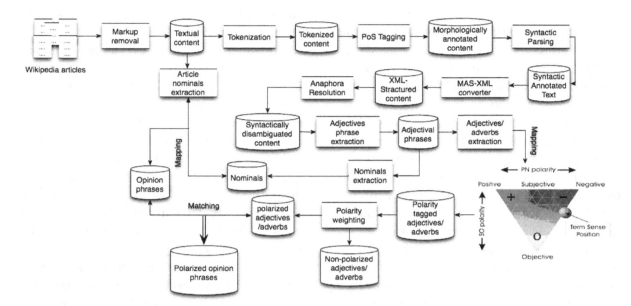

and how to provide links from Wikipedia articles to external (outside Wikipedia) resources. The quest in establishing structural and contextual editing guidelines is to help Wikipedia contributors supply content that is reliable, neutral, verifiable via cited sources, complete and useful for the covered subjects. Above all, it is critical that articles communicate encyclopedic knowledge that would distinguish Wikipedia as an encyclopedia from other information sources.

However, Wikipedia's open nature, lacking coordinated editing, is susceptible to transforming its hosting articles from sources of reliable and trustworthy information to sources of biased and/or malicious content. This is mainly because editors might rely on resources of disputable content for writing an article, or they might manipulate their offered editing freedom and treat it as an opportunity to express their personal viewpoints to a worldwide audience. Both situations result into articles of biased content that is mostly intended for expressing polarized opinions than for informing the readers about the topics they elaborate. Therefore, in both situations, users are hindered

from obtaining accurate and objective information in the article contents and the overall Wikipedia quality is harmed. Driven by the desire to capture information credibility within the Wikipedia articles, we carried out the present study. The aim of our work is to explore the information polarity in Wikipedia articles in order to deduce the amount of credible information in their contents. We believe that the findings of our study will give useful insights regarding the articles' quality and will assist Wikipedia moderators determine effective article review and maintenance policies. In the following paragraphs, we discuss the details of our approach for quantifying and interpreting polarity in Wikipedia articles.

## Identifying Opinion Phrases in Wikipedia Articles

To capture information credibility in the contents of Wikipedia articles, we examine the degree to which articles contain polarized phrases within their contextual elements. Our speculation is that the degree of the articles' information credibility is conversely analogous to the degree of their content polarity, in the sense that the more polarized content an article contains the less credible information it communicates about the topic it discusses.

The method we employ for estimating information polarity in the Wikipedia articles operates upon articles that contain adjectival and/or adverbial phrases referring to the articles' discussed entities. The reason for focusing on such articles is because, according to the observations of Hatzivassiloglou and McKeown (1997) and Turney and Littman (2003), people use adjectives and adverbs to evaluate a topic or verbalize their opinions. Therefore, trying to capture polarization across the entire Wikipedia articles, i.e., even those that do not contain adjectives/adverbs or those whose adjectives/adverbs do not refer to the discussed topic, would significantly increase the overhead and the computational complexity of our measurements without adding much value to the delivered results.

To identify articles of polarized content, we proceed as follows. We rely on the Wikipedia released dumps and we download the contents of articles. We parse the xml file of every article in order to remove markup and we apply tokenization to identify word tokens in the article's textual body. We then pass the tokenized articles through a syntactic parser that annotates every word token with an appropriate grammatical and syntactic category label, with the latter signifying the syntactic role of every lexical entry within its contextual elements. To identify polarized phrases in the morpho-syntactically annotated text, we rely on articles containing at least one adjective or adverb and we apply syntactic dependency parsing and anaphora resolution to their annotated textual content in order to detect the nominal to which every identified adjective/adverb refers.

Depending on the adjective-adverbs referential entities, we discriminate two types of articles as follows. If the identified adjectives/adverbs refer to a nominal that does not describe the article's topic,

we assume that the respective article is neutral (i.e., non-polarized) in the sense that it contains no opinions about the topic it elaborates. Articles identified as neutral via the above process are no longer evaluated. Conversely, if the identified article's adjectives/ adverbs are found to refer to the nominal discussing the article's topic, we further process it in order to determine whether the detected adjectives and/or adverbs have a polarized sentiment orientation or not. In our model, adjectives and/or adverbs referring to the topic of their corresponding article constitute the so-called opinion phrases of the article. Opinion phrases are practically adjectival or adverbial phrases whose head constituents refer to the topic of the article in which they appear. Having identified opinion phrases within the content of Wikipedia articles, our next step is to analyze such phrases in order to derive whether these communicate a polarized opinion or not.

## Detecting Polarized Opinion Phrases

Given that the objective of our study is to identify Wikipedia articles of polarized content, we essentially need a method for determining whether the identified opinion phrases in an article have a neutral or polarized sentiment orientation. Note that by polarized orientation we connote both positive and negative orientations, since both polarity labels entail subjectivity. To discriminate between opinion phrases of neutral and polarized sentiments, we rely on SentiWordNet (Baccianella, et al., 2010), a lexical resource for opinion mining that assigns to every WordNet synset three sentiment scores: positivity (+), negativity (-), and objectivity (=).

In particular, we map the adjectives and adverbs contained in the identified opinion phrases against the SentiWordNet nodes in order to extract the polarity values of their orientations. But, SentiWordNet computes polarity orientations for senses, not words. Therefore, it assigns to every adjective and adverb values for all possible orientations (i.e., positive, negative, and neutral) including the zero value to denote the absence of a polarity in a sense. Moreover, a significant fraction of adjectives and adverbs demonstrate according to SentiWordNet dual orientations, i.e. either positive and neutral or negative and neutral, while the striking majority of the remaining adjectives/adverbs demonstrate a neutral only polarity orientation. As a consequence, SentiWordNet delivers more than one polarity sentiment for every adjective and adverb examined, with the most commonly delivered polarity being the neutral one. This imposes a considerable limitation to our study, which is to identify a single orientation for every opinion phrase identified.

To overcome this limitation, we computed the weighted average polarity orientations across adjective and adverb senses and retained the polarity of the highest average as the dominant orientation of the term considered. That is, we estimate the average positive, average negative and average neutral polarity across all term senses and we retain the polarity of the maximum average score as the term's polarity orientation. This way, we end up with a single polarity orientation for every adjective and adverb contained in the identified opinion phrases.

Based on the above steps, we extract from every Wikipedia article its contained opinion phrases that discuss the article's topic and we assign to every extracted opinion phrase a suitable polarity orientation label based on the information provided in SentiWordNet. Our next step is to deduce the overall articles' polarity, i.e. to estimate the degree to which the article contents are polarized.

## Quantifying Polarity in Article Contents

Having identified in every Wikipedia article the polarized phrases that refer to the article's topic, our next step is to measure the overall polarity of the article in order to infer whether the information it communicates is overall biased (i.e., polarized) or not (i.e., reliable).

In our proposed approach, we measure the polarity in an article by accounting for the distribution of polarized opinion phrases in its contents and the degree of polarity every opinion phrase entails. Recall that by opinion phrase we denote an adjectival or adverbial phrase, which has as referent the nominal that represents the topic of the article. To estimate the articles' polarity, we proceed as follows. We segment the textual body of every article into sequences of $50^3$ consecutive word tokens and we start by computing the distribution of polarized opinion phrases in the article's segments. The distribution of polarity in an article $a_i$ is deduced by the fraction of polarized segments it contains, given by:

$$\text{Polarity Distribution } (a_i) = \frac{\left|\text{\# polarized segments}(a_i)\right|}{\left|\text{\# segments}(a_i)\right|}$$

(1)

Based on the above, we deduce how polarized content spans the article contents so that increased values of *Polarity Distribution* indicate stronger evidence on the polarized nature of the article in the sense that polarized phrases are distributed throughout the article's body.

However, *Polarity Distribution* alone is not sufficient for indicating the degree of polarized content in an article, as it does not account for the amount of opinion phrases contained in articles. To account for the strength of polarized content, we essentially count the fraction of polarized opinion phrases from all opinion phrases contained in the examined articles, as given by:

$$\text{Polarity Strength } (a_i) = \frac{\left|\text{\# polarized opinion phrases in }(a_i)\right|}{\left|\text{\# opinion phrases in }(a_i)\right|}$$

(2)

*Polarity Strength* values indicate the amount of polarized opinions within the article contents, so that the more subjective opinions are expressed across articles the stronger the polarity orientation of the latter. Based on the above metrics, we quantify both the distribution and the strength of the polarized opinion phrases within the article contents. As a final step, we combine the two values (i.e. polarity distribution and polarity strength) into a metric that computes the overall Polarity Value of the article, as:

$$\text{Polarity Value } (a_i) = \text{Polarity Distribution } (a_i) \bullet \text{Polarity Strength } (a_i)$$

(3)

*Polarity values* indicate the degree to which the information supplied in Wikipedia about the topic of an article is polarized and accounts for both the amount and the distribution of polarized opinion phrases within the article's textual body. Therefore, the increased polarity value an article demonstrates the more biased information it provides for its discussed topic and as such the less trustworthy (i.e. credible) this information is. Having quantified the degree of polarized content in an article, we may easily deduce the article's information credibility as:

$$\text{Information Credibility } (a_i) = 1 - \text{Polarity Value } (a_i)$$

(4)

As the formula indicates information credibility of an article is conversely analogous to the polarity value of its information so that the less polarized content in its body the increased its information credibility. Considering that information credibility is a quest in the articles' editing process, the more credible information Wikipedia contains the better quality it bears.

To validate the above assumption and to assess our method's effectiveness in identifying and computing polarity in the Wikipedia collection, we carried out a preliminary experimental study reported next.

## EXPERIMENTAL EVALUATION AND RESULTS

To capture information polarity in the Wikipedia collection, we relied on the October 2009 dump of the English Wikipedia, a 24.5 GB xml corpus, which we processed in order to extract its contained articles. Having processed the Wikipedia corpus, we extracted a sample of 5,208 articles based on the following selection criteria: extracted articles should contain enough textual content (i.e., their size in terms of word tokens should be around the average size of Wikipedia articles, which amounts to 1,000 words), and they should contain a satisfactory amount of adjectives and/or adverbs (experimentally set to 8%) within their textual content. The above selection criteria were imposed for two main reasons: firstly, in order not to waste resources by trying to capture polarized content in articles that do not contain words of sentiment orientation, i.e. adjectives and adverbs, and secondly, in order to ensure that our findings could be generalized for a large part of the Wikipedia collection and would not be influenced by too long or too short Wikipedia articles. Based on the above selection criteria, we sampled a total set of 5,208 articles that satisfy both requisites and we used those articles as the experimental dataset against which we applied our information polarity measurements.

To apply our measurements, we operated as follows. We processed the contents of the selected articles as previously described in order to track opinion phrases referring to the articles' topics. Based on the identified opinion phrases, we extracted their contained adjectives and adverbs and we looked them up in SentiWordNet in order to obtain their sentiment orientations. For associating every adjective and adverb with a single (i.e. the dominant) polarity label, we explored the sentiment orientation of the maximum average weighted polarity value as previously described.

*Table 1. Experimental dataset statistics*

| Collection ID | October 2009 Wikipedia dump |
|---|---|
| Number of examined articles | 5,208 |
| Number of distinct opinion phrases | 180,530 |
| Opinion phrases/article | 34.66 |
| Number of distinct polarized opinion phrases | 13,230 |
| Polarized opinion phrases/article | 2.54 |

dominant neutral sentiment orientation. Table 1 reports the statistics of our experimental dataset.

As the table indicates in the 5,208 articles examined, we encountered 180,530 distinct opinion phrases referring to their discussed topics, with an average of 34.66 opinion phrases per article. In addition, 0.07% (i.e. 13,230 out of the 180,530) of the identified opinion phrases are polarized in the sense that they carry either a positive or a negative stance against their referring topic, which implies that Wikipedia does contain polarized content.

Thereafter, we propagated the polarity label of every adjective and adverb to their corresponding opinion phrase, ending up with annotated opinion phrases according to sentiment orientation. We then clustered the sentiment-annotated opinion phrases into two groups: (1) polarized opinion phrases, i.e., those whose head adjectives/adverbs entail a dominant positive or negative sentiment orientation, and (2) non-polarized opinion phrases, i.e. those whose head adjectives/adverbs entail a

However, to quantify the amount of polarized information in Wikipedia, we applied our polarity measurements (cf. Section 3.4) and estimated the distribution of polarized opinion phrases across the considered articles (*Polarity Distribution* metric), the strength that polarity entails in the considered articles' contents (*Polarity Strength* metric) as well as the overall polarity in the articles body (*Polarity Value* metric). The results delivered after applying each of the above three metrics are

*Figure 2. Distribution of polarized content in the examined articles*

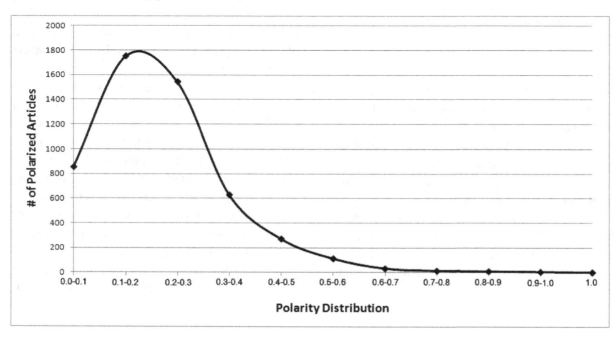

*Figure 3. Average polarity strength in the examined articles*

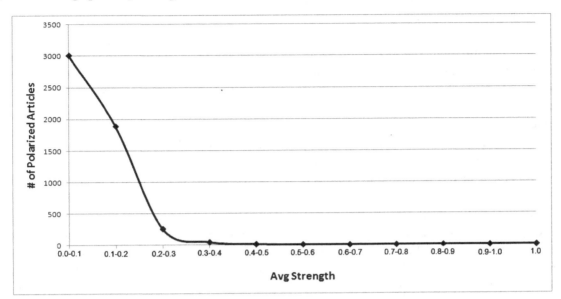

depicted in Figures 2, 3 and 4 respectively. In all figures the *x*-axis reports polarity scores for each metric used and the *y*-axis reports the amount of articles at each polarity score.

As Figure 2 illustrates, polarized opinion phrases follow a normal distribution in the examined articles. This indicates that the majority of articles with polarized content span polarity across their contents, with less than half of their textual segments being polarized. Conversely, only a few articles have all their segments polarized and a few articles contain a single polarized segment.

*Figure 4. Overall polarity in the contents of the examined articles*

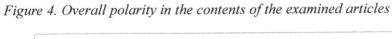

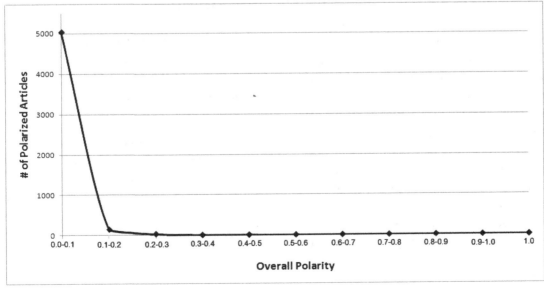

According to Figure 3, most of the Wikipedia articles with polarized content do not contain very strong opinions about their discussed topics. This implies that although Wikipedia editors do not always adopt the guideline of not revealing their personal views about the subjects of their writings, when they do they are generally modest about them.

Finally, based on the overall polarity values across the Wikipedia articles (cf. Figure 4) we observe that most of the articles with polarized content contain few polarized opinions and most of those opinions are of reduced strength. Therefore, we may conclude that Wikipedia exhibits low levels of content bias (i.e. subjectivity), which in turn translates into high levels of information credibility. Although, our proposed quality assessment model merits further validation against a large Wikipedia dataset, the findings of our preliminary experiment reported in this study demonstrate that information bias could and should be employed as indicator of the Wikipedia's content quality.

## CONCLUDING REMARKS AND FUTURE WORK

In this chapter, we have proposed the exploitation of information credibility as a novel indicator of quality for the Wikipedia articles. In the course of our study, we determine the credibility of information an article bears as the inverse value of the article's polarized content. With that in mind, we designed and implemented a model that identifies opinion phrases in the Wikipedia articles. The application of our model to a subset of the Wikipedia corpus revealed that although most of the information provided via the Wikipedia articles is credible, there exist articles that suffer from subjectivity. This suggests that Wikipedia needs undergo further quality assessment control methods in order to stand as a high quality resource of encyclopedic knowledge.

Our measurements, especially those indicating articles of highly polarized content, could help Wikipedia administrators set more precise editing guidelines so that editors contribute information that is accurate and reliable instead of communicating personal opinions. Moreover, our findings could assist Wikipedia moderators implement contextual filtering and peer review mechanisms that would enable editors determine the accuracy of their supplied content.

In the future, we plan to extend our preliminary study and capture information polarity cross the entire Wikipedia collection in order to infer its overall quality. Moreover, we plan to enrich our method with additional features that signify quality in the articles' content such as the frequency of content revisions, the number of article contributors, their authors' reputation, etc. Finally, it would be interesting to delve into the semantics of the polarized article contents and examine whether certain article topics invoke increased levels of subjectivity. Likewise, it would be interesting to attest whether the opinions expressed via polarized articles represent a common sense understanding of the article topics or rather they are susceptible to be spammed content.

## REFERENCES

Adler, B., & de Alfaro, L. (2007). A content-driven reputation system for the Wikipedia. In *Proceedings of the International World Wide Web Conference*, (pp. 261-270). ACM.

Baccianella, S., Esuli, A., & Sebastiani, F. (2010). SentiWordNet 3.0: An enhanced lexical resource for sentiment analysis and opinion mining. In *Proceedings of the Language Resources and Evaluation Conference*, (pp. 2200-2204). IEEE.

Blumenstock, J. E. (2008a). *Automatically assessing the quality of Wikipedia articles*. UBCiSchool Report 2008-021. UBCiSchool.

Blumenstock, J. E. (2008b). Size matters: Word count as a measure of quality in Wikipedia. In *Proceedings of the 17th International World Wide Web Conference*. ACM.

Buriol, J., Castillo, C., Donato, D., Leonardi, S., & Millozzi, S. (2006). Temporal evolution of the wiki graph. In *Proceedings of the Web Intelligence Conference*. IEEE.

Cross, T. (2006). Puppy smoothies: Improving the reliability of open, collaborative wikis. *First Monday, 11*(9).

Emigh, W., & Herring, S. (2005). Collaborative authoring on the web: A genre analysis of online encyclopedias. In *Proceedings of the 38th Hawaii International Conference on System Sciences*. IEEE.

Fellbaum, C. (1998). *WordNet: An electronic lexical database*. Cambridge, MA: MIT Press.

Giles, J. (2005). Internet encyclopedias go head to head. *Nature, 438,* 900–901. doi:10.1038/438900a

Hatzivassiloglou, V., & McKeown, K. R. (1997). Predicting the semantic orientation of adjectives. In *Proceedings of the 35th Annual Meeting of the Association for Computational Linguistics and the 8th Conference of the European Chapter of the ACL*, (pp. 174-181). ACL.

Hu, M., Lim, E. P., Sun, A., Lauw, H., & Vuong, B. Q. (2007). Measuring article quality in Wikipedia: Models and evaluation. In *Proceedings of the International Conference on Knowledge and Information Management*. IEEE.

Kamps, J., & Koolen, M. (2009). Is Wikipedia's link structure different? In *Proceedings of the 2nd International Conference on Web Search and Data Mining*. IEEE.

Kittur, A., Suh, B., Pendleton, B., & Chi, E. (2007). He says, she says: Conflict and coordination in Wikipedia. In *Proceedings of the International Conference on the Special Interest Group on Computer Human Interaction*, (pp. 453-462). IEEE.

Koolen, M., & Kamps, J. (2009). What's in a link? From document importance to topical relevance. In *Proceedings of the 2nd International Conference on Theory of Information Retrieval*, (pp. 313-321). IEEE.

Lim, E. P., Vuong, B. Q., Lauw, H., & Sun, A. (2006). Measuring qualities of articles contributed by online communities. In *Proceedings of the International Conference on Web Intelligence*. IEEE.

Nielsen, F. A. (2007). Scientific citations in Wikipedia. *First Monday, 12*(8).

O'Reilly, T. (2005). What is web 2.0. *O'Reilly Network*. Retrieved from http://oreilly.com/web2/archive/what-is-web-20.html

Potthast, M., Stein, B., & Gerling, R. (2008). Automatic vandalism detection in Wikipedia. *Lecture Notes in Computer Science, 4956,* 663–668. doi:10.1007/978-3-540-78646-7_75

Rieche, D. (2005). How and why Wikipedia works? An interview. In *Proceedings of the ACM Wikisym*. ACM Press.

Stvilia, B., Twidale, M. B., Gasser, L., & Smith, L. C. (2005b). Information quality discussions in Wikipedia. In *Proceedings of the International Conference on Knowledge Management*. IEEE.

Stvilia, B., Twidale, M. B., Smith, L. C., & Gasser, L. (2005a). Assessing information quality of a community-based encyclopedia. In *Proceedings of the International Conference on Information Quality*. IEEE.

Turney, P. D., & Littman, M. L. (2003). Measuring praise and criticism: Inference of semantic orientation from association. *ACM Transactions on Information Systems*, *21*(4), 315–346. doi:10.1145/944012.944013

Voss, J. (2005). Measuring Wikipedia. In *Proceedings of the 10th International Conference of the International Society for Scientometrics and Infometrics*. IEEE.

Vuong, B. Q., Lim, E. P., Sun, A., Le, M. T., Lauw, H. W., & Chang, K. (2008). On ranking controversies in Wikipedia: Models and evaluation. In *Proceedings of the 1st International Conference on Web Search and Data Mining*. IEEE.

Wilkinson, D. M., & Huberman, B. A. (2007). Assessing the value of cooperation in Wikipedia. *First Monday*, *12*(4).

## KEY TERMS AND DEFINITIONS

**Information Credibility:** Accurate and true information that can inspire belief and trust.

**Opinion Mining:** A research area that aims to determine the attitude of a speaker or writer with respect to some topic by leveraging tools and methods coming from the broader areas of text mining, natural language processing, and data mining.

**Polarized Articles:** The process by which the opinions expressed in the contents of an article go to the extremes.

**SentiWordNet:** A lexical resource signs to every WordNet synset three sentiment scores: positivity, negativity and objectivity.

**Wikipedia:** A free encyclopedia built collaboratively using wiki software.

## ENDNOTES

1.  It is also known as valence in the linguistics literature.
2.  http://sentiwordnet.isti.cnr.it/
3.  The window size of segments was experimentally set to 50 consecutive terms as this was found to correspond to the average size of a paragraph in Wikipedia articles.

# Chapter 15
# Ontology-Based Optimization in Search Engine

**Leonardo Balduzzi**
*Universidad Nacional del Centro de la Provincia de Buenos Aires, Argentina*

**Ignacio Cuesta**
*Universidad Nacional del Centro de la Provincia de Buenos Aires, Argentina*

## ABSTRACT

*The major aim of the chapter is to propose and study the use of ontology-based optimization for positioning websites in search engines. In this sense, using heterogeneous inductive learning techniques and ontology for knowledge representation, a knowledge-based system which is capable of supporting the activity of SEO (Search Engine Optimization) has been designed and implemented. From its knowledge base, the system suggests the most appropriate optimization tasks for positioning a pair (keyword, website) on the first page of search engines and infers the positioning results to be obtained. The system evolution and learning capacity allows optimizing the productivity and effectiveness of the SEO process.*

## INTRODUCTION

Online marketing is known as the study of techniques of using the Internet to advertise and sell products and services. This marketing activity has shown the highest growth in recent years driven by the exponential growth of Internet users. Looking further into the future, in US market, the interactive marketing (search marketing, email marketing, social media, display advertising, and mobile marketing) will account for 21% ($55bn) of all marketing spend by 2014 (Forrester Research, 2009).

The large volume of information available on the Internet has accentuated the need to order it, so users can easily and effectively access to such information. For this reason, search engines have become the most popular websites on the Internet. Google (www.google.com) is the most popular website worldwide according to Alexa

DOI: 10.4018/978-1-4666-2494-8.ch015

Copyright © 2013, IGI Global. Copying or distributing in print or electronic forms without written permission of IGI Global is prohibited.

Rank (Alexa, 2010). Along with this trend, the activity of search engine positioning called SEO (Search Engine Optimization) was born. It consists on the implementation of several actions to a website, aimed at making the search engines to place pages from that website in top positions in their SERP's (Search Engine Result Pages) for certain keywords.

The main objective of online marketing is to generate qualified traffic to a website, being each new obtained visit a potential client. Most of the website's visits come from major search engines like Google, Yahoo, Bing, among others. Besides, visits from search engines are of high quality because users are looking for information related to the website topic. This circumstance explains why a successful online marketing campaign increasingly depends on SEO and why search marketing still leads interactive spend representing 60% of online marketing (Forrester Research, 2009).

The method used by search engines to sort the search results is based on algorithms that are not public knowledge. However, guidelines are known for optimizing a website that involve changing certain factors tending to improve its positioning. Being unknown algorithms, SEO activity is empirical and is based on the experience of experts. Despite the experience, in many cases it is not possible to know exactly which the most effective actions to improve positioning are. Therefore, a "trial-and-error" empirical model is applied, which usually has a very high cost of implementation. The success of the activity is further compromised due to increased competition and constant changes in sorting algorithms of search engines.

The market has several SEO tools that provide values of the factors affecting the positioning of a website. The right analysis, interpretation, and modification of these values may allow the website to be located in the top of the search engines. To do this work, it is essential to have a deep knowledge of the definition of each evaluated factor, know its domain, scope, relevance, metrics and how

to modify it to obtain better positioning. Under these circumstances, the following questions arise: Is it possible to position a website without being an expert in SEO? Is it possible for a SEO tool to indicate what factors should be modified to position a website?

In response to these questions born the idea to develop a SEO application centered on a knowledge-based system and able to:

- Intelligently support the process of positioning in search engines, making the domain knowledge to be dependent on a system, instead of on persons.
- Provide a list of actions to implement in order to position a keyword for a particular website.
- Identify the difficulty of positioning a particular keyword.
- Infer the position to get by the keyword in the search engine after applying the proposed optimizations.
- Estimate the organic traffic that would generate the keyword when the website is positioned.
- Dynamically adapt to changes in the search engine algorithms.
- Rank by relevance the factors affecting positioning.

The mentioned application is Matrix (www.matrixsearch.com) and was developed by Intelligent SEO SL, a company that is part of Inspirit (www.inspirit.net), a pioneer group in the ICT sector. The system consists of a facts base, a knowledge base, an inference engine, an ontology, a core module and a user interface. In this chapter, we focus on studying how the inference engine is capable of supporting the SEO activity using the rules of the knowledge base and the proposed ontology.

The following sections focus on presenting learning modules, ontology creation, and results obtained. Finally, conclusions and future research works are detailed.

## BACKGROUND

SEO is one of the leading and most influential activities in the field of online marketing, which is why there is a wealth of information and tools designed to train and support the community of experts in this activity. Search engines have become Internet gateway, new generation of users state that search engines are the first reference source to find new information; so "convince" them that a page deserves to be among the top results, is a must for any online marketing investment that is expected to be profitable (Domene & Grela, 2009).

The challenge of SEO expert is to position a website in search engines whose sorting algorithms he ignores. Therefore, he faces problems such as high uncertainty about the success of the results, the high cost of scaling his work and slow and costly learning due to the constant changes of search engine algorithms. In Enge et al. (2009), the author states that "SEO is rapidly evolving. Search engines are constantly changing their algorithms, and new media and Technologies are being introduced to the Web on a regular basis" (p. 473).

Most available information focuses on identifying and describing the factors affecting positioning. A factor is a particular feature related to a website, Web page or keyword that must be evaluated through one or more quantitative metrics. For example, the factor "keyword use in <title> tag" can be evaluated through the "density" metric (total number of occurrences of the keyword in the title over total number of words in the title) and the "existence" metric (which can take the value 1 or 0 according to whether the keyword is found or not in the title of the Web page).

In this sense, there are several studies and publications that categorize the factors and describe their metrics, even some of them rank the factors by their relevance on the positioning. For example, every two years, SEOmoz surveys top SEO experts in the field worldwide on their opinions about the algorithmic elements that comprise

search engine rankings (Fishkin, 2009). As a result of the survey, an updated ranking of the factors affecting positioning is published.

There is also bibliography describing quality guidelines for optimizing a website designed to guide Webmasters to create and maintain a website so it is more likely to be well positioned in the search engine for certain keywords. In Google (2008), it is stated that "following the best practices outlined below will make it easier for search engines to both crawl and index your content" (p. 1).

Although different sources have several items in common, there is not still a unified classification of the factors affecting positioning. Analyzing the similarities, factors can be grouped according to the following features:

- **Website's factors:** are those that are related to the structure, organization and updating of a website and its relationship to other websites. For example: "Inbounds links" (number of links pointing to a website from other websites), "Page Rank" (popularity indicator of a website).
- **Web Page's factors:** are those related to the structure, organization and updating of a given Web page and its relationship to other Web pages of the website. For example: "use of subtitle tags <H1>, <H2> ... <Hx>."
- **Keyword's factors:** are those that are related to the nature of the keyword. For example: "Competition" (the number of search results of the keyword in the search engine), "Popularity" (number of times the keyword is searched in the search engine in a given period).

Knowledge of SEO experts can be represented by ontology. A usual definition of ontology is: "Ontology represents an explicit specification of domain conceptualization" (Gruber, 1993, p. 199). Ontology can be interpreted as a hierarchy of concepts with attributes and relationships that determine a standard terminology for a specific domain. For example, ontology on Universities may include concepts such as Faculty, Chair, Teacher, No Teacher, and Student; define relationships such as Teacher of a Chair, Students of a Chair, among others.

Ontologies are used as common models for sharing knowledge and information between different systems and applications. This chapter will present an ontology specifying the concepts involved in SEO domain. The taxonomy and the relationships and constraints between different concepts will be described.

## INDUCTIVE LEARNING

Even though algorithms on which search engines are based to sort search results are a mystery, it is well known that there are certain attributes or factors that influence the positioning of a website. The study of the different factors of an individual website is not enough to infer the different positioning strategies of a search engine. The fundamental problem is to determine how the various relevant factors are related to each other and the relevance they have in the final positioning.

The rule generator inductive models generalize the set of training examples in the form of rules that can be evaluated to classify new instances. A rule is a conditional structure that logically relates the information contained in the antecedent (conditions on the positioning factors) with other information contained in the portion of the consequent (existence in the top 10 search results for a keyword).

This system uses three different models of inductive learning:

- **J48:** Generates decision trees for discrete and continuous attributes, use the gain ratio to select the attribute of each node, and applies pruning strategies to reduce the noise of training data (Quinlan, 1993).

- **JRip:** Implements a proportional rule generator with a new metric to guide the pruning phase, a new stop condition with techniques that optimize the learned rules (Cohen, 1995).
- **Part:** Adopts a separate-and-conquer strategy in which it builds a rule, removes the instances its covers, and continues creating rules recursively for the remaining instances until none is left. In essence, to make a single rule a pruned decision tree is built for the current set of instances, the leaf with the largest coverage is made into a rule, and the tree is discarded (Frank & Witten, 1998).

## LEARNING PROCESS/CRISP-DM

When developing a system based on Data Mining, there are various methodologies of modeling process designed to guide development through successive steps to obtain good results. This system is based on CRISP-DM methodology of free distribution (Cross Industry Standard Process for Data Mining) (Chapman, et al., 1999).

It consists of four levels of abstraction, hierarchically organized from general tasks to specific cases. The process is divided into six phases, each one having many general tasks of second level. General tasks are projected to specific ones, where the actions that must be developed for specific situations are described. As a consequence, we find a general task "cleaning data" in second level; then in third level, those tasks that must be developed for a specific case, as for example "cleaning numerical data" or "cleaning categorical data." In the fourth level, groups of actions, decisions, and results about the specific Data Mining project are collected.

The CRISP-DM methodology structures the life-cycle of a Data Mining project in six phases (Figure 1), which interact with each other iteratively during the project development.

*Figure 1. Phases of CRISP-DM reference model (Chapman, et al., 1999)*

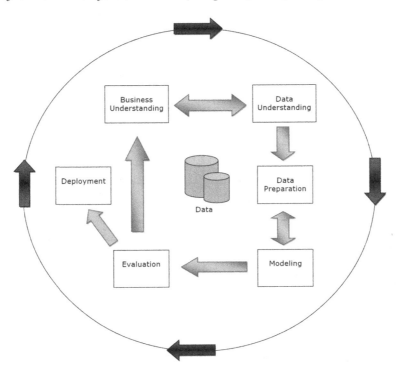

## Clustering of Rules

Clustering is a data mining (machine learning) technique used to place data elements into related groups without advance knowledge of the group definitions. Popular clustering techniques include k-means clustering and Expectation Maximization (EM) clustering (Chapple, 2001).

The first approach considered that each tuple (vector formed by the values of the given factors of a case study [keyword, website]) could evaluate the reliability (positive or negative) of all rules. The problem with this approach is that it causes tuples having different characteristics to those that gave rise to certain rules to make a negative contribution to them. To solve this problem is chosen clustered rules, with the advantage that each tuple only participates in the vote on the reliability of rules pertaining to the same cluster. Another major advantage introduced by clustering is that each tuple only participates in the creation

of rules in the cluster to which it belongs, without affecting the rest of the clusters. This considerably reduces the "noise" that exists when tuples are not clustered and thus obtain more efficient rules.

To perform clustering, the k-means algorithm available in the WEKA package is used (Witten & Frank, 2000). The objective is that the algorithm can identify clusters of data subsets to work with them individually. Clusters are generated by using a subset of factors comprising the 14 factors that provide greater information gain according to the algorithm InfoGainAttributeEval. The result is 5 clusters that group similar tuples.

To determine the membership of a tuple to a cluster, the Euclidean distance between the tuple and the centroid of each cluster is obtained. A tuple will belong to that cluster with which it has lower Euclidean distance.

Once clusters are generated, it is very valuable to analyze the characteristics of each of them to discover their meaning. Cluster meaning should

*Table 1. Comparison of factors involved in clustering*

| Factor | Cluster | | | | |
|---|---|---|---|---|---|
| | 1 | 2 | 3 | 4 | 5 |
| cmpCalculatePRCriterion | > | < | > | < | > |
| AgeOfDocument | = | < | > | < | < |
| cmpAgeOfDocument | > | < | = | < | > |
| InQuotesSearch | = | << | >> | < | > |
| InAnchorSearch | = | < | > | < | > |
| AllInTitleSearch | = | < | > | < | = |
| cmpCalculatePR | = | < | = | < | = |
| WayBackMachineURL | < | < | > | > | > |
| cmpWayBackMachineURL | = | < | = | = | > |
| cmpTotalSitesInboundsYahooCriterion | = | < | > | < | > |
| cmpTotalSitesInboundsYahoo | = | < | = | < | > |
| cmpTotalPagesIndexGoogleCriterion | = | < | = | < | > |
| cmpTotalPagesIndexGoogle | < | < | = | = | > |
| CompetitionGoogle | = | < | > | < | > |

describe the context of each positioning case (tuple) under study. The analysis consists of calculating the average arithmetic of the values of each factor of the tuples of each cluster and compared them to the average arithmetic of the values of each factor of all tuples used for clustering. Table 1 shows the details of this comparison, the highlighted cells indicate points that distinguish each cluster.

When observing in detail the comparison of Table 1, it is possible to see that the factors distinguishing the cluster can be grouped into factors related to the degree of competitors' optimization (with cmp prefix factors) and factors related to the keyword competition (InQuotesSearch, InAnchorSearch, AllInTitleSearch, Competition-Google). Figure 2 shows the meaning of each cluster, taking into account this group.

A major advantage of knowing the meaning of each cluster is to easily identify for which context (cluster) the system gets better results. It also provides the necessary information to intensify the training of the cluster where they obtain the worsen results or there is limited number of rules.

## ONTOLOGY

Although the rules obtained from inductive models allow inferring the possible strategies of search engines to sort search results, there is SEO domain-specific knowledge that cannot be obtained automatically. Obtaining this information is not trivial; a methodology for achieving this is based on interviews and surveys of SEO experts. From these interviews can be determined, conceptualizations, taxonomies of factors, ranges of possible values, relations between them, etc. The best way to represent this information is through an ontology, which be in charge of modeling and conceptualizing the knowledge and has as main objectives to filter and add knowledge to the rules.

### Ontology for Search Engine Optimization

This section will define the ontology for Search Engine Optimization. The main concepts and taxonomy, and some relationships and restrictions between the different concepts will be described.

*Figure 2. Meaning of each cluster*

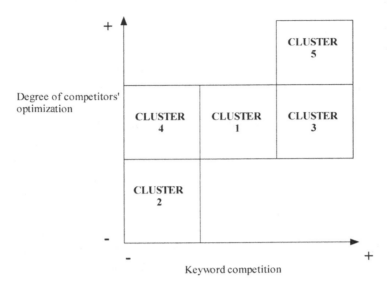

- **Concepts:** The following is a brief description of the main positioning factors taken into account in ontology:
- **CompetitonGoogle:** Amount of search results in Google for the keyword.
- **TotalDMozEntries:** Amount of domain's entries on Dmoz directory.
- **W3CValidation:** Validation of W3C standard of relevant page to optimize source code.
- **CalculatePRCriterion:** Page Rank of the relevant page to optimize.
- **TotalPageIndexesGoogle:** Amount of pages indexed by Google.
- **TotalPageIndexesGoogleCriterion:** Amount of pages indexed by Google that contain the keyword.
- **TotalSiteInboundsYahoo:** Inbound links to the site by Yahoo.
- **TotalSiteInboundsYahooCriterion:** Inbound links to the site by Yahoo that contain the keyword.
- **WayBackMachineUrlAge:** Age of the site in days.
- **CalculatePR:** Page Rank of the home page of the site.
- **AllInTitleSearch:** Amount of results in Google that contain the keyword in the title of the page.
- **InAnchorSearch:** Amount of results in Google containing the keyword at the link's text.
- **InQuotesSearch:** Amount of results in Google from the search of the exact keyword.
- **ExactDensityInTitle:** Number of literal occurrences of the keyword over total words in the Title tag.
- **BroadDensityInTitle:** Sum of occurrences of each one of the words that compose the keyword based on the total of words at Title tag.
- **ExactDensityInBodyText:** Number of literal occurrences of the keywords based on the total of words in Body Text.
- **BroadDensityInBodyText:** Sum of occurrences of each one of the words that compose the keyword based on the total of words at Body tag.

- **ExactDensityInH1Tag:** Number of literal occurrences of the keywords based on the total of words in H1 Tags.
- **BroadDensityInH1Tag:** Sum of occurrences of each one of the words that compose the keyword based on the total of words at H1 tags.
- **ExactDensityInH2Tag:** Number of literal occurrences of the keywords based on the total of words in H2 Tags.
- **BroadDensityInH2Tag:** Sum of occurrences of each one of the words that compose the keyword based on the total of words at H2 tags.
- **ExactDensityInH3Tag:** Number of literal occurrences of the keywords based on the total of words in H3 Tags.
- **BroadDensityInH3Tag:** Sum of occurrences of each one of the words that compose the keyword based on the total of words at H3 tags.
- **ExactDensityInH4Tag:** Number of literal occurrences of the keywords based on the total of words in H4 Tags.
- **BroadDensityInH4Tag:** Sum of occurrences of each one of the words that compose the keyword based on the total of words at H4 tags.
- **BroadExistenceInAltTag:** Existence of all keywords' terms at any Alt tag.
- **ExactExistenceInDomainName:** Literal existence of the keyword in at page domain.
- **BroadExistenceInDomainName:** Existence of all the keywords' terms at domain of the site.
- **ExactExistenceInURL:** Literal existence of the keyword at URL.
- **BroadExistenceInURL:** Existence of all the keywords' terms at URL.
- **BroadExistenceInImageTitles:** Existence of all the keywords' terms at IMG tag.
- **BroadExistenceInBoldStrongTags:** Existence of all keywords' terms at any Bold Strong tag.

- **ExactDensityInMetaDescription:** Number of literal occurrences of the keyword over total words in the tag Meta Description.
- **BroadDensityInMetaDescription:** Sum of occurrences of each one of the words that compose the keyword based on the total of words at MetaDescription tag.
- **ExactExistenceInMetaKeywords:** Literal existence of the keyword at the MetaKewords tag.
- **BroadExistenceInMetaKeywords:** Existence of all the keywords' terms at the MetaKeywords tag.
- **KeywordProminence:** Location of the keyword in the visible content of the relevant page to optimize.
- **ExactExistenceInAnchorText:** Exact existence of the keyword in at least one outbound link of the relevant page to optimize.
- **NumberOfTrailingSlashesInURL:** Amount of trailing slashes "/" at the URL of relevant page to optimize.
- **NumberOfWordInIndexableText:** Indicates the amount of indexable words of the page.
- **URLLength:** Amount of characters that compose the URL.
- **AveragePRExternalLink:** Average Page Rank of external links of the relevant page to optimize.
- **AmountOfExternalLink:** Amount of external links of the relevant page to optimize.
- **AgeOfDocument:** Document age measured in days.
- **Popularity:** Keyword popularity.
- **LinkPopularityDelicious:** Number of entries in the Delicious site.
- **LinkPopularityTechnorati:** Amount of entries in Technorati site.
- **LinkPopularityDigg:** Amount of entries in Digg site.
- **ExistenceOfSitemap:** Existence of Sitemap.

- **ExistenceOfRobots:** Existence of file robots.txt.
- **DeepLevelRelevantPage:** Deep level of relevant page to optimize.
- **OutgoingInternalLink:** Amount of internal out going links from the relevant page.
- **IncomingInternalLink:** Number of incoming internal links to the relevant page.
- **TotalHomeInboundsYahoo:** Amount of external inbounds links to the site home, source Yahoo.
- **TotalPageInboundsYahoo:** Inbound links to the relevant page to optimize according to Yahoo.

*Taxonomy of positioning factors:* Positioning factors can be classified as:

- Website's factors (are those related to the structure, organization and updating of a website and its relationship to other websites) / Web Page's factors (are those re-

lated to the structure, organization and updating of a specific website page and its relationship to other Web pages of the website)/Keyword's factors (are those related to the nature of the keyword).
- Factors of the analyzed site (are those whose values are given by the pair [keyword, website])/Factors of competitors (factors whose values are given by the analysis of the first 5 competitors' websites).
- Modifiable factors (are those whose value can be changed by optimization actions)/ non-modifiable factors (are those whose value cannot be changed by optimization actions).
- Increase factors (are those whose value should be increased)/Decrease factors (are those whose value should be decreased) / Undefined factors (are those whose value is undefined whether to increase or decreased) (see Figure 3).

*Figure 3. Shows the taxonomy stated in the ontology*

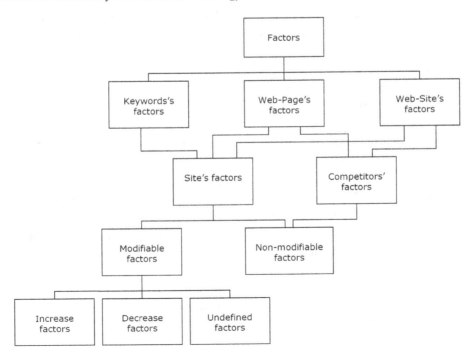

*Restrictions of the factors:* Are conditions on the values of the factors that should be met not causing the rule to be discarded.

- CalculatePRCriterion must be <= a CalculatePR.
- If CalculatePRCriterion value needs to be higher than CalculatePR current value, the value of CalculatePR must be increased.
- For TotalDMozEntries factor, actions that increase its current value over 10 units should not be suggested.
- For URLLength, rule out a change in its value if any one of the following conditions take place:
  ◦ The current position of the keyword is <= 20.
  ◦ The relevant page is the home.
  ◦ The suggested size is smaller than the domain size.
- For NumberOfTrailingSlashesInURL, rule out a change in its value if any one of the following conditions take place:
  ◦ The current position of the keyword is <= 20.
  ◦ The relevant page is the home.
- For CalculatePRCriterion, actions that increase its current value over 2 units should not be suggested.
- For CalculatePR, actions that increase its current value over 2 units should not be suggested.
- For TotalPageIndexesGoogleCriterion, actions that increase its current value over o below 10% should not be suggested.
- For TotalSiteInboundsYahoo, actions that increase its current value over 100% should not be suggested.
- For TotalSiteInboundsYahooCriterion, actions that increase its current value over 100% should not be suggested.

## KNOWLEDGE-BASED SYSTEM APPLIED TO SEO

A knowledge-based system is a software system capable of supporting the explicit representation of knowledge in a specific domain and of exploiting it through appropriate reasoning mechanisms in order to provide a high-level problem-solving performance (Guida & Tasso, 1994). Developed SEO application (Figure 4), centered on a knowledge-based system, comprises:

A facts base that is continuously updated by real positioning cases. For each case, the system calculates a set of factors affecting the positioning and related to a keyword, a website, and competitors' websites. Each case is labeled positioned in the event that the website is among the top 10 search results of that keyword, and is labeled as not positioned otherwise.

A knowledge base that contains the domain knowledge represented by inductive rules. A rule is a conditional structure that logically relates the information contained in the antecedent part with other information contained in the consequent part. The rules of the system are the result of extracting knowledge of facts base using a heterogeneous set of Data Mining models (J48, JRip, and Part).

Each rule obtained through Data Mining models, consists of logical conditions refer to the analyzed positioning factors. The knowledge base only stores those rules that its consequent is to be among the top 10 search results and fulfill its antecedent. Each rule is associated with a cluster and has indicators of reliability, support, estimated position, and cost. Indicators are continuously updated, providing feedback to the system with new knowledge.

An ontology whose function is to conceptualize and model knowledge indicating under what conditions should be considered a rule rather than another. The ontology has as main objectives to filter rules and add knowledge in them.

*Figure 4. System component diagram*

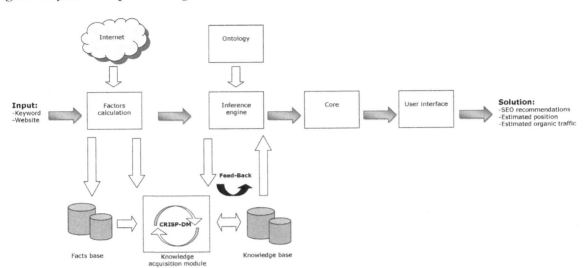

An inference engine that models the human reasoning process from the information in the knowledge base. The engine is in charge of analyzing an input case and determine from all the rules of the knowledge base, which are the candidates to form the solution to be displayed as output. This check will be conducted from the matching between the values of the factors in the entry case and the rules of the knowledge base, while respecting the constraints expressed by the ontology.

A knowledge acquisition module that allows adding, deleting and modifying elements of knowledge (rules) in the system. Being a dynamic context, its presence is essential because the system works properly only if it keeps its knowledge updated. The module allows this maintenance automatically, registering in the knowledge base the changes occurred.

The knowledge acquisition module is responsible for evaluating the rules of the knowledge base and to update their indicators. This feed-back process is carried out using the tuple resulting from the calculation of positioning factors of the input (keyword, website). For each of the rules of the knowledge base the evaluation (positive or negative) is registered and the reliability and sup-

port indicators are updated. For those cases where the evaluation is positive, the estimated position indicator of the rule is updated too. This process of updating knowledge causes that rules whose reliability and support are below the minimum thresholds established are temporarily ignored in the knowledge base.

A core module that gets the data processed by the inference engine and is responsible for identifying the degree of difficulty of the solutions, inferring the position to have the keyword in the search engine after applying the proposed solution, estimating the organic traffic to be generated by the keyword in the analyzed website and getting the ranking factors sorted by relevance.

A user interface that displays in natural language the optimization tasks that should be applied to position a keyword of the analyzed website.

## Run-Time Process

Figure 5 shows the interaction diagram that explains how the system works with the case study detailed below.

Being the input the pair (keyword, website), the Factor Calculation module is responsible for calculating the positioning factors for the website

*Figure 5. System interaction diagram*

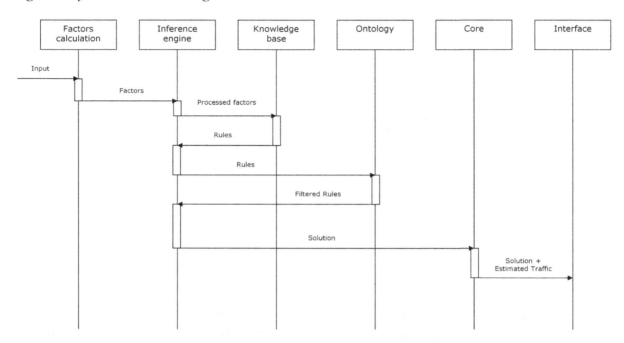

and for five competitors' websites. The websites of the competitors selected are those in the first five results of search engine results page for the keyword entered.

The Inference Engine receives six tuples and condenses them into a single tuple. This tuple consists of the values of website factors and the average value of competitors' websites factors. Using this tuple, the Inference Engine extracts the candidate rules. The Inference Engine discards invalid rules, under the constraints set out by the Ontology. With rules already filtered, the Inference Engine carries out a process called "merge" that involves taking the three rules (if any) that provide greater benefit (value given in terms of the four variables: reliability, support, cost and estimated position). The solution returned by the Inference Engine is generated by combining the rules obtained. To do so, the weight of each solution is considered, always prioritizing the benefit given by each one of them. The main idea is to combine all possible rules in a single one, checking that the rules never contradict one another. In such even, the rule giving a greater

benefit is the one that weighs on the others that generate the conflict, resulting in their removing from the final solution.

The resulting position that is delivered as solution corresponds to the position of the candidate rule with maximum benefit.

The Core calculates the estimated organic traffic of the keyword. The traffic is estimated using mathematical formulas that were deducted after analyzing statistical data for thousands of keywords on hundreds of websites. The extracted data corresponding to visits generated by the chosen keywords from a period of a month. With this information a mathematical formula was created for each one of the positions from 1 to 20 in the search engine result pages. The formulas have as variables the monthly search volume and the estimated position for the keyword.

The Interface returns the final solution that includes a list of SEO recommendations in natural language, the estimated position of the keyword in the search engine after applying the proposal recommendations and the estimated organic traffic that would generate the keyword.

## EVALUATION

In order to evaluate the performance of the system the experiments were based on 42320 training tuples to generate rules for the knowledge base. The rules were tested and evaluated with 27179 cases study.

The following is an analysis of the results obtained in experiments. Analysis is divided into two parts:

- **Evaluation of rules generation:** Analyzing the results in the generation of rules from the used inductive models (J48, JRip, and Part). The evolution of the rules will be analyzed after being evaluated and the behavior of clustered and non-clustered rules will be compared.
- **Evaluation of ontology performance:** Analyzing how ontology acts on the rules selected a priori as solutions and what effect it has on them.

## Evaluation of Rule Generation

Arff files generated from the facts base contain each factor as an attribute and are used as a source to generate inductive models. The files consist of a total of 91 real and numerical attributes plus the nominal attribute "position" whose value is 0 if the tuple is positioned in top10 search results and 1 otherwise. For the creation of inductive models five arff files were generated, it means one per cluster.

For each cluster, the three inductive models were generated (J48 and Part JRip) with the 42320 training tuples. Table 2 shows the overall reliability achieved by each model and the number of rules obtained, all detailed by cluster. In all cases, 10-Fold Cross Validation was used to establish the reliability.

Figure 6 shows the distribution of generated rules with a support higher or equal to 400 in terms of their reliability. Over one month 4634 rules were evaluated by 27179 tuples of real cases, which modify the initial values of reliability and support of each rule. This figure also shows the final rules distribution after the evaluation process mentioned.

Analyzing the graphs, it is possible to observe:

- The presence of a significant number of rules with a support higher than 400 after evaluation. This is due to the large number of instances that have evaluated them and modify their reliability and support values.
- A significant number of rules below an acceptable level of reliability (less than 70%). The use of thresholds allows discarding the rules of low quality when selecting which rules should be considered to provide a solution.

*Table 2. Global reliability for each model and number of rules obtained*

| Cluster | Reliability | | | Number of Rules |
|---|---|---|---|---|
| | **J48** | **JRip** | **Part** | |
| 1 | 75.90% | 78.14% | 75.90% | 404 |
| 2 | 76.50% | 75.79% | 76.60% | 2986 |
| 3 | 73.90% | 78.80% | 73.30% | 104 |
| 4 | 76.30% | 80.30% | 76.20% | 739 |
| 5 | 73.80% | 64.30% | 72.20% | 401 |

*Figure 6. Distribution of rules with support higher or equal to 400*

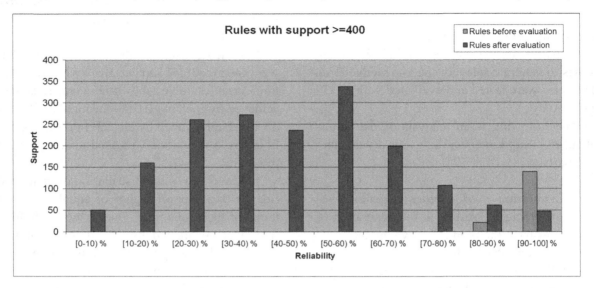

Figure 7 shows a comparison of how the clustered and non-clustered rules evolved after the evaluation process. Notably, there was a marked improvement in the number of rules of acceptable quality (above 70% reliability) of the clustered rules over the non-clustered rules.

## Evaluation of Ontology Performance

The utilization of ontology is essential to add SEO domain expertise knowledge in rules obtained from the knowledge base. The ontology is intended to exclude those rules that are non-applicable for different reasons. Listed below are some of the causes:

*Figure 7. Comparison of the distribution of clustered and non-clustered rules*

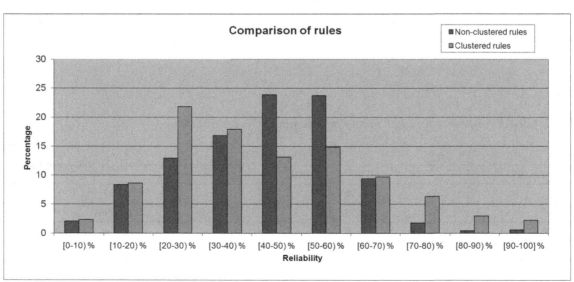

*Table 3. Input tuple*

| CompGoogle. | CPR. | CPRCr. | TSInYahoo. | AllInTSearch. | EDInTitle. | EDInBodyText. | ... | Poss. |
|---|---|---|---|---|---|---|---|---|
| 572000 | 3 | 2 | 24 | 42300 | 0 | 0 | ... | 1 |

- The impossibility of performing an action to change the value of a "non-modifiable" factor.
- The impossibility of performing an action of an absurd change. It means the requirement of changing the value of a factor in the opposite direction to its optimal value.
- The impossibility of performing an action that not comply with "business rules." For example, requiring changing the value of a factor whose implementation means a huge economic effort.

The following example shows how the ontology discards rules from the knowledge base.

Being the input the tuple displayed in Table 3.

The rules of the knowledge base that match with the input tuple are:

- **Rule 1:** CompetitonGoogle < 1356000; CalculatePR < 2; ExactDensityInTitle >= 0.66 -> Position = 0; Reliability: 0.81%; Support: 320.
- **Rule 2:** CompetitonGoogle < 2532000; CalculatePRCriterion >= 2; TotalSiteInboundsYahoo >= 4230 -> Position = 0; Reliability: 0.79%; Supporte: 510.
- **Rule 3:** AllInTitleSearch < 159000; ExactDensityInTitle >= 0.33; ExactDensityInBodyText >= 0.14 -> Position = 0; Reliability: 0.78%; Support: 492.

Rule 1 is discarded by the ontology as it requires modifying the Page Rank of the site below 2 when currently value is 3. CalculatePR is an Increase factor; so its value only should be changed for a value over the current one, otherwise would be an absurd.

Rule 2 is discarded by the ontology as it requires increasing the number of incoming links to the site (TotalSiteInboundsYahoo) over 4230, which would entail a non-admissible effort in hours according with the business rules.

Rule 3 is accepted by the ontology since there are no restrictions on the actions to implement. Requires increasing the exact density in the title of the page (ExactDensityInTitle) over 0.33 and increasing the exact density in the text of the page (ExactDensityInBodyText) over 0.14.

Therefore, without the application of the ontology on the rules obtained from the knowledge base, it would be possible to return non-applicable rules. Ontology adds to the system the representation of SEO expert knowledge that is indispensable for its quality.

## FUTURE RESEARCH DIRECTIONS

It has been presented a knowledge-based system that uses an ontology to support decision making in SEO domain.

In the short term, it is planned to focus on the following lines of research with the aim to improve solutions' reliability:

- To create inductive rule using only competitor's factors data.
- To change the inference engine to take into account the current context of the case study. This means to measure the Euclidean distance between case study's factor values and current competitors' factor values, to then obtain the closest solution.

- To use sequential decision trees, as the LMT algorithm, to consider time factor. The main idea is evaluate changes of factor values according to positioning changes over the time.

It is scheduled to continue incorporating knowledge to the proposed ontology through interviews with SEO experts, in order to enhance relationship between factors and concepts constraints. In addition, to include new SEO factors that affect positioning as inputs of the data mining models to improve solutions.

## CONCLUSION

This chapter has proposed using ontology-based optimization for positioning websites in search engines. For this purpose, a knowledge-based system has been designed and implemented which is capable of supporting the activity of SEO through heterogeneous inductive learning techniques and an ontology for knowledge representation.

An ontology for SEO domain has been specified, defining different concepts, its taxonomy and relationships between them. Although the rules obtained from inductive models allow inferring the possible strategies of search engines to sort search results, the knowledge of SEO domain experts that cannot be extracted automatically must be represented. The best way to represent this information is through an ontology.

The results obtained allow concluding that the use of a defined ontology decisively improves the quality of the system. Failure to use the ontology for the system would bring the risk of absurd solutions to an SEO expert, either because of going against the logic of domain knowledge, or being impossible to implement because of its high cost.

The results obtained in the cases analyzed were positive. The ability of system evolution and learning allows optimizing the productivity and effectiveness of the SEO process.

## REFERENCES

Alexa. (2010). *Top sites*. Retrieved May 3, 2010, from http://www.alexa.com/topsites

Chapman, P., Clinton, J., Khabaza, T., Reinartz, T., & Wirth, R. (1999). *The crisp-DM process model*. Technical Report, CRISM-DM Consortium. Retrieved October 13, 2009, from http://www.crisp-dm.org/CRISPWP-0800.pdf

Chapple, M. (2001). *Clustering*. Retrieved February 11, 2010, from http://databases.about.com/od/datamining/g/clustering.htm

Cohen, W. W. (1995). *Fast effective rule induction*. Paper presented at the Twelfth International Conference on Machine Learning. Tahoe City, CA.

Domene, F., & Grela, J. (2009). *Posicionamiento en buscadores edición 2009*. Madrid, Spain: Ediciones Anaya Multimedia.

Enge, E., Spencer, S., Stricchiola, J., & Fishkin, R. (2009). *The art of SEO mastering search engine optimization*. Sebastopol, CA: O'Reilly Media.

Fishkin, R. (2009). *Search engine ranking factors 2009*. Retrieved February 13, 2010, from http://www.seomoz.org/article/search-ranking-factors

Forrester Research. (2009). *US interactive marketing forecast, 2009 To 2014*. Retrieved February 15, 2010, from http://www.forrester.com/rb/Research/us_interactive_marketing_forecast,_2009_to_2014/q/id/47730/t/2

Frank, E., & Witten, I. H. (1998). *Generating accurate rule sets without global optimization*. Paper presented at the Fifteenth International Conference on Machine Learning. San Francisco, CA: Morgan Kaufmann Publishers.

Google. (2008). *Google's search engine optimization starter guide*. Retrieved February 11, 2010, from http://www.google.com/webmasters/docs/search-engine-optimization-starter-guide.pdf

Gruber, T. (1993). *A translation approach to portable ontologies*. London, UK: Academic Press.

Guida, G., & Tasso, C. (1994). *Design and development of knowledge- based systems: From life cycle to methodology*. Chichester, UK: John Wiley and Sons Ltd.

Quinlan, R. (1993). *C4.5: Programs for machine learning*. San Mateo, CA: Morgan Kaufmann.

Witten, I. H., & Frank, E. (2000). *Data mining, practical machine learning tools and techniques with java implementations*. San Francisco, CA: Morgan Kaufmann.

## ADDITIONAL READING

Agrawal, R., Imielinski, T., & Swami, A. (1993). *Mining association rules between sets of items in large databases*. Washington, DC: ACM Press.

Blankson, S. (2008). *Search engine optimization (SEO): How to optimize your web site for internet search engines: Google, Yahoo! MSN Live, AOL, Ask, Altavista, Fast, Gigablast, Snap, Looksmart, and more*. London, UK: Blankson Enterpise Ltd.

Breiman, L. (2003). *Random forest*. Retrieved February 5, 2010, from http://www.stat.berkeley.edu/users/breiman/RandomForests/cc_home.htm#overview

Choi, N., Song, I.-Y., & Han, H. (2006). *A survey on ontology mapping*. Philadelphia, PA: ACM Press.

Davies, J., Studer, R., & Warren, P. (2006). *Semantic web technologies: Trends and research in ontology-based systems*. London, UK: John Wiley & Sons. doi:10.1002/047003033X

Landwehr, N., Hall, M., & Frank, E. (2003). *Logistic model trees*. Retrieved February 2, 2010, from http://www.cs.waikato.ac.nz/~ml/publications/2003/landwehr-etal.pdf

Ledford, J. L. (2009). *SEO: Search engine optimization bible*. Indianapolis, IN: John Wiley & Sons.

Li, Y., & Zhong, N. (2004). Web mining model and its applications for information gathering. *Knowledge-Based Systems*, *17*, 175–230. doi:10.1016/j.knosys.2004.05.002

Russell, S., & Norving, M. (2004). *Artificial intelligence: A modern approach*. London, UK: Prentice-Hall.

Sparck Jones, K., & Willett, P. (1997). *Readings in information retrieval*. San Francisco, CA: Morgan Kaufmann Publishers.

Williams, R., & Stuart, M. (2009). *Demand for ROI drives growth in online advertising across Europe*. Retrieved February 20, 2010, from http://eiaa.net/news/eiaa-articles-details.asp?lang=1&id=206

# Chapter 16
# Mining Sentiment Using Conversation Ontology

**Priti Srinivas Sajja**
*Sardar Patel University, India*

**Rajendra Akerkar**
*Vestlandsforsking, Norway*

## ABSTRACT

*The research in the field of opinion mining has been ongoing for several years, and many models and techniques have been proposed. One of the techniques that can address the need for automated information monitoring to help to identify the trends and patterns that matter is sentiment mining. Existing approaches enable the analysis of a large number of text documents, mainly based on their statistical properties and possibly combined with numeric data. Most approaches are limited to simple word counts and largely ignore semantic and structural aspects of content. Conversation plays a vital role in expressing and promoting an opinion. In this chapter, the authors discuss the concept of ontology and propose a framework that allows the incorporation of information on conversation structure in the models for sentiment discovery in text.*

## INTRODUCTION

The vision of the Semantic Web is to enable machines to interpret and process information in the World Wide Web to provide quality support to the mankind in carrying out their various tasks with the information and communication technology.

The challenge of the Semantic Web is to provide necessary information with well-defined meaning, understandable for different parties as well as machines in such a way that applications are able to provide customized access to information by taking the individual needs and requirements of the users into account. Several technologies have

DOI: 10.4018/978-1-4666-2494-8.ch016

Copyright © 2013, IGI Global. Copying or distributing in print or electronic forms without written permission of IGI Global is prohibited.

been developed for shaping, constructing, and developing the Semantic Web. Ontology plays an important role for the Semantic Web as a source of formally defined terms for communication. The prime objective of ontology is to facilitate knowledge sharing and reuse on the distributed platform. Typically, ontology includes taxonomy of terms and details about representation scheme. Ontology creation consists of defining all ontology components through an ontology definition language. Such a creation of ontology is initially done informally using either natural language or diagram technique, and further the ontology is encoded in a formal knowledge representation language such as RDF Schema or Web Ontology Language.

In today's world, there is a demand for mechanized information monitoring tools that make easier to discover the issues and patterns that matter and that can follow and predict emerging events in day-to-day processes. One of the techniques that can address this need is sentiment mining. In the literature, existing approaches enable the analysis of a large number of text documents, mainly based on their statistical properties and possibly combined with numeric data. Moreover, such approaches are limited to simple word counts. There is a need for understanding semantic and structural features of content. Human conversation plays a significant role in expressing and promoting an opinion.

The chapter begins with ontology fundamentals. The aim is to discuss ontology concepts at a certain level of details. The chapter is organized as follows: Besides providing definition and necessary introduction, the chapter presents terminology for taxonomy, thesauri, and ontology. Further, various issues related to ontology such as type of ontology, and parameters construction of ontology are discussed. Next section presents general introduction of sentiment mining and, the interrelated notions of text mining and sentiment mining. Further, we focus on discovery of conver-

sation structures. Finally, a framework that allows the incorporation of information on conversation structure in the models for sentiment discovery in text is presented.

## ONTOLOGY FUNDAMENTALS

In the broader context of the Semantic Web, applications need to understand by machine, which is being done with the help of the meaning associated with each component stored on the Web. Such capability of understanding is not covered by the traditional tools like mark up languages and protocols utilized on World Wide Web platform. There is a requirement of a component representation scheme called Ontology. Ontology interweaves human and computer understanding of symbols. These symbols, also known as terms, can be interpreted by both humans and machines. Ontology are means for conceptualizing and structuring knowledge. They are used for semantic annotation of resources in order to support information retrieval, automated inference, and interoperability among services and applications across the Web.

### What is Ontology

Ontologies provides in depth properties and classes such as inverses, unambiguous properties, unique properties, lists, restrictions, cardinalities, pair wise disjoint lists, data types, and so on. Ontologies are often able to provide an objective specification of domain information by representing a consensual agreement on the concepts and relations that characterize the manner knowledge in that domain is expressed. This specification can be the first step in building semantically aware information systems to support diverse enterprise, government, and personal activities.

The original definition of ontology comes from the field of philosophy. It is included in the Webster's revised unabridged dictionary.

*Definition 1:* That department of the science of metaphysics which investigates and explains ontology as the nature and essential properties and relations of all beings, as such, or the principles and causes of being.

Another definition can be given as follows:

*Definition 2:* Ontology is an abstract model, which represents a common and shared understanding of a domain.

The word "ontology" has a very long history in philosophy starting with the Aristotle's works. Defined as "the science of being," it comes from the Greek "ontos" which means being and "logos" for both language and reason. Ontology is then the branch of metaphysics that deals with the nature of being. From the point of view of phenomenology, a more modern philosophy started with the 19th century German philosophers, an ontology is a systematic account of existence. However, according to phenomenological approach, the status of being and existence are different notions, and cannot be combined/thought simultaneously. While philosophers build ontology from the top down, in the field of computer science, an ontology is usually built bottom-up.

As a matter of fact, one can retain three dimensions in an ontology: knowledge, language and logic. In others words: language to speak about the world, conceptualization for understanding the world, and representation for the manipulation of our understanding.

Ontology is well known for many years in the artificial intelligence and knowledge representation communities. It addresses ways of representing knowledge so that machines can reason about it to make valid deductions and inferences. Ontology generally consists of a list of interrelated terms and inference rules and can be exchanged between users and applications. They may be defined in a more or less formal way, from natural language to description logics. The Web Ontology Language (OWL) belongs to the latter category. OWL is built upon RDF and RDFS and extends

them to express class properties. The pioneer definition of ontology in the sense of Semantic Web is proposed by Tom Gruber (1993), which is given as follows:

*Definition 3:* Ontology is a formal explicit specification of a shared conceptualization.

In nineties, knowledge engineers borrowed the term of ontology focusing more on a systematic account of existence rather than a metaphysical approach of the nature of being. As a matter of fact, for artificial intelligence systems, what exists is that which can be represented in a declarative language. Ontology is then an explicit formal specification of how to represent objects, concepts, and relationships that are assumed to exist in some area of interest. It is what Gruber called "*a specification of a conceptualization*" description (just as a formal specification of a program) of the concepts and relationships that can exist for an agent or a community of agents.

A conceptualization is an abstract simplified view of the world that one wish to represent for some purpose. The ontology is a specification because it represents the conceptualization in a concrete form. It is explicit because all concepts and constraints used are explicitly defined. Formal means the ontology should be machine understandable. Shared indicates that the ontology captures consensual knowledge.

Ontology based semantic structures replace the jumbles of ad hoc rule based techniques common to earlier knowledge representation systems. This makes knowledge representation languages easy to manage combining logic and ontology.

In the context of Semantic Web, we can further modify the ontology definition as follows:

*Definition 4:* Computer ontology are formally specified models of known knowledge in a given domain.

Metadata and ontology are complementary and constitute the Semantic Web's building blocks. They avoid meaning ambiguities and provide more precise answers. In addition to a better accuracy of query results, another goal of the Semantic Web is to describe the semantic relationships between these answers.

Any general ontology model represents only a consensual agreement on the concepts and relations that characterize the way knowledge in the domain is expressed. Higher-level ontology may just model common knowledge instead of specific data. Important notions in connection with Web-related ontology are a vocabulary of basic terms and a precise specification of what those terms mean. The consensus standard vocabularies can be handled by defining reusable vocabularies, and customizing and extending them.

Some well-known ontologies from linguistics and knowledge engineering areas are:

- **WordNet:** It is a top-down ontology (in upper layer) in linguistic domain containing structured vocabulary of English language with lexical categories and semantic relations.
- **Cyc:** It is a common ontology consisting of knowledge captured from different domains.

- **SENSUS:** It is a linguistic domain ontology built by extracting and merging information from existing electronic resources for the purpose of machine translation.

## Taxonomy, Thesauri, and Ontology

Taxonomy is a science of classification that provides guidelines about how to categorize, organizes label and arrange information in hierarchical fashion. It can be considered as classification based on similarities. Taxonomy includes presentation of vocabularies, application profile, and development of metadata scheme if any. Taxonomies and thesauri do not appear on the Semantic Web stack, as they were not specifically designed for the Web; they, however, belong to the Semantic Web picture. The taxonomy can be defined as follows:

*Definition 5:* Taxonomy is a hierarchically organized controlled vocabulary. The world has number of taxonomies, because human beings naturally classify things. Taxonomies are semantically weak and are commonly used when navigating without a precise research goal in mind.

*Figure 1. Hierarchical representation of tour attractions*

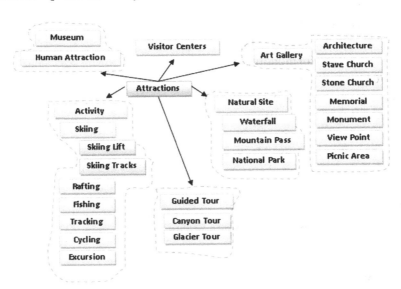

As an example, sample taxonomy from a typical tourism area is presented in this section. A tourism destination is primarily described in terms of an enumeration of the items that it possesses. However, since this is only a collection of names, each item must be characterized in order that the description carries interesting information about the destination. To do this we must possess a vocabulary of terms that represent relevant concepts. A common but not complete vocabulary that might serve this purpose is given by the following list (see Figure 1) where the relative meaning of the terms is reflected in the ordering as taxonomy:

The leaf terms in taxonomy shown in Figure 1 are the primary terms. The other terms are secondary terms that can be introduced by terminological definitions.

Purpose of a thesaurus is to facilitate documents retrieval. The WordNet thesaurus organizes English nouns, verbs, adverbs and adjectives into a set of synonyms and defines relationships between synonyms.

*Definition 6:* Thesaurus is a "controlled vocabulary arranged in a known order and structured so that equivalence, homographic, hierarchical, and associative relationships among terms are displayed clearly and identified by standardized relationship indicators"

The thesaurus can be modeled in two techniques (1) concept-oriented and (2) term-oriented models. ISO provides two standards that deal with for thesaurus namely (1) ISO2788 for monolingual thesauri and (2) ISO5964 for multilingual thesauri.

Figure 2 provides a partial of thesaurus example (sorted alphabetically) for a typical tourism industry system.

Both taxonomies and thesauri provide vocabulary of terms and simple relationships between these terms. Therefore, taxonomies and thesauri are above XML, namespaces and controlled vocabulary in the Semantic Web stack. However, the relationships they express are not as rich as the ones provided by RDF or Topic Maps and consequently by ontology. In general, ontology consists of a taxonomy combined with some relationships, constraints, and rules. These rules may be used in conjunction with RDF or Topic Maps.

Ontology enables us to agree upon the meaning of terms used in a precise domain, knowing that several terms may represent the same concept (synonyms) and several concepts may be described by the same term (ambiguity). Ontology consists in a hierarchical description of important concepts of a domain, and in a description of each concept's properties. Ontology is at the heart of information retrieval from nomadic objects, from the Internet and from heterogeneous data sources. The address can be modeled as shown in Figure 3:

In semantic based information retrieval, ontology directly specifies the meaning of the concepts to be searched for. Whereas, XML based systems are very limited in utility in this context unless the independent site-content authors happen to agree on the semantics of the term they embed in source metadata. Ontology reduces such semantic ambiguity by offering a single interpretation

*Figure 2. An example of thesaurus*

| Accommodation | Bed & breakfast |
| --- | --- |
| | Cabin |
| | Farm house |
| | Hotel |
| | Pension |
| Activity | Climbing |
| | Cycling |
| | Fishing |
| | Kayaking |
| | Rafting |
| | Ski lift |
| | Ski tracks |
| | Skiing |
| | Walking |
| ......... | .......... |
| Events | Cultural |
| | Sport |
| Excursion | Canyon tour |
| | Fjord tour |
| | Glacier tour |
| | Guided tour |
| | Railway |

*Figure 3. An example of address ontology*

resource. Further ontology can also enable software to map and transform information stored using variant terminologies.

Some researchers adopt modeling terminology and consider ontology as a meta-model. A meta-model is an explicit description of the constructs and rules needed to build specific models within a domain of interest. It can be seen from numerous perspectives:

- A set of terms and conceptual primitives: e.g. entity types/classes, relationships, attributes and rules. A specific model can be created by instantiating the types, and relating instances to each other according to the relationships in the meta-model.
- A model of the domain.
- An instance of a more general model, i.e. a meta-meta model.

In order for a meta-model to be ontology, the following properties must hold:

- **Formalization:** It must be expressed in a formal language to enable consistency checks and automated reasoning.
- **Consensuality:** Must be agreed upon by a community. This excludes most database conceptual models, which do not require explicit consensus by the users. Some researchers consider shareability as a distinctive feature of an ontology.
- **Identifiability:** Must be unambiguously identified and ubiquitously accessible over the Net.

## Properties and Characteristics

Some of the key characteristics of ontology can be given as follows (Kavi & Sergei, 1995):

- **Ease of use:** Ontology should be ease to representation, use and supports conversion of content from one ontology to another.
- **Comprehensibility and simplicity:** In addition to being a computational entity, the ontology must be easy to browse and present; it should facilitate acquirer training.
- **Well-formedness:** Ontology should completely describe the intended content along with internally consistent structure, naming conventions, etc. as per well developed guidelines.
- **Utility:** It must ultimately aid language processing in resolving a variety of ambiguities and making necessary inferences.
- **Limited proliferation:** Situated development limits the size of the ontology though presumably any piece of knowledge could be useful for the task in question. The ontology is not limited to its domain but is more developed in the chosen domain.
- **Reliance on technology:** Acquisition and utilization is made more tractable by the deployment of latest technologies: faster machines, color graphical user interfaces, graphical browsers, and editors, on-line lexicons, corpora, and other ontology, as well as semi-automated tools for consistency maintenance and interfaces for lexicographer interactions.

## Types of Ontology

The ontology can be classified by type of the knowledge conveyed by the ontology (Akerkar, 2009):

- A generic ontology, also known as top ontology, specifies general concepts defined independently of a domain of application and which can be used in different application domains. Time, space, mathematics... are examples of general concepts.

- A domain ontology is dedicated to a particular domain which remains generic for this domain and which can be used and reused for particular tasks in the domain. Chemical, medicine, enterprise modeling, etc. are domain ontology.
- An application ontology gathers knowledge dedicated to a particular task including more specialized knowledge of the experts for the application. In general, it is not reusable.
- A meta-ontology, or representation ontology, specifies the knowledge representation principles used to define concepts of domain and generic ontology e.g. what is a class, a relation, a function.

Ontology can also be classified as heavy weight and light weight ontology according to their expressiveness of the content. The parameters for such expressiveness are introduced by McGuinness (2003) and summarized as shown in Table 1.

According to Corcho et al. (2003), the lightweight ontology includes concepts, properties that describe concepts, relationships between concepts and concept taxonomies. Heavyweight ontology are complex and include axioms and constraints also. A systematic evaluation of ontology and related technologies might lead to a consistent level of quality and thus acceptance by industry. For the future, this effort might also lead to standardized benchmarks and certifications.

## Parameters to Build an Ontology

Because of the complexity of the task and the many demands on ontology in terms of usability and reusability, many ontology engineering methodologies have been developed. As stated earlier, ontology quality is measured in terms of criteria like clarity, coherence, extendibility, minimal encoding bias, minimal ontological commitment, etc. are considered (Gruber, 1995; Kalfoglou, 2000). Table 2 describes the criteria in brief.

*Table 1. Parameters of expressiveness of ontology*

| Controlled vocabulary | A list of terms |
|---|---|
| Thesaurus | Relations between terms, such as synonyms, are provided |
| Informal taxonomy | There is an explicit hierarchy (generalization and specialization are supported), but there is no strict inheritance; an instance of a subclass is not necessarily also an instance of the super class |
| Formal taxonomy | There is strict inheritance |
| Frames | A frame (or class) contains a number of properties and these properties are inherited by sub-classes and instances. |
| Value restrictions: | Values of properties are restricted (e.g. by a data type) |
| General logic constraints | Values may be constraint by logical or mathematical formulas using values from other properties |
| First-order logic constraints | Very expressive ontology languages allow first order logic constraints between terms and more detailed relationships such as disjoint classes, disjoint coverings, inverse relationships, part-whole relationships, etc. |

Besides this, to gain the maximum benefit from using ontology, ontology needs to be shared and reused. Existing ontology can be combined in order to create new ontology. This makes the ontology independent, reusable, and sharable within different applications.

These parameters are also need to be considered while engineering ontology. For design and evaluation of ontology many models have been utilized. A classical 'Skeletal model' given by Uschold and King (1995) present a framework for the design and evaluation of ontology. The steps are given as follows:

1. Identifying purpose and scope.
2. Building the ontology.
   a. Ontology capture.
   b. Ontology coding.
   c. Integrating existing ontology.
3. Evaluation.
4. Documentation.

Uschold et al. (1996, 1998) further modified the approach, which can be given as follows:

1. Scoping.
   a. Brainstorming to produce all potentially relevant terms and phrases.
   b. Grouping the terms into work areas.
2. Producing definitions.
   a. Deciding what to do next.
3. Determining the meta-ontology.
4. Address each work area in turn.
5. Define terms.
   a. Reaching agreement in natural language.
6. Reviewing and revise definitions.
7. Developing a meta-ontology.

*Table 2. Design criteria for ontology engineering*

| Clarity | The intended meaning of the term should be clear and does not have many interpretations. |
|---|---|
| Coherence | The ontology must be consistent logically and formally. |
| Extendibility | It should be easy to add new terms/extend definition without having to revise the existing definitions. |
| Minimal encoding bias | Ontology should be as independent as possible from the applications/implementation tools, which will use the ontology. It is independent of formatting schemes. |
| Minimal ontological commitment | Even if the ontology are independent of the platform of implementation and formatting schemes, it can be reusable if the content represented though the ontology is less committed. |

## BACKGROUND OF SENTIMENT MINING

Assessing attitudes to a range of artifacts, including films and cars, banking institutions and holiday destinations (Turney, 2002) has been referred to as sentiment analysis or opinion analysis, or affect analysis or opinion mining (Grefenstette, et al., 2004). Researchers have trained classifiers on corpora of movie reviews (Pang & Lee, 2004; Pang, et al., 2002), and used sentiment extraction for reviews of music and digital cameras (Yi, et al., 2003). Sentiment analysis techniques may be useful for Customer Relationship Management (Roussinov, et al., 2003) and identifying abusive postings in Internet newsgroups (Spertus, 1997). More socially beneficial applications include measuring the "reassurance gap," the difference between crime rates and the public perception of crime, and discovering "internal war," where conflicts may have a historical basis and rely on collective memory or be based on a reinvention of identities. Product sentiment analysis tends to be quite focused.

The domain as well as the object (within the selected domain for which sentiments are being expressed) needs to be fixed prior to the mining process. It may be the movie, or the product, or the company. There may be some deviations from the item—comparisons and so forth. Durbin et al. (2003) differentiate between "analytic methods (e.g. named entity extraction) that provide specific items of information, and synthetic methods (e.g. topic identification) that provide a global characterization." According to these authors, much of the current work on sentiment analysis, opinion analysis, and affective rating fits into this second category. Financial sentiment, however, does not seem to fit such a simple distinction. Financial news may be about a single company, but may also be identifying sentiments about other companies in the same sector. It may contain sentiment about an item such as oil prices rising that have a negative impact on oil-related industries such as the aviation industry but perhaps have a positive impact on the profits of petroleum companies: oil prices rise, profits rise, profits fall. It may contain positives but with a negative outlook. We need to be able to accurately identify the thing about which we are extracting the sentiment, and at the same time, at a more broad level, we desire the global characterization for, for example, a company, an industry sector, a price index or a currency, or any number of these. Extracting financial sentiment, then, appears to demand a hybrid approach.

Turney's (2002) approach to sentiment analysis seeks the "Semantic Orientation": all phrases matching manually selected part-of-speech patterns are scored according to their proximity to either of the words "excellent" or "poor" in a proxy for general language—the AltaVista search engine. Turney claims classification accuracy of bank and car reviews of 80-84% based on 410 articles, but has difficulty classifying movie reviews: his approach classifies the full text as positive or negative, and for movie reviews "the whole is not necessarily the sum of the parts." This is a useful benchmark experiment; however, the scientific repeatability is problematic: firstly, the additional indexing of information by a search engine is likely to change the scoring over time; secondly, this particular experiment cannot now be repeated due to changes to the function of the AltaVista Engine. The uses of ontology has the potential to refine and improve the process of sentiment mining by identifying specific properties of a domain as well as relationships between different concepts from that domain.

## EXTRACTING KNOWLEDGE FROM TEXT

Past few years, a significant amount of research has been focusing on automated techniques for understanding from text by means of text mining. Text mining is a broad term that encapsulates many definitions, which appear to be distributed in a continuum between two extremes. On one hand, text mining refers to retrieving information that already is in the text (typically using predefined patterns). On the other hand, text mining could refer to a more inductive approach, where patterns are to be discovered in textual data. The model follows the data. Many definitions of text mining exist, yet the common denominator is that text mining seeks to extract high-quality information from unstructured data, which is textual in nature, where quality is often conceptualized as a measure of relevance. The dispersion of conceptualizations of text mining is reflected in the terminology used to refer to text mining.

With respect to text mining in its broadest sense, literature exhibits a rough distinction between three stages: preprocessing, processing, and presentation. Feldman and Sanger (2006) provide an extensive overview of preprocessing routines, pattern-discovery algorithms, and presentation-layer elements. Most text mining tools utilize their own framework for processing texts with the purpose of extracting information. However, GATE (Cunningham, 2002), is an architecture, development environment, and framework for building systems and components that process human language, has become popular due to its exibility and extensibility. Amongst supported linguistic analyses are tokenization, Part-Of-Speech (POS) tagging, and semantic analysis. Tools like GATE could prove useful in a setting in which economic discourse is to be analyzed for interesting patterns. However nowadays, patterns in raw text are not enough anymore; insight in (patterns of) associated sentiment is crucial for decision makers.

## Sentiment Mining

The field of sentiment mining is relatively new. Mining sentiments is different from regular text mining as direct keywords cannot be used for searching opinions or sentiments. This is because sentiments or opinions are not usually directly evident. Though sentiments themselves are domain independent, the words used to describe sentiments can vary from domain to domain. Sentiments are expressed in different ways: with overall scores (star ratings) such as pros and cons on features/aspects of the object of opinion, rants and raves, etc. Opinions are subjective and comparative in nature and multiple opinions are expressed in a single passage. Therefore, the process of identifying opinions, classifying them, extracting them, and summarizing them is unique and demanding enough that specialized systems are needed.

The discovery of sentiment is normally focused on reviews of products, movies, etc. The focus of work on analyzing online discussions and blogs is more on distinguishing opinions from facts than on extracting and summarizing opinions. Existing toolkits are limited to simple word counts and relevant linguistic resources are absent or do not always fit into the applied framework. Today's text analytical tools are unprepared to deal with highly dynamic domains, because they have been developed without adaptation in mind and until recently largely ignore structural aspects of content.

## DISCOVERING CONVERSATION STRUCTURES

By using conversation structure and elements such as specific metaphors, analogies, vocabularies, or supportive non-textual data, a specific mood or opinion can be expressed and promoted. For instance, the use of analogies or vocabularies invoking negative associations in means of communication concerning change processes may lead people to have negative expectations. Our framework starts from the hypothesis that sentiment mining in day-to-day conversation can be improved if the information in the structural elements of a text can be gathered.

Conversation is pivotal in any discourse. Humans discuss and argue by exchanging information in natural language. In all societies, there is a tendency for idle, free-owing exchange of ideas and thoughts, which is called conversation. In general, conversation is considered to convey direct information, either in the form of imperatives (e.g. issuing orders) or in the form of information that is actionable (e.g. by revealing private information). Conversation provides a mechanism to diffuse asymmetric information. In addition to the direct information content, argumentation and persuasion are important aspects of linguistic communication. People exchange ideas with a goal. Argumentation is incorporated to convince the listener of the validity of the reasoning. Anyone engaged in argumentation selects and presents information in a particular way that enhances the acceptance of the argument. Hence, oratory, conversation structures, and presentation styles are very important since they facilitate persuasion.

## CONVERSATION ONTOLOGY DRIVEN SENTIMENT MINING

In order to be able to extract sentiment from text sources, we need an information system capable of inferring specific information on sentiment from natural language sentences. The purpose of such a system is to analyze a given text collection and determine the sentiment in the texts. Our system is to take into account conversation structures, which can be detected automatically.

We propose a sentiment mining system, which divides specific roles and tasks amongst different components that are interconnected by their inputs and outputs. Such a system facilitates stepwise abstraction from raw text to useable, formalized chunks of linguistic data and enables effective text processing, as each component can be optimized for a specific task. As shown in Figure 4, we propose to employ the general purpose GATE framework, which allows for easy usage, exten-

sion, and creation of individual components. For preliminary lexico-syntactic analysis of input text (i.e., operations not specific to our envisaged sentiment mining approach), we propose to use some of the existing components from GATE's default system. Provided with GATE is a set of reusable processing resources for common NLP tasks. These are packaged together to form AN-NIE, A Nearly New Information Extraction system, but can also be used individually or coupled together with new modules in order to create new applications. For example, many other NLP tasks might require a sentence splitter and POS tagger, but would not necessarily require resources more specific to Information Extraction tasks such as a named entity transducer. The system is in use for a variety of Information Extraction and other tasks, sometimes in combination with other sets of application-specific modules.

At the outset, we simplify documents from redundant artifacts such as tags, by means of a 'document hander' component.

Subsequently, we employ an English Tokenizer, which splits text into separate tokens (e.g. numbers, punctuations, symbols, and words). The aim is to limit the work of the tokenizer to boost efficiency, and enable greater flexibility by placing the responsibility of analysis on the grammars. Next, a Sentence Splitter is used, which splits the input sentences into simplified sentences. It is a cascade of finite state transducers, which segments the text into sentences. This module is required for the tagger. Then a POS Tagger component is utilized in order to determine the part-of-speech of words within a text collection. The GATE POS tagger is a customized version of the Brill tagger, which produces a part-of-speech tag as an annotation on each word or symbol. Neither the splitter nor the tagger is a mandatory part of the system, but the annotations they produce can be used by the grammar, in order to increase its power and coverage. After these basic syntactic operations, semantic analysis is to be performed by several components. We use a Conversation Gazetteer

*Figure 4. Sentiment mining system*

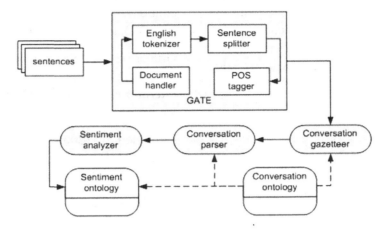

for identifying conversation markers, i.e., key terms related to conversation. To do this, we offer to use a populated conversation ontology that contains definitions of these conversation markers and their relations to conversation text elements (e.g., arguments, supports, conclusions), which are also defined in this ontology. Guided by the annotated conversation key terms found by the gazetteer, the Conversation Parser subsequently identifies text segments and determines their role in a document's conversation structure, hereby utilizing the conversation ontology. Ultimately, the Sentiment Analyzer identifies the sentiment in the individual text segments and connects the sentiment of these segments to the associated conversation structure. Based on their role in the conversation structure, text segments are assigned different weights in their contribution to the overall sentiment. The output of this process is an ontology to represent knowledge of the current sentiment in the text collection. This sentiment ontology in turn utilizes the conversation ontology in order to enable a connection between conversation and sentiment, hereby facilitating insight in opinion genesis. New knowledge on sentiment is stored in the ontology, thus enabling reasoning and inference of knowledge in order to support decision-making processes.

## CONCLUSION

The present human lives are affected by the Web. Adding semantic to the ordinary syntactic Web with different ontology increases power and applicability of the Web and makes the Web more meaningful. Such semantic knowledge representation can be done with different ontologies. Besides development of the domain specific ontologies, techniques for ontology learning, mapping, and merging can be through for further research.

Ontologies are important for application integration and implementation for generic problem solving as they provide a shared and common understanding of data (and, in some cases, services, and processes) that exists within an application integration problem domain. This may help in organizing the tremendous heap of information on the Web in more effective and meaningful way.

The disparate fields of text mining and sentiment mining on the one hand, and conversation discovery on the other hand, offer a wide range of possibilities in order to advance discourse analysis. Firstly, text mining techniques, and more specifically sentiment mining techniques, can help researchers and decision makers to track important trends in the conversation. Secondly, conversation discovery techniques can facilitate insight in the reasoning utilized in dialogue. Hence, we have proposed a sentiment-mining framework that combines insights from these disparate fields by linking conversation structures in discourse to the associated sentiment, which could offer researchers and decision makers another viewpoint on the origins of sentiment.

## REFERENCES

Akerkar, R. A. (2009). *Foundation of the semantics web: XML, RDF & ontology*. Oxford, UK: Alpha Science International.

Corcho, O., Fernández-López, M., & Gómez-Pérez, A. (2003). Methodologies, tools and languages for building ontologies: Where is their meeting point? *Data & Knowledge Engineering, 46*(1), 41–64. doi:10.1016/S0169-023X(02)00195-7

Cunningham, H. (2002). GATE: A general architecture for text engineering. *Computers and the Humanities, 36*(2), 223–254. doi:10.1023/A:1014348124664

Durbin, S. D., Richter, J. N., & Warner, D. (2003). A system for affective rating of texts. In *Proceedings of the 3rd Workshop on Operational Text Classification Systems (OTC 2003)*. Washington, DC: OTC.

Feldman, R., & Sanger, J. (2006). *The text mining handbook: Advanced approaches in analyzing unstructured data*. Cambridge, UK: Cambridge University Press. doi:10.1017/CBO9780511546914

Grefenstette, G., Qu, Y., Shanahan, J. G., & Evans, D. (2004). Coupling niche browsers and affect analysis for an opinion mining application . In *Proceedings of Recherche d'Information Assistée par Ordinateur (RIAO)*. RIAO.

Gruber, T. R. (1993). A translation approach to portable ontology specifications. *Knowledge Acquisition, 5*(2), 199–220. doi:10.1006/knac.1993.1008

Gruber, T. R. (1995). Towards principles for the design of ontologies used for knowledge sharing. *International Journal of Human-Computer Studies, 43*(5-6), 907–928. doi:10.1006/ijhc.1995.1081

Kalfoglou, Y. (2000). *Deploying ontologies in software design*. (PhD Thesis). University of Edinburgh. Edinburgh, UK.

Kavi, M., & Sergei, N. (1995). A situated ontology for practical NLP. In *Proceedings of the Workshop on Basic Ontological Issues in Knowledge Sharing, International Joint Conference on Artificial Intelligence (IJCAI 1995)*. Montreal, Canada: IJCAI.

McGuinness, D. L. (2003). Ontologies come of age . In Fensel, D., Hendler, J., Lieberman, H., & Wahlster, W. (Eds.), *Spinning the Semantic Web: Bringing the World Wide Web to Its Full Potential*. Cambridge, MA: MIT Press.

Pang, B., & Lee, L. (2004). A sentimental education: Sentiment analysis using subjectivity summarization based on minimum cuts. In *Proceedings of the ACL*, (pp. 271-278). ACL.

Pang, B., Lee, L., & Vaithyanathan, S. (2002). Thumbs up? Sentiment classification using machine learning techniques. In *Proceedings of EMNLP*, (pp. 79-86). EMNLP.

Roussinov, D., & Zhao, J. L. (2003). Message sense maker: Engineering a tool set for customer relationship management. In *Proceedings of 36th Annual Hawaii International Conference on System Sciences (HICSS)*. IEEE.

Spertus, E. (1997). Smokey: Automatic recognition of hostile messages. In *Proceedings of Conference on Innovative Applications of Artificial Intelligence,* (pp. 1058-1065). Menlo Park, CA: AAAI Press.

Turney, P. D. (2002). Thumbs up or thumbs down? Semantic orientation applied to unsupervised classification of reviews. In *Proceedings of 40th Annual Meeting of the Association for Computational Linguistics (ACL)*, (pp. 417-424). Philadelphia, PA: ACL.

Uschold, M., & Grüninger, M. (1996). Ontologies: Principles methods and applications. *The Knowledge Engineering Review*, *11*(2), 93–155. doi:10.1017/S0269888900007797

Uschold, M., & King, M. (1995). Towards a methodology for building ontologies. In *Proceedings of the IJCAI 1995 Workshop on Basic Ontological Issues in Knowledge Sharing.* Montreal, Canada: IJCAI.

Uschold, M., King, M., Morale, S., & Zorgios, Y. (1998). The enterprise ontology. *The Knowledge Engineering Review*, *13*(1), 31–89. doi:10.1017/S0269888998001088

Yi, J., Nasukawa, T., Bunescu, R., & Niblack, W. (2003). Sentiment analyzer: Extracting sentiments about a given topic using natural language processing techniques. In *Proceedings of the Third IEEE International Conference on Data Mining (ICDM)*, (pp. 427-434). IEEE Press.

## KEY TERMS AND DEFINITIONS

**Conversation Ontology:** In all societies, there is a tendency for idle, free-owing exchange of ideas and thoughts, which is called conversation. The ontology which represents such conversation is called conversion ontology.

**Meta-Ontology:** A meta-ontology, or representation ontology, specifies the knowledge representation principles used to define concepts of domain and generic ontology.

**Ontology Mapping:** Ontology Mapping is the process whereby two ontologies are semantically related at conceptual level, and the source ontology instances are transformed into the target ontology entities according to those semantic relations.

**Ontology:** It is a rigorous and exhaustive organization of some knowledge domain that is usually hierarchical and contains all the relevant entities and their relations.

**Sentiment Analysis:** It refers to the application of natural language processing, computational linguistics, and text analytics to identify and extract subjective information in source materials. Sentiments/Opinions can be positive, negative, or neutral.

**Sentiment Mining:** It is the area of research that attempts to make automatic systems to mine human opinions from text written in natural language. It is also known as opinion mining.

**Text Mining:** Text mining seeks to extract high-quality information from unstructured data which is textual in nature, where quality is often conceptualized as a measure of relevance.

# Chapter 17
# Automatic Sentiment Analysis on Web Texts for Competitive Intelligence

**Stanley Loh**
*Lutheran University of Brasil (ULBRA), Brazil &
Technology Faculty Senac Pelotas, Brazil*

**Fabiana Lorenzi**
*Lutheran University of Brasil (ULBRA), Brazil*

**Paulo Roberto Pasqualotti**
*University FEEVALE, Brazil*

**Sabrina Ferreira Rodrigues**
*Lutheran University of Brasil (ULBRA), Brazil*

**Luis Fernando Fortes Garcia**
*Lutheran University of Brasil (ULBRA), Brazil &
Dom Bosco Faculty of Porto Alegre, Brazil*

**Valesca Persch Reichelt**
*Lutheran University of Brasil (ULBRA), Brazil*

## ABSTRACT

*This chapter presents a software tool that helps the Competitive Intelligence process by collecting and analyzing texts published on the Internet. The goal is to automatically analyze indicators of the sentiment present in texts about a certain theme, whether positive or negative. The sentiment analysis is made through a probabilistic process over keywords present in the texts, using as reference a task ontology with positive and negative words defined with a degree of confidence.*

## INTRODUCTION

Nowadays organizations have to evaluate their competitive environment, collecting and analyzing external information. This information may be collected from different sources. Among these, Internet is an easy and broad source of information. In this way, organizations and people are measuring the public opinion (repercussion) about facts related to their market or actions by analyzing information published in the Internet. One example is the analysis of news. News are formal sources while there are other many ways for people externalizing their opinions in informal sources, like blogs, forums, twitter, communities and social networks. For organizations, it is important to identify the main informal actors, their sentiment about the facts and how they influence

DOI: 10.4018/978-1-4666-2494-8.ch017

Copyright © 2013, IGI Global. Copying or distributing in print or electronic forms without written permission of IGI Global is prohibited.

other people. However, the success depends on the capacity and velocity of collecting, selecting, and analyzing information that can lead to strategic and valuable decisions.

This work presents a software tool that helps people and organizations in collecting and analyzing texts published in the Web about certain subjects. From a given theme (represented by keywords), texts are collect in different sources as blogs, news, websites and twitter. After that, the tool performs a sentiment analysis over the texts, that is, it analyzes keywords present in the text and compares with a task ontology in order to identify indicators of positive or negative sentiment. Using a probabilistic reasoning process, the tool determines the main sentiment of the text (whether positive, negative, or neutral). The tool also allows selecting the kind of source to be analyzed (or all kinds).

This chapter is structured as follows. Section 2 presents some related work about sentiment analysis. Section 3 presents the software tool, its functionalities, methods, and techniques. Section 4 describes the process of creating the task ontology for the purpose of sentiment analysis, besides explaining the structure of the task ontology if one wishing to apply it on other subject. Section 4 presents an experiment carried out with the tool and the evaluation of the process. Section 5 finishes with concluding remarks and future work.

## RELATED WORK

Automatic Sentiment Analysis is the analysis of affective states made by machines over documents written in natural language, based on emotion categories like positive and negative (Gregory, et al., 2006). Other authors utilize synonyms as "opinion mining" (Pang & Lee, 2008). This kind of work is applied for analysis of customers´ satisfaction about products and services, for identification of attitudes on reports of employees and so on.

Ma et al. (2005) presents experiments with sentiment analysis over chat messages. Emotions are estimated based on keywords present in the text. The work of Genereux and Evans (2006) classifies weblogs according to their affective content, using a two-dimensional space with axes "positive or negative" and "active or passive."

Godbole et al. (2007) assigns scores indicating positive or negative opinion to each distinct entity in texts from newspapers and blogs. They expand a small candidate list of positive and negative words into a sentiment dictionary using path-based analysis of synonyms and antonyms in WordNet.

Pang and Lee (2008) presents a survey about the main techniques used for opinion mining and sentiment analysis in texts, besides concerning other issues in this theme. They expose the difficulty of analyzing sentiments based only on words present in the text. They report an accuracy of 60% for the use of lists of keywords created by humans within a straightforward classification policy. In contrast, "word lists of the same size but chosen based on examination of the corpus' statistics achieves almost 70% accuracy" and "applying machine learning techniques based on unigram models can achieve over 80% in accuracy."

Ortony, Clore, and Colins (Ortony, et al., 1988) presents a psychological and cognitive model of emotions, containing emotions resulting from the description of cognitive processes and real world interpretations by a human subject. The model contains 22 kinds of emotions: "happy for," "resentment," "gloating," "pity," "joy," "distress," "pride," "shame," "admiration," "reproach," "love," "hate," "hope," "fear," "satisfaction," "fears-confirmed," "relief," "disappointment," "gratification," "remorse," "gratitude," and "anger." Table 1 shows the emotions and their corresponding adjectives.

*Table 1. Emotions of the OCC model and the corresponding adjective*

| Emotion | Adjectives |
|---|---|
| Happiness | Happy-for |
| Resentment | Resentful |
| Gloating | (no corresponding) word |
| Pity | Pitiful |
| Joy | Joyful |
| Distress | Distressed |
| Pride | Proud |
| Shame | Shameful |
| Admiration | Admired |
| Reproach | Reproached |
| Love/loving | Loved |
| Hate | Hateful |
| Hope | Hopeful |
| Fear | Fearful |
| Satisfaction | Satisfied |
| Relief | Relieved |
| Disappointment | Disappointed |
| Gratification | Gratificated |
| Remorse | Remorseful |
| Gratitude | Grateful |
| Anger | Angry |

What the works cited above lack is a broad analysis of different kinds of texts published in the Web. Each tool is specialized in a kind of text and this difficult the analysis of competitive information. The tool proposed in this chapter analyzes texts from blogs, news, Twitter, and ordinary webpages.

Furthermore, instead of creating a list of words through human effort, the creation of the task ontology follows a combination of different techniques, as for example, machine learning, dictionaries, thesauri, and language translation.

## PRESENTATION OF THE SOFTWARE TOOL

The current conditions of the Internet have allowed the growing number of users and information through blogs, Web sites for complaints, social networks, posts of Twitter, among others. This kind of sources allows people to explain their views, experiences, and frustrations easily and quickly. In addition, this information may be accessed anywhere by anyone. Thus it became very difficult to filter all this content in order to retrieve only what is of interest and also be able to assess whether what is being said is good or not.

The creation of systems capable of performing the summarization of subjective texts like the cited above, have been a great challenge for Computer Science research. This is due to the fact that computers do not have the ability to understand the nuances of human language that can use irony or phrases whose meaning depends on the entire context.

Thinking of this purpose, the software tool presented in this chapter was developed. Its goal is not to understand humans but simply indicate the kind of sentiment present in a text. In this chapter, only positive and negative sentiments are being considered. However, the tool, the process and the ontology structure allows the analysis of different sentiments.

The developed tool performs information search on the Internet to support Competitive Intelligence activities. After retrieving the content, the tool generates conclusions that aid decision-making processes. Information obtained with this tool is organized into numeric indicators that serve to provide the user with an insight into the impact that the themes and publications of interest are having on the Internet.

The tool receives, as entry, keywords representing a theme or subject, as in a traditional information retrieval system. Then it searches in the Web for texts where the keywords appear. The special feature is that the tool analyzes Web pages, blogs, news and twitter posts. Using meta-search processes on well-known search engines like Google and Yahoo, the tool retrieves the html codes of Web pages found with the parameters. Then, the tool filters html tags resulting in files with only text.

For each text found, the tool analyzes all the words present and compares them against lists of terms from a task ontology. A positive sentiment represents approving the theme and a negative one expresses the disapproval about the theme. Using a probabilistic reasoning process, candidate words are analyzed including their frequency in the texts.

The main screen of the tool, presented in Figure 1, has 4 main parts: in the upper left there is the search form where the user gives keywords about the theme of interest. The user may also selects if he/she wishes the search to be made in blogs, news, Web pages, Twitter, or all. For each type of search it has to be informed the maximum number of results to be analyzed. This must be set due the limitation of search engines APIs (Application Programming Interface). The search in Google returns the maximum of 64 results for each type of search. Twitter has the limitation of 1500 messages as results for a search, and the posts should be a maximum of up to ten and a half days of the date of search.

The search terms have no limitation, and may include any types of characters and may use operators in order to refine the search. The accepted parameters and their descriptions can be found in http://www.google.com.br/intl/pt-BR/help/basics.html for Google searches and in http://search.twitter.com/operators for searches on Twitter.

For each new analysis, the screen shows the progress (main steps) of the process in bottom left, keeping the user informed about the stages. Important information as possible errors in the retrieval of texts is presented (for example, not found pages or denied access). Through this panel, the user can monitor the amount of texts that have

been analyzed so far and it is possible to cancel the execution any time and still check the results so far collected.

The numeric indicators about each sentiment can be seen in the "Results" box, which displays a summary of the total number of positive, negative and neutral texts. Immediately below are listed the information for each text analyzed and their specific results. These lists are organized in tabs according to the classification of texts after analysis. For each text are displayed its main identification information (title and URL) and the specific results of analysis of this item. Clicking on the URL the user can access the original source through the browser and check the contents.

Besides the indicators of each kind of sentiment, the tool also shows the total number of unique domains for each category. In the case of Twitter, instead of single domains, the tool presents the number of unique users. This numbers help users to understand how many people or entities are responsible for the dissemination of the theme in the Internet.

## The Process of Sentiment Analysis

The process of sentiment analysis consists in identifying the trends or repercussion of a theme or subject in public opinion. Although the identification of emotions in texts is nowadays a difficult task, there are techniques of text mining and natural language processing that can help the process. The final goal is not to understand human communication but solely the kind of sentiment present in the text. In the present chapter, we discuss the identification of one of two sentiments: a positive or a negative sentiment.

In a simplified manner, the task consists in identifying the presence of one class in a text, distinguishing the main class from others. The process needs a list of predefined classes and indicators that will help in identifying each class in the text. This a classification task and may be developed with the help of task ontologies, where

*Figure 1. Main screen of the tool*

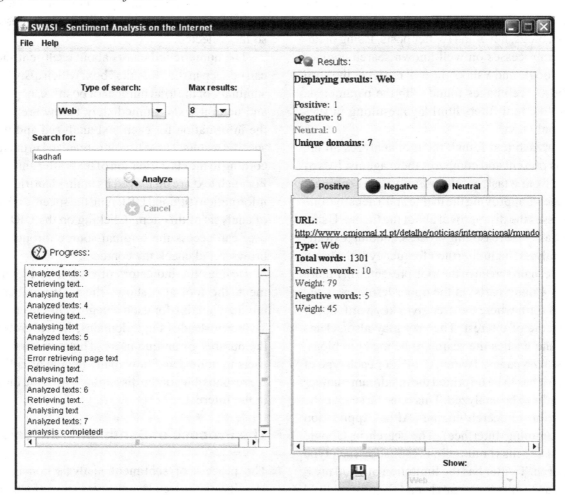

classes and indicators will be defined. As will be explained in the next section, the indicators are terms (single words or expressions), each one associated with a numeric weight, representing the strength of the term for indicating the kind of sentiment.

The process of reasoning about the presence of classes is based on probabilistic paradigms. The assumption is that many terms from different classes may be present in a text. Thus, the process must distinguish what is the main class, by using mathematical formulas about numeric values that represent the strength of each term inside a class

and the degree of importance of the term inside the text.

Figure 2 presents the algorithm for sentiment analysis of a given text. Resuming, the first step is to identify indicators of classes in the text, i.e., terms of the text that are associated with one or more classes in the task ontology. The weights (defined in the task ontology) of each term found in text are summed separately for each class (sentiment). If a term appears more than once in a text, its strength for indicating the class is multiplied by its frequency in the text (the number of appearances).

*Figure 2. Algorithm for the sentiment analysis*

```
For each occurrence of the word in the text
        Search for the word in the ontology
        If the word is positive in the ontology
                Sum the weight of the word in the ontology to the total positive weights
        If the word is negative in the ontology
                Sum the weight of the word in the ontology to the total negative
weights
        If total of positive weights > total of negative weights
                The text is classified as positive
        If total of positive weights < total of negative weights
                The text is classified as negative
        If total of positive weights = total of negative weights
                The text is classified as neutral
```

The final result, that is, if the text has a positive or a negative trend, depends on the numeric total for each class. The class with the greater value wins. If the result is tied, the tool returns a neutral answer. In this case, the tool assumes that is not possible to identify a dominant sentiment. In many texts, it is possible to find positive and negative sentiments. For example, one person may publish his/her opinion about a product, reporting advantages or problems. In these cases, the tool tries to found the dominant sentiment, that is, the one with more presence or more emphasis.

As shown in Figure 1, the tool presents the final count of positive and negative terms and the final sum of weights for each side. That helps users to decide on what to believe and thus the software acts as a support-decision tool.

## THE TASK ONTOLOGY

An ontology contains concepts about a knowledge area, relations among these concepts and a vocabulary (lexicon) used to express the concepts in texts. The software tool utilizes a task ontology (Guarino, 1988), because it is limited to a singular situation or a predefined task: the identification of human sentiments in texts. The role of the task ontology is to represent the different kinds of sentiments that appear in Web texts and how these opinions can be identified inside the Web texts. For these reason, the task ontology is composed by a list of words and expressions (multiwords), each one identified by the corresponding sentiment and a numeric weight. For the tool, the task ontology is structured as a textual file (.txt) with many lines, each one containing a word (or expression) and the sentiment and weight separated by the symbol ";".

The weights are limited to integer numbers between 1 and 10. This scale represents the importance of the word in determining the sentiment present in the text. A high weight means that the word indicates a sentiment without confusion. A low weight means that the word may indicate a sentiment but it may also be used in other context. It is important to state that a term may be associated to one or more classes in the task ontology. Since the process of sentiment analysis is not concerned on the presence of a single term but in the analysis of the context (a group of terms), this is not a problem. Many words have more than one meaning and this (ambiguity) may solved by probabilistic methods.

For the experiments of this chapter, the task ontology was defined with two kinds of sentiments: positive or negative. The same structure may be used in the future to represent other kinds of sentiments. Borod (2000) presents a classification of affective states representing emotions, mood, personal and interpersonal attitudes, personality traits and so on, that can be used for other tasks or to make the identification of more precise or refined sentiments.

The choice of words and expressions present in the task ontology was made by different ways: a process of supervised learning over texts extracted from the Web and the reutilization and integration of Websters and synonyms dictionaries and affective lexicons as WordNet and WordNet Affect. As the task ontology is suited to texts in Portuguese, it was necessary to translate all words and expressions from English to Portuguese. Verbal conjugations were included as variations of the words.

Following, the process of constructing the task ontology is described in details.

## Affect Base

The Affect Base contains terms referring to the domain of affective states. It was created manually by researchers from the "The Cognitive and Communication Technologies" group (http://tcc.itc.it/). The main structure of this base is composed by grammatical classes from WordNet: nouns, verbs, adjectives, and adverbs. Each term has slots with different kinds of information. There are slots for synonyms and antonyms, definitions, related terms with different grammatical classes. In special, the slot "Elliot" identifies one of the 24 categories of emotions proposed by Elliot (1992) and the slots "valence" and "arousal" represent respectively positive and negative affective values (and the degree of excitation of the emotion).

Most information in the Affect Base was collected using dictionaries and scientific documents about psychology of the emotions. Other information was included by hand by the authors of the base and revised by psychologists and lexicography experts.

## WordNet Affect

From the slot "Ortony" in the Affect Base, a second base was created by the same group: the WordNet Affect. It is part of the base WordNet Domains and contains synsets annotated in an additional hierarchy called "affective domain" (http://wndomains.itc.it).

The WordNet Affect Base indicates to what affective class the term belongs according to affective states defined by Ortony et al. (1987). Table 2 presents examples of terms and corresponding affective states.

The task ontology used in the present work utilized the class "Emotion" and other information was added to this base from relations with Word-Net and the OCC Model. A total of 1433 synsets were added to the WordNet Affect, looking forward to maintain the semantic relation to the affective meaning.

*Table 2. Examples of terms for affective states*

| Affective State | Examples |
|---|---|
| emotion | substantive "anger," verb "to fear" |
| mood | substantive "animosity," adjective "amiable" |
| trait | substantive "aggressiveness," adjective "competitive" |
| cognitive state | substantive "confusion," adjective "dazed" |
| physical state | substantive "illness," adjective "all in" |
| edonic signal | substantive "hurt," substantive "suffering" |
| emotion- situation eliciting | substantive "awkwardness," adjective "out of danger" |
| emotional response | substantive "cold sweat," verb "to tremble" |
| behavior | substantive "offense," adjective "inhibited" |
| attitude | substantive "intolerance," noun "defensive" |
| sensation | substantive "coldness," verb "to feel" |

## Translation of the Final Word List

The final list of terms in each kind of emotion was translated to Portuguese by professionals with experience. The process was divided in 3 phases. The first one, when each translator worked separately upon the terms. In the second phase, terms and translations were cross validated among the translators. The final phase was characterized by discussions among the translators for a final decision, especially solving inconsistencies.

The orientation giving to the translators was to be broad, not restricting the isolated meaning of the words. For this task, glossaries of each synset from the WordNet were also translated.

## Machine Learning

Examples of texts where sentiments were present were extracted by human effort from the Web (especially from blogs, news, Twitter). These texts were analyzed by a text mining software tool called Text Mining Suite (www.intext.com.br) for identifying most frequent words and expressions, resulting in two lists: one list with positive words and expressions and other list with negative words.

A special attention was giving to multi-words or expressions, because the previous glossaries only address single words.

## The Final Composition of the Task Ontology

In the context of this chapter, only two kinds of sentiments are being considered: positive and negative. For this reason, the final list of emotional terms created from the bases Affect and WordNet Affect was grouped in two classes (positive and negative). Some terms were disregarded, because it was not possible to classify the term as positive or negative.

After that, this list of terms was combined with the list of terms from the machine learning stage. Duplicities were removed.

The final step was to determine the weight of each term for indicating the level of the sentiment. In this case, human determined the weights using a 1-10 scale, but using as parameter a numeric degree calculated by the Text Mining Tool in the machine-learning step. This numeric degree is based on the frequency of the word inside each class (relative frequency inside each text and frequency in the texts of the training collection).

The resulting task ontology is composed by 3733 terms (single words and expressions), being 1160 positive and 2573 negative.

## EXPERIMENTS AND EVALUATION

This section presents the experiments carried out with the tool applied on texts extracted from the Web and using the task ontology (final list of terms) described in the previous section.

A total of 488 texts were collected from webpages, blogs, and news and 588 texts from twitter posts. Keywords used to retrieve the texts were defined by each user that participated in the experiment (a total of 8 individuals with graduation in Computer Science). The first orientation to these users was to utilize keywords with different lengths in queries using the tool being evaluated.

The second orientation for participants was to read each text in the results of a query with the tool and to verify the correctness of the classification (whether positive or negative).

Table 3 presents the results of the evaluation, showing the number of correct and wrong cases for each kind of query. A query may be conducted only in one kind of source (Web or blog or news or Twitter) or considering a group (Web + blog + news). Analyzing these results, it is possible to

*Table 3. Results of the tool evaluation*

| Source | Correct | % | Wrong | % |
|---|---|---|---|---|
| Web | 46 | 78% | 13 | 22% |
| Blogs | 32 | 71% | 13 | 29% |
| News | 27 | 84% | 5 | 16% |
| Web + Blogs + News | 269 | 76% | 83 | 24% |
| Twitter | 512 | 87% | 76 | 13% |

verify an average accuracy of 79.2% in correct results. This number shows the feasibility of the approach, using the tool and the task ontology created for the experiments.

The worst accuracy was found with blogs. We believe that the way how people write in blogs (informal language) may be the root for the main mistakes. The best performance was achieved with twitter and news. The result with news is considered normal since this kind of text is well formed and is usually revised by many professionals. The result with twitter is against our expectation, especially because posts are short (maximum of 140 characters) and because people publish their posts generally in a hurry. We believe that the good result with twitter posts is due to the use of clear and precise words (since users should use few words, they choice better words).

We consider that mistakes are due to the difficulty of understanding the context of texts published in the Internet. Words may assume different meanings depending on the context. Even when analyzing multi-words or expressions, the context is suitable to pragmatic use of the language. People may utilize humor and jokes to express opinions. Even a phrase like "I like Mondays" may have a contradictory meaning depending on the situation. Furthermore, many webpages treat different kinds of themes and subjects, confusing the analysis method that considers a unique theme inside a same page.

## CONCLUSION

The importance of interpreting the opinions of Internet users is a major challenge for professionals in the area of Competitive Intelligence faced with an immense source of data to be exploited, especially due to the rise of short texts posts (blogs and Twitters) and social networks with very different goals.

The main motivation for developing this tool was to create a way to facilitate the understanding of this huge data published in the Internet. The tool works by helping decision makers to classify texts as positive, negative, or neutral. Although computers are not capable of understanding the subjectivity of human communication, experiments discussed in this chapter demonstrated that analytical techniques may be effective in identifying positive and negative sentiments present in texts. An average accuracy of 79% with texts extracted from Web encourages the research in this area.

The probabilistic process embedded in the tool was efficient for identification of positive and negative sentiments. We believe that the classification in other sentiments is feasible if using a similar process for creating the task ontology. Although the chapter presents a task ontology with only two kinds of sentiment (positive and negative), the techniques embedded in the tool and the ontology structure allows creating more specialized sentiments like the ones present in the OCC model. Future works may investigate the analysis of more precise sentiments.

The classification mistakes resulting from the process may be due to language particularities but they must be investigated with future experiments. The weights utilized in the task ontology may be revised. One assumption is that more precise weights may generate better results if determined by machine learning processes.

Other difficulty when working with texts includes spelling errors, that are hard to be considered in an ontology. In particular, texts from Web tend to have abbreviations, slang, and informal constructions.

Some limitations on the search results are established by the APIs of Google and Twitter. For searches at Google, there is a limitation of 64 results by category and a maximum of 1500 messages at Twitter.

People from different areas can benefit from the knowledge provided by the proposed software, as for example stock market investors who seek to know the image of a company in today's market, consumers interested in a product that want to know the opinion of other people; tourists interested in travel reviews, in order to know the perception of others about places, hotels and tourism services, voters for analyzing public personalities, and so on.

Future work will also include the possibility of research in different languages, using the same probabilistic process and ontology structure. The way the tool was constructed allows the creation of different task ontologies for different languages or kinds of sentiments.

# REFERENCES

Borod, J. C. (Ed.). (2000). *The neuropsychology of emotion.* Oxford, UK: Oxford University Press.

Elliot, C. D. (1992). *The affective reasoner: A process model of emotions in a multi-agent system.* (Ph.D. Thesis). Northwestern University. Evanston, IL.

Genereux, M., & Evans, R. (2006). Towards a validated model for affective classification of texts. In *Proceedings of the Workshop on Sentiment and Subjectivity in Text*, (pp. 55–62). Sydney, Australia: Association for Computational Linguistics.

Godbole, N., Srinivasaiah, M., & Skiena, S. (2007). Large-scale sentiment analysis for news and blogs. In *Proceedings of the International Conference on Weblogs and Social Media (ICWSM)*. Boulder, CO: ICWSM.

Gregory, M. L., Chinchor, N., Whitney, P., Carter, R., Hetzler, E., & Turner, A. (2006). User-directed sentiment analysis: Visualizing the affective content of documents. In *Proceedings of the Workshop on Sentiment and Subjectivity in Text*, (pp. 23–30). Sydney, Australia: Association for Computational Linguistics.

Guarino, N. (Ed.). (1998). Formal ontology and information systems. In *Proceedings of the Formal Ontology in Information Systems*, (pp. 3-15). Amsterdam, The Netherlands: IOS Press.

Ma, C., Prendinger, H., & Ishizuka, M. (2005). A chat system based on emotion estimation from text and embodied conversational messengers. *Lecture Notes in Computer Science*, *3711*, 535–538. doi:10.1007/11558651_56

Ortony, A., Clore, G. L., & Colins, A. (1988). *The cognitive structure of emotions.* Cambridge, UK: Cambridge University Press. doi:10.1017/CBO9780511571299

Ortony, A., Clore, G. L., & Foss, M. A. (1987). *The referential structure of the affective lexicon.* Urbana-Champaign, IL: Universiry of Illinois at Urbana-Champaign.

Pang, B., & Lee, L. (2008). Opinion mining and sentiment analysis. *Foundations and Trends in Information Retrieval, 2*(1-2).

# KEY TERMS AND DEFINITIONS

**Competitive Intelligence:** Area of Business Administration inside Organizations responsible for identifying and monitoring competitors (competing companies) and market evolution.

**Ontology:** Contains concepts about a knowledge area, relations among these concepts and a vocabulary (lexicon) used to express the concepts in texts.

**Opinion Mining:** A synonym for sentiment analysis in the context of computer-based text analysis.

**Sentiment Analysis:** Is the analysis of affective states made by machines over documents written in natural language, based on emotion categories like positive and negative.

**Task Ontology:** An ontology limited to a singular situation or a predefined task.

**Text Mining:** The same as textual data mining, i.e., the application of statistical techniques on content present inside texts.

**Textual Analysis:** Qualitative and/or quantitative analysis of textual content, examining words present in the texts, syntax relations and other techniques for semantic understanding.

**WordNet:** A worldwide ontology available publicly.

# Chapter 18
# Ontology–Based Opinion Mining

**Rajendra Akerkar**
*Western Norway Research Institute, Norway*

**Terje Aaberge**
*Western Norway Research Institute, Norway*

## ABSTRACT

*In this chapter, the authors discuss an ontology-based approach to opinion mining exploiting the possibility to represent commonly shared meaning of linguistic relations by ontologies. The ontology definitions are used as a standard to which sentences extracted from texts are compared. Unlike conventional text mining, which is based on objective topics aiming to discover common patterns of user opinions from their textual statements automatically or semi-automatically, it will extract opinion from subjective locations.*

## INTRODUCTION

The rapid growth in Internet applications has led to an enormous amount of personal reviews on the Web covering many subject areas. These reviews appear in different forms like BBS, blogs, Wiki or forum websites and present information valuable to both the general public searching providers of services and providers trying to adapt to public demands. An intrinsic problem of the overwhelming information, however, is information overloading as users are simply unable to access and read all the available information. Query functions in search engines like Yahoo and Google help users to find reviews but the identification of relevant information from returned pages might demand more effort than worthwhile.

The totality of reviews on an offer may be assumed to represent public opinion concerning its quality. The importance of knowledge of public opinion makes methods of extraction, i.e. opinion mining and sentiment analysis, enjoy a burst research activity. Opinion Mining is the field that deals with the mining of subjective statements from

DOI: 10.4018/978-1-4666-2494-8.ch018

Copyright © 2013, IGI Global. Copying or distributing in print or electronic forms without written permission of IGI Global is prohibited.

texts, the identification of opinions, the estimation of opinion orientation and the extraction of arguments that relate to opinions. Mining opinions in online discussions requires an appropriate representation. It is distinctively different from traditional text mining in that the latter is based on declarative descriptions while the opinion mining must take into account the additional level of description of subjective experience. Specifically, traditional text mining focuses on specific topics (e.g., business, travel) as well as topic shifts in text whereas opinion mining is much more difficult than those for topic mining. This is partially attributed to the fact that topics are represented explicitly with keywords while opinions are expressed with subtlety. Opinion mining requires deeper understanding of language characteristic and textual context (Pang, et al., 2002).

In the past few years, many researchers studied the problem. Most of the existing works are based on product reviews because a review usually focuses on a specific product and contains little irrelevant information. The main tasks are to discover properties that have been commented on and to decide whether the opinions are positive or negative. In this chapter, we discuss the property identification problem by employing ontology structure. Ontology allows us to analyse a review at a finer granularity based on shared meaning.

An ontology provides knowledge about domains that is understandable by developers and can be handled by computers. It is prevalent in annotating documents with metadata, improving the performance of information retrieval and reasoning, and making data interoperable between different apps (Akerkar, 2009). Ontology-based text analysis seems promising for opinion mining.

## BACKGROUND

There are two fundamental research efforts in opinion mining area that have been given attention, namely sentiment classification and property-level opinion mining. Traditional document classification methods are often employed in sentiment classification; the entire document is classified as positive, negative, or neutral. However, these methods must be considered too vague. In most cases, both positive and negative opinions can appear in the same document, for example, "Overall, the accommodation is super, the glacier-hike is thrilling, but the food is tasteless." There are some works focused on sentiment classification. They are based on manually or half-manually constructed a priori knowledge dictionary which contains polarity words. Some classic machine learning methods (Naive Bayes, Maximum Entropy, and SVM) have been tested by Pang et al. (2002) who point out that machine learning methods are more effective than manually labelling. Hearst (1992) proposed a model-based approach trying to analyze the structure of the document more deeply, but the method is so far not supported by experimental data.

In the property level opinion mining critic extraction-related sub-tasks were identification of properties and extraction of opinions associated with these properties. Existing works on identifying object properties discussed in reviews often rely on the simple linguistic heuristic that properties are represented by nouns or noun phrases. Popescu and Etzioni (2005) consider product properties to be predicates forming relationships with the product (for example, for a tour planning, transport is one of its properties) and try to identify the properties connected with the product name. Their approach does not involve opinion mining but simply focuses more on the task of identifying different types of properties. Hu and Liu (2004a) propose the idea of opinion mining and summarization. They use a lexicon-based method to determine whether the opinion expressed on a product property is positive or negative. In a later paper Hu and Liu (2004b) follows the intuition that frequent nouns or noun phrases are likely to be properties. They identify frequent properties through association mining and then apply heuristic-guided pruning aimed at removing multi-word candidates in which the words do not appear together in a certain order and single-word candidates for which subsuming super-strings have been collected. This method is improved by Ding and Liu (2007) using a more sophisticated method based on holistic lexicon and linguistic rules to identify the orientations of context dependent opinion words. The approach works with many special words, phrases, and language constructs which have impacts on opinions based on their linguistic patterns such as "negation" rules, "but" clauses rules, intra-sentence conjunction rule etc. Yi et al. (2003) consider three increasingly strict heuristics to select from noun phrases based on POS tag patterns. Kanayama and Nasukawa (2006) used conjunction rules to find words from large domain corpora. The conjunction rule basically states that when two opinion words are linked by a conjunction in a sentence, their opinion orientations are the same. Godbole et al. (2007) estimated the polarity scores for a large set of named entities. However, they measured the scores by the co-occurrences of named entities and opinion words, so the opinionated sentences, which did not contain named entities, were skipped.

## TOWARDS AN ONTOLOGY-BASED OPINION MINING

To analyse a document means to extract terms that refer to subjects spoken about and predicates that convey meaning of the sentences. The sentences can then be translated into sentences of a formal language. If these sentences are to be processable the computer has to be given the syntactic role of the words, whether a word is a term or a predicate. The final implementation language must therefore be an ontology language, i.e. a metalanguage with respect to the object language that describes the individuals of the domain. In the case of opinion mining there is another reason for the use of metalanguage; an opinion is described by a valuation predicate that applies to object language sentences.

Given a description of the object language vocabulary in the ontology language a comparison with the text of a document using standard methods of text analysis will pick the terms and predicates and form the appropriate descriptive formal language sentences. Moreover, if the vocabulary of the metalanguage also contains the valuation predicates, a comparison will also pick the relevant ones and sentences expressing opinions can be formed. A condition for the method to work is that the vocabularies are sufficiently furnished to permit comparison.

The vocabulary of the language worked with must thus for practical reasons be much richer than is strictly needed for its expressibility. This extra richness can be made explicit by the formulation of an ontology, i.e. supplement the vocabulary with a set of:

- Axioms
- Intensional definitions
- Extensional definitions

An axiom is an implicit definition that relates the primary words of the vocabulary of the object language. The axioms picture structural properties of the domain and express restrictions on the possible meaning of predicates. The intensional and extensional definitions are terminological. They define secondary predicates that serve to facilitate the discourse from the primary words, e.g. instead of having to repeat the properties that an individual must possess to be of a certain kind an intensional definition will introduce a predicate to denote the kind. An intensional definition of a predicate (definiendum) is thus the conjunction of atomic sentences (definientia) stating which properties that an individual must possess for the predicate to apply. When the meaning of the definientia is given the definition explains the meaning of definiendum. An extensional definition of a predicate on the other hand, is simply the list of the names of the individuals that constitute its extension. When the individuals referred to are known, the extension of the predicate representing its meaning is given. From an intensional definition of a predicate, an extensional one can be derived; the extension of the predicate is the class of individuals that satisfies definientia in the intensional definition. It follows that the interpretation of the vocabulary is determined by the interpretation of the primary vocabulary.

The task is therefore to formulate two ontologies, an object language ontology, and a valuation ontology that both are to be implemented in the metalanguage/ontology language.

## Principles of Ontology Construction

The definition indicates that there is an ideal method for the construction of an ontology that consists of accomplishing the following tasks:

1.  Delimit the domain of discourse.
2.  Identify a primary vocabulary.
3.  Establish the axioms.
4.  Introduce secondary words by intensional definitions.
5.  Introduce further secondary words by extensional definitions.

Task number one is preliminary but important because if we do not delimit the domain properly we cannot establish a language of description with a well defined vocabulary. It is the nature of the individuals of the domain that determines the predicates needed for their descriptions. The primary vocabulary consists of the names of the individuals and predicates that represent properties and relations needed to describe the individuals. The structural properties of the domain are described by axioms in words of the primary vocabulary. The formulation of axioms will in general not use the name, but a variable that is representing an individual of a certain kind as in the following example:

"if x is the SonOf y and y is the BrotherOf z then z is the UncleOf x"

which is an axiom relating the predicates "SonOf," "BrotherOf," and "UncleOf." x, y and z are here understood to represent unidentified persons. If ... then is a logical connective. Notice that this axiom is picturing a structural property of family relations for a domain of persons. At the same time, it expresses implicit dependencies of the possible meaning of the predicates.

Task number four consists in formulating intensional definitions to introduce secondary predicates. These are predicates whose extensions are classes. Examples could be "Hotel," "Pension," "Bed&Breakfast," etc. Finally, (task number five) establish further secondary words by extensional definitions. An example of such a definition in informal language is "an accommodation is a Hotel or an accommodation is a Pension or an accommodation is a Bed&Breakfast" that defines Accommodation. The secondary vocabulary is constructed from the primary words.

The numbering of the tasks does not refer to the ordering of their execution. One better keeps in mind the different tasks to be accomplished and work iteratively. Moreover, it might be difficult or not practical to try to fully attain the ideal suggested by the work description. For different reasons one may be forced to compromise.

The construction of an ontology must also take into account its intended use. The vocabulary of an ontology used for text or opinion mining must contain the vocabulary encountered in texts concerning the individuals of the domain to be considered. To accomplish this, the construction might be assisted by automated computational linguistics using existing vocabularies like SentiWordNet. The applicability of the method is limited to the analysis of texts relevant to the individuals of the domain chosen.

## FORMAL DESCRIPTION LANGUAGE

### Object Language

The domain of discourse for a language is assumed to consist of individual objects possessing properties and relations. The attribution of a property to an individual or a relation to a pair of individuals is an atomic fact expressed by an atomic sentence that is the juxtaposition of a name or names and a predicate. There are two ways of conceiving the relation between language and domain; either the structure of the domain is mapped into the language or the structure of the language is mapped into the domain. The first of these corresponds to Wittgenstein's picture theory in Tractatus (1961) the second one is attributed to Tarski (1983) being the standard view in semantics of first order formal languages.

The way of conceiving the structure of the domains is different in the two cases. In the first case, the domain is modelled as a directed graph. An individual is then represented by a node and a relation by an arrow; in the second case, it is modelled as a set consisting of individuals, sets of individuals, sets of ordered pairs of individuals, etc. These conceptualisations are the basis for the intensional and extensional interpretations respectively. The intensional interpretations are represented by maps, a naming map that maps the individuals (or relations) to names, and observables that map an individual (or relation) to a predicate representing a property (or relation). The extensional interpretations are represented by a map that maps names to the individuals, a

one-place predicate to the set of individuals possessing the property referred to by the predicate, a two-place predicate to the set of ordered pairs of individuals possessing the relation denoted by the predicate, etc.

The notion of observable is a fundamental building block in the intensional interpretation scheme. An observable is simulating a kind of measurements the results of which are predicates representing properties of individuals or relations between individuals. It simulates the act of measurement and is associated with an operational definition, i.e. the specification of a standard of measure, laws on which the measurement is based and rules determining the actions to be performed to make the measurement. The possible values (predicates) of an observable represent mutual exclusive properties of individuals or relations between two individuals. Individuals cannot be red and green at the same time. Thus, colour is an observable. Other observables are temperature, weight, position in space, etc.

The result of a measurement on an individual or relation is expressed by a predicate and stated by a sentence that relates the name of the individual or individuals partaking in the relation. These are the atomic sentences of the language. The truth conditions are therefore particularly simple. An atomic sentence is true if it states the result of a measurement. This is expressed in the model of the domain of the metalanguage by a set of commutative diagrams (Aaberge, 2009):

$$N \xrightarrow{\pi} P$$
$$v \uparrow \nearrow \delta \qquad \text{i.e.} \quad \pi\big(\nu\big(d\big)\big) = \delta\big(d\big), \quad \forall d \in D$$
$$D$$

$$(1)$$

where $D$ denotes the domain, $N$ the names, $P$ the predicates, $\nu$ is the naming map $\delta$ is an observable and $\pi$ is defined by the commutativity of a diagram (In the case text analysis of linked data information resources, $D$ is the set of URIs and $N$ the proper names of entities. Otherwise, $D$ is identified with $N$.). The diagram relates the simulation of measurements determining atomic facts assigning properties to an individual (or relation to a pair of individuals) and the formulation of an atomic sentence expressing such a fact. by the juxtaposition of names and predicates, e.g. the sentence pn where n is the name of the individual $d$ and $p$ the predicate referring to a property of $d$ expresses a fact about $d$ if, for $\nu(d) = n$ and $\delta(d) = p$. $\pi(\nu(d)) = \delta(d)$ is therefore a truth condition. It equates a proposition about the system $d$ with a statement of the result of a measurement on $d$ with respect to the observable $\delta$. To be able to express evaluations the absolute notion of truth of sentences in a declarative language has to be graded, i.e. the truth predicate is replaced by a set of predicates that express to which degree a property is present.

## The Metalanguage

Let $L_D(N \cup V, P)$ stand for the object language for a domain $D$, i.e. the set of names, predicates, variables, and sentences. $N$ denotes the set of names, $V$ the set of variables, $P$ the set of one-place and two-place predicates.

The metalanguage for the object language is denoted $L_{M_D}(G \cup W, Q)$ where the domain $M_D$ consists of the set of diagrams (1) and with well formed formulae as isolated nodes, $W$ the set of variables, and $G = D \cup L_D(N \cup V, P)$ the names of the nodes and relations q $(arrows\ d \mapsto n)$ etc. in (1)) and $Q$ the predicates of the metalanguage. The naming map $\eta$ is identity on the nodes of $G$ and maps arrows to the ordered 2-tuples constituted by the names of its source and target, e.g.

$$\eta : M_D \to G; \left(\alpha(n) = p\right) \mapsto \eta\left(\delta(n) = p\right) = (n, p)$$
(2)

The meta-observable $\alpha : M_D \to Q$ associating properties of the nodes in $M_D$ to predicates takes the values $D$, $D^{(2)}$, $N$, $N^{(2)}$, $V$, $P$, $P^{(2)}$, $S$, $H$, $P_\nu, P_\pi, P_{\pi}P_\pi{}^{(2)}, P_\delta, P_\delta{}^{(2)}$ informally defined by

1. $Dm$, m is an individual.
2. $D^{(2)}m$, m is a relation.
3. $Nm$, $m$ is the name of an individual.
4. $N^{(2)}m$, $m$ is the name of a relation.
5. $Vm$, $m$ is a variable.
6. $Pm$, $m$ is a 1-ary predicate.
7. $P^{(2)}m$, $m$ is a 2-ary predicate.
8. $Sm$, $m$ is a sentence.
9. $Hm$, $m$ is a formula.
10. $P_\nu m_1 m_2$, $m_1$ is named $m_2$.
11. $P_\pi m_1 m_2$, $m_1$ is $m_2$.
12. $P_{\pi^{(2)}} m_1 m_2$, $m_1$ is $m_2$.
13. $P_\delta m_1 m_2$, $m_1$ possesses the property represented to by $m_2$.
14. $P_{\delta^{(2)}} m_1 m_2$, $m_1$ is the relation represented by $m_2$.

The operational definition is given by the syntactic rules and interpretation of the language and the semantic value of a symbol are determined by inspection. It should be noticed that these predicates can serve to characterise names and predicates of the object language and thus makes possible a map that to a sentence associates a syntactic description of the sentence.

The commutativity conditions (1) are expressed by

$$\forall_{m_1} \exists_{m_2} \exists_{m_3} \left( \begin{matrix} (Dm_1 \wedge Nm_2 \wedge Pm_3 \wedge P_\nu m_1 m_2 \wedge \\ P_\pi m_2 m_3) \Leftrightarrow P_\delta m_1 m_3 \end{matrix} \right)$$
(3)

The truth conditions are

$$(Dm_1 \wedge Nm_2 \wedge Pm_3 \wedge P_\nu m_1 m_2 \wedge P_\delta m_1 m_3) \Leftrightarrow Tm_2 m_3$$
(4)

where the predicate $T$ expresses the of truth of the atomic sentence. This is the general form of the truth condition. In text analysis not involving linked data it simplifies to

$$\left( Nm_1 \wedge Pm_2 \wedge P_\pi m_1 m_2 \right) \Leftrightarrow Tm_2 m_1 \qquad (5)$$

which tells that a sentence has an evaluation. These conditions should be interpreted as follows: the sentence $Dm_1 \wedge Nm_2 \wedge Pm_3 \wedge (P_\nu m_1 m_2 \wedge P_\delta m_1 m_3)$ or $Nm_1 \wedge Pm_2 \wedge P_\pi m_1 m_2$ is extracted from the text analysis. In the following we will restrict our discussion to the case (5).

## Ontology Language

Predicates of the metalanguage are Individual, Property, Type, Class, and Sent (for sentence) that express properties of the elements of its domain and $\pi_i Of$ that express (semantic) relations.

In first order logic notation a complete representation of the object language atomic sentence pn in the metalanguage, including statements about syntactic values and semantic relations, is

$$Individual\left(n\right) \wedge Class\left(p\right) \wedge \pi_1 Of\left(p,n\right) \qquad (5)$$

Thus, the evaluation conditions for atomic object language sentences are of the form

$$Individual\left(n\right) \wedge Class\left(p\right) \wedge \pi_1 Of\left(p,n\right) \Rightarrow Tpn \qquad (6)$$

The sentences of $L_G$ are uniquely expressible in a N3 representation by blocks of RDF triples. Thus, (5) translates to

$$\text{ol} : \text{n owl} : \text{Type owl} : \text{Individual}$$
$$\text{ol} : \text{p owl} : \text{Type owl} : \text{Class} \qquad (6)$$
$$\text{ol} : \text{p ml} : \pi_1 Of \, \text{ml} : \text{n}$$

and

$$\text{ol} : \text{p}^2 \text{owl} : \text{Type owl} : \text{Property}$$
$$\text{ol} : \text{n}_s \, \text{owl} : \text{Type owl} : \text{Individual}$$
$$\text{ol} : \text{n}_t \, \text{owl} : \text{Type owl} : \text{Individual} \qquad (7)$$
$$\text{ol} : \text{p}^2 \, \text{ml} : \pi_2 Of \, \text{ol} : (\text{n}_s, \text{n}_t)$$

is a translation of a corresponding sentence involving a relation. The prefixes ol, ml, and owl refer to the object language, metalanguage and OWL namespaces respectively. The triples of the kind

$$\text{ol:p ml:}\pi_1 Of \, \text{ol:n}$$
$$\text{ol:p}^2 \, \text{ml:}\pi_2 Of \, \text{ol:}(\text{n}_s, \text{n}_t)$$

are sentences in the ontology language that describe properties and relations of the individual named n.

## A FRAMEWORK FOR ONTOLOGY-BASED OPINION MINING

We focus on how to improve property level opinion mining by employing ontology. The proposed method integrates word segmentation, part-of-speech tagging, ontology development, property identification, and sentiment classification. The framework is illustrated in Figure 1.

The functions of main components are as follows:

1. **Preprocessing of data:** The preprocessing includes words segmentation and POS tagging. Since several predicates cannot be found in standard dictionary, this part is achieved with the help of ontology development which improves the accuracy of word segmentation.

2. **Property identification:** The ontology improves the accuracy of property extraction.

3.  **Opinion identification:** The approach to polarity measurement relies on a lexicon of tagged positive and negative sentiment terms, which are used to quantify positive/negative sentiment. Here, SentiWordNet (http://sentiwordnet.isti.cnr.it/) is the appropriate lexical resource that provides a readily identifiable positive and negative polarity value for a set of "affective" terms.

4.  **Summary:** This analysis is produced by converting the polarity obtained from the ealier step to more precise one by analyzing the context (say, "negation" rules) and with the help of ontology makes it possible to compute the polarities of the nodes through the hierarchy relationship.

The goal is to extract the predicates with a seeds set from hotel reviews as follows:

-   **Part 1:** Select the relevant sentences including value predicates.
-   **Part 2:** Extract the value predicates from those sentences.

We choose the sentences according to two conditions. The first one is that the sentence contains a conjunction. The second one is that the sentence contains at least one predicate seed. The reason is that the phrases in the conjunction structure have the same characteristics. For example, the sentence "*the special offers and the scenic cruise are very good,*" we already know the "*scenic cruise*" is a property, but do not know "*special offers.*" If applying the conjunction strategy, we will easily get that "*special offers*" is also a property. At the initial stage, we use some manually labelled properties as seeds. The whole process will end when no new candidates predicate emerges.

## PREDICATE IDENTIFICATION

The main idea for predicate identification is to use ontology terminologies to extract reference to properties. The workflow is shown in Figure 2. Starting with a preprocessed tour review, we can identify related sentences which contain the ontology terminologies. From those sentences, we can easily extract the predicates.

## OPINION IDENTIFICATION

The approach described in this chapter is influenced by SentiWordNet, a lexical resource for opinion mining. In SentiWordNet, to each

*Figure 1. A framework for ontology-based opinion mining*

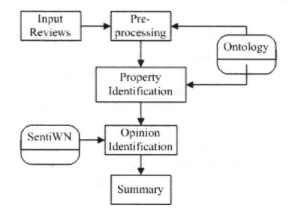

*Figure 2. An interaction between ontology and property identification*

synset (logical groupings) of WordNet, a triple of polarity scores is assigned i.e., a positivity, negativity and objectivity score. The sum of these scores is always 1. For example the triple {0, 1, 0} (positivity, negativity, objectivity) is assigned to the synset of the term "bad." The sum of all scores of this synset is 1. SentiWordNet has been created automatically by means of a combination of linguistic and statistic classifiers. It has been applied in different opinion-related tasks, i.e. for subjectivity analysis and sentiment analysis with promising results.

The document polarity is calculated from the sentence polarities. Therefore, a document is firstly dissected into sentences. Then, for each sentence the polarity is determined by means of SentiWordNet. Each word is stemmed and tagged, stop words are removed. If a stemmed word belongs to one of the word classes "adjective," "verb" or "noun," it is looked up in SentiWordNet. The scores of corresponding synsets are collected. Provided that $n$ corresponding synsets for a word $A$ with part of speech $o$ exist, a sentiment score triple ($score_{pos}$, $score_{neg}$, $score_{obj}$) is determined by means of:

$$score_{pos}(A) = \frac{1}{n} \sum_{i=1}^{n} score_{pos}(i) \qquad (1)$$

$$score_{neg}(A) = \frac{1}{n} \sum_{i=1}^{n} score_{neg}(i) \qquad (2)$$

$$score_{obj}(A) = \frac{1}{n} \sum_{i=1}^{n} score_{obj}(i) \qquad (3)$$

with $score_{\{pos|neg|obj\}}(i)$ = {positivity | negativity |objectivity}—score of synset $i$ for term $A$ and $n$ = number of synsets of term $A$. The scores of all terms within a sentence are in turn added and divided by the number of terms with scores.

## Example

Considering the sentence "The fjord tour, though, is good." that is stemmed, stop words are removed.

The resulting string is "tour good." These two words are searched in SentiWordNet for corresponding synsets. For the input term "tour," SentiWordNet provides only synsets with positivity = 0, negativity = 0, objectivity = 1. For the input term "good," SentiWordNet contains 33 synset entries. After summing up the different scores and dividing the sum by the number of synsets, the resulting values are: positivity = 0.57, negativity = 0.03, objectivity = 0.4. The sentence score triple results from summing up the score triple of each term and dividing each score by the number of considered terms. The resulting triple for this sentence is: positivity = 0.285, negativity = 0.015, objectivity = 0.7.

The mentioned procedure results in a triple of {positivity, negativity, objectivity}-values for each sentence. To determine a score-triple for a document, the sentence score triples are added and normalized by the number of sentences (in the same manner as in above Formulas 1-3). The scores are used in two different ways to classify a document "positive" or "negative." One approach (b) applies a classification rule according to which each document whose positivity score is larger than or equal to the negativity score is classified as "positive." Otherwise, it is considered "negative."

Using the final lists of positive, negative, and neutral words or phrases, we analyze the opinion orientation expressed on each property. Actually, we limit the sentiment analysis on the node of the model, because, some people are not very interested about properties, they just want to know the general information about the hotel. E.g., maybe people do not understand much terminologies in this area, they just wants to know the overall opinion about one hotel, this is obviously, what this user wants to know is a high-level predicate but not the information of a node. In this case, we need to use the hierarchy structure to calculate the opinion of high-level predicate.

## RESULTS

We have analysed the proposed idea to see how effective it is for opinion mining. The proposed method has been evaluated the review data set, which contains around 1350 hotel review documents randomly selected from diy travel (guide. diytravel.co.uk) for analyzing. Half of the hotel reviews are positive and the other half negative. We randomly select 25 positive review documents and 25 negative reviews to test. For the 50 documents, we label the properties as shown in Table 1.

In this analysis, we consider the properties as baseline in contrast to the results from the proposed method, which is combined with ontology.

The findings signify that the accuracy is satisfied, and it is sufficient to compute the score by the proposed method. As the selected dataset is already labeled, we use the origin class label (pos and neg) as baseline, which is contrast to the result output from the proposed method. We inspect every property in each sentence, and analyze the opinion associated with them. By using the analysis mentioned in this chapter, we can get not only the opinion for the entire review, but also each opinion on each property. The proposed technique can detect the properties, which are terminologies in the domain, and the opinions on them.

## FUTURE RESEARCH DIRECTIONS

Ontology development and review parsing mostly rely on manual resources. The next step will be the automatic creation of such resources. Ontology learning is a process of learning an ontology automatically from related textual documents and resources. In addition, subjectivity analysis can be conducted to differentiate subjective expressions from objective facts using some lexical resources. Further, text decomposition in accordance with semantics-based text themes is an important future challenge.

*Table 1. Examples for properties*

| Review sentence | Properties |
|---|---|
| You need to have a sea view to really appreciate this Hotel, as the views must be amongst the best in Benidorm. | Sea view |
| The rooms are old but clean, and we found fantastic service. | Fantastic, clean, old |
| A lot of hassle in hotel street and do not buy cigarettes in hotel they are terrible. The place is too hot in August. | Terrible |

The research efforts considered in this chapter highlight the sensitivity, ambiguity, and variety of natural languages that people use in expressing their opinions. There clearly is a need to further refine properties indicating semantic divergence for unsupervised techniques. First, generic semantic lexicons can be customized for specific domains. Moreover, domain lexicons or dictionaries may add to disambiguation.

Many opinion mining and sentiment analysis approaches are lexicon-based, and many use the popular "bag of words" representation that ignores lexical relationships between words. Given the complexities of human language, these techniques can take us only so far. Because of the complex nature of sentiments, more sophisticated tools are needed to fully take advantage of semantic information in text. Some work has been done, but still much to come in adopting tools developed for other tasks for Sentiment Analysis. Moreover, opinion mining can be used to address larger problems like opinion tracking.

## CONCLUSION

Ontology is a predicate model that describes system at the level of semantics and knowledge. It aims to access knowledge of a domain in a general way and provides a common understanding for predicates in the domain so as to realize knowledge. Opinion mining is a demanding problem, which is to analyze opinions which appear in a series of texts and given by users towards different properties, and determine whether these opinions are positive, negative, or neutral and how strong they are. In this chapter, we focus on employing ontology to mining tour planning reviews. Because ontology aims to provide knowledge about specific domains that are understandable by both developers and computers. In the course of discussion we demonstrate how it is rational and effective to employ ontology to opinion mining.

# REFERENCES

Aaberge, T. (2009). On intensional interpretations of scientific theories. In *Proceedings of the 32nd International Wittgenstein Symposium, LWS.* LWS.

Aaberge, T. (2010). Picturing semantic relations. In *Proceedings of the 33nd International Wittgenstein Symposium, LWS.* LWS.

Akerkar, R. (2009). *Foundations of the semantic web – XML, RDF & ontology.* Oxford, UK: Alpha Science.

Carenini, G., Ng, R., & Pauls, A. (2006). Interactive multimedia summaries of evaluative text. In *Proceedings of the 11th International Conference on Intelligent User Interfaces,* (pp. 124–131). ACM Press.

Dave, K., Lawrence, S., & Pennock, D. (2003). Mining the peanut gallery: Opinion extraction and semantic classification of product reviews. In *Proceedings of the 12th International Conference on World Wide Web,* (pp. 519–528). ACM Press.

Ding, X., & Liu, B. (2007). The utility of linguistic rules in opinion mining. In *Proceedings of SIGIR 2007.* SIGIR.

Gamon, M., Aue, A., Corston-Oliver, S., & Ringger, E. (2005). Pulse: Mining customer opinions from free text. *Lecture Notes in Computer Science, 3646,* 121–132. doi:10.1007/11552253_12

Godbole, N., Srinivasaiah, M., & Skiena, S. (2007). LargeScale sentiment analysis for news and blogs. [ICWSM.]. *Proceedings of ICWSM, 2007,* 219–222.

Gruber, T. R. (1993). A translation approach to portable ontology specifications. *Knowledge Acquisition, 5,* 199–220. doi:10.1006/knac.1993.1008

Hearst, M. A. (2001). Direction-based text interpretation as an information access refinement . In *Text-Based Intelligent Systems* (pp. 257–274). Hillsdale, NJ: Lawrence Erlbaum Associates Inc.

Hu, M., & Liu, B. (2004a). Mining and summarizing customer reviews. In *Proceedings of ACM SIGKDD Conference.* ACM Press.

Hu, M., & Liu, B. (2004b). Mining opinion features in customer reviews. In *Proceedings of AAAI,* (pp. 755–760). AAAI.

Jacquemin, C. (2006). *Spotting and discovering terms through natural language processing.* Cambridge, MA: MIT Press.

Kanayama, H., & Nasukawa, T. (2006). Fully automatic lexicon expansion for domain oriented sentiment analysis. In *Proceedings of the Conference on Empirical Methods in Natural Language Processing, EMNLP 2006.* EMNLP.

Kobayashi, N., Inui, K., & Matsumoto, Y. (2004). Collecting evaluative express for opinion extraction. In *Proceedings of the International Joint Conference on Natural Language Processing, IJCNLP.* IJCNLP.

Pang, B., & Lee, L. (2005). Seeing stars: Exploiting class relationships for sentiment categorization with respect to rating scales. In *Proceedings of ACL 2005, 43rd Meeting of Categorization with Respect to Rating Scales.* Ann. Arbor, MI: ACL.

Pang, B., Lee, L., & Vaithyanathan, S. (2002). Thumbs up? Sentiment classification using machine learning techniques. In *Proceedings of the Conference on Empirical Methods in Natural Language Processing, EMNLP 2002.* EMNLP.

Popescu, A. M., & Etzioni, O. (2005). Extracting product features and opinions from reviews. In *Proceedings of the Conference on Empirical Methods in Natural Language Processing, EMNLP 2005*. EMNLP.

Riloff, E., & Wiebe, J. (2003). Learning extraction patterns for subjective expressions. In *Proceedings of the Conference on Empirical Methods in Natural Language Processing (EMNLP 2003)*, (pp. 105–112). EMNLP.

Tarski, A. (1983). *Logics, semantics, metamatematics*. Indianapolis, IN: Hackett Publishing Company, Inc.

Turney, P., et al. (2002). Thumbs up or thumbs down? Semantic orientation applied to unsupervised classification of reviews. In *Proceedings of the 40th Annual Meeting of the Association for Computational Linguistics*, (pp. 417–424). ACL.

Yi, J., Bunescu, T. N., & Niblack, R. W. (2003). Sentiment analyzer: Extracting sentiments about a given topic using natural language processing techniques. In *Proceedings of IEEE International Conference on Data Mining, ICDM 2003*. IEEE Press.

## KEY TERMS AND DEFINITIONS

**Ontology:** *Ontology* is the theory of objects and their ties. It provides criteria for distinguishing different types of objects (concrete and abstract, existent and nonexistent, real and ideal, independent and dependent) and their ties (relations, dependencies and predication).

**Ontology for an Object Language:** An ontology for an object language is a set of axioms, intensional definitions, and extensional definitions.

**Opinion Mining:** Opinion Mining is about automatically getting to know what people think on an item (brand, product, anything) from their explicit opinions in blogs, comments to blogs posts and news stories, Social Networks, elsewhere in the Web. It involves Natural Language Processing of texts in order to identify the polarity of opinions (like, dislike, neutral), and many more.

**Sentiment Analysis:** Sentiment analysis aims to determine the attitude of a speaker or a writer with respect to some topic or the overall tonality of a document. The attitude may be his or her judgment or evaluation, affective state, or the intended emotional communication.

# Chapter 19
# Intermediary Design for Collaborative Ontology– Based Innovation Monitoring

**Jan Zibuschka**
*Fraunhofer IAO, Germany*

**Uwe Laufs**
*Fraunhofer IAO, Germany*

**Wolf Engelbach**
*Fraunhofer IAO, Germany*

## ABSTRACT

*This chapter presents the architecture of an intermediary platform for networked open innovation management, as well as a surrounding sustainable business ecosystem. The instantiation presented here is tailored towards SMEs, both as stakeholders in the platform and as contributors in the modular ecosystem. It enables SMEs to work together in creating innovative products, increasing both reach and agility of their innovation processes. The chapter also describes to some detail the technical realization of the system, including the representation and automatic acquisition of relevant information. Selected business aspects are also addressed. It specifically focuses on the role of ontologies and how they contribute to the overall business value of the system.*

## INTRODUCTION

Innovations are becoming more and more crucial to the success of an enterprise due to the increasing competitiveness of the globalised economy. The development of new technologies, products, and services offers an effective means to differentiate against competitors. However, to avoid leapfrogging and imitation, innovative enterprises need to be agile and flexible in bringing innovations to the market (Horii & Iwaisako, 2007). Information systems have the potential to significantly contribute to enterprises' success in this context (Dhillon, Stahl, & Baskerville, 2009).

DOI: 10.4018/978-1-4666-2494-8.ch019

Copyright © 2013, IGI Global. Copying or distributing in print or electronic forms without written permission of IGI Global is prohibited.

While the adoption of Open Innovation practices in SMEs is growing, it is much lower than in larger enterprises, depriving them of a central strategy for increased growth and competitiveness (van de Vrande, de Jong, Vanhaverbeke, & de Rochemont, 2009). Some SMEs are active in value creation networks, but those are often geographically limited by collocation factors, a barrier not faced by multinational enterprises (Davenport, 2005).

This chapter presents a design for an intermediary system supporting innovation managers from SMEs and related stakeholders, fostering dialogue in networked innovation management and hopefully involving more SMEs in wider-ranging Open Innovation activities. The platform addresses directly involved stakeholders (innovation funders, innovation intermediaries, innovation explorers), but also offers a broader ecosystem (in the sense of Peltoniemi [2004] a sustainable value network in which enterprises "work co-operatively and competitively to support new products, satisfy customer needs, and eventually incorporate the next round of innovations") for suppliers of related applications, such as product lifecycle management.

We present the design of an intermediary platform, used for monitoring innovations based on information sources from the Web, illustrate its business value, and show how ontologies contribute to it both from a technological and business perspective.

## BACKGROUND

There have been several papers investigating the deployment of Web 2.0 technologies in the context of innovative SMEs and SME networks, such as the ones by Lindermann, Valcárcel, Schaarschmidt, and von Kortzfleisch (2009) as well as Blinn, Lindermann, Fäcks, and Nüttgens (2009). Those papers offer a requirements analysis and first steps in a design science approach, but no resulting artifact has been presented yet. Duin et al. (2008)

present components for such a system, but do not integrate them or discuss their business value. We are not the first to use ontologies in innovation management; similar approaches are presented by Li, Wang, Li, and Zhao (2007).

We use a combination of social and semantic Web to mitigate the chicken-egg effect. This is discussed in much more detail by Ankolekar, Krötzsch, Tran, and Vrandecic (2008). However, we introduce it to innovation management and illustrate its value in this use case.

## INTERMEDIARY DESIGN

### Issues, Controversies, Problems

While existing approaches focus either on the participating SMEs, and supporting communications between them, capturing the knowledge of the non-executive workers, or capturing the users' knowledge, business perspectives on integrated platforms for innovation management are few, far in between, and often not satisfactory documented from a scientific perspective. We present in this work an approach integrating a wider set of stakeholders in the Open Innovation process, tools for innovation management, and underlying technologies. We document it by presenting a reference architecture for an innovation management intermediary integrating a comprehensive set of components, and demonstrate overall viability and fit of the components in a wider business platform supporting innovation management in SMEs. We specifically focus on the contributions of ontologies in creating business value as basis technology for the platform and by enabling integration within the ecosystem.

### Solutions and Recommendations

We propose as pivotal element of an Open Innovation ecosystem an intermediary platform integrating a broad set of stakeholders (see Figure 1), as also proposed by e.g. Lichtenthaler and

*Figure 1. Overview of system architecture*

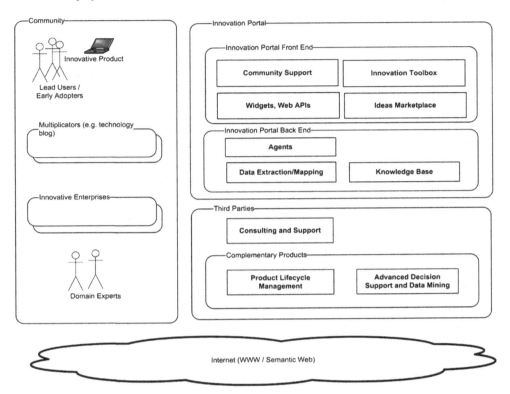

Ernst (2008). The intermediary architecture has several advantages in this context. Intermediaries are a viable business architecture for SMEs that do not have the capabilities or resources to deploy their own enterprise systems (Lockett & Brown, 2005), in this case facilities for managing Open Innovation projects.

Specifically, they have the potential to aggregate common and field-specific knowledge bases. They also aid in acceleration and standardization of innovation-related information exchange, and support the formation of temporary virtual organizations (Carlsson, Corvello, & Migliarese, 2009). Additionally, the hosted application service provider paradigm also shared by our Web based intermediary platform is identified as the most viable means of engaging SMEs in complex e-business activities in the area of innovation. One advantage of intermediary deployments is that they enable participating SMEs to benefit from

the feedback provided by the customers of competing products (Sawhney, Verona, & Prandelli, 2005).

Additionally, the intermediary platform supports various deployment possibilities, allowing for neutral parties or trusted parties within an ecosystem to deploy the platform, increasing trustworthiness. Potential candidates for operation of the platform include independent organizations not themselves competing in the business domains of the participating SMEs (e.g. dedicated start-ups or research organizations), as well as SME networking organizations or cooperatives.

This work presents results from an ongoing research project aiming at implementing a platform supporting innovation management. Implementation of the design and establishment of the surrounding ecosystem is ongoing; however, the components described here have already been implemented in cooperation with various stakeholders. Interviews with those stakeholders have also informed the platform design, which has evolved over several iterations, and has been discussed in the context of several application fields.

## System Architecture

An overview of the overall proposed architecture is given in Figure 1. The intermediary platform offers several core services supporting the networked innovation management process. We can only give an overview of the components here, we refer the interested reader to Bullinger (2009), which describes many of the components in considerable detail. We also give additional related work for the components here, to allow for a convincing representation while preserving the overall structure of this contribution.

The main components of the envisioned core innovation intermediary platform are:

- A community portal, acting as the entry point, hosting community support services and information and gathering a community of practice consisting of innovative businesses and early adopters taking advantage of social networking features (e.g. discussion forums, facilities for defining and maintaining their social graph and contacts). Those features integrate with a project and partner matching component, aiding participants e.g. in identifying interesting project fields, or identifying potential partners for projects in certain areas.
- A set of agents extracting information from available external data sources on the WWW or Semantic Web, such as software agents extracting information from publication databases, technology blogs, or semantic services on the Internet of knowledge. Semantic technologies will be implemented to assess the relevance of what they sense and subsequently, filter information.

- Semantic Knowledge Base aggregating information from agents, user feedback, experiences from previous projects and data mining. This data will be the base for e.g. technology forecasting and decision support in different phases of network-centric innovation processes.
- Widgets and Web APIs supporting innovation management, such as the ones described in Huber, Bretschneider, Leimeister, and Krcmar (2009) and Zhu and Porter (2002), ousourcing control of AI learning processes for the data processing and aggregation steps, to improve the foresight capabilities of the intermediary platform. Offering tools to users to motivate them to contribute in open innovation processes is discussed in some detail in von Hippel and Katz (2002).
- An Innovation Toolbox, based on the trademarked process described in Cooper (2008) and Ettlie and Elsenbach (2007), guiding the user's through the phases of the early innovation process. The toolbox integrates available widgets, APIs, and the Ideas Marketplace, as mandated by the identified phase of the innovation process.
- An open product/service Ideas Marketplace bringing product and service ideas, users and enterprises together in a bazaar-like environment to form both general market solutions and specialised, customised services. This component is based on existing commercial idea marketplaces, e.g. by Innocentive (Innocentive, 2010). The incentive model is based on research by Järvilehto, Leppälä, and Similä (2008), however, the component is designed to be flexible and extensible.

Additionally, we have identified several areas where the portal functionality can be supplemented by third party services, applications, or software components, giving an impression of the ecosystem we hope to form around the innovation intermediary. Of course, we hope that innovative contributors will come up with additional components we do not foresee at this time, which is part of the value of the ecosystem approach (Peltoniemi, 2004). We provide the following illustrative examples:

- A protocol definition allowing collaboration tools implementing it to be able to become part of a temporary network of businesses or individuals within a innovative product/service ecosystem (see Figure 2), based on the enterprise collaboration protocols investigated in the EU projects TRUSTCOM (Wilson, et al., 2006) and SYNERGY (Popplewell, et al., 2008). The portal-only mode is aimed at small SMEs, leveraging a software as a service approach to lower the barriers they are facing when

entering enterprise collaboration systems (Brown & Lockett, 2007).

- Based on that, an integrated product/service lifecycle management tool (Sharma, 2005), supporting a team built around an innovation idea in the later phases of innovation and product lifecycle management. Such a tool can integrate into the intermediary platform by extending the approach established for the innovation management cockpit (Ettlie & Elsenbach, 2007; Bullinger, 2009) and described in more detail in section 5.

- A data mining component (Finzen, Kintz, Kett, & Koch, 2009), providing inputs from additional data sources (beyond the extracting agents mentioned above) and laying the basis for an advanced decision support infrastructure with regard to e.g. technology forecasting or ex-ante valuation of innovations.

*Figure 2. Interoperable collaboration protocol*

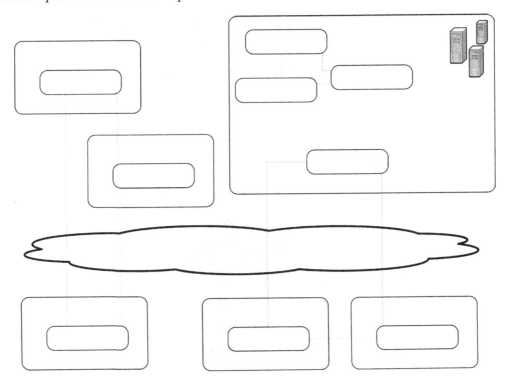

## Process Overview

Our platform supports involves various stakeholders. We assume the following roles: a platform developer providing the basic software, a platform operator hosting the platform for a specific domain or SME network (which may or may not be the same as the software developer), a participating organization, and an end-user giving feedback to the platform. We also considered several additional multiplication roles contributing indirectly to the platform, e.g. by using its widgets (see Figure 1). The platform itself as well as the ecosystems it tries to support stakeholder inclusion to support agility in development at many levels. Ontologies contribute significantly to this approach: they enable the software developer to provide a tweakable software platform to the platform operator, who in turn can meet the requirements of his specific business domain and participating organizations.

The structural architecture of the platform can be illustrated by its two main components, front end and back end. The back end provides knowledge acquisition and knowledge base functionalities as well as a module for processing and integrating acquired information. Aggregated information is presented to the user by the front end (see Figure 3), which also provides feedback to the back end for input to the data processing and aggregation components. The main steps are:

*Automatic Knowledge Acquisition:* Within the World Wide Web already a lot of structured or semi-structured information exists which can be queried using standardized interfaces. For example, the Open Search interface provides access to several content management systems, blogging systems, and search engines, and can be used to retrieve information from many existing sources in the Web. Information sources without a dedicated external interface often can also be accessed using bots and parsers with additional effort for interfacing, extraction and additional maintenance efforts in case of changing structures of the information sources. The platform focuses on the acquisition of time variant indicator data retrieved from the Web. These indicators include:

- Results from search engines returned for a specified term (e.g. generic search engines or specialized search engines for scientific papers, blogs, books, or domain specific catalogues). Data is automatically extracted via the Web interface.
- Data retrieved via dedicated interfaces (e.g. Web services provided by online book dealers)

*Figure 3. Web data extraction and processing*

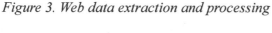

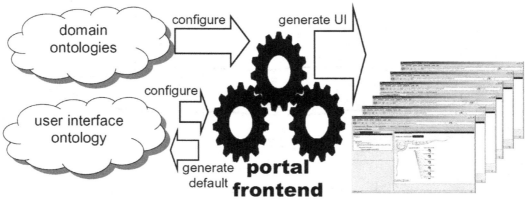

- Data semi-automatically extracted from charts by image processing (e.g. usage statistics provided by search engines)

*Knowledge Base:* In the domain of innovation, different kinds of information are available in different formats, systems and with a varying grade of formalization ranging from plain text to highly structured information. Against the background of proprietary implementations and heterogeneous data structures as well as semantic differences there is a need for an integrative way to represent this data.

We use ontologies to integrate information from various platform-internal and external sources (see Knowledge Acquisition, above) as well as across platform components (Ideas Market, Innovation Toolbox, etc.).

*Visualization and User Feedback:* The portal provides customizable templates for information presentation and community inclusion (see the Front End section), which are essential in the context of Web-mining approaches to realize collaborative feedback mechanisms for calibrating the Web mining Artificial Intelligence (AI) used for information aggregation. Current AI approaches are not capable of producing convincing results for all domains without supervision. Outsourcing this control of the learning process to stakeholders, such as groups of domain experts or customer

end users from the Web and integrating applicable components into the workflows of the portal (e.g. the innovation marketplace) is a valuable contribution to the viability of ontology-based mining processes, realizing a semi-supervised learning in the sense of Chang, Kayed, Girgis, and Shaalan (2006).

Ontologies contribute significantly on all the process steps shown in Figure 4.

*Data source description ontologies (Automatic Knowledge Acquisition):* To enable appropriate processing of automatically acquired information, ontologies are used to describe relevant properties of data sources and the information they provide. For example, blogs provide up-to-date information while information in books often can be regarded as less up-to-date but more credible. In addition, information sources can differ regarding their relevance in different knowledge domains. Therefore, the data source ontology plays a key part in making it easy to integrate various information sources on the Web, and significantly lowers barriers associated with integrating data sources existing within the platform into new domains. It also enables a structured process for integrating new data sources, reducing configuration costs. Finally, user interfaces for these steps can be derived from the ontology, minimizing platform implementation costs.

*Figure 4. Ontologies in the system*

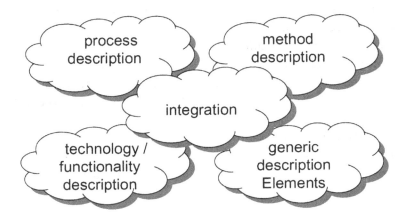

*Innovation domain description ontologies (Knowledge Base):* Regarding the different domains in which the platform may be used, domain specific aspects are modeled in domain specific ontologies. The focus of these ontologies is on categorizing retrieved results as well as on providing domain specific configuration information for data processing. They contribute to the adaptability of the system to different innovation domains, significantly broadening its appeal, and reducing configuration costs. They also assist in the categorization of innovative technologies, leading to a common taxonomy shared by system stakeholders, which reduces friction and leads to an increased agility of innovation processes. Storing relevant information using ontologies makes it possible to compare and potentially aggregate stored information from different sources and domains, enabling a reduction to human-understandable dimensions, which can be passed to the frontend for visualization, and enables effective gathering of feedback. Automatically retrieved information is aggregated to different indicators, e.g. as a measure of maturity of innovations.

*User interface customization ontologies (Visualization and User Feedback):* Ontologies also assist in the customization of the user interface, supporting a semi-automatic generation of the system front-end from domain ontologies for various innovation domains (which in turn address various data sources). This leads to a high configurability of the front-end to end-user requirements while minimizing costs for minor changes. The Java Platform Enterprise Edition (JEE) and an ontology-based knowledge base are used to create Web-based user interfaces semi-automatically from existing ontologies, which leads to reduced implementation efforts and increased flexibility regarding future portal changes.

The following sections will dive deeper into implementation details to further illustrate the role and implementation of ontologies.

## Portal Back-End Implementation

The portal backend is based on JEE. In our architecture, portal backend is responsible for providing required basic. The portal back end is sub-divided into two modules, one for ontology access and management, the other for ontology and individual analysis.

Based on HPs Jena Framework, ontology individuals can be stored in files and be processed in memory as well as in relational databases. This makes possible to choose between high runtime performance and the ability to store large amounts of information. The ontology access and management module also abstracts the implementation based on Jena, which allows replacing the implementation if required. In principle, any data storage system could be integrated to store or retrieve information via the given interface. This especially can be valuable feature regarding the virtual (read only) integration of existing data sources like e.g. enterprise resource planning systems. The ontology access and management module is heavily used for storing and retrieving information of the domain description ontologies as well as the user interface customization ontology.

The ontology analysis module provides analysis functionality regarding the ontologies used in the portal. It implements basic analysis functionality for ontology meta-structures:

- Analysis of ontology concept hierarchies, cardinalities, restrictions.
- Analysis regarding data type or object properties contained in ontologies.

The provided analysis functionality is required especially for ontology and rule based user interface default generation described in the following section.

The module also integrates the Pellet reasoner, which offers a large amount of analysis functionality. Reasoning and basic analysis functionality is heavily used for analysis of domain taxonomies provided by the platform operators or semi-supervised by users.

While information source and credibility are described by the data source description ontologies, the derived domain specific individuals are validated by the community members to achieve higher knowledge quality stored in the innovation domain ontologies as individuals. Based on this information, queries and rules are used to derive additional information. This information is also validated by the community.

The configured or derived domain description ontologies are used as a basis for the storage format of information in the knowledge base. They also serve as a basis for the frontend data display as configured by the UI ontologies. They also serve as a base for the interoperability protocol and communication within the platform.

## Portal Front-End Implementation

Regarding the given dynamic in the field of innovation, user interfaces have to be adaptable to frequent changes induced by the domain requirements. The approach to achieve this and the components involved are described in the following section.

The platform offers a wide range of user interface components, which can be combined to complex Web based user interfaces. There are several elements, which allow structuring of the User Interface (UI) components.

- **Perspectives:** Perspectives are a well-known concept, which allow customization of full screen content and also switching between various views.
- **Containers, Frames, and Framesets:** Perspectives can be subdivided using Frames and framesets. Within frames, UI elements can be grouped and organized in containers.

- **Elements:** Elements include all non-structuring standalone user interface components such as widgets (buttons, text fields, etc.).

The User Interface configuration module realizes the functionality required for providing configurable user interfaces on the domain ontologies. For new or changed domain ontologies, default user interface configurations are created. Missing configurations are created "on the fly" and can be refined afterwards. User interface configurations are realized and stored in user interface ontologies (see Figure 5).

Figure 6 shows a default user interface generated from a non-customized domain ontology. The default user interface ontology provides an instantly working scaffolding mechanism and allows browsing and modification operations on the whole domain ontology.

The generation of default user interface configuration can be adjusted using rules, which are formulated in a UI ontology. Rules can be based on domain ontology content or meta-information, e.g. it can be stated as a rule that specific widgets that visualize textual properties of domain ontologies shall be used based on any of the following criteria:

- Class of the domain ontology concept.
- XML datatype of the property.
- Defined restrictions defined in the domain ontology.
- Defined cardinalities.
- Specific URIs of specific domain ontology elements.

Specific changes to all parts of the generated user interface configurations can be applied in detail. Figure 7 shows a configured Web based user interface. In the illustrated case, an individual of the concept "technology" is displayed for editing and browsing of related items. The generated

*Figure 5. Customization and fallback to defaults during user interface aggregation*

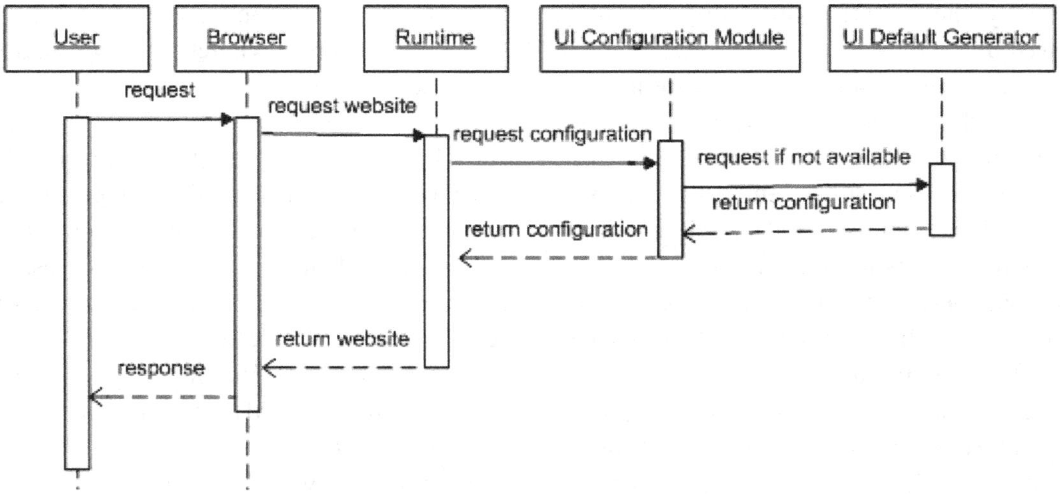

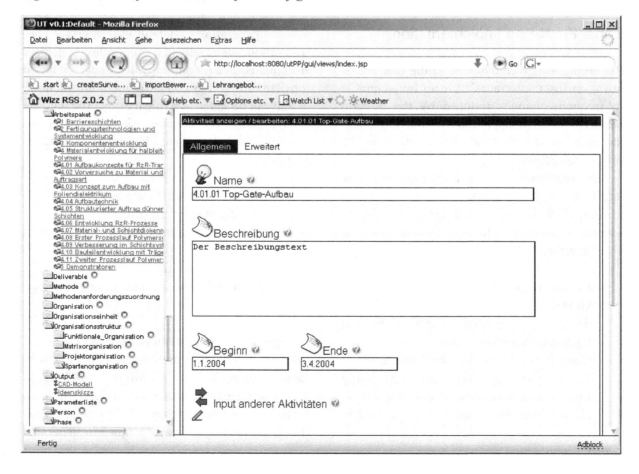

*Figure 6. User interface based on default configuration*

*Figure 7. Customized user interface*

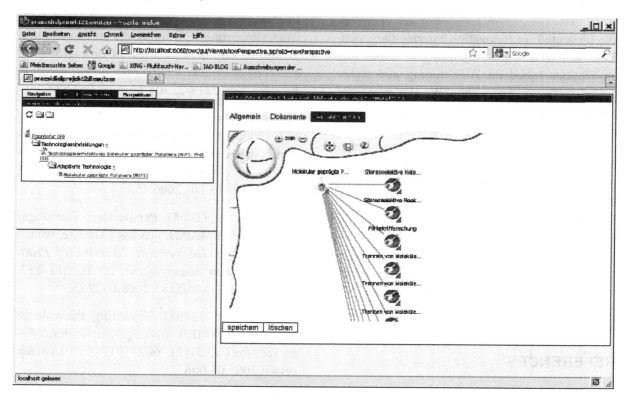

configuration is modified regarding the navigation on the left. In addition, a flash-based viewer is added which shows the dependencies between the individual and related manufacturing methods.

## FUTURE RESEARCH DIRECTIONS

While the design of the platform is already based on stakeholder interviews, an integrated version of the system will again be evaluated by application partners to provide feedback about the applicability of the resulting instantiation. While technological viability has already been demonstrated, this will give final feedback about business viability before the final deployment.

In addition, different implementation details of the platform can only be fully evaluated in the final design, such as user interfaces for feedback into the mining steps or secure data integration mechanisms (the current state of the art has been surveyed here, but for the first demonstrator, underlying security mechanisms were not implemented).

With regard to the business value of ontologies, comparative quantitative investigations should be enabled when the platform presented here is instantiated in different application fields. This will allow for direct quantification of the contribution to flexibility. The first instantiation which has already been performed indicates that the implementation effort may well have been reduced by 80% (or about one person year) due to UI ontologies and code generation alone. It remains to be seen whether this is applicable to all application fields. Similarly, the data source ontologies have only been implemented for one instantiation with quite encouraging results, however, we will only be able to evaluate their reusability after additional instantiations.

# CONCLUSION

We presented an innovation intermediary platform architecture for monitoring of trends and innovations based on Web mining and stakeholder inclusion approaches. We also presented a comprehensive set of integrated components, and demonstrated overall viability and fit of the components in a wider business platform supporting innovation management in SMEs. We specifically focused on the contributions of ontologies in creating business value as basis technology for the platform and by enabling integration within the ecosystem, determining dimensions of business value potentially applicable beyond the innovation management use case. We presented selected implementation details to further highlight the role of ontologies in the system.

# REFERENCES

Ankolekar, A., Krötzsch, M., Tran, T., & Vrandecic, D. (2008). The two cultures: Mashing up web 2.0 and the semantic web. *Web Semantics: Science. Services and Agents on the World Wide Web, 6*(1), 70–75. doi:10.1016/j.websem.2007.11.005

Blinn, N., Lindermann, N., Fäcks, K., & Nüttgens, M. (2009). Web 2.0 in SME networks - A design science approach considering multi-perspective requirements. In *Proceedings of Value Creation in E-Business Management* (pp. 271–283). Academic Press. doi:10.1007/978-3-642-03132-8_22

Brown, D. H., & Lockett, N. (2007). E-business, innovation and SMEs: The significance of hosted services and firm aggregations. *International Journal of Entrepreneurship and Innovation Management, 7*(1), 92–112. doi:10.1504/IJEIM.2007.012175

Bullinger, H. (2009). *Fokus technologie.* München, Germany: Carl Hanser Verlag.

Carlsson, S., Corvello, V., & Migliarese, P. (2009). Enabling open innovation: Proposal of a framework supporting ICT and KMS implementation in web-based intermediaries. In *Proceedings of the 17th European Conference on Information Systems,* (pp. 2218-2230). Verona, Italy: ECIS.

Chang, C., Kayed, M., Girgis, M. R., & Shaalan, K. F. (2006). A survey of web information extraction systems. *IEEE Transactions on Knowledge and Data Engineering, 18*(10), 1411–1428. doi:10.1109/TKDE.2006.152

Cooper, R. G. (2008). Perspective: The stage-gate(R) idea-to-launch process - Update, what's new, and NexGen systems. *Journal of Product Innovation Management, 25*(3), 213–232. doi:10.1111/j.1540-5885.2008.00296.x

Davenport, S. (2005). Exploring the role of proximity in SME knowledge-acquisition. *Research Policy, 34*(5), 683–701. doi:10.1016/j.respol.2005.03.006

Dhillon, G., Stahl, B., & Baskerville, R. (2009). Creativity and intelligence in small and medium sized enterprises: The role of information systems. In *Proceedings of the Information Systems – Creativity and Innovation in Small and Medium-Sized Enterprises,* (pp. 1-9). IEEE.

Duin, H., Geven, A., Dittenberger, S., Tscheligi, M., Hesmer, A., & Thoben, K. D. (2008). A toolset to support the early stage of innovation. *Towards New Challenges for Innovative Management Practices, 2*(1), 111–118.

Ettlie, J. E., & Elsenbach, J. M. (2007). Modified stage-gate® regimes in new product development. *Journal of Product Innovation Management, 24*(1), 20–33. doi:10.1111/j.1540-5885.2006.00230.x

Finzen, J., Kintz, M., Kett, H., & Koch, S. (2009). Strategic innovation management on the basis of searching and mining press releases. In *Proceedings of the Fifth International Conference on Web Information Systems and Technologies.* Lisbon, Portugal: INSTICC Press.

Horii, R., & Iwaisako, T. (2007). Economic growth with imperfect protection of intellectual property rights. *Journal of Economics*, *90*(1), 45–85. doi:10.1007/s00712-006-0222-6

Huber, M., Bretschneider, U., Leimeister, J., & Krcmar, H. (2009). Making innovation happen: Tool-support for software related communities for innovations. In *Proceedings of the Open Design Spaces Supporting User Innovation*, (pp. 22-32). Bonn, Germany: IISI.

Innocentive. (2010). *Website*. Retrieved from http://www.innocentive.com/

Järvilehto, M., Leppälä, K., & Similä, J. (2008). Communicative incentives in consumer innovation brokering. In *Proceedings of the Hawaii International Conference on System Sciences*, (p. 418). Los Alamitos, CA: IEEE Computer Society.

Li, Y., Wang, J., Li, X., & Zhao, W. (2007). Design creativity in product innovation. *International Journal of Advanced Manufacturing Technology*, *33*(3), 213–222. doi:10.1007/s00170-006-0457-y

Lichtenthaler, U., & Ernst, H. (2008). Intermediary services in the markets for technology: Organizational antecedents and performance consequences. *Organization Studies*, *29*(7), 1003–1035. doi:10.1177/0170840608090531

Lindermann, N., Valcárcel, S., Schaarschmidt, M., & von Kortzfleisch, H. (2009). SME 2.0: Roadmap towards web 2.0-based open innovation in SME-networks. In *Proceedings of Creativity and Innovation in Small and Medium-Sized Enterprises*, (pp. 28-41). Academic Press.

Lockett, N. J., & Brown, D. H. (2005). An SME perspective of vertical application service providers. *International Journal of Enterprise Information Systems*, *1*(2), 37–55. doi:10.4018/jeis.2005040103

Peltoniemi, M. (2004). Cluster, value network and business ecosystem: Knowledge and innovation approach. In *Proceedings of Organisations, Innovation and Complexity: New Perspectives on the Knowledge Economy*, (pp. 9–10). NEXSUS.

Popplewell, K., Stojanovic, N., Abecker, A., Apostolou, D., Mentzas, G., & Harding, J. (2008). Supporting adaptive enterprise collaboration through semantic knowledge services. [Springer.]. *Proceedings of Enterprise Interoperability*, *III*, 381–393. doi:10.1007/978-1-84800-221-0_30

Sawhney, M., Verona, G., & Prandelli, E. (2005). Collaborating to create: The internet as a platform for customer engagement in product innovation. *Journal of Interactive Marketing*, *19*(4), 4–17. doi:10.1002/dir.20046

Sharma, A. (2005). Collaborative product innovation: Integrating elements of CPI via PLM framework. *Computer Aided Design*, *37*(13), 1425–1434. doi:10.1016/j.cad.2005.02.012

van de Vrande, V., de Jong, J. P., Vanhaverbeke, W., & de Rochemont, M. (2009). Open innovation in SMEs: Trends, motives and management challenges. *Technovation*, *29*(6-7), 423–437. doi:10.1016/j.technovation.2008.10.001

von Hippel, E., & Katz, R. (2002). Shifting innovation to users via toolkits. *Management Science*, *48*(7), 821–833. doi:10.1287/mnsc.48.7.821.2817

Wilson, M., Arenas, A., Chadwick, D., Dimitrakos, T., Doser, J., Giambiagi, P., et al. (2006). The TrustCoM approach to enforcing agreements between interoperating enterprises. In *Proceedings of the Interoperability for Enterprise Software and Applications Conference (I-ESA 2006)*, (pp. 365–375). I-ESA.

Zhu, D., & Porter, A. (2002). Automated extraction and visualization of information for technological intelligence and forecasting. *Technological Forecasting and Social Change, 69*, 495–506. doi:10.1016/S0040-1625(01)00157-3

## ADDITIONAL READING

Bügel, U., Knaf, H., & Laufs, U. (2012). Technologieentwicklung: Theoretische und praktische unterstützung mit data mining. *HMD – Praxis Wirtschaftsinformatik, 268*, 21-34.

Bughin, J., Chui, M., & Johnson, B. (2008, June). The next step in open innovation. *The McKinsey Quarterly*, 1–8.

Bullinger, H. (2006). *Fokus innovation*. München, Germany: Carl Hanser Verlag.

Bullinger, H. (2009). *Fokus technologie*. München, Germany: Carl Hanser Verlag.

Chesbrough, H., Vanhaverbeke, W., & West, J. (2006). *Open innovation: Researching a new paradigm*. Oxford, UK: Oxford University Press.

Cooper, R. G. (2001). *Winning at new products: Accelerating the process from idea to launch* (3rd ed.). New York, NY: Basic Books.

Dhillon, G., Stahl, B., & Baskerville, R. (2009). *Information systems – Creativity and innovation in small and medium-sized enterprises*. Berlin, Germany: Springer. doi:10.1007/978-3-642-02388-0

Ettlie, J. E., & Elsenbach, J. M. (2007). Modified stage-gate® regimes in new product development. *Journal of Product Innovation Management, 24*(1), 20–33. doi:10.1111/j.1540-5885.2006.00230.x

Gibbert, M., Leibold, M., & Probst, G. (2002). Five styles of customer knowledge management, and how smart companies use them to create value. *European Management Journal, 20*(5), 459–469. doi:10.1016/S0263-2373(02)00101-9

Hopkins, M. S. (2010). The 4 ways IT is driving innovation. *MIT Sloan Management Review,, 10*.

Levien, R., & Iansiti, M. (2004). *The keystone advantage: What the new dynamics of business ecosystems mean for strategy, innovation, and sustainability*. Columbus, OH: McGraw-Hill Professional.

Li, M., Kürümlüoglu, M., Mazura, M., & van den Berg, R. (2009). *Future internet enterprise systems (FInES) cluster position paper final version (version 3.0)*. Brussels, Belgium: European Commission.

Lichtenthaler, U., & Ernst, H. (2008). Intermediary services in the markets for technology: Organizational antecedents and performance consequences. *Organization Studies, 29*(7), 1003–1035. doi:10.1177/0170840608090531

Mahemoff, M. (2006). *Ajax design patterns*. New York, NY: O'Reilly Media, Inc.

Massa, S., & Testa, S. (2008). Innovation and SMEs: Misaligned perspectives and goals among entrepreneurs, academics, and policy makers. *Technovation, 28*(7), 393–407. doi:10.1016/j.technovation.2008.01.002

Nambisan, S., & Sawhney, M. (2007). *The global brain: Your roadmap for innovating faster and smarter in a networked world*. Philadelphia, PA: Wharton School Publishing.

Normann, R., & Ramírez, R. (1993). From value chain to value constellation: Designing interactive strategy. *Harvard Business Review, 71*(4), 65–77.

O'Reilly, T., & Battelle, J. (2012). Web squared: Web 2.0 five years on. In *Web 2.0 Summit*. New York, NY: O'Reilly.

Peltoniemi, M. (2004). Cluster, value network and business ecosystem: Knowledge and innovation approach. In *Organisations, Innovation and Complexity: New Perspectives on the Knowledge Economy*, (pp. 9–10). NEXSUS.

Porter, M. E. (1990). *The competitive advantage of nations*. New York, NY: Free Press.

Prahalad, C. K., & Ramaswamy, V. (2000). Co-opting customer competence. *Harvard Business Review*, *78*(1), 79–90.

Sawhney, M., Verona, G., & Prandelli, E. (2005). Collaborating to create: The internet as a platform for customer engagement in product innovation. *Journal of Interactive Marketing*, *19*(4), 4–17. doi:10.1002/dir.20046

Shavinina, L. V. (2003). *The international handbook on innovation*. London, UK: Elsevier.

Smits, R. (2002). Innovation studies in the 21st century - Questions from a user's perspective. *Technological Forecasting and Social Change*, *69*, 861–883. doi:10.1016/S0040-1625(01)00181-0

Toffler, A. (1980). *The third wave*. New York, NY: Bantam Books.

## KEY TERMS AND DEFINITIONS

**Innovation:** The development of new products, services or business models, particularly if based on non-obvious ideas. The platform aims to support truly novel approaches that may not be obvious for stakeholders directly by using AI and Web mining approaches.

**Intermediation:** Providing a product, service, platform, or information to several stakeholders mediating between them. In this case, the intermediary usually refers to the platform operator.

**Monitoring:** The platform supports monitoring (continuous supervision) of trends using schedulers, push Web apps, and pull operations initiated by the user, depending on agent configuration.

**Ontology:** An ontology provides a shared vocabulary for knowledge representation. In this chapter, we use the term ontology for both concepts and individuals of configurations, products, processes, services, or business models, defined using a ontology description language like OWL.

**Stakeholder:** We use stakeholder analysis in an interorganizational setting, so our main unit of analysis is the participating organization. However, there is a strong user involvement in many modules, making Web end users also an important stakeholder, and giving related multiplicators such as blogs a strong impact.

**Trend:** A value representing the development of a property of an entity over time. In our context, an aggregation of timing, content and other properties of information extracted from Web sources for a product or service of a platform participant.

# Compilation of References

Aaberge, T. (2009). On intensional interpretations of scientific theories. In *Proceedings of the 32nd International Wittgenstein Symposium, LWS.* LWS.

Aaberge, T. (2010). Picturing semantic relations. In *Proceedings of the 33nd International Wittgenstein Symposium, LWS.* LWS.

Aalmink, J., & Marx Gómez, J. (2009). Enterprise tomography - An efficient approach for semi-automatic localization of integration concepts in VLBAs . In Cruz-Cunha, M. M. (Ed.), *Social, Managerial and Organizational Dimensions of Enterprise Information Systems.* Hershey, PA: IGI Global. doi:10.4018/978-1-60566-856-7.ch012

Aalmink, J., & Marx Gómez, J. (2011). Enterprise tomography - An efficient application lifecycle management approach supporting semiautomatic localization, delta-tracking and visualization of integration ontologies in VLBAs . In Kumar, S., Bendoly, E., & Esteves, J. (Eds.), *Frontiers of Research in Enterprise Systems.* Thousand Oaks, CA: SAGE.

Abadi, D., Lindner, W., Madden, S., & Schuler, J. (2004). An integration framework for sensor networks and data stream management systems. In *Proceedings of the Thirtieth International Conference on Very Large Data Bases,* (pp. 1361-1364). Toronto, Canada: IEEE.

Abadi, D. J. (2008). *Query execution in column-oriented database system.* Cambridge, MA: MIT.

Abadi, D. J., Madden, S. R., & Hachem, N. (2008). Column-stores vs. row-stores: How different are they really? [ACM Press.]. *Proceedings of SIGMOD, 2008,* 967–980. doi:10.1145/1376616.1376712

Abascal, J., & Nicolle, C. (2005). Moving towards inclusive design guidelines for socially and ethically aware HCI. *Interacting with Computers, 17,* 484–505. doi:10.1016/j.intcom.2005.03.002

Abels, S., Haak, L., & Hahn, A. (2005). Identification of common methods used for ontology integration tasks: Interoperability of heterogeneous information systems. In *Proceedings of the First International Workshop on Interoperability of Heterogeneous Information Systems,* (pp. 75-78). Bremen, Germany: ACM Press.

Abouzeid, A., Bajda-Pawlikowski, K., Abadi, D., Silberschatz, A., & Rasin, A. (2009). HadoopDB: An architectural hybrid of MapReduce and DBMS technologies for analytical workloads. *Proceedings of the VLDB Endowment, 2*(1).

Abramson, M., & Goldinger, S. D. (1997). What the reader's eye tells the mind's ear: Silent reading activates inner speech. *Perception & Psychophysics, 59,* 1069–1068. doi:10.3758/BF03205520

Adams, A.-M., & Gathercole, S. E. (1996). Phonological working memory and spoken language development in young children. *The Quarterly Journal of Experimental Psychology, 49,* 216–233.

Adar, E., & Adamic, L. A. (2005). Tracking information epidemics in blogspace. In *Proceedings of the IEEE/WIC/ACM International Conference on Web Intelligence.* IEEE/WIC/ACM.

Adler, B., & de Alfaro, L. (2007). A content-driven reputation system for the Wikipedia. In *Proceedings of the International World Wide Web Conference,* (pp. 261-270). ACM.

Agarwal, N., & Son, S. H. (1993). *Experiences with the development of a multimedia information system for medical applications. Technical Report*. Charlottesville, VA: University of Virginia.

Agina, A. M., & Kommers, P. A. M. (2008). The positive of violent games on children's self-regulation learning. In *Proceedings of the IADIS Multi Conference on Computer Science and Information Systems*, (pp. 141-145). Amsterdam, The Netherlands: University of Twente Press.

Agina, A. M., Kommers, P. A., & Steehouder, F. (2011). The effect of the external regulator's absence on children's speech use, manifested self-regulation, and task performance during learning tasks. *Computers in Human Behavior*. Retrieved from http://doc.utwente.nl/76592/

Agina, A. M., Kommers, P. A., & Steehouder, F. (2011). The effect of nonhuman's versus human's external regulation on children's speech use, manifested self-regulation, and satisfaction during learning tasks. *Computers in Human Behavior*. Retrieved from http://doc.utwente.nl/76593/

Agina, A. M., Kommers, P. A., & Steehouder, F. (2011). The effect of the nonhuman external regulator's answer-until-correct (AUC) versus knowledge-of-result (KR) task feedback on children's behavioral regulation during learning tasks. *Computers in Human Behavior*. Retrieved from http://www.deepdyve.com/lp/elsevier/the-effect-of-the-nonhuman-external-regulator-s-answer-until-correct-dKZHxc0Ehi

Agina, A. M. (2008). Towards understanding self-organization: How self-regulation contributes to self-organization? *International Journal of Continuing Engineering Education and Lifelong Learning, 18*, 366–379. doi:10.1504/IJCEELL.2008.018838

Agina, A. M., Kommers, P. A., & Steehouder, F. (2011). The effect of nonhuman's external regulation on detecting the natural development process of young children's self-regulation during learning tasks. *Computers in Human Behavior, 28*(2), 527–539. doi:10.1016/j.chb.2011.10.025

Agrawal, S., Narasayya, V., & Yang, B. (2004). Integrating vertical and horizontal partitioning into automated physical database design. In *Proceedings of the 2004 ACM SIGMOD International Conference on Management of Data*. Paris, France: ACM Press.

Akerkar, R. A. (2009). *Foundation of the semantics web: XML, RDF & ontology*. Oxford, UK: Alpha Science International.

Alexa. (2010). *Top sites*. Retrieved May 3, 2010, from http://www.alexa.com/topsites

Alexander, P. A., & Judy, J. E. (1988). The interaction of domain-specific and strategic knowledge in academic performance. *Review of Educational Research, 58*, 375–404.

Allen, M. H., Lincoln, A. J., & Kaufman, A. S. (1991). Sequential and simultaneous processing abilities of high functioning autistic and language-impaired children. *Journal of Autism and Developmental Disorders, 21*, 483–502. doi:10.1007/BF02206872

Alvarez-Sabucedo, L., Anido-Rifon, L., Corradini, F., Polzonetti, A., & Re, B. (2010). Knowledge-based platform for egovernment agents: A web-based solution using semantic technologies. *Expert Systems with Applications, 37*(5), 3647–3656. doi:10.1016/j.eswa.2009.10.026

Ambler, S. W. (2010). *Surveys: What they tell us, 2010 IT project success rates*. Retrieved from http://drdobbs.com/architecture-and-design/226500046

Anderson, R. E. (1982). Speech imagery is not always faster than visual imagery. *Memory & Cognition, 10*, 371–380. doi:10.3758/BF03202429

Andersson, B., Bergholtz, M., Edirisuriya, A., Ilayperuma, T., Johannesson, P., & Gordijn, J. … Weigand, H. (2006). Towards a reference ontology for business models. In *Proceedings of the 25th International Conference on Conceptual Modeling*. Berlin, Germany: Springer-Verlag.

Ankolekar, A., Krötzsch, M., Tran, T., & Vrandecic, D. (2008). The two cultures: Mashing up web 2.0 and the semantic web. *Web Semantics: Science . Services and Agents on the World Wide Web, 6*(1), 70–75. doi:10.1016/j.websem.2007.11.005

Annett, J. (1969). *Feedback and human behavior*. Oxford, UK: Penguin Books.

Anton, M., & DiCamilla, F. J. (1999). Socio–cognitive functions of L1 collaborative interaction in the L2 classroom. *Modern Language Journal, 83*, 233–247. doi:10.1111/0026-7902.00018

Appel, G., & Lantolf, J. P. (1994). Speaking as mediation: A study of L1 and L2 text recall tasks. *Modern Language Journal*, *78*, 437–452. doi:10.1111/j.1540-4781.1994.tb02062.x

Ardila, A., & Rosseli, M. (1994). Development of language, memory, and visual spatial abilities in 5- to 12-year-old children using a neuropsychological battery. *Developmental Neuropsychology*, *10*, 97–120. doi:10.1080/87565649409540571

Asrim, A. M., Ibrahim, A., & Hunt, A. (2006). An HCI model for usability of sonification applications. In *Proceedings of the 5th International Conference on Task Models and Diagrams for Users Interface Design (TAMODIA 2006)*, (pp. 245-258). Berlin, Germany: Springer-Verlag.

Aßmann, U., Zschaler, S., & Wagner, G. (2006). Ontologies, meta-models, and the model-driven paradigm . In Calero, C., Ruiz, F., & Piattini, M. (Eds.), *Ontologies for Software Engineering and Software Technology* (pp. 249–273). Berlin, Germany: Springer. doi:10.1007/3-540-34518-3_9

Asunci, G., & Mez, P., & Rez. (2002). Ontology specification languages for the semantic web. *IEEE Intelligent Systems*, *17*, 54–60. doi:10.1109/5254.988453

Auer, S., & Lehmann, J. (2010). Creating knowledge out of interlinked data. *Semantic Web*, *1*(1), 97–104.

Azevedo, R., Ragan, S., Cromley, J. G., & Pritchett, S. (2002). *Do different goal-setting conditions facilitate students' ability to regulate their learning of complex science topics with RiverWeb?* Paper presented at the Annual Conference of the American Educational Research Association. New Orleans, LA.

Azevedo, R., & Cromley, J. G. (2004). Does training of self-regulated learning facilitate student's learning with hypermedia? *Journal of Educational Psychology*, *96*, 523–535. doi:10.1037/0022-0663.96.3.523

Azevedo, R., Guthrie, J. T., & Seibert, D. (2004). The role of self-regulated learning in fostering students' conceptual understanding of complex systems with hypermedia. *Journal of Educational Computing Research*, *30*, 87–111. doi:10.2190/DVWX-GM1T-6THQ-5WC7

Baccianella, S., Esuli, A., & Sebastiani, F. (2010). SentiWordNet 3.0: An enhanced lexical resource for sentiment analysis and opinion mining. In *Proceedings of the Language Resources and Evaluation Conference*, (pp. 2200-2204). IEEE.

Baddeley, A. D. (1986). *Working memory*. Oxford, UK: Oxford University Press.

Baddeley, A. D. (2002). Is working memory still working? *European Psychologist*, *7*, 85–97. doi:10.1027//1016-9040.7.2.85

Baddeley, A. D. (2003). Working memory and language: An overview. *Journal of Communication Disorders*, *36*, 189–208. doi:10.1016/S0021-9924(03)00019-4

Baddeley, A. D., & Della Sala, S. (1998). Working memory and executive control . In Roberts, A. C., & Robbins, T. W. (Eds.), *The Prefrontal Cortex: Executive and Cognitive Functions* (pp. 143–162). Oxford, UK: Oxford University Press. doi:10.1093/acprof:oso/9780198524410.003.0002

Baddeley, A. D., Emslie, H., Kolondny, J., & Duncan, J. (1998). Random generation and the executive control of working memory. *Quarterly Journal of Experimental Psychology*, *51*, 819–852.

Baddeley, A. D., & Hitch, G. (1974). Working memory . In Bower, G. A. (Ed.), *Recent Advances in the Psychology of Learning and Motivation* (*Vol. 8*, pp. 263–302). New York, NY: Academic Press.

Baddeley, A., Gathercole, S., & Papagno, C. (1998). The phonological loop as a language learning device. *Psychological Review*, *105*, 158–173. doi:10.1037/0033-295X.105.1.158

Bader, D. A., Kintali, S., Madduri, K., & Mihail, M. (2007). Approximating betweeness centrality. *Lecture Notes in Computer Science*, *4863*, 124–134. doi:10.1007/978-3-540-77004-6_10

Badley, G. (2009). Academic writing as shaping and reshaping. *Teaching in Higher Education*, *14*(2), 209–219. doi:10.1080/13562510902757294

Baeza-Yates, R., & Ribeiro-Neto, B. (1999). *Modern information retrieval*. Harlow, MA: Addison Wesley.

Baeza-Yates, R., & Ribeiro-Neto, B. (2011). *Modern information retrieval: The concepts and technology behind search* (2nd ed.). Reading, MA: Addison-Wesley Professional.

Bailey, D. B. Jr, Hatton, D. D., Mesibov, G., Ament, N., & Skinner, M. (2000). Early development, temperament, and functional impairment in autism and fragile X syndrome. *Journal of Autism and Developmental Disorders*, *30*, 49–59. doi:10.1023/A:1005412111706

Bain, S. K. (1993). Sequential and simultaneous processing in children with learning disabilities: An attempted replication. *The Journal of Special Education*, *27*, 235–246. doi:10.1177/002246699302700206

Baker, L. (1991). Metacognition, reading, and science education . In Santa, C. M., & Alvermann, D. E. (Eds.), *Science Learning-Processes and Applications* (pp. 2–13). Newark, DE: International Reading Association.

Baker, S. R. (2006). Towards an idiothetic understanding of the role of social problem solving in daily event, mood and health experience: A prospective daily diary study. *British Journal of Health Psychology*, *11*, 513–531. doi:10.1348/135910705X57647

Bakhtin, M. M. (1986). *Speech genres & other late essays*. Austin, TX: University of Texas Press.

Balamore, U., & Wozniak, R. H. (1984). Speech–action coordination in young children. *Developmental Psychology*, *20*, 850–858. doi:10.1037/0012-1649.20.5.850

Balasubramanian, V., Bieber, M., & Isakowitz, T. (2001). A case study in systematic hypermedia design. *Information Systems*, *26*(4), 295–320. doi:10.1016/S0306-4379(01)00022-9

Balthazar, C. H. (2003). The word length effect in children with language impairment. *Journal of Communication Disorders*, *36*, 487–505. doi:10.1016/S0021-9924(03)00033-9

Banko, M., Cafarella, M. J., Soderland, S., Broadhead, M., & Etzioni, O. (2007). Open information extraction from the web. In *Proceedings Of The 20th International Joint Conference On Artificial Intelligence,* (pp. 2670–2676). San Francisco, CA: Morgan Kaufmann Publishers Inc.

Barnes, S. B. (2006). A privacy paradox: Social networking in the United States. *First Monday*, *11*(9).

Barnes, T. A., Pashby, I. R., & Gibbons, A. M. (2006). Managing collaborative R&D projects development of a practical management tool. *International Journal of Project Management*, *24*(5), 395–404. doi:10.1016/j.ijproman.2006.03.003

Barry, C., & Lang, M. (2001). A survey of multimedia and web development techniques and methodology usage. *IEEE MultiMedia*, *8*(2), 52–60. doi:10.1109/93.917971

Barry, C., & Lang, M. (2003). A comparison of traditional and multimedia information systems development practices. *Information and Software Technology*, *45*(4), 217–227. doi:10.1016/S0950-5849(02)00207-0

Bartsch, K., & Estes, D. (1996). Individual differences in children's developing theory of mind and implications for metacognition. *Learning and Individual Differences*, *8*, 281–304. doi:10.1016/S1041-6080(96)90020-5

Bateman, S., Brooks, C., & McCalla, G. (2006). Collaborative tagging approaches for ontological metadata in adaptive e-learning systems. In *Proceedings of the International Workshop on Applications of Semantic Web Technologies for E-Learning (SW-EL 2006)*, (pp. 3-12). Dublin, Ireland: SW-EL.

Beaudichon, J. (1973). Nature and instrumental function on private speech in problem solving situations. *Merrill-Palmer Quarterly*, *19*, 117–135.

Beer, D., & Burrows, R. (2007). Sociology and, of and in Web 2.0: Some initial considerations. *Sociological Research Online*, *12*(5). doi:10.5153/sro.1560

Beggs, W. D. A., & Howarth, P. N. (1985). Inner speech as a learned skill. *Journal of Experimental Child Psychology*, *39*, 396–411. doi:10.1016/0022-0965(85)90048-7

Behrend, D. A., Rosengren, K. S., & Perlmutter, M. (1989). A new look at children's private speech: The effects of age, task difficulty, and parent presence. *International Journal of Behavioral Development*, *12*, 305–320.

Behrend, D. A., Rosengren, K., & Perlmutter, M. (1992). The relation between private speech and parental interactive style . In Diaz, R. M., & Berk, L. E. (Eds.), *Private Speech: From Social Interaction to Self-Regulation* (pp. 85–100). Hillsdale, NJ: Erlbaum.

Beitzel, S. M., Jensen, E. C., Lewis, D. D., Chowdhury, A., & Frieder, O. (2007). Automatic classification of web queries using very large unlabeled query logs. *ACM Transactions on Information Systems*, *25*(2). doi:10.1145/1229179.1229183

Belew, R. (2000). *Finding out about: a cognitive perspective on search engine technology and the WWW*. Cambridge, UK: Cambridge University Press.

Benz, D., Hotho, A., & St, S. (2010). Semantics made by you and me: Self-emerging ontologies can capture the diversity of shared knowledge. In *Proceedings of the 2nd Web Science Conference (WebSci 2010)*. Raleigh, NC: WebSci.

Berk, L. E. (1986). Relationship of elementary school children's private speech to behavioral accompaniment to task, attention, and task performance. *Developmental Psychology*, *22*, 671–680. doi:10.1037/0012-1649.22.5.671

Berk, L. E. (1992). Children's private speech: An overview of theory and the status of research . In Diaz, R. M., & Berk, L. E. (Eds.), *Private Speech: From Social Interaction to self-Regulation* (pp. 17–53). Hillsdale, NJ: Erlbaum.

Berk, L. E., & Garvin, R. A. (1984). Development of private speech among low-income Appalachian children. *Developmental Psychology*, *20*, 271–286. doi:10.1037/0012-1649.20.2.271

Berk, L. E., & Landau, S. (1993). Private speech of learning disabled and normally achieving children in classroom academic and laboratory contexts. *Child Development*, *64*, 556–571. doi:10.2307/1131269

Berk, L. E., & Potts, M. K. (1991). Development and functional significance of private speech among attention-deficit hyperactivity disordered and normal boys. *Journal of Abnormal Child Psychology*, *19*, 357–377. doi:10.1007/BF00911237

Berk, L. E., & Spuhl, S. T. (1995). Maternal interaction, private speech, and task performance in preschool children. *Early Childhood Research Quarterly*, *10*, 145–169. doi:10.1016/0885-2006(95)90001-2

Berk, L. E., & Winsler, A. (1995). *Scaffolding children's learning: Vygotsky and early childhood education*. Washington, DC: National Association for the Education of Young Children.

Bernardini, S. (1999). *Using think-aloud protocols to investigate the translation process: Methodological aspects*. Bologna, Italy: University of Bologna.

Berners-Lee, T., Hendler, J., & Lassila, O. (2001). The semantic web. *Scientific American*, *284*(5), 34–43. doi:10.1038/scientificamerican0501-34

Berrueta, D. (2006). *MORFEO-MyMobileWeb: Tecnologías avanzadas de software abierto para el desarrollo de la Web Móvil: 1.0, 2.0 y 3.0*. CETIC Fundation.

Biggs, J. (1987). *Student approaches to learning and studying*. Hawthorn, Australia: Australian Council for Educational Research.

Bilodeau, E. A. (1969). *Principles of skill acquisition*. New York, NY: Academic Press.

Birch, D. (1966). Verbal control of nonverbal behavior. *Journal of Experimental Child Psychology*, *4*, 266–275. doi:10.1016/0022-0965(66)90027-0

Bishop, D. V. M., Aamodt-Leeper, G., Creswell, C., McGurk, R., & Skuse, D. H. (2001). Individual differences in cognitive planning on the Tower of Hanoi task: Neuropsychological maturity or measurement error? *Journal of Child Psychology and Psychiatry, and Allied Disciplines*, *42*, 551–556. doi:10.1111/1469-7610.00749

Bishop, D. V. M., North, T., & Dnlan, C. (1996). Nonword repetition as behavioural marker for inherited language impairment: Evidence from a twin study. *Journal of Child Psychology and Psychiatry, and Allied Disciplines*, *37*, 391–404. doi:10.1111/j.1469-7610.1996.tb01420.x

Bivens, J. A., & Berk, L. E. (1990). A longitudinal study of the development of elementary school children's private speech. *Merrill-Palmer Quarterly*, *36*, 443–463.

Bjorklund, D. F., & Douglas, R. N. (1997). The development of memory strategies . In Cowan, N. (Ed.), *The Development of Memory in Childhood* (pp. 201–246). Hove, UK: Psychology Press.

Blinn, N., Lindermann, N., Fäcks, K., & Nüttgens, M. (2009). Web 2.0 in SME networks - A design science approach considering multi-perspective requirements . In *Proceedings of Value Creation in E-Business Management* (pp. 271–283). Academic Press. doi:10.1007/978-3-642-03132-8_22

Blochdorn, S., & Hotho, A. (2004). Text classification by boosting weak learners based on terms and concepts. In *Proceedings of the 4th IEEE International Conference in Data Mining,* (pp. 331-334). Brighton, UK: IEEE Press.

Bloom, B. (1976). *Human characteristics and school learning*. New York, NY: McGraw-Hill.

Blumenstock, J. E. (2008). *Automatically assessing the quality of Wikipedia articles*. UBCiSchool Report 2008-021. UBCiSchool.

Blumenstock, J. E. (2008). Size matters: Word count as a measure of quality in Wikipedia. In *Proceedings of the 17th International World Wide Web Conference*. ACM.

Bock, C., & Grüninger, M. (2005). PSL: A semantic domain for flow models. *Software & Systems Modeling, 4*(2), 209–231. doi:10.1007/s10270-004-0066-x

Bodea, C., & Dascalu, M. (2009). Designing project management tests based on semantic nets and concept space graphs. In *Proceedings of the 12th International Business Information Management Association Conference (IBIMA),* (pp. 1232-1236). Kuala Lumpur, Malaysia: IBIMA.

Bodea, C., & Dascalu, M. (2009). A parameterized web-based testing model for project management. In *Proceedings of the 8th International Conference on Advances in Web Based Learning,* (pp. 68-72). Aachen, Germany: Springer.

Bodea, C., & Lipai, A. (2009). Development of a meta-search tool for the web using a clustering algorithm. In *Proceedings of the 12th International Business Information Management Association Conference (IBIMA),* (pp. 729-733). Kuala Lumpur, Malaysia: IBIMA.

Bodea, C., Trandafir, I., & Borozan, A. M. (2008). Assessment of project management knowledge using semantic networks in the SinPers system. In *Proceedings of the 22nd IPMA World Congress on Project Management*. Rome, Italy: IPMA.

Bodrova, E., & Leong, D. J. (2006). Self-regulation as key to school readiness: How early childhood teachers promote this critical competency . In Zaslow, M., & Martinez-Beck, I. (Eds.), *Critical Issues in Early Childhood Professional Development* (pp. 203–224). Baltimore, MD: Brookes.

Boehm, B. (1986). A spiral model of software development and enhancement. *SIGSOFT Software Engineering Notes, 11*(4), 14–24. doi:10.1145/12944.12948

Boekaerts, M. (1996). Self-regulated learning and the junction of cognition and motivation. *European Psychologist, 1*, 100–112. doi:10.1027/1016-9040.1.2.100

Boekaerts, M. (1997). Self-regulated learning: A new concept embraced by researchers, policy makers, educators, teachers and students. *Learning and Instruction, 7*, 161–186. doi:10.1016/S0959-4752(96)00015-1

Boekaerts, M. (1999). Self-regulated learning: Where we are today. *International Journal of Educational Research, 31*, 445–457. doi:10.1016/S0883-0355(99)00014-2

Boekaerts, M., & Corno, L. (2005). Self-regulation in the classroom: A perspective on assessment and intervention. *Applied Psychology, 54*(2), 199–231. doi:10.1111/j.1464-0597.2005.00205.x

Boekaerts, M., Otten, R., & Simons, R. (1997). Een onderzoek naar de bruikbaarheid van de ILS leerstijlen in de onderbouw van het voortgezet onderwijs. [Exploring the utility of Vermunts' ILS learning style construct for high school students]. *Tijdschrift voor Onderwijsresearch, 22*, 15–36.

Boekaerts, M., Pintrich, P. R., & Zeidner, M. (Eds.). (2000). *Handbook of self-regulation*. San Diego, CA: Academic Press.

Bonabeau, E. (2009). Decisions 2.0: The power of collective intelligence. *MIT Sloan Management Review, 50*(2), 45–52.

Borkowski, J. G., & Muthukrishna, N. (1992). Moving metacognition into the classroom: "Working models" and effective strategy teaching . In Pressley, M., Harris, K. R., & Guthrie, J. T. (Eds.), *Promoting Academic Competence and Literacy in School* (pp. 477–501). Toronto, Canada: Academic Press.

Borod, J. C. (Ed.). (2000). *The neuropsychology of emotion*. Oxford, UK: Oxford University Press.

Bothos, E., Apostolou, D., & Mentzas, G. (2009). Collective intelligence for idea management with internet-based information aggregation markets. *Internet Research*, *19*(1), 26–41. doi:10.1108/10662240910927803

Boud, D., & Keogh, R. (1985). Promoting reflection in learning: A model. In D. Boud, R. Keogh., & D. Walker (Eds.), *Reflection: Turning Experience into Learning*, (pp. 18-40). London, UK: Kogan.

Brabham, D. C. (2008). Crowdsourcing as a model for problem solving: An introduction and cases. *Convergence: The International Journal of Research into New Media Technologies*, *14*(1), 75–90. doi:10.1177/1354856507084420

Bracken, C. C., & Lombard, M. (2004). Social presence and children: Praise, intrinsic motivation, and learning with computers. *The Journal of Communication*, *54*, 22–37. doi:10.1111/j.1460-2466.2004.tb02611.x

Bransford, J., Brown, A. L., & Cocking, R. R. (Eds.). (2000). *How people learn: Brain, mind, experience, and school*. Washington, DC: Academic Press.

Braten, I., & Olaussen, B. S. (2005). Profiling individual differences in student motivation: A longitudinal cluster-analytic study in different academic contexts. *Contemporary Educational Psychology*, *30*, 359–396. doi:10.1016/j.cedpsych.2005.01.003

Brehm, N., Lübke, D., & Marx Gómez, J. (2007). Federated enterprise resource planning (FERP) systems . In Saha, P. (Ed.), *Handbook of Enterprise Systems Architecture in Practice* (pp. 290–305). Hershey, PA: IGI Global. doi:10.4018/978-1-59904-189-6.ch017

Brehm, N., Marx Gómez, J., & Rautenstrauch, C. (2006). An ERP solution based on web services and peer-to-peer networks for small and medium enterprises. *International Journal of Information Systems and Change Management*, *1*(1), 99–111. doi:10.1504/IJISCM.2006.008288

Breslin, J. G., O'Sullivan, D., Passant, A., & Vasiliu, L. (2010). Semantic web computing in industry. *Computers in Industry*, *61*(8), 729–741. doi:10.1016/j.compind.2010.05.002

Brewster, C., Ciravegna, F., & Wilks, Y. (2003). Background and foreground knowledge in dynamic ontology construction: Viewing text as knowledge maintenance. In *Proceedings of the Semantic Web Workshop, SIGIR August 2003*. Toronto, Canada: SIGIR.

Brian, H.-S. (2008). *Connecting powertypes and stereotypes*. Retrieved from http://www.jot.fm/issues/issue_2005_09/article3.pdf

Bridges, F. A., & Cicchetti, D. (1982). Mothers' ratings of the temperament characteristics of Down syndrome infants. *Developmental Psychology*, *18*, 238–244. doi:10.1037/0012-1649.18.2.238

Brin, S., & Page, L. (1998). The anatomy of a large-scale hypertextual web search engine. In *Proceedings of the Seventh International World Wide Web Conference*, (pp. 107-117). Brisbane, Australia: Elsevier Science Publishers.

Brodwin, M. G., Star, T., & Cardoso, E. (2004). Computer assistive technology for people who have disabilities: Computer adaptations and modifications. *Journal of Rehabilitation*, *70*, 28–33.

Bronson, M. B. (2000). *Self-regulation in early childhood: Nature and nurture*. New York, NY: Guilford.

Bronson, M. B. (2000). Recognizing and supporting the development of self-regulation in young children. *Young Children*, *55*, 32–37.

Brown, A. L. (1978). Knowing when, where and how to remember: A problem of metacognition . In Glaser, R. (Ed.), *Advances in Instructional Psychology* (pp. 165–177). Hillsdale, NJ: Erlbaum.

Brown, A. L. (1987). Metacognition, executive control, self-regulation, and other more mysterious mechanisms . In Weinert, F. E., & Kluwe, R. H. (Eds.), *Metacognition, Motivation, and Understanding* (pp. 65–116). Hillsdale, NJ: Erlbaum.

Brown, D. H., & Lockett, N. (2007). E-business, innovation and SMEs: The significance of hosted services and firm aggregations. *International Journal of Entrepreneurship and Innovation Management*, *7*(1), 92–112. doi:10.1504/IJEIM.2007.012175

Bullinger, H. (2009). *Fokus technologie*. München, Germany: Carl Hanser Verlag.

Bunke, H., Dickinsion, P. J., Kraetzl, M., & Wallis, W. D. (2007). *A graph-theoretic approach to enterprise networks dynamics* (pp. 71–117). Birkhäuser, Switzerland: Birkhäuser Verlag.

Burgess, N., & Hitch, G. L. (1992). Towards a network model of the articulatory loop. *Journal of Memory and Language, 31*, 429–460. doi:10.1016/0749-596X(92)90022-P

Buriol, J., Castillo, C., Donato, D., Leonardi, S., & Millozzi, S. (2006). Temporal evolution of the wiki graph. In *Proceedings of the Web Intelligence Conference*. IEEE.

Bush, V. (1945). As we may think. *Atlantic Monthly, 176*(1), 101–108.

Butler, D. L., & Cartier, S. C. (2005). *Multiple complementary methods for understanding self-regulated learning as situated in context*. Paper presented at the Annual Meeting of the American Educational Research Association. Montreal, Canada.

Butler, D. L. (1998). Metacognition and learning disabilities . In Wong, B. Y. L. (Ed.), *Learning about Learning Disabilities* (2nd ed., pp. 277–307). Toronto, Canada: Academic Press.

Butler, D. L. (2002). Qualitative approaches to investigating self-regulated learning: Contributions and challenges. *Educational Psychologist, 37*, 59–63.

Butler, D. L., & Winne, P. H. (1995). Feedback and self-regulated learning: A theoretical synthesis. *Review of Educational Research, 65*, 245–281.

Butler, D. L., & Winne, P. H. (2005). Feedback and self-regulated learning: A theoretical synthesis. *Review of Educational Research, 65*, 245–281.

Byrne, D. (1971). *The attraction paradigm*. New York, NY: Academic Press.

Calero, M. D., García-Martín, M. B., Jiménez, M. I., Kazén, M., & Araque, A. (2007). Self-regulation advantage for high-IQ children: Findings from a research study. *Learning and Individual Differences, 17*(4). doi:10.1016/j.lindif.2007.03.012

Cameron, J., & Pierce, W. D. (1994). Reinforcement, reward, and intrinsic motivation: A meta-analysis. *Review of Educational Research, 64*, 363–423.

Campbell, M. C., & Kirmani, A. (2000). Consumers' use of persuasion knowledge: The effects of accessibility and cognitive capacity on perceptions of an influence agent. *The Journal of Consumer Research, 27*, 69–83. doi:10.1086/314309

Cardoso, J. (2007). The semantic web vision: Where are we? *IEEE Intelligent Systems, 22*(5), 22–26. doi:10.1109/MIS.2007.4338499

Carenini, G., Ng, R., & Pauls, A. (2006). Interactive multimedia summaries of evaluative text. In *Proceedings of the 11th International Conference on Intelligent User Interfaces*, (pp. 124–131). ACM Press.

Carlsson, S., Corvello, V., & Migliarese, P. (2009). Enabling open innovation: Proposal of a framework supporting ICT and KMS implementation in web-based intermediaries. In *Proceedings of the 17th European Conference on Information Systems*, (pp. 2218-2230). Verona, Italy: ECIS.

Carnegie, D. (1964). *How to win friends and influence people*. New York, NY: Simon & Schuster.

Carr, M. (1998). Metacognition in mathematics from a constructivist perspective . In Hacker, D., Dunlosky, J., & Graesser, A. (Eds.), *Metacognition in Educational Theory and Practice* (pp. 69–81). New York, NY: Academic Press.

Carroll, D. J., Apperly, I. A., & Riggs, K. J. (2007). Choosing between two objects reduces 3-year-olds' errors on a reverse-contingency test of executive function. *Journal of Experimental Child Psychology, 98*, 184–192. doi:10.1016/j.jecp.2007.08.001

Carstensen, P. H., & Vogelsang, L. (2001). Design of web-based information systems —New challenges for systems development? In *Proceedings Ninth European Conference on Information Systems*. Bled, Slovenia: IEEE.

Carver, C. S., & Scheier, M. F. (1981). *Attention and self-regulation: A control-theory approach to human behavior*. New York, NY: Springer-Verlag.

Carver, C. S., & Scheier, M. F. (1990). Principles of self-regulation: Action and emotion . In Higgins, E. T., & Sorrentino, R. M. (Eds.), *Handbook of Motivation and Cognition: Foundations of Social Behavior* (*Vol. 2*, pp. 3–52). New York, NY: Guilford.

Cassidy, C., Christie, D., Coutts, N., Dunn, J., Sinclair, C., & Skinner, D. (2007). Building communities of educational enquiry. *Oxford Review of Education, 34*(2), 217–235. doi:10.1080/03054980701614945

Cassidy, C., Christie, D., Coutts, N., Dunn, J., Sinclair, C., & Skinner, D. (2007). Building communities of educational enquiry. *Oxford Review of Education, 34*(2), 217–235. doi:10.1080/03054980701614945

Castellanos-Nieves, D., Fernández-Breis, J. T., Valencia-García, R., Martínez-Béjar, R., & Iniesta-Moreno, M. (2011). Semantic web technologies for supporting learning assessment. *Information Sciences, 181*(9), 1517–1537. doi:10.1016/j.ins.2011.01.010

Catano, V. M. (1975). Relation of improved performance through verbal praise to source of praise. *Perceptual and Motor Skills, 41*, 71–74. doi:10.2466/pms.1975.41.1.71

Chakrabarti, S., Berg, M. V. D., & Dom, B. (1999). Focused crawling: A new approach to topic-specific web resource discovery. *Computer Networks: The international Journal of Computer and Telecommunications Networking, 31*(11-16), 1623-1640.

Chang, C., Kayed, M., Girgis, M. R., & Shaalan, K. F. (2006). A survey of web information extraction systems. *IEEE Transactions on Knowledge and Data Engineering, 18*(10), 1411–1428. doi:10.1109/TKDE.2006.152

Chang, E. C. (2003). A critical appraisal and extension of hope theory in middle-aged men and women: Is it important to distinguish agency and pathways components? *Journal of Social and Clinical Psychology, 22*, 121–143. doi:10.1521/jscp.22.2.121.22876

Chang, E. C., & D'Zurilla, T. J. (1996). Relations between problem orientation and optimism, pessimism, and trait affectivity: A construct validation study. *Behaviour Research and Therapy, 34*, 185–194. doi:10.1016/0005-7967(95)00046-1

Chang, E. C., D'Zurilla, T. J., & Sanna, L. J. (2004). Introduction: Social problem solving for the real world . In Chang, E. C., D'Zurilla, T. J., & Sanna, L. J. (Eds.), *Social Problem Solving: Theory, Research, and Training* (pp. 3–7). Washington, DC: American Psychological Association. doi:10.1037/10805-000

Chang, E. C., Downey, C. A., & Salata, J. L. (2004). Social problem solving and positive psychological functioning: Looking at the positive side of problem solving . In Chang, E. C., D'Zurilla, T. J., & Sanna, L. J. (Eds.), *Social Problem Solving: Theory, Research, and Training* (pp. 99–116). Washington, DC: American Psychological Association. doi:10.1037/10805-006

Chang, E. C., Sanna, L. J., Riley, M. M., Thornburg, A. T., Zumberg, K. M., & Edwards, M. C. (2007). Relations between problem-solving styles and psychological adjustment in young adults: Is stress a mediating variable? *Personality and Individual Differences, 42*, 135–144. doi:10.1016/j.paid.2006.06.011

Chang, F., & Burns, B. (2005). Attention in preschoolers: Associations with effortful control and motivation. *Child Development, 76*, 247–263. doi:10.1111/j.1467-8624.2005.00842.x

Chapman, P., Clinton, J., Khabaza, T., Reinartz, T., & Wirth, R. (1999). *The crisp-DM process model*. Technical Report, CRISM-DM Consortium. Retrieved October 13, 2009, from http://www.crisp-dm.org/CRISPWP-0800.pdf

Chapple, M. (2001). *Clustering*. Retrieved February 11, 2010, from http://databases.about.com/od/datamining/g/clustering.htm

Chen, C. (1992). Understanding multimedia information systems: Consequences for today and possibilities for tomorrow. In *Proceedings of NIT 1992: The 5th International Conference on New Information Technology*, (pp. 49-62). Hong Kong, China: NIT.

Chen, H., & Dumais, S. (2000). Bringing order to the web: Automatically categorizing search result. In *Proceedings of the SIGCHI Conference on Human Factors in Computing Systems CHI 2000*. The Hague, The Netherlands: ACM Press.

Cherry, K. E., Matson, J. L., & Palawskyj, T. R. (1997). Psychopathology in older adults with severe and profound mental retardation. *American Journal of Mental Retardation*, *101*, 445–458.

Cheung, P. P. P., & Siu, A. M. H. (2009). A comparison of patterns of sensory processing in children with and without developmental disabilities. *Research in Developmental Disabilities*, *30*, 1468–1480. doi:10.1016/j.ridd.2009.07.009

Chi, N. L. (2003). *A tolerance rough set approach to clustering web search results.* (Master Thesis). Warsaw University. Warsaw, Poland.

Chiang, H. M. (2009). Differences between spontaneous and elicited expressive communication in children with autism. *Research in Autism Spectrum Disorders*, *3*, 214–222. doi:10.1016/j.rasd.2008.06.002

Childs, C. P., & Greenfield, P. M. (1980). Informal modes of learning and teaching: The case of Zinacanteco weaving. In Warrenk, N. (Ed.), *Studies in Cross-Cultural Psychology* (Vol. 2, pp. 269–316). London, UK: Academic Press.

Chirita, P.-A., Nejdl, W., Paiu, R., & Kohlschütter, C. (2005). Using ODP metadata to personalize search. In *Proceedings of the 28th Annual International ACM SIGIR Conference on Research and Development in Information Retrieval.* Salvador, Brazil: ACM Press.

Cho, J. (2001). *Crawling the web: Discovery and maintenance of large-scale web data.* (PhD Thesis). Stanford University. Stanford, CA.

Ciocoiu, M., Nau, D. S., & Gruninger, M. (2001). Ontologies for integrating engineering applications. *Journal of Computing and Information Science in Engineering*, *1*(1), 12–22. doi:10.1115/1.1344878

Ciravegna, F. (2001). Challenges in information extraction from text for knowledge management. In *Proceedings of the IEEE Intelligent Systems and their Applications.* IEEE Press.

Clarke-Stewart, K. A., Allhusen, V. D., McDowell, D. J., Thelen, L., & Call, J. D. (2003). Identifying psychological problems in young children: How do mothers compare with child psychiatrists? *Applied Developmental Psychology*, *23*, 589–624. doi:10.1016/S0193-3973(03)00006-6

Cleary, T. J., & Zimmerman, B. J. (2004). Self-regulation empowerment program: A school-based program to enhance self-regulation and self-motivation cycles of student learning. *Psychology in the Schools*, *41*, 143–168. doi:10.1002/pits.10177

Cohen, W. W. (1995). *Fast effective rule induction.* Paper presented at the Twelfth International Conference on Machine Learning. Tahoe City, CA.

Collies, B., DeBoer, W., & Slotman, K. (2001). Feedback for web-based assignments. *Journal of Computer Assisted Learning*, *17*, 306–313. doi:10.1046/j.0266-4909.2001.00185.x

Colomo-Palacios, R., García-Crespo, Á., Soto-Acosta, P., Ruano-Mayoral, M., & Jiménez-López, D. (2010). A case analysis of semantic technologies for R&D intermediation information management. *International Journal of Information Management*, *30*(5), 465–469. doi:10.1016/j.ijinfomgt.2010.05.012

Connelly, F. M., Clandinin, D. J., & He, M. F. (1997). Teachers' personal practical knowledge on the professional knowledge landscape. *Teaching and Teacher Education*, *13*(7), 665–674. doi:10.1016/S0742-051X(97)00014-0

Cook, A. M., & Hussey, S. M. (2002). *Assistive technologies: Principles and practice.* St. Louis, MO: Mosby.

Cooper, R. G. (2008). Perspective: The stage-gate(R) idea-to-launch process - Update, what's new, and NexGen systems. *Journal of Product Innovation Management*, *25*(3), 213–232. doi:10.1111/j.1540-5885.2008.00296.x

Copeland, A. P. (1979). Types of private speech produced by hyperactive and nonhyperactive boys. *Journal of Abnormal Child Psychology*, *7*, 169–177. doi:10.1007/BF00918897

Corcho, O., Fernández-López, M., & Gómez-Pérez, A. (2003). Methodologies, tools and languages for building ontologies: Where is their meeting point? *Data & Knowledge Engineering*, *46*(1), 41–64. doi:10.1016/S0169-023X(02)00195-7

Corkum, P., Humphries, K., Mullane, J. C., & Theriault, F. (2008). Private speech in children with ADHD and their typically developing peers during problem-solving and inhibition tasks. *Contemporary Educational Psychology*, *33*, 97–115. doi:10.1016/j.cedpsych.2006.12.003

Corno, L. (2001). Volitional aspects of self-regulated learning . In Zimmerman, B. J., & Schunk, D. H. (Eds.), *Self-Regulated Learning and Academic Achievement: Theoretical Perspectives* (2nd ed., pp. 191–226). Mahwah, NJ: Erlbaum.

Cover, T. M., & Hart, P. E. (1967). Nearest neighbour pattern classification. *IEEE Transactions on Information Theory, 13*(1), 21–27. doi:10.1109/TIT.1967.1053964

Cowan, N., & Kail, R. (1996). Covert processes and their development in STM . In Gathercole, S. E. (Ed.), *Models of Short-Term Memory* (pp. 29–50). Hove, UK: Psychology Press.

Cox, M. T. (2005). Metacognition in computation: A selected research review. *Artificial Intelligence, 169*, 104–141. doi:10.1016/j.artint.2005.10.009

Crapo, A. W., Waisel, L. B., Wallace, W. A., & Willemain, T. R. (2000). Visualization and the process of modeling: A cognitive-theoretic view. In *Proceedings of the 6th ACM SIGKDD International Conference on Knowledge Discovery and Data Mining*. New York, NY: ACM Press.

Cross, D. R., & Paris, S. G. (1988). Developmental and instructional analysis of children's metacognition and reading comprehension. *Journal of Educational Psychology, 80*, 131–142. doi:10.1037/0022-0663.80.2.131

Cross, T. (2006). Puppy smoothies: Improving the reliability of open, collaborative wikis. *First Monday, 11*(9).

Cunningham, H. (2002). GATE: A general architecture for text engineering. *Computers and the Humanities, 36*(2), 223–254. doi:10.1023/A:1014348124664

Cutting, D. R., Karger, D. R., Pedersen, J. O., & Tukey, J. W. (1992). Scatter/gather: A cluster-based approach to browsing large document collections. In *Proceedings of the 15th International Conference on Research and Development of Information Retrieval (SIGIR)*, (pp. 318-329). Copenhagen, Denmark: ACM.

D'Zurilla, T. J. (1986). *Problem-solving therapy: A social competence approach to clinical intervention*. New York, NY: Springer.

D'Zurilla, T. J., & Maydeu-Olivares, A. (1995). Conceptual and methodological issues in social problem-solving assessment. *Behavior Therapy, 26*, 409–432. doi:10.1016/S0005-7894(05)80091-7

D'Zurilla, T. J., Nezu, A. M., & Maydeu-Olivares, A. (2004). Social problem solving: Theory and assessment . In Chang, E. C., D'Zurilla, T. J., & Sanna, L. J. (Eds.), *Social Problem Solving: Theory, Research, and Training* (pp. 11–27). Washington, DC: American Psychological Association. doi:10.1037/10805-001

Da Fonseca, D., Santos, A., Bastard-Rosset, D., Rodan, C., Poinso, F., & Deruelle, C. (2009). Can children with autistic spectrum disorders extract emotions out of contextual cues? *Research in Autism Spectrum Disorders, 3*, 50–56. doi:10.1016/j.rasd.2008.04.001

Damon, W. (1981). *The social world of the child*. San Francisco, CA: Jossey-Bass.

Darling, S., Sala, S., Gray, C., & Trivelli, C. (1998). Putative functions of the prefrontal cortex . In Mazzoni, G., & Nelson, T. (Eds.), *Metacognition and Cognitive Neuropsychology* (pp. 42–69). Mahwah, NJ: Erlbaum.

Daugherty, M., White, C., & Manning, B. (1994). Relationships among private speech and creativity measurements of young children. *Gifted Child Quarterly, 38*, 21–26. doi:10.1177/001698629403800103

Dave, K., Lawrence, S., & Pennock, D. (2003). Mining the peanut gallery: Opinion extraction and semantic classification of product reviews. In *Proceedings of the 12th International Conference on World Wide Web*, (pp. 519–528). ACM Press.

Davenport, S. (2005). Exploring the role of proximity in SME knowledge-acquisition. *Research Policy, 34*(5), 683–701. doi:10.1016/j.respol.2005.03.006

David, P., Lu, T., & Cai, L. (2002). *Computers as social actors: Testing the fairness of man and machine*. Paper presented to the Fifth Annual International Workshop, Presence 2002, Universidade Fernando Pessoa. Porto, Portugal.

de Geurrero, M. C. M. (2004). Early stages of L2 inner speech development: What verbal reports suggest. *International Journal of Applied Linguistics, 14*, 90–112. doi:10.1111/j.1473-4192.2004.00055.x

de Guerrero, M. C. M. (1994). Form and functions of inner speech in adult second language learning . In Lantolf, J. P., & Appel, G. (Eds.), *Vygotskian Approaches to Second Language Research* (pp. 83–115). Upper Saddle River, NJ: Ablex Pub.

de Guerrero, M. C. M. (1999). Inner speech as mental rehearsal: The case of advanced L2 learners. *Issues in Applied Linguistics, 10*, 27–55.

De La Ossa, J. L., & Gauvain, M. (2001). Joint attention by mothers and children while using plans. *International Journal of Behavioral Development, 25*, 176–183. doi:10.1080/01650250042000168

De Troyer, O. M. F., & Leune, C. J. (1998). WSDM: A user centered design method for web sites. In *Proceedings of Seventh International World Wide Web Conference*. Brisbane, Australia: ACM.

De Troyer, O., & Casteleyn, S. (2003). Modeling complex processes for web applications using WSDM. In *Proceedings of the Third International Workshop on Web-Oriented Software Technologies*. Oviedo, Spain: IEEE.

De Troyer, O. (2001). Audience-driven web design . In *Information Modeling in the New Millennium* (pp. 442–461). Hershey, PA: IGI Global. doi:10.4018/978-1-878289-77-3.ch022

De Troyer, O. (2008). Audience-driven design approach for web systems . In *Encyclopedia of Information Science and Technology* (2nd ed., pp. 274–278). Hershey, PA: IGI Global. doi:10.4018/978-1-60566-026-4.ch047

Deci, E. L., & Ryan, R. M. (1985). *Intrinsic motivation and self-determination in human behavior*. New York, NY: Plenum Press.

Dede, C. (2009). *Determining, developing and assessing the capabilities of 'future-ready' students*. Retrieved from http://www.fi.ncsu.edu/assets/research_papers/brown-bag/determining-developing-and-assessing-the-capabilities-of-future-ready-students.pdf

Deed, C., & Edwards, A. (2010). Using social networks in learning and teaching in higher education: An Australian case study. *International Journal of Knowledge Society Research, 1*(2), 1–12. doi:10.4018/jksr.2010040101

Deed, C., & Edwards, A. (2011). The role of outside affordances in developing expertise in online collaborative learning. *International Journal of Knowledge Society Research, 2*(2), 27–38. doi:10.4018/jksr.2011040103

Deed, C., & Edwards, A. (2011). Unrestricted student blogging: Implications for active learning in a virtual text-based environment. *Active Learning in Higher Education, 12*(1). doi:10.1177/1469787410387725

Deed, C., & Edwards, A. (2012). Knowledge building in online environments: Constraining and enabling collective intelligence . In de Pablos, P. O., Lytras, M. D., Tennyson, R. D., & Gayo, J. E. L. (Eds.), *Cases on Open-Linked Data and Semantic Web Applications*. Hershey, PA: IGI Global.

Dello, K., Nixon, L., & Tolksdorf, R. (2008). Extending the makna semantic wiki to support workflows. In *Proceedings of the 3rd Semantic Wiki Workshop*. IEEE.

Dengler, F., Lamparter, S., Hefke, M., & Abecker, A. (2009). Collaborative process development using semantic MediaWiki. In *Proceedings of the 5th Conference of Professional Knowledge Management*. Solothurn, Switzerland: IEEE.

Deniz, C. B. (2004). Early childhood teachers' beliefs about, and self-reported practices toward, children's private speech. *Dissertation Abstracts International. A, The Humanities and Social Sciences, 64*(9-A), 3185.

Denzin, N. K. (1978). *The research act: A theoretical introduction to socio-logical methods*. New York, NY: McGraw-Hill.

Desoete, A., Roeyers, H., & Buysse, A. (2001). Metacognition and mathematical problem solving in grade 3. *Journal of Learning Disabilities, 34*, 435–449. doi:10.1177/002221940103400505

Devedzi, V. (2002). Understanding ontological engineering. *Communications of the ACM, 45*(4), 136–144. doi:10.1145/505248.506002

Dev, P. C. (1997). Intrinsic motivation and academic achievement: What does their relationship imply for the classroom teacher? *Remedial and Special Education, 18,* 12–19. doi:10.1177/074193259701800104

DeVries, R., & Zan, B. (1992). *Social processes in development: A constructivist view of Piaget, Vygotsky, and education.* Paper presented at the annual meeting of the Jean Piaget Society. Montreal, Canada.

DeVries, R. (2000). Vygotsky, Piaget, and education: A reciprocal assimilation of theories and educational practices. *New Ideas in Psychology, 18,* 187–213. doi:10.1016/S0732-118X(00)00008-8

Dewey, J. (1916). *Democracy and education.* New York, NY: MacMillan.

Dhillon, G., Stahl, B., & Baskerville, R. (2009). Creativity and intelligence in small and medium sized enterprises: The role of information systems. In *Proceedings of the Information Systems – Creativity and Innovation in Small and Medium-Sized Enterprises,* (pp. 1-9). IEEE.

Diamond, K. E. (1993). The role of parents' observations and concerns in screening for developmental delays in young children. *Topics in Early Childhood Special Education, 13,* 68–81. doi:10.1177/027112149301300108

Diaz, R. M., & Berk, L. E. (1995). A Vygotskian critique of self-instructional training. *Development and Psychopathology, 7,* 369–392. doi:10.1017/S0954579400006568

Diaz, R. M., & Berk, L. E. (Eds.). (1992). *Private speech: From social interaction to self-regulation.* Hillsdale, NJ: Erlbaum.

Diaz, R. M., Winsler, A., Atencio, D. J., & Harbers, K. (1992). Mediation of self-regulation through the use of private speech. *International Journal of Cognitive Education and Mediated Learning, 2,* 1–13.

Dichtelmiller, M., Meisels, S. J., Plunkett, J. W., Bozynski, M. E. A., Claflin, C., & Mangelsdorf, S. C. (1992). The relationship of parental knowledge to the development of extremely low birth weight infants. *Journal of Early Intervention, 16,* 210–220. doi:10.1177/105381519201600302

Dick, W., Carey, L., & Carey, J. O. (2001). *The systematic design of instruction.* New York, NY: Addison, Wesley, Longman.

Dietz, J. L. G. (2006). *Enterprise ontology: Theory and methodology.* Berlin, Germany: Springer Verlag. doi:10.1007/3-540-33149-2

Ding, X., & Liu, B. (2007). The utility of linguistic rules in opinion mining. In *Proceedings of SIGIR 2007.* SIGIR.

Ding, Y. (2010). Semantic web: Who is who in the field — A bibliometric analysis. *Journal of Information Science, 36*(3), 335–356. doi:10.1177/0165551510365295

Dixon, W. A., Heppner, P. P., & Anderson, W. P. (1991). Problem-solving appraisal, stress, hopelessness, and suicide ideation in a college population. *Journal of Counseling Psychology, 38,* 51–56. doi:10.1037/0022-0167.38.1.51

Domene, F., & Grela, J. (2009). *Posicionamiento en buscadores edición 2009.* Madrid, Spain: Ediciones Anaya Multimedia.

Dorn, C., Burkhart, T., Werth, D., & Dustdar, S. (2010). Self-adjusting recommendations for people-driven ad-hoc processes . In Hull, R., Mendling, J., & Tai, S. (Eds.), *Business Process Management.* Berlin, Germany: Springer-Verlag. doi:10.1007/978-3-642-15618-2_23

Drucker, P. F. (1969). *The age of discontinuity: Guidelines to our changing society.* London, UK: Heinemann.

Duin, H., Geven, A., Dittenberger, S., Tscheligi, M., Hesmer, A., & Thoben, K. D. (2008). A toolset to support the early stage of innovation. *Towards New Challenges for Innovative Management Practices, 2*(1), 111–118.

Dumais, S. T., & Chen, H. (2000). Hierarchical classification of web content. In *Proceedings of the 23rd Annual International ACM SIGIR Conference on Research and Development in Information Retrieval.* Athens, Greece: ACM Press.

Duncana, R. M., & Cheyne, J. A. (2002). Private speech in young adults task difficulty, self-regulation, and psychological predication. *Cognitive Development, 16,* 889–906.

Duncan, D., Matson, J. L., Bamburg, J. W., Cherry, K. E., & Backley, T. (1999). The relationship of self-injurious behavior and aggression to social skills in persons with severe and profound learning disability. *Research in Developmental Disabilities, 20,* 441–448. doi:10.1016/S0891-4222(99)00024-4

Duncan, R. M., & Pratt, M. W. (1997). Microgenetic change in the quantity and quality of preschoolers' private speech. *International Journal of Behavioral Development, 20*, 367–383. doi:10.1080/016502597385388

Durbin, S. D., Richter, J. N., & Warner, D. (2003). A system for affective rating of texts. In *Proceedings of the 3rd Workshop on Operational Text Classification Systems (OTC 2003).* Washington, DC: OTC.

Ehrich, J. F. (2006). Vygotskian inner speech and the reading process. *Australian Journal of Educational & Developmental Psychology, 6*, 12–25.

Elin, L. (2000). *Designing and developing multimedia: A practical guide for the producer, director, and writer.* Needham Heights, MA: Allyn & Bacon, Inc.

Ell, B., Dengler, F., Djordjevic, D., Garzotto, F., Krötzsch, M., & Siorpaes, K. … Wögler, S. (2010). *Conceptual models for enterprise knowledge – Final models and evaluation.* New York, NY: ACTIVE Project.

Elliot, C. D. (1992). *The affective reasoner: A process model of emotions in a multi-agent system.* (Ph.D. Thesis). Northwestern University. Evanston, IL.

Ellis-Weismer, S. E., Tomblin, J. B., Zhang, X., Buckwalter, P., Chynoweth, J. G., & Jones, M. (2000). Nonword repetition performance in school-age children with and without language impairment. *Journal of Speech, Language, and Hearing Research: JSLHR, 43*, 865–878.

Embregts, P. J. C. M., Didden, R., Schreuder, C., Huitink, C., & van Nieuwenhuijzen, M. (2009). Aggressive behavior in individuals with moderate to borderline intellectual disabilities who live in a residential facility: An evaluation of functional variables. *Research in Developmental Disabilities, 30*, 682–688. doi:10.1016/j.ridd.2008.04.007

Emigh, W., & Herring, S. (2005). Collaborative authoring on the web: A genre analysis of online encyclopedias. In *Proceedings of the 38th Hawaii International Conference on System Sciences.* IEEE.

Emig, J. (1977). Writing as a mode of learning. *College Composition and Communication, 28*(2), 122–128. doi:10.2307/356095

Emirbayer, M., & Mische, A. (1998). What is agency? *American Journal of Sociology, 103*, 962–1023. doi:10.1086/231294

Enge, E., Spencer, S., Stricchiola, J., & Fishkin, R. (2009). *The art of SEO mastering search engine optimization.* Sebastopol, CA: O'Reilly Media.

Engestrom, Y. (1987). *Learning by expanding: An activity-theoretical approach to developmental research.* Helsinki, Finland: Orienta-Konsultit.

Engestrom, Y., Brown, K., Christopher, L. K., & Gregory, J. (1997). Coordination, cooperation and communication in the courts: Expansive transitions in legal work . In Cole, M., Engestrom, Y., & Vasquez, T. (Eds.), *Mind, Culture and Activity: Seminal Papers from the Laboratory of Comparative Human Cognition.* Cambridge, UK: Cambridge University Press.

Entwistle, N. (2001). *Scoring key for the approaches and study skills inventory for students (ASSIST).* Unpublished paper. Edinburgh, UK: University of Edinburgh.

Entwistle, N. (1988). Motivational factors in student's approaches to learning . In Schmeck, R. R. (Ed.), *Learning Strategies and Learning Styles* (pp. 21–51). New York, NY: Plenum.

Enyedy, N., & Hoadley, C. M. (2006). From dialogue to monologue and back: Middle spaces in computer-mediated learning. *Computer-Supported Collaborative Learning, 1*, 413–439. doi:10.1007/s11412-006-9000-2

Epstein, A. (2004). *Parallel hardware architectures for the life science.* (Doctoral Thesis). Delft University. Delft, The Netherlands.

Ericsson, K. A., & Simon, H. A. (1993). *Protocol analysis: Verbal reports as data* (2nd ed.). Cambridge, MA: MIT Press.

Ermolayev, V., Keberle, N., & Matzke, W.-E. (2008). An upper level ontological model for engineering design performance domain. In *Proceedings of the 27th International Conference on Conceptual Modeling.* Berlin, Germany: Springer-Verlag.

Ermolayev, V., Ruiz, C., Tilly, M., Jentzsch, E., & Gomez-Perez, J. M. (2010). A context model for knowledge workers. In *Proceedings of the 2nd International Workshop on Context, Information and Ontologies (CIAO 2010)*. Retrieved from http://ceur-ws.org/

Ermolayev, V., Dengler, F., Fortuna, C., Tajner, T., Bösser, T., & Melchior, E.-M. (2011). Increasing predictability and sharing tacit knowledge in electronic design . In Warren, P., Simperl, E., & Davies, J. (Eds.), *Context and Semantics in Knowledge Management* (pp. 189–212). Berlin, Germany: Springer Verlag. doi:10.1007/978-3-642-19510-5_10

Ermolayev, V., Jentzsch, E., & Fortuna, C. (2010). *Requirements for fully functional prototype*. New York, NY: ACTIVE Project.

Esbensen, B. M., Taylor, M., & Stoess, C. (1997). Children's behavioral understanding of knowledge acquisition. *Cognitive Development, 12*, 53–84. doi:10.1016/S0885-2014(97)90030-7

Ester, M., Kriegel, H.-P., & Schubert, M. (2004). Accurate and efficient crawling for relevant websites. In *Proceedings of the 30th International Very Large Data Bases Conference*. Toronto, Canada: Morgan Kaufmann.

Ettlie, J. E., & Elsenbach, J. M. (2007). Modified stage-gate® regimes in new product development. *Journal of Product Innovation Management, 24*(1), 20–33. doi:10.1111/j.1540-5885.2006.00230.x

Faber, A., & Mazlish, E. (1995). Praise that doesn't demean, criticism that doesn't wound. *American Educator, 19*, 33–38.

Farmer, C. A., & Aman, M. G. (2009). Development of the children's scale of hostility and aggression: Reactive/proactive (C-SHARP). *Research in Developmental Disabilities, 30*, 1155–1167. doi:10.1016/j.ridd.2009.03.001

Farquhar, A., Fikes, R., & Rice, J. (1996). The ontolingua server: A tool for collaborative ontology construction. *Knowledge Systems, 46*, 707–727.

Farson, R. E. (1963). Praise reappraised. *Harvard Business Review, 41*, 61–66.

Fazio, B. B. (1996). Serial memory in children with specific language impairment: Examining specific content areas for assessment and intervention. *Topics in Language Disorders, 17*, 58–71. doi:10.1097/00011363-199611000-00007

Feldman, R., & Sanger, J. (2006). *The text mining handbook: Advanced approaches in analyzing unstructured data*. Cambridge, UK: Cambridge University Press. doi:10.1017/CBO9780511546914

Fellbaum, C. (1998). *WordNet: An electronic lexical database*. Cambridge, MA: MIT Press.

Fennell, C. T., & Werker, J. F. (2004). *Applying speech perception to word learning at 14 months: Effects of word knowledge and familiarity*. Paper presented at the 28th Annual Boston University Conference on Language Development. Boston, MA.

Fensel, D. (2002). *Ontologies: A silver bullet for knowledge management and electronic commerce*. Berlin, Germany: Springer-Verlag.

Fernadez-Duque, D., Baird, J., & Posner, M. (2000). Awareness and metacognition. *Consciousness and Cognition, 9*, 324–326. doi:10.1006/ccog.2000.0449

Fernandez-Breis, J., Castellanos-Nieves, D., & Valencia-García, R. (2009). Measuring individual learning performance in group work from a knowledge integration perspective. *Information Sciences, 179*(4), 339–354. doi:10.1016/j.ins.2008.10.014

Fernyhough, C., & Fradley, E. (2005). Private speech on an executive task: Relations with task difficulty and task performance. *Cognitive Development, 20*, 103–120. doi:10.1016/j.cogdev.2004.11.002

Ferragina, P., & Gulli, A. (2005). A personalized search engine based on web-snippet hierarchical clustering. In *Proceedings of the Special Interest Tracks and Posters of the 14th International Conference on World Wide Web*. Chiba, Japan: ACM Press.

Fidler, D. J., Most, D. E., Booth-LaForce, C., & Kelly, J. F. (2006). Temperament and behaviour problems in young children with Down syndrome at 12, 30, and 45 months. *Down Syndrome . Research & Practice, 10*, 23–29.

Finzen, J., Kintz, M., Kett, H., & Koch, S. (2009). Strategic innovation management on the basis of searching and mining press releases. In *Proceedings of the Fifth International Conference on Web Information Systems and Technologies*. Lisbon, Portugal: INSTICC Press.

Fischer, M., Rolf, J. E., Hasazi, H. E., & Cummings, I. (1984). Follow-up of a preschool epidemiological sample: Cross-age continuities and predictions of later adjustment with internalizing and externalizing dimensions of behavior. *Child Development, 55*, 137–150. doi:10.2307/1129840

Fishkin, R. (2009). *Search engine ranking factors 2009*. Retrieved February 13, 2010, from http://www.seomoz.org/article/search-ranking-factors

Fitts, P. M. (1962). Factors in complex skill training . In Glaser, R. (Ed.), *Training Research and Education* (pp. 177–197). Pittsburgh, PA: University of Pittsburgh Press.

Flavell, J. H. (1966). Le langage privé. *Bulletin de Psychologie, 19*, 698–701.

Flavell, J. H. (1976). Metacognitive aspects of problem solving . In Resnick, L. B. (Ed.), *The Nature of Intelligence* (pp. 231–236). Hillsdale, NJ: Erlbaum.

Flavell, J. H. (1977). *Cognitive development*. Englewood Cliffs, NJ: Prentice-Hall.

Flavell, J. H. (1979). Metacognition and cognitive monitoring—A new era of cognitive-developmental inquiry. *The American Psychologist, 34*, 906–911. doi:10.1037/0003-066X.34.10.906

Flavell, J. H. (1987). Speculations about the nature and development of metacognition . In Weinert, F. E., & Kluwe, R. H. (Eds.), *Metacognition, Motivation, and Understanding* (pp. 21–29). Hillsdale, NJ: Erlbaum.

Flavell, J. H., Beach, D. R., & Chinsky, J. M. (1996). Spontaneous verbal rehearsal in a memory task as a function of age. *Child Development, 37*, 283–299. doi:10.2307/1126804

Fogg, B. J. (2002). *Persuasive technology: Using computers to change what we think and do*. San Francisco, CA: Kaufmann.

Forman, G. (2003). An extensive empirical study of feature selection metrics for text classification. *Journal of Machine Learning Research, 3*, 1289–1305. Retrieved from http://jmlr.csail.mit.edu/papers/volume3/forman03a/forman03a_full.pdf

Forrester Research. (2009). *US interactive marketing forecast, 2009 To 2014*. Retrieved February 15, 2010, from http://www.forrester.com/rb/Research/us_interactive_marketing_forecast,_2009_to_2014/q/id/47730/t/2

Fowler, M. (1997). *Analysis patterns, reusable object models*. Reading, MA: Addison Wesley Longman.

Francis, H. (1982). *Learning to read*. London, UK: Allen & Unwin.

Frank, E., & Witten, I. H. (1998). *Generating accurate rule sets without global optimization*. Paper presented at the Fifteenth International Conference on Machine Learning. San Francisco, CA: Morgan Kaufmann Publishers.

Franstrom, F., & Lewis, J. (2000). *CiteSeer*. Retrieved December 27, 2009, from http://citeseerx.ist.psu.edu/viewdoc/summary?doi=10.1.1.36.7008

Frauenglass, M. H., & Diaz, R. M. (1985). Self-regulatory functions of children's private speech: A critical analysis of recent challenges to Vygotsky's theory. *Developmental Psychology, 21*, 357–364. doi:10.1037/0012-1649.21.2.357

Frawley, W., & Lantolf, J. P. (1985). Second language discourse: A Vygotskian perspective. *Applied Linguistics, 6*, 19–44. doi:10.1093/applin/6.1.19

Frawley, W., & Lantolf, J. P. (1986). Private speech and self-regulation: A commentary on Frauenglass and Diaz. *Developmental Psychology, 22*, 706–708. doi:10.1037/0012-1649.22.5.706

Fredricks, J. A., Blumenfeld, P. C., & Paris, A. H. (2004). School engagement: Potential of the concept, state of the evidence. *Review of Educational Research, 74*(1), 59–109. doi:10.3102/00346543074001059

Freinet, C. (1969). *Pour l'ecole du peuple: Guide pratique pour l'organisation materielle, technique et pedagogique de l'ecole populaire* [For a school of the people: A practical guide for the material, technical, and pedagogical organization of a popular school]. Barcelona, Spain: Editorial Laia.

Freinet, C. (1969). *Pour l'ecole du peuple: Guide pratique pour l'organisation materielle, technique et pedagogique de l'ecole populaire* [For a school of the people: A practical guide for the material, technical, and pedagogical organization of a popular school]. Barcelona, Spain: Editorial Laia.

Frommholz, I. (2001). Categorizing web documents in hierarchical catalogues. In *Proceedings of the 23rd European Colloquium on Information Retrieval Research (ECIR 2001)*. Darmstadt, Germany: British Computer Society

Fuson, K. C. (1979). The development of self-regulating aspects of speech: A review. In Zivin, G. (Ed.), *The Development of Self-Regulation through Private Speech* (pp. 135–217). New York, NY: Wiley.

Gabrilovich, E. (2006). *Feature generation for textual information retrieval using world knowledge*. (PhD Dissertation). Israel Institute of Technology. Haifa, Israel. Retrieved from http://www.cs.technion.ac.il/~gabr/pubs.html

Gamon, M., Aue, A., Corston-Oliver, S., & Ringger, E. (2005). Pulse: Mining customer opinions from free text. *Lecture Notes in Computer Science*, *3646*, 121–132. doi:10.1007/11552253_12

García Díaz, V., & Cueva Lovelle, J. M. (2010). *Ingeniería dirigida por modelos* [presentations]. Oviedo.

García-Crespo, A., Colomo-Palacios, R., Gómez-Berbís, J. M., & Ruiz-Mezcua, B. (2010). SEMO: A framework for customer social networks analysis based on semantics. *Journal of Information Technology*, *25*(2), 178–188. doi:10.1057/jit.2010.1

García-Crespo, Á., López-Cuadrado, J. L., Colomo-Palacios, R., González-Carrasco, I., & Ruiz-Mezcua, B. (2011). Sem-fit: A semantic based expert system to provide recommendations in the tourism domain. *Expert Systems with Applications*, *38*(10), 13310–13319. doi:10.1016/j.eswa.2011.04.152

García-Magariño, I., Fuentes-Fernández, R., & Gómez-Sanz, J. J. (2009). Guideline for the definition of EMF metamodels using an entity-relationship approach. *Information and Software Technology*, *51*(8), 1217–1230. doi:10.1016/j.infsof.2009.02.003

Garcia, R., Perdrix, F., Gil, R., & Oliva, M. (2008). The semantic web as a newspaper media convergence facilitator. *Journal of Web Semantics*, *6*(2), 151–161. doi:10.1016/j.websem.2008.01.002

Garcia-Sanchez, F., Fernandez-Breis, J., Valencia-Garcia, R., Gomez, J., & Martinez-Bejar, R. (2008). Combining semantic web technologies with multi-agent systems for integrated access to biological resources. *Journal of Biomedical Informatics*, *41*(5), 848–859. doi:10.1016/j.jbi.2008.05.007

Gardner, W., & Rogoff, B. (1990). Children's deliberateness of planning according to task circumstances. *Developmental Psychology*, *26*, 480–487. doi:10.1037/0012-1649.26.3.480

Gartstein, M. A., Marmion, J., & Swanson, H. L. (2006). Infant temperament: An evaluation of children with Down syndrome. *Journal of Reproductive and Infant Psychology*, *24*, 31–41. doi:10.1080/02646830500475237

Garzotto, F., Mainetti, L., & Paolini, P. (1995). Hypermedia design, analysis, and evaluation issues. *Communications of the ACM*, *38*(8), 74–86. doi:10.1145/208344.208349

Garzotto, F., & Paolini, P. (1993). HDM—A model-based approach to hypertext application design. *ACM Transactions on Information Systems*, *11*(1), 1–26. doi:10.1145/151480.151483

Gaskill, M. N., & Díaz, R. M. (1991). The relation between private speech and cognitive performance. *Infancia y Aprendizaje*, *53*, 45–58.

Gathercole, S. E., Willis, C. S., Baddeley, A. D., & Emslie, H. (1994). The children's test of nonword repetition: A test of phonological working memory. *Memory (Hove, England)*, *2*, 103–127. doi:10.1080/09658219408258940

Gauch, S., Chaffee, J., & Pretschner, A. (2003). Ontology-based personalized search and browsing. *Web Intelligence and Agent System*, *1*(3-4), 219–234.

Genereux, M., & Evans, R. (2006). Towards a validated model for affective classification of texts. In *Proceedings of the Workshop on Sentiment and Subjectivity in Text*, (pp. 55–62). Sydney, Australia: Association for Computational Linguistics.

Gervilliers, D., Bertellot, C., & Lemery, J. (1977). *Las correspondencias escolares*. Barcelona, Spain: Editorial Laia.

Ghidini, C., Kump, B., Lindstaedt, S., Mahbub, N., Pammer, V., Rospocher, M., & Serafini, L. (2009). Moki: The enterprise modelling wiki . In *The Semantic Web: Research and Applications*. Berlin, Germany: Springer-Verlag. doi:10.1007/978-3-642-02121-3_65

Giarratano, J. C., & Riley, G. D. (2005). *Expert systems: Principles and programming*. Pacific Grove, CA: Brooks/Cole Publishing Co.

Giles, J. (2005). Internet encyclopedias go head to head. *Nature*, *438*, 900–901. doi:10.1038/438900a

Gillam, R. B., Cowan, N., & Day, L. S. (1995). Sequential memory in children with and without language impairment. *Journal of Speech and Hearing Research*, *38*, 393–402.

Gillespie, L. G., & Seibel, N. L. (2006). Self-regulation: A cornerstone of early childhood development. *Journal of the National Association for Education of Young Children*, *12*, 142–161.

Gilmore, L., Cuskelly, M., & Hayes, A. (2003). Self-regulatory behaviors in children with Down syndrome and typically developing children measured using the Goodman lock box. *Research in Developmental Disabilities*, *24*, 95–108. doi:10.1016/S0891-4222(03)00012-X

Girbau, D. (2002). A sequential analysis of private and social speech in children's dyadic communication. *The Spanish Journal of Psychology*, *52*, 110–118.

Glascoe, F. P. (1994). It's not what it seems: The relationship between parents' concerns and children with global delays. *Clinical Pediatrics*, *33*, 292–296. doi:10.1177/000992289403300507

Glascoe, F. P., & MacLean, W. E. (1990). How parents appraise their child's development. *Family Relations*, *39*, 280–283. doi:10.2307/584872

Godbole, N., Srinivasaiah, M., & Skiena, S. (2007). Large-scale sentiment analysis for news and blogs. In *Proceedings of the International Conference on Weblogs and Social Media (ICWSM)*. Boulder, CO: ICWSM.

Godbole, N., Srinivasaiah, M., & Skiena, S. (2007). LargeScale sentiment analysis for news and blogs. [ICWSM.]. *Proceedings of ICWSM*, *2007*, 219–222.

Gómez-Pérez, A., Fernández-López, M., & Corcho, O. (2003). *Ontological engineering*. Berlin, Germany: Springer-Verlag.

Goodman, S. H. (1981). The integration of verbal and motor behavior in preschool children. *Child Development*, *52*, 280–289. doi:10.2307/1129241

Google. (2008). *Google's search engine optimization starter guide*. Retrieved February 11, 2010, from http://www.google.com/webmasters/docs/search-engine-optimization-starter-guide.pdf

Gopnik, A., & Graf, P. (1988). Knowing how you know: Young children's ability to identify and remember the sources of their beliefs. *Child Development*, *59*, 1366–1371. doi:10.2307/1130499

Gospodnetić, O., & Hatcher, E. (2005). *Lucene in action*. Greenwich, CT: Manning Publications.

Gottfried, A. E., Fleming, J., & Gottfried, A. W. (1994). Role of parental motivational practices in children's academic intrinsic motivation and achievement. *Journal of Educational Psychology*, *86*, 104–113. doi:10.1037/0022-0663.86.1.104

Goudena, P. P. (1992). The problem of abbreviation and internalization of private speech . In Diaz, R. M., & Berk, L. E. (Eds.), *Private Speech: From Social Interaction to Self-Regulation* (pp. 215–224). Hillsdale, NJ: Erlbaum.

Grace-Martin, M., & Gay, G. (2001). Web browsing, mobile computing and academic performance. *Journal of Educational Technology & Society*, *4*(3), 95–107.

Grebner, O., Ong, E., Riss, U., Brunzel, M., Bernardi, A., & Roth-Berghofer, T. (2006). *Task management model*. NEPOMUK Project.

Greenberg, J., & Pattuelli, M. (2001). Author-generated Dublin core metadata for web resources: A baseline study in an organization. *Journal of Digital Information*, *2*, 38–46.

Greenhow, C., Robelia, B., & Hughes, J. E. (2009). Web 2.0 and classroom research: What path should we take now? *Educational Researcher*, *38*(4), 246–259. doi:10.3102/0013189X09336671

Greeno, J. G. (1994). Gibson's affordances. *Psychological Review*, *101*(2), 336–343. doi:10.1037/0033-295X.101.2.336

Grefenstette, G., Qu, Y., Shanahan, J. G., & Evans, D. (2004). Coupling niche browsers and affect analysis for an opinion mining application. In *Proceedings of Recherche d'Information Assistée par Ordinateur (RIAO)*. RIAO.

Gregory, M. L., Chinchor, N., Whitney, P., Carter, R., Hetzler, E., & Turner, A. (2006). User-directed sentiment analysis: Visualizing the affective content of documents. In *Proceedings of the Workshop on Sentiment and Subjectivity in Text*, (pp. 23–30). Sydney, Australia: Association for Computational Linguistics.

Grinsven, L., & Tillema, H. (2006). Learning opportunities to support student self-regulation: Comparing different instructional formats. *Educational Research*, *48*, 77–91. doi:10.1080/00131880500498495

Gronau, N., Müller, C., & Korf, R. (2005). KMDL – Capturing, analysing, and improving knowledge-intensive business processes. *Journal of Universal Computer Science*, *11*(1), 452–472.

Grosky, W. I. (1994). Multimedia information systems. *IEEE MultiMedia*, *1*(1), 12–24. doi:10.1109/93.295262

Group, O. M. (2007). *MOF 2.0/XMI mapping, version 2.1.1* (p. 120). Object Management Group.

Gruber, T. (2007). Collective knowledge systems. In *Proceedings of the 5th International Semantic Web Conference*. IEEE.

Gruber, T. (1993). *A translation approach to portable ontologies*. London, UK: Academic Press.

Gruber, T. R. (1993). A translation approach to portable ontology specifications. *Knowledge Acquisition*, *5*(2), 199–220. doi:10.1006/knac.1993.1008

Gruber, T. R. (1995). Towards principles for the design of ontologies used for knowledge sharing. *International Journal of Human-Computer Studies*, *43*(5-6), 907–928. doi:10.1006/ijhc.1995.1081

Grüninger, M., Atefy, K., & Fox, M. S. (2000). Ontologies to support process integration in enterprise engineering. *Computational & Mathematical Organization Theory*, *6*(4), 381–394. doi:10.1023/A:1009610430261

Grünwald, C., & Marx Gómez, J. (2007). Conception of system supported generation of sustainability reports in a large scale enterprise. In J. Marx Gomez, M. Sonnenschein, M. Müller, H. Welsch, & C. Rautenstrauch (Eds.), *Information Technologies in Environmental Engineering: ITEE 2007 - Third International ICSC Symposium*, (pp. 60-68). Berlin, Germany: Springer Verlag.

Guarino, N. (Ed.). (1998). Formal ontology and information systems. In *Proceedings of the Formal Ontology in Information Systems*, (pp. 3-15). Amsterdam, The Netherlands: IOS Press.

Guida, G., & Tasso, C. (1994). *Design and development of knowledge- based systems: From life cycle to methodology*. Chichester, UK: John Wiley and Sons Ltd.

Guizzardi, G. (2007). On ontology, ontologies, conceptualizations, modeling languages, and (meta)models. In *Proceedings of the 2007 Conference on Databases and Information Systems IV: Selected Papers from the Seventh International Baltic Conference*. IEEE.

Guizzardi, G. (2005). *Ontological foundations for structural conceptual models*. Enschede.

Guizzardi, G. (2005). *Ontological foundations for structural conceptual models. CTIT*. Centre for Telematics and Information Technology.

Gunawardena, C., & Zittle, F. (1997). Social presence as a predictor of satisfaction within a computer mediated conferencing environment. *American Journal of Distance Education*, *11*, 8–26. doi:10.1080/08923649709526970

Guterman, E. (2003). Integrating written metacognitive awareness guidance as a 'psychological tool' to improve student performance. *Learning and Instruction*, *13*, 633–651. doi:10.1016/S0959-4752(02)00070-1

Guy, M., & Tonkin, E. (2006). Folksonomies tidying up tags? *D-Lib Magazine*, *12*, 1–14.

Haak, L., & Brehm, N. (2008). *Ontologies supporting VLBAs semantic integration in the context of FERP*. In *Proceedings of the 3rd International Conference on Information and Communication Technologies: From Theory To Applications, ICTTA 2008*, (pp. 1-5). ICTTA.

Hadwin, A., & Winne, P. (2001). CoNoteS2: A software tool for promoting self-regulation. *Educational Research and Evaluation*, *7*, 313–334. doi:10.1076/edre.7.2.313.3868

Hagedoorn, J., Link, A. N., & Vonortas, N. S. (2009). Research partnerships. *Research Policy*, *29*(4-5), 567–586. doi:10.1016/S0048-7333(99)00090-6

Hagel, J., & Rayport, J. F. (1997). The coming battle for customer information. *Harvard Business Review*, *75*(1), 53–65.

Hale, S., Bronik, M. D., & Fry, A. F. (1997). Verbal and spatial working memory in school-age children: Developmental differences in susceptibility to interference. *Developmental Psychology*, *33*, 361–371. doi:10.1037/0012-1649.33.2.364

Hale, S., Myerson, J., Rhee, S. H., Weiss, C. S., & Abrams, R. A. (1996). Selective interference with the maintenance of location information in working memory. *Neuropsychology*, *10*, 228–240. doi:10.1037/0894-4105.10.2.228

Harter, S. P. (1992). Psychological relevance and information science. *Journal of the American Society for Information Science American Society for Information Science*, *43*(9), 602–615. doi:10.1002/(SICI)1097-4571(199210)43:9<602::AID-ASI3>3.0.CO;2-Q

Haste, H. (1987). Growing into rules . In Bruner, J., & Haste, H. (Eds.), *Making Sense* (pp. 163–195). New York, NY: Metheun.

Hatano, G., & Inagaki, K. (1986). Two courses of expertise . In Stevenson, H., Azuma, H., & Hakuta, K. (Eds.), *Child Development and Education in Japan* (pp. 262–272). New York, NY: W. H. Reeman and Company.

Hatzivassiloglou, V., & McKeown, K. R. (1997). Predicting the semantic orientation of adjectives. In *Proceedings of the 35th Annual Meeting of the Association for Computational Linguistics and the 8th Conference of the European Chapter of the ACL*, (pp. 174-181). ACL.

Haveliwala, T. H. (2002). Topic-sensitive PageRank. In *Proceedings of the 11th International Conference on World Wide Web (WWW 2002)*. Honolulu, HI: ACM Press.

Hearst, M. A. (2001). Direction-based text interpretation as an information access refinement . In *Text-Based Intelligent Systems* (pp. 257–274). Hillsdale, NJ: Lawrence Erlbaum Associates Inc.

Hearst, M. A., Dumais, S. T., Osuna, E., Platt, J., & Schölkopf, B. (1998). Support vector machines. *IEEE Intelligent Systems*, *13*(4), 18–28. doi:10.1109/5254.708428

Heflin, J., & Hendler, J. (2001). A portrait of the semantic web in action. *IEEE Intelligent Systems*, *16*(2), 54–59. doi:10.1109/5254.920600

Henderlong, J. (2000). *Beneficial and detrimental effects of praise on children's motivation: Performance versus person feedback*. (Unpublished Doctoral Dissertation). Stanford University. Palo Alto, CA.

Henderson-Sellers, B. (2011). Bridging metamodels and ontologies in software engineering. *Journal of Systems and Software*, *84*(2), 301–313. doi:10.1016/j.jss.2010.10.025

Hendler, J. (2001). Agents and the semantic web. *IEEE Intelligent Systems*, *16*(2), 30–37. doi:10.1109/5254.920597

Hennessey, G. (1999). *Probing the dimensions of metacognition: Implications for conceptual change teaching-learning*. Paper presented at annual meeting of the national association for research in science teaching. San Francisco, CA.

Hepp, M., De Leenheer, P., & de Moor, A. (2007). *Ontology management: Semantic web, semantic web services, and business applications*. Berlin, Germany: Springer.

Hepp, M., & Roman, D. (2007). An ontology framework for semantic business process management . In Oberweis, A., Weinhardt, C., Gimpel, H., Koschmider, A., Pankratius, V., & Schmizler, B. (Eds.), *eOrganisation: Service-Prozess, Market-Engineering* (*Vol. 1*). Karlsruhe, Germany: Universitaetsverlag Karlsruhe.

Heppner, P. P. (1988). *The problem-solving inventory*. Palo Alto, CA: Consulting Psychologist Press.

Heppner, P. P., & Peterson, C. H. (1982). The development and implications of a personal problem solving inventory. *Journal of Counseling Psychology*, *29*, 580–590. doi:10.1037/0022-0167.29.6.580

Heuser, L., Alsdorf, C., & Woods, D. (2007). Enterprise 2.0 - The service grid –User-driven innovation - Business model transformation. In *Proceedings of the International Research Forum 2007, Potsdam, SAP Research*. Evolved Technologist Press.

Heuser, L., Alsdorf, C., & Woods, D. (2008). The web-based service industry – Infrastructure for enterprise SOA 2.0, potential killer applications - Semantic service discovery. In *Proceedings of the International Research Forum 2008, Potsdam, SAP Research*. Evolved Technologist Press.

Higgins, E. T. (1997). Beyond pleasure and pain. *The American Psychologist*, *52*, 1280–1300. doi:10.1037/0003-066X.52.12.1280

Hinshaw, S. P. (1994). Conduct disorder in childhood: Conceptualizing, diagnosis, comorbidity, and risk status for antisocial functioning in adulthood . In Fowles, D., Sutker, P., & Goodman, S. (Eds.), *Progress in Experimental Personality and Psychopathology Research: Special Focus on Psychopathology and Antisocial Personality, a Developmental Perspective* (pp. 3–44). New York, NY: Springer.

Hitz, M., & Werthner, H. (1993). Development and analysis of a wide area multimedia information system. In *Proceedings of the 1993 ACM/SIGAPP Symposium on Applied Computing: States of the Art and Practice (SAC 1993)*, (pp. 238-246). New York, NY: ACM Press.

Hitzler, P., & Janowicz, K. (2011). Semantic web tools and system. *Semantic Web*, *2*(1), 1–2.

Hoffman, L. M., & Gillam, R. B. (2004). Verbal and spatial information processing constraints in children with specific language impairment. *Journal of Speech, Language, and Hearing Research: JSLHR*, *47*, 114–125. doi:10.1044/1092-4388(2004/011)

Holding, D. H. (1965). *Principles of training*. Oxford, UK: Pergamon Press.

Horii, R., & Iwaisako, T. (2007). Economic growth with imperfect protection of intellectual property rights. *Journal of Economics*, *90*(1), 45–85. doi:10.1007/s00712-006-0222-6

Horridge, M., & Bechhofer, S. (2009). *The OWL API: A Java API for working with OWL 2 ontologies*. Paper presented at the 6th OWL Experiences and Directions Workshop. Chantilly, VA.

Horrocks, I. (2008). Ontologies and the semantic web. *Communications of the ACM*, *51*(12), 58–67. doi:10.1145/1409360.1409377

Hotho, A., Maedche, A., & Staab, S. (2001). Ontology-based text clustering . In *Proceedings of Text Learning: Beyond Supervision, IJCAI*. Seattle, WA: IJCAI.

Howels, J. (2006). Intermediation and the role of intermediaries in innovation. *Research Policy*, *35*(5), 715–728. doi:10.1016/j.respol.2006.03.005

Hu, M., & Liu, B. (2004). Mining and summarizing customer reviews. In *Proceedings of ACM SIGKDD Conference*. ACM Press.

Hu, M., & Liu, B. (2004). Mining opinion features in customer reviews. In *Proceedings of AAAI*, (pp. 755–760). AAAI.

Hu, M., Lim, E. P., Sun, A., Lauw, H., & Vuong, B. Q. (2007). Measuring article quality in Wikipedia: Models and evaluation. In *Proceedings of the International Conference on Knowledge and Information Management*. IEEE.

Huber, M., Bretschneider, U., Leimeister, J., & Krcmar, H. (2009). Making innovation happen: Tool-support for software related communities for innovations. In *Proceedings of the Open Design Spaces Supporting User Innovation*, (pp. 22-32). Bonn, Germany: IISI.

Hudson, J. A., Shapiro, L. R., & Sosa, B. B. (1995). Planning in the real world: Preschool children's scripts and plans for familiar events. *Child Development*, *66*, 984–998. doi:10.2307/1131793

Innocentive. (2010). *Website*. Retrieved from http://www.innocentive.com/

Isaki, E., & Plante, E. (1997). Short-term and working memory differences in language/learning disabled and normal adults. *Journal of Communication Disorders*, *30*, 327–437. doi:10.1016/S0021-9924(96)00111-6

Isakowitz, T., Kamis, A., & Koufaris, M. (1997). Extending the capabilities of RMM: Russian dolls and hypertext. In *Proceedings of 30th Hawaii International Conference on System Sciences (HICSS-30)*. Maui, HI: IEEE.

Isakowitz, T., Stohr, E. A., & Balasubramanian, P. (1995). A RMM: Methodology for structured hypermedia design. *Communications of the ACM, 38*(8), 34–44. doi:10.1145/208344.208346

Ivers, K. S., & Baron, A. (2002). *Multimedia projects in education: Designing, producing, and assessing.* Wesport, CT: Teacher Ideas Press.

Jääskeläinen, R. (1999). *Tapping the process: An explorative study of the cognitive and affective factors involved in translating.* Joensuu, Finland: University of Joensuu.

Jacobson, M., & Archodidou, A. (2000). The design of hypermedia tools for learning: Fostering conceptual change and transfer of complex scientific knowledge. *Journal of the Learning Sciences, 9*, 149–199. doi:10.1207/s15327809jls0902_2

Jacquemin, C. (2006). *Spotting and discovering terms through natural language processing.* Cambridge, MA: MIT Press.

Jansen, B. J., & Spink, A. (2006). How are we searching the world wide web? A comparison of nine search engine transaction logs. *Information Processing & Management, 42*(1), 248–263. doi:10.1016/j.ipm.2004.10.007

Järvilehto, M., Leppälä, K., & Similä, J. (2008). Communicative incentives in consumer innovation brokering. In *Proceedings of the Hawaii International Conference on System Sciences,* (p. 418). Los Alamitos, CA: IEEE Computer Society.

Jiang, X., & Tan, A. H. (2009). Learning and inferencing in user ontology for personalized semantic web search. *Information Sciences: An International Journal, 179*(16), 2794–2808.

Jiang, Z., Joshi, A., Krishnapuram, R., & Yi, L. (2000). *Retriever: Improving web search engine results using clustering.* Baltimore, MD: University of Maryland Baltimore County.

Jing, L., Zhou, L., Ng, M., & Huang, J. Z. (2006). Ontology-based distance measure for text mining. In *Proceedings of the Sixth SIAM International Conference on Data Mining (SDM)*. Bethesda, MD: SIAM.

Joachims, T. (1998). Text categorization with support vector machines: Learning with many relevant features. In *Proceedings of the 10th European Conference on Machine Learning (ECML 1998)*. Chemnitz, Germany: Springer-Verlag.

John-Hattie, J., & Timperley, H. (2007). The power of feedback. *Review of Educational Research, 77*(1), 81–112. doi:10.3102/003465430298487

Jonassen, D. (1996). *Computers as mind tools for schools.* Columbus, OH: Merrill.

Jones, M. G., Farquhar, J. D., & Surry, D. W. (1995). Using metacognitive theories to design user interfaces for computer-based learning. *Educational Technology, 35*, 12–22.

Just, M., & Carpenter, P. (1992). A capacity theory of comprehension: Individual differences in working memory. *Psychological Review, 99*, 122–149. doi:10.1037/0033-295X.99.1.122

Kalfoglou, Y. (2000). *Deploying ontologies in software design.* (PhD Thesis). University of Edinburgh. Edinburgh, UK.

Kamii, C., & DeVries, R. (1980). *Group games in early education: Implications of Piaget's theory.* Washington, DC: National Association for the Education of Young Children.

Kamps, J., & Koolen, M. (2009). Is Wikipedia's link structure different? In *Proceedings of the 2nd International Conference on Web Search and Data Mining.* IEEE.

Kanayama, H., & Nasukawa, T. (2006). Fully automatic lexicon expansion for domain oriented sentiment analysis. In *Proceedings of the Conference on Empirical Methods in Natural Language Processing, EMNLP 2006.* EMNLP.

Kanellopoulos, D., Kotsiantis, S., & Pintelas, P. (2006). Ontology-based learning applications: A development methodology. In *Proceedings of the 24th IASTED International Multi-Conference Software Engineering,* (pp. 27-32). Innsbruck, Austria: IASTED.

Kangasoja, J. (2002). *Complex design problems: An impetus for learning and knotworking.* Retrieved 21 May, 2011, from http://www.edu.helsinki.fi/activity/publications/files/47/ICLS2002_Kangasoja.pdf

Kärkkäinen, J., Sanders, P., & Burkhardt, S. (2006). Linear work suffix array construction. *Journal of the ACM, 53*(6), 918–936. doi:10.1145/1217856.1217858

Katz, I., Assor, A., Kanat-Maymon, Y., & Bereby-Meyer, Y. (2006). Interest as a motivational resource: Feedback and gender matter, but interest makes the difference. *Social Psychology of Education, 9*, 27–42. doi:10.1007/s11218-005-2863-7

Kau, A. S. M., Reider, E. E., Payne, L., Meyer, W. A., & Freund, L. (2000). Early behavior signs of psychiatric phenotypes in fragile X syndrome. *American Journal of Mental Retardation, 105*, 286–299. doi:10.1352/0895-8017(2000)105<0286:EBSOPP>2.0.CO;2

Kavi, M., & Sergei, N. (1995). A situated ontology for practical NLP. In *Proceedings of the Workshop on Basic Ontological Issues in Knowledge Sharing, International Joint Conference on Artificial Intelligence (IJCAI 1995).* Montreal, Canada: IJCAI.

Kay, J., Li, L., & Fekete, A. (2007). *Learner reflection in student self-assessment.* Paper presented at the Ninth Australasian Computing Education Conference (ACE 2007). Ballarat, Australia.

Kayed, A., El-Qawasmeh, E., & Qawaqneh, Z. (2010). Ranking web sites using domain ontology concepts. *Information & Management, 47*, 350–355. doi:10.1016/j.im.2010.08.002

Kayem, J. J. (2004). Making scents: Aromatic output for HCI. *Interaction, 11*(1), 48–61.

Kazdin, A. E. (1993). Treatment of conduct disorder: Progress and directions in psychotherapy research. *Development and Psychopathology, 5*, 277–310. doi:10.1017/S0954579400004399

Keenan, K., Shaw, D. S., Delliquadri, E., Giovannelli, J., & Walsh, B. (1998). Evidence for the continuity of early problem behaviors: Application of a developmental model. *Journal of Abnormal Child Psychology, 26*, 441–454. doi:10.1023/A:1022647717926

Keenan, K., & Wakschlag, L. S. (2000). More than the terrible twos: The nature and severity of behavior problems in clinic-referred preschool children. *Journal of Abnormal Child Psychology, 28*, 33–46. doi:10.1023/A:1005118000977

Keen, P. G. W. (1991). Relevance and rigor in information systems research: Improving quality, confidence, cohesion and impact . In *Information Systems Research: Contemporary Approaches and Emergent Traditions* (pp. 27–49). Amsterdam, The Netherlands: Elsevier Science Publishers.

Kim, S. G., Kim, J. W., & Lee, C. W. (2007). Implementation of multi-touch tabletop display for HCI (human computer interaction). In *Proceedings of the 12th International Conference on Human-Computer Interaction: Interaction Platforms and Techniques (HCI 2007)*, (pp. 854-863). Berlin, Germany: Springer-Verlag.

Kittur, A., Suh, B., Pendleton, B., & Chi, E. (2007). He says, she says: Conflict and coordination in Wikipedia. In *Proceedings of the International Conference on the Special Interest Group on Computer Human Interaction*, (pp. 453-462). IEEE.

Klas, C.-P., & Fuhr, N. (2000). A new effective approach for categorizing web documents. In *Proceedings of the 22nd Annual Colloquium of the British Computer Society Information Retrieval Specialist Group (BCSIGSG 2000)*. Cambridge, UK: British Computer Society.

Kleinberg, J. M. (1999). Authoritative sources in a hyperlinked environment. *Journal of the ACM, 46*(5), 604–632. doi:10.1145/324133.324140

Klein-Tasman, B. P., & Mervis, C. B. (2003). Distinctive personality characteristics of 8-, 9-, and 10-year-olds with Williams syndrome. *Developmental Neuropsychology, 23*, 269–290.

Kleppe, A., Warmer, J., & Bast, W. (2003). *MDA explained: The model driven architecture™: Practice and promise.* Reading, MA: Addison Wesley.

Kluger, A. N., & DeNisi, A. (1996). The effects of feedback interventions on performance: A historical review, a meta-analysis, and a preliminary feedback intervention theory. *Psychological Bulletin, 119*, 254–284. doi:10.1037/0033-2909.119.2.254

Kobayashi, N., Inui, K., & Matsumoto, Y. (2004). Collecting evaluative express for opinion extraction. In *Proceedings of the International Joint Conference on Natural Language Processing, IJCNLP*. IJCNLP.

Koch, N., Kraus, A., Cachero, C., & Meliá, S. (2003). Modeling web business processes with OOH and UWE. In *Proceedings of the Third International Workshop on Web-oriented Software Technology (IWWOST 2003)*, (pp. 27-50). IWWOST.

Koenemann-Belliveau, J., Carroll, J. M., Rosson, M. B., & Singley, M. K. (1994). *Comparative usability evaluation: Critical incidents and critical threads, in human factors in computing systems*. New York, NY: ACM Press.

Kogilavani, A. A., & Balasubramanie, P. (2009). Ontology enhanced clustering based summarization of medical documents. *International Journal of Recent Trends in Engineering, 1*.

Kohlberg, L., Yaeger, J., & Hjertholm, E. (1968). Private speech: Four studies and a review of theories. *Child Development, 39*, 691–736. doi:10.2307/1126979

Kolesnikov, O., Lee, W., & Lipton, R. (2003). *Filtering spam using search engines*. Retrieved from ftp://ftp.cc.gatech.edu/pub/coc/tech_reports/2003/GIT-CC-03-58.pdf

Konstantareas, M. M., & Stewart, K. (2006). Affect regulation and temperament in children with autism spectrum disorder. *Journal of Autism and Developmental Disorders, 36*, 143–154. doi:10.1007/s10803-005-0051-4

Koolen, M., & Kamps, J. (2009). What's in a link? From document importance to topical relevance. In *Proceedings of the 2nd International Conference on Theory of Information Retrieval*, (pp. 313-321). IEEE.

Kopp, C. B. (1982). Antecedents of self-regulation: A developmental perspective. *Developmental Psychology, 18*, 199–214. doi:10.1037/0012-1649.18.2.199

Korfiatis, N., Poulos, M., & Bokos, G. (2006). Evaluating authoritative sources using social networks: An insight from Wikipedia. *Online Information Review, 30*(3), 252–262. doi:10.1108/14684520610675780

Kouijzer, M. E. J., de Moor, J. M. H., Gerrits, B. J. L., Congedo, M., & van Schie, H. T. (2009). Neurofeedback improves executive functioning in children with autism spectrum disorders. *Research in Autism Spectrum Disorders, 3*, 145–162. doi:10.1016/j.rasd.2008.05.001

Krafft, K. C., & Berk, L. E. (1998). Private speech in two preschools: Significance of open-ended activities and make-believe play for verbal self-regulation. *Early Childhood Research Quarterly, 13*, 637–658. doi:10.1016/S0885-2006(99)80065-9

Krahmer, E., & Ummelen, N. (2004). *Thinking about thinking aloud: A comparison of two verbal protocols for usability testing*. Tilburg, The Netherlands: Tilburg University.

Kramarski, B., & Gutman, M. (2006). How can self-regulated learning be supported in mathematical e-learning environments? *Journal of Computer Assisted Learning, 22*, 24–33. doi:10.1111/j.1365-2729.2006.00157.x

Kramarski, B., & Mevarech, Z. R. (2003). Enhancing mathematical reasoning in the classroom: Effects of cooperative learning and metacognitive training. *American Educational Research Journal, 40*, 281–310. doi:10.3102/00028312040001281

Kramarski, B., & Mizrachi, N. (2006). Online discussion and self-regulated learning: Effects of four instructional methods on mathematical literacy. *The Journal of Educational Research, 99*(4), 218–230. doi:10.3200/JOER.99.4.218-231

Krötzsch, M., Vrandecic, D., Völkel, M., Haller, H., & Studer, R. (2007). Semantic wikipedia. *Journal of Web Semantics, 5*(4), 251–261. doi:10.1016/j.websem.2007.09.001

Kuhl, J. (2000). The volitional basis of personality systems interaction theory: Applications in learning and treatment contexts. *International Journal of Educational Research, 33*, 665–703. doi:10.1016/S0883-0355(00)00045-8

Kuhl, J. (2001). *Motivation und persönlichkeit: Interaktionen psychischer systeme*. Göttingen, Germany: Hogrefe.

Kules, B., Kustanowitz, J., & Shneiderman, B. (2006). Categorizing web search results into meaningful and stable categories using fast-feature techniques. In *Proceedings of the 6th ACM/IEEE-CS Joint Conference on Digital Libraries (JCDL 2006)*. Chapel Hill, NC: ACM Press.

Kunder, M. D. (2012). *World wide web size*. Retrieved january 2012, from http://www.worldwidewebsize.com/

Labrou, Y., & Finin, T. (1999). Yahoo! as an ontology - Using Yahoo! categories to describe documents. In *Proceedings of the Eighth International Conference on Information and Knowledge Management, 1999*. Kansas City, MO: ACM Press.

Lakes, K. D., & Hoyt, W. R. (2004). Promoting self-regulation through school-based martial arts training. *Applied Developmental Psychology, 25*, 283–302. doi:10.1016/j.appdev.2004.04.002

Lankshear, C., & Knobel, M. (2007). Researching new literacies: Web 2.0 practices and insider perspectives. *E-Learning and Digital Media, 4*(3).

Lankshear, C., & Knobel, M. (2007). Researching new literacies: Web 2.0 practices and insider perspectives. *E-Learning and Digital Media, 4*(3).

Laurillard, D. (2009). The pedagogical challenges to collaborative technologies. *Computer-Supported Collaborative Learning, 4*, 5–20. doi:10.1007/s11412-008-9056-2

Lazarević, B., Marjanović, Z., Aničić, N., & Babarogić, S. (2006). *Databases*. Faculty of Organizational Sciences. Belgrade, Serbia: University of Belgrade.

Lee, E.-J. (1999). The effects of five-year-old preschoolers' use of private speech on performance and attention for two kinds of problems-solving tasks. *Dissertation Abstracts International. A, The Humanities and Social Sciences, 60*(6-A), 1999.

Lee, E.-J. (2003). Effects of gender of the computer on informational social influence: The moderating role of task type. *International Journal of Human-Computer Studies, 58*, 347–362. doi:10.1016/S1071-5819(03)00009-0

Lee, M. R., & Lan, Y. (2007). From web 2.0 to conversational knowledge management: Towards collaborative intelligence. *Journal of Entrepreneurship Research, 2*(2), 47–62.

Lee, S., Beamish, P., Lee, H., & Park, J. (2009). Strategic choice during economic crisis: Domestic market position, organizational capabilities and export flexibility. *Journal of World Business, 44*(1), 1–15. doi:10.1016/j.jwb.2008.03.015

Lee, S., Neve, W. D., Plataniotis, K. N., & Ro, Y. M. (2010). MAP-based image tag recommendation using a visual folksonomy. *Pattern Recognition Letters, 31*, 976–982. doi:10.1016/j.patrec.2009.12.024

Leontiev, A. A. (1978). Some new trends in Soviet psycholinguistics . In Wertsch, J. V. (Ed.), *Recent Trends in Soviet Psycholinguistics* (pp. 10–20). White Plains, NY: Sharpe.

Leouski, A., & Croft, W. (1996). *An evaluation of techniques for clustering search results*. Amherst, MA: University of Massachusetts.

Lepper, M. R., Greene, D., & Nisbett, R. E. (1973). Undermining children's intrinsic motivation with extrinsic reward: A test of the "overjustification" hypothesis. *Journal of Personality and Social Psychology, 28*, 129–137. doi:10.1037/h0035519

Lepper, M. R., & Woolverton, M. (2002). The wisdom of practice: Lessons learned from the study of highly effective tutors . In Aronson, J. (Ed.), *Improving Academic Achievement: Contributions of Social Psychology* (pp. 135–158). Orlando, FL: Academic Press. doi:10.1016/B978-012064455-1/50010-5

Lepper, M. R., Woolverton, M., Mumme, D. L., & Gurtner, J. (1993). Motivational techniques of expert human tutors: Lessons for the design of computer-based tutors . In Lajoie, S. P., & Derry, S. J. (Eds.), *Computers as Cognitive Tools* (pp. 75–105). Hillsdale, NJ: Erlbaum.

Lesley, M. (2007). Social problem solving training for African Americans: Effects on dietary problem solving skill and DASH diet-related behavior change. *Patient Education and Counseling, 65*, 137–146. doi:10.1016/j.pec.2006.07.001

Lester, J., Converse, S., Kahler, S., Barlow, S., Stone, B., & Bhogal, R. (1997). The persona effect: Affective impact of animated pedagogical agents. In *Proceedings of CHI 1997*, (pp. 359-366). ACM Press.

Leuf, B., & Cunningham, W. (2001). *The wiki way: Collaboration and sharing on the internet*. Reading, MA: Addison-Wesley.

Leuski, A., & Allan, J. (2000). Improving interactive retrieval by combining ranked list and clustering. In *Proceedings of RIAO,* (pp. 665-681). Paris, France: RIAO.

LeVine, R. A. (1989). Cultural environments in child development . In Damon, W. (Ed.), *Child Development Today and Tomorrow* (pp. 52–68). San Francisco, CA: Jossey-Bass.

Levy, P. (1997). *Collective Intelligence: Mankind's Emerging World in Cyberspace* (Bononno, R., Trans.). New York, NY: Plenum.

Lichtenthaler, U., & Ernst, H. (2008). Intermediary services in the markets for technology: Organizational antecedents and performance consequences. *Organization Studies, 29*(7), 1003–1035. doi:10.1177/0170840608090531

Liebermann, D., Giesbrecht, G. F., & Muller, U. (2007). Cognitive and emotional aspects of self-regulation in preschoolers. *Cognitive Development, 22,* 511–529. doi:10.1016/j.cogdev.2007.08.005

Lim, E. P., Vuong, B. Q., Lauw, H., & Sun, A. (2006). Measuring qualities of articles contributed by online communities. In *Proceedings of the International Conference on Web Intelligence*. IEEE.

Lin, T., Etzioni, O., & Fogarty, J. (2009). Identifying interesting assertions from the web. In *Proceeding of the 18th ACM Conference on Information And Knowledge Management,* (pp. 1787–1790). New York, NY: ACM Press.

Lindermann, N., Valcárcel, S., Schaarschmidt, M., & von Kortzfleisch, H. (2009). SME 2.0: Roadmap towards web 2.0-based open innovation in SME-networks. In *Proceedings of Creativity and Innovation in Small and Medium-Sized Enterprises,* (pp. 28-41). Academic Press.

Ling-Yi, L., Cherng, R., Lee, I., Chen, Y., Yang, H., & Chen, Y. (2011). The agreement of caregivers' initial identification of children's developmental problems with the professional assessment in Taiwan. *Research in Developmental Disabilities, 32,* 1714–1721. doi:10.1016/j.ridd.2011.02.026

Li, Y., Wang, J., Li, X., & Zhao, W. (2007). Design creativity in product innovation. *International Journal of Advanced Manufacturing Technology, 33*(3), 213–222. doi:10.1007/s00170-006-0457-y

Lockett, N. J., & Brown, D. H. (2005). An SME perspective of vertical application service providers. *International Journal of Enterprise Information Systems, 1*(2), 37–55. doi:10.4018/jeis.2005040103

Loper, A. B. (1980). Metacognitive development: Implications for cognitive training. *Exceptional Education Quarterly, 1,* 1–8.

Lovaas, O. I. (1961). Interaction between verbal and nonverbal behavior. *Child Development, 32,* 329–336.

Lovaas, O. I. (1964). Cue properties of words: The control of operant responding by rate and content of verbal operants. *Child Development, 35,* 245–256.

LoVullo, S. V., & Matson, J. L. (2009). Comorbid psychopathology in adults with autism spectrum disorders and intellectual disabilities. *Research in Developmental Disabilities, 30,* 1288–1296. doi:10.1016/j.ridd.2009.05.004

Lowe, D., & Hall, W. (1999). *Hypermedia and the web: An engineering approach*. Chichester, UK: Wiley.

Lubeck, S. (1996). Deconstructing child development knowledge and teacher preparation. *Early Childhood Research Quarterly, 11,* 147–167. doi:10.1016/S0885-2006(96)90003-4

Lula, P., & Paliwoda-Pekosz, G. (2008). An ontology-based cluster analysis framework. In *Proceedings of the First International Workshop on Ontology-Supported Business Intelligence,* (pp. 1-6). Karlsruhe, Germany: IEEE.

Luria, A. R. (1959). The directive functions of speech in development and dissolution: Part 1: Development of the directive functions of speech in early childhood. *Word, 15,* 341–352.

Luria, A. R. (1961). Chapter . In Tizard, J. (Ed.), *The Role of Speech in the Regulation of Normal and Abnormal Behavior* (pp. 163–197). New York, NY: Liveright.

Lytras, M. D., & García, R. (2008). Semantic web applications: a framework for industry and business exploitation - What is needed for the adoption of the semantic web from the market and industry. *International Journal of Knowledge and Learning*, *4*(1), 93–108. doi:10.1504/IJKL.2008.019739

Ma, C., Prendinger, H., & Ishizuka, M. (2005). A chat system based on emotion estimation from text and embodied conversational messengers. *Lecture Notes in Computer Science*, *3711*, 535–538. doi:10.1007/11558651_56

Mackay, D. G. (1981). The problem of rehearsal or mental practice. *Journal of Motor Behavior*, *13*, 274–285.

MacNeil, B. M., Lopes, V. A., & Minnes, P. M. (2009). Anxiety in children and adolescents with autism spectrum disorders. *Research in Autism Spectrum Disorders*, *3*, 1–21. doi:10.1016/j.rasd.2008.06.001

Mainela-Arnold, E., & Evans, J. L. (2005). Beyond capacity limitations: Determinants of word recall performance on verbal working memory span tasks in children with SLI. *Journal of Speech, Language, and Hearing Research: JSLHR*, *48*, 897–909. doi:10.1044/1092-4388(2005/062)

Malcom, E. (1994). *SSADM version 4: A user's guide* (2nd ed.). New York, NY: McGraw-Hill, Inc.

Manning, C. D., Raghavan, P., & Schütze, H. (2008). *Introduction to information retrieval*. Cambridge, UK: Cambridge University Press. doi:10.1017/CBO9780511809071

Marmolin, H. (1991). Multimedia from the perspectives of psychology. In *Proceedings of the Eurographics Workshop on Multimedia*, (pp. 39-52). Springer-Verlag.

Martic, J. (2004). Self-regulated learning, social cognitive theory and agency. *Educational Psychologist*, *39*, 135–145. doi:10.1207/s15326985ep3902_4

Martin, N., & Saffran, E. M. (1997). Language and auditory-verbal short-term memory impairment: Evidence for common underlying processes. *Cognitive Neuropsychology*, *14*, 641–682. doi:10.1080/026432997381402

Martin, R. C., Lesch, M. F., & Bartha, M. C. (1999). Independence of input and output phonology in word processing and short-term memory. *Journal of Memory and Language*, *41*, 3–29. doi:10.1006/jmla.1999.2637

Marton, F., & Sa'ljo", R. (1984). Approaches to learning . In Marton, F., Hounsell, D., & Entwistle, N. (Eds.), *The Experience of Learning* (pp. 36–55). Edinburgh, UK: Scottish Academic Press.

Marton, K., & Schwartz, R. G. (2003). Working memory capacity and language processes in children with specific language impairment. *Journal of Speech, Language, and Hearing Research: JSLHR*, *46*, 1138–1153. doi:10.1044/1092-4388(2003/089)

Marx Gómez, J. (2009). Corporate environmental management information systems - CEMIS 2.0. In D. Davcev & J. Marx Gómez (Eds.), *Proceedings of the ICT Innovations Conference 2009*, (pp. 1-4). Ohrid, Macedonia: Springer Heidelberg.

Mathes, A. (2004). *Folksonomies - Cooperative classification and communication through shared metadata the creation of metadata: Professionals, content creators, users*. Retrieved from http://www.adammathes.com/academic/computer-mediated-communication/folksonomies.html

Mathews, R., Buss, R., Stanley, W., Blanchard-Fields, F., Cho, J., & Druhan, B. (1989). Role of implicit and explicit processes in learning from examples: A synergistic effect. *Journal of Experimental Psychology. Learning, Memory, and Cognition*, *15*, 1083–1100. doi:10.1037/0278-7393.15.6.1083

Matson, J. L., & Shoemaker, M. (2009). Intellectual disability and its relationship to autism spectrum disorders. *Research in Developmental Disabilities*, *30*, 1107–1114. doi:10.1016/j.ridd.2009.06.003

Matson, J. L., Smiroldo, B. B., Hamilton, M., & Baglio, C. S. (1997). Do anxiety disorders exist in persons with severe and profound mental retardation? *Research in Developmental Disabilities*, *18*, 39–44. doi:10.1016/S0891-4222(96)00036-4

Matthew, C. T., & Sternberg, R. J. (2009). Developing experience-based (tacit) knowledge through reflection. *Learning and Individual Differences*, *19*, 530–540. doi:10.1016/j.lindif.2009.07.001

Matuga, J. M. (2003). Children's private speech during algorithmic and heuristic drawing tasks. *Contemporary Educational Psychology*, *28*, 552–572. doi:10.1016/S0361-476X(02)00061-9

Mayer, R., Menzel, C., Painter, M., Witte, P. D., Blinn, T., & Perakath, B. (1995). *Information integration for concurrent engineering (IICE) IDEF3 process description capture method report*. New York, NY: Knowledge Based Systems Inc.

Maynard, A. (2002). Cultural teaching: The development of teaching skills in Maya sibling interactions. *Child Development*, *73*, 969–982. doi:10.1111/1467-8624.00450

Mazzoni, G., & Nelson, T. (Eds.). (1998). *Metacognition and cognitive neuropsychology*. Mahwah, NJ: Erlbaum.

McCaslin, M., & Hickey, D. T. (2001). Educational psychology, social constructivism, and educational practice: A case of emergent identity. *Educational Psychologist*, *36*, 133–140. doi:10.1207/S15326985EP3602_8

McClelland, M. M., Cameron, C. E., Connor, C. M., Farris, C. L., Jewkes, A. M., & Morrison, F. J. (2007). Links between behavioral regulation and preschoolers' 705 literacy, vocabulary, and math skills. *Developmental Psychology*, *43*, 947–959. doi:10.1037/0012-1649.43.4.947

McCutchen, D., & Perfetti, C. (1982). The visual tongue-twister effect: Phonological activation in silent reading. *Journal of Verbal Learning and Verbal Behavior*, *21*, 672–687. doi:10.1016/S0022-5371(82)90870-2

McGuinness, D. L., & Van Harmelen, F. (2004). Owl web ontology language overview: W3C recommendation 10 Feb 2004. *World Wide Web Consortium*. Retrieved from http://www.w3.org/TR/owl-features/

McGuinness, D. L. (2003). Ontologies come of age . In Fensel, D., Hendler, J., Lieberman, H., & Wahlster, W. (Eds.), *Spinning the Semantic Web: Bringing the World Wide Web to Its Full Potential*. Cambridge, MA: MIT Press.

McIlraith, S. A., Son, T. C., & Honglei, Z. (2001). Semantic web services. *IEEE Intelligent Systems*, *16*(2), 46–53. doi:10.1109/5254.920599

McKay, J. (1992). Building self-esteem in children . In McKay, M., & Fanning, P. (Eds.), *Self-Esteem* (2nd ed., pp. 239–271). Oakland, CA: New Harbinger.

McQuillan, J., & Rodrigo, V. (1995). A reading "din in the head": Evidence of involuntary mental rehearsal in second language readers. *Foreign Language Annals*, *28*, 330–336. doi:10.1111/j.1944-9720.1995.tb00802.x

Meichenbaum, D., & Goodman, J. (1969). Reflection-impulsivity and verbal control of motor behavior. *Child Development*, *40*, 785–797.

Meichenbaum, D., & Goodman, J. (1969). The developmental control of operant motor responding by verbal operants. *Journal of Experimental Child Psychology*, *7*, 553–565. doi:10.1016/0022-0965(69)90016-2

Melchior, E.-M., & Bösser, T. (2011). *Results of the field trials: User acceptance, business benefits, and organizational impact of ACTIVE technology*. ACTIVE Project.

Merriman, W. E., & Schuster, J. M. (1991). Young children's disambiguation of object name reference. *Child Development*, *62*, 1288–1301. doi:10.2307/1130807

Meskendahl, S. (2010). The influence of business strategy on project portfolio management and its success -- A conceptual framework. *International Journal of Project Management*, *28*(8), 807–817. doi:10.1016/j.ijproman.2010.06.007

Metcalfe, J. (1994). A computational modeling approach to novelty monitoring, metacognition, and frontal lobe dysfunction . In Metcalfe, J., & Shimamura, A. (Eds.), *Metacognition: Knowing about Knowing* (pp. 211–263). Cambridge, MA: MIT Press.

Metcalfe, J., & Shimamura, A. (Eds.). (1994). *Metacognition: Knowing about knowing*. Cambridge, MA: MIT Press.

Mevarech, Z. R., & Kramarski, B. (1997). IMPROVE: A multidimensional method for teaching mathematics in heterogeneous classrooms. *American Educational Research Journal*, *34*, 365–394.

Meyer, D. K., & Turner, J. C. (2002). Using instructional discourse analysis to study the scaffolding of student self-regulation. *Educational Psychologist*, *37*, 5–13.

Micarelli, A., Gasparetti, F., Sciarrone, F., & Gauch, S. (2007). Personalized search on the world wide web . In Brusilovsky, P., Kobsa, A., & Nejdl, W. (Eds.), *The Adaptive Web* (pp. 195–230). Berlin, Germany: Springer-Verlag. doi:10.1007/978-3-540-72079-9_6

Mikroyannidis, A., & Theodoulidis, B. (2010). Ontology management and evolution for business intelligence. *International Journal of Information Management*, *30*(6), 559–566. doi:10.1016/j.ijinfomgt.2009.10.002

Minasian, J. R. (1969). Research and development, production functions, and rates of return. *The American Economic Review*, *59*(2), 80–85.

Miniwastts Marketing Group. (2012). *Internet world stasts*. Retrieved 01 20, 2012, from http://www.internetworldstats.com/stats.htm

Mitchell, T. M. (1997). *Machine learning*. New York, NY: McGraw-Hill Companies.

Mladenic, D. (1998). Turning Yahoo into an automatic web-page classifier. In *Proceedings of the 13th European Conference on Artificial Intelligence Yong Research Paper*. Brighton, UK: John Wiley & Sons.

Moens, M. (2003). *Information extraction: Algorithms and prospects in a retrieval context*. Berlin, Germany: Springer-Verlag.

Montenegro-Marin, C. E., Cueva-Lovelle, J. C., Sanjuan-Martinez, O., & Neñez-Valdes, E. R. (2011). Towards an ontology to describe the taxonomy of common modules in learning management systems. *International Jorunal of Interactive Multimedia and Artificial Intelligence*, *1*, 47–53.

Montenegro-Marin, C. E., Cueva-Lovelle, J. M., Martínez, O. S., & García-Díaz, V. (2012). Domain specific language for the generation of learning management systems modules. *Journal of Web Engineering*, *11*(1), 23–50.

Montgomery, J. W. (2000). Verbal working memory and sentence comprehension in children with specific language impairment. *Journal of Speech, Language, and Hearing Research: JSLHR*, *43*, 293–308.

Montgomery, J. W. (2000). Relation of working to off-line and real-time sentence processing in children with specific language impairment. *Applied Psycholinguistics*, *21*, 117–148. doi:10.1017/S0142716400001065

Montgomery, J. W. (2003). Working memory and comprehension in children with specific language impairment: What we know so far. *Journal of Communication Disorders*, *36*, 221–231. doi:10.1016/S0021-9924(03)00021-2

Montgomery, J. W. (2004). Sentence comprehension in children with specific language impairment: Effects of input rate and phonological working memory. *International Journal of Language & Communication Disorders*, *39*(1), 115–133. doi:10.1080/13682820310001616985

Moon, Y., & Nass, C. (1996). How "real" are computer personalities? Psychological responses to personality types in human-computer interaction. *Communication Research*, *23*, 651–674. doi:10.1177/009365096023006002

Moshinskie, J. F. (1998). A survey of multimedia developers concerning the use of automated instructional design software. *Journal of Instruction Delivery Systems*, *12*(2), 26–32.

Mueller, C. M., & Dweck, C. S. (1998). Praise for intelligence can undermine children's motivation and performance. *Journal of Personality and Social Psychology*, *75*, 33–52. doi:10.1037/0022-3514.75.1.33

Müller, U., Zelazo, P. D., Hood, S., Leone, T., & Rohrer, L. (2004). Interference control in a new rule use task: Age-related changes, labeling, and attention. *Child Development*, *75*, 1594–1609. doi:10.1111/j.1467-8624.2004.00759.x

Munde, V. S., Vlaskamp, C., Ruijssenaars, A. J. J. M., & Nakken, H. (2009). Alertness in individuals with profound intellectual and multiple disabilities: A literature review. *Research in Developmental Disabilities*, *30*, 462–480. doi:10.1016/j.ridd.2008.07.003

Muraven, M. (2010). Building self-control strength: Practicing self-control leads to improved self-control performance. *Journal of Experimental Social Psychology*, *46*, 465–468. doi:10.1016/j.jesp.2009.12.011

Murphy, O., Healy, O., & Leader, G. (2009). Risk factors for challenging behaviors among 157 children with autism spectrum disorders in Ireland. *Research in Autism Spectrum Disorders*, *3*, 474–482. doi:10.1016/j.rasd.2008.09.008

Murugesan, S., Deshpande, Y., Hansen, S., & Ginige, A. (1999). Web engineering: A new discipline for development of web-based systems. In *Proceedings of First ICSE Workshop on Web Engineering, International Conference on Software Engineering (ICSE 1999)*. Los Angeles, CA: ACM.

Nanard, J., & Nanard, M. (1995). Hypertext design environments and the hypertext design process. *Communications of the ACM*, *38*(8), 49–56. doi:10.1145/208344.208347

Nass, C., Steuer, J. S., & Tauber, E. (1994). Computers are social actors. In *Proceedings of the CHI Conference,* (pp. 72-77). Boston, MA: CHI.

Nass, C., Fogg, B. J., & Moon, Y. (1996). Can computers be teammates? *International Journal of Human-Computer Studies, 45,* 669–678. doi:10.1006/ijhc.1996.0073

Nass, C., & Steuer, J. (1993). Voices, boxes, and sources of messages: Computers and social actors. *Human Communication Research, 19,* 504–527. doi:10.1111/j.1468-2958.1993.tb00311.x

Natalya, F. N., & Deborah, L. M. (2005). *Ontology development 101: A guide to creating your first ontology.* Palo Alto, CA: Stanford.

Nation, K., Adams, J. W., Bowyer-Crane, C. A., & Snowling, M. J. (1999). Working memory deficits in poor comprehenders reflect underlying language impairments. *Journal of Experimental Child Psychology, 73,* 139–158. doi:10.1006/jecp.1999.2498

Navathe, S., Ceri, S., Wiederhold, G., & Dou, J. (1984). Vertical partitioning algorithms for database design: A graphical algorithm. *ACM Transactions on Database Systems, 9*(4), 680–710. doi:10.1145/1994.2209

Nelson-Legall, S. (1987). Necessary and unnecessary help-seeking in children. *The Journal of Genetic Psychology, 148,* 53–62. doi:10.1080/00221325.1987.9914536

Nelson, T., & Narens, L. (1990). Meta-memory: A theoretical treatment and new findings . In Bower, G. (Ed.), *The Psychology of Learning and Motivation* (*Vol. 26,* pp. 125–140). New York, NY: Academic Press.

Neuhaus, M., & Bunke, H. (2006). A random walk kernel derived from graph edit distance. *Lecture Notes in Computer Science, 4109,* 191–199. doi:10.1007/11815921_20

Newman, R. S., & Schwager, M. T. (1992). Student perceptions and academic help seeking . In Schunk, D. H., & Meece, J. L. (Eds.), *Student Perceptions in the Classroom* (pp. 123–146). Hillsdale, NJ: Erlbaum.

New, R. (1994). Culture, child development, and developmentally appropriate practices . In Mallory, B., & New, R. (Eds.), *Diversity and Developmentally Appropriate Practices* (pp. 65–83). New York, NY: Teachers College Press.

Nezu, A. M. (1986). Negative life stress and anxiety: Problem solving as a moderator variable. *Psychological Reports, 58,* 279–283. doi:10.2466/pr0.1986.58.1.279

Nezu, A. M. (2004). Problem solving and behavior-therapy revisited. *Behavior Therapy, 35,* 1–33. doi:10.1016/S0005-7894(04)80002-9

Nezu, A. M., Nezu, C. M., & Perri, M. G. (1989). *Problem-solving therapy for depression: Theory, research, and clinical guidelines.* New York, NY: Wiley.

Nezu, A. M., & Ronan, G. F. (1988). Social problem solving as a moderator of stress-related depressive symptoms: A prospective analysis. *Journal of Counseling Psychology, 35,* 134–138. doi:10.1037/0022-0167.35.2.134

Nielsen, F. A. (2007). Scientific citations in Wikipedia. *First Monday, 12*(8).

Nielsen, J., Clemmensen, T., & Yssing, C. (2002). Getting access to what goes on in people's heads? Reflections on the think-aloud technique . In *Proceedings of NordiCHI.* NordiCHI.

Nonaka, I., & Takeuchi, H. (1995). *The knowledge-creating company.* Oxford, UK: Oxford University Press.

Norrelgen, F., Lacerda, F., & Forssberg, H. (2002). Temporal resolution of auditory perception and verbal working memory in 15 children with language impairment. *Journal of Learning Disabilities, 35,* 540–546. doi:10.1177/00222194020350060501

Nulens, R. (2006). *Sequentie analyse.* (Doctoral Thesis). Transnationale Universiteit Limburg. Maastricht, The Netherlands.

Numminem, H., Service, E., Ahonen, T., & Ruoppila, I. (2001). Working memory and everyday cognition in adults with Down syndrome. *Journal of Intellectual Disability Research, 45,* 157–168. doi:10.1046/j.1365-2788.2001.00298.x

Nygaard, E., Smith, L., & Torgersen, A. M. (2002). Temperament in children with Down syndrome and in prematurely born children. *Scandinavian Journal of Psychology, 43,* 61–71. doi:10.1111/1467-9450.00269

O'Leary, K. D., & O'Leary, S. G. (1977). *Classroom management: The successful use of behaviour modification* (2nd ed.). New York, NY: Pergamon Press.

O'Reilly, T. (2005). What is web 2.0. *O'Reilly Network.* Retrieved from http://oreilly.com/web2/archive/what-is-web-20.html

OECD. (1993). *Proposed standard practice for surveys of research and experimental development: Frascati manual* (5th ed.). Paris, France: OECD.

Okonkwo, C., & Vassileva, J. (2001). Affective pedagogical agents and user persuasion . In Stephanidis, P. (Ed.), *Universal Access in Human-Computer Interaction* (pp. 397–401). New Orleans, LA: UAHCI.

Oliver, J. A., Edmiaston, R., & Fitzgerald, L. M. (2003). Regular and special education teachers' beliefs regarding the role of private speech in children's learning. In Winsler, A. (Ed.), *Awareness, Attitudes, and Beliefs Concerning Children's Private Speech.* Tampa, FL: Academic Press.

Open Directory Project. (2008). *Website.* Retrieved from www.dmoz.org

Oracle White Paper. (2009). *Advanced performance and scalability for semantic web applications.* Oracle.

O'Reilly, T. (2007). What is web 2.0: Design patterns and business models for the next generation of software. *Communications & Strategies, 65,* 17–37.

Ortony, A., Clore, G. L., & Colins, A. (1988). *The cognitive structure of emotions.* Cambridge, UK: Cambridge University Press. doi:10.1017/CBO9780511571299

Ortony, A., Clore, G. L., & Foss, M. A. (1987). *The referential structure of the affective lexicon.* Urbana-Champaign, IL: Universiry of Illinois at Urbana-Champaign.

Osiński, S. (2003). *An algorithm for clustering of web search results.* (Master Thesis). Poznań University of Technology. Poznań, Poland.

Osswald, K. (2003). *Konzeptmanagement: Interaktive medien – interdisziplinäre projekte.* Berlin, Germany: Springer.

Padiya, T., Ahir, M., Bhise, M., & Chaudhary, S. (2012). Data partitioning for semantic web. *International Journal of Computer and Communication Technology, 3*(2), 32–35.

Page, L., Brin, S., Motwani, R., & Winograd, T. (1998). *The pagerank citation ranking: Bring order to the web.* Retrieved from http://citeseer.ist.psu.edu/page98pagerank.html

Palincsar, A. S. (1998). Social constructivist perspectives on teaching and learning. *Annual Review of Psychology, 49,* 345–375. doi:10.1146/annurev.psych.49.1.345

Palincsar, A. S., & Herrenkohl, L. R. (2002). Designing collaborative learning contexts. *Theory into Practice, 41*(1), 26–32. doi:10.1207/s15430421tip4101_5

Palincsar, A., & Brown, A. (1984). Reciprocal teaching of comprehension fostering and monitoring activities. *Cognition and Instruction, 1,* 117–175. doi:10.1207/s1532690xci0102_1

Panaoura, A., & Philippou, G. (2007). The developmental change of young pupils' metacognitive ability in mathematics in relation to their cognitive abilities. *Cognitive Development, 22,* 149–164. doi:10.1016/j.cogdev.2006.08.004

Panchenko, O. (2007). Concept location and program comprehension in service-oriented software. In *Proceedings of the IEEE 23rd International Conference on Software Maintenance: Doctoral Symposium, ICSM,* (pp. 513-514). Paris, France: IEEE Press.

Pang, B., & Lee, L. (2004). A sentimental education: Sentiment analysis using subjectivity summarization based on minimum cuts. In *Proceedings of the ACL,* (pp. 271-278). ACL.

Pang, B., & Lee, L. (2005). Seeing stars: Exploiting class relationships for sentiment categorization with respect to rating scales. In *Proceedings of ACL 2005, 43rd Meeting of Categorization with Respect to Rating Scales.* Ann. Arbor, MI: ACL.

Pang, B., & Lee, L. (2008). Opinion mining and sentiment analysis. *Foundations and Trends in Information Retrieval, 2*(1-2).

Pang, B., Lee, L., & Vaithyanathan, S. (2002). Thumbs up? Sentiment classification using machine learning techniques. In *Proceedings of the Conference on Empirical Methods in Natural Language Processing, EMNLP 2002.* EMNLP.

Paniagua-Martín, F., García-Crespo, Á., Colomo-Palacios, R., & Ruiz-Mezcua, B. (2011). SSAAMAR: Semantic annotation architecture for accessible multimedia resources. *IEEE MultiMedia, 18*(2), 16–25. doi:10.1109/MMUL.2010.43

Pappas, S., Ginsburg, H., & Jiang, M. (2003). SES differences in young children's metacognition in the context of mathematical problem solving. *Cognitive Development*, *18*, 431–450. doi:10.1016/S0885-2014(03)00043-1

Pardillo, J., & Cachero, C. (2010). Domain-specific language modelling with UML profiles by decoupling abstract and concrete syntaxes. *Journal of Systems and Software*, *83*(12), 2591–2606. doi:10.1016/j.jss.2010.08.019

Paris, S. G., & Winograd, P. (2001). *The role of self-regulated learning in contextual teaching: Principles and practices for teacher preparation.* Retrieved from http://www.ciera.org/library/archive/2001-04/0104parwin.htm

Paris, S. G., & Byrnes, J. P. (1989). The constructivist approach to self-regulation and learning in the classroom. In Zimmerman, B. J., & Schunk, D. H. (Eds.), *Self-Regulated Learning and Academic Achievement: Theory, Research, and Practice* (pp. 281–321). New York, NY: Springer-Verlag. doi:10.1007/978-1-4612-3618-4_7

Paris, S. G., & Paris, A. H. (2001). Classroom applications of research on self-regulated learning. *Educational Psychologist*, *36*, 89–101. doi:10.1207/S15326985EP3602_4

Paris, S. G., & Winograd, P. (1990). Promoting metacognition and motivation of exceptional children. *Remedial and Special Education*, *11*, 7–15. doi:10.1177/074193259001100604

Paris, S., & Newman, R. (1990). Developmental aspects of self-regulated learning. *Educational Psychologist*, *25*, 87–102. doi:10.1207/s15326985ep2501_7

Pask, G. (1975). *Conversation, cognition and learning: A cybernetic theory and methodology.* Amsterdam, The Netherlands: Elsevier.

Pask, G. (1988). Learning strategies, teaching strategies, and conceptual or learning style. In Schmeck, R. R. (Ed.), *Learning Strategies and Learning Styles* (pp. 83–100). New York, NY: Plenum.

Pastor, D. A., Barron, K. E., Miller, B. J., & Davis, S. L. (2007). A latent profile analysis of college students' achievement goal orientation. *Contemporary Educational Psychology*, *32*, 8–47. doi:10.1016/j.cedpsych.2006.10.003

Patrick, H., & Middleton, M. J. (2002). Turning the kaleidoscope: What we see when self-regulated learning is viewed with a qualitative lens. *Educational Psychology*, *37*, 27–39.

Pawlikowski, K., Abadi, D., Silberschatz, A., & Paulson, E. (2011). Efficient processing of data warehousing queries in a split execution environment. In *Proceedings of the 2011 International Conference on Management of Data, SIGMOD 2011.* ACM Press.

Peltoniemi, M. (2004). Cluster, value network and business ecosystem: Knowledge and innovation approach. In *Proceedings of Organisations, Innovation and Complexity: New Perspectives on the Knowledge Economy,* (pp. 9–10). NEXSUS.

Pérez, A. G. (1995). Some ideas and examples to evaluate ontologies. In *Proceedings of the Eleventh Conference on Artificial Intelligence for Applications,* (pp. 299-305). IEEE Press.

Perugini, S. (2008). Symbolic links in the open directory project. *Information Processing & Management*, *44*(2), 910–930. doi:10.1016/j.ipm.2007.06.005

Piaget, J. (1959). *The language and thought of the child.* London, UK: Routledge.

Piaget, J. (1965). *The moral judgement of the child.* London, UK: Free Press.

Piaget, J. (1968). *Le langage et la pensée chez l'enfant: Études sur la logique de l'enfant* (7th ed.). Neuchâtel, Switzerland: Delachaux et Niestlé. [The language and thought of the child]

Picard, R., & Klein, J. (2001). Computers that recognize and respond to user emotion: Theoretical and practical implications. *Interacting with Computers*, *3*, 3–14.

Pierce, E. W., Ewing, L. J., & Campbell, S. B. (1999). Diagnostic status and symptomatic behavior of hard-to-manage preschool children in middle childhood and early adolescence. *Journal of Clinical Child Psychology*, *28*, 44–57. doi:10.1207/s15374424jccp2801_4

Pintrich, P. (1999). The role of motivation in promoting and sustaining self-regulated learning. *International Journal of Educational Research*, *31*, 459–470. doi:10.1016/S0883-0355(99)00015-4

Pintrich, P. R. (2000). The role of goal orientation in self-regulated learning . In Boekaerts, M., Pintrich, P. R., & Zeidner, M. (Eds.), *Handbook of Self-Regulation* (pp. 451–502). San Diego, CA: Academic Press. doi:10.1016/B978-012109890-2/50043-3

Pintrich, P. R. (Ed.). (1995). Current issues in research on self-regulated learning: A discussion with commentaries. *Educational Psychologist*, *30*, 171–232. doi:10.1207/s15326985ep3004_1

Pintrich, P. R., & De Groot, E. V. (1990). Motivational and self-regulated learning components of classroom academic performance. *Journal of Educational Psychology*, *82*, 33–40. doi:10.1037/0022-0663.82.1.33

Pintrich, P. R., Roeser, R., & De Groot, E. (1994). Classroom and individual differences in early adolescents' motivation and self-regulated learning. *The Journal of Early Adolescence*, *14*, 139–161. doi:10.1177/027243169401400204

Pintrich, P. R., & Zusho, A. (2002). The development of academic self-regulation: The role of cognitive and motivational factors . In Wigfield, A., & Eccles, J. S. (Eds.), *Development of Achievement Motivation* (pp. 249–284). San Diego, CA: Academic Press. doi:10.1016/B978-012750053-9/50012-7

PISA. (2003). *Literacy skills for the world of tomorrow*. Paris, France: PISA.

Pitkow, J., Schütze, H., Cass, T., Cooley, R., Turnbull, D., & Edmonds, A. (2002). Personalized search: A contextual computing approach may prove a breakthrough in personalized search efficiency. *Communications of the ACM*, *45*(9), 50–55.

Plattner, H. (2009). A common database approach for OLTP and OLAP using an in-memory column database. In *Proceedings of the 35th SIGMOD International Conference on Management of Data*. Providence, RI: ACM Press.

Pohl, K. (2006). Perspective models as a means for achieving true representational accuracy. In *Proceedings of the IEEE Aerospace Conference*. Big Sky, MT: IEEE Press.

Popescu, A. M., & Etzioni, O. (2005). Extracting product features and opinions from reviews. In *Proceedings of the Conference on Empirical Methods in Natural Language Processing, EMNLP 2005*. EMNLP.

Popplewell, K., Stojanovic, N., Abecker, A., Apostolou, D., Mentzas, G., & Harding, J. (2008). Supporting adaptive enterprise collaboration through semantic knowledge services. [Springer.]. *Proceedings of Enterprise Interoperability*, *III*, 381–393. doi:10.1007/978-1-84800-221-0_30

Potthast, M., Stein, B., & Gerling, R. (2008). Automatic vandalism detection in Wikipedia. *Lecture Notes in Computer Science*, *4956*, 663–668. doi:10.1007/978-3-540-78646-7_75

Powell, W. W., & Snellman, K. (2004). The knowledge economy. *Annual Review of Sociology*, *30*, 199–220. doi:10.1146/annurev.soc.29.010202.100037

Presley, M., & Ghatala, E. S. (1990). Self-regulated learning: Monitoring learning from text. *Educational Psychologist*, *25*, 19–33. doi:10.1207/s15326985ep2501_3

Pressley, M. (1986). The relevance of the good strategy user model to the teaching of mathematics. *Educational Psychologist*, *21*, 139–161.

Pressley, M. (1995). More about the development of self-regulation: Complex, long-term, and thoroughly social. *Educational Psychologist*, *30*, 207–212. doi:10.1207/s15326985ep3004_6

Pressman, R. S., Lewis, T., Adida, B., Ullman, E., DeMarco, T., & Gilb, T. (1998). Can internet-based applications be engineered? *IEEE Software*, *15*(5), 104–110. doi:10.1109/MS.1998.714869

Price, G. (2004). *Reducing information overkill*. Retrieved January 28, 2010, from http://searchenginewatch.com/showPage.html?page=3415071

Puustinen, M. (1998). Help-seeking behavior in a problem-solving situation: Development of self-regulation. *European Journal of Psychology of Education*, *13*, 271–282. doi:10.1007/BF03173093

Puustinen, M., & Pulkkinen, L. (2001). Models of self-regulated learning: A review. *Scandinavian Journal of Educational Research*, *45*, 21–46. doi:10.1080/00313830120074206

Quinlan, R. (1993). *C4.5: Programs for machine learning*. San Mateo, CA: Morgan Kaufmann.

Reder, L., & Schunn, C. (1996). Metacognition does not imply awareness: Strategy choice is governed by implicit learning and memory. In Reder, L. (Ed.), *Implicit Memory and Metacognition* (pp. 63–92). Mahwah, NJ: Erlbaum.

Reeves, B., & Nass, C. (1996). *The media equation: How people treat computers, television, and new media like real people and places*. Cambridge, UK: Cambridge University Press.

Reich, S. (2005). What do mothers know? Maternal knowledge of child development. *Infant Mental Health Journal, 26*, 143–156. doi:10.1002/imhj.20038

Relph, E. (1976). *Place and placelessness*. London, UK: Pion.

Renger, S. (2006). *Evaluation eines trainings zur selbststeuerung*. [Evaluation of a training program in self-government]. (Unpublished Masters Thesis). University of Osnabrück. Osnabrück, Germany.

Rheinberg, F., Vollmeyer, R., & Rollett, W. (2002). Motivation and self-regulated learning: A type analysis with process variables. *Psychologia, 45*, 237–249. doi:10.2117/psysoc.2002.237

Richman, N., Stevenson, J., & Graham, P. (1982). *Preschool to school: A behavioral study*. New York, NY: Academic Press.

Rieche, D. (2005). How and why Wikipedia works? An interview. In *Proceedings of the ACM Wikisym*. ACM Press.

Riedl, C., Blohm, I., Leimeister, J. M., & Krcmar, H. (2010). Rating scales for collective intelligence in innovation communities: Why quick and easy decision making does not get it right. In *Proceedings of the 31st International Conference on Information Systems*. IEEE.

Riloff, E., & Wiebe, J. (2003). Learning extraction patterns for subjective expressions. In *Proceedings of the Conference on Empirical Methods in Natural Language Processing (EMNLP 2003)*, (pp. 105–112). EMNLP.

Roberts, K. (2002). Children's ability to distinguish between memories from multiple sources: Implications for the quality and accuracy of eyewitness statements. *Developmental Review, 22*, 403–435. doi:10.1016/S0273-2297(02)00005-9

Rodríguez-González, A., García-Crespo, Á., Colomo-Palacios, R., Guildrís-Iglesias, F., & Gómez-Berbís, J. M. (2011). CAST: Using neural networks to improve trading systems based on technical analysis by means of the RSI financial indicator. *Expert Systems with Applications, 38*(9), 11489–11500. doi:10.1016/j.eswa.2011.03.023

Rodriguez, M. A., & Shinavier, J. (2009). Exposing multi-relational networks to single-relational network analysis algorithms. *Journal of Informetrics, 4*(1), 29–41. doi:10.1016/j.joi.2009.06.004

Roebuck, R. (1998). *Reading and recall in L1 and L2: A sociocultural approach*. Stamford, CT: Ablex Publishing.

Rose, E., Bramham, J., Young, S., Paliokostas, E., & Xenitidis, K. (2009). Neuropsychological characteristics of adults with comorbid ADHD and borderline/mild intellectual disability. *Research in Developmental Disabilities, 30*, 496–502. doi:10.1016/j.ridd.2008.07.009

Rosenblum, D. (2007). What anyone can know: The privacy risks of social networking sites. In *Proceedings of the IEEE Security and Privacy*, (pp. 40-49). IEEE Press.

Rosenquist, C., Conners, F. A., & Roskos-Ewoldsen, B. (2003). Phonological and visuo-spatial working memory in individuals with intellectual disability. *American Journal of Mental Retardation, 108*, 403–413. doi:10.1352/0895-8017(2003)108<403:PAVWMI>2.0.CO;2

Rossi, G., & Schwabe, D. (2001). Object-oriented web applications modeling . In *Information Modeling in the New Millennium* (pp. 463–483). Hershey, PA: IGI Global. doi:10.4018/978-1-878289-77-3.ch023

Roussel, P. A., Saad, K. N., & Erickson, T. J. (1991). *Third generation R&D: Managing the link to corporate strategy*. Boston, MA: Harvard Business School Press.

Roussinov, D., & Zhao, J. L. (2003). Message sense maker: Engineering a tool set for customer relationship management. In *Proceedings of 36th Annual Hawaii International Conference on System Sciences (HICSS)*. IEEE.

Rozendaal, J. S., Minnaert, A., & Boekaerts, M. (2003). Motivation and self-regulated learning in secondary vocational education: Information-processing type and gender differences. *Learning and Individual Differences, 13*, 273–289. doi:10.1016/S1041-6080(03)00016-5

Russell, S., & Norvig, P. (2009). *Artificial intelligence: A modern approach* (3rd ed.). Upper Saddle River, NJ: Prentice Hall Press.

Russo, N. L., & Graham, B. R. (1999). A first step in developing a web application design methodology: Understanding the environment. In *Proceedings of Sixth International BCS Information Systems Methodologies Conference*. London, UK: Springer.

Rutter, M. (1989). Pathways from childhood to adult life. *Journal of Child Psychology and Psychiatry, and Allied Disciplines, 30,* 23–52. doi:10.1111/j.1469-7610.1989.tb00768.x

Ryan, K. (2008). *What's wrong with being cuil?* Retrieved February 13, 2010, from http://searchenginewatch.com/showPage.html?page=3630382

Ryan, A. M., Pintrich, P. R., & Midgley, C. (2001). Avoiding seeking help in the classroom: Who and why? *Educational Psychology Review, 13,* 93–114. doi:10.1023/A:1009013420053

Ryu, K., & Yücesan, E. (2007). CPM: A collaborative process modeling for cooperative manufacturers. *Advanced Engineering Informatics, 21*(2), 231–239. doi:10.1016/j.aei.2006.05.003

Sadoski, M., & Paivio, A. (2001). *Imagery and text: A dual coding theory of reading and writing*. Mahwah, NJ: Lawrence Erlbaum Associates.

Sahaym, A., Steensma, H. K., & Barden, J. Q. (2010). The influence of R&D investment on the use of corporate venture capital: An industry-level analysis. *Journal of Business Venturing, 25*(4), 276–388. doi:10.1016/j.jbusvent.2008.12.001

Salisbury-Glennon, J. D., Gorrell, J., Sanders, S., Boyd, P., & Kamen, M. (1999). *Self-regulated learning strategies used by the learners in a learner-centered school*. Paper presented at the Annual Meeting of the American Educational Research Association. Montreal, Canada.

Salton, G. (1989). *Automatic text processing: The transformation, analysis and retrieval of information by computer*. Reading, MA: Addison-Weslay Logman Publishing.

Sanchez-Alonso, S., & Vovides, Y. (2007). Integration of metacognitive skills in the design of learning objects. *Computers in Human Behavior, 23,* 2585–2595. doi:10.1016/j.chb.2006.08.010

Santrock, J. (1997). *Life-span development* (6th ed.). Dubuque, IA: Brown & Benchmark Publishers.

Sawhney, M., Prandelli, E., & Verona, G. (2003). The power of innomediation. *MIT Sloan Management Review, 44*(2), 76–82.

Sawhney, M., Verona, G., & Prandelli, E. (2005). Collaborating to create: The internet as a platform for customer engagement in product innovation. *Journal of Interactive Marketing, 19*(4), 4–17. doi:10.1002/dir.20046

Schall, U., Johnston, P., Lagopoulos, J., Jüptner, M., Jentzen, W., & Thienel, R. (2003). Functional brain maps of Tower of London performance: A positron emission tomography and functional magnetic resonance imaging study. *NeuroImage, 20,* 1154–1161. doi:10.1016/S1053-8119(03)00338-0

Scheer, A.-W., & Jost, W. (2002). *ARIS in der praxis*. Berlin, Germany: Springer Verlag. doi:10.1007/978-3-642-55924-2

Schlick, M. (1939). *Problems of ethics*. New York, NY: Prentice-Hall.

Schmeck, R., Geiser-Bernstein, E., & Cercy, S. (1991). Self-concept and learning: The revised inventory of learning processes. *Educational Psychology, 11,* 343–362. doi:10.1080/0144341910110310

Schmitt, E. (2010). US tells WikiLeaks to return Afghan war logs. *New York Times*. Retrieved from http://www.nytimes.com/2010/08/06/world/asia/06wiki.html

Schneider, W. (1998). The development of procedural metamemory in childhood and adolescence. In Mazzoni, G., & Nelson, T. (Eds.), *Metacognition and Cognitive Neuropsychology* (pp. 143–171). Mahwah, NJ: Erlbaum.

Schoenfeld, A. H. (1992). Learning to think mathematically: Problem solving, metacognition, and sense making in mathematics. In Grouws, D. A. (Ed.), *Handbook of Research on Mathematics Teaching and Learning* (pp. 165–197). New York, NY: MacMillan.

Schommer, M. (1990). Effects of beliefs about the nature of knowledge on comprehension. *Journal of Educational Psychology, 82*, 498–504. doi:10.1037/0022-0663.82.3.498

Schon, D. (1983). *The reflective practitioner: How professionals think in action.* New York, NY: Basic Books. doi:10.1080/07377366.1986.10401080

Schön, D. A. (1983). *The reflective practitioner.* New York, NY: Basic Books.

Schön, D. A. (1987). *Educating the reflective practitioner.* San Francisco, CA: Jossey-Bass.

Schraw, G. (1994). The effect of metacognitive knowledge on local and global monitoring. *Contemporary Educational Psychology, 19*, 143–154. doi:10.1006/ceps.1994.1013

Schraw, G., & Dennison, R. S. (1994). Assessing metacognitive awareness. *Contemporary Educational Psychology, 19*, 460–475. doi:10.1006/ceps.1994.1033

Schreiber, G., Akkermans, H., Anjewierden, A., de Hoog, R., Shadbolt, N., van de Velde, W., & Wielinga, B. (1999). *Knowledge engineering and management: The CommonKADS methodology.* Cambridge, MA: MIT Press.

Schunk, D. H. (1986). Vicarious influences on self-efficacy for cognitive skill learning. *Journal of Social and Clinical Psychology, 4*, 316–327. doi:10.1521/jscp.1986.4.3.316

Schunk, D. H. (1994). Self-regulation of self-efficacy and attributions in academic settings . In Schunk, D. H., & Zimmerman, B. J. (Eds.), *Self-Regulation of Learning and Performance: Issues and Educational Applications* (pp. 75–99). Hillsdale, NJ: Erlbaum.

Schunk, D. H. (2005). Self-regulated learning: The educational legacy of Paul R. Pintrich. *Educational Psychologist, 40*, 85–94. doi:10.1207/s15326985ep4002_3

Schunk, D. H., & Zimmerman, B. J. (1988). *Self-regulated learning: From teaching to self-reflective practice.* New York, NY: Guilford.

Schwabe, D., Guimaraes, R. M., & Rossi, G. (2002). Cohesive design of personalized web applications. *IEEE Internet Computing, 6*(2), 34–43. doi:10.1109/4236.991441

Schwabe, D., & Rossi, G. (1995). The object-oriented hypermedia design model. *Communications of the ACM, 38*(8), 45–48. doi:10.1145/208344.208354

Schwabe, D., & Rossi, G. (1998). An object oriented approach to web-based applications design. *Theoretical Practice and Object Systems, 4*(4), 207–225. doi:10.1002/(SICI)1096-9942(1998)4:4<207::AID-TAPO2>3.0.CO;2-2

Schwartz, D. L., Bransford, J. D., & Sears, D. (2005). Efficiency and innovation in transfer . In Mestre, J. (Ed.), *Transfer of Learning from a Modern Multidisciplinary Perspective* (pp. 1–51). Greenwich, CT: Information Age Publishing.

Sekatzek, P. E., & Krcmar, H. (2009). Measurement of the standard proximity of adapted standard business software. *Business and Information Systems Engineering, 1*(3), 234–244. doi:10.1007/s12599-009-0045-4

Sektnan, M., McClellanda, M., Acocka, A., & Morrisonb, J. (2010). Relations between early family risk, children's behavioral regulation, and academic achievement. *Early Childhood Research Quarterly.* Retrieved from http://www.ncbi.nlm.nih.gov/pmc/articles/PMC2953426/

Sethi, A., Mischel, W., Aber, J. L., Shoda, Y., & Rodriguez, M. L. (2000). The role of strategic attention deployment in development of self-regulation: Predicting preschoolers' delay of gratification from mother-toddler interactions. *Developmental Psychology, 36*, 767–777. doi:10.1037/0012-1649.36.6.767

Shanahan, M., Roberts, J., Hatton, D., Reznick, J., & Goldsmith, H. (2008). Early temperament and negative reactivity in boys with fragile X syndrome. *Journal of Intellectual Disability Research, 52*, 842–854. doi:10.1111/j.1365-2788.2008.01074.x

Sharma, A. (2005). Collaborative product innovation: Integrating elements of CPI via PLM framework. *Computer Aided Design, 37*(13), 1425–1434. doi:10.1016/j.cad.2005.02.012

Sharples, M., Taylor, J., & Vavoula, G. (2007). A theory of learning for the mobile age . In Andrews, A., & Haythornthwaite, C. (Eds.), *The Sage Handbook of e-Learning Research* (pp. 221–247). London, UK: Sage Publications Ltd.doi:10.1007/978-3-531-92133-4_6

Shen, D., Pan, R., Sun, J.-T., Pan, J. J., Wu, K., Yin, J., & Yang, Q. (2006). Query enrichment for web-query classification. *ACM Transactions on Information Systems*, *24*(3), 320–352. doi:10.1145/1165774.1165776

Shih, C. (2011). Assisting people with developmental disabilities to improve computer pointing efficiency through multiple mice and automatic pointing assistive programs. *Research in Developmental Disabilities*, *32*, 1736–1744. doi:10.1016/j.ridd.2011.03.002

Shih, C., Shih, C. T., & Pi, P. (2011). Using an extended automatic target acquisition program with dual cursor technology to assist people with developmental disabilities in improving their pointing efficiency. *Research in Developmental Disabilities*, *32*, 1506–1513. doi:10.1016/j.ridd.2011.01.043

Shonkoff, J., & Phillips, D. (2000). *From neurons to neighborhoods: The science of early childhood development*. Washington, DC: National Academies Press.

Shvachkin, N. K. (1973). The development of phonemic speech perception in early childhood . In Ferguson, C., & Slobin, D. (Eds.), *Studies of Child Language Development* (pp. 91–127). New York, NY: Holt, Rinehart, & Winston.

Siegler, R. S., & Stern, E. (1998). Conscious and unconscious strategy discoveries: A microgenetic analysis. *Journal of Experimental Psychology. General*, *127*, 377–397. doi:10.1037/0096-3445.127.4.377

Siemens, G. (2005). *Connectivism: A learning theory for the digital age*. Elearnspace.

Simonds, J., Kieras, J. E., Rueda, M. R., & Rothbart, M. K. (2007). Effortful control, executive attention, and emotional regulation in 7–10-year-old children. *Cognitive Development*, *22*, 474–488. doi:10.1016/j.cogdev.2007.08.009

Sivell, J. (Ed.). (1994). *Frienet pedagogy: Theory and practice*. New York, NY: The Edwin Mellen Press.

Slaats, A. (1999). Learning styles in secondary vocational education: Disciplinary differences. *Learning and Instruction*, *9*, 475–492. doi:10.1016/S0959-4752(99)00007-9

Sokolov, A. N. (1972). *Inner speech and thought*. New York, NY: Plenum. doi:10.1007/978-1-4684-1914-6

Soto-Acosta, P., Casado-Lumbreras, C., & Cabezas-Isla, F. (2010). Shaping human capital in software development teams: The case of mentoring enabled by semantics. *IET Software*, *4*(6), 445–452. doi:10.1049/iet-sen.2010.0087

Spekman, R. E., Isabella, L. A., MacAvoy, T. C., & Forbes, T. III. (1996). Creating strategic alliances which endure. *Long Range Planning*, *29*(3), 346–357. doi:10.1016/0024-6301(96)00021-0

Sperling, R. A., Howard, B. C., Miller, L. A., & Murphy, C. (2002). Measures of children's knowledge and regulation of cognition. *Contemporary Educational Psychology*, *27*, 51–79. doi:10.1006/ceps.2001.1091

Spero, M. (1978). Thoughts on computerized psychotherapy. *Psychiatry*, *41*, 279–288.

Spertus, E. (1997). Smokey: Automatic recognition of hostile messages. In *Proceedings of Conference on Innovative Applications of Artificial Intelligence,* (pp. 1058-1065). Menlo Park, CA: AAAI Press.

Spivack, G., Platt, J. J., & Shure, M. B. (1976). *The problem-solving approach to adjustment*. San Francisco, CA: Jossey-Bass.

Stager, C. L., & Werker, J. F. (1997). Infants listen for more phonetic detail in speech perception than in word-learning tasks. *Nature*, *388*, 381–382. doi:10.1038/41102

Stanford Center for Biomedical Informatics Research. (2010). *Protege ontology library*. Retrieved Nov, 2010, from http://protegewiki.stanford.edu/wiki/Protege_Ontology_Library

Starkey, L. (2010). Teachers' pedagogical reasoning and action in the digital age. *Teachers and Teaching: Theory and Practice*, *16*(2), 233–244. doi:10.1080/13540600903478433

Stefanowski, J., & Weiss, D. (2003). Carrot2 and language properties in web search results clustering. In *Proceedings of the First International Web Intelligence Conference,* (pp. 240-249). Madrid, Spain: Springer.

Sternberg, R. J. (1999). Intelligence as developing expertise. *Contemporary Educational Psychology*, *24*, 359–375. doi:10.1006/ceps.1998.0998

Sternberg, R. J. (2003). What is an "expert student?". *Educational Researcher, 32*(5), 5–9. doi:10.3102/0013189X032008005

Sternberg, R. J., & Horvath, J. A. (1995). A prototype view of expert teaching. *Educational Researcher, 24*(6), 9–17.

Stipek, D., Recchia, S., & Mcclintic, S. (1992). Self-evaluation in young children. *Monographs of the Society for Research in Child Development, 57*, 84–87. doi:10.2307/1166190

St-Laurent, D., & Moss, E. (2002). Le developpement de la planification: Influence dune attention conjointe. *Enfance, 4*, 341–361. doi:10.3917/enf.544.0341

Stoneman, Z. (2007). Examining the Down syndrome advantage: Mothers and fathers of young children with disabilities. *Journal of Intellectual Disability Research, 51*, 1006–1017. doi:10.1111/j.1365-2788.2007.01012.x

Stright, A. D., Neitzel, C., Sears, K. G., & Hoke-Sinex, L. (2001). Instruction begins in the home: Relations between parental instruction and children's self-regulation in the classroom. *Journal of Educational Psychology, 93*, 456–466. doi:10.1037/0022-0663.93.3.456

Studer, R., Benjamins, V. R., & Fensel, D. (1998). Knowledge engineering: Principles and methods. *Data & Knowledge Engineering, 25*(1-2), 161–197. doi:10.1016/S0169-023X(97)00056-6

Stvilia, B., Twidale, M. B., Gasser, L., & Smith, L. C. (2005). Information quality discussions in Wikipedia. In *Proceedings of the International Conference on Knowledge Management*. IEEE.

Stvilia, B., Twidale, M. B., Smith, L. C., & Gasser, L. (2005). Assessing information quality of a community-based encyclopedia. In *Proceedings of the International Conference on Information Quality*. IEEE.

Suchanek, F., Vojnovic, M., & Gunawardena, D. (2008). Social tags: Meaning and suggestions. In *Proceeding of the 17th ACM Conference on Information and Knowledge Management,* (pp. 223-232). New York, NY: ACM Press.

Sulis, W. (1997). Fundamental concepts of collective intelligence. *Nonlinear Dynamics Psychology and Life Sciences, 1*(1), 35–53. doi:10.1023/A:1022371810032

Sun, R. (1999). Accounting for the computational basis of consciousness: A connectionist approach. *Consciousness and Cognition, 8*, 529–565. doi:10.1006/ccog.1999.0405

Sun, R. (2002). *Duality of the mind.* Mahwah, NJ: Erlbaum.

Sun, R., & Mathews, R. (2003). Explicit and implicit processes of metacognition . In Shohov, S. (Ed.), *Advances in Psychology Research* (pp. 3–18). Hauppauge, NY: Nova Science Pub.

Sun, R., Merrill, E., & Peterson, T. (2001). From implicit skills to explicit knowledge: A bottom-up model of skill learning. *Cognitive Science, 25*, 203–244. doi:10.1207/s15516709cog2502_2

Sun, R., Slusarz, P., & Terry, C. (2005). The interaction of the explicit and the implicit in skill learning: A dual-process approach. *Psychological Review, 112*, 159–192. doi:10.1037/0033-295X.112.1.159

Sun, R., Zhang, X., & Mathew, R. (2006). Modeling metacognition in a cognitive architecture. *Cognitive Systems Research, 7*, 327–338. doi:10.1016/j.cogsys.2005.09.001

Sweller, J. (1998). Cognitive load during problem solving: Effects on learning. *Cognitive Science, 12*, 257–285. doi:10.1207/s15516709cog1202_4

Tang, H.-F. L., & Dewei, L. (2009). Towards ontology learning from folksonomies. In *Proceedings of the 21st International Joint Conference on Artificial Intelligence (IJCAI)*, (pp. 2089-2094). IJCAI.

Tang, C. M., Bartsch, K., & Nunez, N. (2007). Young children's reports of when learning occurred. *Journal of Experimental Child Psychology, 97*, 149–164. doi:10.1016/j.jecp.2007.01.003

Tanudjaja, F., & Mui, L. (2002). Persona: A contextualized and personalized web search. In *Proceedings of the 35th Hawaii International Conference on System Sciences (HICSS-35 2002)*. Big Island, HI: IEEE Computer Society.

Tarski, A. (1983). *Logics, semantics, metamatematics*. Indianapolis, IN: Hackett Publishing Company, Inc.

Taylor, M., Esbensen, B. M., & Bennett, R. T. (1994). Children's understanding of knowledge acquisition: The tendency for children to report that they have always known what they have just learned. *Child Development, 65*, 1581–1604. doi:10.2307/1131282

Taylor, R. (1987). Selecting effective courseware: Three fundamental instructional factors. *Contemporary Educational Psychology*, *12*, 231–243. doi:10.1016/S0361-476X(87)80028-0

Thiessen, E. D. (2007). The effect of distributional information on children's use of phonemic contrasts. *Journal of Memory and Language*, *56*, 16–34. doi:10.1016/j.jml.2006.07.002

Thomas, C. F., & Griffin, L. S. (1998). Who will create the metadata for the internet?. *First Monday: A Peer-Reviewed Journal on the Internet, 3*.

Thorndike, E. L. (1913). *Educational psychology: The psychology of learning*. New York, NY: Teachers College Press. doi:10.1037/13051-000

Tilly, M. (2010). *Dynamic models for knowledge processes: Final models*. ACTIVE Project.

Tinsley, V. S., & Waters, H. S. (1982). The development of verbal control over motor behavior: A replication and extension of Luria's findings. *Child Development*, *53*, 746–753. doi:10.2307/1129388

Tisdelle, D. A., & St. Lawrence, J. S. (1986). Interpersonal problem-solving competency: Review and critique of the literature. *Clinical Psychology Review*, *6*, 337–356. doi:10.1016/0272-7358(86)90005-X

Tiun, S., Abdullah, R., & Kong, T. E. (2001). Automatic topic identification using ontology hierarchy. In *Proceedings, Computational Linguistic and Intelligent Text Processing, Second International Conference CICLing*, (pp. 444-453). Mexico City, Mexico: Springer.

Trigwell, K., Martin, E., Benjamin, J., & Prosser, M. (2000). Scholarship of teaching: A model. *Higher Education Research & Development*, *19*(2), 155–168. doi:10.1080/072943600445628

Tsao, R., & Kindelberger, C. (2009). Variability of cognitive development in children with Down syndrome: Relevance of good reasons for using the cluster procedure. *Research in Developmental Disabilities*, *30*, 426–432. doi:10.1016/j.ridd.2008.10.009

Tu, C. H., & McIsaac, M. S. (2002). An examination of social presence to increase interaction in online classes. *American Journal of Distance Education*, *16*, 131–150. doi:10.1207/S15389286AJDE1603_2

Turney, P. D. (2002). Thumbs up or thumbs down? Semantic orientation applied to unsupervised classification of reviews. In *Proceedings of 40th Annual Meeting of the Association for Computational Linguistics (ACL)*, (pp. 417-424). Philadelphia, PA: ACL.

Turney, P. D., & Littman, M. L. (2003). Measuring praise and criticism: Inference of semantic orientation from association. *ACM Transactions on Information Systems*, *21*(4), 315–346. doi:10.1145/944012.944013

Upton, T. A., & Lee-Thompson, L. (2001). The role of the first language in second language reading. *Studies in Second Language Acquisition*, *23*, 469–495.

Uschold, M., & King, M. (1995). Towards a methodology for building ontologies. In *Proceedings of the IJCAI 1995 Workshop on Basic Ontological Issues in Knowledge Sharing*. Montreal, Canada: IJCAI.

Uschold, M., & Grüninger, M. (1996). Ontologies: Principles methods and applications. *The Knowledge Engineering Review*, *11*(2), 93–155. doi:10.1017/S0269888900007797

Uschold, M., King, M., Moralee, S., & Zorgios, Y. (1998). The enterprise ontology. *The Knowledge Engineering Review*, *13*(1), 31–89. doi:10.1017/S0269888998001088

Ushakova, T. N. (1994). Inner speech and second language acquisition: An experimental theoretical approach . In Lantolf, J. P., & Appel, G. (Eds.), *Vygotskian Approaches to Second Language Research* (pp. 135–156). Upper Saddle River, NJ: Able.

Vacura, M., & Svatek, V. (2010). Ontology based tracking and propagation of provenance. [NDT.]. *Proceedings of NDT, 2010*, 489–496.

Van Daal, J., Verhoeven, L., van Leeuwe, J., & Balkom, H. (2007). Working memory limitations in children with severe language impairment. *Journal of Communication Disorders*, *41*(2), 85–107. doi:10.1016/j.jcomdis.2007.03.010

van de Vrande, V., de Jong, J. P., Vanhaverbeke, W., & de Rochemont, M. (2009). Open innovation in SMEs: Trends, motives and management challenges. *Technovation*, *29*(6-7), 423–437. doi:10.1016/j.technovation.2008.10.001

Vansteenkiste, M., & Deci, E. L. (2003). Competitively contingent rewards and intrinsic motivation: Can losers remain motivated? *Motivation and Emotion, 27*, 273–299. doi:10.1023/A:1026259005264

Vargas-Vera, M., Domingue, J., Motta, E., Buckingham Shum, S., & Lanzoni, M. (2001). Knowledge extraction by using an ontology based annotation tool. In *Proceedings of the Workshop on Knowledge Markup and Semantic Annotation (K CAPA 2001)*. Victoria, Canada: K CAPA.

Veenman, M. V. J. (2005). The assessment of metacognitive skills: What can be learned from multi-method designs? In Moschner, B., & Artelt, C. (Eds.), *Lernstrategien und Metakognition: Implikationen für Forschung und Praxis* (pp. 75–97). Berlin, Germany: Waxmann.

Veenman, M., Wilhelm, P., & Beishuizen, J. (2004). The relation between intellectual and metacognitive skills from a developmental perspective. *Learning and Instruction, 14*, 89–109. doi:10.1016/j.learninstruc.2003.10.004

Vermunt, J. (1992). *Leerstijlen en sturen van leerprocessing in het hoger onderwijs: Naar procesgerichte instructie en zelfstandig denken* [Learning styles and regulation of learning processes in higher education: Towards process-guided instruction and independent reasoning]. Amsterdam, The Netherlands: Swets & Zeitlinger.

Vermunt, J., & Verloop, N. (1999). Congruence and friction between teaching and learning. *Learning and Instruction, 9*, 257–280. doi:10.1016/S0959-4752(98)00028-0

Vieillevoye, S., & Nader-Grosbois, N. (2007). Self-regulation during pretend play in children with intellectual disability and in normally developing children. *Research in Developmental Disabilities, 29*(3), 256–272. doi:10.1016/j.ridd.2007.05.003

von Hippel, E., & Katz, R. (2002). Shifting innovation to users via toolkits. *Management Science, 48*(7), 821–833. doi:10.1287/mnsc.48.7.821.2817

Voss, J. (2005). Measuring Wikipedia. In *Proceedings of the 10th International Conference of the International Society for Scientometrics and Infometrics*. IEEE.

Vossen, G., Lytras, M., & Koudas, N. (2007). Editorial: Revisiting the (machine) semantic web: The missing layers for the human semantic web. *IEEE Transactions on Knowledge and Data Engineering, 19*(2), 145–148. doi:10.1109/TKDE.2007.30

Vrba, P., Radakovic, M., Obitko, M., & Marik, V. (2011). Semantic technologies: Latest advances in agent-based manufacturing control systems. *International Journal of Production Research, 49*(5), 1483–1496. doi:10.1080/00207543.2010.518746

Vuong, B. Q., Lim, E. P., Sun, A., Le, M. T., Lauw, H. W., & Chang, K. (2008). On ranking controversies in Wikipedia: Models and evaluation. In *Proceedings of the 1st International Conference on Web Search and Data Mining*. IEEE.

Vygotsky, L. S. (1987). Thinking and speech. In Rieber & A. Carton (Eds.), *The Collected Works of L. S. Vygotsky: Vol 1: Problems of General Psychology*, (pp. 39–285). New York, NY: Plenum Press.

Vygotsky, L. S., Luria, A., Leontiev, A., & Levina, R. (1929). The function and fate of egocentric speech. In *Proceedings of the 9th International Congress of Psychology*. Princeton, NJ: Psychological Review.

Vygotsky, L. S. (1978). Chapter . In Cole, M., John-Steiner, V., Scribner, S., & Souberman, E. (Eds.), *Mind in Society: The Development of Higher Mental Processes* (pp. 36–47). Cambridge, MA: Harvard University Press.

Vygotsky, L. S. (1978). *Mind in society: The development of higher psychological processes*. Cambridge, MA: Harvard University Press.

Vygotsky, L. S. (1986). *Thought and language*. Cambridge, MA: MIT Press.

W3. (2001). SWAD-Europe deliverable 10.1: Scalability and storage: Survey of free software / open source RDF storage systems. Retrieved from http://www.w3.org/2001/sw/Europe/reports/rdf_scalable_storage_report/

Wager, W., & Wager, S. U. (1985). Presenting questions, processing responses, and providing feedback in CAI. *Journal of Instructional Development, 8*(4), 2–8. doi:10.1007/BF02906047

Wal, T. V. (2007). *Folksonomy*. Retrieved january 2012, from http://vanderwal.net/folksonomy.html

Walther, J. B. (1992). Interpersonal effects in computer-mediated interaction: A relational perspective. *Communication Research, 19*, 52–90. doi:10.1177/009365092019001003

Wang, J., Ding, Z., & Jiang, C. (2005). An ontology-based public transport query system. In *Proceedings of the International Conference on Semantics, Knowledge and Grid (SKG 2005)*. IEEE Press.

Wang, J., & Hwang, W. L. (2007). A fuzzy set approach for R&D portfolio selection using a real options valuation model. *Omega, 35*(3), 247–257. doi:10.1016/j.omega.2005.06.002

Warren, P., Kings, N., Thurlow, I., Davies, J., Bürger, T., & Simperl, E. (2009). Improving knowledge worker productivity – The ACTIVE integrated approach. *BT Technology Journal, 26*(2), 165–176.

Web1. (2011). *A development process for a multimedia project*. [Web log]. Retrieved from http://www.squidoo.com/multimedia-development-process

Web2. (2011). *Multimedia development life cycle: DI-MACC interactive media project*. Retrieved from http://www.dimacc.com/lifecycle.shtml

Web3. (2010). *A CA technologies survey, balancing agility with governance: A survey of portfolio management for agile IT*. Retrieved from http://www.ca.com/~/media/files/supportingpieces/ppm-summit-agile-research-oct-2010.aspx

Wegner, D., & Bargh, J. (1998). Control and automaticity in social life . In Gilbert, D., Fiske, S. T., & Lindzey, G. (Eds.), *Handbook of Social Psychology* (4th ed., pp. 446–496). New York, NY: McGraw-Hill.

Weikum, G., & Theobald, M. (2010). From information to knowledge: Harvesting entities and relationships from web sources. In *Proceedings of the Twenty-Ninth ACM SIGMOD-SIGACT-SIGART Symposium on Principles of Database Systems of Data*, (pp. 65–76). New York, NY: ACM Press.

Weiss, D. (2001). *A clustering interface for web search results in Polish and English*. (Master's Thesis). Poznan University of Technology. Poznan, Poland.

Welch, T. A. (1984). A technique for high-performance data compression. *Computer, 17*(6), 8–19. doi:10.1109/MC.1984.1659158

Wendel, W. B. (2000). Value pluralism in legal ethics. *Washington University Law Quarterly, 78*, 113–213.

Werker, J. F., Fennell, C. T., Corcoran, K. M., & Stager, C. L. (2002). Infants' ability to learn phonetically similar words: Effects of age and vocabulary size. *Infancy, 3*, 1–30.

Wiener, N. (1954). *The human use of human beings: Cybernetics and society*. Oxford, UK: Houghton Mifflin.

Wikileaks. (2010). Afghan war diary. *Wikileaks Organization*. Retrieved from http://wikileaks.org/wiki/Afghan_War_Diary,_2004-2010

Wilkinson, D. M., & Huberman, B. A. (2007). Assessing the value of cooperation in Wikipedia. *First Monday, 12*(4).

Williamson, M. (2003). *Using DMOZ open directory project lists with novell bordermanager*. Retrieved from http://www.novell.com/coolsolutions/feature/7930.html

Wilson, M., Arenas, A., Chadwick, D., Dimitrakos, T., Doser, J., Giambiagi, P., et al. (2006). The TrustCoM approach to enforcing agreements between interoperating enterprises. In *Proceedings of the Interoperability for Enterprise Software and Applications Conference (I-ESA 2006)*, (pp. 365–375). I-ESA.

Wimalasuriya, D. C., & Dou, D. (2010). Ontology-based information extraction: An introduction and a survey of current approaches. *Journal of Information Science, 36*(3), 306–332. doi:10.1177/0165551509360123

Winne, P. H., Hadwin, A. F., Stockley, D. B., & Nesbit, J. C. (2000). *Traces versus self-reports of study tactics and their relations to achievement*. Unpublished.

Winne, P. H. (1995). Inherent details in self-regulated learning. *Educational Psychologist, 30*, 173–187. doi:10.1207/s15326985ep3004_2

Winne, P. H. (2001). Self-regulated learning viewed from models of information processing . In Zimmerman, B., & Schunk, D. (Eds.), *Self-Regulated Learning and Academic Achievement: Theoretical Perspectives* (pp. 153–189). Mahwah, NJ: Erlbaum.

Winne, P. H., & Perry, N. E. (2000). Measuring self-regulated learning . In Boekaerts, M., Pintrich, P. R., & Ziedner, M. (Eds.), *Handbook of Self-Regulation: Theory Research and Applications* (pp. 531–566). San Diego, CA: Academic Press.

Winnykamen, F. (1993). Gestion socio-cognitive du recours a` l'aide d'autrui chez l'enfant. *Journal of Instructional Psychology*, *28*, 645–659. doi:10.1080/00207599308246949

Winsler, A., Fernyhough, C., McClaren, E. M., & Way, E. (2005). *Private speech coding manual*. Fairfax, VA: George Mason University. Retrieved from http://classweb.gmu.edu/awinsler/Resources/PsCodingManual.pdf

Winsler, A. (1998). Parent-child interaction and private speech in boys with ADHD. *Applied Developmental Science*, *2*, 17–39. doi:10.1207/s1532480xads0201_2

Winsler, A., Abar, B., Feder, M. A., Schunn, C. D., & Rubio, D. A. (2007). Private speech and executive functioning among high-functioning children with autistic spectrum disorders. *Journal of Autistic Development Disorder*, *37*, 1617–1635. doi:10.1007/s10803-006-0294-8

Winsler, A., Carlton, M. P., & Barry, M. J. (2000). Age-related changes in preschool children's systematic use of private speech in a natural setting. *Journal of Child Language*, *27*, 665–687. doi:10.1017/S0305000900004402

Winsler, A., De Le'on, J. R., Wallace, B., Carlton, M. P., & Willson-Quayle, A. (2003). Private speech in preschool children: Developmental stability and change, across-task consistency, and relations with classroom behavior. *Journal of Child Language*, *30*, 583–608. doi:10.1017/S0305000903005671

Winsler, A., & Diaz, R. M. (1995). Private speech in the classroom: The effects of activity type, presence of others, classroom context, and mixed-age grouping. *International Journal of Behavioral Development*, *18*, 463–488.

Winsler, A., Diaz, R. M., Atencio, D. J., McCarthy, E. M., & Chabay, L. A. (2000). Verbal self-regulation over time in preschool children at risk for attention and behavior problems. *Journal of Child Psychology and Psychiatry, and Allied Disciplines*, *41*, 875–886. doi:10.1111/1469-7610.00675

Winsler, A., Diaz, R. M., McCarthy, E. M., Atencio, D. J., & Chabay, L. A. (1999). Mother-child interaction, private speech, and task performance in preschool children with behavior problems. *Journal of Child Psychology and Psychiatry, and Allied Disciplines*, *40*, 891–904. doi:10.1111/1469-7610.00507

Winsler, A., Diaz, R. M., & Montero, I. (1997). The role of private speech in the transition from collaborative to independent task performance in young children. *Early Childhood Research Quarterly*, *12*, 59–79. doi:10.1016/S0885-2006(97)90043-0

Winsler, A., Manfra, L., & Diaz, R. M. (2007). Should I let them talk? Private speech and task performance among preschool children with and without behavior problems. *Early Childhood Research Quarterly*, *22*, 215–231. doi:10.1016/j.ecresq.2007.01.001

Winsler, A., & Naglieri, J. (2003). Overt and covert verbal problem-solving strategies: Developmental trends in use, awareness, and relations with task performance in children aged 5 to 17. *Child Development*, *74*, 659–678. doi:10.1111/1467-8624.00561

Witten, I. H., & Frank, E. (2000). *Data mining, practical machine learning tools and techniques with java implementations*. San Francisco, CA: Morgan Kaufmann.

Woitsch, R., & Karagiannis, D. (2005). Process oriented knowledge management: A service based approach. *Journal of Universal Computer Science*, *11*(4), 565–588.

Wong, A. W. K., Chan, C. C. H., Li-Tsang, C. W. P., & Lam, C. S. (2009). Competence of people with intellectual disabilities on using human-computer interface. *Research in Developmental Disabilities*, *30*, 107–123. doi:10.1016/j.ridd.2008.01.002

Wozniak, R. (1972). Verbal regulation of motor behavior: Soviet research and non-Soviet replications. *Human Development*, *44*, 13–47. doi:10.1159/000271226

Wozniak, R. H. (1975). A dialectical paradigm for psychological research: Implications drawn from the history of psychology in the Soviet Union. *Human Development*, *18*, 18–34. doi:10.1159/000271473

Wright, M., Clarysse, B., Lockett, A., & Knockaert, M. (2008). Mid-range universities' linkages with industry: Knowledge types and the role of intermediaries. *Research Policy*, *37*(8), 1205–1223. doi:10.1016/j.respol.2008.04.021

Wróblewski, M. (2003). *A hierarchical WWW pages clustering algorithm based on the vector space model*. (Master Thesis). Poznań University of Technology. Poznań, Poland.

Yaden, D. B. Jr. (1984). Inner speech, oral language, and reading: Huey and Vygotsky revisited. *Reading Psychology: An International Quarterly, 5,* 155–166. doi:10.1080/0270271840050118

Yates, A., Cafarella, M., Banko, M., Etzioni, O., Broadhead, M., & Soderland, S. (2007). TextRunner: Open information extraction on the web. In *Proceedings of Human Language Technologies: The Annual Conference of the North American Chapter of the Association for Computational Linguistics,* (p. 25–26). Morristown, NJ: ACL.

Yelland, N., Cope, B., & Kalantzis, M. (2008). Learning by design: Creating pedagogical frameworks for knowledge building in the twenty-first century. *Asia-Pacific Journal of Teacher Education, 36*(3), 197–213. doi:10.1080/13598660802232597

Yi, J., Bunescu, T. N., & Niblack, R. W. (2003). Sentiment analyzer: Extracting sentiments about a given topic using natural language processing techniques. In *Proceedings of IEEE International Conference on Data Mining, ICDM 2003.* IEEE Press.

Yi, J., Nasukawa, T., Bunescu, R., & Niblack, W. (2003). Sentiment analyzer: Extracting sentiments about a given topic using natural language processing techniques. In *Proceedings of the Third IEEE International Conference on Data Mining (ICDM),* (pp. 427-434). IEEE Press.

Zamir, O. (1999). *Clustering web documents: A phrase-based method.* (PhD Thesis). University of Washington. Seattle, WA.

Zamir, O., & Etzioni, O. (1998). Web document clustering: A feasibility demonstration. In *Proceedings of the 19th International Computer Research and Development of Information Retrieval (SIGIR),* (pp. 46-54). Melbourne, Australia: ACM.

Zeanah, C. H., Boris, N. W., & Scheeringa, M. S. (1997). Psychopathology in infancy. *Journal of Child Psychology and Psychiatry, and Allied Disciplines, 38,* 81–99. doi:10.1111/j.1469-7610.1997.tb01506.x

Zeidner, M., Boekarts, M., & Pintrich, P. R. (2000). Self-regulation: Directions and challenges for future research . In Boekaerts, M., Pintrich, P., & Seidner, M. (Eds.), *Self-Regulation: Theory, Research, and Applications* (pp. 749–768). Orlando, FL: Academic Press.

Zeng, H.-J., He, Q.-C., Chen, Z., Ma, W.-Y., & Ma, J. (2004). Learning to cluster web search results. In *Proceedings of the 27th Annual International ACM SIGIR Conference on Research and Development in Information Retrieval.* Sheffield, UK: ACM Press.

Zhao, Y. (2007). A dynamic model of active portfolio management with benchmark orientation. *Journal of Banking & Finance, 31*(11), 3336–3356. doi:10.1016/j.jbankfin.2007.04.007

Zhu, D. (2007). *Improving the relevance of search results via search-term disambiguation and ontological filtering.* (Master Dissertation). Curtin University of Technology. Perth, Australia. Retrieved from http://adt.curtin.edu.au/theses/available/adt-WCU20080331.163016

Zhu, D., & Dreher, H. (2009). Discovering semantic aspects of socially constructed knowledge hierarchy to boost the relevance of web searching. *Journal of Univeral Computer Science, 15*(8), 1685–1710.

Zhu, D., & Porter, A. (2002). Automated extraction and visualization of information for technological intelligence and forecasting. *Technological Forecasting and Social Change, 69,* 495–506. doi:10.1016/S0040-1625(01)00157-3

Zimmerman, B. J. (1989). A social cognitive view of self-regulated academic learning. *Journal of Educational Psychology, 81,* 329–339. doi:10.1037/0022-0663.81.3.329

Zimmerman, B. J. (1995). Self-regulation involves more than metacognition: A social cognitive perspective. *Educational Psychologist, 30,* 217–221. doi:10.1207/s15326985ep3004_8

Zimmerman, B. J. (1998). Academic studying and the development of personal skill: A self-regulatory perspective. *Educational Psychologist, 33,* 73–86.

Zimmerman, B. J. (2000). Attaining self-regulation: A social-cognitive perspective . In Boekaerts, M., Pintrich, P., & Seidner, M. (Eds.), *Self-Regulation: Theory, Research, and Applications* (pp. 13–39). Orlando, FL: Academic Press.

Zimmerman, B. J. (2000). Self-efficacy: An essential motive to learn. *Contemporary Educational Psychology*, *25*, 82–91. doi:10.1006/ceps.1999.1016

Zimmerman, B. J. (2001). Theories of self-regulated learning and academic achievement: An overview and analysis . In Zimmerman, B. J., & Schunk, D. H. (Eds.), *Self-Regulated Learning and Academic Achievement: Theoretical Perspectives* (2nd ed., pp. 1–38). Mahwah, NJ: Erlbaum.

Zimmerman, B. J., & Martinez-Pons, M. (1990). Student differences in self-regulated learning: Related grade, sex, and giftedness to self-efficacy and strategy use. *Journal of Educational Psychology*, *82*, 51–59. doi:10.1037/0022-0663.82.1.51

Zimmerman, B. J., & Schunk, D. H. (1989). *Self-regulated learning and academic achievement*. New York, NY: Springer-Verlag. doi:10.1007/978-1-4612-3618-4

Zimmerman, B. J., & Schunk, D. H. (2001). Reflections on theories of self-regulated learning and academic achievement . In Zimmerman, B. J., & Schunk, D. H. (Eds.), *Self-Regulated Learning and Academic Achievement: Theoretical Perspectives* (2nd ed., pp. 289–307). Mahwah, NJ: Erlbaum.

Zimmerman, B. J., & Schunk, D. H. (Eds.). (2001). *Self-regulated learning and academic achievement: Theoretical perspectives* (2nd ed.). Mahwah, NJ: Erlbaum.

Zorilla, M., Mora, E., Corcuera, P., & Frenandez, J. (1999). Vertical partitioning algorithms in distributed databases. In *Proceedings on Computer Aided Systems Theory, EUROCAST 1999*. EUROCAST.

Zumberg, K. M., Chang, E. C., & Sanna, L. J. (2008). Does problem orientation involve more than generalized self-efficacy? Predicting psychological and physical functioning in college students. *Personality and Individual Differences*, *45*, 328–332. doi:10.1016/j.paid.2008.04.017

# About the Contributors

**Patricia Ordóñez de Pablos** is a Professor in the Department of Business Administration in the Faculty of Economics and Business of the University of Oviedo, Spain. Her teaching and research interests focus on the areas of strategic management, knowledge management, intellectual capital, organizational learning, human resources management, information technologies, and Semantic Web. She serves as Associate Editor of *Behavior and Information Technology*. She is the author of numerous papers published in leading academic journals such as *Computers in Human Behavior*, *Journal of Knowledge Management*, *Information Management Systems*, *International Journal of Technology Management*, *Journal of Universal Computer Science*, etc. She has published books with Springer and IGI Global.

**Héctor Oscar Nigro** received a Systems Engineer degree from UNICEN (Universidad Nacional del Centro de la Provincia de Buenos Aires), Tandil, Argentina; Magister degree in Sociology and Political Sciences from FLACSO (Facultad Latinoamericana de Ciencias Sociales); and is a PHD candidate in Computational and Industrial Mathematics at UNICEN. He is a full Professor in the Department of Computer Sciences and Systems in the Exact Sciences Faculty—UNICEN. He is the director of MERAIS IV Project (UNICEN). In addition, he has realized consulting activities related to data mining, data analysis, and knowledge management for the last 20 years. His research interests are in databases, data warehouses, data mining, knowledge management, and OLAP. He has published book chapters and articles presented at various professional conferences on his research activities. Prof. Nigro has co-edited the book *Data Mining with Ontologies: Implementations, Findings, and Frameworks*, published by IGI Global (2008).

**Robert D. Tennyson** is Professor of Educational Psychology at the University of Minnesota. He is Editor of a professional journal, *Computers in Human Behavior*. He also serves on editorial boards for seven other peer-reviewed journals. His research and publications include topics on problem solving, concept learning, intelligent systems, testing and measurement, instructional design, and advanced learning technologies. He has directed sponsored workshops and advanced study institutes in Germany, Greece, Norway, Spain, and Taiwan. He has authored over 300 journal articles, books, and book chapters.

**Sandra Elizabeth González Císaro** was born in Mar del Plata, Argentina. She received a Systems Engineer degree from UNICEN (Universidad Nacional del Centro de la Provincia de Buenos Aires), Tandil, Argentina, and is a PHD candidate in Computational and Industrial Mathematics at UNICEN. She is an Assistant Professor at Department of Computer Sciences and Systems in the Exact Sciences Faculty, UNICEN, and she is also working on MERAIS IV Project (UNICEN). Her research interests are in databases, data warehouses, data mining, knowledge management, OLAP, symbolic data analysis, and management expert systems. She has published book chapters and articles presented at various professional conferences related with her research activities. She has co-edited the book *Data Mining with Ontologies: Implementations, Findings, and Frameworks*, published by IGI Global (2008). Eng. González Císaro is an IEEE Computer Society member.

**Waldemar Karwowsk** is Professor and Chairman, Department of Industrial Engineering and Management Systems at the University of Central Florida, USA. Executive Director, Institute for Advanced Systems Engineering, University of Central Florida, Orlando, Florida (8/1/2008-present). He holds an M.S. (1978) in Production Engineering and Management from the Technical University of Wroclaw, Poland, and a Ph.D. (1982) in Industrial Engineering from Texas Tech University. He was awarded D.Sc. (dr habil.) degree in Management Science by the State Institute for Organization and Management in Industry, Poland (2004). He also received Honorary Doctorate degrees from three European universities. He is the author or coauthor of over 380 scientific publications. His research interests focus on human systems integration, human performance, cognitive engineering, activity theory, knowledge management, systems engineering, human-computer interaction, fuzzy logic, and neuro-fuzzy modeling applications of nonlinear dynamics to human performance, and neuroergonomics. Dr. Karwowski was named the J. B. Speed School of Engineering Alumni Scholar for Research, University of Louisville (2004–2006). He is Past President of the International Ergonomics Association (2000-2003) and past President of the Human Factors and Ergonomics Society (2007). Dr. Karwowski currently serves on the Board on Human Systems-Integration, National Research Council, the National Academies, USA (2007–2011). Currently, he is Editor of the *Human Factors and Ergonomics in Manufacturing Journal,* and Editor-in-Chief of *Theoretical Issues in Ergonomics Science Journal.*

\* \* \*

**Terje Aaberge** is a Researcher at Western Norway Research Institute, Norway. He was employed by the Department of Theoretical Physics at this university from 1973 to 1982 and has since been Visiting Researcher at the department with almost yearly visits financed by the Fonds National Suisse until 2006. He is primarily working in the domains of logic and semantic technologies.

**Jan Aalmink** was born in 1967, Nordhorn, Northern Germany. His interest in computer science began in the early 80s. He received the university-entrance diploma in 1987 from Fachgymnasium Technik in Nordhorn. He studied both Informatics and Mathematics at Technical University of Clausthal. After receiving degrees Dipl.-Inf. and Dipl.-Math from Technical University of Clausthal in 1991, he entered the business IT world. After 3 years in IT consulting industry as a freelancer, he joined SAP AG in 1994. Prior to his recent appointment to Senior Software Architect, he was responsible for enterprise systems engineering in the areas of logistics-controlling, cost containment, financial services, foundation, manufacturing industries, and supply chain management. In addition to SAP, he joined the research Department VLBA—Very Large Business Applications—at University of Oldenburg as an external PhD student in 2008. His research interests include enterprise systems engineering and diagnostics, enterprise tomography, cloud computing, in-memory computing, search engine technology, algorithm engineering, graph-theory, and development efficiency.

**Adel M. Agina** is a Computer Programmer (B.Sc), holds a Master degree in Educational Technology (TAET) and a PhD in Communication Studies (Technical and Professional Communication). Among the three areas of knowledge, he developed the first computer-based methodology, which is currently known as Aginian's methodology in which all of his published journal articles are currently known as Aginian's studies. His main interest topic of research is the young children's developmental processes with nonhuman external regulators.

**Rajendra Akerkar** is a Senior Researcher and Professor at Western Norway Research Institute (Vestlandsforsking), Norway. He is also a Chairman of Technomathematics Research Foundation, Kolhapur, India. He has authored 13 books and more than 90 research articles. His current research focuses on intelligent information management, semantic technologies, and Web mining.

**Rocío Vega Alonso** is a Consultant at PMOpartners, Spain. She obtained a Computer Science degree by Universidad Pontificia Comillas (ICAI), Madrid (2009). She is author of an R&D project about treatment and encoding digital video signals for transmission and behavior with a specific codec. Before consultancy, she worked in bank and insurance companies in the IT department. In her 2 years of consultancy experience, she has been involved in project and portfolio management projects with different tools for national and international customers in bank and communications sectors. In Sem-IDI project, she has been responsible for tools evaluation, requirement definition, and integration with sematics module.

**Jose María Alvarez** (PhD ABD) is Master of Computer Science (2007) and Bachelor of Computer Science (2005) by the University of Oviedo. In June 2008, he was rewarded with the "Best Final Degree Project in Computer Science" by the Official Association of Computer Engineers of Asturias (Spain) thanks to this project "Activation of Concepts in Ontologies through the Spreading Activation Technique." From 2005 to 2010, he worked at the R&D Department in the Semantic Technologies area within CTIC Foundation; more specifically, he worked in projects related to Semantic Web services, rule based systems, search systems, linked data, etc. During this stage, he participated in several research projects in different research programmes: PRAVIA project-PCTI Asturias cod. IE05-172 (Regional scope), PRIMA-Plan Avanza-cod. TSI-020302-2008-32 (National scope), and ONTORULE-FP7 cod. 231875 (European scope). Now he holds a position as Assistant Professor at the Department of Computer Science within the University of Oviedo, and he is also Senior Researcher at WESO Research Group (University of Oviedo). He is waiting to defend his PhD dissertation about e-Procurement and Linked Data supervised by Dr. José Emilio Labra Gayo.

**César Luis Alvargonzález** (MSc) is a student at the Master of Computer Science and Bachelor of Computer Science (2011) by the University of Oviedo. He has worked as IT Services Intern in the Education Faculty at the University of Oviedo and as Web Developer at the Advanced Analytic Intelligence Cathedra. Nowadays, he works as researcher at WESO Research Group (University of Oviedo).

**Hisham Assal** received his Ph.D. in Computer-Aided Design from the University of California, Los Angeles (UCLA), in 1996. As the Director of Research, Dr. Assal designs and develops distributed, collaborative decision support systems for military and industry applications. His interests include knowledge representation, knowledge management, intelligent agents, and complex systems. Dr. Assal has written and contributed to numerous publications on the subjects of intelligent design, knowledge representation, and system architecture.

**Leonardo Balduzzi** is Co-Founder and Director of Region Global SA, an IT company in charge of creating hyperlocal e-commerce websites, such as www.region20.com.ar. He worked at ITC group Inspirit (www.inspirit.net) for 3 years as Project Manager. He graduated as System Engineer from UNICEN University (Tandil, Buenos Aires, Argentina). His thesis topic was "Knowledge-Based System applied to SEO" as result of specialization in Data Mining and Data Warehouse issues. For 5 years, he managed several IT projects linked to Internet, for the company Intercomgi. He worked in the development of a SEO product, Matrix (www.matrixsearch.com), as head of the development team.

**Jeries Besharat** is a Ph.D. candidate at the Computer Engineering and Informatics Department of Patras University. His area of expertise is Web metrics, data mining, and natural language processing. He received his diploma from the Department of Information and Communication Systems Engineering of the Aegean University and his M. Sc from the Computer Engineering and Informatics Department of Patras University.

**Minal Bhise** obtained her ME and PhD in Computer Science from BITS, Pilani. She has been working in distributed databases, Semantic Web, and cloud databases. She is a faculty at DA-IICT, Gandhinagar, India.

**Constanța-Nicoleta Bodea** is Professor at the Academy of Economic Study Bucharest (ASE), Faculty of Cybernetics, Statistics and Economic Informatics, Economic Informatics Department. Currently, she teaches Artificial Intelligence, Data Mining, and Project Management. She coordinates numerous research projects at national level and achieved a high expertise in managing projects with multiple consortia. She is author of 11 books and more than 50 papers on project management, information systems, and artificial intelligence, being honored by IPMA with the Outstanding Research Contributions in 2007.

**Sanjay Chaudhary** obtained his PhD in Computer Science from Gujarat Vidyapeeth. His research areas are distributed computing, service-oriented computing, and ICT applications in agriculture. He is a Professor and Dean (Academic Programs) at Dhirubhai Ambani Institute of Information and Communication Technology (DA-IICT), Gandhinagar, India.

**Ricardo Colomo-Palacios** is an Associate Professor at the Computer Science Department of the Universidad Carlos III de Madrid. His research interests include applied research in information systems, software project management, people in software projects, and Social and Semantic Web. He received his PhD in Computer Science from the Universidad Politécnica of Madrid (2005). He also holds an MBA from the Instituto de Empresa (2002). He has been working as a software engineer, project manager, and software engineering consultant in several companies including Spanish IT Leader INDRA. He is also an Editorial Board Member and Associate Editor for several international journals and conferences and Editor in Chief of *International Journal of Human Capital and Information Technology Professionals*.

**Ruben González Crespo** is a research manager in accessibility and usability in Web environments for people with severe disabilities. BS in Computer Management from the Polithecnical University of Madrid and Computer Engineering from the Pontifical University of Salamanca. Master in Project Management from the same university. PhD from the Pontifical University of Salamanca in 2008 and PhD Extraordinary Award given by the UPSA, where he is a Professor at the School of Computing (Madrid Campus) since 2005. Currently, he is the Director of the Master in Project Management, is Professor of Doctoral Programs organized by the University and Master's programs in GIS, Software Engineering, and Security.

**Ignacio Andrés Cuesta** is Co-Founder and CEO of Region Global SA, an IT company in charge of creating hyperlocal e-commerce websites, such as www.region20.com.ar. He worked at ITC group Inspirit (www.inspirit.net) for 7 years, the last 2 as Chief Technology Officer of a SEO product, Matrix (www.matrixsearch.com). He graduated as System Engineer from UNICEN University (Tandil, Buenos Aires, Argentina). During his studies, he has specialized in data mining issues and developed his thesis in knowledge-based system applied to SEO. He has been active in the area of online marketing for 5 years as head of SEO team at online marketing agency Atraczion. He was a member of several organization and communities, such as SEMPO, Online Marketing Latam, Search Marketing Argentina. His international experience includes works and consultancies in Argentina, Spain, and USA.

**Maria-Iuliana Dascălu** has a Master Degree in Project Management from the Academy of Economic Studies, Bucharest, Romania (2008), and a Bachelor Degree in Computer Science from the Alexandru-Ioan Cuza University, Iasi, Romania (2006). She is a PhD from the Academy of Economic Studies, combining her work experience as a programmer with numerous research activities. Her research relates to computer-assisted testing with applications in e-learning environments for project management, competencies development systems, and their benefits to adult education. Maria Dascălu is a Certified Project Management Associate (2008). She also conducted a research stage at the University of Gothenburg, Sweden, from October 2009 to May 2010.

**Craig Deed** is a Senior Lecturer in the Faculty of Education, La Trobe University, Australia. He has written extensively in the areas of student engagement, learner agency though multi-modal representation of personal reflection, the application of Web 2.0 tools in contemporary learning environments, and innovative pedagogy to address learning preferences and capacities of today's students. Current research projects include the use of flexible and virtual learning spaces; design and application of teacher-as-researcher as a means of building practical knowledge; new models of pre-service teacher education; and self-regulated learning for personal learning design.

**Frank Dengler** is a Research Associate at the Institute of Applied Informatics and Formal Description Methods (Institute AIFB), Karlsruhe Institute of Technology (KIT). He was involved in the ACTIVE project. Before joining the AIFB team, Frank worked as IT professional service consultant at Intel. He was involved in different data center and healthcare projects. Frank received his diploma in Information Engineering and Management from the Universitдt Karlsruhe (TH). His research focuses on business processes management, informal processes, and collaborative process development using semantic technologies.

**Heinz Dreher** is Professor of Informatics in the School of Information Systems, Curtin Business School, at Curtin University, Perth, Western Australia. He has published in the information systems and educational technology domains through conferences, journals, invited talks, and seminars. He is currently the holder of Australian National Competitive Grant funding for a 4-year e-learning project and a 4-year project on automated essay grading technology development, trial usage and evaluation. He has received numerous industry grants for investigating hypertext-based systems in training and business scenarios, and is an experienced and accomplished teacher, receiving awards for his work in cross-cultural awareness and course design. In 2004, he was appointed Adjunct Professor for Computer Science at TU Graz, and continues to collaborate in teaching and learning and research projects with European partners. Dr. Dreher's research and development programme is conducted within the Semantic Analysis and Text Mining for Business and Education research cluster in the Curtin Business School (www.eaglesemantics.com). Research funding for individual projects is also sought, including for mining vast repositories of heterogeneous data such as from the natural resources industries.

**Anthony David Edwards** is currently Director of Education at Liverpool Hope University in the UK. He gained both his Doctorate and Masters Degrees from Liverpool University. His publications include work on e-learning and education, the use of technology in education, the historical link between technology and the economy and education, displaced communities and education, and a series of school textbooks on technological subjects. He is currently researching and writing on the link between technology and creativity.

**Wolf Engelbach**, Head of the Department for Information Management holds a PhD. in Civil Engineering. His publication activities concentrate on enterprise collaboration and mobile media. Among others, he has lead the collaborative EU project AMI-SME (Analysis of Market Information for SME), the conception work package in the ITEA-project LOMS, and is currently in charge of the conception work package in the German project VeRSiert that addresses cooperation of different stakeholders in the area of civil security in public transport.

**Vadim Ermolayev** is an Associate Professor at the Department of Information Technologies of Zaporozhye National University, and the Head of Intelligent Systems Research Group. He received his PhD from Zaporozhye University. Vadim is also an independent research consultant in knowledge engineering and management, semantic technologies, intelligent software systems, distributed artificial intelligence. Prof. Ermolayev has been involved in the ACTIVE Project as a part of the Case Study Partner Team of Cadence Design Systems GmbH. Vadim is a professional member of the ACM.

**Alberto López Fernández** holds a Computer Science Engineer degree, by Universidad Pontificia de Salamanca, and finished a Project Management (PMP, CMMI, ITIL) Master. He is ITIL Foundation v2 certificated and ITIL Foundation v3 trained. Prior to joining PMOpartners, he worked in an IT department as analyst, programmer, and system administrator. In his 3 years of consultancy experience, he has been involved in several project and portfolio management implementations (HP PPM and Daptiv PPM) and Quality Assurance (QA) tools in finance and public sectors. In Sem-IDI project, he has been involved in requirement definition and PPM tool customization.

**Luis Fernando Fortes Garcia** has a Bachelor degree in Computer Science obtained in Catholic University of Rio Grande do Sul (1994), a Master degree (1997) and a Doctor Degree (2005) in Computer Science from Federal University of Rio Grande do Sul. He has professional and academic experiences in software engineering, distance education, computer networks, mobile computing, software quality, it governance, knowledge management, and text summarization. He is a Professor in Lutheran University of Brasil (ULBRA) and Dom Bosco Faculty.

**B. Cristina Pelayo Garcia-Bustelo** is a Lecturer in the Computer Science Department of the University of Oviedo. Ph.D. from the University of Oviedo in Computer Engineering. Her research interests include object-oriented technology, Web engineering, e-government, modeling software with BPM, DSL, and MDA.

**Joaquín Fernández-González** is the CEO of EgeoIT, Spain, and Agricultural Engineer in the Universidad Politécnica de Madrid, Executive MBA in the Instituto de Empresa de Madrid, and Specialist in R&D Projects Management and International Actions in the Universidad Politécnica de Madrid.

**Jorge Marx Gómez** studied Computer Engineering and Industrial Engineering at the University of Applied Science of Berlin (Technische Fachhochschule). He was a Lecturer and Researcher at the Otto-von-Guericke-Universität Magdeburg where he also obtained a PhD degree in Business Information Systems with the work "Computer-Based Approaches to Forecast Returns of Scrapped Products to Recycling." In 2004, he received his habilitation for the work "Automated Environmental Reporting through Material Flow Networks" at the Otto-von-Guericke-Universität Magdeburg. From 2002 until 2003, he was a Visiting Professor for Business Information Systems at the Technical University of Clausthal. In 2005, he became a Full Professor of Business Information Systems at the Carl von Ossietzky University Oldenburg. He is the Chair of the Department Very Large Business Applications. His research interests include environmental management information systems, material flow management systems, federated ERP-systems, environmental data warehousing, recycling program planning, disassembly planning and control, life cycle assessment, simulation and neuro-fuzzy-systems. Jorge Marx Gómez is a member in the following institutions: German Association of Computer Science (Gesellschaft für Informatik e.V., in short GI), OFFIS e.V. (Oldenburg Institute of Informatics), SAP Roundtable for Business Intelligence, German Association of University Professors and Lecturers (Deutscher Hochschulverband, in short DHV), German Forum of Interoperability (in short DFI), German Oracle Users Group e.V. (in short DOAG), and reviewer and expert in DAAD selection committee for Latin-American research proposals.

**Weena Jimenez** (MSc) is Master of Computer Science (2012) by the University of Oviedo; Bachelor of Computer Science (2007) by Institute of Management and Technology, Venezuela; Bachelor of Social Communication (2002) by Catholic University Andres Bello, Venezuela. She has worked as a Web Master in Venezolana TV Chanel from 2004 to 2009. Nowadays, she works as researcher at WESO Research Group (University of Oviedo).

**Diego Jiménez-López** is an R&D Consultant in EgeoIT, Spain, and PhD candidate in the Computer Science Department at Universidad Carlos III de Madrid. He holds an MSc in Computer Science from Universidad Carlos III de Madrid. He has been involved in several research projects related to Semantic Web, e-learning, project management, and finances.

**Nikos Kirtsis** is a Postgraduate Researcher at the Computer Engineering and Informatics Department of Patras University. His area of expertise is Web data analysis, data mining, Web search refinement, and natural language processing. He received his diploma and M.Sc from the Computer Engineering and Informatics Department of Patras University.

**Piet A. M. Kommers** is an Associate Professor at the University of Twente. His major topic of concern is the "media society" and the ways it affects networking, learning, and citizenship. In his position as UNESCO Honorary Professor, he focuses on ICT in teacher education and its further development towards multicultural attitudes. He was recently invited to be a member of the Ministerial Advisory Boards in Singapore and Taiwan on projects for Advanced Learning Technologies. He has authored journal articles, journal editorials, monographs, and edited books, edited proceedings, proceedings contributions, reports, and presentations.

**Franz J. Kurfess** joined the Computer Science Department of California Polytechnic State University in the summer of 2000, after a short stay with Concordia University in Montreal, Canada, and a longer stay with the New Jersey Institute of Technology. Before that, he spent some time with the University of Ulm, Germany, the International Computer Science Institute in Berkeley, CA, and the Technical University in Munich, where he obtained his M.S. and Ph.D. in Computer Science. His main areas of research are artificial intelligence and human-computer interaction, with particular interest in the usability and interaction aspects of knowledge-intensive systems.

**José Emilio Labra** is Associate Professor at the Department of Computer Science, (University of Oviedo) from 1992. In 2001, he obtained his PhD in Computer Science. Since 2004, he holds the position as Dean of Computer Engineering School at the University of Oviedo. From a research point view, he is focused on the application and development of innovative solutions with semantic technologies. In this context, he is the main researcher of the WESO Research Group at the Department of Computer Science, and he is involved in several research projects with different scopes: regional, national, and European. Finally, he is the author of more than 50 scientific publications and member, reviewer, and part of the program committee of the main conferences and journals in his research area like International Conference on Web Engineering, Social Data on The Web, Workshop on Web Services, and ACM. He is currently editor of different special issues of the IGI Global journal.

**Uwe Laufs** is a Researcher and Project Leader, and he works at Fraunhofer-Institute for Industrial Engineering (IAO) in Stuttgart, Germany. He studied Computer Science and Media at University of Applied Sciences Stuttgart and Computer Science at University Hagen. His main areas of work are software engineering and software management, including the realisation of Semantic Web applications for industrial purposes and for innovation management. Uwe Laufs also works on innovative user interface technologies und automatic user interface generation, including multi-touch user interfaces. He also is involved in the development of "Multitouch for Java" (MT4j), which is one of the leading open source development platforms for multi-touch applications.

**Adina-Lipai** is working as a Software Developer. She has a Bachelor Degree in Informatics from the Academy of Economic Studies, Bucharest, Romania. Adina Lipai earned a PhD in Economic Cybernetics and Statistics at the Academy of Economic Studies. Her research relates to the Web search engines, the innovative approaches for increasing the search performance.

**Stanley Loh** is a Professor in the Catholic University of Pelotas, in the Lutheran University of Brazil and in the Senac Technology Faculty. He has a Ph.D. degree in Computer Science (2001). He also has Computer Science Master degree and Bachelor degree. He works as Consultant in IT companies (Invenio, InText Mining, and ADS Digital). His interests include recommendation systems, text mining, Web search, knowledge management, business intelligence, and competitive intelligence.

**Fabiana Lorenzi** has a Ph.D. degree in Computer Science from Federal University of Rio Grande do Sul (UFRGS), and she is a Professor in Lutheran University of Brazil (ULBRA). She works as Consultant at Invenio Softare Inteligente, and her interests include recommendation systems, case-based reasoning, and multi-agent systems.

**Juan Manuel Cueva Lovelle** is a Mining Engineer from Oviedo Mining Engineers Technical School in 1983 (Oviedo University, Spain). Ph. D. from Madrid Polytechnic University, Spain (1990). From 1985, he is a Professor at the Languages and Computers Systems Area in Oviedo University (Spain). ACM and IEEE voting member. His research interests include object-oriented technology, language processors, human-computer interface, Web engineering, modeling software with BPM, DSL, and MDA.

**David Mayorga Martin** is a Project Manager at PMOpartners, Spain. He holds a Business Administration degree by Universidad Pontificia Comilla de Madrid (1998), and a Law degree by Universidad Nacional de Educación a Distancia (2002). He is a PmP certified (#1391209) and Project Management Institute (PMI) member. In his 11 years of consultancy experience, he has been involved in several system implementation projects of Customer Relationship Management (CRM), Project and Portfolio Management, and Quality Assurance (QA) tools for national and international customers. Before Sem-IDI project, he took part in an R&D project to develop an IT solution to manage social coverage of Spanish dependant citizens.

**Óscar Sanjuán Martínez** is a Lecturer in the Computer Science Department of the University of Oviedo. Ph.D. from the Pontifical University of Salamanca in Computer Engineering. His research interests include object-oriented technology, Web engineering, software agents, modeling software with BPM, DSL, and MDA.

**Miloš Milovanović** is a Teaching Assistant at the University of Belgrade, School of Business Administration. He is also member of Laboratory for Multimedia Communications. Recently, he acquired a Masters degree in Information Technologies and became a PhD student in the same area. His research interests include game-based learning, distributed informational systems, and multimedia.

**Miroslav Minović** is Assistant Professor of Informational Technology at University of Belgrade, School of Business Administration. He is also Active Member of Laboratory for Multimedia Communications. His research interests include human-computer interaction as well as the development of advanced user interfaces in education and games. Minovic received his PhD in Informational Technology from University of Belgrade in 2010.

**Carlos E. Montenegro-Marin** is a Lecturer in the Faculty of Engineering of the Distrital University "Francisco José de Caldas", Colombia. Ph.D. from the University of Oviedo in Computer Engineering. His research interests include programming languages, cloud computing, and model driving engineering.

**Trupti Padiya** is now a postgraduate research student at DAIICT-Gandhinagar, India. Her research interest includes Semantic Web, databases, and distributed computing.

**Paulo Roberto Pasqualotti** is graduated in Computer Science with postgraduate studies in the field of Computing and Education. He has a Master degree in Artificial Intelligence. His master dissertation was in the area of affective computing involving the development of an affective lexicon called WordNet Affect BR, for the Portuguese language, presenting a list of words with emotional meaning. He is a Researcher and a Professor at the University FEEVALE, teaching Computing and Education disciplines and training teachers to use technology as a resource for teaching and learning. He has published papers in the field of information technology in education and the digital inclusion of seniors, researching the use of technology for improving quality of life.

**Kym Pohl**, In a career that spans industry as well as research, Kym has over two decades of experience in the design and development of agent-based, decision-support systems. Throughout these years, Kym has led numerous projects within various domains including logistical supply-chain management, command and control (C2), building design, and border security. Kym is well versed in agent-based computing as well as ontological modeling, maintaining a strong working knowledge of agent technologies and representational paradigms. Leveraging his expertise and experience, Kym often provides technical consultation to various groups within academia, industry, and government. In addition, Kym is a frequent contributor to various publications and conferences, valuing the opportunity to share thoughts and insights with others.

**Valesca Persch Reichelt** is graduated in Business Administration by Federal University of Rio Grande do Sul (UFRGS) and has Master degrees in Business Administration at Getulio Vargas Foundation (São Paulo, Brazil) and at Stockholm School of Economics (Sweden). She also has a Doctor degree in Business Administration with emphasis in Marketing, at Getulio Vargas Foundation (2007). She coordinates Business bachelor and MBA courses at ULBRA (Lutheran University of Brasil) and actuates as Visitor Professor at several Brazilian educational institutions. She has experience in marketing and sales, in companies related to the construction and editorial sector. She is a business consultant in the fields of relationship management, marketing, communication, sales, and business plan.

**Sabrina Ferreira Rodrigues** is a Business Intelligence (BI) Analyst in NeoGrid Company and holds a Computer Science Bachelor degree from the Lutheran University of Brazil (ULBRA) in 2010. Currently, she is making postgraduate studies in Knowledge Management and Information Technology in ULBRA. She has experience in database management and business intelligence tools, system development in Java, and as a teacher of basic and intermediate informatics. She is a MCTS Certified (Microsoft Certified Technology Specialist) in SQL Server.

**Marcos Ruano-Mayoral** is a Consultant at EgeoIT, Spain. Formerly, he was a Research Assistant of the Computer Science Department at Universidad Carlos III de Madrid. He holds a BSc in Computer Systems from Universidad de Valladolid and a MSc in Computer Science from Universidad Carlos III de Madrid. He has been involved in several research projects as information management engineer and software consultant.

**Priti Srinivas Sajja** joined the faculty of the Department of Computer Science, Sardar Patel University, India, in 1994, and presently works as an Associate Professor. Her research interests include knowledge-based systems, soft computing, multiagent systems, and software engineering. She has more than 100 publications in books, book chapters, journals, and in the proceedings of national and international conferences. She is co-author of "Knowledge-Based Systems" and "Intelligent Technologies for Web Applications."

**Emily Schwarz** is a Doctoral Student at the University of Oregon pursuing a degree in Computer Science and specializing in Bioinformatics and Scientific Computing. She received her Master of Science degree in Computer Science from California Polytechnic State University, San Luis Obispo, in 2011, and her Bachelor of Science from San Diego State University in 2007. Her other research interests include artificial intelligence and human-computer interaction.

**John Seng** is an Associate Professor in the Computer Science Department at California Polytechnic State University, San Luis Obispo. His research interests include high performance embedded systems, high performance microprocessors, and also low-power processors as well. Most of his previous work has been aimed at reducing the power consumption of general-purpose microprocessors while maintaining a high-level of performance. He also worked in the areas of robotics, machine vision, and natural language processing.

**Sofia Stamou** is a Lecturer at the Department of Archives and Library Science of the Ionian University. Her area of expertise is text analysis and language processing with an emphasis on semantic analysis of textual data. Her research interests include Web searching, personalization, ontologies, text mining, and data organization. She received her Ph.D. and M.Sc. degrees from the Computer Engineering and Informatics Department of Patras University and her B.A. in Philosophy from the University of Ioannina.

**Dušan Starčević** is a full Professor at the School of Business Administration, University of Belgrade, and a Visiting Professor at the university's School of Electrical Engineering. He is also Vice-Dean for Scientific Research at the School of Business Administration. His main research interests include distributed information systems, multimedia, and computer graphics. He received a PhD in Information Systems from the University of Belgrade.

**Velimir Štavljanin** is Assistant Professor of Marketing and Communications at University of Belgrade, School of Business Administration. He is also Active Member of Laboratory for Multimedia Communications. His research interests include multimedia systems development.

**Paraskevi Tzekou** is a Ph.D. candidate at the Computer Engineering and Informatics Department of Patras University. Her area of expertise is text summarization, natural language processing, Web data management, and text mining. She received her diploma and M.Sc. from the Computer Engineering and Informatics Department of Patras University.

**Pablo Abella Vallina** (MSc) is Master of Computer Science specializing in Web Engineering (2011) and Bachelor of Computer Science (2009) by the University of Oviedo. He works in the WESO Research Group since December 2010, taking part in different national projects collaborating with some companies. He is also part of the Gamelab, which is the biggest International Show of Video Games and Interactive Entertainment here in Spain that is held every year in June in Barcelona.

**Timo von der Dovenmühle** was born in 1973. As a teenager in the 80s/90s his first contact to computers was affected by numbers like 6502 or 68000. Subsequently, he started to work as an electronic technician. From 2006 – 2012, he studied Business Information Systems at the Department VLBA (Very Large Business Applications) of the University of Oldenburg under supervision of Professor Marx Gómez. At this time, his interest in research work was promoted by his professor and department members. As a result, he started to work as an external PhD student in 2012. His research interests include service oriented architectures, IT-service management, and benchmarking of service providers.

**Dengya Zhu** is a PhD. from School of Information System, Curtin University, Australia. He received his Master of Information System by research degree at Curtin University, and Bachelor's degree in Information System Engineering at National University of Defense Technology in China. He used to be a Lecturer, Senior Engineer, and Manager of a software company in China, and has extensive industry experience. His research fields include information retrieval, Web data mining, machine learning, search engine, natural language process, semantic analysis, database systems design, open source software development, and object-oriented programming/design. He is a reviewer of several conferences and edited books, and has published many papers.

**Jan Zibuschka** holds a diploma in Computer Science from Technical University of Darmstadt. Currently, he is working as a Senior Researcher and Project Leader at Fraunhofer IAO, Stuttgart, Germany. He participated in several national and international research projects dealing with security and privacy, such as FP ICT projects PRIME, PrimeLife, and FIDIS, and national projects such as civil security project VeRSiert. He has published in the areas of information intermediation in distributed value networks and interorganisational information infrastructures, covering both technical and economic aspects. He also published in several areas of security, including the design of market-compliant solutions for privacy in location-based services and cost-efficient approaches for Web identity management and single sign on.

# Index